THE INTERNATIONAL ENCYCLOPEDIA OF DOGS

Edited by Anne Rogers Clark
and Andrew H. Brace

With Special Contributions by Renée Sporre-Willes

Howell Book House
1633 Broadway
New York, NY 10019

THE INTERNATIONAL ENCYCLOPEDIA OF DOGS

Howell Book House
A Simon & Schuster Macmillan Company
1633 Broadway
New York, NY 10019

MACMILLAN is a registered trademark of Macmillan, Inc.

This is a Cynthia Parzych Publishing book created by
Mirabel Books Ltd., P.O. Box 1214, London SW6 7XF

Edited by: Nicky Thompson
Text design by: Dalia Hartman
Jacket design by: George Berrian

Library of Congress Cataloging-in-Publication Data
Clark, Anne Rogers.
    The international encyclopedia of dogs/Anne Rogers Clark,
Andrew H. Brace.
        p.   cm.
    Includes bibliographical references (p.   ) and index.
    ISBN 0-87605-624-9
    1. Dogs --Encyclopedias.   I. Brace, Andrew H. II. Title.
SF422.C58 1995
636. 7 003--dc20   95-30193
                                                  CIP

Separations by H&Y Printing Limited, Hong Kong
Manufactured in Hong Kong by South China Printing Company (1988) Limited

10 9 8 7 6 5 4 3 2 1

CONTENTS

HOW TO USE THIS BOOK

The authority and international character of this encyclopedia are its most pervasive features. Both the editors and their supporting contributors and consultants are drawn from a worldwide circle of experts. The number of breeds described is one of the most ambitious ever attempted in an encyclopedia with descriptions of dogs from every corner of the world. The encyclopedia is divided into three parts.

The chapters which form the first section provide both the general reader and those people professionally involved with dogs, with information and guidance on a wide range of canine topics.

The second section of the book describes over 300 breeds of dogs, ordered alphabetically.

BREED RECOGNITION

All the breeds recognized by the American Kennel Club, the Canadian Kennel Club, the Fédération Cynologique Internationale and the Kennel Club of Great Britain are included in the book. If a dog is recognized by one or more of these registries this is indicated at the end of the breed entry by the identifying initials of the registry: AKC, CKC, FCI, KC. Only breeds which had achieved full recognition by one of these registries at the time the book went to press will carry the appropriate registry initials in the entry. As it happens, two breeds – the Brazilian Terrier and the Korean Gindo Dog – gained FCI recognition after the press date had passed. Descriptions and photographs of these two breeds will be included in subsequent editions of this book.

The affiliations of particular breeds to certain national registries – the Australian National Kennel Council, the New Zealand Kennel Club and the Kennel Union of South Africa have not been specified as the majority of these breeds are recognized by and follow the Standards of the Kennel Club in the United Kingdom, or in certain cases, those of the American Kennel Club or the Fédération Cynologique Internationale.

There are some breeds described which are not recognized by any of the four major registries but by one or more national registries, because of the breed's importance in these countries. Please see, for example, the Dingo entry on page 203. There are also breeds described that are not recognized by any registry and that may be rare. They qualify for inclusion in the book as they are known to specialists or to the general public in certain areas of the world.

FORMAT OF THE BREED ENTRIES

The name (or names) given to a breed is dictated by the four registries that recognize it and the name the particular registry (or registries) gives to the breed.

If the AKC and the KC recognize the same breed but call it by a different (even slightly different) name, then the AKC name precedes the KC name at the head of the entry. If the FCI name for a breed differs from that of the AKC or KC then the FCI name is given as well. The FCI name is normally the one given to a breed in its country of origin. However, there are occasions where the FCI has two names for the same breed – that of the country of origin and another, usually anglicized, name for ease of recognition in English-speaking countries. See, for instance the entry for the Ainu/Hokkaido on page 74. In cases like this both names are given at the head of the entry. The index provides a full cross-reference of all breed names.

LENGTH OF ENTRY

The length of each breed entry is governed by the popularity of the breed. A breed's popularity, in turn, has been determined by the number of annual registrations.

ESSENTIALS OF THE BREED

The details of a breed's Standard are dealt with, where space permits, in the sub-entry: Essentials of the Breed. The information here represents a précis and an extrapolation of the official Standard. Where there are differences in the Standard for the same breed between registries, these differences are pointed out. If no Standard exists for a breed, the ideal physical features of the dog are described.

BREED ILLUSTRATIONS

Each breed entry is illustrated with one or more photographs. The sources are some of the world's finest dog photographers, and individual owners and breeders of championship quality dogs. Most of the photographs have been selected because they are first-rate examples of each breed in its natural setting. The same breed sometimes has a different "look" in, say, the United States than in Europe. Consequently, two examples of the same breed are sometimes shown to illustrate a difference. Not all the breed photographs were chosen with an eye to the Standard. In the case of most of the Australian working dogs, for example, the photographs are of the dogs working at their traditional roles in their natural settings. These dogs do not necessarily conform to the ideal of their breed Standard.

In the third section of the book the reader will find a full glossary of canine terms and details of how to contact dog clubs, registries and welfare associations. There is also a fully cross-referenced index.

ORIGINS, DESIGN, FUNCTIONS AND GENETICS OF THE DOG

All potential dog owners and breeders will find that their understanding of a particular breed increases dramatically when they have as much background information as possible on the canine world, past and present. How a dog came into being, its historical origins, its original purpose and role, how breeders have sought to develop aspects in certain types of dog, and how genetics play their part have all had considerable influence on the vast range of dog breeds that exist today.

EARLY DEVELOPMENTS

The dog is generally accepted as the first species to be domesticated by man and this link goes back between 10,000 and 12,000 years. Popular belief is that primitive man found a litter of wolf cubs and took them home to domesticate and use as aids in hunting. In reality the domestication of the dog may have occurred for a variety of reasons with hunting support being only one. Pet ownership is well documented in even primitive tribes so the early "wolf-dogs" may just as readily have

Today's German Shepherd Dog, like all types of dogs, evolved from some type of wolf. If properly trained this breed has a steady and solid temperament.

been intended as pets, bedwarmers or even as a source of food.

Although various suggestions have been put forward as to the origins of the dog, it now seems to be generally accepted that the dog, of whatever breed, has developed from some form of wolf. The wolf, like the coyote and golden jackal, possesses thirty-nine pairs of chromosomes and so does the dog. In fact, there are relatively few differences between the wolf and dog in genetic terms. Matings between wolf and dog have occurred and do result in viable fertile hybrids because their chromosome numbers are identical and the chromosomes of both animals are compatible.

VARIETY IN BREEDS

More than any other species, the dog shows enormous differentiation in respect of breeds and sizes. The Saint Bernard, weighing in at more than most men, is vastly different from the Chihuahua, which easily fits into a pocket, yet both have the same chromosome make-up and are capable of intermating, albeit with some practical difficulties.

Although dog breeders often claim great antiquity for their breeds, the truth is that many breeds are relatively new in terms of years. Dogs similar to modern English Toy Spaniels can be seen in sixteenth-century paintings while dogs akin to the Saluki or Afghan Hound have been identified in Assyrian wall paintings dating back over 4,000 years. However, modern breeds cannot claim lines of unbroken descent back to these times.

Undoubtedly man has been breeding dogs for specific purposes for several thousand years and as a consequence has brought about differentiation into distinct physical shapes so that sighthound/Greyhound types were developed as well as smaller, child substitute, animals. Nevertheless accurate control of pedigrees is a relatively modern innovation dating back really to the establishment of the English Kennel Club in 1873 which is considerably later than the establishment of the first cattle and horse stud books. Most other kennel clubs were formed in the two decades following the English Kennel Club formation.

In the strictest sense, dog breeds date back only to the last couple of decades of the nineteenth century or to more recent decades in this century but distinct types of dogs existed centuries earlier. It is important not to claim great age for breeds though it is quite legitimate to claim considerable antiquity for certain types of dogs.

BREED CLASSIFICATION

According to J.A. Peters in the *Journal of the American Veterinary Medical Association* (1969), the earliest classification of dog breeds and types in the English language was published in 1486 and was allegedly based on one made some seventy or eighty years earlier. This classification included gaze-hounds, scent hunters, bull-baiting animals, giant dogs (Mastiffs) and toys.

These types of dog had clearly taken a long time to evolve and had been developed for a variety of purposes. The forerunner of the modern Saluki probably goes back to around 7000 B.C. and originated in the Mediterranean region. Some others among the sighthounds

The English Foxhound, a scenthound well known for its deep melodic voice in pursuit of quarry, was developed and reared by horsemen to be followed by mounted hunters.

were developed from around 3000-4000 B.C. to chase game but, like the Saluki, came from the same general region in the world.

Other hound types that use scent rather than sight to hunt are more recent. They developed in different places, with the Bloodhound probably the earliest of these. Elkhound ancestors were Viking dogs. The forerunners of the Rhodesian Ridgeback were native dogs of the South African veldt.

Ancient fighting or war dogs were probably the ancestors of the giant breeds like the English Mastiff and from these developed other large breeds like the Great Dane and Saint Bernard, possibly from Roman times. Functional breeds like terriers were of largely unknown ancestry but used for killing rats as well as "unearthing" other animals like fox and badger. They developed as small active animals and only in relatively modern times have they evolved (in some cases) into "exhibition" animals, some with overlarge heads and rather lengthy bodies no longer suitable for their original tasks.

Many working breeds developed as herding dogs though sheep work has led to the development of two kinds of dog. Genuine herders like the Border Collie and the Kelpie developed in locations where predators were of minimal importance. In contrast, in central Europe livestock protection types were larger than herders. They were usually, though not inevitably, white and were produced to protect flocks against predators such as the wolf. Today, in many of the western United States, predation, mainly from coyotes but also bears, mountain lions, bobcats and foxes can account for lamb losses approaching one million per year. Livestock protection breeds such as the Maremma, Anatolian Shepherd, Kuvasz and Great Pyrenees have been and are being successfully used to reduce these lamb losses.

Some breeds developed as tiny pets or child substitutes. The Chihuahua comes from dogs that lived in the ancient Mayan territories (now modern Mexico), the Pekingese from China and the Spitz types from ancient Arctic/Viking animals.

Many breeds now known as gun dogs

Ancient fighting or war dogs, such as these hunting wild boar, were probably developed in Roman times from giant breeds. They are depicted in Co-Emperor Maximian's Villa Imperiale floor mosaics of the 4th century A.D. at Casale near Piazza Armerina in Sicily.

(Pointers, Setters, Spaniels and Retrievers) were formed in the early 1900s and show some more modern derivations into so-called distinct breeds while some European versions of the Pointer probably have hound ancestry.

Even before kennel clubs were established, specific breeds were known to exist and were classified into particular groups or categories. Modern classifications by kennel clubs vary according to club but usually comprise Gun Dogs, Hounds, Working, Terriers, Toys and so-called Utility or Non-Sporting. This class-ification used by the English Kennel Club is not always favored elsewhere (North America, for instance) where the Working group is subdivided into two categories comprising pastoral (known as Herding) and guard and draft (known as Working) types. The Herding group comprises all sheep/cattle herding breeding while Working covers all other working types. A similar classification exists with the Fédération Cynologique Internationale (FCI) which is the body covering most of the world outside the United Kingdom and North America. In their case the Working group is further subdivided to separate Mastiff types.

DESIGN AND FUNCTION

Dogs are mammals and have a physiology much like other quadruped mammals. The skeletal system gives rigidity to the body with bones acting as levers, stores of minerals and sites for blood formation. Long bones are mainly used in locomotion and include the humerus, radius and ulna of the foreleg and the femur, tibia and fibula of the hind leg. The skull of the dog shows greater variation than in other species ranging from the "compressed" (brachycephalic) format of the bull breeds through to the narrow long skull of the sighthounds. Tail length also shows great variation.

The dog's circulatory system has a four-chambered heart similar to that of man. It is also subject to some of the same inherited diseases including patent ductus arteriosus and conotruncal septal defects. In essence arteries carry oxygenated blood from the heart and veins carry unoxygenated blood back to the heart.

The digestive system starts with a mouth containing twenty-eight deciduous teeth which are gradually replaced in early puppy-hood by forty-two permanent teeth (twelve incisors, four canines, sixteen premolars and ten molars). There is a simple stomach and a small and large intestine — the large one is the shortest and simplest of all domestic animals. The dog is a carnivore but less genuinely than the cat. It is more like an omnivore.

In the wolf the reproductive system is monoestrus — the animal comes into season once a year. Domestic dogs usually cycle twice a year. Puberty begins when puppies are about six to nine months. The estrus cycle consists of a proestrus period (about nine days), an estrus (five to twenty days) and a metestrus (eighty to ninety days). Pregnancy lasts about sixty-three days. Litter size in the wolf is usually four cubs. In the dog it varies over a wide range. In broad terms litter size is positively influenced by body weight and/or wither height. Small breeds

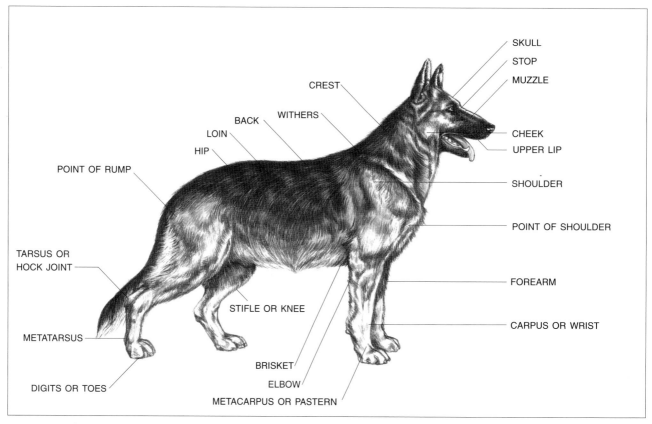

Features of the dog

have from one to four pups and larger breeds have anything up to twenty-two. A breed the size of the German Shepherd has a range up to seventeen pups, with 7.7 on average.

THE DEVELOPMENT OF STANDARDS

Dog breeds were initially developed to undertake activities and accordingly their supporters sought to perfect particular features deemed to be desirable. So-called Toy breeds, developed primarily as pets or child substitutes, were required to be small for easy handling with coat length and type developed to create an object of "beauty." Most other breeds were bred for working purposes and thus the physical shape sought was based upon man's perception of the characteristics required for the work to be done. Few breeds can be credited to the work of specific breeders. Most were developed by members of a club. In the German Shepherd Dog, for example, the principal enthusiast was a cavalry captain Max von Stephanitz, and his Standard (drawn

up in the late 1890s) called for a square dog with a ninety degree shoulder. Function has led to the development of a slightly longer dog with a shoulder closer to one hundred degrees. The developers of particular breeds have, in modern times, drawn up a kind of written blueprint of what the breed should look like. This has been called a Standard against which each breed should be compared or judged. The originators of these Standards were not always knowledgeable about anatomy. Over the years, the need to revise, reword and improve the Standards has been necessary.

Herding breeds diverged from livestock protection breeds in a variety of ways. Medium to large size was desirable in a dog being used to see off predators but was undesirable in a genuine herding breed which needed to be agile and highly mobile. Herders were proportioned 10:9 in terms of body length to wither height. Protection dogs could develop in squarer shapes. Depending upon location, coat length would vary from the very short coat of the Kelpie

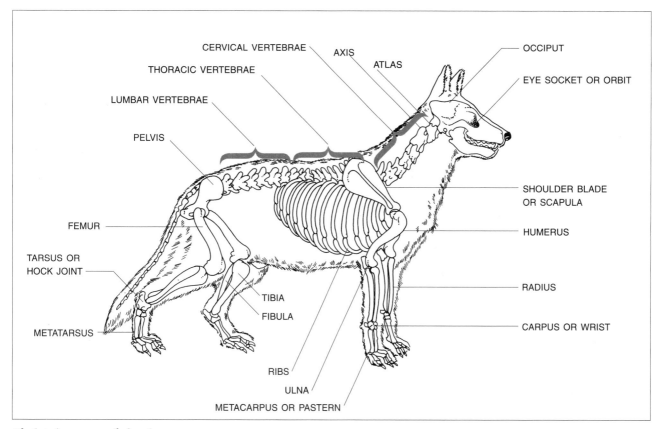

CERVICAL VERTEBRAE
AXIS
ATLAS
OCCIPUT
EYE SOCKET OR ORBIT
THORACIC VERTEBRAE
LUMBAR VERTEBRAE
PELVIS
SHOULDER BLADE OR SCAPULA
HUMERUS
FEMUR
TARSUS OR HOCK JOINT
RADIUS
TIBIA
FIBULA
CARPUS OR WRIST
METATARSUS
RIBS
ULNA
METACARPUS OR PASTERN

Skeletal system of the dog

developed in the hot dry regions of Australia to the medium-length coat of the Border Collie which worked in the cold Scottish hills. Similarly color, though largely esthetic, was also important. Protection animals were preferably white like the sheep they frequently protected whereas all-white herding breeds were undesirable because they were more difficult to identify and control on snow-covered hills.

Herding breeds are, from an early stage, interested in retrieving games and stalking, while protection breeds spend their puppy-hood playing antagonistic "games." If Border Collies and Maremmas are reared together, they will stick to their distinct breed groups because they have differing instincts and hence different puppy games. Protection dogs have an innate instinct but they still have to be conditioned by rearing them with sheep from an early age if they are to carry out their role successfully. In contrast a herding breed, even if reared among sheep, is unlikely to develop the livestock protection abilities because its

instincts are quite different from a Komondor, Anatolian Shepherd or Maremma.

THE SIZE OF DOGS

Gun dogs were developed in varying sizes from relatively small spaniels to medium-sized setters, retriever and pointers. With the exception of the Pointer and the relatively modern Labrador, most gun dogs developed in the United Kingdom (the Clumber Spaniel and Golden Retriever, for instance) have medium to longish coats whereas several European ones (like the German Wire and Shorthaired Pointers, the Hungarian Vizla and Weimaraner) have short or wiry coats. Nearly all have developed shapes that are slightly longer than they are tall with sleek ribbing and limited depth of chest. Coat color may vary because it is considered relatively unimportant.

Sighthounds were developed along Grey-hound lines for speed at the gallop. An absence of massive bone or great substance, plenty of lung room and good eyesight were

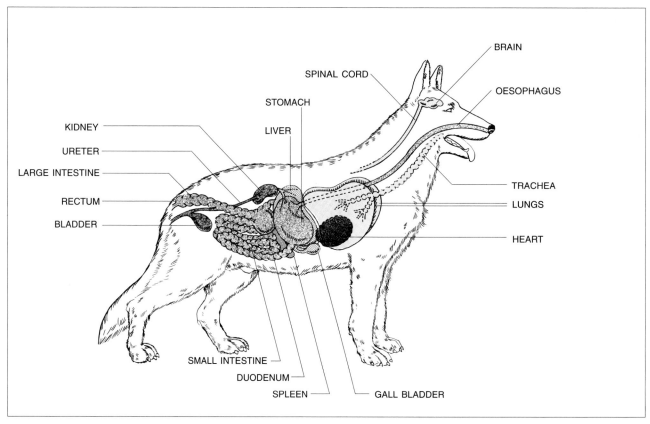

KIDNEY

URETER

LARGE INTESTINE

RECTUM

BLADDER

STOMACH

LIVER

SPINAL CORD

BRAIN

OESOPHAGUS

TRACHEA

LUNGS

HEART

SMALL INTESTINE

DUODENUM

SPLEEN

GALL BLADDER

Major systems of the dog

desirable. Such breeds have relatively long legs and considerable "tuck-up" in the loin. Other hounds were usually short-coated dogs selected for their pronounced scenting ability and were of various sizes depending upon the prey sought. Speed was a minor consideration other than in Foxhounds that were always geared toward endurance.

Terriers were essentially small, somewhat square dogs without the layback of shoulder sought in most other breeds. Originally, terriers were specifically used down holes or in confined spaces where speed of movement was not required.

Some breeds were developed as bull- or bear-baiting animals. They needed to be shortcoated with small ears and fairly short tails but with massive jaws, often undershot to allow the dog to grip but still breathe. They were medium sized and agile with good length of leg and very muscular. When these barbaric sports were banned the "bull breeds" developed in no set direction since their role had disappeared.

But Bull Terriers, Boxers, Bulldogs and American Pit Bulls are descendants of these original baiting breeds. Of course, fighting potential had been selected into such breeds and, once their roles changed, these potentials had to be modified in other less fearsome directions. In the same way, since fighting was no longer undertaken, agility became less necessary. Exaggeration by man led to such extreme types as the Bulldog, now vastly different from its bull-baiting progenitors.

MORE RECENT DEVELOPMENTS

Many of the dogs placed in the Working Group are relatively new to the dog scene. Breeds like the German Shepherd Dog developed from a motley assortment of German sheepdogs around the end of the nineteenth century. The Doberman was a guard breed developed by judicious crossing around the same time and was followed, a little later, by the Boxer. In the development of some of the more modern breeds older

A Border Collie guarding Navajo sheep in Monument Valley, Utah. Herding breeds, like this one, are bred to be of small to medium size and to be agile and highly mobile.

breeds were used as crosses prior to selection for the new type.

Most of the selection undertaken in the development of breeds was done by trial and error. Those animals that did a job well were used to produce the next generation. Failures were discarded from breeding programs. In the twentieth century, breed Standards have been used as yardsticks by which breeds are judged. As a consequence most dog breeds have been selected for so-called physical excellence regardless of function.

For example, early Bernese Mountain Dog breeders sought a cleft nasal palate in the

Bull Terriers are just one of the breeds that are descendants of bull- or bear-baiting dogs. Fighting potential had been selected into these breeds, but once their roles changed in modern times, the potential to fight had to be modified in other, less fearsome directions.

belief that it made the dog look more ferocious when, in fact, such a feature was harmful to the dog's health and eventually selected against. Similarly, the breed Standard called for a chest coming "at least to the elbow" and thus, in theory, permitted a chest that reached to the ground. The Bulldog Standard sought a head as large as possible, seemingly oblivious to the fact that this was inevitably going to lead to a high percentage of Caesarean births. Most Standards were drawn up in the country where the breed developed and simply translated into other languages as the breed spread. In modern times collaboration between kennel clubs has meant that many flaws in Standards have been removed, although many breeders may still be seeking to reproduce dogs that conform to ideals that no longer hold good and were not sound in the first instance.

The dog has been changed more in the last one hundred years than it had changed in the thousands of years preceding this century. Much of the momentum for change has stemmed from the show ring and the desire of breeders to produce animals of a specific breed or type which would win in the ring. Although it would not be true of every breed, present-day examples of certain breeds have little in common with their ancestors of a century ago. The modern Chow Chow bears minimal resemblance to those of 1900, in the same way that the Bulldog no longer resembles its bull-baiting ancestors. In contrast, the Border Terrier of today is little changed from those which originally formed the breed. Similarly modern German Shepherd Dogs generally have better characters and are more athletic and functionally correct than those which were introduced to the United Kingdom in 1918. Much of this change has only occurred in the past two decades.

In some breeds there has been a dichotomy between the dogs used for working and those bred primarily for the show ring. This is perhaps most obvious in some, though not all, breeds of gun dog. Labrador Retrievers used for working purposes tend to be smaller, lighter and faster than the dogs seen in the show ring although, as in any breed, there are exceptions to this general rule. If the working and show types were to be bred apart with little or no intermixing then in due course they would emerge as two distinct breed types of differing appearance, behavior and quite distinct bloodlines in the immediate generations.

SIMPLE GENETIC PRINCIPLES

Dogs have been and are selected for a variety of features or traits. These can be classified into the broad groups shown in Table 1 on page 15.

Before examining these groups, the concept of heritability should be considered. The heritability of a trait is usually expressed as a percentage and measures the degree to which any superiority or inferiority in the parents can be passed on to the offspring. It is thus a predeterminant of the speed of genetic progress that is feasible. (See Table 2 on page 16.)

In broad terms low heritabilities are values below 20 percent, medium are from 20-40 percent and high values are in excess of 40 percent with very few traits being above 70 percent. Heritabilities really apply to traits that are called polygenic, i.e., traits controlled by many genes. Each gene may have minimal influence but collectively genes can influence

major characteristics. However, such traits are not usually 100 percent genetic — they are also influenced by environmental factors such as nutrition and exercise.

Although heritabilities can be expressed in mathematical terms, they can best be understood by a breeder in more practical terminology. If a character is 40 percent heritable then this means that 40 percent of any superiority of parents (over the average of the population) would be transmitted to the next generation. If, for example, wither height in a breed averaged 25 inches/64 cm and the breeder decided to breed from parents which together averaged 26 inches/67 cm in wither height, then the parental superiority is 26 minus 25 inches, or 67 minus 64 cm , i.e. 1 inch or 3 cm. If heritability was 40 percent then only 40 percent of 1 inch or 3cm would be transmitted to the offspring which would thus measure just under 25 1/2 inches/65.2 cm.

Clearly this is a broad generalization and on small numbers things might not work out exactly as planned. But over larger numbers heritabilities are important in predicting the results of selection. Although widely known and used in farm livestock, few heritabilities have been calculated in dogs. Nevertheless the fact that dog breeders may be ignorant of such

The early Bulldog Standard required a head as large as possible, not taking into account that a large head would lead to a high percentage of Caesarean births.

factors does not alter the genetic principles involved. Traits that have low heritabilities such as reproductive traits will be very difficult to select for and thus, however skillful the breeder, progress will be slow.

Anyone breeding only from bitches that have large litters would not necessarily see a rapid increase in litter size in the stock because the trait is of low heritability. In contrast, selecting stock that are tall in stature would lead to quite a rapid increase in wither height. A trait like fear is quite highly inherited. Dogs that are fearful are much more likely to bite than dogs with a stable character and breeders should be firm in selecting against animals of poor character. Conformational traits are those concerned with almost all aspects of conformation and all are traits controlled by many genes and are often moderately heritable. Thus the alteration of certain aspects of shape can be achieved relatively quickly. This is of course equally true in selecting for poor as well as good construction.

Qualitative traits like coat color, coat type, ear carriage and so on are relatively simple in their mode of inheritance, with few genes involved in each feature. These traits are, in effect, Mendelian traits named after an Austrian monk, Gregor Mendel (1822-84), the founder of the modern science of genetics. Although Mendelian traits are often important in certain breeds, they tend to be features that are not crucial to the health and well-being of the dog. In fact, they are largely esthetic and breeders or judges should not seek to place excessive influence on such easily changed features.

Anomalies or defects are traits that are not desired but are actually best avoided. Some of them, such as progressive retinal atrophy, are known to be Mendelian and controlled by a single gene. Others, including hip dysplasia and osteochondrosis dissecans (OCD − a faulty conversion of cartilage to bone that occurs in the shoulder and elbow at about four to five months of age), are polygenic and are thus controlled to a greater or lesser degree by inheritance, as well as being influenced by external features such as nutrition and exercise.

Breeders are perpetually seeking to improve fitness traits, enhance constructional features and produce good behavioral responses while at the same time hoping to reduce the incidence of inherited defects to minimal levels. Progress actually depends upon the degree to which a trait is inherited and the extent to which it is selected for. If the trait is of high heritability then progress is potentially high, but it is important that breeders select the best possible stock from which to breed.

SELECTION IN BREEDING

The old adage of breeding the best to the best is good sound genetics but it is important that

TABLE 1. FEATURES SELECTED FOR IN DOGS

TYPE OF TRAIT	TYPICAL EXAMPLES	HERITABILITY
Fitness	Fertility, litter size, viability, longevity	Low
Behavioral	Temperament, working potential, innate instinct	Low to Medium
Conformational	Most aspects of construction	Low to high
Qualitative	Coat color, coat type, eye color	Mendelian
Anomalies	Progressive retinal atrophy, hip dysplasia, hereditary cataract	Some are Mendelian, others are polygenic

breeders know what the best is. All too often breeders are inclined to think that the best are the dogs which they own. If breeders are right then they will make progress by breeding from these dogs. If, however, they are wrong then breeding from such animals will ultimately retard progress. Since much of what is considered good is decided in the show ring, it is imperative that judges do indeed select only the best specimens since it is from among the leading winners that most breeding selection will take place. Judges therefore have a crucial role to play. If judges are not skilled, they will inevitably give high awards to the wrong dogs and could therefore lead the breed down the wrong road. The same is true if judges either cannot assess or if they ignore weak characters and thus allow fearful or, worse still, overly aggressive animals to win. Breeders are not, of course, obliged to follow judges and skilled breeders often will not. But most dog breeders are involved for relatively short periods of time (five to seven years)

and many will follow fashion simply because they are not knowledgeable.

A breeder, in whatever breed, has to formulate an idea of what it is he or she is trying to achieve. To do this, a breeder must fully understand the breed Standard since this should form a blueprint for the ideal being sought. However, character as well as construction must be considered since the majority of dogs are sold to pet owners and for them a sound character is, in the long term, more important than mere physical beauty. Owners have to live with the real dog not the prizes that it has won.

Of course, no dog is perfect and inevitably breeding takes place using animals which might fail in a particular feature while excelling in others. The dog breeder must use a system of selection to which he or she can easily adhere. The principal one used by breeders involves independent culling. Using this technique, the breeder sets a specific limit for a series of important features of the dog below which

TABLE 2. TRAITS AND HERITABILITY

CATEGORY	TRAIT	HERITABILITY (PERCENTAGE)*
Reproductive traits	Fertility	less than 15
	Gestation length	40
	Litter size	less than 20
Conformational traits	Body length	20-40
	Body weight	20-40
	Rear pastern length	30-60
	Wither height	40-60
Behavioral traits	Fear	50
	Retrieve (young pup)	20
Anomalies	Elbow problems	40-60
	Hip dysplasia (varies with breed/scheme)	25-55
	Panosteiosis	20

* The percentages given here are only guides to possible percentages and may not apply in any specific breed or population. Nevertheless they are educated guesses based on such data as do exist and knowledge of the situation in other livestock.

he or she will not go. It might be decided, for example, to breed only from males that are at least 25 inches/64 cm in height; that have well laid back shoulders; broad well-angulated thighs; 10:9 proportions and a chest depth that is one-half of the wither height. These might be some of the criteria set. Each dog would be evaluated against these standards. Those falling below the required minimal level in any one feature would be eliminated from breeding. Thus all breeding stock will meet a certain basic minimum level of excellence.

Clearly the more traits that are listed and the tougher the imposed limits, the more likely the breeder will find that all dogs will fail in something. It is thus important that breeders set a sensible and plausible standard in each trait and that only really important features are sought. There would, for instance, be little logic in culling an otherwise outstanding animal simply because its eye color was slightly too light. Given sensible standards and a limited number of attainable goals, a breeder will be able to make progress depending upon the extent to which the traits involved are heritable. In most breeds only about ten percent of males and thirty percent of females are used for breeding, so a high proportion of dogs are not and should not be bred from at all — no matter how much a breeder might like to have a puppy from a favorite pet.

There is an element of luck involved in all dog breeding but the better the breeders' knowledge and understanding of the Standard and the greater their ability to recognize merit (and shortcomings) in examples of the breed concerned, the more likely they are to succeed. The breeder who cannot distinguish, for example, a correctly laid scapula from a forward-placed one is going to run into difficulties sooner or later and breed from inadequate stock, creating poorer shoulder construction as a consequence.

In polygenic traits such as most conformational aspects there is some truth in the view that like begets like. If tall animals are

bred from then, gradually and perceptibly, the breed will get taller. If early maturing animals are bred from by using those animals which appear "finished" while still only puppies or yearlings, then the breed will become more early maturing. These things occur because the genes involved have a collective influence even though the individual genes are not in themselves very important. The more heritable the trait examined and the greater the selection practiced, the more successful selection will be in moving the breed in a given direction. Very often breed advancement does not occur but this is usually because breeders

The character of a dog and its construction should be of equal concern to breeders. The Bloodhound, bred for scent-trailing, is a very large, but gentle companion that requires human contact and early socialization.

are not all selecting for the same things or not all in the same direction.

HERITABLE DEFECTS

Certain anomalies need to be considered depending upon the breed. In breeds where hip dysplasia is known to be a definite problem, breeders are required to have their potential breeding stock assessed through the appropriate scheme such as that of the British Veterinarian Association/Kennel Club in the United Kingdom, the Orthopedic Foundation for Animals (OFA) in the United States or the Australian Veterinary Association (AVA) in Australia. Most countries with kennel clubs have recognized schemes and dogs which do not measure up well to breed averages should be discarded. Similarly, if progressive retinal atrophy is known to exist in the breed all would-be breeding stock should be eye-tested every twelve months during their breeding life and culled from breeding if they fail. A German Shepherd Dog breeder should not use a male until it has been cleared for hemophilia A. In the same way a Bernese Mountain Dog breeder should not be using dogs that have not had their elbows checked through a recognized scheme. These are necessary rules of thumb that breeders in specific breeds need to apply if they are to breed litters which they will sell to others.

Progress in hip dysplasia control is often slow despite the fact that in some breeds the heritability is around 40 percent. The fault lies not with the inherited nature of hip dysplasia or even failure to screen dogs but rather from the fact that, having screened animals, some breeders still breed from the dogs that are worse than the breed average or they continue to use sires which have been shown to be producers of poor hips.

GENETIC INFLUENCE ON BREEDING

When considering an individual mating, both sire and dam are equally influential though one may offer "better" genes than the other. However, in considering breeds as a whole,

sires are generally much more important than dams. This is because fewer sires than dams are needed and thus potential for selection is greater through sires. In most breeds it is probable that about seventy percent of progress will stem from the selection of sires. While it is undoubtedly true that bitches are the strength of a kennel, it is equally true that careful attention to the selection of the very best sires will bring about the greatest advances.

In the case of simple Mendelian traits, like does not necessarily breed like. For instance, if two smooth-coated Chihuahuas are mated they could give rise to some long-coated progeny if both parents are "carriers" of the long-coated gene. If the smooth-coated gene is designated as L and the long coat as l then smooth-coated dogs can be either LL or Ll but long coats are always ll. Table 3 below shows the results which might occur from various combinations of matings. Although this applies to smooth and long coats in this instance, the basic rules apply to any simple Mendelian recessive trait.

In Table 3 the percentages are accurate in

TABLE 3. MATING RESULTS FOR LONG/ SHORT COAT (PERCENTAGE OF PROGENY SEEN)

L = smooth-coated gene   l = long-coated gene

MATING PARENTS	PROGENY		
	LL (short)	Ll (short)	ll (long)
1 LL x LL (short x short)	100	0	0
2 LL x Ll (short x short)	50	50	0
3 LL x ll (short x long)	0	100	0
4 Ll x Ll (short x short)	25	50	25
5 Ll x ll (short x long)	0	50	50
6 ll x ll (long x long)	0	0	100

matings 1, 3 and 6 but in the other three the percentages only apply given sufficient numbers of animals. Note that because short coat is dominant to long coat it will totally mask long coat so that an LL and an Ll animal would appear identical to look at as far as coat length is concerned. Note also that only when the gene l is carried by *both* parents can long-coated stock result (matings 4, 5 and 6). The most usual mating which brings to light a hidden recessive is mating 4 when, perhaps unwittingly, a breeder mates together two carrier animals resulting in some 25 percent (on average) of the pups showing the recessive trait. In the case of long and short coats these may both be acceptable in some breeds but in the case of other traits the equivalent of long coat may be undesirable. There are many such traits in the dog ranging over coat color, eye disease and a variety of other anomalies.

BREEDING SYSTEMS

In broad terms the dog breeder is, by definition, a breeder of purebred stock. Thus the many advantages of crossbreeding are not available to him or her. He or she can, in fact, breed either from related animals within the same breed (inbreeding) or from unrelated animals (outbreeding). In a sense all dogs within a given breed will show some degree of relationship since all will have descended from the same source animals. This apart, close relationships may be relatively low in dogs that are widely separated in terms of location (different countries) or are members of numerically large breeds. Relationships will be closer in numerically small populations.

Inbreeding, which in its less extreme form may be called linebreeding, is a powerful tool that carries with it certain difficulties. The more that dogs are inbred (i.e., the closer the relationships between breeding stock) the greater the risks that arise. These risks involve firstly the occurrence of hidden anomalies. If a breeder mates together dogs that closely relate to some famous ancestor and that

ancestor carried some deleterious recessive (known or unknown to the breeder) then the chances of puppies which carry a double dose of this recessive, and thus exhibit the problem, is increased. The same is true of more polygenic traits. For example, if the famous ancestor was poor in shoulder placement then inbreeding to that ancestor might increase the chances of poor shoulder placement in the puppies.

Thus, inbreeding should only be undertaken in very outstanding animals with few faults and, as far as one can tell, no major deleterious Mendelian features. However, even with this proviso there are still risks attached to inbreeding. Traits concerned with fitness (reproduction) which are low heritability but may be controlled by combinations of genes do have problems with inbreeding. Inbred dogs are, among other things, likely to be less fertile and give rise to smaller litters as a consequence, although this is not necessarily inevitable.

Inbreeding is something that should not be done lightly and dogs should preferably not be bred too closely. However the nature of some breeds means that breeders cannot avoid mating distantly related animals together because all members of the breed will have specific ancestors way back in their pedigrees. Boxers all trace back to Lustig v Dom, Bernese Mountain Dogs all go back to the Newfoundland Pluto v Erlengut and German Shepherd Dogs all go through Erich v Grafenwerth. These ancestors are unavoidable in all specimens of these breeds.

Most breeders will try to mate dogs that look alike — type to type mating. This is a sound policy but because dogs do have flaws it is important to try to avoid mating dogs that both have the same flaws. If a dog is too short in the foreleg then it should not be mated to an animal that is also short in foreleg. In this instance, there should be an attempt to use a longer-legged mate in the hope that this compensatory mating will give a more acceptable leg length in the progeny.

SELECTING A DOG

It is always exciting when the decision is made to bring a dog into the family. However, owning a dog is a major commitment and the reasons for wanting a dog, family needs and home environment must all be carefully evaluated before any decision is taken. Dog ownership is a responsibility for all members of the family.

Any family considering purchasing a dog should set aside a few hours to ask themselves the following twenty questions. With all family members present, many important issues will be raised, and the ensuing dialog will help to set realistic parameters for the future pet.

Questions for the Family to Consider

1. Has any family member owned a dog before?
2. Will someone be at home at all times?
3. Will the dog live in the house?
4. Will a fenced-in yard be provided?
5. Does any family member suffer from allergies to pets?
6. The initial cost of a dog is modest compared to its maintenance and care. Is the family able to meet the financial commitment?
7. Is the dog's size a consideration?
8. Is a vocal or quiet dog preferred?
9. Is any family member prepared to groom the dog's coat frequently?
10. What are the five essential traits this pet should possess?
11. Must this be a puppy and, if so, why?
12. If an adult dog is preferred, what are the age parameters: one year, two years?
13. Is the family familiar with an adult dog of the chosen breed?
14. Has a fancier been consulted about the breed's basic characteristics?
15. Has a veterinarian been consulted about the care and cost of a healthy dog?
16. Is there a preference for a male or female dog and, if so, why?
17. Is breeding the reason for owning a dog and, if so, will a responsible approach be taken toward this issue?
18. Is the pet to be neutered or spayed?
19. Will the animal be trained to be a good canine citizen?
20. Is there a true family commitment to taking care of the pet throughout all its years?

If the idea of owning a dog is still as appealing after considering these questions, then the size of responsibility will be understood. These issues should not be frightening nor diminish the pleasure of dog ownership but only increase awareness of the special bond that can be built between the dog and the family.

Finding Out About a Breed

The breed descriptions and photographs in this book will serve to whet the appetite once the decision to acquire a dog is made. It is important to find out as much as possible about the breed in question and to see the breed in real life. Local newspapers and pet stores are often sources of information on nearby dog shows, Obedience Trials or Performance Events. It is well worth spending time to attend some of these events. The more information gathered, the more educated a choice of breed will be.

The American Kennel Club (AKC) has overseen the production of videos in nearly all the AKC recognized breeds. Although they aim to teach prospective judges how to evaluate breeds by following the AKC's Standards, they also give information on a breed's origins and past and present uses, so the videos may be helpful for prospective owners. Color, coat type, how the breed performs its particular function, as well as information on its adaptability, temperament and special care requirements are also usually included. The videos are for sale direct to the public from the AKC (see page 487 for address) or they may be available through libraries. At the moment, the Canadian Kennel Club, British Kennel Club and Fédération Cynologique Internationale do not produce videos. However, the KC will provide members of the public on request with a list of breeders with puppies for sale.

DOGS VERSUS BITCHES

It is very important to consider whether the dog should be male or female. The male of almost every breed is just a little bolder, more independent and a little more active than the female. Many people like this attitude and will therefore opt for a male. Generally, females are a little sweeter, more dependent and less rambunctious. The female is also usually thought to be easier to housetrain, but this really depends on the attitude of the person who is in charge of the housetraining.

The female has twice yearly heat periods. At these times, she must be carefully protected from being bred inadvertently. In the case of pet dogs, the spaying of females and neutering of males is strongly recommended. Spaying females before their first season almost guarantees a life without the threat of mammary cancer. Neutering males early in life reduces their urges to mark territory by leg-lifting and to roam in search of mates. No purebred dogs may be shown in AKC conformation classes if they have been spayed or neutered; the KC does allow them to be exhibited.

SHOW PROSPECT OR PET?

Whether the puppy is to be a family pet or a show prospect is of course another vital consideration. Very few top-flight kennels will sell a very good show prospect to the first-time dog owner. Breeders spend many years perfecting a family of their favorite breed. So it is natural that they should want show prospects to go to buyers who have acquired an expertise in the raising, training and conditioning of well-adjusted, healthy dogs.

Pet and show prospects must be assured a safe place to live, preferably inside the buyer's house. The animal must also have a safe exercise area — a secure, well-fenced yard —

or long, regular walks on a leash. It will need training to become housetrained, to respond to simple obedience commands, to ride sensibly in a car, and to assume a place in its human family. A dog must be monitored every step of the way.

A show prospect, even with a short, "no care" coat, has certain requirements to look its best. Nutrition plays a large part in a glossy, gleaming coat, as does grooming and keeping the dog free of ticks, fleas, skin eruptions and diseases. Long-coated breeds will require frequent, intelligent brushing, grooming, washing and drying with a hair dryer. A grooming table, the correct brushes and knowledge of the correct brushing techniques are all essential. Several hours weekly must be spent on these grooming chores and although there are short cuts, none of these work in the long run. The trimmed breeds like the Poodle and most terriers, and very hairy breeds like the Old English Sheepdog, Briard and Bouvier des Flandres, require an even greater dedication to grooming — though for many it becomes a fascinating hobby. But this hobby does require week in, week out care. If the coat is allowed to become wet, dirty, matted or infested with fleas, then a whole year's work may be lost and will have to begin all over again.

Owning a show dog requires extra hours devoted to weekly grooming and conditioning.

ASK THE EXPERTS

Once the choice is narrowed as to breed, age and sex, friends who own dogs should be consulted for guidance, while local vets and commercial or boarding kennels should be able to provide lists of breeders. Healthy, well-bred dogs are rarely found in local pet stores, so it is wise to deal with an expert who knows a breed's background, and what it can and cannot provide. An expert can provide life-long guidance for both dog and owner. It is helpful to visit local shows (breed specialty shows are ideal) and to talk to breeders who are producing the type of dog that appeals. When they have finished showing, most breeders will be happy to discuss the availability of puppies and their experiences with the breed.

BREED CHARACTERISTIC

Every breed has certain inbred characteristics. Sporting dogs, such as spaniels and retrievers, enjoy outdoor activity, have keen ears and noses, are generally easy to train, and are comparatively healthy so long as they are well cared for and properly exercised. There are two groups of hounds: sighthounds, whose ability to hunt is primarily centered in extremely keen sight; and scenthounds, that use their noses in search and rescue or tracking tasks. Hounds are inclined to be independent and since they respond to the senses of sight or smell should be trained early to come on command.

Working dogs enjoy being useful, respond well to training, and in general make very good pets if they are well trained and have adequate space and exercise.

Giant breeds (such as the Great Dane, Newfoundland, Great Pyrenees and Saint Bernard) live shorter lives, require a larger expenditure for care and feeding, and should not be considered for apartments or small homes.

Terriers vary in size from the king of the terriers (the Airedale) to the Norfolk and Norwich breeds. They are active and bright, and tend to be long lived. They occur in many coat lengths and textures and many require a great deal of coat care. Toys have been bred to be pets. They are small in physical size but they do not seem to be aware of this. They are not the best choice for a young family with small children or a family in the planning.

Choosing a dog from the Non-sporting Group (called companion dogs in many countries) is like shopping in a department store. From the neat little Schipperke to the glamorous, bright Standard Poodle, there is something for everyone. Two new breeds in this group, the Chinese Shar-Pei and the Shiba Inu, have a small gene pool, can be expensive, and should only be purchased after much thought and investigation. Dogs in the Herding Group have helped farmers to maintain boundaries with flocks for centuries. They seem happiest when set a task, train comparatively easily, and like close interaction with their families.

BREED REGISTRATION

Many purebred dogs are not yet registered with the American Kennel Club or the English Kennel Club, while some breeds have their own registry. The Fédération Cynologique Internationale (FCI), which is the coordinating body used by most foreign countries in the world of purebred dogs, does not register dogs but its member countries run their own national registries. The FCI's list of breeds is considerably larger than that of the American, Canadian and English Kennel Clubs, and appears to be growing daily, with new breeds gaining recognition as more countries with native breeds become accepted.

The English Kennel Club recognizes 183 breeds or varieties of dog but not all have been registered or shown in sufficient numbers to warrant being awarded Challenge Certificates (CCs) and championship status. CCs are awarded to twenty-three Gun Dog (Sporting) breeds, twenty-nine Working breeds, twenty-three Terrier breeds, twenty-four Hound breeds, nineteen Toy breeds and twenty Utility (Non-Sporting) breeds. The Kennel Club treats the Dachshund as six different breeds but the

It is important to look at practical considerations before deciding to acquire any particular breed. For instance, giant breeds, such as the Saint Bernard, live shorter lives and require a larger expenditure for care and feeding.

Belgian Sheepdog as one when CCs are awarded.

Each registration body maintains carefully documented breeding records, provides services, and usually holds events of some sort to acquaint fanciers with these breeds. All have business offices, keep records and schedule events. In any country, breeders and fanciers can provide the addresses to prospective puppy buyers.

FINDING A DOG

It is essential not to rush into a purchase. A litter of puppies may not be available when needed. Or an older dog may not have appeared on the market. This does not mean that preparations cannot be made for the dog's arrival. The purchase of a portable kennel or crate will provide a haven for the new dog in the home and is a safe way of transporting it from its original home and to and from the vet. Holes should be plugged, fences repaired and if there is no fence, a portable barrier

should be on hand so that the dog will become accustomed to being enclosed. If a coated breed has been selected, the necessary grooming tools should be purchased. A family should decide in advance on words to be used in training the pup, who will be the source of correction, as well as who will care for a rapidly growing pup.

It may take weeks, months or a year to find the right dog. Owners should feel comfortable with the breeder, have access to pictures of the parents of the dog selected, and have some idea of its genetic make-up. The rarer the breed, the longer the probable waiting period.

WHEN TO BRING A NEW DOG HOME?

A well-socialized, correctly raised pup should go to its new home no later than ten weeks of age. By this time it will have had at least its first two immunization shots, will know its name, and will have some idea of being clean in its quarters. Mentally, at this stage, it should be unafraid, become quickly used to a car, be ready to bond to its owner and learn very quickly what is expected of it. After ten weeks, if the pup stays with its litter mates, it will be more dog oriented than people oriented — a disadvantage for a dog that is to be a pet. At ten weeks, positive show qualities cannot be guaranteed but a good breeder should be able to make a qualified statement as to the good points of a dog and its less positive aspects. Questions about teeth, mouth formation, growth and showmanship will have to wait until the pup matures.

If acquiring an older dog, care should be taken as to how it has been raised to date. A totally kennel-raised pup seldom makes the transition to a house well. A dog that has been house-raised, taught a few lessons and has a good disposition is worth considering. Occasionally an older female may become available. She may have put in her time, been shown and completed her championship, been bred and had two or three litters, and is now ready to be spayed and settled in a good home. Such a dog is a real find, as any such female will have learned much about life and will adjust comfortably into most situations.

The new pet should not be introduced to the home during times of stress or excitement. For example, if it is to be a Christmas present, the gift may be announced on Christmas Day but the puppy or dog should be brought home a week or so later when the household has resumed its normal routine. Too much excitement for any animal will only muddle it and make adjustment difficult. It needs a stress-free environment in which to settle down and adapt to a new regime in a sensible way.

Advice From Breeders

Each breeder should supply the new owner with instructions for care, a history of health problems, proof of testing and inoculations and a schedule for future immunizations. Good breeders will also give friendly, knowledgeable support from the day the dog is selected to the day the owner shares the dog's death with the breeder. The first three months will certainly require some interaction and caring breeders generally feel and act responsibly for each puppy they breed.

The Cost of a Dog

The initial cost of a dog is only a small part of what is to come. Care, feeding, training, vet's fees, medications, grooming and boarding are all factors that must be considered before the decision to purchase a dog is made. Always buy from a breeder with a good reputation.

Generally, breeders have different attitudes toward pricing. In Andrew Brace's experience, the best breeders are those who say, "My puppies cost this much and for this I am willing to sell you a typical, sound, healthy puppy with quality breeding. If the pup turns into a great show dog, that is a bonus, but I am not selling you any guarantees in that direction." Some breeders will price puppies in a litter on a sliding scale, with "show puppies" double what "pet puppies" cost, but in reality it is impossible to grade puppies like this and such breeders should be given a wide berth.

Buying a Show Dog

A top show dog can command almost any price, because it will have proved itself in the ring. This is especially true of a dog that is in the hands of a very wise breeder or a knowledgeable professional handler. Anyone who wants a show dog of this caliber will have to part with a sizeable amount of money, and in all probability will be unable to take the dog home. The dog will remain with a professional to further its career, and the owner will be left with bills for its board, training, grooming, vet fees, showing and advertising. The rewards for this are the pleasure of owning a fine animal, seeing its name in print and starting a collection of ribbons and trophies. When the star is retired, it may come to live with its owner, unless it is decided that it would be better for it to remain with the person with whom it has lived for the duration of its show career.

Buying a young prospect as a companion and show dog involves an element of risk and this is where a mentor of some sort can be extremely helpful. An expert with a good reputation can generally be found to advise, provided that money and time are no object. The most useful advice is to try to buy the best dog that can be afforded and to seek the advice of the best mentor available. Showing dogs is a fascinating sport but it can also be all-consuming and its rewards are very rarely financial ones.

In Andrew Brace's opinion, when selecting a puppy as a show dog, he would want to see it at between six and eight weeks of age. This is when the puppy looks like a miniature version of the mature adult. At this stage puppies have the proportions and balance that they will show later in life. Once they get beyond this age, they will grow disproportionately — lengthen in the back, appear higher at the rear than at the withers and so on — only to return to their former promise with full maturity. The puppies should be seen running together because far more can be deduced than if they are seen "stacked" singly on a table.

Essentially, it is important that a puppy should look like its breed even though it is a baby. Character and a strong personality should be visible. A puppy that catches the eye because it has a certain "swagger" is the one which will develop "style" as an adult. Most importantly, the puppy should simply catch the new owner's eye. If it does that, it will also be likely to catch a judge's eye later in life.

REGISTERED PUPPIES AND DOGS

Whether a dog can be registered with a kennel club depends on the country in which it is being registered. In the United States and Canada, all purebred dogs are eligible for registration if their parents are registered with the American Kennel Club or the Canadian Kennel Club. In these countries, when a dog is purchased, the seller must provide an application for registration. The new owner must complete the form stating whether full registration or a non-breeding, non-showing application is being applied for.

If the dog has already been registered, the

When selecting a puppy as a show dog it is best in some breeds to see it between six and eight weeks of age when the puppy looks like a miniature version of the mature adult. Pictured here is Ch. Potterdale Classic of Moonhill with her pup.

seller must endorse the back of the registration certificate to the new owner, who must send the form to the address indicated with the stated fee. The governing body will then register the dog in the new owner's name and send a certificate verifying this.

When the dog's name has been decided, the application has been completed and sent to the kennel club with the fee, in due course the dog will be registered in the new owner's name and a certificate will issued. A rule recently introduced in the United States requires that, in most cases, registrations must be complete by the time a dog is six months old.

Registration papers should be thoroughly discussed and explained at the time of purchase. All terms of the sale should be made clear to the new owner and proper documentation of the transaction should be provided. Any restrictions on breeding, arrangements allowing a dog to be shown, or anything that ties the purchaser and the seller to an agreement should be clearly documented. It is advisable to seek a legal opinion on the validity of the document. Both seller and buyer should keep a copy of the agreement. The breeder should supply a pedigree, showing the dog's family tree. If this is not forthcoming, for a fee the registering kennel club will supply a copy of this interesting document.

In the United Kingdom, registration must be within twelve months of the birth. The onus of registering a dog with the Kennel Club lies with the breeder. At the time of mating the bitch, the breeder must obtain an official Kennel Club form from the owner of the stud dog, which certifies that the mating took place on a certain date. Following the birth of a litter, this form must be completed by the breeder, specifying full details about the sire and dam, and the number, color and sex of the puppies. Puppies must be named at this stage by the breeder. In the past, buyers could register puppies that they had bought unregistered.

In FCI countries, registration demands vary from country to country and, under some registration bodies, certain health certificates must be held by the parents before registration is granted. These certificates document such things as hip dysplasia, progressive retinal atrophy and so on — and this all varies from breed to breed.

SELECTING A PUPPY

Buying a dog will probably affect the next ten years, so patience is well warranted. If there is any doubt about having found the right breeder or the right dog, the buyer should not feel pressured into making a purchase that feels wrong. Appointments with breeders should be made in advance and preferably limited to one a day. Buyers should not be surprised if they are asked endless questions. Any conscientious breeder will want to have a great amount of information about anyone keen to buy one of their puppies.

Young puppies are vulnerable and breeders may be reluctant to allow them to be handled out of concern for their health. It is helpful to watch the interaction between litter mates so that a puppy can be measured against the others. Each puppy has its own complex genetic make-up and personality and as they play it is easy to pick out the shy one, the bully, the one who asks to be looked at. Puppies

Each dog has its own personality and genetic make-up. A good way to size up a dog is to watch its interaction with its litter mates.

should be eager, outgoing, healthy and happy. The biggest mistake a buyer can make is to feel sorry for a weak-looking or nervous puppy and take it home. This will end in misery. It is important to take the time to observe the puppies and ask questions of the breeder who has watched them since their birth.

If feasible, the puppy should be seen along with its dam and its sire, though this may not be possible. It is important to check that the bitch has a sound temperament and is a good looking specimen — making allowances for the inevitable loss of condition following whelping.

New owners should take the puppy to the vet as soon as possible. The puppy should be transported in a carrier. Bring all the puppy's records. While the vet carries out the examination, take details of the vet's hours, staff, who to call in emergencies, and note any differences between the vet's and the breeder's recommendations on pet care. Once home, details of the visit to the vet should be reported by telephone to the breeder. If upon examination the vet detects a defect or problem that would render the puppy unfit for sale, the usual procedure is to return the puppy. The purchase price should be refunded.

BUYING AN OLDER DOG

When a dog of six months or older is being purchased, it will need more time to become part of the family. The adjustment will be easier if the dog's accustomed routine is followed. Management is extremely important for an older dog, which should not be left unattended for long periods of time. Even though the dog may appear to have bonded, a strange voice or a frightening sound may make it take off — and most dogs can outrun their owners.

LONG DISTANCE PURCHASES

There are times when a puppy or dog cannot be purchased locally. Then it will be necessary to resort to purchasing by phone or by mail. Clearly state your needs. Keep a record of what you have requested and of anything promised. When writing, be explicit and demand the same of the breeder who is selling. Most people have a mental picture of their ideal dog but the breeder may have a completely different picture. These days, many breeders use video cassettes to show their stock. If videos are not available, ask for pictures of both the mother and father and of the other puppies in the litter.

The new pup should be taken home on a flight or in a car but the travel arrangements should be comfortable. As soon as the puppy is home, it should be taken directly to the vet. Then the seller should be given a report.

Few breeders will ship puppies to strangers. In fact, Andrew Brace feels that if a puppy buyer cannot be bothered to collect a puppy personally then the buyer cannot be that keen to own it.

A WORD OF WARNING

There are a few miscellaneous cautions about purchasing a dog. First of all, never buy a dog as a surprise gift: it may not be welcome, in which case it is likely to be given away. Even if someone would definitely welcome such a present, selecting the dog or puppy should be a joint project. The person on the receiving end should be allowed to make the

Young children and dogs can become inseparable but care should be taken in supervision.

final decision. When buying a dog as a child's gift, the child should be allowed to make the choice within reason. It is usually wise to wait until the child is six before taking such a step. Younger children and dogs can become inseparable but supervision is needed to ensure proper care. It is advisable to wait until the child and pup have adjusted to each other and their initial excitement has calmed down before imposing any serious control.

Often a family is so taken with a puppy that they decide to own two, thinking that the pups will keep each other company. This is true to a degree but two dogs will never bond as intimately with an owner as will one dog. If two dogs sound tempting, remember that it is far better to own one well-raised dog and then to let the first dog raise the second one, acquired later, itself.

TAKING IN AN UNWANTED DOG

In modern society, many wonderful dogs end up in animal shelters. If you would like to provide a home for an unwanted dog, it is worth contacting and investigating a shelter. Good shelters will give an honest evaluation, spay or neuter dogs if required, and provide good care for animals. Few will be able to supply a complete history of each dog. Nonetheless, many truly fine pets may be found in humane shelters.

Patience, a desire to help a dreadful situation that is growing throughout the world, and a sincere love of dogs are several of the many reasons why pets might be selected from a shelter. Anyone who decides to choose a pet from a shelter should still seek the advice of a vet and abide by his or her evaluation of the chosen dog.

A DOG IS FOR LIFE

No matter how many dogs you will ever own, each is different. The choice of dog lies with you, its future owner, but once you have made the decision, it will be your friend for life. Enjoy the dog, treasure it and never let it down. It will never disappoint you.

HEALTH, GENERAL CARE AND FEEDING

Bringing a new puppy into the home requires careful preparation. Before a purchase is made, any owner must decide what to expect from the dog and why the dog is wanted. Responsibility for feeding, exercise, training and veterinary care should also be established well in advance.

SAFE AREAS FOR THE PUPPY

A comfortable shipping crate or box helps the puppy and human members of the household to live together in harmony — it also helps with housetraining. Any crate should be large enough for the dog when it is fully grown. This is a great way to give the pet a place to eat and sleep and provides a safe haven from service people and unruly children.

The puppy will also need an exercise area. An ideal arrangement is to erect double fencing that gives protection from teasing youngsters and any traffic noise. It also helps to prevent the puppy from barking excessively at outside distractions. A second fence will stop the puppy if it tries to escape, perhaps when a

A cardboard box is a perfect place for the newly acquired puppy. This Norfolk Terrier pup will eat, sleep and find a safe haven in its comfortably fitted-out box.

meter reader or others inadvertently leave an inner gate open. This type of fencing also insulates legitimate visitors from an angry dog guarding the home. An entrance from the inside yard into the house through a doggy door will allow the dog to exercise when it chooses while also enabling it to perform its duty as a watch dog.

THE EARLY DAYS AT HOME

When the puppy arrives in its new home depends a little on circumstances, but bitches usually wean litters between the ages of six and eight weeks. Owners find it difficult to raise anything younger. Animal behaviorists have learned that training at this early age has a favorable effect. For the first few days, excessive petting and handling by children should be limited.

Any puppy should only be purchased subject to a veterinarian's health examination — few legitimate breeders will object to this. The new puppy should visit the vet as soon as possible. He or she will determine its health status, test for parasites, and prepare an immunization schedule. The first visit is the time to ask about cost and any other relevant questions.

Most breeders recommend a feeding program for the puppies that they sell. Even if the diet seems unusual, it should be adhered to for a week or two. The new home thrusts many adjustments on a puppy and strange foods often trigger attacks of diarrhea.

TEETH, TOYS AND TRAINING

At three months of age, adult teeth will begin to erupt and push out a puppy's baby teeth. New owners should be prepared for it to chew on shoes, slippers, socks, furniture and anything handy. Giving a puppy its own well-designed toys will go some way to diverting its attention from expensive oriental carpets, antique chairs or other valuables. Toys should be chosen carefully, however.

Puppies should be introduced as soon as possible to a soft leather collar and a leash.

The new puppy should be introduced to a soft collar and leash as soon as possible — the collar will need to be changed frequently as the dog grows. It is important to start obedience training early and there are many helpful books on this subject. Once the owner has learned how to control the puppy on its leash and the puppy has completed the initial round of immunizations, it may be walked in safe areas where it can meet adults, children and other dogs. This form of socializing develops the puppy's confidence and prepares it for an environment inhabited mostly by humans.

Children with dogs can bring joy to parents but they can also create major problems. Growing up with a dog provides invaluable training for a child and caring for the pet teaches him or her responsibility. It is essential that children are taught that a pet is not a toy but a living being with feelings like their own. Most youngsters are not ready for a puppy until they reach about six years of age. If a dog is living with a couple before the birth of a first child, careful supervision of both the dog and new baby will be necessary. If breeding the house pet is purely to help to educate the children, owners should think seriously about

the fate of the puppies, and then probably abandon any ideas about breeding. Surgical sterilization is a reliable method of birth control in dogs. Both the American Veterinary Medical Association and the American Kennel Club endorse spaying and castration any time after eight months of age. A vet may recommend postponing surgery until later but it should be done before the female's first heat period.

DISEASE AND PREVENTION

A number of infectious diseases affect dogs and there are many vaccines that prevent them. There are also numerous ailments and other categories of disease of which the prudent owner should be aware. The study of genetic defects in dogs is now receiving much attention. As elimination of these problems from breeding stock becomes more feasible and a reality, it will ultimately lead to healthier and happier pets.

Vets have the academic training and experience in disease prevention to design immunization schedules for all dogs in the community. They may also recommend protection against other infectious diseases in addition to those described in Table 4 on page 30.

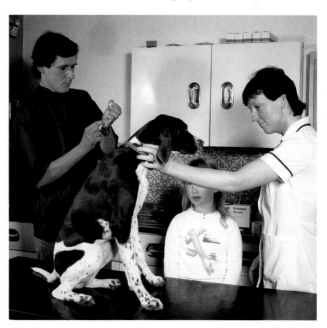

The vet can design an immunization program for any breed of dog and recommend protection against infectious diseases.

TABLE 4. DISEASES AND DISORDERS

DISEASE/ AILMENT	SYMPTOMS	CAUSE	CURE
Canine Distemper	Begins with signs of respiratory problems and can attack any system.	A virus passed between dogs.	Preventative vaccines exist and must be administered yearly; recovery is rare from virus that attacks nervous system.
Canine Hepatitis	Fever	Viral disease	Immunization
Fleas	Itching, irritated skin	Fleas live in dog's coat and cause irritation or allergies	Application of Insect Growth Control Regulators (IGR), non-toxic sterilizers kill adult fleas.
Gastric Torsion	Gas, bloat, attempted vomiting	Build up of gas that dilates and twists the stomach. Possible displacement of spleen and other organs.	Dogs with large stomach cavities are thought to be most prone. Monitor water intake, avoid feeding soy products, feed small meals, encourage rest after feeding. Prompt surgery required.
Heartworm Disease	Difficulty in breathing, swelling, collapse after slight exertion	Worms infect heart and major blood vessels causing Heartworm Disease. Infection commonly spread by mosquitos.	Larvicides are administered daily or once a month; should not be administered without a blood test.
Parvo or Corona Virus	Vomiting, fever, diarrhea	Inflammation of stomach or bowel (Gastroenteritis) caused by Parvo or Corona Virus.	Replace lost fluids, control nausea and diarrhea. Parvo Virus is usually fatal. Yearly vaccination can prevent Parvo. Contact with infected feces spreads infection so carefully control.
Tapeworm	Bad coat, weight loss	One type transmitted by fleas; another by rabbits.	Prevent dog from eating game. Treat with effective medication.
Ticks	Fever, nasal and eye discharge, loss of appetite	Ticks transmit infections such as Lyme Disease and Ehrlichiosis	After walks in areas that may be infected, check coat for ticks and remove them.
Whip, Hook, Round Worms (Ascarid)	Bad stools, thin coats (Whip Worms)	Worms get into dog's gut.	Regular stool examinations help to control as does removal of feces so dogs do not come into contact with it.

ACCIDENTS

Accidents do happen so all dog owners should ensure that exercise yards are kept free of rakes, sharp instruments and objects that dogs might swallow. In addition, when a dog is being walked on a leash, the owner should be wary of any loose dog that approaches. The best policy is to freeze until the stray's intentions can be determined.

All dog owners should prepare a first aid kit and keep it in an accessible place. The vet can suggest items that are appropriate for the dog and its environment.

Every summer, dogs locked up in hot automobiles die of heat strokes. Ambient temperatures may measure a pleasant 80°F/26°C but a lethal 140°F/60°C inside a vehicle. Heat stroke can also strike dogs inside and outdoors when exposed to direct sunlight. Dogs must always have access to plenty of fresh water.

If a dog is panting with its tongue lolling and seems restless, move it to a cooler spot. If possible, place an ice cube in its mouth and splash it with cold water. Rush it to the nearest vet unless these measures give immediate relief. These signs and a temperature over 104°F/40°C signal approaching heat stroke.

DENTAL CARE

Mouth infections can cause serious health problems and should be prevented. Daily care should begin on a routine basis when the puppy starts to teethe. Pet supply stores sell canine toothbrushes and paste – dogs object to those designed for humans. Owners should begin by rubbing the teeth and gums with a 2 x 2 inch/5 x 5 cm piece of gauze saturated with 3 percent hydrogen peroxide. If this does not work, play with the dog's mouth, massaging the gums and teeth with bare fingers. The gauze alone may then be introduced and finally, peroxide added.

As dogs mature, they require professional dental care. Ultrasound instruments and dental scalers will remove tartar before it can injure teeth and gums. An annual examination

Dental care is important for every dog and special canine toothbrushes and toothpaste help to make the job a little easier.

of the teeth and gums is adequate for most dogs, but older ones may require more frequent dental care. These measures will prevent serious complications.

EYE CARE

The eyes of healthy dogs rarely need attention, but may require periodic cleaning. If a dog gathers discharge at the edges of the lids on a windy day, its face should be washed with clean warm water. When the discharge is thick or causes discomfort, professional help should be sought without delay. Injury or a foreign body lodged behind the third eyelid can cause severe pain. This type of problem is compounded because a dog will usually scratch or rub its face.

Today, veterinary ophthalmologists are able to suture tears expertly and successfully remove thorns or splinters which become buried in the cornea. They also routinely remove cataracts and can even replace a lens with an artificial one.

CANCER

Cancer is as much a growing problem for canines as for humans. It is the owner's responsibility to recognize signs that indicate a need for precise diagnosis. The American Veterinary Medical Association publishes a useful brochure, *Cancer in Animals,* that lists common signs. Some member countries of the Fédération Cynologique Internationale also publish leaflets on diseases. Essentially, the common signs of cancer that alert owners should look out for in their dogs are:

1. Lumps or bumps that persist or grow
2. Sores that do not heal
3. Weight loss
4. Loss of appetite
5. Bleeding or discharge from any body opening
6. Offensive odor
7. Difficulty in eating or swallowing
8. Loss of stamina or a reluctance to exercise
9. Persistent lameness or stiffness
10. Difficulty in breathing, urinating, defecating

Other disorders can cause one or more of these signs but unless there is an obvious explanation, it is wise to get a professional opinion. Early diagnosis and treatment can save lives.

NUTRITION

Food quality and genetic background help to determine a dog's state of health and length of life. Many pet food companies offer a variety of preparations that will fit the needs and budgets of most people. However, interpreting advertising claims and label information can confuse even the best informed. A vet or breeder is probably the best informed source of advice about food or diet. The following information will also help owners to make a good choice of diet for their dogs.

There are seven basic ingredients which must be incorporated into a complete diet:

1. **Protein** must include ten essential amino acids that canine digestive systems can synthesize. Fish and meat contain high quality protein. Some dog foods include meat or meat by-products that contain bone, tendon, poultry heads, feet, necks and backs. These provide low-quality protein that is not easily digested.
2. **Fat** must contain all necessary fatty acids.
3. **Carbohydrates** (biscuit, dog meal, toast, crackers etc.) should provide much of the caloric requirement. Protein (from meat, eggs, fish, cheese and milk) and fat provide the rest.
4. **Vitamins** (supplements should be given to puppies, working dogs, show animals, stud dogs, pregnant and lactating bitches).
5. **Minerals**
6. **Fiber** provides no nutrients but its bulk helps to regulate healthy bowel movements. Nutritionists suggest that beet pulp, a waste product of the sugar industry, is an ideal source of fiber. It is popular in weight-reducing diets because it provides no calories. A healthy dog's food should include about 4 percent fiber.
7. **Water**, although the last on this list, is most important.

Manufacturers cannot sell foods that dogs refuse to eat. Tests have shown that canines prefer a formula with additional salt, fat and protein. Vets advise a minimum of these ingredients for dogs suffering from cardiovascular and kidney disease. Experts recommend that most humans should limit these substances in their own diet but no one has yet proven that excesses harm healthy animals.

PUPPY DIETS

Most puppies will begin to taste their mother's food at five weeks of age when they begin to explore outside the whelping box. Weaning usually begins in earnest at five weeks of age and reaches completion at six to eight weeks. Growing dogs require greater quantities of key ingredients. Good commercial puppy diets offer easily digested protein that includes the ten essential amino acids. The food should contain about 26 percent crude protein.

Many breeders prefer homemade weaning

diets. These should include a quality animal source protein; a soft, cooked cereal; vegetable oil; and a vitamin mineral supplement. Puppies will eat these preparations if they are moist, well cooked and warm. Sometimes the only way to introduce a puppy to its new diet is by placing a bit of food in its mouth.

Puppies should be given plenty of clean water. Nutritionists do not recommend milk after weaning. Breeders usually keep puppies on the special formula for about two weeks and then change to a commercial puppy food.

Most good, commercially prepared food will have an analysis of its content and recommended quantities to feed on the container label. This information should be used as a guide. Keeping a chart of an animal's daily intake of food and measuring its weight regularly is a good way to keep a reliable report on progress. The amount of food provided may have to be adjusted to avoid obesity. Any unexplained loss in weight may either indicate sickness or the need for more food.

An Adult Dog's Diet

Adult maintenance diets contain approximately 16 percent crude protein and usually contain less carbohydrate and fat. Active dogs need more calories. Others often like the easy life and prefer eating to exercise. They should receive maintenance or reducing diets.

As dogs age, maintaining a good balance between exercise and diet becomes more important. Obesity decreases a dog's life expectancy and makes its life less enjoyable. A sensible exercise program and controlled food intake help to control a pet's weight. Weight-reducing diets on the market provide balanced nutrition, more fiber and lower energy content.

Hard working dogs, those used for hunting, police duty and exhibition in dog shows, require food with high levels of protein and energy. Manufacturers prepare diets for them with 30 percent crude protein and more high-calorie fat. Some handlers and owners supplement these with a good canned meat product or fresh meat.

A good balance between diet and exercise should be maintained as dogs age.

Diet in Aging Dogs

A dog's nutritional needs change as it ages. It exercises less and requires fewer calories. Most dogs over five years old experience some loss of renal and cardiac function. Authorities believe that diets containing adequate but not excessive amounts of protein, phosphorous and sodium slow the progression of renal and cardiac failure. The limited amount of protein must include readily digestible, essential amino acids that are found in a balanced diet. It is wise to consult the vet to ensure that the older dog is getting all it needs from its food.

Obesity increases handicaps in the aged dog. Weak muscles, creaking joints and an inability to cope with the added load lead to inactivity and more weight gain. Aging dogs need a minimum amount of easily digested fat that includes adequate amounts of necessary fatty acids. Fat is high in calories. Fiber contains no calories but older animals have less efficient digestive tracts and so should receive moderate amounts.

Food companies offer special diets for elderly dogs but some owners believe that it is possible to provide more quality for less money with home-prepared diets. A vet can help to insure that the recipe includes proper proportions of essential ingredients. Weighing the dog regularly helps to prevent obesity. If the aging dog is ever fed "treats" between meals, these additional calories should be included when calculating daily intake. Older dogs get set in their ways and resent abrupt changes, so their diet and exercise routines should be adjusted with caution.

DEVELOPMENTS IN OLD AGE

As a dog ages it experiences a partial loss of vision, hearing, taste and some sense of smell. The family's response to a pet's altered behavior is as important as a correct diet. A handicapped dog should always be protected when it is away from home or outside a fenced yard, and only taken out when leashed.

Small children should be taught to approach an aging pet cautiously because a blind, deaf dog might bite if startled. Also, if the position of furniture is changed, the dog should be introduced to the new arrangement. A veteran is best confined to its crate or kept out of the way when visitors who are unfamiliar with dogs are being entertained.

HEALTH PROBLEMS

A toothache or inflammation of the ear can make any dog feel under par. An aging dog's mouth should be regularly inspected and dental care provided when needed. A dog with toothache may mouth its food, drop it back into the pan and paw at its lips. Most owners will recognize dogs with an aching ear — the animal will hold the bad ear down and scratch at it. Inspection under the ear flap will frequently reveal a foul odor, discharge or swelling, and the vet should be consulted.

Aged dogs may suffer from incontinence — the inability to retain urine. Also, excessive thirst associated with kidney disease can cause lack of control. Often the sphincter muscles that regulate the passage of urine from the bladder grow weak and can result in bed wetting. The vet may find a correctable cause.

If therapy does not solve the problem, the dog should be exercised outdoors frequently. When inside, it should be confined to rooms with easily cleaned floors. Pet stores stock beds with washable, waterproof covers that protect sensitive elbows and hocks from hard surfaces.

Some people have an amazing amount of tolerance for an old dog that dribbles urine in the house. Others find the situation unacceptable. An old dog who has lost control suffers from shame and punishment is inappropriate. Four-legged companions need as much help in adjusting to retirement and old age as people. They appreciate generous applications of tender, loving care and attention.

COPING WITH LOSS

The term euthanasia comes from the Greek word meaning "easy death." Members of the veterinary profession pledge to prevent pain and suffering in animals, not to terminate lives. However, sometimes the latter is the only way to prevent the former. Seeing a beloved pet finally at peace and completely free of pain can offer comfort to members of the family.

The human/companion animal bond has developed over thousands of years. Only in the last twenty or thirty years have psychologists tried to help people to cope with the loss of a cherished pet. They describe four different stages of bereavement: denial, anger, grief and resolution.

Professional help is available in many communities but some mourners prefer to go it alone. They find solace in silent contemplation and often in volunteer work for humane or animal welfare organizations. Psychologists agree unanimously on one aspect: it is healthy and normal to grieve. When nothing else helps, it may be best to go for a walk in the park or sit alone on a bench. Owners should try to reflect on all the good times that they have enjoyed with their wonderful companion, and to remember that there is nothing wrong with shedding tears.

BREEDING

The first question that potential breeders should consider is "Why breed?" There are many unwanted dogs, including purebreds, that end up homeless or in shelters. No one should breed just so that their children can witness the miracle of birth, or to have a pup from a favorite pet.

POINTS TO CONSIDER

The only valid reason for allowing a male or female to reproduce should be to further the enhancement of the breed. A purebred should be evaluated for its worth and value as a producer by a professional — either a breeder or a handler/trainer or judge. The animal in question must be evaluated against the breed's Standard, with emphasis on temperament and absence of serious or disqualifying factors. Next, a three-generation pedigree should be analyzed to determine the quality of the animal's ancestors with type, temperament and health the key considerations.

The third very important part of this decision concerns health, age and testing for heritable

When considering whether to breed your purebred, an evaluation by a professional - a breeder, handler or judge - is of the utmost importance. This judge sizes up a Manchester Terrier at the Windsor Show held annually in the United Kingdom.

defects. Generally, a bitch under the age of eighteen months should not be bred — and ideally should be at least two years old. Any bitch over the age of six should not be bred for the first time unless there are extenuating circumstances. The risk of loss is too great, and the birthing process too painful and traumatic to an older bitch, particularly if she has been a family pet.

CHECKING FOR HERITABLE DEFECTS

X-raying for hip problems in almost all breeds is a necessity. This cannot be done for certification until the age of two years. The patella and elbows may also be certified at this stage. Eye examinations for progressive retinal atrophy, cataracts and narrow or non-existent optic nerves should be done early. Blood testing for Von Willebrand's disease (a bleeding disorder) should be done periodically. Skin punch testing for sebaceous adenitis is another annual procedure. A breeder or vet will be able to advise about other heritable problems that are breed specific. No dogs with apparent epilepsy, large umbilical hernias, inverted eyelids, skin disorders or temperament problems of any sort should be bred.

A BREEDER'S RESPONSIBILITIES

It is essential that the potential breeder carries out all the above checks, is fully aware of what is involved and plans the breeding carefully. It is also most important to remember that breeding is not a money-making venture. Most breeders are lucky if they manage to break even on a litter. The dangers in breeding a bitch should also not be forgotten. She may die during whelping or in a Caesarean section. Similarly, males after being used at stud may be less clean in house manners than before.

FINANCIAL IMPLICATIONS

In addition to paying for the tests for heritable problems, for a complete physical examination of the bitch and bringing all inoculations up to date, there are other costs which should be taken into account. There is the expenditure involved when taking or shipping the bitch to the chosen stud dog or, in the case of using cooled semen, the cost of obtaining semen from the dog, the shipment of the sperm, and the implantation by the vet.

A stud fee must also be paid at the time the bitch is bred or at a later date, if specified in the breeding contract. If the stud fee involves the choice of the litter being returned to the owner of the stud dog, the bitch's owner is responsible for all the expenses incurred by this puppy (physical examinations, inoculations, wormings and so on) until the puppy is delivered. Many behaviorists and writers advise that a puppy should be placed in its new home by the age of seven weeks, but this is up to the breeder. Some wait until the puppy is older and well socialized before selling.

The bitch also incurs further expense. She must be taken to the vet after breeding to be palpated at about three or four weeks or to have a sonogram to ensure that she is indeed in whelp. Special food is required as well. If problems arise with the whelping, emergency vet fees, possibly including the charge for a Caesarean section, will have to be met.

The new mother and her puppies must be seen by the vet within twenty-four hours of the birth. The vet will examine for heritable defects such as cleft palate, hernias and so on. After the birth, the mother should be given a shot of oxytocin to clear the birth canal and uterus of placental residue, retained after-births or even a reluctant puppy. This is best administered by the vet since it is an intramuscular injection with some risk involved.

At five days, puppies must have their dewclaws and tails dealt with, if part of the breed Standard, thus incurring yet another vet's fee. Worm checks on the puppies, and required inoculations should start ten days to two weeks after they are weaned. This all involves quite a large outlay of money, plus a great deal of time. Not to breed may often be the best choice.

KEEPING RECORDS

It is important for breeders to keep records. In the United States it is a requirement of the American Kennel Club. Breeding dates, complete identification of the dog bred to, its owner's name and address, the litter birth date, the sexes of the puppies, when and to whom the puppies were sold, and the dates when the registration papers were transferred are all part of correct record keeping. The person who has bred the litter should be prepared to accept total responsibility for the puppies. This means being willing to take them back and find new homes if the original homes do not work out.

REASONS FOR BREEDING

Of course, the show ring is not the only reason to be interested in breeding dogs. The Standard of perfection as set down for every breed is not based on beauty but on designing an animal that can function best at what it was designed to do. Breeds vary tremendously. There are the magnificent bird hunters, pointers, setters, spaniels — whose attitude, temperament, wonderful legs, angulation, feet, hard toplines, good mouths and keenness enable them to hunt for hours. There are also breeds like the Pekingese. With its expressive

The Bloodhound, a scent-trailing hound, is designed so that the luxuriant wrinkles about its head and neck entrap the scent of the target.

face, glamorous coat and fringes and its short legs, it fits the bill as a child substitute in looks, while its short legs prevent it from straying too far. The Obedience ring is a proving ground, with tests to establish mental ability, stamina and soundness in jumping and retrieving. There are dogs that compete in Agility, guard and herding dogs, police workers, drug sniffers, search and rescue dogs and therapy dogs – all these types benefit from correct breeding practices.

BREED STANDARDS

It is the responsibility of the parent club of each breed, or of the Kennel Club itself, to write, up-date and clarify the relevant Standard. Also the Standards can differ from country to country. Very early dog enthusiasts may not have had insights about genetic problems but they were certainly animal people. The Standards that they therefore originally conceived were written to convey in words the description of a perfect specimen, which was well suited in conformation as well as in coat, color and temperament to perform the tasks for which it was bred.

The balance and symmetry of the Pointer, when it is covering the ground with its tail held high and nostrils flared, make it the aristocrat of all Sporting dogs.

The breed Standards were written to describe a perfect specimen. This Afghan Hound, a Cruft's Best in Show winner, comes close to the description in the American Standard calling for, "An aristocrat, his whole appearance one of dignity and aloofness...."

FINDING THE PERFECT STUD

Once a potential breeder has decided that he or she can afford the time and money to breed, the right mate for the bitch must be found. The first step is to contact the breeder who supplied the bitch. In all probability, he or she will be interested. Contacting the national breed club of the breed in question is also a good first step. Usually, a letter of inquiry to the breed club will generate a list of local club members who may prove helpful in the search.

Another course of action is to visit dog shows. These will be attended by interested, knowledgeable people. With persistence, it is usually possible to find someone who will allow his or her dog to be used for breeding, but the reasons given for not breeding should always be carefully weighed. Anyone who does enter into an agreement should always make sure that everything is in writing.

CHOOSING A STUD DOG

The breeder is entitled to extensive information about the potential stud dog. The stud dog must undergo the same testing as the bitch.

Choosing a stud dog is both a visual and

Dog shows, attended by interested and knowledgeable people, are good places to search for the perfect mate for your dog. The Montgomery County Kennel Club show is held annually in the United States.

mental process. Some breeders rely on looks alone while others are swayed by a strict analysis of the pedigree. The most consistently successful choices are made by balancing all the factors and considering all the information to hand. The breeder must have both a correct mental picture of the breed and the ability to be a visionary with the will to improve. Breeders need to acquire important scientific knowledge to help with their decisions. If the bitch is a maiden, it is best to breed her with an experienced stud. A proven brood bitch may be bred to a young inexperienced dog.

TYPES OF BREEDING

There are three basic ways to select a breeding partner and which type is chosen will largely depend on the individual breeder's commitment and enthusiasm for the job to hand. The three are known as outcrossing, linebreeding and inbreeding.

OUTBREEDING

This method involves breeding to an unrelated animal of the same breed. It is of course based on the visual physical attributes of the animals involved as well as their compatibility. But this is not a balancing act. A small bitch to a large dog will not necessarily result in all the off-spring being medium sized. With a small bitch, the best result is most likely to come from

breeding to a male that is the correct breed Standard size. It is always wise to investigate what the male has produced before — whether it has proved dominant and strong in producing its correct size.

LINE BREEDING

The second way to select a partner is to breed the most perfect specimen possible, which has the same exceptional common ancestor in the first three generations. This is the route that most successful breeders take. The reason this works is that all factors are taken into consideration: conformation, temperament and health matters. A well-known and successful family of any breed is known for its strengths and its weaknesses. It is obviously not clever to reintroduce to a family a dog that shows signs of the family's faults such as poor feet, light eyes, a poor coat or an incorrect croup and tail set. Breeders should aim to consolidate a family's strengths — temperament, intelligence, correct size, and longevity.

INBREEDING

The third method is inbreeding — breeding father to daughter, brother to sister or mother to son. This type of selection naturally played an important part in the formation of different breeds but responsibility increases dramatically. Close inbreeding has been used to uncover the hidden or recessive genes in a family i.e., light eyes, incorrect placement of teeth, incorrect coats, bad temperament. The resulting litter should be carefully evaluated. If the results are poor, those puppies that have good dispositions and are healthy should be neutered and allowed to go to homes as pets. The remainder should be humanely destroyed. This type of breeding is obviously not for the uneducated breeder, the fainthearted or those with limited resources.

PREPARATIONS

The next step is to draw up a contract. A contract and breeding agreement should state the names of the couple to be bred, as well as those of their respective sire and dam. It should also include the names of the owners of both bitch and dog, their addresses and phone numbers, the names of the handler and of the witness to the breeding, the dates of the breeding, the stud fee and payment date, or whether a choice of litter puppy is to be taken in lieu of the fee. A complete list of charges should include handling the breeding, the board of the bitch, any charge for trips to the airport for shipping and returning, any vet's fees involved, the number of puppies that constitutes a live litter, whether there will be a return service if the bitch does not whelp or if none of the puppies survive the whelping. The contract should be drawn up in duplicate and signed by both parties.

Next, a vet must give the bitch a complete physical examination and medical evaluation. About two to three months (and no later than one month) before she is due in season, steps should be taken to prepare the bitch for breeding. Checks should be made for both internal and external parasites and if found, should be eliminated.

One month before her cycle, the vet should give the bitch boosters to her immunizations as this will help to protect the whelps from disease. The bitch must also have a test for brucellosis (an almost incurable, infectious disease spread by sexual secretions that causes spontaneous abortions) and be cleared for any specific breed health problems (hip dysplasia, eye defects etc.). These tests should include screening for genetic disease in the systems including orthopedics, eyes, cardio-vascular (for heart and lung disease), neuro-logical, skin and temperament. The maiden bitch should be examined for vaginal strictures that might restrict copulation.

The stud dog must also have testing for communicable diseases, and have the quality and quantity of its sperm tested. Like the bitch, it must be tested for the genetic diseases.

Most bitches cycle or come into heat twice a year, often in the spring and fall. The Basenji is an exception coming into heat only once a year in the fall. The Toys and smaller breeds have their first cycle at about eight months of age, while the larger breeds usually start later — even up to fourteen or fifteen months. It is not advisable to breed a young bitch at her first season but better to wait until the second when she will be more physically mature. The lining of the uterus becomes a little thicker with each addditional season making it slightly more difficult for the bitch to conceive. Breeding a bitch for the first time when she is healthy and best able to carry her young is preferable to waiting until she is four or five years old.

ANATOMY AND PHYSIOLOGY

The dog's major reproductive organs are external — the testes and the penis. These are connected by ducts inside the abdomen. The two testes are located in the scrotum, a divided pouch of skin that lies between the thighs. The testes are responsible for producing sperm and secreting testosterone, the hormone responsible for male sex characteristics. Nature has arranged them outside the body to keep the sperm cool — it does not tolerate body temperature for long. The penis is enclosed by a sheath of skin (known as the sheath or prepuce), and is composed of soft erectile tissue and a small central bone. At the base of the penis is an area called the bulbous glandis. This quickly swells into a large, hard mound when the penis engorges and becomes rigid. This, together with a constrictive, muscular ridge at the opening of the bitch's vulva, is responsible for the interlocking of the two animals during copulation — known as a "tie."

Except for the mammary glands and the vulva, the bitch's major reproductive organs are internal. They are comprised of a pair of ovaries and fallopian tubes, plus the uterus, cervix and vagina. The two ovaries lie behind the kidneys at about the last rib. The ovaries produce the eggs (or ova) and also the hormones responsible for the female sex characteristics. Each ovary is enclosed by a tiny fallopian tube that connects the ovary to the upper end of a uterine tube. The uterus is bi-horned or Y-shaped above the short, main body, and it is in each "horn" that the embryo will develop. The mouth of the uterus or cervix is tightly closed except when the bitch is in heat or in the act of whelping. The cervix opens into the vagina which ends externally in the vulva. This is made up of erectile tissue which swells and softens during heat or estrus, thus facilitating the act of breeding.

THE FEMALE CYCLE

There are four stages in the bitch's reproductive cycle: proestrus, estrus, diestrus and anestrus. The cycle begins with the proestrus — a time when the vulva begins to swell and the start of a bloody discharge may be seen. This stage can last from as few as three days to as many as eighteen, with the average being about nine days. The bloody discharge comes from the congestion and discharge of the mucous membrane lining of the uterus, the endometrium. As this point the uterus is preparing to accept eggs. At the end of proestrus, the bitch goes into a standing stage that generally lasts about nine days but again may vary from three days to three weeks. It is during this period that the bitch will accept the dog and fertilization may take place.

Some bitches continue with a bloody discharge but the majority have a diminished discharge and the color lightens gradually from red to a straw color when the bitch is ready to breed. The vulva continues to swell and also becomes soft. It is now that the bitch will become flirtatious and will stand for the dog to mount — hence the term "standing heat." The bitch will usually flag at this time — pulling her tail up and off to the side away from the vulva. She will do this as a response to the mounting action of the dog or even when touched or rubbed at the base of the tail.

Ovulation is most likely to occur somewhere between the tenth and fourteenth day of the cycle, and this is when most successful breedings take place. However, these time scales are all averages and may not necessarily be the "normal" time frame for an individual bitch.

The diestrus stage in the cycle is approximately sixty days after the estrus, when the bitch will usually refuse a dog. The anestrus is the period of sexual inactivity which leads up to the proestrus.

All of this activity revolves around the secretion of the female hormones by the ovaries. The level of estrogen, which initiates the proestrus period, generally starts about one month before and gradually rises, peaks, and then falls just below proestrus. At that time, the progesterone (the hormones required for maintaining pregnancy) starts to rise, peaks and stays at a higher level until either labor or a false pregnancy develop. The level of luteinizing hormone (known as LH) suddenly surges when the estrogen level falls and the progesterone level rises, and it is this surge that stimulates the ovaries to release their eggs. Two to three days after the stimulation, the eggs are released and travel through the fallopian tubes to the uterus. They then take another two or three days to mature and become ready for possible fertilization by the millions of sperm that swim around and brush against each ovum after the coupling has taken place. Once a sperm has entered a mature egg and it has its full set of chromosomes, no other sperm can enter that egg. However, there are still plenty of other eggs left which might become fertilized by different sperm.

One or two breedings to the stud does not mean that all fertilization has indeed taken place, so the breeder must not allow the bitch into contact with other males until well into her diestrus when she will definitely reject all dogs. If in the interim she mates by accident with a second dog, none of the offspring will be eligible for registration because there is no way to identify the sire of each whelp. It is possible for a bitch to be fertilized by a number of dogs during one season.

The simplest way to find the right breeding date is to allow dogs to mate at their natural calling time. Another is to analyze slides prepared from the lining of the vagina.

Hormonal action precipitates changes in the appearance and condition of the epithelial cells in the vagina but, to be accurate to any degree, it is essential to have a series of slides that run from the latter part of the proestrus on into estrus. Some vets are able to determine the best breeding time through vaginal inspections. Also, simple blood tests (progesterone assays) determine when a bitch has ovulated by charting the sudden rise in the progesterone level (coinciding with the LH surge) or whether or not she is maintaining a high enough level to sustain pregnancy.

COPULATION

Normally when the actual breeding takes place the bitch is sent to the dog. The animals should not be fed or heavily watered before mating. When brought into the room with the bitch, the experienced stud knows exactly when and what to do. If by chance he should drop to the floor and show no interest, it is probably because she has caught his eye and said something like, "OK, Big Boy, one step closer and I'll bite your head off!" It is probable that the animals know more about the timing than the humans involved.

There should be at least three people present to assist with the mating: one to control the bitch, which should always be muzzled; one to assist the dog; a third person for general help or emergencies. The person who assists the dog must be known to the animal and the dog should be trained to accept help, usually by having the helper manipulate the vulva and getting the dog "on target." If a lubricant is to be used to facilitate the breeding, it should obviously not be a spermicide.

With an inexperienced or young dog, a short time may be allowed for flirting. The dog mounts the bitch from the rear and positions himself high on the back and starts slow, probing thrusts. When he has found the entrance, he begins thrusting more rapidly and treads with his back feet. Usually this is accompanied by a much stronger thrust, or even a jump, at which time, the penis is pushed entirely inside the vagina. The bulbous glandis swells quickly, locking the two in the act. The dog will stop thrusting at this point and will ejaculate.

As the tie can last from as short as a few to more than twenty or thirty minutes, the breeding pair should be controlled. Soon after the tie the dog will probably try to turn himself by lifting one leg over the bitch's back, leaving them with their rears facing each other. It is perfectly acceptable to help the dog to turn. This is nature's way of giving the animals protection while they cannot separate.

The bitch should be supported at all times so that she cannot sit down and injure the stud. Small dogs can be bred on a table, if they are accustomed to standing in this way, while medium to large-sized dogs are usually bred on the ground or floor. If there is a height discrepancy, rolled-up rugs, mats or towels or even risers or boxes may be used under the shorter animal. The footing should be secure and not slippery, so that the dog has good traction. While they are tied, mating dogs should *never* be forcibly separated. This could cause severe injury and it could wreck the stud's career.

AFTER THE COUPLING

Seminal fluid is made up of three fractions — the first helps to lubricate and contains some sperm, the second is rich with sperm and the third also contains sperm but mainly acts as a life support and swimming medium for the sperm. Sperm are probably only effective during the first twenty-four to thirty-six hours.

After the tie is broken, one of the attendants should monitor the stud and make sure that the penis slips back into the sheath correctly. Occasionally it is too enlarged. Cold, damp or wet towels should be placed around it so that the mucous membrane does not dry out. Sometimes the sheath or prepuce will turn inward and catch as the penis is returning to the sheath. This can be very painful for the dog in future breeding. Care should always be taken that the penis is not injured while it is engorged as consequent bleeding would be profuse and even life threatening. Similarly, while the breeding process is not a completely sterile acitivity, any human intervention should be as clean or sterile as possible. After breeding the dog should be returned to his box and allowed to calm down.

Sometimes the bulbous glandis swells before the tie is complete. If the manipulator is quick enough the dogs can be held together tightly until the ejaculation is finished. In that case the bitch's hindquarters should be raised and held up for at least ten minutes giving the sperm time to start their journey. At this time, a gloved finger inserted in the vagina will stimulate the bitch to have a series of contractions further aiding the seminal fluid on its way.

ARTIFICIAL INSEMINATION

If the natural act does not work out, the vet can artificially inseminate the bitch. With both animals present, the ejaculate is collected by the vet with special equipment. The vet collects the fluid and with special tubes deposits the sperm in the bitch near the cervix.

If it is impossible for the bitch and stud to be together then modern science has made it possible for a vet to breed dogs using chilled or frozen semen. With the help of overnight shipping systems, semen can now be flown worldwide. Frozen semen is viable twenty years after the collection and freezing period. Each year a new record is being set for increasing lengths of potency. Before these methods are employed, breeders should check with the ruling kennel club as to what is allowed and how to keep proper records. Some kennel clubs do not yet allow this type of breeding.

WATCHING FOR WHELPING

The average time for a bitch to whelp is nine weeks (sixty-three days). The exact time can be fairly accurately determined by keeping running vaginal smears and to note the date that diestrus started. Whelping should occur fifty-seven days after this, based on the fact that ovulation usually occurs six days before diestrus begins.

There are several ways to determine whether the bitch is in whelp. The first is by watching for behavioral symptoms. It is possible that the bitch will develop symptoms of morning sickness between the third and fourth weeks. She may go off her food for a while. This can be a fairly reliable indication of pregnancy. Some believe that this nausea and occasional vomiting is caused by a hormonal release of encysted worms in the body tissue and the migration of these through the blood stream.

Another sign is when a mucous plug develops in the vagina or by palpation of the abdomen. Palpation should be done on about the twenty-eighth day of the supposed pregnancy. Only a vet should carry out the procedure as fetuses can be injured if it is done incorrectly.

Ultrasound is another reliable option. Ultrasound can provide early confirmation of a pregnancy and has no known effects on the fetus. Like all the other pregnancy-testing options, it is not a reliable way to establish when the bitch will actually give birth.

The fourth method involves radiography. Early use of this could cause damage to a fetus, although, in theory, it is safer late in the pregnancy (after the forty-second day). X-rays are particularly helpful in revealing possible delivery problems and to check after whelping that there are no late arrivals or whelps left unborn.

DIET IN PREGNANCY

After it has been established that the bitch is pregnant, her food should be increased gradually to twice the normal amount. All this time she should be fed a high-quality puppy food. Avoid giving the pregnant bitch medications if possible, with the exception of heartworm medication which should not be stopped. The vet should have the final word about what should or should not be administered.

As the gestation period advances and the bitch becomes heavier, it is wise to split her meals into smaller ones provided more often, to make her feel comfortable. The bitch needs moderate exercise at this time, but she should be prevented from jumping. If she must be

A pregnant West Highland White Terrier. When it has been established that a bitch is in whelp, special attention should be given to her diet.

a normal pregnancy is sixty-three days to term, a pregnancy of fifty-nine days is not unusual.

USEFUL EQUIPMENT

When it is certain that the bitch is carrying pups, the breeder should begin preparing. The first thing is to prepare a whelping box and plan the best place to locate it. Ideally, it should be put in a quiet, draft-free and warm place, conveniently located to be well supervised. It should also be somewhere that offers a few human comforts too, as someone will be spending many hours nearby. The chosen spot must be large enough for a box that will allow both the bitch and whelps to move around and must have space for human intervention.

Whelping boxes can be bought ready made but it is not difficult to construct one. It must have a removable pig-rail. This is a railing that runs around the interior of the whelping box. This will provide a safe place for the newborn so that the mother cannot inadvertently press them against the sides of the whelping box. The sides should be high enough to contain the pups and protect against drafts and yet be low enough to allow the bitch to escape from the puppies from time to time. Newspaper can be used in the box when the bitch is whelping and for a day or so afterwards, while she still has a heavier discharge. In time the paper should be replaced with flooring that gives better traction to the pups while they nurse, crawl around and eventually start to walk. A piece of plywood with a large towel or bed pad wrapped around it is a perfect solution. The bitch will try to scratch up the towel but the plywood will hold it down and she will soon give up.

SOURCES OF HEAT

Whelps need an environment of around 85°F/ 30°C or even as high as 90°F/32°C because they are unable to maintain their own body heat until they are about seven to ten days old so a heat source should be arranged. One possibility is an infra-red heat lamp with a reflector. If a heat lamp is used, great care must be taken to

lifted, her abdomen should be supported without hands or fingers digging into her sides. Longhaired breeds should be trimmed and bathed earlier than scheduled.

As early as possible, plans should be made for a possible Caesarean birth in brachycephalic and some Toy breeds, where the head is often too large to pass though the birth canal. Any breed that has been developed into an abnormal size or shape can easily run into problems in delivery and all care should be taken to protect the bitch. Advance planning is the first step. The bitch should be checked daily for any signs of vaginal discharge which could indicate an impending problem. A close watch should also be kept for any abnormal behavior that indicates illness of any sort. The breeder should also keep a count of the days because, although

This Golden Retriever litter enjoys the pleasure of their whelping box with its roomy size, pig-rail for protection, soft and grippable flooring and heating lamp.

delivering, when the whelping box is being cleaned or while traveling to the vet's is very useful. A "birthing kit" should be prepared and contain scissors, a hemostat, cotton thread, dental floss, a clock, a notebook and pen, an ear syringe, sterile gloves, an eye dropper, a rectal thermometer, milk replacer, a nursing kit, absorbent cotton, hydrogen peroxide (3 percent), alcohol, feeding tubes, petroleum jelly, the vet's phone number and Pedialyte. Pedialyte is the brand name for a liquid used to supply water and electrolytes to young animals with diarrhea.

WHELPING

One week before the bitch is due to whelp it is wise to take her to the whelping box so that she can establish residence and become familiar with it. At this time, she should be cleaned up by scissoring or clipping off long hair around the vulva and around the teats. It is also important to keep an eye on her outdoor activities. As a dog is naturally a den animal, she may be secretly building her own house underground or in a corner out of the way. The bitch should be encouraged to nest, but only in the clean whelping box, padded with newspaper that she can shred to her heart's content.

The bitch's temperature should also be monitored twice a day as she approaches whelping. If her temperature rises above 103°F/39°C, the vet should be consulted. If it drops to 99°F/37°C or below it is time to prepare for the exciting event. If her temperature drops a full degree and remains constant until the next reading, she is likely to start whelping within the next twenty-four hours, so the vet should be notified and put on call to aid in an emergency. It is imperative that the novice breeder have an experienced helper to give assistance. Extreme restlessness, nesting in her box, shivering when her temperature drops, wanting human company, rejecting food, tearing her bed, panting, concern with the area of the vulva, clear mucous discharge and ultimately pushing with the abdomen or visible contractions are all signs that whelping time is close.

ensure that it is securely fastened or it may become a fire hazard. Wires should be kept out of the reach of both bitch and pups. A heating pad made specifically for animals can be used. It should be encased in a hard cover, with all wires shielded, so that it cannot be scratched or chewed. Another fairly safe heating device is an oil radiator. Whatever method of heating used, it is important that the bitch and whelps have an area to which they can move to prevent them from becoming too warm and risking dehydration. The box must be protected from drafts.

Other items that will be needed include plenty of clean, rough towels and baby or food scales for weighing the pups. A cardboard box to hold the pups while the bitch is

The Stages of Labor

There are three parts of active labor. The first stage when the passages are dilating and relaxing can last for what may feel like an eternity, but will actually not be longer than forty-eight hours. The second stage begins with the first signs of pushing or contractions, and coincides with the full dilation of the cervix. This stage can be voluntarily suppressed by the bitch if there are too many distractions. She must be kept quiet with only the breeder and helper present. The contractions help to push the whelps along in the birth canal. Each whelp is contained in a water sac or membrane and is attached by a cord (the umbilicus) to the placenta, which is in turn attached to the wall of the uterus.

With strong contractions, the first pup may be born within half an hour but with weaker contractions it can take up to three hours. Arrival times vary — fifteen to twenty minutes apart could be a good average — and sometimes one will arrive immediately after another. Pups usually come from the alternate "horns" of the uterus and the bitch will change her position from side to side to accommodate this. There often seems to be a longer wait about half way through. This can be a good time to offer the bitch some water and to suggest that she stretches her legs. A short outing on a leash can help if she is showing no signs of activity, but it is important to keep a close eye on her. If it is night, take a flashlight and examine anything that she deposits outside. Whatever the circumstances, never let active labor go for more than three hours without notifying the vet.

What to Expect

The first signs of birth are likely to be a bubble coming from the vulva — that is, the sac containing both the whelp and fluid. It will often break and help to lubricate the canal. If it does break, there is less time in which to be sure that the air passages of the whelp are clear so that it can start breathing. While the pup is still attached to the placenta and is in the sac there is a little more leeway before breathing must start. If the placenta does not arrive with the pup in sac — and often it does not — it is important to watch carefully for it and to be sure that it is expelled. Often this will be just before the next delivery.

There is no need for the domesticated dog to eat the placentas, so they can be removed from the box. However, they must all be counted because a retained placenta can cause serious or even fatal infection in the dam. The dam herself will usually (unless it is her first time) help to lick up the fluids and will nudge and lick the whelps. This stimulates them to breathe, and helps them to find a teat and suckle. It is good to help the pups to suckle as this stimulates the bitch to more contractions, helping the birthing process. It also encourages the flow of milk to the mammaries in a natural manner. The expulsion of the placenta is actually the third stage of labor but it usually occurs simultaneously with the second stage. Just before each imminent birth, the newborns that have already arrived should be placed in a separate cardboard box in a warm, secure place, and then put back with the dam again.

Providing the Dam With Help

If the bitch needs human help in extracting a pup, great care must be taken not to cause it

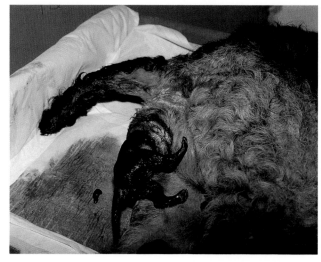

Breech births are just as common as when the whelp arrives head first, but the bitch in this case, an Airedale, may require some help.

any injury. The aim should be to pull gently downward and forward, toward the bitch's head. Whenever possible, this pulling should be in time with the contractions so that the bitch aids the process. If the sac has broken and the presentation is head first, try to clean the nose and mouth of the whelp so that it can start to breathe on its own. Breech presentations (when the whelp comes out feet first) are just as common as when the whelp arrives head first, but they are slightly more difficult if the legs get in the way.

AFTER THE BIRTH

When the pup is delivered, dry it thoroughly on a clean towel, making sure that the mucous is removed from the nose and throat. An ear syringe may be used to do this but great care should be taken not to suction too strongly and risk injuring the nose passage or the lungs. The umbilical cord should be removed and a hemostat should be clamped on the cord about 1 inch/2.5 cm from the pup's body. It is important not to tug on the cord because this may cause a hernia. The clamping action of the hemostat bruises the cord in the same way as a bitch's chewing would, crushing the blood vessels and helping to stem the bleeding. When the blood flow has reduced, the hemostat should be removed and reclamped about 1/2 inch/1 cm further away from the body. The cord should be cut with scissors on the side of the hemostat away from the whelp's body and thrown away, along with the placenta if it is still attached. Next the cord should be tied with dental floss or cotton thread dipped in alcohol just to the body side of the hemostat, between it and the area first crushed. The ends of the floss or cotton should be short so that they cannot be caught on little toes or stepped on.

It is important for all the puppies to suckle the "first milk." This is called colostrum and is a little thicker and yellower than regular milk. It contains antibodies which when absorbed by the pups will protect them against infectious disease for about four to six weeks. As a result of the mother licking them or of an attendant toweling each puppy, the whelps will produce their first dark stool called the meconium — this is very dark with yellow staining and is the contents of the alimentary canal before birth. The new mother must keep the puppies clean and stimulate their excretory organs by licking their abdomens. If she is hesitant about this, put a little petroleum jelly or butter under their tails and on their lower abdomens and she, by licking it off, will accomplish the same aim.

During whelping, the dam should be offered water. As soon as she has finished whelping, and has relieved herself during a closely watched walk, she should be offered food. The broth and meat from a plump chicken, soft foods such as creamed soup, broth, French toast, macaroni and cheese may be offered for a few days, while gradually getting her back on a regular schedule. She should have as much as three times the normal amount of food while she is nursing. Calcium supplements such as powdered non-fat milk should be added to the diet, especially if the litter is large.

It is most important that all the puppies and the dam should be taken to the vet for examination within twenty-four hours of the last pup being born, though a lucky breeder will have a vet who makes house calls. The vet will examine for retained placentas and give a shot of oxytocin to help to clean out the bitch if necessary. The vet will also examine the puppies for any birth defects, like a cleft palate.

The bitch will have a discharge and bleeding for a few days after delivery. This is normal and will gradually change to a more watery, less bloody discharge and then stop. As soon as the discharge is less messy, the paper in the whelping box can be replaced with something that provides a good footing and can be washed each day. The bitch's temperature should be monitored and her breasts checked daily after the birth. Her temperature will rise slightly while she is actively nursing so it is best to check it between feedings. The puppies' nails should be kept trimmed so that they do not scratch the bitch's teats or catch in the flooring.

DEVELOPMENT AND TRAINING

A healthy new litter of puppies is not just something to dream over, but will need a great deal of care. Whether a puppy has been bred to be a show winner, Obedience dog, shooting dog, retriever, a seeing eye/guide dog, or any one of a number of other aspects of the purebred dog, it is the breeder's awesome responsibility to ensure that the puppies are brought to their fullest use at maturity.

Hopefully, a new breeder will have found a wise and sharing person to be a confidant and mentor. A mentor should be able to provide guidance and advice as the litter progresses, drawing on past experience to help the new breeder so the best possible things are done for the new pups.

It is important to keep notes on everything to do with the litter including weight, when the eyes open and even the color. Soft Coated Wheaten puppies, for instance, are dark apricot in color at birth. It is difficult to believe that as they mature, the color will lighten to a clear, golden wheaten color.

NOTING PROGRESS

It is extremely important, as mentioned in the last chapter, to keep a diary on everything to do with the litter and the mother. Record the date of birth. Note the weight of each puppy daily during the first week, and then weekly thereafter. Other useful pieces of information include the puppies' color, markings, when the tails and dewclaws are dealt with (if appropriate) and by whom, how the tails were measured, when the eyes open, and when and how weaning is started. It is wise to note the general health of the litter and mother during the first few weeks after the birth. Keep a record of the mother's temperature daily for the first week to monitor possible infections.

Keep the vet's address and phone number handy, along with that of the helpful mentor. When subsequent litters are born, the breeder will be glad to have everything written down as a source of reference. The vet's and mentor's comments, when the litter is seen for the first time, should also be recorded.

Breeders have the responsibility of ensuring that each puppy in a litter is brought to its full use. These Alaskan Malamute pups are getting their first experience with snow and will train to be sled dogs.

If a litter is very large, the puppies should be rotated so they each get a fair chance at nursing. This Australian Cattle Dog appears to have her brood well-organized.

THE EARLY DAYS

The first three weeks of a puppy's life are critical. This time determines its survival chances. From birth, newborns should be handled daily so that the dog-human bond begins. It is vital that the pups start to nurse as soon as possible so that they acquire the mother's protective immunities. Newborns are born with their eyes closed — they open on about the tenth day, and usually bitch puppies open their eyes a day ahead of the males. At birth, the ears are also closed, so the puppies cannot hear at first. But they can crawl, seek warmth, and want to suckle and sleep.

A puppy that cries incessantly is too hot or too cold, not getting enough to eat, or its mother has not stimulated its bowel movement. If a pup is too cold, its digestive process is slowed. This can cause death in only a short time, so a careful check should be made of its body temperature. If the litter is large, the newborns should be rotated so that they get a fair chance at nursing. If a puppy is hungry, bitch's milk replacer is available commercially and should be used to supplement the feeding.

It is important not to overfeed as this is just as harmful as underfeeding. A puppy twitching in its sleep is quite normal and an indication that all is going well.

CONSULTING AN EXPERT

Very shortly after the birth, a knowledgeable breeder should evaluate the litter, scrutinizing evenness of size, quality of color and markings, general vigor and health. There are certain qualities of conformation, apparent to a knowing breeder, that will portend plusses and minuses at maturity. These are more obvious before the pup starts to put on its "baby fat" in the first week or ten days.

In breeds where docking is the norm, the puppy's tail should be docked between the second and fifth day. It is best to rely on the breeder's opinion as to the proper length of

As soon as possible after birth, a knowledgeable breeder should evaluate the litter. This is best done in the first week to ten days. For Chinese Shar-Pei puppies, timing is important because they have twice as much skin as they need and they quickly grow into it.

If a litter is large and all one color, like this litter of six West Highland White Terriers, it is important to identify each puppy in some way.

the tail, because not all vets are up to date on what is currently considered correct. Some breeds normally require ear cropping, too (this is illegal in the United Kingdom and some European countries). Consult the breeder about the best age to do this. It is usually done after the first shots are given. Young pups should have their toenails clipped twice a week to protect the mother's mammary glands from being scratched, and once they are weaned their nails should be tipped off once a week.

The breeder's opinions should be recorded in the diary. If the litter is large and one color, it can be difficult to distinguish puppies, so it is important to mark each one. With coated breeds, scissors can be used to cut the coat in different places on the puppies' backs or legs. Nail polish may also be used as a marker.

WEANING PUPPIES

The second critical stage in development is the third to the seventh week. Environment now becomes an important part in its life because by this time it can see, hear and smell. Feeding a pup solid food should start at about three weeks. If the mother is fed a nutritious soft food in a flat pan placed in the whelping box,

the pups will investigate and then eat the food. Many breeders begin by feeding small meatballs of ground raw beef once or twice a day by hand.

As feeding progresses, commercially prepared puppy food mixed with warm water — and perhaps with cottage cheese, or ground meat or cooked eggs — is suggested as a suitable food. Milk is not recommended because it loosens the puppies' stools. The puppies will

If the mother is fed a nutritious, soft food from a flat pan placed in the whelping box, the puppies, like these Cavalier King Charles Spaniels, will eat the food, too, usually starting in their third week.

still be nursing at this stage anyway.

Puppies must be fed four times a day at first, at the same time each day. When they are about eight weeks, this should be reduced to three times a day, depending on the breed. As the pups mature, this should be decreased to twice a day until they are one year old. It is up to the owner to establish a feeding routine but, generally, food should be fed at the same time and in the same place daily. An evening meal should not be fed too late. Medium-sized and small breeds will do well on just one meal a day throughout their lives, but Toy and giant breeds will do better on two meals. The weight of a dog compared with its size should always be a determining factor. Obesity is undesirable and harmful. It may injure a young dog's bones and ligaments. Supplements should never be given to a puppy or dog without a vet's advice. And water should be available early in the weaning process.

A stool sample should be procured from several pups in the litter and taken to the vet for examination. If worms are present, the vet will offer advice on medications and procedures. If the first checks are done as soon as the puppies are on solid food, it will allow time for a second check before they go to their new homes. Ideally, a puppy should always be free of worms when it is delivered to its new owner.

TEETH AND IMMUNIZATIONS

At three weeks the first teeth start to show. At this time the dam will probably want to leave the pups for periods of time — this is quite natural. The pup's teeth should be examined to check for proper bites and the findings recorded in the diary. Permanent teeth do not start to set in until about four months. By this age, puppies should be used to having their mouths examined and have their teeth checked twice weekly to ensure that the baby teeth are shedding properly. Occasionally some baby teeth will need to be pulled by the vet so that the second teeth are correctly positioned. The whole teething process continues until

the large molars arrive at about six months.

The vet will recommend when the puppies should receive their first immunization shots. This is important because there are several killer diseases that may be carried from puppy to puppy. When a pup leaves to go to its new home, its medical record should be provided with its pedigree, registration papers and the breeder's record of its socialization to date.

BEFORE LEAVING HOME

It is up to the breeder to teach a puppy some form of socialization before it leaves for its new home. The puppy should also have some idea about housetraining. If the young dog is allowed to wander outside its sleeping box to defecate and urinate, this activity will become instilled in it. An inside pen with a dog door leading to the outside will give the puppy the

This Afghan Hound puppy is learning to sit. At an early stage all puppies should be taught to respond to simple commands.

opportunity to housetrain itself.

A puppy should also be well acquainted with a crate. An airline crate which is the correct size for the particular breed is useful for these crates are lightweight, portable and easy to clean. A crate with soft bedding, placed in an enclosed inside pen, will soon become a comfy haven for the den-loving canine.

INITIAL TRAINING

A puppy is responsive and should be taught to learn as much as possible before it is ten weeks old. It should be introduced to a leash. It is best to use a soft web or fabric leash — choke collars are not recommended. When done early, leash training is very easy. The pup should have a simple, informal "call" name and should respond to the trainer's voice. At first it should simply be taught to understand simple commands like "come," "no" and "wait" — and be rewarded lavishly with praise as well as a treat. It will enjoy playing games such as retrieving a toy or a ball.

Puppies must also be introduced to traveling by car. It is much safer for both driver and puppy if it is always in a crate when out for a drive. If car riding is started early, motion sickness is rarely a problem.

THE BREEDER'S RESPONSIBILITY

The breeder should try to determine the potential adult temperament of each puppy before it is sold. It is always best to try to match a pup to the new owner's needs. This will help to reduce the likelihood of a pup being "returned" or ending up in a shelter. A potentially aggressive pup should not be sold to a family with young children. It should be neutered as soon as possible. A shy, retiring pup should go to a quiet home without young children.

From the third to seventh weeks of its life, a puppy's brain and nervous system are developing to full capacity. The puppy will form attachments to the others in the litter and will begin to develop a bond with humans through daily handling. This is the period when puppies

These English Setters, in their first few months of life, are already beginning to establish an order of dominance. Between three to seven weeks after birth, it is important to step in and teach the puppy its place in your "pack".

start to play, fight and establish an order of dominance. The breeder should now start to teach a puppy. If a puppy is taken from its home in this development stage it can survive, but it is likely to bond only with people, and may not show any interest in dog activities, including sexual matters. Removing a puppy at this time can make a dog aggressive.

The mother should not be forgotten as her puppies take the limelight. They each require individual attention, grooming and playtimes to keep the human bond strong.

Although the excitement and focus naturally tends toward the puppies as they grow older and learn new things, the mother should not be forgotten, for it is thanks to her that the litter has been produced. It is important to keep her clean and well-groomed, and to give her long walks and playtimes on her own. Although the mother and her pups share many moments together, it is vital that they are all given individual attention — yet another reason why the time-consuming dedication required for breeding should be considered carefully well in advance.

Settling Into the New Home

By about ten weeks the puppies should go to their new homes. This gives the new owners time to bond with the puppy, to continue housetraining and simple obedience. Bringing a puppy into a home with children can be a rewarding experience. However, children must be taught to be kind and gentle with the puppy during these critical development stages, otherwise the dog may turn out to be aggressive or dominant. Children must allow the pup time by itself to eat, chew and sleep. A child should never be given total responsibility for a dog — an adult should oversee things. Since the dog is a pack animal, a puppy must be taught that it comes at the bottom of the pack in the hierarchy of its new family.

Socially acceptable behavior must be established and kept with a gentle firmness. Dogs need to know the limits of what is and is not allowed. This should be conveyed with no conflicting signals. Praise should be given when the puppy is successful. Discipline should be gentle and accompanied by speaking. A dog will readily sense displeasure and will respond to a firm "no" or "shame." A dog should not be hit with the hand or a rolled up newspaper, shouted at or have its head threatened. It is important that the dog acts bravely when subjected to loud noises, such as thunder, and not be shy.

The crate is an ideal spot to put the puppy when the owner is out or otherwise occupied. The crate should not be used as a punishment. Two of the best locations for the crate are in a fenced-off area in the kitchen or in a close-by laundry room.

Successful Housetraining

With proper perseverance, housetraining can probably be accomplished in two weeks. Consistency is the key word to all training. The pup should always be fed at the same time of day and should be taken outside to the same spot and through the same door. The pup will want to eliminate after waking, after eating and after playing. Other times may be a little more difficult to predict but the puppy will hint at its intentions through body language such as sniffing and circling. The puppy should be hustled outside. Someone should stay with the pup and give praise when it has finished.

A very young puppy should be taken out as soon as it wakes up and immediately after it has eaten. At first this will be many times

To achieve success in housetraining a puppy should be taken to its "spot" and praised well when it has finished.

during the day (and night) but as it grows up and can control its bladder for longer periods of time, the trips outside will dwindle to three or four times a day. Praise for its accomplishments is essential for the training to be effective. There is no short cut to this training but if the owner is assiduous at the beginning it will pay off with a quickly housetrained dog.

A puppy should never be allowed to eliminate in the house — paper training is a waste of time and a bad habit. If the pup starts inside, it should be quickly scooped up and told "no" loudly, carried to its spot outside and then praised well when it has finished. It is pointless to punish a dog for a past mistake because dogs have no sense of time and will not relate to the accident unless is is actually caught in the act.

FURTHER TRAINING

From the seventh to twelfth weeks, the puppy should be expanding its horizons and absorbing all that it can. It should have a real name and respond to it and to its owner with dedication and interest. Training during this period should not last for longer than half an hour. Plenty of praise should be given when the puppy responds well. At this age, the puppy has its best attitude toward direction and will respond to what it is told. It is a time when the dog-human relationship will grow.

From twelve to sixteen weeks the puppy starts to declare its independence and the owner and dog establish who is boss. This period is when physical and social development run parallel. It is also the time when puppies cut their second teeth, and can be thought of as teenagers. Their mouths bother them and their attention span is short. Puppies should still be treated kindly at this time.

After sixteen weeks the learning process that has already been established should continue. If the original foundations of training are not well founded, it will be difficult to train the dog to accomplish more. It is important to remember that the first sixteen weeks of a puppy's life is when its socialization between humans and other dogs takes place. Time and effort spent during this time are well worth the trouble. A puppy brought on in the best way possible will ensure that the next twelve or so years are both pleasant and productive for both the owner and dog.

GROOMING POTENTIAL SHOW DOGS

Any puppy that is considered a show prospect should spend time on the grooming table in order to have its teeth checked, ears cleaned and toe nails clipped. Short-coated breeds should be groomed with a damp towel and given a good brush with a mitt fitted with bristles, called a hound glove. Dogs with long coats that must be trimmed or plucked, or washed and brushed dry under a dryer, should have all this attended to on a grooming table. Occasionally, ears need some attention after cropping and terrier ears may need to be set. This is another job for the grooming table.

None of the tasks at the grooming table should be a chore for the owner or dog. The dog should enjoy the attention. The owner should learn how to prepare a dog for the show ring. An experienced person who has knowledge of showing the breed will be invaluable in helping the novice to groom a dog so that the process is easy and pleasant.

Essentially, the making of a show dog involves teaching it how to walk on a leash, pose on both a table and the ground and rise to the occasion. If the breeder bonds strongly with a young hopeful it will try hard to please. The more that both owner and dog learn and share, the more fulfilling the dog-human relationship becomes.

THE TRANSFORMATION OF PUPPIES

As the pup grows older, many changes occur. Size and strength increase and sexual maturity begins. A bitch pup may come into her first season any time after she reaches eight months and the consensus of opinion among vets is that she should be spayed before this season starts. Spaying is probably the greatest safeguard against cancer of the mammary glands at a later age. The operation involved is also safer and simpler at this stage than after a season or two.

A bitch's body matures and develops more rapidly than that of a male dog, and early spaying will probably not affect its growth. In the United States, a bitch kept for show may not be spayed and care must be taken to observe and record its first season. In contrast, a dog often does not become sexually mature or become "bodied up" until it is two or more years old. It may be sexually active from around six months on and may be used at stud after the age of eight or nine months. A dog of this age is too young for proper results in tests that should take place before breeding. If a dog is not to stand at stud, it should be neutered before it has any contact with a bitch in season. If it has a retained testicle, this should be removed to prevent any possible cancer later in life. Toy breeds reach physical maturity much earlier than larger breeds.

BASIC TRAINING

To be a good citizen and an ideal companion, a minimal amount of training is required. Dogs enjoy a sense of purpose. Just like people, they thrive on praise and they are happiest when they are being useful. This is only natural since it was the dog's usefulness that originally made him man's companion.

The basic lessons a dog should learn are to "heel" while walking on a leash, sit, stay, come and lie down. Many clubs and organizations will help new owners to train a dog. Dog-training clubs frequently advertise in local newspapers when classes are held. If the new owner wants to do the training without outside help, there are many self-help books that can assist. The vet may also be able to help by recommending classes or by advising the owner on a dog's progress and making suggestions if behavior problems develop. Unruly puppies are a nuisance, just like unruly children. Training sessions for puppies should be very short, maybe five minutes at a time,

and training should not be at the same time and place as play time. Puppies will learn the difference very quickly.

Anne Rogers Clark believes, and scientific studies have proven, that dogs have a definite adolescence. This varies by breed and sex of dog; females generally show adolescent behavior a few months before males. A change in attitude can be detected and dogs need special attention at this time. If there is a tendency toward either shyness or aggression it will appear most strongly during adolescence, and this is the time to deal with it through training.

LIVING WITH OTHERS

Being a good citizen applies not only to a dog. An owner who picks up the dog (size and strength permitting), or instructs it to sit when strangers approach during a walk, is being a considerate neighbor.

People own dogs for all sorts of reasons. But whatever the underlying factor, the bond between a dog and its human owner makes people more of what they are. In an understanding relationship people rise to a higher level of responsibility, communication and compassion. They become more aware of and more in harmony with nature. A native American saying is, "God had a friend and it was a dog."

Not only dogs, but their owners, too, must learn to be good citizens, particularly when a dog is taken into public places. This is when the dog's training is tested.

THE COMPETITIVE DOG

Dogs shows came into existence because sportsmen and stockmen wanted to evaluate their own animals against those of their peers. As various types of dog evolved to serve particular functions for their owners, selective breeding became an important part of fixing breed type. Fanciers who were keen to breed a dog with certain valuable features were naturally interested in finding dogs that possessed these features and incorporating them into their breeding programs.

THE EARLY DAYS

There are conflicting reports as to when the first recorded dog show took place. As long ago as 1775 a huntsman named John Warde organized hound shows outside the hunting season in an attempt to maintain contact with others who shared his love of fox hunting. In the early 1800s, many London public houses contained "pits" where dogs were expected to dispatch rats, an activity that satisfied the gamblers' instincts, and undoubtedly some notorious venues such as the Westminster Pit played host to dog fights.

As these barbaric sports became more frowned upon, the concept of the dog show evolved — and show dogs were referred to as "fancy pets." By the middle of the nineteenth century, British dog fanciers began to meet and compare the quality of their dogs. Initially these meetings were informal but later they became more organized competitions.

In June 1859 a well-organized poultry show at Newcastle-upon-Tyne included for the first time two classes for dogs, one for Setters and one for Pointers. The driving force behind the innovation was a Mr. Pape, a local gunsmith. In November of that year, Richard Brailsford ran a show in Birmingham that continues to this day as the "Birmingham National."

The ideal vehicle for improvement of stock is regular competition where the best specimens of the breed can be evaluated by knowledge-able and experienced people. Early dog breeders started with a good idea that today has grown into a popular pastime internationally. The first British dog shows catered for sporting dogs — gundogs, hounds and terriers — and soon other types were included such as the popular Toy breeds, kept purely for companionship and entertainment.

Interestingly, dog shows have long been attended by all levels of society and to this day the sport remains one of the least class conscious of hobbies. Since such shows began, lowly working people used to hold competitions in backstreet alehouses, while the nobility was patronizing similar events.

THE FOUNDING OF KENNEL CLUBS

As the breeds began to develop, shows increased in size and in 1873 the Kennel Club was formed in the United Kingdom. Its aim was to maintain a registry of all purebred dogs

In 1873 the British Kennel Club was established and it also held its first show at Crystal Palace, London in June of that year. Today's Cruft's show is the preeminent dog show in the United Kingdom. Pictured here is the 1991 Best in Show winner, Show Champion Raycroft Socialite, a Clumber Spaniel.

The American Kennel Club was formed in 1884 and today, the most important show it approves annually is the Westminster show. Shown here with judge Anne Rogers Clark (left) is 1978 Westminster Best in Show winner, Ch. Cede Higgens, a Yorkshire Terrier.

FCI, the coordinating body for kennel clubs in most of Europe, Australasia, Africa, Central and South America, was founded in 1911. Its main event, the World Show, is held each year in a different country. The 1994 World Show was held in Bern, Switzerland and was won by the Siberian Husky, Ch. Artic Blue's Red Senator.

and act as a coordinating body for competitive shows. As shows had become more popular, various irregularities and scandals occurred, and it was apparent that a rigid controlling body was necessary which could legislate and make rules and regulations. Sewallis Evelyn Shirley was the driving force behind the formation of the Kennel Club. In April 1873 he saw his dream realized. Shirley became the Kennel Club's first chairman, a position he held for twenty-six years. The Kennel Club ran its first actual show in June of that year, when 975 entries were received at the Crystal Palace venue. Soon it devised the Challenge Certificate as the highest award obtainable. These contribute to a dog's Championship.

The American Kennel Club was formed in 1884, and the Canadian Kennel Club was established four years later. The Fédération Cynologique Internationale (FCI) was not founded until 1911, its original member countries being Germany, Austria, Belgium, France and Holland. This is more of a coordinating body than a governing body, and it does not operate any registration system for dogs. Each year the number of its member countries increases and under its auspices a "World Show" is held each year in a different country.

ORGANIZATIONAL DIFFERENCES

Perhaps the most fundamental difference between the Kennel Club in the United Kingdom and the American Kennel Club is that the British governing body maintains its role as a traditional gentleman's social club, though since 1979, full membership has been granted to women. The American Kennel Club is not a social club but a huge, non-profit organization with paid staff, as well as a body of some 300 delegates from the many dog clubs throughout the United States. It is from these delegates that a board of directors and president are elected. The AKC's primary function is to be a registry body. However, its charter is very broad and gives the organization the right and power to oversee all aspects of the sport. As shows have become larger and the sport has escalated, there has been a need for more input and direction from the AKC.

Spectators in both countries frequently question the level of democracy present in these systems. Neither seems as open as, for example, Scandinavian kennel clubs where anyone who participates at kennel club functions must first become a member.

Today dog shows are organized in all countries of the world. Each country implements a system with some fundamental differences from country to country.

In the United Kingdom, for example, a dog has to win three Challenge Certificates (CCs) under three different judges to become a Champion. At least one of these certificates must be won when the dog is more than one year old. The CC is awarded to the dog and bitch considered the best by the judge at a Championship show where CCs are on offer, and all dogs of a specific breed are in competition together, including existing Champions.

In the United States, however, Championship-making points are only won with non-Champions in competition, the best dog and best bitch are declared Winners Dog and Winners Bitch. These dogs then go forward to meet the established Champions in the Best of Breed class. There is no minimum age limit for a Champion to "finish"' (complete a dog's Championship) in the United States. The points system is quite complex. To become a Champion, a dog needs to win a minimum of 15 points, and 5 points is the maximum number a dog can win at one show. Points are allocated at the various shows based on both the location of the show (venues fall into different "zones"), the breed and sex of the dog, and the number of dogs in competition. To complete its American Championship a dog must have won at least two "majors" (3 points or more) under two different judges. The balance of points may be won in smaller numbers. As with the British system, the minimum number of shows a dog needs to attend to gain its title is three. However, the American system becomes further complicated

in that a dog can increase its points won by acquitting itself well at Group level, where it competes with other breeds within its Group. Thus, if a dog wins no points because it is the only dog of its breed entered, but then goes on to win the Group or Best in Show where it defeats dogs which have themselves won points or majors within the breed competition, it too will be given the same number of points as the dog it has defeated. The defeated dog retains its points, however.

The Canadian system is very similar to that found in the United States. In Canada a dog must defeat at least one other entry and ten points are required for a championship. In countries affiliated to the FCI, once the dogs have been judged, the awarding of Certificates depends very much on the age of the winners and the level of their previous wins. Consequently an International Certificate (Certificate d'Aptitude, Championship Internationale de Beauté) is often awarded to a dog that may not be standing first, or even second, because the dogs that have beaten it are either too young or alternatively are already International Champions. However, awarding Certificates, in whatever country, is always at the judge's discretion and it is often felt that some judges tend to be overgenerous in their reluctance to

Judging a Great Dane at a Canadian show. Canadian dog shows are run and judged in a very similar way to those held in the United States.

withhold top awards when the presented dogs are clearly lacking in outstanding merit. Around the world, some smaller countries often combine aspects of both the American and British systems, even though they may be affiliated to the FCI.

TYPES OF DOG SHOWS

There are various levels of dog shows in all countries with Championship shows always the highest. At a lower level there are Match shows in the United States and Open shows, Limited shows, Sanction shows, Primary shows and Exemption shows in the United Kingdom. These shows tend to be structured in such a way that entry is restricted to dogs which have not won a given amount of prizes at previous shows, and so the level of competition will vary.

Regardless of level, there are primarily two types of competition in the conformation ring — breed and variety. Breed competition involves dogs of the same breed competing through the various classes until a Best Dog, Best Bitch and eventually Best of Breed is determined. In Variety competition, dogs of different breeds compete together, either in a class or a group situation. For example, a class could be scheduled at a show for "Any Variety Terrier," that class being open to all terriers. In the Terrier Group competition, however, only those terriers which have won Best of Breed in their respective breed classes are eligible to compete. One of the most difficult aspects of dog shows for the inexperienced observer to understand is the principle behind variety competition, and a frequently posed question is "How can you judge a Chihuahua against a Great Dane?"

This question is addressed below, but first it is useful to consider the principles of breed competition, i.e., competition confined to a single breed. Each breed of pedigree dog, when it was first recognized by the canine governing body of the country, had a breed Standard or written description of perfection drawn up. Every breed Standard describes the various points in detail. The descriptions of the requirements for each aspect of the overall animal invariably had the breed's function, rather than what was the fashion, as its foundation. Copies of breed Standards are readily available from parent breed clubs and national kennel clubs, and are usually included in books on specific breeds.

THE BREED STANDARDS

Essentially all breed Standards consist of specific descriptions under the following headings: General Appearance, Characteristics, Temperament, Head and Skull, Eyes, Ears, Mouth, Neck, Forequarters, Body, Hindquarters, Feet, Tail, Gait/Movement, Coat, Color, Size and Faults. In recent years specific faults have been deleted from the British breed Standards whereas their European and American counterparts continue to list what are considered disqualifying faults.

Over the years, breed Standards have been honed, streamlined or simply changed because governing bodies have tried to establish international similarity. Breed clubs, often run by breeders who wish to change fashions, have pressured for change. Streamlining the often verbose originals into more standardized formats has also brought change.

The breed Standard is the most valuable tool of dog judges. Coupled with their natural eye for quality and balance, their assumed integrity and strength of character, it is all they should require if they are to assess an entry of dogs and make justified and logical placings. Happily for the dog exhibitor, breed Standards allow great freedom on the part of the judge for personal interpretation. Furthermore, while many of the original Standards were set out in such a way that a percentage of points were allocated to particular aspects of the overall animal, the whole adding up to 100, the current formats are much less rigid and encourage appreciation of the whole dog, rather than "dissecting" it.

While the breed Standards aim to paint a word picture of perfection for each breed,

JUDGING THE AMERICAN COCKER SPANIEL

The American Cocker Spaniel Standard is based on its ability to function in the field. An initial impression should be taken of its total profile standing, when its type, size, proportion and balance may be assessed. Then its profile should be assessed in motion. The hardest dog to breed is one with a short body which can move. All aspects of the dog should be considered against the Standard. The table examination is useful because tabling reveals all the details of structure.

Back on the ground, the Cocker's coming and going movement must be scrutinized. It should be of high station, short back and high top, with a good reach and drive and an ability to cover the ground effortlessly in a straight line. Ideally, the Cocker should be moved swiftly (not running) on a fairly loose leash. The typical animal should be free of any exaggeration. Judging is a matter of comparison to the Standard and compromise on any shortcomings of each entrant. The Cocker in the ring, constructed to do a super job in the field and temperamentally attuned to work, will finish high in the ribbons, so long as its head, coat, color and size fall within reasonable limits. The Cocker must have the ability and will to function.

---

they tend to be rather clinical — especially the more modern, streamlined versions. Some original Standards may have been considered florid in language, but many of the expressions used conveyed subtle nuances very succinctly. As an example, changing the requirement of the Pekingese head to be "large" rather than "massive" loses the sense of great size. As newly worded Standards are handed down from generation to generation, there is the danger that essential breed characteristics may be lost along the way.

PICKING A WINNER

A further disadvantage of the written breed Standards is that they make no reference to the one intangible that every judge hopes to find in his or her top winners — charisma, star quality or presence. When it is present it will be recognized, and it is a virtue possessed by all the great dogs. They sem to have an aura about them. For the dedicated judge, finding — or even seeing — such a dog, is one of the most fulfilling pleasures.

Andrew Brace recalls, "The memory of seeing truly outstanding dogs never fades, and those blessed with this air of supremacy hap-

pen only once every so often. The first dog to make such an impression on me was the Bull Terrier, Ch. Abraxas Audacity, who won Best

One disadvantage of written breed Standards is the difficulty they present in describing the special, intangible qualities that every judge hopes to find in top winners. This photo seems to capture the charisma or star quality, that this Fox Terrier, on the right, appears to possess.

Anne Rogers Clark was the handler for Ch. Karlena's Musical Rattler, the Best of Breed Coonhound, at the Westminster Show held February 8-9, 1960 in New York.

in Show at Cruft's in 1972. I remember him making his entrance into the "big ring" as if it were yesterday, a gleaming white beast, rippling with perfectly honed muscle, and yet so clean in outline. He stepped on to the red carpet, just shook himself once or twice, looked down his nose and strode the length of the huge arena, tail wagging and with just a hint of mischief in his eye. He was the very essence of this magnificent breed, he shone with condition and his every move reflected personality. It was no surprise when he walked off with the Big One!

"Of the great dogs I have judged, none has impressed me more than the magnificent Lhasa Apso, Ch. Saxonsprings Fresno, who really did justify the hackneyed phrase of becoming a legend in her own lifetime. I had the pleasure of judging her at a small limited show in Sheffield when she was very much an uncooperative teenager, but from the start she had "the look," a definite statement that she was something special, and when I got her on the table she was an absolute joy to handle,

with perfect conformation, and everything fitting and flowing. Despite her waywardness on the day I made her Best in Show, and after she had broken all records it was with pleasure I awarded her the Challenge Certificate and Best of Breed at her retirement show."

Anne Rogers Clark has vivid memories of the thrill that working with and judging dogs can generate. She comments: "Judging dogs is like... finding pearls in oysters, or a gold nugget...the excitement is palpable, real and remembered when you find the next great one. My first experience was before I became a judge and was a professional handler. A client, the great financier and poodle enthusiast Clarence Dillon, had gone to England and purchased a promising black Miniature Poodle bitch from a well-known kennel. He brought her back to the States and, as he did not have a regular handler at the time, she just sat in his lovely kennel for several months while he surveyed the available handlers who might be interested. I was quite young at the time, but was well on the way in my profession, and was delighted to be asked to review his stock. The bitch was overgrown with hair but looked promising, and I took her home for further study. After several days of bathing, brushing, clipping and shaping, the most beautiful young Miniature bitch appeared that anyone — including myself — had ever seen. She went on to great heights. In 1959 we won the Westminster Show together and her blood lives on today through her descendents, including the Non-Sporting Group winner at the 1995 Westminster. Her name was Dunwalke's Ch. Fontclair Festoon.

"There have been many others, joys to find, thrilling to watch fulfill their destiny both in the show ring and as producers. This is what gets you out of bed on a dark, rainy morning to judge outdoors all day in less than perfect conditions. The next one in the ring may be the one we have been looking for."

No matter how much one reads breed Standards, or studies the written word, the ability to appreciate greatness is an instinctive thing, a gift if you like, and not given to all.

THE MAKING OF A JUDGE

One of the most frequently asked questions in the dog world is how to become a judge. The process varies dramatically from country to country. Regardless of nationality, it would be unthinkable for anyone to contemplate judging before he or she has a thorough knowledge of their chosen breed and also the practicalities of controlling a show ring. Before taking the step to become a judge, excellent practical experience can be gained by acting as ring steward for experienced judges. This teaches ring procedure and how to maintain the necessary paperwork, such as the judge's book and the steward's sheet. It also gets the candidate used to handling a degree of authority "center stage".

Some judges combine their activities and exhibit and handle show dogs. Despite a busy judging schedule Andrew Brace handled his Beagle, Ch. Dialynne Tolliver of Tragband, to complete its Championship in three consecutive shows during the 1995 show season.

In the United Kingdom there is no facility for anyone to apply to become a judge, because potential judges are issued with an invitation to judge from a canine society. Breed clubs maintain lists of potential judges at various levels, the lowest of which would include the names of people who have been successful breeders, and who would be considered ready to start judging at the smallest shows. Eventually, after a minimum of five years' judging at this level, an invitation may be forthcoming for a Championship event. Permission has to be given by the Kennel Club for anyone to award Challenge Certificates, and a detailed question- naire has to be completed by the invited judge. This is studied by the Kennel Club Judges Committee and the opinions of the relevant breed clubs may be sought. The Kennel Club will then approve the judge for that appoint- ment only. Alternatively, if they do not grant approval, they give no reason. In the United Kingdom, since judges are approved for one show only they must go through the same process with every additional breed they judge. This slow process explains why in 1995 there was only one person in the United Kingdom who had been approved to judge all breeds.

In the past, judges were drawn from the ranks of highly successful breeders and stock- men present in the British Fancy. Officials would invite them because of their accepted knowledge. Such people did not have to acquire the same level of "hands-on" experience as the present-day judges in the United Kingdom,

THE GREAT JUDGES

The older generation of all-rounder judges, who judged dogs and all types of livestock, was rich in "characters," some of whose reputations suggest that they would be far from acceptable to today's governing body. Stories are told of how some judges actually handled dogs in the ring while smoking a cigar, and it is reputed that Countess Howe once judged Labradors from a wheelchair, selecting her winners by pointing with her walking-stick.

Recent years have seen all-rounders, like

Catherine Sutton, in the Best in Show ring at the Santa Barbara Kennel Club Show. This judge was considered the ultimate professional.

Joe Braddon and Bill Siggers. Both shared a mischievous sense of humor which would perhaps not be appreciated today, but there was no denying that their knowledge of all breeds was vast, and their eye for picking a great one as a youngster was well known.

The ranks of British all-rounders in the past few years have sadly been depleted. R. M. "Bobby" James achieved universal acclaim for his exceptional eye and his wonderfully fulsome judge's critiques; Lily Turner had raven black hair and a constant, benevolent grin; Stanley Dangerfield had a ramrod-straight figure and famous pastel jackets; Herbert Essam wore a plastic orchid and matching collars-and-ties — long before they became fashionable; Catherine Sutton was the ultimate professional at everything she attempted; Joe Cartledge always had a kind word for youngsters and novices; Reg Gadsden's severe expression belied the gentle soul that hid beneath; the well-loved all-rounder, Judy DeCasembroot, was always confident and invariably right. These and many more have been taken from the British dog scene, with few possible replacements.

Other judges, like the internationally respected Gwen Broadley have chosen to retire while still physically active. Her loss was acutely felt, though she remains as keen and successful a breeder of Labradors as ever.

It has perhaps been left to Scandinavia to develop popular all-rounder judges who combine great knowledge with lively personalities; Finland's Hans Lehtinen and Denmark's Ole Staunskjaer spring to mind as obvious examples.

The most loved, respected and revered judge in the United States was Alva Rosenberg, a quiet man with a wonderful mind, a calm hand on a dog and the most incredible memory about dogs that he had judged and found worthy. His name became synonymous with quality and type, and the aim of breeders was to breed dogs that would please Alva. Another dog man through and through was Percy Roberts, an Englishman who settled in the United States. He became a very famous handler and an importer of dogs for American clients, and won Best in Show at the Westminster Show four times — a record. He ran a great ring with total control, and when the dogs were placed everyone knew exactly where they stood and why they stood there.

Some governing bodies may strive to produce a generation of judges which is in many ways cloned, but it is to be hoped that individuals will be allowed to flourish, provided their knowledge, integrity and dedication is what the role of dog judge demands.

THE AMERICAN SYSTEM

In the United States, judges can apply to judge and they are assessed at a practical level by more experienced judges. The American Kennel Club grants judges approval to judge breeds and may grant experienced judges more than one breed at a time. They often grant approval for a sub-group of similar breeds at the same time. This is where the breeders, judges and future handlers find their proving ground. Their skill, intuition, manners and abilities are what count in this competition, not the attributes and conformation of their dogs.

The AKC continually refines its judging procedures to the benefit of all concerned. James Edward Clark was the first person in the United States to organize a seminar on a specific breed to help educate breeders and aspiring judges. Held in Pittsburgh, Pennsylvania in the early 1960s, it was a great learning experience. The principle of holding teaching seminars caught on. Many breed seminars are now held annually in the United States.

The American Kennel Club has started to hold two AKC Judges Institutes yearly. These are extremely popular "teach-ins" that last for a week. All aspects of judging are examined including how to run a ring, understanding the Standards, rules and regulations, giving written and verbal critiques, evaluating a class, weighing and measuring a dog, touching a dog correctly when judging it — in fact, everything a judge needs to know. The instructors often learn as much as the students.

In the United States a person may apply to judge a specific breed if he or she has bred that breed for at least ten years, has bred at least four litters and produced at least two Champions. The applicant must also have judged at six Sanction Match Shows or Sweepstake classes of the breed, and been a steward at no less than five AKC licenced shows. All potential breeders must complete a detailed and lengthy form. If the application is approved by the AKC board of directors, the applicant is required to take a written test on the breed in question. An AKC representative interviews the applicant if the test is passed. The interview allows the applicant to demonstrate further knowledge of the breed and judging skills. The board of directors reviews all reports and results. If its decision is favorable, the applicant is granted the status of provisional judge.

Provisional judges must wait until a club invites them to judge and complete five provisional assignments while being observed by an AKC field representative. If all goes well, the reports are put to the board for approval. This procedure takes about six months. Once a person has judged a number of shows application can be made to judge another breed. Applicants who have been judges in another country and who live in the United States may apply to judge more than one breed or a Group, on their first application. The growth of interest in purebred dogs and the attendant dog shows in the United States has meant that increasing numbers of judges are required to take care of the many annual dog shows. The AKC is continually reviewing the best way to identify and reward the talents necessary for superior judging.

THE CANADIAN SYSTEM

In Canada, those who wish to apply to be a judge must have bred at least one Champion that was finished ten years ago, plus one other that was finished at any time. Applicants must also have bred at least four litters and be a member of the Canadian Kennel Club. Other requirements are at least thirty hours of ring stewarding (at least three hours each session), and applicants must have judged a minimum of five CKC sanctioned matches within the last five years. Aspiring judges must give details of their background in dogs and pass a written exam when making an application. The results are sent to a committee for evaluation. Those who succeed may accept one assignment, at which they are observed. After this hurdle, any number of assignments to judge the permitted breeds may be accepted and judges will be observed at three of these. If no negative comments have been made, judges may go on the approved list. New approvals may be applied for yearly.

FCI Judges

FCI related countries generally attach great importance to study and examinations, both practical and theoretical. Often intensive courses must be attended, ensuring that the candidate judge is well versed in basic canine anatomy, before going on to more detailed study of breed characteristics and type. A student judge system operates by which potential judges have the opportunity to handle and write critiques on dogs which are being judged by a more experienced judge. At the end of the day, the student's opinions are studied and compared with those of the judge who will make a recommendation that the student is sufficiently knowledgeable to judge that breed, or otherwise.

In assessing any breed, judges will base their evaluation on personal experience gained as breeder and exhibitor, the level of quality to which they have been exposed, and knowledge of the written breed Standard. While the Standard may describe perfection, any judge's perception of that level of quality will be very much colored by his or her own particular background.

As an example, if a judge has been a breeder of Boxers and has previously had great problems with light eyes in his or her own particular bloodlines, this judge will be more aware of the difficulty experienced in breeding that fault out than will a judge who has never encountered the problem.

Exhibiting for the First Time

Showing a dog against other specimens of its own breed is the logical place to start, and it is best to begin in the lower classes where youth and inexperience will be common to most of the competing dogs. It is important that even the newest of exhibitors be aware from the outset that their dog is unlikely to be a Champion. Many owners of companion dogs find themselves being talked into showing their pet by a self-appointed sage who has assured the owner that the dog is a potential winner.

Exhibiting for the first time can be an enlightening but nerve-rattling experience. Starting at a young age builds confidence.

It is not wise to take such advice. If the dog has been bought as a companion, it may have some minor flaw that in no way detracts from its overall appearance and ability to perform the function of much-loved pet, but the flaw might handicap it in the show ring. It is wise to get the breeder's advice as to whether the puppy they sold is likely to have show potential when it matures. If the dog is not well above average quality, it is pointless to pursue on a show career. It is far better to consider the dog a treasured companion and, if the interest in showing is strong, get some experience at dog shows as a spectator and then buy a dog that has possibilities as a winner.

While showing can become an absorbing and enjoyable hobby, there is little point in spending money on competing with an inferior specimen. The vital ingredient of a successful show dog is breed type. The dog must look like its breed — it must walk into the ring and shout "I am a Boxer" or "I am a Poodle." The instant recognition of a particular breed is as much a matter of temperament and "attitude" as it is of the physical requirements of the breed Standard. Other essentials are soundness of mind and body, condition and handling.

Handling in the Ring

In Britain and Europe dog showing remains very much the province of the dedicated amateur. Most breeders still handle their own dogs in the ring and derive much pleasure from so doing. There are few professional handlers who show other people's dogs for a living, although they are noticeably on the increase in some countries.

In the United States, on the other hand, and in Canada to a certain extent, where vast distances are often covered by campaigned show dogs, professional handlers are frequently used and dogs are often boarded with a handler for several months or years at a time, to fit in a busy show schedule.

Certainly professional handlers have an advantage over beginners, since years of experience will have taught them how to present the coat of various breeds, how best to emphasize virtues and disguise faults, and how to gait any dog to create the best impression of typical movement. However, few professional handlers have the time to build up the rapport which many long-serving "amateur" breeder/exhibitors can, and the fact that such people are living with their show dogs twenty-four hours a day means that they get a much closer insight into a dog's personality and what makes it tick.

If an owner chooses to show his or her dog, it should be very clear what he or she hopes

Two Show Views

To illustrate the difference a handler can make, here are two pictures of the same top winning English Cocker Spaniel shown in 1952. In the picture at left, the dog is posed by its handler to show it off to its best advantage, and indeed it is winning Best of Breed at the world-famous Morris and Essex Kennel Club dog show in the United States, under breed authority Raymond Beale. In the picture at right, taken ten minutes later, it is shown posed by its breeder/owner Harry Anyon.

Anyon had this photo taken because he felt that the first picture did not depict an English Cocker in the way that he felt was correct. The same dog is shown in each photo but presented differently.

The same dog is photographed here ten minutes later. The dog is being posed by the breeder and owner, Harry Anyon, in the manner he felt showed the English Cocker to its best advantage.

Ch. Cartref Canyon being posed by its handler, Anne Rogers Clark, at the Morris and Essex Kennel Club Show in 1952, where this English Cocker Spaniel won Best of Breed.

to achieve. It is important to always be realistic and know enough about the breed to realize where the dog fails and excels. An owner must also be sufficiently open-minded to see the virtues and faults of competing dogs. Showing dogs as a social activity may seem a good idea, but few people can handle being long-term losers. Everyone, if they are honest, wants to win, and for this reason it is important to take the best available dog into the ring in search of that goal.

PREPARING A DOG FOR A SHOW

Any show dog, no matter how outstanding, in terms of the breed Standard, must be shown to its advantage. It should be in peak condition (which comes through an ongoing program of diet, exercise and grooming), well presented

Competing in the show ring involves much work and devotion, as can be seen in the pre-show preparations of this owner of an Afghan Hound.

(which cannot be achieved simply the day before) and well handled. All show dogs should be trained to allow a strange judge to handle their intimate parts, must move at the optimum pace when required to, and be able to adopt a traditional show stance for the breed for an indefinite period of time. To achieve this, much preparation must take place before the show, and few newcomers manage to succeed without help from more experienced competitors.

COMPETING AROUND THE WORLD

In breed judging in many countries such as the United Kingdom, the United States, Australasia and Canada, classes of the same breed are judged against each other, and at the same time, are assessed against their breed's Standard. Of ten dogs, for instance, competing in the same class, a judge will be expected to place the winning dogs in order — First, Second, Third, etc. This continues until all the dogs of one breed have been judged and a Best of Breed winner is chosen. In the United Kingdom, this will be determined from the Best Dog and Best Bitch. In the United States on the other hand, Best of Breed will be chosen from the Best Dog and Best Bitch of the non-Champions (Winners Dog and Winners Bitch) alongside all the Champions.

In most member countries of the FCI the competition is more complex as it takes place on fundamentally two different levels. Firstly, dogs are judged in isolation against the breed Standard. They are given an individual, written, detailed critique and are then given a Quality Grading. This will be Excellent/First; Very Good/Second; Good/Third, etc. The actual nomenclature depends on the country in which the dog is judged. Once all the dogs in a particular class have been graded, then only those receiving a First or Excellent grading are called back into the ring. Those with lesser gradings leave the ring with their critiques, never to return again. Once a judge has placed those dogs selected as Excellent in order, he or she is then invited to give further honors, if desired, by attesting that some of the placed dogs are of "Certificate Quality."

This kind of system involves much more work on the part of the judges, the stewards, the kennel clubs and the organizers in general, but it has great advantages. In the first instance every exhibitor gets the judge's actual opinion. This is not the case in the United Kingdom and the United States, for example, where it is highly feasible that a judge might leave a dog out of the placings which, had it been judged under a grading system, would have comfortably achieved an Excellent. Further, if the owner is a newer exhibitor, he or she is told the dog's shortcomings as well as its virtues. This is very educational as these critiques tend to be quite forthright. Newer exhibitors quickly become accustomed to appreciating the dog as it is, faults and all. Because these critiques are a major part of the competition system in Scandinavia, they have contributed largely to the rapid advances made in these countries in both the breeding and judging spheres.

In any country, Championship titles can only be won against competition in the same breed, whether this is achieved through Certificates or a points system, although in the United States final points may be achieved via success at Group level. In breed judging it is imperative that the judge's major consideration be rewarding the best specimen in the breed, by virtue of its correct type, measured against the breed Standard, and its physical and mental soundness.

It is important that judges and owners appreciate that different breeds have different temperaments, and in some breeds what is actually typical temperament for the breed may not coincide with what is generally perceived as an ideal "show" temperament. A real extrovert character with relentless showmanship may be extremely eye-catching to both ringside and judge, but at all times a major consideration must be whether a dog exhibits temperament that is typical for its breed.

Once a dog has won Best of Breed it will progress through to its respective Group where it will be competing against other Best of Breed winners of basically similar type.

Variety judging of this nature is a far less exact form of judging than standard breed judging, because the comparisons necessary are not direct. In other words, the Best of Breed Beagle will be assessed against the Beagle breed Standard while the Best of Breed Whippet will be judged against its Standard. Whichever comes closest to its breed ideal should, in theory, win.

When judging a single breed, the judge is comparing each dog against the same breed Standard. In variety judging, however, it is impossible to compare like with like. Each dog is evaluated against its own particular breed Standard, and then compared with the other breeds in competition. The judge's results will be based on the closeness of each breed to its own Standards. Once group winners have been established, they all then compete for the ultimate accolade of Best in Show, and again variety judging takes place.

It is a sad fact of life, and perhaps a poor reflection on the knowledge of some judges, that certain breeds tend to score over others, simply because they are perceived to be "better Group dogs," in other words they have more

A Miniature Poodle is shown being put through its paces during an Obedience trial.

"glamor" or "showiness" than others. In theory, any breed should be capable of winning top honors, provided its closeness to its own breed Standard is much higher than that of any of its competitors.

SPECIAL ACTIVITIES

The American Kennel Club has encouraged the development of the utilitarian side of purebred Sporting, Hound, Working, Terrier and Herding breeds by sponsoring field trials, hunting tests and working trials. For those dogs that pass the trials and tests, accreditation is provided indicating that these beautiful hunting and working breeds are not only structurally and mentally attuned for work, but can indeed perform the work for which each breed was developed. The AKC sanctions such events as Beagle trials, lure coursing for Sighthounds, earthdog tests for Terriers and Dachshunds, all sorts of Obedience classes, working certificates for Retrievers and herding tests for Herding breeds. There is strong support in the fancy for Agility tests that attract all breeds. Many Sporting breeds such as the German Shorthaired Pointer, Brittany and Viszla, boast dual Champions in the field and on the bench.

The Canadian Kennel Club and the Kennel Club in the United Kingdom also sponsor working trials and tests for Sporting and Working breeds. The Kennel Club sponsors Working, Field, Agility, Bloodhound and Obedience trials. In fact gun dogs and Border Collies in the United Kingdom must earn three Champion Certificates to become a Show Champion plus earn and maintain a working qualification to become a full Champion.

Tests and trials for both hunting and Working breeds have been held in most west European and Scandinavian countries since the early 1900s. They are usually run by kennel clubs in FCI countries. These clubs train and educate judges for the different breed trials and tests. In many FCI countries it is necessary to have a test or trial result if a Working or hunting breed is to qualify as a Show Champion. It is also necessary in these countries that Conformation awards be earned for a dog to attain a Trial or Working Champion title.

Internationally, judges for field events can be Conformation judges or they may only be licensed or approved for trial judging. Tests and trials are judged on performance of the dogs alone and not on Conformation, although ideally the best-constructed dog should have the most stamina and ability to do its job well. Judges look for courage, a good nose, and intelligence when judging these trial events.

LOWER LEVELS OF SHOWS

While Champions can only be created at Championship shows, in various countries there are lower levels of shows which are utilized to the full by exhibitors who wish to gain experience for themselves, their dogs, or who simply do not feel it is advisable to compete against the very uppermost level of competition. These shows can take various forms. Some are very much lower-key versions of the Championship events. Others are considerably less formal events, sometimes with entries being taken on the day, as in the case of the British exemption show. These shows are usually held in aid of a charity and are frequently held in conjunction with a village fair or country show. Apart from a handful of pedigree classes, there are invariably novelty classes which include such titles as "Dog with the waggiest tail" or "Dog most like its owner." Often non-pedigree dogs will be found competing in such classes, and while they may be considered a little beneath the dignity of more seasoned exhibitors, these classes can prove excellent training grounds for young stock before their show careers start in earnest.

Whatever type of dog show an exhibitor enters, it is essential that he or she should keep the whole business in perspective. Pearls of wisdom to be remembered include: "There is always another show and always another judge," and "The dog you take home with you is the same dog you brought that morning."

AFFENPINSCHER

ORIGIN AND DEVELOPMENT

Even the cognoscenti who have been involved with Toy dogs for many years will agree that there is only a small amount of information on this rare breed. Though known from about the year 1600, very little historical material on the Affenpinscher exists. What is known, as the roots of the name reveal, is that the breed was developed in Germany where, at a time when it was larger in size than is now preferred, these dogs were used as ratters in stables and on farms. Most were 12-14 inches/30-35 cm in height, and black, reddish black, or salt and pepper in color.

Smaller sized dogs were preferred by some and these were bred as mousers for use in the home. Old sources say that it was a man living near Lubeck, Germany, who first concentrated on producing a distinct, small breed. At the

Affenpinscher with natural (uncropped) ears

same time, others were breeding a larger dog used to kill rats. Most canine historians believe that these dogs were the predecessors of the breed now known as the Miniature Schnauzer.

The *Schoshunderassen* (which loosely means pet dog) with their monkeylike expression, naturally clean nature, minimum of coat care, and intelligent behavior, quickly worked their way into the hearts of early breeders. The Dutch Pug, then immensely popular, was infused into the early blood of these dogs, as was the smooth-haired German Pinscher and another breed referred to as the German Silky Pinscher. These crosses are the root of the great variety in colors.

Some paintings by Old Masters depict a small, rough-coated, bearded dog which seems likely to be an early example of the Affenpinscher.

Temperament

These dogs are normally quiet, inquisitive and non-argumentative, although they will fiercely defend their owners and homes from the largest transgressor.

Health Matters

Serious health matters do not seem to trouble the Affenpinscher. However, it is a Toy dog, so care must be taken with its fine bones. It should be prevented from jumping off furniture as this can lead to broken bones. Its coat must be kept tidy and clean to forestall skin problems. Similarly, its face and eyes should be checked daily and washed and cleaned if necessary. This is because the coat on the head is profuse and may interfere with the Affenpinscher's eyesight if not attended to.

Special Care and Training

The Affenpinscher needs no more special attention than any small dog. Obedience training, like walking to heel and coming when called, is best started at an early age.

Adaptability

The breed went through a period of greatly diminished popularity but continued to hold

The Affenpincher's monkey-like expression is the breed's signature.

a core of devoted fanciers. Some superior specimens in the show ring have attracted a recent rebirth of interest in the breed, and more are now being seen. Its ease of care, quick to learn attitude and ability to charm swiftly those in its company are certain to assure the Affenpinscher a new wave of devotees.

Essentials of the Breed

Today's Affenpinscher is about 10 1/4 inches/ 26 cm high, with a harsh, dense coat which should look neat but shaggy. Black or black with gray shading are the most dominant colors and, generally, the most desired. Black-and-tan, silver-gray, red and mixtures of these are also found. The signature of the breed is its monkeylike expression which is attained through a combination of its small head with a broad brow and the shaggy, standoff coat on its head, neck, and shoulders. The ears — small, high set and carried erect if cropped — complete the picture.

Registry: AKC, CKC, FCI (Group 2), KC

AFGHAN HOUND

ORIGIN AND DEVELOPMENT

The Afghan Hound is a glamorous show dog, an arrogant yet mischievous companion, and an extraordinarily agile hunter. It belongs to the family of sighthounds or gazehounds (those who hunt by sight). This grouping ranges from the imposing, stately, Irish Wolfhound to the speedy Whippet — some people also include the dainty Italian Greyhound. The Afghan Hound falls into the intermediate range of this family. It has greater breadth of body and larger feet than other gazehounds, of which the Greyhound is the prototype. In addition, the Afghan is more angular than curvy or sinuous.

The Afghan Hound was unknown to Western civilization until the late nineteenth century, when members of the British military took several specimens of the breed home with them and began to exhibit them at local pet shows. The earliest reference to the Afghan Hound in pictures is in a work by Thomas Duer Broughton entitled, *Letters Written in a Mahretta Camp During the Year 1809*. This book was published in London in 1813 and shows a colored plate entitled, "A Meenah of Jajurh", a native soldier with quite a small Afghan Hound, probably one of the dogs kept

Afghan Hound

in military camps used as a guard dog.

Before this, however, the Afghan Hound's origin and history is mainly conjecture. There has been vast research into its background, but the history of the breed is part myth, part legend, and the remainder derives from the combined history of several Greyhound breeds from Afghanistan and the surrounding countries. It is generally acknowledged that the Afghan Hound and Saluki are descendants from a common source, and may even have been interbred. The controversy about which came first is longstanding and will probably never be resolved.

The diversity within the two breeds varies and is probably due more to geography than selection. The Afghan Hounds of the lowlands of southern and western Afghanistan, toward Iran or Baluchistan, tend to have a sparse coat and a leaner, more racy appearance which is similar to the Salukis of that region. In the rugged mountain terrain of the Hindu Kush range, however, Afghan Hounds tend to be shorter, more powerfully built and to have shaggy coats. From this area, specifically in the mountains around Kabul, developed the modern notion of the "mountain type" Afghan Hound, with a full coat and profuse topknot. Discovery of these shaggy beasts has sparked the ever-continuing argument about which is the elder statesman of the breed: the powerfully built heavily coated Afghan Hound or the sparsely coated, lighter built Saluki.

In 1856, Lt. Col. Kullmar, who was attached to the American Embassy in Kabul, acquired an Afghan Hound and set out to research the breed's history in its native land. He met a native Afghani general who agreed to peruse the historical archives. He learned that the breed had found favor with a local ruler, Sultan Muhamud Ghaznawe. The Sultan utilized Afghan Hounds in his campaigns as couriers, guards and hunters. He also considered them lucky talismans. He referred to them as Tazi dogs and even named a region for them. The general also noted, "...There are two types of Tazi found in Afghanistan: the longhaired (called the most pure and most valued) and the shorthaired. The longhaired Tazi lives in the north and northwestern parts of Afghanistan. The shorthaired Tazi lives principally in the eastern, southern and western parts of the country."

Much of the modern history of the Afghan Hound is due to the work of Major Amps and his wife, Mary, who were transferred from their native England to the area of Kabul soon after the 1919 Afghan War. They established their kennel, "Ghazni," in the hill country of Afghanistan and they became influential in determining the breed's future. Their Sirdar of Ghazni and Khan of Ghazni are found in most American Afghan Hound pedigrees, and Mary Amps researched the breed and wrote prolifically on the subject.

The Amps returned to England with their hounds and competed with the stock of the Bell-Murray contingent, who had brought in the rangier, sparsely coated "desert type" of hound. By 1926, Afghan Hounds of both "types" found their way to the United States. It did not hurt the breed's popularity that the comedian Zeppo Marx and his wife brought some carefully selected stock back from England and that Marion Florsheim sold war bonds with her Afghan Hound always by her side.

TEMPERAMENT

Afghan Hounds are naturally eye-catching with their exotic looks, luxuriant coats and aristocratic mien. Their regal bearing notwithstanding, there beats the heart of irrepressible exuberance and puckish humor with those they know well. When newly introduced, the Afghan Hound is reserved and aloof, needing time to become acquainted before letting down its guard.

HEALTH MATTERS

The Afghan Hound is a healthy breed, often living into its teens. There has been some evidence of juvenile cataracts and a few cases of hip dysplasia, but these are rare.

SPECIAL CARE AND TRAINING

The Afghan Hound requires daily exercise to keep fit. The Afghan coat, like human hair, needs to be brushed and washed on at least a weekly basis.

ADAPTABILITY

Afghan Hounds are amazingly adaptable, versatile and have a sense of the ridiculous. Primarily sighthounds, they have been known to follow a track, retrieve and herd, and hunt independently — their hallmark. As a broken-field runner, the Afghan Hound has no equal.

The Afghan Hound was designed to be a swift, sharp-turning and independent hunter. This breed enjoys doing what is asked of it, but frequently reminds its owner that it has ideas of its own.

ESSENTIALS OF THE BREED

The Afghan Hound's characteristics are described well in the American Standard calling for: "An aristocrat, his whole appearance one of dignity and aloofness with no trace of plainness or coarseness. His head must be "proudly-carried... eyes gazing into the distance as if in memory of ages past." To hunt it needs to be far-sighted, so will pull back its head to see something under its nose. The American Standard lists the "striking characteristics of the breed — exotic, or Eastern expression, large feet, and the impression of somewhat exaggerated bend of stifle due to profuse trouserings..." Once seen, its breathtaking, free-floating powerful stride and springing gait, is never forgotten.

The Afghan Hound's square, angular outline distinguishes it from its cousins, the Greyhound, Scottish Deerhound and Whippet, which have more sinuous curves. The Afghan stands about 25-27 inches/63-68 cm high and weighs about 50-60 pounds/22-27 kg. It is not heavily bodied and the hip bones should be prominent. It may be any solid color, black-and-tan, and also domino, (a dark coat on the saddle and face with pale leg furnishings and top-knot). White markings are not desirable on the head but white shirt frontings are allowed.

Registry: AKC, CKC, FCI (Group 10), KC

AÏDI/CHIEN D'ATLAS

This very rare breed is a Moroccan herding dog that is said to be closely related to European mountain dogs. It has a reputation as a serious guard dog but is mainly used as a working dog.

The height at its withers should be about 20-24 inches/52-62 cm. The medium Aïdi should have a rustic appearance and be strongly built. Its ears are semi- erect, as in the Border Collie, and its tail is long. The coat should be moderately long, except on the neck and tail where it is longer, thick and somewhat coarse in texture. The color should be white or cream, but wolf gray or white with gray flecks are also permissible.

Registry: FCI (Group 2)

Aïdi

AINU/HOKKAIDO

The Hokkaido is a Japanese spitz breed rarely seen outside that country. It was originally called Ainu after a tribe that has existed in Japan for thousands of years. The Ainu people, who live on Hokkaido, the most northern Japanese island, keep very much to their old traditions, and they still use their hunting dog as a working animal. The breed is hardy, self-confident and a ferocious hunter and guard dog. The Hokkaido is very suspicious of strangers, and most loyal and devoted to its master.

Japan has six native spitz breeds, the main difference between them being their size. The Hokkaido is about 17 1/2-20 1/2 inches/45-52 cm at its withers. The breeds' common features are a wedge-shaped head with pronounced cheeks, decidedly slanted eyes and hooded ears. However, the Hokkaido is more strongly built than the other middle-sized breeds. Its coat should be short and harsh, standing out from the body and a little longer on the tail and buttocks. It is most often white or red with cream markings.

Registry: FCI (Group 5)

Ainu

AIREDALE TERRIER

ORIGIN AND DEVELOPMENT

The majority of terriers were evolved in Great Britain, and almost all were engendered and fully developed in the northern regions. The exact origins of the modern-day terrier go back a long way and stem from the old, wirehaired Black and Tan Terrier that played a major role in its development. There is considerable supportive testimony to this and it is conceivable that the Black and Tans were themselves descendants of the dogs mentioned in early writings as "teroure" (1570) and "terrores," depicted as "dogges serving ye pastime of hunting beastes."

The geography of an area usually determined the work of the sporting terrier, many being designated a parochial or regional denomination from where they originated. The Airedale Terrier is one such example. It probably came into existence around 1840, and was primarily introduced by workers in the wool industry and miners of the West Riding of Yorkshire, England, which encompassed Bingley, Otley, Shipley and smaller places along the course of the Aire and Wharfe Rivers. The breed owes its inception to the passion for otter-hunting of the residents of this region. The Airedale's prowess was that of a surface and waterside hunter, passing through various vicissitudes in its formative period, from contributions by the Old English Black and Tan, Irish, and White English Terriers. The Otterhound also played a major part in the Airedale's ancestry, coming from an area where Otterhounds worked alongside contemporary hard-bitten dogs about the size of a Fox Terrier.

Broken-haired terriers were first exhibited in the 1860s at agricultural shows around Yorkshire, materializing by 1875 as the Waterside, Bingley or Wharfedale Terrier. Following a meeting of like-minded fanciers, held at the Airedale Agricultural Society show of 1882, by popular acclaim the breed became known as the

Airedale Terrier

Airedale Terrier. The Birmingham National Show in the following year scheduled three classes for the Airedale. Then in 1886 the breed was added to the Kennel Club Stud Book. The register shows that out of thirty registrations, eighteen possessed pedigrees. The breed gradually became better known outside its native Yorkshire, and with selective breeding the Airedale became more uniform, taking on terrier characteristics, shape and type. The majority weighed upward of 45 pounds/20 kg. The length of their legs was paramount to their work, enabling them to leap from river bank to river bank without swimming and to clamber over Yorkshire stone walls without assistance.

TEMPERAMENT

The Airedale, truly the king of terriers, has a temperament par excellence. It is intelligent, biddable, utterly reliable and versatile, finding itself in many roles from hunting to guarding and security work to simply being a companion. Unfortunately in some European countries, Airedales are encouraged to display aggression. This is thoroughly undesirable since its natural temperament is beyond reproach.

HEALTH MATTERS

Like the majority of terriers, the Airedale is extremely hardy, with few if any health problems. Visits to the vet are usually confined to minor matters and routine inoculations. Airedales that are to be used for breeding purposes should be X-rayed for hip dysplasia.

SPECIAL CARE AND TRAINING

The Airedale is very responsive to training, probably the easiest of all in the Terrier Group, and it reacts well to basic obedience routines. Regular grooming is essential because they have two coats — a soft undercoat and a hard-textured outer jacket. It is better if Airedales can be hand-stripped, at least twice yearly, usually in the spring and fall. This method is painless, removes dead hair and helps to maintain the correct color and texture of the coat. Clipping, while quick, economical and effective to a degree, eventually debases both the beautiful natural color and texture of the coat. Airedales do not cast their coat naturally.

ADAPTABILITY

The Airedale is just as much at ease in town or country, but because of its size it requires space and exercise. They are not ideal dogs for apartment-dwellers. They are blessed with inherent good sense and seldom "get under their owners' feet". They are absolutely devoted companions, their protective instincts are well developed, and yet they do not give voice unnecessarily. The Airedale is an all-round sporting dog that can be readily trained to the gun — such is its versatility.

ESSENTIALS OF THE BREED

With the exception of weight, there has been very little change in the fundamental breed Standard. Setting aside the size and color, the Airedale has many analogous points with the Wire Fox Terrier, but the Airedale has none of the exaggerated characteristics that the Wire often has. Its expression is one of intelligence and beauty. The head is long, the eye dark and full of terrier expression. The jaw is punishing with teeth that close with a vice-like hold. The correct earset is essential to convey the typical expression. The topline of the forward-folded ear should be above the level of the skull, the ear being small yet in proportion to the size of the dog. Pendulous, houndy ears destroy the true Airedale expression. The quality Airedale has a reachy neck which is clean, free from throatiness, gradually widening towards the shoulders. These should be long, well laid back, sloping obliquely into the back. The front is straight, the elbows perpendicular to the body. The legs have round bone, finishing with tight catlike and well-padded feet. The back is short, with a well-sprung, deep rib cage affording ample heartroom. In the well ribbed up, or short-coupled animal there is little space between the back rib and thigh. The topline should be level, with no suggestion of slackness. The tail is set high (resulting in the terrier phrase "plenty of dog behind the tail") and is customarily docked. The hindquarters should be long and muscular, the second thigh well developed, the hocks well let down and parallel when viewed from the rear.

The Airedale must be upstanding, smart and symmetrical. The coat texture should be hard, wiry and dense. The body color should be black or black-grizzle. The head and ears should be of a rich tan, the ears often being slightly darker. The legs up to the shoulder and thigh should also be tan, a rich mahogany shade being much favored. Measured at the withers, Airedale dogs should stand around 23-24 inches/ 58-61 cm, with bitches 1 inch/2.5 cm less. Weight should be commensurate with height and type and should convey the impression of great strength and substance but not at the expense of quality.

Registry: AKC, CKC, FCI (Group 3), KC

AKBASH

The Akbash originates from the great plains of Turkey. It is a large dog mainly used by shepherds to guard flocks of sheep against predators. In its country of origin, the breed is known to be a serious guard dog that is confident, an independent worker and very suspicious of strangers.

The Akbash is about 28-34 inches/70-86 cm high and is built on more elegant lines than are usually associated with big flock guardians of this kind. Its coat should be white and lie flat on the body. It should be considerably longer on the chest and neck, almost forming a mane and it should also be long on the tail and buttocks. Sometimes the Akbash is shorthaired. Both coat varieties should have a double coat with a thick undercoat.

Registry: Not recognized by the AKC, CKC, FCI or KC.

The Rough-coated Akbash is used in Turkey to guard flocks of sheep against predators and is built more elegantly than most big flock guardians.

AKITA/JAPANESE AKITA

ORIGIN AND DEVELOPMENT

This much loved Japanese breed takes its name from the prefecture of Akita in northern Japan. The Akita dates back some three hundred years and today resembles the Japanese dog found carved in early Japanese tombs. Its ears, carriage and distinctive tail are unmistakable.

The Akita is the largest dog of any breed surviving in Japan today. In July 1931 the Japanese government designated the Akita as a National Monument and as one of Japan's national treasures. Used in its homeland as a guard dog, and as a hunter of bear, deer and wild boar, the Akita was also put to work as a retriever of waterfowl from land and water. The Akita was used as a fighting dog until that unfortunate sport was outlawed. It was not unusual for the Akita to be revered as a pet in Japanese households and when they died very often their pelts were hung in the house in memory of the departed dog.

In type, the Akita mirrors its northern heritage, seen in the so-called spitz breeds. Its head, erect ears, heavy curled tail, wonderfully thick and luxurious double coat make it a recognizable part of this family. In October 1973 they were classified as Working Dogs at American Kennel Club Shows.

TEMPERAMENT

The Akita is apt to be very aggressive toward other dogs. The answer to this is early obedience training which should then be maintained through its entire life. The breed tends to be obstinate, but is very cooperative once the message is firmly made clear.

If the Akita is going to be in a household with children, it should be brought up with them from puppyhood. It must have exercise for both its well-being and training — this will stretch both mind and intelligence. Always remember that the Akita is primarily a guard dog, and because of its great size and strength must be taught to obey implicitly if it is to be an integral part of the home life of its owners. The breed as such does not have a bad temper — but it can display the temperament that it was bred to have. Care must be taken with discipline and it should be firm. However, severity will be reacted against by these dogs.

Akita or Japanese Akita as it is known in the United Kingdom

HEALTH MATTERS

The Akita is a type of northern dog that it is considered a very natural breed — as such it tends to be quite healthy. As a precaution, the hips should be X-rayed on breeding stock after the age of two since hip dysplasia is well known in the breed. In fact, almost all dogs of this size (irrespective of breed) are subject to varying degrees of hip laxity. Hypothyroidism is known in the breed as well as some forms of inherited eye problems. Always buy from reputable breeders since they should have kept health records for several generations. Dealing with reliable breeders reduces the chances of buying a puppy susceptible to hip displasia, hypothyroidism or other problems.

Skin problems may be kept to a minimum by caring for the Akita's coat and skin meticulously. Since the Akita has a very thick double coat, keeping it in a warm environment, either indoors or out, is not in the best interest of the animal. The Akita should become accustomed to having its teeth examined as a puppy so that it can be checked that the baby teeth are being shed according to schedule. This will teach it to have manners in relation to its mouth when the time comes to begin brushing its new teeth to keep them clean and prevent mouth odors.

Likewise the Akita's nails should be trimmed just a little every week with a dog nail cutter so that it will allow this to be done all its life with little or no fuss. If the nails are always kept short, there will never be a time when nail cutting will hurt the dog and it will become used to the procedure. The ears of this erect-eared breed are rarely a problem. If there is a noticeable odor coming from the ear opening or if the dog shakes or paws at its ears, you should consult a veterinarian.

SPECIAL CARE AND TRAINING

The Akita has a thick double coat typical of its northern dog heritage. In warm weather the coat will shed and should be encouraged to do so by mild shampooing in warm baths, followed by careful drying and brushing. Obedience training is essential — the dog must know to obey its owners. The Akita is widely known for its loyalty.

ADAPTABILITY

Adequate space is essential because the Akita is such a large dog. In its homeland, Japan, where space is not always available, a single Akita may be kept as a pet in a very small house; however, it has humans at its beck and call to grant its every wish, be it a walk or a romp. A Japanese scholar has written, "the character of these dogs suggests the ancient Japanese people, austere, valiant, faithful, good natured, gentle and sensitive to the kindness of their masters."

ESSENTIALS OF THE BREED

The Akita is large, slightly longer from breast to rear than from top of its shoulders to the ground. Males usually top off at 26-28 inches/ 66-71 cm tall, with females 1-2 inches/2.5-5 cm smaller. The Akita has moderate angles in fore and hindquarters, a large wedge-shaped head, erect and expressive ears carried slightly forward (when folded forward the ear tip just reaches the eye), small deep-set eyes that appear triangular, heavy bones, a thick double coat of various colors. This is finished off with a well-placed and carried thick, heavy curled tail.

The white Akita used to be the most well thought of, with its black pigmented nose, mouth and toe pads. This color is not the most favored in the American dog scene today, with solid reds, brindles and all manner of colors with white in pleasing patterns now more often shown in competition. The Fédération Cynologique Internationale's Standard varies dramatically from the American and British versions and the Japanese-inspired FCI Standard does not allow the particolor that is accepted in the States and Britain. All over the world, however, the Akita has a majesty and bearing that is unmistakable.

Registry: AKC, CKC, FCI (Group 5), KC

ALASKAN MALAMUTE

ORIGIN AND DEVELOPMENT

The use of dogs as draft or hunting animals in the far north has been a part of northern peoples' culture since the Stone Age. The Alaskan Malamute was developed by a tribe of Nomadic, industrious and skilled Inuit people called Mahlemuts, who lived in the upper part of western Alaska, across from Siberia along the shores of Kotzebue Sound. The Mahlemuts wanted a large, strong, sled-pulling dog that was not a speedster but a heavy hauler so that they could use them as draft animals. In the harsh and bitter cold, dogs were the only domestic animals that could survive. In the summer when sleds could not be used to carry heavier loads, Malamutes were used as pack dogs. In the nineteenth century, European explorers and Russian whalers used to tell of the Mahlemut tribe having dogs of great beauty and endurance.

As the white man settled in Alaska from 1750 to 1900, dogs were used for hunting and hauling in large numbers with little attention paid to type. Further, the emerging sport of

Alaskan Malamute

dog sled racing did the Malamute breed no favors as many crosses were made to other breeds in a vain attempt to make them faster. The Eskimos kept their dogs true to type and fortunately the breed became interesting to United States breeders, among them the legendary "Short" Seely, a breeder in New Hampshire. "Short" Seely obtained good specimens, bred them wisely, and sent them off with Admiral Byrd on his Antarctic voyage.

TEMPERAMENT

The Malamute is family oriented, loves to be with people and has a friendly, open demeanor. It is a wonderful companion and lives very well with children. It is happiest when pulling a sled or a wheeled cart and the children of the family will enjoy this aspect. The Malamute also makes a good jogging companion.

HEALTH MATTERS

The Alaskan Malamute is quite healthy as befits a natural breed, although it is known to suffer from a condition where the growth of the limbs is reduced (known as dwarfism, achondroplasia or chondrodystrophia). The Malamute's hips should be X-rayed if the animal is to be used for breeding. Teeth and nails should also be attended to throughout its life. This breed should not be allowed to become obese.

SPECIAL CARE AND TRAINING

Obedience training is very important to Malamutes for it gives their minds a sense of purpose and the exercise is good for them. Many Malamute owners train their dogs for weight-pulling contests. The dogs take to this very well and are able to shift one-ton loads over short distances. They are not city dogs and need good exercise, either sledding, jogging or in an enclosed safe yard. A bored Malamute is noisy and destructive. Their coats are heavy and unique — a harsh topcoat and a heavy plush undercoat. Shedding in warm weather is natural and the Malamute coat must be kept clean and brushed weekly. Parasites (fleas and ticks) can cause skin problems, so careful attention should be paid to keeping the Malamute free of these pests.

ADAPTABILITY

Well suited to colder climates, the Alaskan Malamute prefers outdoor living and is definitely not comfortable in hot, humid weather. This breed is not suited to city living as it needs space in which to exercise and do its own thing — pulling sleds and being a playful companion.

ESSENTIALS OF THE BREED

A substantial, powerful breed, Malamutes are a good size — males are 25 inches/64 cm and 85 pounds/38.5 kg; females are 23 inches/59 cm and 75 pounds/34 kg. The breed has heavy bones, good feet and a well-knit body.

The head of the Alaskan Malamute is large and wedge shaped; the eyes should preferably be dark and must not be blue. The ears should be well furred and erect. Its tail is long, bushy and carried over the back. Many colors are permissible, usually light gray to black with a white underbody and white markings on the face, feet and legs. The head may have cap-like markings or a mask. The breed should have a thick double coat and a proud carriage. The Malamute should not have any problems that would prevent it from heavy duty, such as hauling freight through ice and snow.

Registry: AKC, CKC, FCI (Group 5), KC

ALPINE DACHSBRACKE/ ALPENLANDISCHE DACHSBRACKE

The Alpine Dachsbracke comes from the alplands of Austria where it is mainly used for deer hunting. Fanciers of the Alpine Dachsbracke also find them useful for hunting fox and hare and for retrieving and tracking wounded prey. The breed is rarely seen outside its home country.

Alpine Dachsbracke

The dog was developed from old breeds that were generally intended to be hardy and useful for working in very rough terrain. The Alpine Dachsbracke was recognized in the 1880s and is still mainly kept and used as a hunting dog.

The Alpine Dachsbracke's body should be a definite rectangular shape, with strong, fairly short legs but not so short as to give an impression of being lowlegged. The height at its withers should be 14-15 inches/36-38 cm. The head should be shaped like that of East European hounds i.e. a broad skull, high-set ears that are wide at the base and without folds. Its coat should be close fitting, coarse in texture and about 1 inch/2.5 cm long. The color should be deep red, usually with black tips. Although black and tan are not mentioned as a permitted color in the Standard, the breed is also known to carry this color.

Registry: FCI (Group 6)

AMERICAN ESKIMO DOG

Americans have been used to seeing the forerunner of this new American breed in and around the larger cities in the United States for years. Before World War I the German Spitz was frequently seen, kept as a house pet by German émigrés around New York City. These small white dogs became more and more numerous, all of them descending from the larger German Spitz, the Wold Spitz or Keeshond (from Holland), the white Pomeranian and the Italian spitz breed, Volpino Italiano. After World War II some of the breeders may have incorporated crosses to the Japanese Spitz.

Across the United States, these small white dogs became known as the American Spitz. In 1917 the breed was renamed the American Eskimo Dog, with Eskie as its nickname. No one seems to know why the breed name was chosen except that some of the native American Eskimos produced a spitz-type working sled dog. The Eskie seems to be a miniaturized version of these dogs. In 1985 the American Eskimo Dog Club of America was formed to work toward American Kennel Club recognition for the breed. It is now recognized and competes in the Non-Sporting Group. It is the fifth Nordic or spitz breed to compete in this

American Eskimo Dog

group, the others being the Finnish Spitz, the Keeshond, the Shiba Inu and the Chow Chow.

The Eskie is typical of a small dog that has been bred to be a house dog, companion and watch dog. Its warning bark to signal the approach of a stranger is never followed by aggression. It is watchful, alert, intelligent and friendly. The American Eskimo Dog is wonderful with its human family and includes all ages in its circle — shyness is rare. The Eskie will also quickly learn all the established tricks that people teach to pet dogs.

A remarkably healthy dog, the Eskie needs attention paid to its eyes and tear ducts. The breed's thick double coat should be kept clean and free of fleas that can cause dermatitis.

Bred as a house dog and companion, the Eskie is an "indoor" breed. Housetraining and an introduction to plenty of human companionship should be done as early as possible in its life. The Eskie must be groomed weekly, well brushed, bathed as necessary, and its teeth and nails attended to regularly.

The Eskie comes in three sizes, measured at the top of the shoulder. The Toy is 9 inches/ 23 cm up to and including 12 inches/30 cm; the Miniature is over 12 inches/30 cm up to and including 15 inches/38 cm; and the Standard is over 15 inches/38 cm up to and including 19 inches/48 cm. This means that there is an Eskie for all interests and house sizes. They love to walk and should be well exercised either on a leash or in a safely enclosed yard.

Eskies always have a white coat, or white with biscuit or cream markings. Their skin is pink or gray; black is the preferred color of the pigment in their eyelids, gums, nose and pads.

The shape of an Eskie is like that of a spitz breed, it is slightly longer than tall, has the spitz or Nordic-type face with erect triangular-shaped ears and a wedge-shaped head with muzzle and skull about the same length. Its neck is well carried, topline good and level, tail well placed and carried arched over the body when at attention. Good legs and feet allow the Eskie to trot with bold energetic action. Its thick white or biscuit-colored double coat should not be trimmed with the exception of neatening any stray hairs about its feet and up the back of its hocks. The coat on the American Eskimo Dog should have no curl or wave; the undercoat should be thick and plush with the harsher outer coat growing up through it.

No colors other than those described above are allowed. The eyes must not be blue and no Eskie may be shown if it is under 9 inches/23cm or over 19 inches/48cm. The breed has many admirers and it has withstood the test of time.

Registry: AKC

AMERICAN PIT BULL TERRIER

A fairly old breed by American standards, the American Pit Bull Terrier's ancestors were introduced to the United States in the mid-1800s by Boston-Irish immigrants. These dogs were combined with stock from England and Scotland which dated back to before 1900 in their native lands and were early forebears of the Staffordshire Bull Terrier. American Pit Bulls were bred to be fighting dogs and their abilities were honed for that purpose by early breeders — blood sports played an important part in the development of the breed. These dogs have strong assertive personalities so owners have a responsibility to train the breed carefully.

Because of the breed's characteristics, there are laws concerning ownership in some countries. In Great Britain, for instance, the Dangerous Dogs Act introduced in 1991 does not allow import or ownership of Pit Bulls unless a Certificate of exemption has been obtained. This involves neutering the dog and implanting in the dog an identifying transponder. Owners must hold a third party insurance policy and the dog must be recorded on the index of Exempted Dogs. The dog must be kept in secure conditions, be muzzled in public places and held on the leash by someone who is at least sixteen years of age. Infringement of the Act results in a fine and/or imprisonment of the owner, and in many cases, an order for the destruction of the dog.

The American Pit Bull Terrier weighs between 35-60 pounds/16-27 kg and is muscularly built with a deep chest and well-sprung ribs. The coat is short, glossy, and stiff and can be of any color or combination. Its skull should be flat, wide and brick-like and its ears may be natural or cropped.

Famed for their intelligence and loyalty, American Pit Bull Terriers make excellent companions despite the unfair press the breed sometimes receives. Given their strong personality, obedience training is highly recommended.

Registry: not recognized by the AKC, CKC, FCI or KC.

American Pit Bull Terrier

AMERICAN STAFFORDSHIRE TERRIER

ORIGIN AND DEVELOPMENT

This noble terrier, of American design, was only recognized relatively recently as a distinct breed. It descends from the dogs that were imported to the United States for the "sport" of dog fighting at the time of the American Civil War. The breed's roots stem from the fighting pits of England and those in America, dating from the early 1800s when Bulldog and Terrier breeding began.

A great variety of breeds have been credited with the development of the "Amstaff" as it is known today, including the Bull Terrier, the Old English White Terrier, the Black and Tan, the Bulldog, the Mastiff, the Pointer, the Dalmatian and, of course, the Staffordshire Bull Terrier.

The American Kennel Club recognized the Staffordshire Terrier as a distinct breed in 1935. Its name was changed to the American Staffordshire Terrier in 1972 and in 1974 the AKC admitted the Staffordshire Bull Terrier, its English cousin, to the Stud Book.

Americans diverted from the old Staffordshire Bull Terrier-type dog through varied infusions. There was not so much emphasis on breeding a distinct type as there was in developing a great fighting machine. The resulting dog is one of tremendous stamina, legendary courage, adaptability and intelligence and yet it is not inclined toward viciousness. The breed's fighting background has imparted courage and a protective nature. This combination makes the Amstaff an excellent guard dog. Many dog enthusiasts have come to appreciate the Amstaff's numerous physical and temperamental assets. This breed has taken a secure place in the dog show world and there have been many specimens that have made great wins in the strongest all-terrier and all-breed competitions.

TEMPERAMENT

Those familiar with the breed laud its easy going nature, devotion to family and friends, and its gentle ways with children. However, they may show aggressive responses to cats, rabbits and household pets. It is attentive to all that is happening around it, not prone to look for trouble but well able to handle any that might arise. During World War II, posters featuring this dog as a symbol of American courage and determination were commonly found.

HEALTH MATTERS

The Amstaff suffers from no hereditary illnesses. It is prone to hives caused by stress or insect bites. This may be treated with antihistamines under the direction of the vet. Also, a bored Amstaff that is kenneled for long periods of time may lick its legs out of boredom and cause an unsightly redness on its white markings. The dog and its surroundings should always be kept very clean. It will benefit from increased "quality time" with walks, obedience training and companionship. As with any muscular, active dog, correct feeding of a balanced nutritious diet is essential.

SPECIAL CARE AND TRAINING

This breed requires no special coat care. It requires special training because of its aggressive nature. Since it is intelligent, it will be quick to learn anything that its owner chooses to teach it. It needs an assertive training regimen.

ADAPTABILITY

This breed will live happily in both an urban or country setting, and is equally at ease in an apartment or in a home with larger grounds.

ESSENTIALS OF THE BREED

Muscular and remarkably agile rather than leggy or racy, Amstaffs run from 17-19 inches/ 43-48 cm at the withers, depending upon their sex. The neck is heavy and of medium length; the chest is deep and strong; the ribs are well sprung; the front is rather wide. Its legs are straight with large, round bones supported on

American Staffordshire Terrier with natural (uncropped) ears

well-arched and compact feet. Strength of jaw is of great importance and it should be well defined with obvious musculature, while the teeth should meet in a scissors bite capable of great punishing power.

The ears may be cropped or preferably natural, short and held rose, or half pricked. If cropped, they are short, erect and set on high.

The short, glossy and stiff coat can be found in all colors and may be solid, patched or multi-colored but should not be more than 80 percent white, black-and-tan or liver. The eye rims, nose and lips should have complete pigment, preferably in black.

Registry: AKC, CKC, FCI (Group 3)

ANATOLIAN SHEPHERD DOG

This large mastiff-type breed originated in Turkey where it was used primarily as a guardian of flocks. When first recognized in the United Kingdom, the breed was known as the Anatolian Karabash, a move that proved controversial with some breeders who claim that the Karabash, a fawn dog with black points, is the only true Anatolian Shepherd and that dogs of other colors are not pure. The Anatolian is a steady and bold dog that should not be aggressive. It is as well, however, to respect its guarding origins and appreciate these when considering ownership.

The coat is short and dense with a thick undercoat and so requires minimal grooming — a weekly thorough brushing is usually sufficient. Like all working breeds of this size, these active dogs need a lot of exercise and also mental stimulation to avoid boredom. It will live happily with humans but will do better in an outdoor situation than in a town house.

The Anatolian has a large skull, broad and flat between the ears, and males have a noticeably wider head than females. The muzzle should be one-third the total length, and the lips are slightly pendulous giving a square profile. The nose, lips and eye rims should be black. The eyes are rather small and deep set; the ears triangular in shape but rounded at the tips and moderate in size.

The Anatolian's body should be balanced and indicate power and strength; its movement should be supple and powerful. Typical of the breed is the low head carriage which shows the head, neck and topline being level when moving, creating an impression that the dog is stalking. The Anatolian Shepherd Dog should stand between 28-32 inches/71-81 cm at the shoulder and can weigh in excess of 140 pounds/63.5 kg.

Registry: FCI (Group 2), KC

Anatolian Shepherd Dog

ANGLO-FRANÇAIS AND FRANÇAIS HOUNDS

Listed under this heading are seven of the twenty-two French hound breeds that are recognized by the Fédération Cynologique Internationale. These are the Grand Anglo-Français Tricolore, Grand Anglo-Français Blanc et Noir, Grand Anglo-Français Blanc et Orange, Français Tricolore, Français Blanc et Noir, Français Blanc et Orange and Anglo-Français de Petit Vénerie.

As the breed name indicates, these French hounds are crossbreeds between the English (i.e. Anglo) Foxhound and several of the very old French hound breeds. The crossbreeding began seriously in the nineteenth century though it had been attempted earlier. The English Foxhound was originally developed by breeding from French hounds. Before 1957, when it was decided to call all varieties with Foxhound blood "Anglo-Français," most of the "crossbreeds" had very long breed names that stated all the breeds that combined to make up a pack (and which often eventually become a breed).

The larger types of Anglo-Français and the Français Hounds (no crossing with Foxhounds) are mainly used as pack hounds. Their prey might be stag, deer, boar or fox. "Grand" does not necessarily stand for the size of the hound — in most cases it is simply a label for a pack that is used for larger game, "Chien de Grand Vénerie." They are used for a hunting form called "Chasse-à-Courre" which means that the pack follows the prey and kills it. The other form is called "Chasse-à-Tir" where one, or several, or a pack of hounds chases the prey toward the guns. This form of hunting is mainly used for prey like boar and hare. The French expression for hounds used for smaller game, "Chiens de Petite Vénerie", is also part of the breed name in some cases, as in Anglo-Français de Petite Vénerie. The above breeds are strictly used for hunting and are rarely seen outside hunting kennels. The French

Grand Anglo-Français Tricolore

hounds are of the so-called West European hound type — they have a rather long, narrow head with a slightly convex nose ridge, low-set folded ears and a very noble expression. The breeds described here all have a smooth coat.

The height at the withers and color of the coat varies slightly: Grand Anglo-Français Tricolore is about 24-28 inches/60-70 cm and colored as its name suggests. Grand Anglo-Français Blanc et Noir is 24 1/2-28 inches/62-72 cm and mainly black with white trimming and pale tan markings. Grand Anglo-Français Blanc et Orange, Français Tricolore and Français Blanc et Orange are all about 24-28 inches/60-70 cm, and also colored as their names indicate. Français Blanc et Noir is about 24 1/2-28 inches/ 62-72 cm and is mainly black with white trimmings and pale tan markings. Anglo-Français de Petit Vénerie is is about 19-23 inches/46-58 cm and can be colored as the Tricolore, Blanc et Noir or Blanc et Orange.

Registry: FCI (Group 6)

APPENZELL CATTLE DOG/
APPENZELLER SENNENHUND

The Appenzell Cattle Dog was developed in the Swiss district of Appenzell and is believed to be a descendent of cattle dogs left there by the Romans. The modern Appenzeller, recognized in 1898, is still used as a cattle dog today. It is a self-assured dog, known to be a fearless farm or guard dog, that is affectionate to its family but slightly suspicious of strangers.

The breed should stand 20-22 inches/50-56 cm high and be square in build, with a tightly curled tail and ears hanging close to its cheeks. The coat should be close fitting and either black or Havana brown with symmetrical tan and white markings. Problems to look out for are a wall eye, a tail that is straight or has a kink, a single coat and colors other than those above.

Registry: FCI (Group 2)

Appenzell Cattle Dog

ARIÈGEOIS

The Ariègeois is a French breed, rarely seen outside France, that comes from the Ariège region near the Pyrenees in the south. It is one of the few French hounds that has not been crossed with the English Foxhound and its ancestors are supposed to be the Gascon Saintongeois and Grand Bleu de Gascogne. The Ariègeois is mainly used for hunting small game like rabbit, hare and fox. The breed is hardy, known for its good tracking ability and is strictly kept as a hunter.

At its withers the Ariègois is about 21-24 inches/ 53-60 cm. As in most French hounds, its typical features are a rather long, narrow head with a slightly convex nose ridge, low-set folded ears and a very noble expression. Its coat should be short, smooth and white, with large black patches. Its ears and the sides of its head should always be black with pale tan markings.

The Ariègeois, used in France to hunt small game, is rarely seen outside of the Ariège region near the Pyrenees.

Registry: FCI (Group 6)

AUSTRALIAN CATTLE DOG

ORIGIN AND DEVELOPMENT

The Australian Cattle Dog was bred to support the establishment of the cattle industry in Australia. Working dogs imported into Australia from other countries initially proved good for smallholdings or family farms. However, in around 1813 after the Great Dividing Range had been crossed, the settlers had hundreds of smallholdings with thousands of square miles that were often unfenced. Not surprisingly, cattle were quite difficult to control on such properties. Many different dogs were used by drovers, but they found that they could not withstand the high temperatures and long distances. The principal requirement in the desired cattle dog was that it should be a strong biter with exceptional stamina and resilience. It also had to be capable of mustering and moving wild cattle.

Early breeders kept few records and there is a difference of opinion as to which breeds contributed to the Australian Cattle Dog as it is today. Nevertheless, it is generally accepted that the breed resulted from the crossing of blue merle Smooth Collies with the dingo, with a later injection of Dalmatian and black-and-tan Kelpie blood. The resulting dogs proved indispensable to the property owners in Queensland and they became known as Queensland Blue Heelers. In 1893 Robert Kaleski began breeding Blue Heelers and he started showing them four years later. Kaleski drew up the first breed Standard in 1902 which was subsequently accepted and endorsed by the original Kennel Club of New South Wales in 1903. The official name of the breed was then changed to Australian Cattle Dog.

TEMPERAMENT

The Cattle Dog is tough, hard working, rather aloof with strangers, but to its owner it is eternally loyal, gentle, alert and can be easily trained. It should be a bright and intelligent dog, ready to defend its master and property at all times, and yet still be amenable to handling and discipline. The dog is such a heavy biter that it is much too dangerous to encourage uncontrollable or temperamental specimens.

HEALTH MATTERS

The Cattle Dog is a very tough and hardy animal. It is generally free of any major hereditary defects, like hip dysplasia and other hereditary ailments that often affect larger dogs.

SPECIAL CARE AND TRAINING

Cattle Dogs are sharply alert but they can be headstrong. It is essential that they are taught to obey their owners' commands early in life. Grooming requirements are minimal.

ADAPTABILITY

Cattle Dogs make wonderful guard or watchdogs and they can also be extremely loyal friends. They make excellent companions and are becoming increasingly popular as pets, but they require a definite amount of physical and mental exercise for their own well-being. If their minds are insufficiently stretched, they can become a liability.

ESSENTIALS OF THE BREED

The Cattle Dog is a strong biter and it needs a broad skull that offers better leverage to the jaw than a narrow one. A slight but definite stop is called for so that, should a dog be kicked by a steer, the hoof is more likely to deflect off its head. The foreface should be well filled in under the eyes and there should be a gradual taper to the nose. A strong, deep muzzle of medium length, together with a good underjaw and tight, clean lips are necessary for it to carry out its job of driving and turning the cattle by biting their heels.

Australian Cattle Dogs are born white, usually with black or red markings, depending on their future body color. The coloring begins to show through at around three weeks of age. The new pup's skin pigmentation is usually the best indication of future coloring. The Cattle Dog's color and markings should be blue, blue mottled or blue speckled, with or without black, blue or tan markings on the head, or red speckled with or without darker red markings on the head. Ideally, the Australian Cattle Dog's head markings should be evenly distributed all over.

To the drovers on the old stock routes, color had a very practical value. A dark dog was almost invisible at night and could patrol a mob of cattle virtually without being seen.

A lighter colored brush on the tail gave the watchful stockman an indication of where his dog was. Very pale dogs were more visible at night and during the day, and hence more likely to be kicked by cattle. The Australian Cattle Dog is a dog that exemplifies normality and lack of exaggeration. A good specimen of the breed has a correct balance between skeletal structure and structural relationships. It is a dog of moderation, orientated towards maximum exercise, tolerance and without physical exaggeration.

Registry: AKC, CKC, FCI (Group 1), KC

Australian Cattle Dog

AUSTRALIAN KELPIE

The Kelpie is an Australian breed, developed and maintained as a working sheepdog to cope with the local geographical and climatic conditions — it is the only dog which can handle sheep in the vast, rugged country areas of Australia. It is reasonably certain that the Australian Kelpie originated from shorthaired, pricked or semi-prick-eared dogs from the border counties of England and Scotland and these might well have been known as a breed of Collie. Some say that these dogs were mated with a dingo (the most intelligent and cunning dog known to man) and that this is why the Kelpie has such an amazing stamina and endurance compared to other dogs. However, as with many breeds, no true record has been kept which relates the true evolution of the Kelpie.

The Kelpie is not, and never should be, a biting dog when working, but it often barks when mustering or yarding sheep. It is said that the Kelpie does the work of six to eight mounted horsemen and that without its help the cost of Australia's wool clip would be prohibitive.

The Kelpie is extremely alert, eager and highly intelligent, with a mild, tractable disposition, a seemingly inexhaustable supply of energy and a marked loyalty and devotion to duty. It is also one of the most social breeds of the canine species and needs companionship almost more than food. The Kelpie's ability as a working sheepdog is legendary — it is equally easy to train for obedience or tracking, as a show dog or companion. However, a Kelpie owner does need patience and understanding for the breed can be obstinate.

Typical of most Australian breeds, the Kelpie is a hardy dog, free of major hereditary diseases. If kept as a house pet, the Kelpie will need plenty of room, but its devotion, loyalty and instinct to guard property is outstanding. No specialized grooming is necessary.

The Kelpie has a typical soft sheepdog expression and is not required to have the Cattle Dog's strength of jaw. Its medium-sized

Australian Kelpie

almond brown eyes are typical of a Collie, being both bright and intelligent with an eager but kindly expression. The head gives the Kelpie its true appearance; it must be in proportion to the size of the dog, broad and slightly rounded between the medium-sized, pricked ears. The muzzle is slightly shorter than the forehead and the profile has parallel planes divided by a pronounced stop with slightly chiseled rounded cheeks. The teeth should be sound and strong, meeting in a scissors bite with tight lips.

The Kelpie is not a square dog but is a dog of moderate length with a level topline and a deep, rather than wide, chest. It has a short, dense undercoat and a weather-resistant outercoat of hard, close, straight hair lying flat to the body which can be of any of the following colors: red, red-and-tan, black, black-and-tan, chocolate, fawn and smoke blue. The Kelpie must be perfectly sound in construction and movement to produce the almost unlimited stamina demanded of a working sheepdog in the wide open spaces. In size the male Kelpie tends to stand about 18-20 inches/46-50 cm, with bitches being 1 inch/2.5 cm smaller.

Registry: AKC, FCI (Group 1), KC

AUSTRALIAN SHEPHERD

ORIGIN AND DEVELOPMENT

Despite its name, the Australian Shepherd did not in fact come from Australia. It is believed that some early specimens spent time in Australia on their way from Spain where they are assumed to have originated. Around the year 1875, Basque sheep herders began to migrate to the United States bringing their sheep-dogs with them. At that time the breed developed into the Australian Shepherd as it is known today.

The Canadian and Mexican Kennel Clubs gave full recognition to the Australian Shepherd in 1976. Unification of Australian Shepherd clubs and the development of a Standard in the United States for the breed occurred in the same year. Australian Shepherds were admitted to the Miscellaneous class in 1991 and attained regular American Kennel Club breed status on January 1, 1993. After the breed's recognition, it became a virtual "overnight success" in the American show ring with a gratifying number making their presence strongly felt in the Herding Group and in the Best in Show competition as well. Happily, American fanciers have not forgotten the breed's original purpose and many still work stock.

TEMPERAMENT

This breed was originally bred to have strong herding and sheep-guarding instincts. It is not prone to immediate friendships and it treats strangers with reserve, although it recognizes them after a proper introduction. It is dependable, persistent, independent in nature and a tireless worker with complete devotion to its owner. Ask anything of the breed and it will deliver.

HEALTH MATTERS

The Australian Shepherd is a healthy, sturdy breed, relatively free of any special medical problems. Two diseases of the eye can affect the breed: progressive retinal atrophy and Collie eye anomaly. Both these disorders are hereditary defects of the retina. The incidence of hip dysplasia (malformation of the hip joint) is relatively low for medium-sized dogs.

ADAPTABILITY

The basic instinct to herd is inherent in this breed — once in a pen with sheep, ducks or chickens, the dog will immediately go to work. Its medium texture, weather-resistant coat enables the Australian Shepherd to adapt to different climates and weather conditions. They have the stamina to withstand many hours of hard work and they make loyal companions.

SPECIAL CARE AND TRAINING

Because of the nature of their work, Australian Shepherds require daily exercise to acquire and maintain good muscle tone. When used as working herding dogs they benefit from stock dog training. Obedience training comes easily and they excel in competition. Special attention to grooming is necessary after each outing, since their coats pick up burrs, foxtails and other weed seeds.

ESSENTIALS OF THE BREED

Australian Shepherds come in four basic colors. These are blue merle, black, red merle and all red with or without white markings and/or tan points. White on this breed's body between the withers and the tail, on the sides between the elbows and on the back of the dog's hindquarters is not allowed. If there is a white hairline on the neck as a collar, this should then not extend beyond the point of the withers.

The dog's body has substance with moderate bone and a natural or docked tail. The breed's size ranges from 18-23 inches/46-58 cm at the withers. A good Australian Shepherd is intelligent and very alert so judges should severely penalize shyness. A dog with a mouth under or overshot more than 1/8 inch/2.5 mm or showing white body splashes would be disqualified in a show.

Registry: AKC, KC

Australian Shepherd

AUSTRALIAN TERRIER

ORIGIN AND DEVELOPMENT

The Australian Terrier is basically a product of Australia, although it has been derived from stock that was undoubtedly British in origin. First known as the Broken-haired Terrier, the Australian Terrier in many ways resembles the early type Scotch Terrier (not to be confused with today's Scottish Terrier), early Cairn, Shorthaired Skye Terrier and Dandie Dinmont Terrier, which all had common ancestors. The Australian has inherited many of their qualities including a harsh coat, softer topknot and strong jaws. Later, Yorkshire and Irish Terriers were introduced to obtain the desired color and size, but no crossing with any other breed is definitely recorded.

The Australian Terrier's rugged and sturdy appearance is well suited to the harsh terrains

Australian Terrier

of its homeland where it was used to guard mines and tend sheep. The breed's finest attribute is that it is a great hunter of vermin.

The Australian Terrier Club was initially formed in Australia in 1887. The breed was presented for the first time at a show in Melbourne in 1903, and was shortly afterwards introduced into Great Britain, being officially recognized by the British Kennel Club in 1933. It was not until 1960 that the Australian Terrier obtained American Kennel Club recognition.

In recent years type in British Australian Terriers has been improved and the gene pool increased through the importation of several significant dogs from both Australia and New Zealand. Nowadays, top class Australian Terriers can be seen in the show rings of Great Britain, United States and the Scandinavian countries where visiting Australian judges have frequently commented on the surprisingly high level of quality to be found within the breed.

TEMPERAMENT

The "Aussie," as it is affectionately known, is one of the smallest in the Terrier Group. It is a tough, cheeky little fellow with the courage of a much larger dog. The Aussie has boundless energy, is very loyal, shows great affection for its immediate family and its extraordinary intelligence makes it a responsive and very protective companion.

HEALTH MATTERS

The Australian Terrier enjoys life, has a keen sense of hearing and smell, is hardy, healthy and economical to feed. It is long lived and free of any major hereditary diseases.

SPECIAL CARE AND TRAINING

This is a low-maintenance breed but it still requires regular bathing and a good vigorous brushing to remove any dead hair. Any untidy hair on the ears and around the tail should be removed and long hair on the feet should be trimmed up to the wrist joints. The nails should be kept short. The Australian

Terrier is easily trained for both breed and Obedience competition, or simply to be a well-mannered companion.

ADAPTABILITY

The Australian Terrier will live in all conditions and climates and is equally happy in a city apartment as on a country estate. It is very loyal and affectionate — and excellent with children. This is a small dog that requires little conscious effort for its welfare, fitting well into all aspects and conditions of modern living.

ESSENTIALS OF THE BREED

A small, well-balanced dog, the Australian Terrier is full of terrier character, with a strong muzzle the same length as its flat skull. It has small dark eyes with a keen expression. Its body should be long in proportion to its height, with a firm level topline.

The Standard calls for the Aussie to stand 10 inches/25 cm at the shoulder and weigh 14 pounds/6 kg. Its ribs should extend well back with strong loins and a deep flank, and its tail should be set high and traditionally docked to give a well-balanced outline. It has well-turned stifles that are very strong and well muscled.

The Australian Terrier is a double-coated dog with a harsh, dense, weather-resistant topcoat and a softer undercoat. There are two distinct coat colorings in the Australian: blue (silver or dark) with tan, and solid red (sometimes called sandy). In the reds the color must be quite clear and not carry any shading or smuttiness. The blue-and-tans should have a blue, steel-blue or dark gray-blue coat with good rich tan markings on the face, ears, under the body, on the lower legs and feet and around the vent. The richer the color and more clearly defined, the better. The topknot of the Australian Terrier can be blue, silver or a lighter shade than the dog's head color.

Registry: AKC, CKC, FCI (Group 3), KC

AUSTRIAN GRAND BRACKES

Austria's three large hounds are listed under this heading — all three breeds are rarely seen outside their native country. The Austrian Brackes are scenthounds strictly kept for hunting hare and fox. They are also very reliable tracking hounds used for searching out wounded or dead game.

The Austrian Shorthaired Bracke, sometimes called Brandlbracke, was recognized in 1883 and originates from the old hounds said to have been crossed with the St. Hubert type of Swiss Jura Hound. At its withers, its height should be about 18-23 inches/46-58 cm. Its body should be long, not heavy and its head should be narrow, elongated and with rather low-set ears. The coat should be smooth and glossy, while the color should be black-and-tan or rich tan, with or without black hair-tips — slight white markings are permissible.

The Wirehaired hound, Steirische Rauhhaarige Hochgebirgsbracke, is sometimes also called the Peintinger Bracke after its creator. Mr. Peintinger developed the breed in the 1870s and it was given official recognition in 1889. This breed is used for work in high altitudes and is considered very hardy.

At its withers, it is about 17-23 inches/44-58 cm. The body should be rectangular and strong but not coarse. The head should be a medium length with ears that do not fold. The ears should be carried close to the cheeks. The nose and pigmentation should be black, and the coat should be medium length, wiry and any shade of red.

The Tiroler Bracke is slightly shorter and stronger in build than the Austrian Shorthaired Bracke or the Steirische Rauhhaarige Hochgebirgsbracke. There are two sizes for this type, with the height at its withers either 12-15 inches/30-39 cm or 16-19 inches/40-48 cm. The head should be elongated and the ears high set, broad at the base, with rounded tips and carried flat, close to the cheeks. The coat should be short, hard textured and lie close. The color may be black, red or tan, with or without a black mantle and white markings.

Registry: FCI (Group 6)

The Austrian Shorthaired Bracke is sometimes called the Brandlbracke.

*Steirische Rauhhaarige
Hochgebirgsbracke*

Tiroler Bracke

AUSTRIAN SHORTHAIRED PINSCHER/ OESTERREICHISCHER KURZHAARIGER PINSCHER

The Austrian Pinscher was recognized in 1928 and is thought to originate from German Pinschers and local hounds, though its build is more rectangular and coarse than that of the German Pinscher. It is mainly used as a farm dog and is said to be a good ratter.

The dog is about 13-19 inches/33-48 cm at its withers. Its ears are large, pendant with no folds. The tail is set high, and carried in a slight curl over the back or docked short. The coat is about 1 1/4 inches/3 cm long, harsh in texture and lies close to the body except on the tail where it may be longer. All shades of red or black-and-tan are acceptable colors. The Austrian Pinscher is rarely seen outside its home country.

Registry: FCI (Group 2)

Austrian Shorthaired Pinscher

AZAWAKH

This elegant sighthound breed originates from Mali in Africa — France is its parent country. Azawakhs are used as guard dogs and to hunt antelope and rabbit by the Tuareg tribes. This breed is related to both the Saluki and the Sloughi but it is more aloof than either.

In body, the Azawakh should be square and tall, about 24-29 inches/60-74 cm at its withers. The breed is very elegant and has a smooth, thin and glossy coat which can vary from light to deep red or brindle. Ideally it should have white socks, or at least be white on all four feet. The breed has excited quite an interest since it first arrived in Europe in early 1970, but it is still a rare breed.

Azawakh

Registry: FCI (Group 10)

BALKANSKI GONIC

This scenthound from the Balkan peninsula and mountains, particularly former Yugoslavia, has been true to its type since the nineteenth century. The Balkanski Gonic is used purely as a hunting dog, most often for hare and fox.

The height at its withers should be about 17-21 inches/44-54 cm. It has a rectangular body, well muscled and with good bone. It is similar to many East European hounds in that it has quite a broad head with a flat skull and triangular ears. These should hang close to the cheeks without any folds and not be too long. Its coat should be short, hard and glossy in a rich tan with a black saddle. Before the civil war broke out in former Yugoslavia, the breed could be seen in vast numbers at international shows.

Balkanski Gonic

Registry: FCI (Group 6)

BARBET

A French breed rarely seen outside France, the Barbet is a water retrieving gun dog that is considered one of the oldest water dogs. It is mentioned as the progenitor of several breeds including, for instance, the Poodle.

In build, the Barbet should be more rectangular than square, standing about 18-20 inches/ 45-50 cm at its withers. The tail should be long and not carried over its back. Most significant for the breed, and for all so-called water dogs, is the water-resistant, woolly, wavy or curly coat that covers the whole dog. This coat should have a natural look and not be groomed like a Poodle or shaped with scissors. The color of the Barbet should be either black, grayish black, liver brown or white, with or without patches in these shades.

Barbet

Registry: FCI (Group 8)

BASENJI

ORIGIN AND DEVELOPMENT

The Basenji, known as the African Barkless Dog, is considered by its devotees as unique to the canine species. One of the oldest breeds, Basenji-type dogs are depicted on the tombs of Egyptian pharaohs and date back to as early as 3600 B.C. Today, Basenjis can be found in southern Sudan and in Zaire where they live with the natives in remote forests and are used for hunting purposes. Rather than pointing or retrieving, Basenjis are used to assist beaters in flushing game which is driven into nets strung up against trees.

Basenjis were imported to England in the 1930s and first introduced to America in 1941. After a slow start of some twenty years, they gradually came to be known and appreciated.

TEMPERAMENT

The Basenji's barklessness, convenient size, short shiny coat, absence of odor and meticulous personal habits are definite positive attributes. In addition, its strength, agility, perseverance and independence of the hunter, coupled with a good set of teeth, make the Basenji capable of being very destructive if it is bored, lonesome, thwarted or lacks sufficient exercise to occupy it.

HEALTH MATTERS

All of the Basenjis outside Africa are descended from only a dozen individuals. This very limited gene pool began to allow some physiological anomalies to appear. As with any pure bred dogs, a limited ancestry is bound to result in some undesirable characteristics or allow them to surface. With the cooperation of the Basenji Club of America, two safaris into Zaire in 1987 and 1988 resulted in the importation and subsequent acceptance by the Kennel Club of fourteen Basenjis to enlarge the gene pool.

The primary concerns are fanconis syndrome (a kidney dystrophy), a malabsorption labeled IPSID (immuno proliforative small intestine disease) and progressive retinal atrophy. Hemolytic anemia due to pyravate kinase deficiency in the red blood cells used to be a critical problem. A definitive test for this anemia and careful breeding have almost eliminated it and hopefully other inherited disorders may be addressed just as effectively. As with humans, in canine health surveillance, detection and diagnosis have greatly expanded current knowledge and awareness of disease. Indeed, they have often benefited each other.

SPECIAL CARE AND TRAINING

Those who admire the Basenji's graceful appearance, its almost catlike mannerisms and its delightful sense of humor should be willing to devote enough time to its exercise and training to allow it to fulfill its potential as a unique and charming companion.

As a general rule, Basenjis only come into heat once a year, although there are increasing exceptions to this. About 90 percent of litters are born from October through December. The females are excellent mothers whose litters average from four to six offspring. House-training comes quite readily to these naturally clean creatures but other training requires patience, consistency, affection and humor. They are perhaps not so different from children.

ADAPTABILILTY

Although the Basenji hunts by scent, it has gained recognition as a sighthound through lure coursing competition. Kept primarily as a household pet, the Basenji can still take part in a variety of activities, including conformation competition, obedience, agility, field work and hunting.

ESSENTIALS OF THE BREED

Small and shorthaired, with a foxy face, worried-looking wrinkled brow, upright ears, and tail curled like a doughnut, the Basenji's most unusual characteristic is that it does not bark. It is not mute, however, and although usually quiet, it has a repertoire of sounds that ranges from a pleased throaty crow to a keening wail made when it is lonely or unhappy. Well-balanced, graceful and active, the breed's height of 16-17 inches/40-43 cm allows it to function in an environment devoid of luxury. With the new African blood came an old African color: tiger striped brindle. Previously, the accepted colors were red with white, tricolor (black-and-tan with white) and black with white. Brindle, in varying degrees of intensity set off with white markings, can be very attractive and has provoked considerable interest — it may well be accepted in Great Britain in the near future.

Concerned Basenji fanciers should be commended for the initiative they have exhibited in their dedication to preserving this unique and delightful breed for posterity.

Registry: AKC, CKC, FCI (Group 5), KC

Basenji

BASSET ARTÉSIEN NORMAND

Basset Artésien Normand is one of six recognized French Basset breeds. It is believed that the ancestors of the breed were used as pack hounds in the north of France as early as the thirteenth century. As the breed name indicates, this Basset comes from crossbreeding between Bassets from Artois and from Normandy performed by the Compte le Couteulx de Canteleu from Ètrepagny and Louis Lane from Rouen in the 1850s. Léon Verrier, also from Rouen, continued their work which resulted in the recognition of the breed in 1911. The breed continued to change for several decades after this and it is still mainly used for hunting — but not as pack hounds outside France.

The Basset Artésien Normand is the most elegant of the Basset breeds, with a long, narrow head and very low set ears that are folded. Its height at the withers is about 10-14 inches/ 26-36 cm. The coat should be smooth and

Basset Artésien Normand

glossy and its color is usually tricolor although white with orange patches is also allowed. The breed is best known in Europe and in the Scandinavian countries.

Registry: FCI (Group 6)

BASSET BLEU DE GASCOGNE

The blue mottled Basset from Gascogne in France was almost extinct around the 1890s. It is now rarely seen outside France. One breeder in particular made it his task to save the breed. He used the now extinct Basset Saintongeois and the Grand Bleu de Gascogne and although the breed is still rare it is considered true to the old type. It is mainly used for hunting smaller game.

Basset Bleu de Gascogne has an elegant build and is about 13-16 1/2 inches/34-42 cm at the withers. This hunting breed has a long, narrow head and very low-set ears that are folded. The coat should be smooth and mottled blue in color with black patches and tan markings.

Registry: FCI (Group 6)

The Basset Bleu de Gascogne came close to extinction in the 1890s and now is rarely seen outside France.

BASSET FAUVE DE BRETAGNE

The Basset variety from Bretagne (or Brittany) in France almost became extinct during the nineteenth century. The few true-to-type dogs were crossed with the Bassets Griffon Vendéen and red Wire Dachshunds and thus the breed was saved. Nowadays it is not entirely restricted to being kept as a hunting dog.

The dog's height at its withers is about 12 1/2-14 inches/32-36 cm. Its build is rather robust and its head fairly strong with low-set ears and a broad skull that is not as long as in other Basset breeds. The coat should be wiry but not abundant and the color can be any shade of fawn or red. The breed is still rare but may be seen at dog shows in Europe and in Scandinavia in particular.

Basset Fauve de Bretagne

Registry: FCI (Group 6)

BASSETS GRIFFON VENDÉEN

On the west coast of France, in the *département* (region) of Vendée, is the home of four rough-coated hound breeds. They are all shaggy coated and similar, except for the length of their legs. The smallest is the Petit Basset Griffon Vendéen, followed by Grand Basset Griffon Vendéen, Briquet Vendéen and Grand Vendéen. The word "griffon" is used to describe shaggy — or wiry coated — breeds. Of the two Basset breeds from Vendée, it is believed that the larger is the original type.

The Grand is longer in body, tail, head, ears and coat than the Petit. Both breeds are used for hunting smaller game and deer, but they are rarely used as pack hounds outside France. Centuries ago, the breed used to "go to ground", like terriers. The Petit is now fairly well known for its working abilities and as a show dog in North America, Europe and in Scandinavian countries.

There is a distinct difference in size between the two: at the withers, the Grand is about

Grand Basset Griffon Vendéen

15-17 inches/39-44 cm; the Petit is about 13-15 inches/33-39 cm. Both can be gray, badger color, white or red. Red is permissible but not desired. Most common is white with red, gray, black or badger or a combination of these.

Registry: FCI (Group 6)

BASSET HOUND

ORIGIN AND DEVELOPMENT

The forerunners of the Basset Hound first appeared in the sixteenth century in litters of French stag hounds. They resembled their siblings in every detail except for their stunted limb development. These short-legged hounds assumed a curiosity value and were bred together until a "basset" type of hound became established. The French word *"basset"* means low-set. Gradually several types of Basset evolved, some now extinct, but the modern Basset can be traced to the Basset d'Artois and the Basset Normand.

In 1866 Lord Galway introduced the breed into Britain and shortly afterwards two other prominent sportsmen, Lord Onslow and Sir Everett Millais, became involved. In many ways, it is Millais who can be regarded as the father of the breed in Britain – in 1884 he was a driving force behind the formation of the Basset Hound Club. Queen Alexandra's royal patronage helped to bring the breed further popularity and, by 1886, there were no fewer than 120 Bassets entered at a London dog show where Millais himself judged the breed. Millais realized the dangers of a small gene pool and in 1892 he introduced a Bloodhound cross, which to some extent obviously changed the appearance of the breed. The effect of this cross can still be seen today in so far as the Basset remains much heavier and looser-skinned than its purely French counterpart, the Basset Artésien Normand.

Bassets proved popular as hunting dogs, and several packs in Britain hunted hare on a regular basis. World War I took its toll on the breed in the United Kingdom with only thirty-three hounds being registered from 1913-23. Indeed the Basset Hound Club was closed down in 1921.

Thanks to the efforts of the Heseltine brothers, Mrs. Grew and Mrs. Elms, the breed was saved from extinction, but suffered setbacks with the onset of the World War II. Mrs. Grew and Mrs. Elms remained involved with the breed after hostilities ceased, and were joined by Miss Keevil whose enthusiasm helped the breed through a difficult era when she imported Bassets Artésian Normand to supplement existing breeding stock. One of her imports, Grims Ulema de Barly, had a profoundly positive effect on the breed during the 1940s.

In 1954 the Basset Hound Club was reformed and gradually the breed's popularity increased, dramatically affected by the well-known "Hush Puppies" shoe advertising campaign. Widespread in-breeding posed a threat and in the mid-1950s the Basset Hound Club imported from the United States a stud dog, Lyn Mar Acres Dauntless, which proved of great benefit to the breed. Since that time the breed has seen several imports from various countries many of which have helped to maintain the overall quality which has enabled the breed to be a regular contender in the Best in Show ring.

TEMPERAMENT

Despite its "Hush Puppy" appeal, the Basset is essentially a hunting dog with strong natural instincts and will power. It is generally placid, if sometimes a little stubborn, and should show neither nervousness nor aggression. It can be vocal at times and its rich, baying bark can be quite penetrating.

HEALTH MATTERS

Kept properly exercised and sensibly fed, the Basset should remain fit and healthy, though neglect and over-indulgence can lead to obesity and possible back problems. Entropion can occur in some extreme eye shapes.

SPECIAL CARE AND TRAINING

The Basset is easy to take care of and requires little grooming other than regular brushing to remove dead hair. It should be taught basic obedience from an early age as it can be self-willed,

Basset Hound

and when its natural scenting ability tempts it to go off in hot pursuit, its owner should be confident that it will come when called.

ADAPTABILITY

The Basset needs plenty of exercise. It is best suited to a home where it can enjoy open spaces and keep itself occupied in a natural environment.

ESSENTIALS OF THE BREED

The Basset should have great substance, be strong-boned and relatively low to the ground with moderate length of body. The head is quite long and should show moderate amount of wrinkling on the skull, the skin of the head being very loose. The muzzle is quite lean and heavily flewed. Wrinkles coupled with sagacious brown or hazel eyes and very long ears give the Basset a rather serious expression. Its forechest should be well filled and the forelegs show a distinct crook. The feet are large and well padded; the forefeet may turn slightly out. The topline is level and the tail carried high, scimitar-style. The hindquarters should be very well developed and musculature should be such that from the rear the hound appears to have an "apple bottom." The coat is smooth and close, and is popularly tricolor or lemon/tan-and-white, though all recognized hound colors are allowed. The Basset stands up to 15 inches/39 cm at the withers.

Registry: AKC, CKC, FCI (Group 6), KC

BAVARIAN MOUNTAIN DOG/ BAYERISCHER GEBIRGSSCHWEISSHUND

This breed was developed in the middle of the nineteenth century, probably from crosses between the Hanovarian Schweisshound (Bloodhound) and local scenthounds, in the mountains of Bavaria in southern Germany. The reason was because using large hounds for hunting in the mountains was prohibited, and so the need for good tracking dogs became important. The German word "Schweiss" in its name means blood describing a dog that follows the scent of blood. This is different from the Bloodhound that takes its name from "being of true and noble blood" or "thoroughbred". The Bavarian Mountain Dog always hunts with a tracking line. It is kept strictly as a hunting dog and is rarely seen in any numbers at all-breed dog shows.

In males, the height at the withers should not exceed 20 inches/50 cm and in females 18 inches/ 45 cm. Its body is decidedly rectangular and should never give an impression of being leggy. The ears should be big and broad at the base and never folded. Large ears are an important feature as they are supposed to help to keep the scent close to the dog's nose when it is tracking. The coat should be thick but smooth and glossy. Its color can be any shade of red, from very deep red to light fawn. Deep red with black-tipped hair, especially on the head, ears and tail is very common.

Registry: FCI (Group 6)

Bavarian Mountain Dog

BEAGLE

ORIGIN AND DEVELOPMENT

The Beagle is a scenthound, developed in the British Isles where it hunted mainly rabbit and hare in packs, the huntsmen originally following on foot. In the ancient Celtic, French and Old English languages can be found similar words, each meaning "small" — namely *beag, beigh* and *begle*. One of these may be responsible for the smallest scent-hound's name. Written references to the breed can be found as far back as Chaucer in the fourteenth century and the Beagle has evolved quite naturally since, free of cross-breeding and exaggeration. Huntsmen of the eighteenth century often worked with small Beagles which could fit in their hunting coat pockets, their diminutive size later giving rise to the expression "pocket Beagle" which is used to describe smaller specimens.

As the population of game in parts of the United States and Canada decreased, the Beagle's involvement with hunting became centered more and more on rabbit. Whilst they are sometimes hunted as packs, and accompanied by mounted horsemen, Beagles were originally bred to be followed on foot and largely this practice persists. Larger than typical Beagles have been used with Harriers in some tropical countries to hunt wild cat. The Harrier was specifically developed to hunt hare and is, loosely speaking, a characteristically dish-faced, smaller version of the Foxhound.

The British Kennel Club first recognized the Beagle in 1873, and the original specimens seen in the show ring were pack-bred hounds. With the decline in hunting in the United Kingdom, since the 1950s the Beagle has become increasingly popular as a companion and show dog, as it is in the United States where many field trials are held to this day. The compact size, robust physique and biddable temperament of this smart little hound have contributed to its great popularity as a companion. Sadly these are the very qualities which have found favor with vivisectionists, and it remains a constant cause of concern among Beagle breeders that, without careful vetting of prospective purchasers, their puppies may find their way to laboratories via unscrupulous "middle men." However, many research establishments now breed their own Beagles in sterile surroundings and far fewer dogs are brought in.

In recent years, the American Beagle has contributed significantly to the progress of its British counterpart as a show dog with a number of prepotent imported stud dogs traveling across the Atlantic to the breed's homeland. This has resulted in the British Beagle becoming a more compact, well-knit breed with a better finished muzzle and softer expression, more level topline and greater hind angulation. The "smartness" of the American influence has helped to establish the Beagle as a regular contender in Variety competitions, and since the 1970s the breed has produced many Group and Best in Show winners in the United Kingdom.

The fact that the breed is shown as two different sized varieties in the United States has meant that America's loss has been Britain's gain, with the American maximum height in the larger variety (15 inches/39 cm) being 1 inch/2.5 cm less than its British equivalent. There still remains a tendency for the British show Beagles to be at the upper limits of the breed Standard's requirements for height, which is why there is never any shortage of buyers when a top-class American Beagle "measures out" in the American show ring. The maximum height of 15 inches/39 cm has in many cases been a great asset to breeders in Great Britain and will probably long remain so.

TEMPERAMENT

The Beagle should be amiable and alert, able to cope with any situation and never ill-adjusted. It is an ideal family dog and the perfect children's companion. A Beagle will join in the most boisterous of games, and enjoy any amount of exercise, remaining tolerant and placid no matter what childish indignities are leveled against it. Although not developed as a guard dog, and lacking any aggressive tendencies, it will nonetheless fulfill the role of home protector in that it will soon let its owners know of the presence of strangers, with its unique "baying" bark.

HEALTH MATTERS

Owing to its very "moderate" physique, the Beagle remains free of major hereditary defects. The main reason for consulting a veterinarian is obesity for the Beagle is a natural glutton and its diet should always be sensibly monitored.

SPECIAL CARE AND TRAINING

Beagles respond well to basic obedience. It is essential that the breed is trained to come when called, as this can avert disaster should a potential "hunting" situation arise and its apparently buried natural instincts surface.

ADAPTABILITY

Because of its equable nature, handy size and easily cared for coat, the Beagle adapts well to a home or kennel environment, but owners should always be aware of the breed's hunting instincts, deep-seated though they may be after many generations. One solitary Beagle left in isolation for long periods will soon become

Beagle

bored, and out of sheer frustration may become destructive in the home. Given the company of another human or canine, it will thrive and be quite undemanding.

ESSENTIALS OF THE BREED

Since the Beagle was developed as a hound to be followed on foot, its size is very important. In the United States the breed is shown as two varieties — up to 13 inches/33 cm height at withers and 13-15 inches/33-39 cm. In the United Kingdom the desirable minimum height is 13 inches/33 cm and the maximum 16 inches/40 cm. Only one variety is recognized. The head should be fairly long, slightly domed at the occiput with moderately low-set ears which can reach to the end of the nose. The stop should be moderately well defined, the muzzle square-cut and the large, set-apart eyes should be dark brown or hazel which help to create the unique soft, pleading expression that is so very much a part of the Beagle's charm.

The neck should be long enough to come down easily to scent, the shoulders should be clean and sloping, the chest broad and deep. The back should be short, muscular and strong, with well-sprung ribs and not too much tuck-up. The forelegs should be straight with plenty of bone, pasterns short and straight, and the feet close, round and firm with full and hard pads. The hindquarters should show muscular thighs, well-bent stifles and well-let-down hocks, parallel to each other. The tail (or "stern" in hound parlance) should be high set, but never turned forward over the back, or inclined forward at the root. The tip is traditionally white. The gait should be free striding, long reaching in front without high action, while the hindquarters should exhibit great drive. The coat should be short, dense and weather-proof. The blanketed tricolor is the most popular in the show ring, particularly in the United States, but any recognized hound color is equally correct.

Registry: AKC, CKC, FCI (Group 6), KC

BEAGLE HARRIER

The crossbreeding of Beagle and Harrier, started in France by Baron Gerard Grandin de l'Epriever in the 1920s, was aimed at combining the best of the two breeds' hunting abilities. The formula was to retain only one sex from each cross and then mate that specimen back to a pure Beagle, again with only one sex retained. This was then mated to a Harrier. And so it went on. A very keen hound for hunting smaller game and roe deer was produced.

The Beagle Harrier should stand midway between its two parent breeds, with the height at its withers about 18-20 inches/45-50 cm. It is closer to the Harrier than to the Beagles seen at dog shows. The coat should be smooth and tricolored — they are usually black blanketed.

Registry: FCI (Group 6)

The Beagle Harrier breed was created by crossbreeding the Beagle and the Harrier.

BEARDED COLLIE

ORIGIN AND DEVELOPMENT

Historians speculate that the Bearded Collie developed from the Polski Owczarek Nizinny dog from Poland. Scotland traded with Poland during the sixteenth century and Polish sailors may have traded Nizinny dogs for prized Scottish sheep. The Polish dogs mixed with Highland Collies and later became what is known as the Bearded Collie. The Highland Collie was one of three or four different names given to the working dog of Scotland's hill shepherds.

Beardie history is incomplete and undocumented but the breed is apparently one of Great Britain's oldest. Some evidence has led to the belief that it was established before the Roman invasion but other stories vary somewhat from this theory. A dog that resembled the Beardie appeared in British portraits and writings in the 1700s.

The Highland Collie filled the role of a

Bearded Collie

working companion for Scots instead of performing as a show breed intended to please the fancy of noblemen. Stockmen used these dogs as drovers during the seventeenth and eighteenth centuries. Driving cattle and sheep to market through the windswept hills of Scotland challenged the human drovers and their four-legged assistants. Bearded Collies are swift dogs and carried out their tasks over moorland with skill and grace.

There is a dearth of documentation following this period until 1912 when the first breed Standard was written. Much later, a British lady revived the breed when she obtained a specimen and exhibited it in shows held in England. Her bitch became a British Champion in 1959 and this event created increased interest in the breed.

Some time later, Beardies met with success and popularity in Canada and the United States. The Canadian and American Kennel Clubs accepted them in record time. Fanciers formed the Bearded Collie Club of America in 1969 and the American Kennel Club registered the breed seven years later. The Bearded Collie has a steady following today.

TEMPERAMENT

Because of the high level of intelligence and resourcefulness of Bearded Collies, owners and handlers must keep them busy or they will invent things to keep themselves occupied. They are a forgiving breed and never hold grudges. Beardies are the happiest of dogs and never fail to show it, although sometimes they may display an excess of boisterous behavior. They most certainly have a well-developed, puckish sense of humor. There are a variety of temperaments in the breed from sweet and quiet to the opposite extreme. For these reasons it will not suit everyone. It is not a dog for anyone seeking a companion with a low level of activity.

HEALTH MATTERS

The Beardie is comparatively free of genetic defects but breeders recommend routine radio-

graphs in order to eliminate any chance of introducing hip dysplasia (abnormal hip joints) into breeding stock. The Orthopedic Foundation for Animals certifies X-rays in the United States. The British Veterinary Association Hip Dysplasia Scheme offers the same service in Great Britain.

American breeders also suggest certification of breeding stock by veterinary ophthalmologists to avoid the hereditary problems caused in other breeds by progressive retinal atrophy and juvenile cataract.

ADAPTABILITY

The Bearded Collie has an inherited instinct to herd. This attribute makes it a particularly good family dog because it is expected to gather its flock together. The family members become the flock of sheep that they must guard and watch. The breed readily adapts to family life, yet it has all the qualities of a strong outdoor dog.

Beardies have a highly developed personality required for the job of herding. In addition, history credits the breed with the instincts of a cattle drover. This is a dog capable of either driving cattle or herding sheep — unusual dual talents. Beardies do well in a kennel when given sufficient human contact and opportunites to socialize.

SPECIAL CARE AND TRAINING

Training should begin early because it is difficult to get rid of bad habits once they become ingrained. The Bearded Collie is a sensitive dog. It accepts trainers who use a firm hand, but harsh methods will break its spirit. Handlers must take care to use the right balance of freedom and fun when training their dogs for obedience. Time allowed for play and exercise free of restraint, plus an equal amount of time devoted to disciplined training, is the way to develop a well-adjusted dog.

It is advisable to begin housetraining a Bearded Collie immediately after it has arrived in a new home. People familiar with the breed recommend walking the dog or playing with a ball for two half-hour periods each day.

The Bearded Collie requires special coat care — a grooming method that fanciers call "line-brushing." This involves separating the coat into sections while the dog lies on its side. The groomer then brushes from the skin out to the end of the hair shaft. A well-groomed coat requires this procedure once a week, before each bath and again after drying. Bathing only when necessary helps to conserve the natural oils in the skin and hair. A healthy, well-groomed coat will result.

ESSENTIALS OF THE BREED

The Bearded Collie should be of medium size. It should also be hardy, active and agile. The height of an adult should range between 20-22 inches/50-56 cm at the withers. The Bearded Collie has a double coat consisting of a soft, furry undercoat and a flat, harsh, shaggy outercoat.

The Beardie is a natural looking, working animal, and its coat provides protection from the wet weather, cold and wind typical of the moors. Its color at birth is black, blue, brown or fawn, with or without white markings. White must appear only on the fore-face as a blaze, tail-tip, skull, chest, legs and feet and around the neck. Skin pigmentation of the nose, lips and eye rims should follow the prime coat color. The coat must appear natural, with no trace of trimming. Fanciers prefer that the breed remain free of artificial change of any kind. This maintains the working qualities of the breed without alteration.

Bearded Collies have a supple, powerful and well-balanced gait. As with any herding breed, movement should reflect the need for a lithe, flexible dog capable of changing direction at a moment's notice. The Bearded Collie has a timeless beauty combined with a functional grace and charm that few breeds have maintained over the centuries. This remarkable animal is expected to aid and delight its human companions for centuries to come.

Registry: AKC, CKC, FCI (Group 1), KC

BEAUCERON/BERGER DE BEAUCE

This French herding breed is of a type known for centuries in western Europe and it might be part of the Doberman's ancestry. Today it is still used as a herder and guard dog and is known as a serious working dog.

The Beauceron stands about 25-29 1/2 inches/ 63-75 cm at its withers. Its body is rectangular and stronger in bone and substance than the Doberman. Its ears should be cropped but the tail left long. Dewclaws on the hind legs should be well developed. The coat should be short, but not smooth. In color, it should be black-and-tan, with or without patches of grayish merle-speckling. The latter color is called harlequin. The breed is rare but entries at dog shows have increased.

Registry: FCI (Group 1)

The Beauceron is used in France as a herder and guard dog and may be part of the Doberman's ancestry.

BEDLINGTON TERRIER

ORIGIN AND DEVELOPMENT

The Bedlington Terrier is of British origin like most terrier breeds, probably evolving in Northumberland, England. It was formerly known as the Rothbury, Rodbury or Northumberland Fox Terrier. As the original breed became less used for its original task of going to ground in search of vermin, and was employed more as a catcher of rabbits on the ground, so its form and outline began to change.

Shorter legs were replaced by long ones, and its more rugged frame by a much more elegant outline to which the Whippet undoubtedly contributed.

The breed has had something of a checkered history. The Bedlington's heritage which combined the spunk of a typical terrier with the speed of a sighthound made it an attractive proposition to the poaching fraternity, and the breed originally had a reputation for being a gypsy's dog. However, at the turn of

Bedlington Terrier

the century its elegant appearance and genteel manners helped it find its way into many stately homes as the companion of the nobility. In many ways the Bedlington is the classic example of a canine "social climber" who took readily to its new-found status.

The Bedlington differs emphatically from other terriers, being distinctively shaped, roach-backed, hare-footed and possessing an unusual coat. The breed should have sufficient speed to catch a rabbit, and it is not as lamblike as it might appear. The Bedlington is still very much a terrier at heart. Their coats offer great scope to the hairdressers of the dog world, and a superbly trimmed Bedlington is indeed a joy to behold.

TEMPERAMENT

The Bedlington is rather a quiet dog, quite suitable for family life, making a loyal companion which is affectionate and able to adapt to every mood of its owner. Bedlingtons are not troublemakers and are much more tolerant than most other terriers, yet if need be they will stand their quarter.

HEALTH MATTERS

Breeders are acutely aware of the hereditary fault known as copper toxicosis that occurs in this breed, but affected dogs can strangely live a relatively normal life. Dedicated breeders have their stock biopsied, and test-mate to differentiate the patterns of inheritance, intent on eventual eradication of the problem. Cracked or horny pads have previously been a problem, but are seldom encountered today. Like most terriers, Bedlingtons are generally extremely hardy, rarely requiring other than routine veterinary attention.

SPECIAL CARE AND TRAINING

Bedlingtons are readily kept smart and tidy. Much can be achieved with simple scissorsing, thus avoiding costly visits to the grooming parlor. Regular grooming is required, but the coat does not shed. The coat is thick and of a linty texture. The topknot, which should be regularly groomed and trimmed, remains very much a breed feature.

ADAPTABILITY

The Bedlington is a sporting dog requiring a degree of exercise. The breed thrives on human companionship. It is ideally suited to a domestic existence and is easily trained for obedience.

ESSENTIALS OF THE BREED

The Bedlington's unusual shape, its light springy gait and its graceful, lithe outline attracts much attention to the breed. The head is narrow, the cheeks flat and with unbroken lines. The eye shape should seem triangular and the eye expressive, dark, small and bright. The nostrils should be large, the lips close-fitting and the jaw punishing. The ears are said to be filbert-shaped, lying flat to the cheek. Although its expression is mild and gentle, the breed is not shy. The Bedlington's action is distinctive, springy and light at slower paces. The front legs are set wider at the top than at the feet, giving what is termed a horse-shoe front. Unlike most other terriers, Bedlingtons are hare-footed, with long and slightly sloping pasterns. The neck is long, tapering into flat, sloping shoulders. The body is markedly muscular, flexible, flat-ribbed and deep-chested. The back is roached and the loins decidedly arched. Because of this, the hind legs have the appearance of being longer than the forelegs. The hocks are well let down, showing strength. The tail is thick at the root, tapering and of moderate length. The breed may be blue, sandy, liver, blue-and-tan, sandy-and-tan or liver-and-tan. The tan is found over the eyes, inside the ears, under the tail and found in traces on the insides of the legs. Puppies tend to be born black or brown. Bedlingtons have individual guard hairs in their thick, linty coats. Males stand around 16 inches/40 cm at the shoulder and weigh between 18-23 pounds/8-10 kg. Bitches are slightly smaller.

Registry: AKC, CKC, FCI (Group 3), KC

BELGIAN SHEEPDOGS/
BELGIAN SHEPHERD DOGS

ORIGIN AND DEVELOPMENT

The dogs of the Belgian shepherds share an historical evolution very similar to many of the European herding breeds. However, over the centuries a particular type evolved to meet the specific needs of shepherds in what is now Belgium. These strong, sturdy, agile, intelligent and loyal dogs were so prized by their masters that when the decline of maintaining sheep herds in the area threatened their continued existence, their fanciers banded together to create a breed formally and to develop a breed Standard. Thus, in 1891 the breed, known throughout the world as the Belgian Shepherd Dog was officially created.

In establishing the breed and creating the Standard, these fanciers were able to agree on most aspects of type, structure, character and other breed essentials but there was one area of challenge. What was to be the correct coat and color of this breed? Present in the gene pool of these dogs were dogs with long coats, dogs with short coats and dogs with rough or wire coats. In addition, colors varied. There were dogs with black coats, dogs with dark reddish coats and black masks, and dogs with gray coats and black masks. Fortunately, wisdom prevailed and the fanciers recognized that issues such as type, structure, character, intelligence, working ability and so on were important issues in the establishment and the maintenance of a breed gene pool. Issues such as the diversity of coat type and color would be tolerated and permitted.

Despite this original tolerance of coat type and color diversity, this issue has plagued the development of the breed over the past century and has seen many changes and evolutions in the combination of coat types and colors that are permitted. Today, however, it is generally agreed by most breed authorities that there is

The Groenendael is designated as the Belgian Sheepdog by the American Kennel Club.

The Laekenois is not recognized by the AKC.

one breed of Belgian Shepherd Dog with four varieties. These varieties, named for the area in Belgium where they were developed and most prized are the Groenendael, the Laekenois, the Malinois and the Tervueren.

The Groenendael is a long-coated solid black dog with limited white permitted. The Lakenois is a rough or wire-coated fawn or gray dog. The Malinois is short coated in fawn, red or brown (gray is allowed in some countries) with a black mask and black overlay on the body. Finally, the Tervueren is a long-coated fawn or dark red dog (again, some countries permit gray) also with a black mask and black overlay on the body.

This status of one breed with four varieties is accepted by the Fédération Cynologique Internationale (FCI) and most national kennel clubs. The one exception is the American Kennel Club (AKC) which recognizes only three of the four varieties, namely the Groenendael, designated as the Belgian Sheep-dog; the Tervueren, designated as the Belgian Tervueren; and the Malinois, designated as the Belgian Malinois. The AKC does not recognize the Laekenois. To protect the integrity of the three varieties as separate breeds, the AKC does not permit breeding between the different coat types; it limits registration of imported dogs to those that are products of three generations of

breeding within one coat type; and it registers puppies according to the breed designation of their parents and not according to coat type and color.

Since 1994 the Belgian Shepherd has been regarded as a single breed by the British Kennel Club, with all four coat types competing in the same ring for Best of Breed and free to be interbred with any of the four varieties. This decision was met with great condemnation by Belgian Shepherd breeders in the United Kingdom but to no avail.

The maintenance of the one breed with four coat types and color varieties by the FCI and the rest of the world's kennel clubs has, of course, resulted in a different set of rules and practices. Dogs are always registered on the basis of their coat type and color and not that of their parents. There are no pedigree limitations placed on the registration of imports. Inter-variety breeding, while generally not advocated, is permitted in special circumstances and is used extensively to maintain the essentials of breed type, structure and character in each variety.

Malinois or Belgian Malinois as it is designated by the AKC.

Regardless of variety the Belgian Sheepdog should have a proud carriage of head, as does this Tervueren.

TEMPERAMENT

The breed is very intelligent, lively and activity loving. It excels in an active family environment. Also, the Belgian is an outstanding working dog whether the challenge is obedience, ring sport, herding, agility or tracking.

HEALTH MATTERS

Belgians are normally very healthy dogs that live beyond twelve years of age. The gene pool of the breed is relatively free of major occurrences of heritable diseases and conditions. However, epilepsy, excessive shyness, eye problems and hip dysplasia have been documented in the breed.

SPECIAL CARE AND TRAINING

Belgian Shepherd Dogs should have early socialization. They must be taught from a very early age not to distrust strange situations or people. The breed is a wonderful obedience worker and a natural herder.

ADAPTABILITY

So long as it has space in which to exercise regularly, the Belgian Shepherd Dog will adapt to both an urban and country environment.

ESSENTIALS OF THE BREED

Regardless of variety, the Belgian Shepherd Dog is an extremely elegant, upstanding, square, natural dog with an exceedingly proud carriage of head. Of medium size, males average 25 inches/64 cm in height and 60-70 pounds/ 27-32 kg in weight, while females average 23 inches/58 cm in height and 45-55 pounds/ 20.5 to 25 kg in weight. In addition to the males being larger than the females, they are generally more impressive in appearance. However, females have a refinement and femininity that should never be seen in males. Generally Belgian males shed their undercoats once a year while females normally shed twice a year. But this characteristic can vary between the coat varieties as does the required coat care, which is neither difficult nor extensive.

Registry: AKC (ex Lakenois), CKC, FCI (Group 1), KC

Tervueren or Belgian Tervueren as it is known by the AKC.

BERGER PICARD/ BERGER DE PICARDIE

This French shaggy-coated herding breed is usually referred to as "Picardie." The breed is named after the Picardie region in northeast France. It is believed that sheepdogs of a similar type have existed here since the tenth century. The origin of the Picardie is supposed to be closely linked with that of the two other French herding breeds — the Briard and the Beauceron. All three breeds were shown at the first French dog show in 1863. The Picardie was recognized in 1923.

On the whole, the large sheepdog breeds of northern Europe are all similar, as is clearly visible when comparing the Picardie with, for instance, the four varieties of Belgian Shepherd Dogs and the three from the Netherlands. Although the Picardie is mainly used for herding sheep, a task it still performs with skill in the valleys of the River Somme, it is also regarded as a good guard dog. Its temperament is lively, spontaneous and agile. The Picardie can be seen at most large European dog shows, but not in great numbers. It is still considered a rare breed outside France.

The Picardie should stand about 22-26 inches/ 55-65 cm at its withers. It has a decidedly rectangular body and long, rather narrow head with high-set pricked and pointed ears. Its tail is long and its coat should be shaggy, somewhat wiry in texture and about 2 inches/5 cm long. It should look natural and rustic. The coloring may be any shade of red, with or without black tips. The most common color is fawn grizzle. Grizzle is a description of color and color pattern used for breeds such as the Picardie and Saluki. The same coloring and pattern sometimes is described as wolf or hare colored in other breeds. Grizzle is used to describe hair that has a very light color at the base of the hair, deeper color at the middle and dark or black color at the tip. It describes hair then made up of three different colors or shades of color.

Registry: FCI (Group 1)

Berger Picard

BERGAMASCO

This old sheepdog breed is rarely seen outside Italy. It comes from the mountains around the city of Bergamo, but it has been used as a herder in several other parts of the country too. It is descended from Asian sheepdogs and it is supposed to have arrived in Italy with tradesmen from Phoenicia. Several of the middle-sized sheepdog breeds in Europe are of similar type — the Puli, Schapendoes, Catalan Sheepdog, Pyrenean Sheepdog and the Polish Owczarek Nizinny. Although the cords or mats in the large herding breed, the Komodor, are very distinct, this breed is usually not mentioned in relation to the Bergamasco. Some historians suggest that the Tibetan Terrier might be the ancestor of them all. However, only the Bergamasco and the Puli have a very heavily matted coat.

The Bergamasco is an independent working dog. It should be rectangular in body, strong and very muscular. The Bergamasco stands about 21-24 inches/54-62 cm at the withers and weighs about 59-82 pounds/27-37 kg. Its head should be big and quite long. The breed's most significant feature is its coat, which should be soft, wavy and very long. The coat is longest over the loin where, in an adult dog, it can reach the ground. The coat should be naturally matted not in corded curls but in flat stripes, almost 1 inch/2.5 cm wide. The coat does not become fully matted until the dog is about five years old. On the head and lower parts of its legs the coat should be shorter and less matted. The tail has long shaggy hair that is rarely matted. The color may be all nuances of gray, from very light to grayish black. Solid black is rarely found but this color is also permitted.

Registry: FCI (Group 1)

Bergamasco

BERNESE MOUNTAIN DOG/ BERNER SENNENHUND

ORIGIN AND DEVELOPMENT

The Bernese Mountain Dog traces its ancestry to the Roman invasion of Switzerland 2,000 years ago. Caesar's Mastiffs, used as guard dogs, were crossed with native flock-guarding dogs. These crosses produced animals able to withstand the severe weather found in the Alps. As time went by, the weavers of Berne used the Bernese as draft dogs. The breed became general farm dogs and guardians of the flocks. Market days were work days for the lovable black, tan, and white Bernese as they pulled carts full of baskets and dairy products to the market place.

By the 1800s the breed had all but died out. However, concentrated efforts on the part of Herr Franz Schertenleib and Albert Heim, two celebrated fanciers of the time, saved the breed and today its popularity is ever on the increase.

TEMPERAMENT

Great strides have been made to improve the temperament of the breed, which was a naturally reticent country dog. Today, a sweet, character and really outgoing attitude is found.

Bernese Mountain Dog

HEALTH MATTERS

The Bernese Mountain Dog has had problems with hip dysplasia. X-ray evaluations of the hips must be done with all breeding animals. Gastric torsion has been noted in some families.

SPECIAL CARE AND TRAINING

The Bernese thrives on obedience training. The exercise gained is good for its physique and its mind. The Bernese coat is thick, lustrous and requires regular weekly grooming. Its teeth and nails also benefit from weekly attention. Do not allow the Bernese to become obese.

ADAPTABILITY

The Bernese is primarily a country dog. Not surprisingly, it does not do well in very hot or humid climates because of its heavy coat. It can be kept the city, however, provided that it is given sufficient exercise.

ESSENTIALS OF THE BREED

In the United States, males are 24 1/2-27 1/2 inches/62-70 cm tall while females are 22 1/2-25 1/2 inches/57-65 cm — they should be about 1/2 inch/1 cm taller in the United Kingdom. Males can weigh 80-105 pounds/36-48 kg and females 75-90 pounds/34-41 kg. Both sexes have large bodies, solid toplines, good legs and feet, strong muzzles with good breadth of skull and smallish ears, which are V-shaped and drooped. Its tail should be thick, well furred and carried slightly up. The color is important: the base color should be inky black with tan markings on all four legs, and there should be a spot over each eye. Additionally, it should have white chest markings in the form of a cross, a white tail tip, a white blaze on the face and white toes. Its dark eyes are very expressive and its demeanor is steady and loyal.

Registry: AKC, CKC, FCI (Group 2), KC

BICHON FRISÉ

ORIGIN AND DEVELOPMENT

Even the breed authorities admit that the history of today's Bichon Frisé is at best a well-intended composite of fact, fiction, legend and conjecture that lacks specific dates and its verification remains a challenge to today's leading breeders. However, there is widespread agreement that a small, coated dog — often white — existed even before the time of Christ.

Several theories exist related to the early years of these "small, coated, often-white" dogs. Some authorities view the dog as a direct ancestor of the Maltese, descended from a spitz-type dog in south-central Europe that was found throughout the Mediterranean area. On the other hand, one European authority claims that the people in the southern Mediterranean had a dwarf breed that resulted from crosses of the miniature Spaniel and miniature Poodle or with Cayenne dogs. He sees these breeds as

the foundation which gave rise to the "barbichon," later called the Bichon — and he places its origin in Italy.

The complexity of pinpointing the most likely origin stems from the fact that the "small, coated, often-white" dogs had enduring qualities that made them prized possessions of their owners. As history unfolded and people traveled, they took these dogs with them and various colonies of the dogs' descendants developed. These dogs shared many similar characteristics but also had many significant differences.

So, ultimately, it became evident that several "breeds" carried the name "Bichon": The Dog of Tenerife, the Dog of Havana, the Dog of Bologna, the Dog of Baleares, the Dog of Peru, the Dog of Holland and — according to one French publication — also the Little Lion Dog of Buffon. Another Parisian publication included four categories: the Maltese, the Bolognese, the Tenerife and the Havanese.

An American Bichon Frisé

Both of these French publications date from the 1930s.

Following World War I, both French and Belgian breeders sustained such an active interest in the breed, which was then called Bichon à Poil Frisé or Tenerife Bichon, that a breed Standard was merited. The official Standard was adopted on March 15, 1933 and was written by Madame Bouctovagniez, president of the Toy Club of France, in conjunction with the Friends of the Belgian Breeds.

One related challenge was that of coming up with a single name for the breed. Apparently the discussion was heated concerning the choice of a name and finally Madame Nizet de Leemans, head of the Breed Standards Committee of the Fédération Cynologique Internationale, asked her colleagues in desperation, "What does it look like?" She was told it was a fluffy, little white dog. "Well then," she said, "It shall be called Bichon Frisé (fluffy little dog)." And so it was.

The Bichon Frisé Club of America was founded in 1964 and the breed Standard was approved in October, 1988.

An English Bichon Frisé

TEMPERAMENT

"The Bichon Frisé is a gentle-mannered, sensitive little dog that is playful and affectionate." The breed Standard calls the breed's cheerful attitude the "hallmark of the breed" and encourages breeders and owners to settle for nothing less.

HEALTH MATTERS

This dog is not known to have any heritable problems and in general should be healthy and require no more than the usual inoculations.

SPECIAL CARE AND TRAINING

The only limiting factor in its suitability is that because the breed is white it requires trimming and frequent coat care. People who select this breed should expect to provide regular brushing and periodic trimming. And because of its color, regular bathing will be required with frequency dependent upon the dog's living situation and the owner's desire that the Bichon should look its best.

ADAPTABILITY

Considering its temperament, it is easy to understand that the breed is well suited to people of all ages and in a wide range of living situations.

ESSENTIALS OF THE BREED

The ideal Bichon Frisé is a sturdy, white dog standing 9 1/2-11 1/2 inches/24-29 cm tall (and 1/2 inch/1 cm shorter in the United Kingdom). Measured from the point of the chest to the point of the rump, it is one-fourth longer than its height at the withers. The depth of body (withers to chest) should equal the distance from its chest to the ground.

Viewed from the front, the head portrays a circle of white with three black points: its nose and its round, black (or dark brown) eyes that look directly forward. Black eyes and black halos greatly enhance its expression. The head itself is three parts muzzle to five parts skull. Lines connecting the eyes and nose form an equilateral triangle. Its lips are black, its muzzle blunt, and its ear leather should be short, V-shaped and rather fine. Its ears should be set slightly higher than its eyes and forward on the skull to frame the face. The scissors bite is correct but this will be penalized if it is overshot or undershot. Missing teeth will be severely faulted.

The neck — occiput to withers — should be one third of the body length (point of chest to point of rump). It should be arched and carried proudly because it plays an important part in creating the breed's desired general appearance. The topline should be level with a slight arch over the loin. The ribs are moderately sprung, and the chest is moderately deep and wide enough to enhance movement. The tail of the Bichon Frisé is set on level with the topline, well plumed and carried over the back. The shoulder should be well laid back (at an angle of 45 degrees) with the front leg placed directly under the withers. The well-developed hindquarters match the angulation of the forequarters.

The Bichon coat is composed of a soft, dense undercoat and a coarser, curlier outercoat that stands off the body, giving a powder puff appearance. A wiry coat is not desirable but limp, silky coats or a lack of undercoat is a serious fault. The coat is usually trimmed to the dog's natural body contours — even though the Fédération Cynologique Internationale's breed Standard does not allow trimming of the breed. It should be rounded off in all directions and never cut so short as to be overly trimmed giving a squared-off appearance. The furnishings of the Bichon Frisé's head, the ears and the tail are left long with the head trimmed to create a round, overall look.

The Bichon's desired movement is free and flowing with topline level and head carried somewhat erect. The movement is precise and true, coming and going, with moderate width behind. Fluid movement with good extension front and rear are ideal.

Registry: AKC, CKC, FCI (Group 9), KC

BILLY

This French breed was created in the 1870s at Castle Billy in Poitou. Billy, Grand Bleu de Gascogne and Poitevin represent the truly old French hound breeds, that is, with no Foxhound blood. The Billy was developed from three of the old breeds that are now extinct: Larye, Ceris and Montemboeufs.

After World War II only a couple of Billy were left and these were mated to Poitevins, Porcelains and Harriers and hence new packs were created that kept the original breed name. They usually hunt roe deer, but some packs even hunt boar. The Billy is very rare, even in France. Few are seen on the international show circuit.

The Billy has a fine build; its head should be long with a convex nose ridge. The height at its withers should be about 23-26 inches/58-66 cm. The ears are higher set and not as traditionally folded in French hounds. Its coat should be smooth and fine, while the color should always be white with very pale lemon, orange or café au lait colored patches. Pronounced black eye rims are a typical feature.

Registry: FCI (Group 6)

Billy

BLACK RUSSIAN TERRIER/ TJORNYJ TERJER

This breed was developed in Moscow just after World War II. By crossing Giant Schnauzers with Airedale Terriers, Rottweilers and a local type of dog called the Moscow Retriever, breeders obtained a strong, fearless and hardy working dog. The idea was to produce a useful dog for military and police work and the result lived up to expectations. The Black Russian Terrier is rare but can be seen in small numbers at European and Scandinavian dog shows.

The rustic, hardy Black Terrier resembles the Giant Schnauzer but does not enjoy its more elegant structure. At the withers its height is about 25-28 inches/64-72 cm. Its head is broad and its ears rarely cropped. The tail should be docked short. Its coat should be thick, wiry and 1 1/2-4 inches/4-10 cm long, giving a natural un-trimmed look. It should be black or grayish black in color.

Registry: FCI (Group 2)

Black Russian Terrier

BLOODHOUND

ORIGIN AND DEVELOPMENT

The Bloodhound is a very old breed. Specimens were alive and thriving in Greece long before the coming of Christianity. The dog's name was coined by the English and it has nothing to do with following a blood trail. The breed was nurtured in England by members of high society (the bluebloods), and this is where the name Bloodhound comes from. The Bloodhound has always been used as a scent-trailing hound and the luxuriant wrinkles about its head and neck entrap the scent of the target. This holds it in good stead for locating lost children, the confused elderly or perhaps a camper lost without a compass.

TEMPERAMENT

The Bloodhound has never been used as an attacking animal and it is a gentle family companion. Puppies need to be socialized early and the Bloodhound *must* have human contact to prosper.

HEALTH MATTERS

Inverted eyelids can be a problem and should the condition arise, a vet should be consulted because the eyesight could be damaged. Hounds that have had their eyes surgically corrected may not be shown. Hips of breeding animals should be X-rayed after two years of age. The dog's water intake should be controlled, because the breed has a tendency to what is known as gastric torsion or bloat (correctly this is gastric dilatation-volvulus). With this condition, gas dilates the stomach so that it twists on its axis (or volvus). This puts the spleen and other surrounding organs in danger of being displaced, with death caused by a disrupted blood supply and other factors likely. Surgery will be required — and quickly.

No specific cause is known to be at the root of this problem, which occurs in dogs, humans, cattle and swine. Theories abound — that it runs in families, that it is prevalent in dogs with large stomach cavities, that few measures can be taken to prevent the disaster. However, it is best to avoid soy products (which cause gas) and to feed small meals in preference to a large one. Owners should always consult a vet immediately if the dog seems bloated, full of gas or tries repeatedly to vomit with no results.

SPECIAL CARE AND TRAINING

Bloodhounds are clean dogs by nature but they all tend to drool, distributing saliva over a large area when they shake their heads. The Bloodhound should never be exercised off the lead except in an enclosed area: they never learn that cars are dangerous.

The naturally short smooth coat of the Bloodhound is easily cared for. A rub down with a wet towel several times a week solves the problem of lifting this heavyweight into a tub. Toenails must be filed or clipped weekly because long nails will lead to an unsightly flat foot, which is a weakness of this breed. The Bloodhound's long pendulous ears need weekly care since they tend to dip into everything and the deep folds can harbor mites and ear infections.

Good nutrition is essential. Care should be taken in feeding, with two or more small meals preferable to one large one. Exercise should be limited after eating.

ADAPTABILITY

Since the Bloodhound is a very large dog, with males often weighing more than 100 pounds/ 45 kg and females nearly as much, its owners should have the time, space and knowledge to deal with animals of this size.

ESSENTIALS OF THE BREED

Its huge size of 23-27 inches/58-68 cm, its thin, loose and pliable skin that falls in soft folds around its neck, and its wonderful deep voice are all hallmarks of the Bloodhound. Its head is

Bloodhound

long, with the foreface and backskull of equal length and the latter neither coarse nor cloddy. Its ears are very long and pendulous, which helps the breed to track scent while trailing. Its body is massive, deep and strong with a solid and firm topline. Its tail is long, quite thick (not stringy) and carried up and gaily when the hound is moving. Its neck is long enough to reach the ground easily when trailing. The Bloodhound's eyes are deep set and should be clear. Although there have been mouth problems within the breed — misalignment of teeth and an undershot bite — the perfect mouth should have a normal scissors bite. Its coloring should be black-and-tan, clear red and liver-and-tan. Small amounts of white on the toes or chest are tolerated. A loose swinging but sound gait are typical.

Registry: AKC, CKC, FCI (Group 6), KC

BOLOGNESE

The Bolognese is a breed that has existed in the Mediterranean for thousands of years. It belongs to a group of (usually white) Toy Dogs, known as Barbichons. Its origin is closely related to that of the Maltese. As its name suggests, the breed's development took place in the Italian city of Bologna. The breed is still quite rare outside Italy.

The Bolognese's body structure should be fine and its body proportions square. At its withers, it should stand about 10-12 inches/25-30 cm. Its muzzle should be short and strong. The coat should be long, standing out from the body, with loose curls all over, except on the nose ridge where it should be short. Pigmentation on the nose, lips and eye rims should be black. Pigmentation other than black is considered a serious fault. The overall look should be natural and not scissored; the coat texture should be soft but not woolly. The color should always be white, although light lemon markings on the ears are tolerated. Temperament should be even.

Registry: FCI (Group 9)

Bolognese

BORDER COLLIE

ORIGIN AND DEVELOPMENT

The Border Collie developed over generations from such breeds as Bearded Collies, Harlequins, Bob-tailed Sheepdogs and Smithfields. Possibly the earliest reference to a dog similar to the Border occurs in Dr. John Caius' *Treatise on English Dogges*, written in 1570. He describes the "Shepherd's Dogge" as being "of medium size which answered to his master's will, shaking of fist, or shrill hissing and the dogs would bring sheep to the place of his master's will." Subsequent references confirm that a Border Collie type dog existed in the mid-1700s.

The breed owes its name to the area where it originally evolved — the Border counties of England and Scotland. Records show that similar dogs were found all over the British Isles and Europe, where they were known under other names. The first sheepdog trial was held in Bala, North Wales in 1873, when a dog named Tweed from Scotland won both the trial and the prize for the most handsome dog.

The International Sheepdog Society (ISDS) was founded in 1906 and its Stud Book was first published in 1955. For many years the Border Collie in Britain remained very much the province of the ISDS. In the mid-1960s the Kennel Club began to register Border Collies. In 1982 the breed was awarded its first Challenge Certificates at Cruft's dog show..

Meanwhile, the Border Collie was imported into Australia as a working sheepdog. It found many admirers there. In Australia the breed developed as a showdog much sooner than in Britain and proved equally popular on the show bench in New Zealand. In recent years many leading British show Border Collies have been bred from stock imported from Australasia. The Border has a great ability and enthusiasm to work sheep and to a lesser degree cattle. It must be able to crouch, creep and spring into action if a sheep gets out of line. It needs to be an extremely lithe and agile dog, and have strength, substance and stamina to be an effective working dog. In 1963, the Australian National Kennel Council adopted a Standard for the breed. From October 1, 1995 the breed will be eligable for showing in regular class competition in the United States.

TEMPERAMENT

The Border thrives on constant involvement and stimulation; one of the most intelligent of all dog breeds, it learns quickly and enjoys a challenge. It demonstrates a loyal and faithful nature. While very protective of the family, it should also be kindly disposed toward stock.

HEALTH MATTERS

The Border Collie is quite a healthy dog with no major hereditary diseases. However, progressive retinal atrophy has been a concern in the past and breeders have worked hard to eradicate this eye condition. A genetic disorder called ceriod lipofuscinosis (storage disease) has also been identified in the breed. This affects body cells and nerve cells in particular. It is not contagious and does not normally show up until the animal is about eighteen months old. At the moment, it is considered incurable.

SPECIAL CARE AND TRAINING

Like most working dogs, the Border Collie requires plenty of active exercise and mental stimulation. It thrives on games and is generally willing to please, quick to learn and at times appears to be able to think ahead of its owner — particularly in the Obedience ring which they seem to dominate internationally. Grooming is straightforward and very basic.

ADAPTABILITY

The Border Collie should be a very even-tempered dog and at all times be amenable and very manageable. It is extremely intelligent and easily trained; it listens and wants to please. A very popular competition dog in both breed and Obedience rings, it is increasingly in demand as a pet, but prospective owners should realize that it needs constant physical and mental activity if it is to be at its best.

ESSENTIALS OF THE BREED

The Border should be a graceful dog with perfect balance and a smooth outline, giving the impression that it is capable of a full day's work. Like most working breeds, it is slightly longer than its wither height, and should have plenty of heart room with well-sprung ribs and a moderately broad chest. The skull should be flat when viewed from the side; the muzzle of the same length and of moderate strength. Viewed from above, the head should be wedge shaped with a moderate amount of chiseling to the foreface below the eyes.

The Border's eager expression must give the impression that it is willing to please its owner at all times. While the Australian Breed Standard calls for semi-erect ears, its British counterpart still allows for fully erect ears. Whatever carriage, they should be set well apart on the top of the skull and be highly mobile. The more popular coat of the Border is a weather-resistant double coat of moderate length, with an abundant coat around the neck forming a mane. The British Standard also allows for a smooth coat. The breed comes in a variety of colors where white should never predominate. The more usual base colors include black, blue, chocolate, red, blue merle and black-and-tan. The Border male stands around 19-21 inches/48-53 cm at the withers, with bitches 1 inch/2.5 cm smaller.

Registry: AKC, CKC, FCI (Group 1), KC

Border Collie

BORDER TERRIER

ORIGIN AND DEVELOPMENT

Border Terriers were developed to hunt along-side Foxhounds in the countryside of northeast England. The breed was certainly in existence before the middle of the eighteenth century when Frank Paton painted a portrait of Arthur Wentworth which included two Border Terriers, *Earth Stopper to Tufnell Joliffe's Hounds*. The painting was completed in about 1754. Foxes had been hunted in England since at least 1219 when Henry III gave John Fitz-Robert permission "to keep dogs of his own to hunt foxes and hares in the forest of Northumbria". This hunting was not part of a social, sporting ritual but a necessary means to prevent the destruction of lambs on which Border farmers relied for their livelihood. The hunting of foxes with hounds in Northumbria would be inconceivable without the services of a useful terrier and this is why, from the beginning of the thirteenth century, there must have been terriers in this region.

The history of Border Terriers is inextricably mixed with that of hunting in Northumbria. The Kielder Hounds were favorably noticed in the early 1800s by that most snobbish of sporting reporters, Nimrod. They were hunted by the Robson family who, in 1857, moved the pack to Byrness in Reedwater where they were amalgamated with hounds kept by John Dodd of Catcleugh. The new pack was known as the Reedwater Hounds. In 1869 Jacob Robson's relative, John, took over the mastership of the pack and the name was again changed to the Border Foxhounds. It was within this pack and two neighboring packs, the Liddesdale and the North Tyne, that Border Terriers as they are known today were developed. The area has produced both the Dandie Dinmont and the Bedlington, originally known as the Rothbury Terriers. Neither of these breeds were worked with hounds, although there is undoubtedly a close relationship between them and the Border

Terrier. For work with hounds, the three packs relied on the white Redesdale Terriers, now extinct, and the colored Coquetdale Terriers which have, because of their close association with the Border Foxhounds, since become known as Border Terriers.

The terriers of the region first appeared in the show ring when the newly formed Agricultural Societies began to run shows toward the end of the eighteenth century. Attempts to put Border Terriers on a more formal footing were made in 1895 when John Houliston tried to found a club. His attempts came to nothing as did the first application, made in 1914, for Kennel Club recognition.

In 1920, however, the Kennel Club was finally persuaded, by Captain Hamilton Adams, one of its members who bred Sealyhams in Eastbourne, Sussex, to accept the dogs as an old breed which was in the process of being revived. A breed Standard, which was ignored by breeders, was also approved and the breed looked forward to its new career in the show ring. Prior to recognition, fears had been expressed that the breed would be ruined as a working terrier because the fashionable demands of the show ring were given priority over more essential matters. In order to prevent this, the newly formed Border Terrier Club drew up its own Standard and the one that had been approved by the Kennel Club was quietly scrapped. Even so, not all the breed's supporters were satisfied and some formed the short-lived Northumberland Border Terrier Club, which not only continued to oppose recognition but even went so far as to try to prevent people who did not live in Northumberland from being involved with the breed. By the mid-1920s, the two societies had pooled their resources and had produced a Standard which in all essential respects remains unchanged to this day. Breed clubs continue to place emphasis on the need to preserve the working qualities of the breed, and some do so by issuing working certificates, by putting on classes for working dogs and by education.

The breed is recognized by all the world's kennel clubs and in recent years has become one of the top twenty most popular breeds in United Kingdom. The breed is also popular throughout Scandinavia, where the quality of the best dogs is on a par with anything produced in the United Kingdom. The breed is less popular in other parts of the world where its workaday image and lack of obvious glamor tend to make it a breed best appreciated by dedicated enthusiasts.

TEMPERAMENT

Continued contact with their original purpose in life, as well as the respect shown by the best breeders for the demands exerted by this *raison d'être*, has meant that Border Terriers,

Border Terrier

though well able to look after themselves in any dispute, usually have an amiable outlook on life. Border Terriers were intended to run with Foxhounds and be at hand to worry foxes out from any places in which they might take refuge. They mix freely with hounds — often living in the same kennels; they also run with mounted followers alongside farm stock and must be able to work alongside other terriers at the behest of strangers. There is no room in the hunting field for any terrier which shows the slightest tendency toward the hysterical "terrier spirit" sometimes encouraged in the show ring. The breed's sporting background means that it may be inclined to undertake illicit excursions and, once this interest has been kindled, only very secure fencing and constant vigilance will thwart a determined Border.

HEALTH MATTERS

Obviously a terrier that is expected to run with hounds over wild moorland country in the depth of winter and then to face a foe fighting for its life must be extremely robust. However, growing popularity, which attracts the interest of commercial breeders, may expose the Border Terrier to the risk of health problems in the future, although small, carefully selective breeders will continue to put health at the top of any list of priorities.

SPECIAL TRAINING

Owners should not expect instant obedience from a Border; its origins demanded a strongly independent nature which combines self-reliance with initiative. When summoned from a distance, a Border Terrier will often indicate that it is busy for the moment and will be along in a few minutes. It will usually honor its word but its return may involve a detour or two, to take in places of interest en route. The Border Terrier owner will derive great pleasure from the hours spent training his dog on a one-to-one basis, and the initial hard work will eventually pay great dividends.

ADAPTABILITY

Border Terriers tend to make the most of any situation in which they might find themselves; they are remarkably self-reliant and will contrive to make the best of a home whether in a city apartment or a country mansion. Their equable nature makes them ideal as family pets — they are as much at home by the fireside as on a long country walk. They acquit themselves well in the show ring, make excellent Agility dogs and are much used both as therapy dogs and as assistance dogs for the deaf.

ESSENTIALS OF THE BREED

The broad, strong, otterlike head with its short, powerful jaws makes it easy to distinguish the Border from all other terriers, while the breed's rather houndlike body proportions, its thick, loose pelt, double, weather-resistant coat and short, undocked "carrot" tail are equally important to the connoisseur. The Border Terrier's expression is one of kindly but implacable determination. The eyes are dark, the ears dropping forward close to the cheeks. The teeth are unusually large and strong and meet in a scissors grip. The neck is strong, the shoulders rather long and well laid back, as is necessary for a terrier required both to negotiate rough country and maneuver in restricted underground places.

The Border Terrier should be about 13 inches/ 33 cm at the withers. Its chest is rather deep and narrow and it should never have round ribs. The loin is quite long, flexible and strong, the hindquarters powerful and racy with low-set hocks, producing a moderate degree of rear angulation. The coat, which should not require trimming with knives, razors or scissors, is harsh and lies close to the body over a dense, soft undercoat. The color of the Border may be red, wheaten, gray-and-tan or blue-and-tan with a small amount of white permitted, though white is not encouraged, on the chest.

Registry: AKC, CKC, FCI (Group 3), KC

BORZOI

ORIGIN AND DEVELOPMENT

A native of Russia — indeed, it is also known as the Russian Wolfhound — this tall, exotic looking and luxuriantly coated hound was bred to hunt: to track, run down and dispatch the wolf from wherever it was hiding. Believed to have descended from the extinct Steppe Greyhound with crosses to other breeds, the Borzoi has retained its sighthound silhouette. Its double coat always served it well during brutal Russian winters. The breed has been refined through the years. It is a beautiful animal with flowing lines, sporting an attractive coat which comes in a great variety of colors.

In recent years the Borzoi has been trained to hunt coyotes in the United States. As the sport of lure coursing has become more prominent, it has proven itself to be a willing and eager participant.

TEMPERAMENT

Borzois are gentle but inclined to fun and racing games. They adapt well to a life of ease and enjoyment. However, as with any sporting hound, it must have exercise and training in order to retain its wonderful athletic look. Free exercise should not be chanced as it is a

Borzoi

sighthound and will chase anything it deems as prey. It will not pay attention to its own safety. For example, it will run across or down a road without heed of cars or any danger to itself.

HEALTH MATTERS

The Borzoi is a healthy dog for the most part. There have been cases of progressive retinal atrophy (night blindness) as well as gastric torsion. As with many sighthounds there is a tendency to be sensitive to anesthesia, as well as some other drugs. Care should also be taken with flea collars. Similarly, do not exercise this hound on lawns freshly treated with fertilizers, insecticides or chemical weed killers.

SPECIAL CARE AND TRAINING

The Borzoi is somewhat stubborn to train. Training should begin early — by at least ten weeks. As the breed is a large one, care must be taken to give a youngster every opportunity to take as much free exercise in a safely enclosed yard while not on a leash. This will all aid its growth and experience. Borzois should not be cooped or confined.

ESSENTIALS OF THE BREED

A tall glamorous sighthound, the Borzoi stands 26-28 inches/65-70 cm high in the United States. The British Standard requires males to be 29 inches/73 cm and females 27 inches/68 cm. The Borzoi has sturdy bones, a deep chest, an arched loin, and a low-placed long tail carried in a streaming manner behind the dog when it is trotting or galloping. Its head is quite long, with a distinct Roman finish or downfaced look to the muzzle. The teeth should meet in a scissors or even bite, although the breed frequently lacks pre-molars. The eyes should be dark, and the folded ears thrown back and close to the neck when in repose. When the dog is alert, the ears are thrown out to the sides of the head — still with a fold- and never erect.

The flowing double coat of many colors is very thick. The tail is well covered, as are the neck, chest and backs of the legs. The face and the front of the legs are covered with smooth lying hair.

Registry: AKC, CKC, FCI (Group 10), KC

BOSANSKI OSTRODLAKI GONIC-BARAK

This wirehaired scenthound from Bosnia in former Yugoslavia has been known and true to type since the nineteenth century. It is strictly used to hunt wild boar, hare and fox.

The height at the withers should be about 18-22 inches/46-56 cm. The body should be almost rectangular, well muscled and with good bone. The breed is east European in type, i.e., it has a broad head with a flat skull and triangular, not too long ears hanging close to the cheeks without any folds. The coat should be wiry with a thick undercoat and a shaggy appearance. It is usually pale wheaten with a grayish saddle.

Registry: FCI (Group 6)

Bosanski Ostrodlaki Gonic-Barak

BOSTON TERRIER

ORIGIN AND DEVELOPMENT

A truly American dog, the Boston Terrier is one of a handful of breeds which has been developed in the United States. In the 1900s, the breed was a great favorite as a pet and show dog. The Boston Terrier is a distinctively marked, smooth coated, tidy package, classified as a Non-Sporting Dog. It derives from crosses between the Bulldog and Terrier, which is why it has the short face of the Bulldog's ancestors and the pluck of its Terrier forebears.

TEMPERAMENT

The Boston Terrier was designed to be what it is: a companion, watchdog and Yankee Doodle Dandy. It is good with children, if brought up with them, and loves to go for walks, rides in the car — in fact anything on the agenda is fine with the Boston Terrier.

HEALTH MATTERS

This breed is generally healthy, although its prominent eye can easily be injured. Because of its short nose, it is also inclined to wheeze and snore. Some skin problems do exist. Teeth should be kept clean (they can be brushed, much to the amusement of the Boston) and nails filed or cut weekly. The erect ear, either natural or cropped, makes ear problems rare.

SPECIAL CARE AND TRAINING

Clean as a whistle, a rub down with a damp towel several times weekly keeps the dog clean; a total bath is not needed very often. The Boston Terrier is easily house trained and will learn any trick that its owner has the time and patience to teach it.

ADAPTABILITY

The Boston Terrier was successfully bred for adaptability. Its size, 25 pounds/11 kg or smaller, makes it particularly suitable as a house dog.

ESSENTIALS OF THE BREED

Distinctive white markings on a seal, black or brindle background, a short back with a slightly

Boston Terrier

arched loin, a short tail and a smooth coat are all characteristics of the Boston Terrier. In the show ring, it is classified according to weight: under 15 pounds/7 kg, 15-20 pounds/7-9 kg and 20-25 pounds/9-11 kg. Height is not specified under the breed Standard but as a rule, when measured at the shoulder, males should be about 15 inches/38 cm and females about 1 inch/2.5 cm or so less in height than males. The Boston's head is its hallmark, with its square short muzzle, seemingly square backskull and well-defined stop. The ears of the Boston Terrier are erect and carried stiffly, whether cropped or natural, and its eyes are most expressive. The chest is deep and full and the leg bones are not heavy or cumbersome — all the feet are well formed. Its movement should be quick stepping, free and quite stylish. The Boston is a welcome addition to almost any home.

Registry: AKC, CKC, FCI (Group 9), KC

The Kennel Club Standard requires that the Boston Terrier has uncropped ears in the United Kingdom.

BOUVIER DES ARDENNES

This hardy cattle dog is supposed to be one of the original, old type of Belgian cattle herders. Certainly, it is smaller but in type it is not dissimilar to what the Bouvier des Flandres once looked like. Its reputation is that of a very good guard dog as well as a tough herder. The breed is considered extremely rare. Some say that the Bouvier des Ardennes is on the verge of extinction.

The Bouvier des Ardennes stands about 22 inches/57 cm at the withers. Its body should be square and compact, and its ears should be quite big, pricked and never cropped. Its coat should be harsh and shaggy on the body, shorter on the legs and the breed may be of any color, although grayish black is the most common color.

Registry: FCI (Group 1)

The Bouvier des Ardennes is extremely rare, even in Belgium, its country of origin.

BOUVIER DES FLANDRES

ORIGIN AND DEVELOPMENT

The Bouvier des Flandres originated in the Flanders area of Belgium. This was a dog of many uses which included pulling carts and driving cattle or oxen. In fact, the name Bouvier means: "driver of oxen". Few Bouviers survived World War I, and the breed owes its present numbers to a few dedicated breeders.

The Bouvier des Flandres was imported to the United States in the 1930s. Because of its large size and tough appearance, it makes a good watchdog. In addition to its original role, it also does well as a guide dog for the blind or helping in police work.

TEMPERAMENT

The Bouvier des Flandres is a good family dog. It is good with children when it has been raised with them. It loves the company of people.

HEALTH MATTERS

As with many large to giant-sized breeds, the Bouvier des Flandres is prone to hip dysplasia and so stock should be purchased from reputable breeders who have health and temperament as their primary interest and who have kept health records on several generations. Gastric torsion can be a problem and it is recommended that the Bouvier be given two or three small meals daily, rather than one large one, followed immediately by periods of rest or inactivity. Feeding soy-free products is encouraged.

SPECIAL CARE AND TRAINING

Teeth, nails and ears need weekly attention and, as the coat should be 2 1/2 inches/6.5 cm in length over the entire body, routine weekly brushing and combing are prerequisites. The beard and mustache can grow quite bushy and

Bouvier des Flandres

138

The Bouvier des Flandres must have natural, uncropped ears according to the Kennel Club Standard in the United Kingdom.

long and they may need washing and drying on a regular basis. Full baths should be given as required; regular grooming will remove shedding hair.

ADAPTABILITY

Its large size necessitates ample space in which to exercise. The breed also enjoys being put to work, which keeps its mind active. For these reasons, is is much better suited to country living.

ESSENTIALS OF THE BREED

The Bouvier des Flandres is large, up to 27 1/2 inches/70 cm for the male and 26 1/2 inches/ 67 cm for the female. Under the British Standard, males are 25-27 inches/63-68 cm. On average, the breed weighs 75-95 pounds/34-43 kg. The Bouvier is a square dog with a robust body. It has a large head with either cropped or natural ears. The breed's dark eyes peer out from under profuse eyebrows. It has a short docked tail and a rather tousled coat. Colors range from fawn to black and include gray, brindle, and salt and pepper; white and brown are not acceptable. The Bouvier des Flandres is a big, wonderful, tousled dog with a dependable disposition.

Registry: AKC, CKC, FCI (Group 1), KC

BOXER

ORIGIN AND DEVELOPMENT

The history of the Boxer goes back to the 1880s when a Munich man, Georg Alt, mated a small Bullenbeisser bitch (which he had bought in France) to a local dog and produced a parti-colored bitch called Schenken. The Bullenbeisser was a mastiff-type breed which was used for baiting, guarding and hunting boar and bear. Schenken was subsequently mated to an English Bulldog and a son of this breeding, Flocki, was shown in 1895 at a Munich dog show. He became the first Boxer to be entered in the German Stud Book.

Flocki had a sister named Blanka, who was more instrumental in founding the breed. She

A brindle Boxer

was white and became the dam of a lightly marked brindle-and-white bitch, Meta von der Passage (born in 1898) to which virtually all the leading Boxers in the world can trace their origins. The legacy of Meta and her ancestors is that, to this day, white puppies are often born in Boxer litters. More than one-third white markings are not allowed in the show ring and solid white puppies are usually culled due to the risk of deafness.

The German Boxer Club was formed in 1896 and published the first Boxer breed Standard in 1902. It was a very detailed document and little has been changed in this Standard to this day. One of the major personalities to contribute to the progress of the Boxer was Frau Friederun Stockmann whose von Dom Kennel supplied many key dogs to both Great Britain and the United States. Over the years the breed has become rather more refined in type in these two countries. Modern Boxers in the United Kingdom tend to have a little more elegance and smartness than some of their mid-European counterparts where the Boxer head is considered all-important, almost to the exclusion of everything else. In some countries the breed traditionally has both its tail docked and its ears cropped, though now one or both practices have been outlawed by certain nations.

TEMPERAMENT

The Boxer is the ultimate "people dog." It loves to be with its human family and enjoys nothing more than entertaining them. It is a natural extrovert, inquisitive and active. The Boxer should always be even-tempered and, while capable of standing its ground, should never be unduly aggressive. Nervousness should not be tolerated in this naturally noble and outgoing breed.

HEALTH MATTERS

The Boxer suffered something of a setback, mainly in Britain, with the discovery of the inherited condition of progressive axonopathy, a disease of the central nervous system which proves debilitating. Happily breeders have been diligent in virtually wiping out the condition, but Boxer litters should never be bred without thorough prior research of pedigrees to ascertain whether or not they contain known carriers. Occasional heart murmurs have been discovered in the breed, but in general these dogs remain fit and hardy. This is a relatively healthy breed.

SPECIAL CARE AND TRAINING

The Boxer is a boisterous breed by nature and an unruly adult can be a liability, so it is essential that all puppies receive a grounding in basic obedience. The breed's intelligence and learning capabilities are such that many Boxers have distinguished themselves in Obedience and working trials and it has been known for them to work as guide dogs for the blind. The Boxer is a low-maintenance breed with minimal grooming requirements.

ADAPTABILITY

Boxers will adapt to virtually any home environment, provided they have company. They mix freely with other dogs and children and can live happily in an urban home if they get enough regular exercise.

ESSENTIALS OF THE BREED

The key word in the Boxer breed Standard is "nobility" and the breed should always be proud in its bearing. The head should be distinctive, with a short, well-padded muzzle, great width and strength of underjaw, a slight tilt to the nose and a pronounced stop and rise in the skull, which help to create the classic Boxer profile. The ears are generally cropped in the United States, South America and Canada, adding to the alert expression — but the American Standard does not specifically disqualify an uncropped Boxer. In countries such as the United Kingdom, Australia and Scandinavia, where cropping is prohibited, the ears are of medium size, neither too small nor overly large. They are well set so that the folded ears break just at the top of the skull,

This fawn Boxer has natural, uncropped ears as required by the Kennel Club Standard in the United Kingdom

drop forward and frame the head and eye in an attractive manner. Tail docking is banned in Denmark, Norway and Sweden.

The Boxer should be clean-cheeked and the eyes should be dark and expressive. The neck should be elegantly crested, the topline short and firm, sloping slightly to the rear, with well-angulated quarters with musculature which stands out "plastically" from under the skin. The Boxer should have good depth of brisket, a noticeable tuck-up and high tailset. Its movement should be forceful with a roomy stride. Strongly boned, the Boxer should always be well up on its feet and have a natural style about it.

The Boxer can be brindle or fawn, with or without the white markings which now seem so fashionable — almost to the point of being obligatory — in the show ring. Plain colored dogs with no white markings are still seen winning top honors in Germany and central Europe however. Brindles must have black stripes on the base fawn color, with the stripes being in distinct relief. Far too many Boxers have colors merging, so that the dog appears almost black. While popular with some fanciers, merging colors are incorrect.. The breed should stand 21-25 inches/53-64 cm at the shoulder.

Registry: AKC, CKC, FCI (Group 2), KC

BRACCO ITALIANO

The Bracco Italiano is also called the Italian Pointer. When historians refer to the ancient pointer used for hunting game birds, they mention heavy Spanish hounds. It is believed that the Spanish Pointer, Perdigueiro Burgos and the Bracco Italiano are breeds that most resemble those ancient hounds. The Bracco is said to originate from crossing the Molosser with sighthounds that Phoenician tradesmen brought back from Egypt, some 2,000 years ago.

The Bracco is a very efficient gun dog but it is not used in the same way as the British gun dogs, which set out to search fields at a fast gallop. The Bracco searches in a long, elastic striding trot, with its nose high in the wind. However, it stands and points in traditional fashion. In Italy the Bracco Italiano is strictly used as a hunting dog, but its spectacular looks, pleasant temperament and eye-catching movement have put it in the showring.

The Bracco should be about 22-26 inches/55-67 cm at its withers, and its body should be more rectangular than square. There should be hardly any visible tuck-up. The withers and hipbones should be level but the line of the back should be slightly lower. Its head should be fairly long and narrow with a pronounced occipital bone, marked stop and pendulous lips. The ears should be long, folded and set low. The skull and nose ridge should be slightly diverging when viewed in profile. Its coat should be smooth and fine. Acceptable coloring is white with fine speckling, all shades of roan, from lemon to deep orange, usually with large patches on the back and always on the sides of the head and ears. Black pigmentation is a disqualifying fault.

Registry: FCI (Group 7)

Bracco Italiano

BRAQUE DE L'ARIÈGE

This French pointing gun dog was developed during the twentieth century by crossing Braque Saint-Germain and Braque Français with local dogs, in the Ariège region of the

Braque de l'Ariège

Pyrenees. The local dogs were said to descend from dogs that were crosses of Perdigueiro de Burgos and the Bracco Italiano. The Ariège is strictly used for hunting and is very rare. It ranges in type from heavy, rather "houndy" dogs to elegant more speedy specimens.

This breed is about 24-26 inches/60-67 cm at its withers. Its body should be rectangular, strong and compact with a sloping cross and a docked tail. The head should be strong but not heavy and its ears set high, triangular in shape, rather broad at the base and not folded. The coat should be smooth and white with sparse speckling and larger patches in either orange, liver or chestnut. Any patches on the sides of the head and ears should be solid areas of color.

Registry: FCI (Group 7)

BRAQUE D'AUVERGNE

This strong, substantial pointing gun dog was developed in — and takes its breed name from — the mountain area of Auvergne, in the mid-south

Braque d'Auvergne

of France. Its origin is not clear but the breed is said to be closely related to the Braque Français.

At its withers, the dog should be about 22-25 inches/55-63 cm. Its body should be square, strong and muscular. The head should be quite long with a well-defined stop. The lips should also be well defined and pendulous — small dewlaps are typical. This Braque's ears are long and set in line with the eyes. Its tail should be docked slightly shorter than half its length. The coat should be short, glossy and preferably white with black mottling that gives a blue impression, and with big black patches. The head and ears should always be black although a mottled blaze is permissible. The Braque d'Auvergne is rarely seen outside France, except for the occasional entry at large European dog shows.

Registry: FCI (Group 7)

BRAQUE DU BOURBONNAIS

The pointing gun dog from Bourbonnais was well known two hundred years ago. Considering the breed's frequent rise and fall, it has endured very well — as has its working ability.

The dog stands about 19-22 inches/48-57 cm at its withers. Its body should be square and muscular with strong, well-boned legs. Its skull should be broad and rounded and its ears, set rather high, should be triangular, broad at the base and not folded. Apart from its color, the most significant characteristic of the breed is that it has a natural dock — a very short or stumpy tail. Its coat should be smooth and always white with mottling, almost like fine ticking, in liver brown or reddish liver brown. Its ears should always be a solid color.

Registry: FCI (Group 7)

Braque du Bourbonnais

BRAQUE DUPUY

This very ancient rare breed is elegant and houndlike. Dupuys are referred to in some literature as being almost extinct soon after the French Revolution. There has been little mention of the breed during the twentieth century and few have seen it in modern times.

At its withers, the breed stands to about 26-27 inches/65-69 cm. It should be elegant, rather high on its legs and with a long narrow head, only a slight stop and a convex nose ridge. Its coat should be smooth and white, with chestnut or small liver-colored spots and a few large patches.

Registry: FCI (Group 7)

The Braque Dupuy, depicted in this color print from 1890, is very rare, if not extinct.

145

BRAQUE SAINT-GERMAIN

The Saint-Germain resembles the English Pointer which is not surprising as the Pointer is very much part of its origin, along with a few French gun dog breeds. The alliance is said to have taken place in the 1830s. This is a useful hunting dog that is only kept for work.

At its withers, the dog is about 20-24 inches/ 50-62 cm. Although similar to the Pointer, the Saint-Germain does not have the classic Pointer head because it has a convex nose ridge and only a slight stop. Its coat should be smooth, fine and glossy. The Saint-Germain is always white with a few bright orange patches. Any patches on the side of the head and ears should always be orange.

Registry: FCI (Group 7)

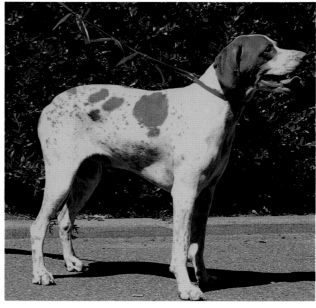

Braque Saint-Germain

BRAQUES FRANÇAISES

The original French pointing gun dog has existed since the fifteenth century. However, breeds from other countries took the hunter's

Braque Français, Pyrénées

fancy and by the end of the nineteenth century the old Braque Français was hard to find. When the restructuring of the breed took place it was found that two types had evolved, with similar characteristics. Both came from the south of France. The slightly taller dog was found in the southwest area of Gascogne and the smaller came from around the Pyrenees. Today, the breed, and both its varieties, have a very good reputation as working dogs and have been successful in field trials. They are able to search out prey at a gallop or trot and are very efficient. The breed can usually be seen at larger European dog shows although it is not well known outside France.

The Gascogne is about 22-27 inches/56-69 cm tall at its withers. Its body should be rectangular with good angulation in the front and hindquarters. Its skull should be almost flat with a lightly marked occipital bone, a shade longer than the muzzle. Its lips should be pendulous so that the muzzle looks square. A tendency to loose skin on the throat is acceptable. The ears should be set in line with the eyes and be long enough to reach the tip of the nose. The Gascogne's coat should be short and somewhat coarse in texture on its body, and fine and smooth on its head and ears. Finally, it should be white with liver brown mottling and one, or several, big brown patches on its body. Solid brown should always cover the sides of the head and ears.

The Pyrénées is smaller, reaching about 18 1/2-23 inches/47-58 cm. In most aspects, except size, the Pyrénées looks very much like the Gascogne. However, there are a few differences. The skull is slightly broader and the occipital bone not as evident. Also, its lips should not be so pendulous as to give a square muzzle. Its ears are set higher and should not reach the nose tip. The coloring of the two types should be the same except that the Pyrénées is usually more mottled brown on its body.

Registry: FCI (Group 7)

Braque Français, Gascogne

BRIARD/BERGER DE BRIE

ORIGIN AND DEVELOPMENT

The Briard's history is said to trace back to the days of the Emperor Charlemagne, and while it is primarily thought of as a herding dog, many tales have been passed down through generations of French folklore telling of the breed's great acts of heroism and courage. The Briard's ancestors were probably rough-coated sheepdogs which were brought to Europe accompanying Asian invaders who waged war in the Middle Ages.

In 1863, a Briard named Charmante won the very first "Exposition de Paris," beating all the other shepherd dogs entered. Four years later, the first breed Standard was formulated and in 1909 the first breed club was founded in France. During both world wars the Briard was used extensively as a war dog. Although an advertisement was placed in Britain's *Dog World* newspaper by a Parisian Briard breeder as long ago as 1937, there is no documented evidence that the breed appeared in Britain before the 1960s, and then the original stock arrived via Ireland. In the hands of a few pioneering breeders the Briard gradually achieved popularity, possibly aided by the publicity given to the pet Briards owned by the popular British singer and TV personality Cilla Black. In parts of Europe and the United States the breed is still mainly shown with cropped ears.

Briard

TEMPERAMENT

The Briard is a big-hearted dog, utterly loyal to its owner who it will guard with its life. It is spirited and a thinker, and feels happy in its own domain, seldom seeking to wander. The breed can be reserved with strangers and rather independent, but to those it knows it is both loving and faithful. For these reasons the Briard may not be the ideal dog for a first-time buyer. However, many experienced dog owners who understand the Briard's special temperament have been totally converted to the breed.

HEALTH MATTERS

A generally sturdy and trouble-free breed, the Briard has been found to suffer occasionally from central progressive retinal atrophy, an eye disorder which has an inherited factor. Responsible breeders are working hard to breed only from clear stock which keeps the condition largely in check. Hip dysplasia has also been found, but this again is something which caring breeders monitor closely in potential breeding stock.

SPECIAL CARE AND TRAINING

The Briard is highly trainable in many disciplines. To be kept happy and healthy, its coat needs careful attention as it will soon become badly matted if it is left unattended. Thorough "to the skin" brushing on a routine basis is essential.

ADAPTABILITY

The Briard is a social dog with its immediate family and has strong guarding instincts. Given adequate exercise of both mind and body, it can exist virtually anywhere.

ESSENTIALS OF THE BREED

The Briard's coat is very dry in texture, long and slightly wavy, with a fine and dense undercoat. The skull and muzzle should form two equal rectangles, with any suggestion of weakness in the foreface considered a bad

The Briard, according to the Kennel Club Standard in the United Kingdom, must have uncropped ears that should be well covered with hair.

fault. The ears may be cropped, in which case they are held erect and well covered with hair, or they may be natural, falling down and forward and also heavily coated. Its nose should be large and square and always black. In color the Briard may be fawn, black or gray, and while there can be individual black hairs in fawn dogs, the black should never be so solid as to create the impression of a demarcation line — this constitutes a bi-color which is unacceptable.

The body should be slightly longer than the shoulder height, the Briard being a strongly boned and well-muscled dog with well-angulated hindquarters on which will be found double dewclaws, a hallmark of the breed. Another valuable breed feature, sadly now seen less and less, is the "crochet-hook" at the tip of the tail, which should always reach at least to the hock. The Briard's movement is ground-covering and effortless. The breed stands between 23-27 inches/58-69 cm at the withers.

Registry: AKC, CKC, FCI (Group 1), KC

BRIQUETS GRIFFON VENDÉEN

On the west coast of France, in the Vendée region, south of Brittany, is the home of four rough-coated hound breeds. The four Vendéen hound breeds are very old breeds that originated from the largest and rarest of them all — the Grand Griffon Vendéen. Large, rough coated hounds were known in Gallo-Roman times and one of the Vendéen hound's forebears, the Gris de St. Louis, is believed to have descended from those early Gallo-Roman dogs. The St. Louis dog was crossed with hounds from Poitou, part of the Vendée region, and is supposed to be an ancestor of the Grand Griffon Vendéen.

After the French Revolution the breeds nearly disappeared, but a few devoted fanciers persisted. Finally in 1907 a breed club was organized.

The four breeds are all shaggy coated and more or less similar, with the exception of the length of their legs. The medium-sized breed is the Briquet — the word describes the same features as the English word "cobby" (meaning stout or square in build). The French word "griffon" is used for shaggy or wiry coated breeds. The Briquet is worked in small packs with only two or three pairs. It is relatively popular and can be seen in numbers at dog shows, especially in France.

The Vendéen hounds are known as hardy, well constructed hunting dogs. Unfortunately they are also known to be very independent and unruly and very hot to pursue and kill prey. These things, together with a lesser voice than other French hounds, have somewhat contributed to keeping their reputation as top hunting dogs down.

The breed is about 19-22 inches/48-55 cm tall at the withers. Its color may be any variation of fawn, white with patches in either gray, badger, orange or black, or tricolored.

Registry: FCI (Group 6)

Briquet Griffon Vendéen

BRITTANY/ÉPAGNEUL BRETON

As far back as 150 A.D., the poet Oppianus wrote of the Bretons' slender dogs and their acute sense of smell. However, the first accurate records are to be found in paintings and tapestries dating from the seventeenth century. A painting by Oudry (1686-1745) shows a liver-and-white Brittany-type dog pointing partridge. Several dogs of the same type in both liver and white, and orange and white appear in Flemish paintings from the school of Jan Steen.

In theory, the first tailless Brittany was born in Pontou in the mid-1800s. Apparently, it proved to be a wonderful hunter for birds and all its litters had some puppies born tailless or stub tailed. By 1850, an English clergyman, the Reverend Davies, wrote of hunting over a small bobtail dog that pointed and retrieved and was very popular with local poachers because the dogs were quick, agile and easily handled.

The breed was exhibited and recognized in France in 1907. In 1931 the Brittany was introduced to the United States where it found favor with local hunters. It took longer for those in field trials to take to it because they were more

Brittany

used to long-tailed pointers and setters; however, by 1939 the first field trial for Brittanys alone had been held in the United States and greatly helped to establish the breed.

The Brittany's popularity and development in the United States has been phenomenal, gaining year by year until it has become the first Field Champion and Dual Champion in a number of pointing breed competitions. With the support of a vast number of hunters who swear by its performance, the Brittany ranks high in the listing of breed registrations at the American Kennel Club. The Brittany is in fact the most popular of all pointing breeds in the field in the United States. As a hunting companion and field trialer, the Brittany has become an integral part of the American hunting scene.

Effective in all weather and in any terrain, the Brittany is a tireless, fast hunter with an acute sense of smell and an outstanding bird sense. An excellent and intelligent personal hunting dog, it easily extends itself as a wide-ranging field trialer that is best followed on horseback.

TEMPERAMENT

Normally a friendly dog, the Brittany's first interest is birds, however, with people second. It is and should be independent, as befits a pointing bird dog, willing to work with (rather than for) its owner.

HEALTH MATTERS

Bred first for function, the Brittany is a healthy, active dog. Some instances of hip dysplasia need to be closely monitored. Skin problems may appear and are sometimes caused by allergies to food or grass. These may be controlled with antihistamines under a vet's supervision, or by keeping the coat and skin very clean and free of fleas and ticks.

SPECIAL CARE AND TRAINING

An intelligent breed, the Brittany needs to be trained with a firm but decidedly soft hand. The Brittany does not usually require a great amount of trimming, although the long hair around the back of the hocks and the feet should be kept tidy, and the toenails should be kept short. Some dogs are shown with their necks slightly trimmed but this is not necessary as the Brittany's coat is not profuse.

ADAPTABILITY

Halfway between the setter and spaniel in size and with an easy-to-care-for coat, the Brittany is an excellent house dog as long as nonstop, boundless energy is acceptable to its owners. The Brittany must have something to work at to be happy, if not in the field then in the Obedience or Agility show ring. Exercise is a must for this breed.

ESSENTIALS OF THE BREED

A compact, closely knit dog of medium size, the Brittany is leggy and somewhat light in bone, as befits its agility, with great ground-covering ability. The breed is square in outline and should be 17 1/2-20 1/2 inches/44-52 cm in height. It should weigh between 30-40 pounds/14-18 kg. It has a short, straight back and a slightly sloping topline. The tail is short, either naturally or docked and is set on as an extension of its spine.

While the Brittany does have the soft expression of a bird dog, it is very eager and alert, and always ready to go hunting. Its short, high-set ears do much to contribute to this alert expression, as do its well-set eyes in varying shades of amber. The Brittany's mouth should have a normal scissors bite and, usually, full dentition.

The Brittany is orange and white, liver and white, or tricolor (liver and white with orange points) in either clear or roan patterns. Black is a disqualification color in the United States. The Brittany's movement or action is of great importance. Its side gait should be smooth, efficient and ground covering, with the hind foot stepping into or beyond the print left by the front foot. Above all the Brittany must be an athlete.

Registry: AKC, CKC, FCI (Group 7), KC

BROHOLMER

The Danish Mastiff-like Broholmer was once well known. During the latter part of the nineteenth century the last of the breed was thought to have been saved, although it was considered extinct after World War II. In 1974 the Danish Kennel Club set out to restore the breed, and in 1982 the Fédération Cynologique Internationale again entered it in its registry as a recognized breed.

The height at the withers varies according to sex: males should be over 29 1/2 inches/75 cm and bitches over 28 inches/70 cm. The body should be rectangular with typical mastiff features. The head should be big and strong, while the skull and nose ridge should be parallel when viewed in profile, with only a slight stop. The muzzle should not be too long and it should have pendulous lips. Dewlaps should be well developed. The Broholmer's coat should be short with a coarse texture. Its coloring may vary from light to dark fawn with a black mask (black is also permissible).

Registry: FCI (Group 2)

Broholmer

BRUSSELS GRIFFON/ GRIFFON BRUXELLOIS

ORIGIN AND DEVELOPMENT

Once the Belgian street urchin but now found frequently living in the lap of luxury, the Brussels Griffon has made a smooth transition into acceptance. The old Griffon d'Ecurie (Stable Griffon) was a street dog that was often found killing rats in stables. Dogs of this type were portrayed by Du Empoli and the Flemish painter Van Dyck (1599-1641).

A famous painting by the French Impressionist Renoir (1841-1919), *Bather with Griffon*, gives a good impression of what the Griffon of his day looked like. The dog shown is similar to an early Welsh Terrier and the artist's talent for transferring life to canvas makes it likely that this was how it actually looked.

The Affenpinscher was bred with these dogs and the blood of the Dutch Pug and Ruby English Toy Spaniel, two well-known and very popular breeds, was introduced to the resulting litters. These infusions brought about several changes. First the breed now developed with both rough and smooth coats ("*griffon*" means rough or wiry). The Smooths were referred to as Le Petit Brabançon. Next, it became a brachycephalic breed which means that it had a rounded skull and short muzzle. Its appearance thus altered, it moved from the stables and streets into homes where

Brussels Griffon with natural (uncropped) ears

it won its way into people's hearts.

In competition the numbers of Brussels Griffons have recently been rising as a new generation discovers their old charm. Once a rarity in the Toy Group, it is now a well-established member and good representatives of the breed are frequently found gathering top awards.

TEMPERAMENT

Griffs, as their English-speaking devotees know them (they *never* refer to them as "Brussels"), with their humanlike, often quizzical expression, large, meaningful eyes and pouty mouths are impish, inquisitive dogs and full of terrier confidence. It is said that puppies and adolescents can be rather sensitive, so care is called for in training to the lead and other essential lessons, to prepare a young dog for a life as a companion or an outgoing show dog. The Griffon must think the training regimen is entirely his own idea.

HEALTH MATTERS

As with any Toy dog, care should be taken not to allow a young Griffon to jump off furniture to prevent it from breaking its legs. Since its eyes are quite prominent, they should be bathed daily and checked for problems, including irritation from eyelashes or head furnishings. Slipping patellas may be a problem in the breed and may be caused by trauma, as well as being a heritable problem. A Griffon's rear legs should never be grabbed or twisted because this might cause patella luxation. With a young puppy, the teeth should be inspected at least weekly to make sure that the baby teeth are shedding properly, and that the second teeth are growing as they should (teeth normally start to shed at three and a half to four months). The vet should be consulted if any problems are noted.

SPECIAL CARE AND TRAINING

These dogs are highly intelligent and quick to learn commands from their owners. In this respect the breed resembles many of the harsh-coated Terriers, but the outer coat is not usually as hard as that of an Irish or Welsh Terrier. The Rough Griffon's coat is a broken-coated type, with long, harsh and wiry outer hairs and a soft undercoat. The outer coat should be plucked gently so that the new coat can grow and replace the dead one. This is good for both the skin and the coat and also reduces scratching and shedding.

ADAPTABILITY

The Brussels Griffon is filled with the joy of life and is at home in any surroundings. Its increasing popularity means that it is very unlikely to find itself relegated back to the stables in the near future.

ESSENTIALS OF THE BREED

Griffs are square in body, usually running to 6-10 pounds/2.7-4.5 kg in weight. Of the two coat varieties the Rough is harsh and wiry with a soft undercoat, while the Smooth has a short, straight and glossy coat with no wire feel to it. The colors are rich red, red and black mingled or black-and-tan. Frosting on the whiskers of mature dogs is common and acceptable. The Fédération Cynologique Internationale has divided the Brussels Griffon into three breeds. These are the Griffon Bruxellois, which is always red and rough coated; the Griffon Belge, which is rough coated, black, black-and-tan or red grizzle in color; and the Petit Brabançon, which is smooth coated red, with or without a black mask, or black-and-tan in color. Some countries also accept solid black.

As might be expected, great emphasis is placed on the head of the Brussels Griffon which should be slightly domed with large, black eyes. In the United States the ears of the Brussels Griffon are usually cropped to stand in small erect points. The cropping process enhances the breed's insouciant expression. The nose is black, short, deeply set and laid back with a slight backward tilt. The nostrils should be large and open; the jaw is undershot, with a strong chin and a wide muzzle that has an upward turn. The teeth and tongue must not show.

Registry: AKC, CKC, FCI, (Group 9), KC

BULLDOG

ORIGIN AND DEVELOPMENT

The Bulldog has its roots firmly planted in British soil and has come to be recognized throughout the world as a symbol of tenacity, stubborn determination and steadfastness. These attributes are truly characteristic of the Bulldog and are doubtlessly a legacy from the breed's distant past. The Bulldog is mentioned in many written works throughout the centuries but not always by the familiar name used today. One of the earliest terms used to describe the breed was "Bandogge." This description was first used in 1576 by Dr. Caius (Queen Elizabeth I's physician) and William Harrison in his *Description of England* of 1586 attributes the use of this name to the fact that dogs of this breed would spend much of their time in "bonds" or, to use his own words "manie of them are tied up in chaines and strong bonds in the daie time for doing hurt abroad, which is an huge dog, stubborn, ouglie, eager, burthenouse of bodie (and therefore of little swiftness), terrible and fearful to behold and oftentimes more fierce and fell than anie Archadian or Corsican cur."

Shakespeare mentions the breed in *King Henry VI*, Act 1; "The time when screech owls and Bandogges howl and spirits walk and ghosts break up their graves". And Shakespeare's friend, Ben Jonson, in his play *The Silent Woman*, first acted in 1609, mentions both Bulldogs and Beardogs. This is believed to be the earliest reference using today's name.

The Bulldog has been kept for a variety of purposes over the years: as a butcher's dog to help control unruly oxen, as a guard, as a hunting dog, but most commonly and certainly the purpose for which the breed gained notoriety, for the so-called "sport" of baiting. The "bait" basically involved the tethering of an animal — bears, bulls, horses, apes and lions were all considered fair game. The object was to send trained dogs in to attack an animal and try to overpower it. In the case of the bullbait, the Bulldog's objective was to grasp the fleshy nose of the bull and thereby "pin" it to the ground. Although a perilous task, many dogs did succeed and large wagers were placed on the outcome. Bullbaiting became popular in England during the early thirteenth century and bearbaiting some 200 years before this. By the end of the thirteenth century, most English market towns had their own "Bull Ring" and at Tutbury in Staffordshire annual baitings continued for five centuries until they were brought to an end by the Duke of Devonshire in 1778.

Although baiting is now regarded to have been a callous and inhumane pastime, it is worth remembering that many of the characteristics so admired by devotees of the breed today came about as a result of breeders trying to produce a dog for the baiting ring and not for the show ring. A short muzzle and undershot jaw were necessary to enable a vicelike grip to be secured on the adversary when the opportunity arose, as a second chance to obtain a hold would be unlikely to occur. The Bulldog was bred to have a nose placed well back into its head to enable the dog to breathe freely while holding the bull by its fleshy nose. So, much of the present-day Bulldog reflects the purpose for which it was originally bred but perhaps in no way more so than its stoical manner.

Since the late 1800s Bulldogs have become popular show dogs around the world. This seems to be particularly true in English-speaking countries and the breed has had a firm foothold in the United States and Canada since the earliest days. The breed has also found favor in Australia, New Zealand and South Africa since the turn of the century, and subsequently in many other countries.

TEMPERAMENT

The Bulldog is truly an ideal pet as it loves to be in the company of its family, and its suitability

Bulldog

as a companion to children is universally acknowledged. Although by no means a noisy breed, it will generally let you know if there is a stranger around and the Bulldog's physical appearance is usually enough to deter any would-be intruder. Although the breed is more than capable of looking after itself, should the situation arise, it is not a troublemaker with other dogs and will generally only retaliate as a last resort.

HEALTH MATTERS

The Bulldog is often attributed with far more health problems than is actually the case. Although it is untrue that the breed is without problems, they are not as common as some would believe. Overheating is a main consideration with the breed. As with any brachycephalic (short-headed) dog, its restricted airways can cause a problem in exceptionally hot or humid weather, but with a little common sense, difficulties can be avoided and once acclimatized most Bulldogs actually enjoy basking in the sun. Bulldogs are rather prone to "itchy" skin, particularly in hot weather, and a close eye should be kept

for any sign of a rash or sore spots. A high percentage of Bulldog puppies are born via Caesarean section.

SPECIAL CARE AND TRAINING

The Bulldog is certainly not a breed designed for the obedience enthusiast. It possesses far too much strength of character to comply with commands without first giving them due consideration. The breed has a reputation for being rather slow-witted, which is most unfair. Please remember that it is not slow, but thinking. As most Bulldogs seem to prefer traveling by car to walking, it is necessary to get them used to a lead from an early age in order to prevent any battle of wills at a later date. The only special care is the powdering of facial folds and wrinkles and under the tail, especially in hot weather since these areas tend to become damp and thereby open to infection.

ADAPTABILITY

The Bulldog must be one of the most adaptable of all breeds as its requirements in life are not great. It enjoys its home comforts but requests very little else. It demands only a small amount of space and will adapt equally well to life in an apartment, with an occasional stroll around the park, as it will to living in a large house and garden. The Bulldog's main priority is that it is with those it cares for and those who care for it.

ESSENTIALS OF THE BREED

The Bulldog should be 55 pounds/25 kg for a dog and 50 pounds/23 kg for a bitch in the United Kingdom, and 50 pounds/23 kg for a dog and 40 pounds/18 kg for a bitch in the United States. The head of the Bulldog is all-important and nearly half of the points contained in the breed Standard are attributed to the head's properties. The short muzzle with its "laid back" nose is a hallmark of the breed and the wide, undershot jaw helps to give the unique expression admired by so many. The eyes should be dark and set well apart with a definite stop between. The skull is divided by the furrow which runs from the stop to the occiput. The Bulldog's front is another trade-mark of the breed with its "tacked on" shoulder and deep brisket giving the appearance of strength and stability — the bone of the foreleg must be straight, however. The slightly arched neck, which should be short rather than long, leads smoothly into the "roach back," another characteristic of the breed. The tail should be low set and carried in a downward direction. The United Kingdom Standard only allows for the straight tail whereas the United States Standard allows for the tail to be either straight or screwed. The belly should be well "tucked up" with the ribs well rounded and deep. The gait should be peculiarly heavy and constrained. It should appear to walk with short, quick steps on the tips of the toes, with the hind feet appearing to skim the ground, and running with one or other shoulder rather advanced. This action should give the characteristic "roll." The coat should be short and straight and all colors are acceptable except black and black-and-tan. The dudley (liver colored) nose is most unacceptable, being a disqualification in the United States and considered highly undesirable in the United Kingdom.

Registry: AKC, CKC, FCI (Group 2), KC

The head of the Bulldog is an important feature, for almost half the points in the Standard concern its properties.

BULLMASTIFF

ORIGIN AND DEVELOPMENT

The Bullmastiff is a relative newcomer. It was only developed in the late nineteenth century by crossings of the Mastiff (60 percent) and the Bulldog (40 percent). Poachers were a plague to gamekeepers on large estates in England, and this powerful, agile resulting cross proved to be a competent colleague. Its mission was to allow the poacher to approach, then throw him down and hold — not savage — him. A brindle color, so obscure at night, was preferred for the job. With increased popularity and the establishment of type, the fawn with dark mask and ears of the Mastiff became more evident. By 1924 the breed had become standardized and was officially recognized as the Bullmastiff in England and then by the American Kennel Club in 1933.

TEMPERAMENT

The Bullmastiff is fearless, loyal and loving. This breed is a natural guardian of the home and a devoted, gentle companion.

HEALTH MATTERS

As in most breeds, hip dysplasia is known. Gastric torsion and cancer are the most frequent causes of premature death. Common complaints are contact dermatitis, alopecia and eczema.

Bullmastiff

SPECIAL CARE AND TRAINING

The Bullmastiff's short coat is easily maintained and adapts to a considerable range of climate. It is worth remembering why the breed was developed and to be fully aware of its impressive stature and strength. Bullmastiffs are compliant and responsive to training. However, it is the owner's obligation to bring its potential to fruition.

ADAPTABILITY

The Bullmastiff has demonstrated its adaptability by making the transition from the gamekeeper's night dog to its primary role of family pet and watchdog. Although a house and some outdoor space is recommended, an owner dedicated to providing adequate exercise can successfully maintain a Bullmastiff as an apartment dweller.

ESSENTIALS OF THE BREED

The Bullmastiff is a powerful dog — muscular, balanced and neatly square. Males stand 25-27 inches/63-68.5 cm at the withers and weigh 110-130 pounds/50-59 kg. Bitches are 1 inch/2.5 cm shorter and 10 pounds/4.5 kg lighter. Substantial bone, breadth throughout and well-developed musculature are covered with a short dense coat of red, fawn or brindle, preferably with dark muzzle. The distinctive head characterizes the breed. The muzzle to skull proportions are one to three, with medium-sized dark eyes and V-shaped ears which are set wide, high and carried close to the well-developed cheeks. Wrinkles appear on the large skull when alert. The nose should be broad and black, and the bite preferably level or slightly undershot. The legs are well boned, with moderately sloping shoulders and matching moderately angled hind quarters. Its medium-sized feet should be round and thick and the tapered tail set on high and strong at the root. The Bullmastiff's appearance is one of active power and symmetry, and its free, straightforward gait enhances this impression of strength and agility. This is a natural breed in which neither ears nor tails have ever been altered.

Registry: AKC, CKC, FCI (Group 2), KC

The Bullmastiff is characterized by its distinctive head.

BULL TERRIER

ORIGIN AND DEVELOPMENT

The Bull Terrier cannot claim an ancestry as a pure breed stretching back many hundreds of years, as can some sighthounds. In the first half of the nineteenth century fanciers began to cross the old English Bulldog with terriers, to produce a lighter, more agile dog both for the pit and to tackle vermin. By the middle of the century the "Bull and Terrier" was well recognized, if variable in weight and conformation. The type became established as the Bull Terrier.

To this day there are no size limitations to the breed; although show dogs nowadays tend to weigh between about 55-70 pounds/25-30 kg and bitches between 45-60 pounds/20-27 kg. The smallest recorded Champion in the breed was a dog weighing 12 pounds/5.4 kg. One concession has been made: the Miniature Bull Terrier is now shown as a separate breed with a height limit of 14 inches/36 cm.

Over the years it has been recognized that previous differentiations between colored, "color-bred" and "pure-bred" whites cannot

Colored Bull Terrier

genetically be justified, and in most countries, including the United Kingdom, all colors and whites are shown together. It is not unusual to get mixed litters of puppies. Under American Kennel Club rules, coloreds and whites — even when born in the same litter — are still shown as separate breeds. Bull Terriers have been dogs with an excellent disposition, particularly good with children and fully adapted to the civilized, not to say luxury, life.

Temperament

Bull Terriers tend to be friendly and amenable to discipline and have a good temperament, They also have a devastating sense of humor. They are outgoing dogs with a dominant nature and substantial body weight. As they are strong in both mind and muscle, they may not be the best choice of breed for the elderly or people who are not experienced with dogs. Like most terrier breeds, they are game for anything. This means that, if they do become involved in a fight, they will not be the first to break away.

Health Matters

Every breed of dog has its recognized problems and this one is known to be prone to sensitive skin. The breed does not thrive in cold and damp conditions and, unless given ample bedding, may develop pressure sores. White Bull Terriers are known to be born deaf occasionally. A program to control this inheritable condition was first instituted for this breed. Research is now in progress to overcome a congenital heart condition and familial kidney disease. Notwithstanding these serious diseases, Bull Terriers are generally healthy, with a lifespan of fourteen or fifteen years.

Special Care and Training

Puppies must be socialized early with humans and other dogs (and animals) in order to prevent their dominance becoming overwhelming. They are not easy to train because they have a mind of their own but basic training should present no special problems.

Adaptability

Bull Terriers are quite prepared to adapt anyone to their lifestyle. They enjoy as much exercise as offered, but are equally happy spending most of their time at home, relaxing in luxurious surroundings. Bull Terriers have a light coat and love warmth and comfort.

Essentials of the Breed

There is no height or weight standard for the Bull Terrier, but it should be strongly built and muscular. The breed Standard states that "there should be the impression of maximum substance for size of dog, consistent with quality and sex." Its head is unique, and characteristically should be egg-shaped from the front and completely filled. The eyes must be dark, appear narrow and have a piercing glint. The ears must be capable of being carried stiffly erect. Although the breed should have a regular scissors bite, some less-than-perfect mouths have been seen in top winners, and this is a shortcoming to which many breeder judges have in the past been rather lenient. The neck must be very muscular, long and arched, tapering smoothly into the shoulders, which should be strong and muscular but without loading. Elbows must be held straight. The forelegs should have strong, round bone and upright pasterns, and they should be perfectly parallel. Feet should be round, compact and with well-arched toes. The body should be well rounded with a marked spring of rib and great depth and a short back. The tail should be short, set on low and carried horizontally. The hind legs should be muscular, with good angulation to stifle and hocks. The dog should stand and move with its hind legs in parallel. Bull Terriers should move with free easy strides, covering the ground well and with the breed's typical jaunty air. White dogs should have a pure white coat, but markings on the head should not be penalized. For coloreds, the color should always predominate. No color is a disqualification but blue and liver are highly undesirable.

Registry: AKC, CKC, FCI (Group 3), KC

CA DE BESTIAR

The origin of this Spanish breed, mainly found in the Balearic Islands, is somewhat uncertain. Some say that it is very old, others that it was

Ca de Bestiar

developed from several different breeds on the island of Majorca in the nineteenth century. It is a breed that is mainly used as guard dog on farms for protecting property and cattle. Its work has always been more important than its looks. Its temperament is reserved with strangers and it becomes fearful if threatened. This very hardy breed is able to work in extreme heat.

The breed stands 24-29 inches/62-73 cm at its withers. The body is rectangular and rather high on the legs. Its head should be triangular in shape, and its ears and tail kept natural. The coat may be either short and smooth or about 2 1/2 inches/7 cm long and slightly wavy. The color should always be black, although a little white on the chest and feet is permissible.

Registry: FCI (Group 1)

CAIRN TERRIER

ORIGIN AND DEVELOPMENT

A number of illustrations from as far back as the fifteenth century portray small rough coated terriers that closely resemble today's Cairn Terriers. By the late 1700s the Highlands of Scotland fairly teemed with small terriers known as "Short Haired or Little Skye Terriers." These little dogs were likely the result of crosses with the old White Terrier and the old Black and Tan Terrier, thought to be the father of all terriers. Although commonly found among the farms and barnyards of the area in these early years, it was not until the early 1900s that these terriers were introduced to the dog show world. It was at this time that the formal name "Cairn Terrier" was designated after the area where they worked hunting fox, otter and badger.

The white dogs of this breed became the forefathers of the West Highland White Terrier. The two breeds had so much in common, in fact, that it was only in 1924 that the British Kennel Club forbade the practice of inter-breeding the Westies and the White Cairn. Although the Cairn was originally developed to be a rough and tumble little sporting terrier, it has become one of the most popular household pets in England and, indeed, in North America. It is also interesting that it frequently is the breed with the most entries at the world-famous Montgomery County All-Terrier Show held in Pennsylvania each October.

TEMPERAMENT

The Cairn is a wonderful family dog but never forget that its ancestry as a "sporting terrier" makes it very active, inquisitive and always "ready to go." Its terrier heritage makes it an ideal single house dog and it is good with children.

SPECIAL CARE AND TRAINING

A rough appearance is essential to a Cairn. Its coat should never be trimmed with scissors (except for shaping the feet), but must be kept tidy by using the finger and thumb. This can be more time consuming than difficult. With good weekly care the Cairn will never look unkempt. Of course, the teeth and nails must be looked at weekly, and attended to as needed. The nails should be clipped back from puppyhood so that the Cairn will accept this as a matter of course. Frequent bathing should be avoided as it softens the coat. Regular brushing and combing with a rub off with a damp towel are all that is required for the coat on the body and head. The belly and legs may be sponged off and then dried.

Cairn Terrier

HEALTH MATTERS

The Cairn is a quite hardy, game little terrier, and is easy to raise if common sense is applied. There are some heritable health problems that exist in the breed, including patella luxation or slipping stifles (kneecaps). The best plan is to purchase stock from a reputable breeder who will have screened the breeding stock for all possible flaws.

Another problem involving the rear legs is called Legg Perthes. This is a malformation of the hip that can be identified by X-ray and that causes lameness. "Lion jaw" can also be a problem with the Cairn and other terriers. This is a malformation of the lower jaw that becomes noticeable as the puppy reaches the age of three to four months. The signs are that it has difficulty in opening and closing its mouth and also with eating.

ADAPTABILITY

Small enough for an apartment, tough enough for a country farm, the Cairn will make itself at home anywhere that it has a friend or a family of which it can be a part. Care is needed to prevent it from digging its way out of a run, bearing in mind that it was bred and trained to dig out its prey — it has never forgotten this.

ESSENTIALS OF THE BREED

The Cairn dog should weigh no more than 14 pounds/6 kg and a bitch should weigh about 1 pound/450 g less. Rugged in appearance, its coat should look shaggy but have a hard longer outercoat (about 2 inches/5 cm) and an abundant soft undercoat. It should have sharply pointed ears that should be kept free of long hair so that its shape may be seen, small intelligent, fairly dark eyes, and large teeth that meet in a scissors or even bite.

The Cairn is slightly longer than it is tall, has a level topline, an undocked tail carried gaily but not over the back. Its front legs should be straight but the front feet may turn out slightly. The rear legs must have a good turn of stifle and good propulsion. Its skull should be large, its foreface no longer than the backskull, and the whole head protected with hard coat to frame the head and give the typical expression. The Cairn comes in a great variety of colors and these will often change drastically from puppyhood to adulthood. Cream varying to deep red, brindle, and light gray to almost totally black are all very acceptable. The only forbidden color is white.

Registry: AKC, CKC, FCI (Group 3), KC

CANAAN DOG

The Canaan Dog is sometimes referred to as the free-living pariah of the Middle East, but it should not be confused with the mongrels and cross-breeds which will be found in towns and villages there. The Canaan is a distinct type which has survived in the desert since pre-biblical times. From ancient paintings and inscriptions, it seems very probable that a dog of similar conformation was domesticated and used for various purposes 2,000 or more years ago. In the 1930s the Israelis began re-domesticating these dogs when they realized their potential as watchdogs and started using them to guard the early Jewish settlements. A breeding program was begun and, whenever possible, new wild stock was incorporated. Today this policy is still followed but with ever-increasing difficulty as a strict rabies control program, together with the "spread of civilization," has resulted in the true, wild Canaan becoming extremely scarce.

Centuries of natural selection in cruel desert conditions have resulted in a resourceful, almost disease-free animal of high intelligence with exceptionally keen hearing, eyesight and

Canaan Dog

scenting ability. They make good companion dogs, that are loyal and affectionate to their "family." Medium-sized, measuring 20-24 inches/ 50-60 cm at the shoulder, they are remarkably strong for their size and exceedingly agile. They have a medium length double coat and come in all shades of desert colors with white markings, as well as black and white. Introduced into America and Canada nearly thirty years ago, they are also now established, as a rare breed, in Great Britain and many other European countries. However small numbers resulted in the Canaan Dog losing its breed classes at the 1995 Cruft's Show where it was thus forced to compete in the "Any Variety Utility Not Separately Classified" section.

Registry: AKC, CKC, FCI (Group 5), KC

CANADIAN ESKIMO DOG

ORIGIN AND DEVELOPMENT

Descended from an aboriginal breed called "Qimmig" by the Inuit, this breed is closely associated with the Thule culture. It comes from the coastal and archipelago areas of North America where its strength and stamina made it an excellent intermediate breed between the Malamute and the Siberian Husky. The existing strain of Canadian Eskimo Dogs is derived primarily from stock bred by the Eskimo Dog Research Foundation in Canada's Northwest Territories, and was based on specimens from the dogs kept by the Inuit of Baffin Island and the Boothia and Melville Peninsulas. The Eskimo dog, as is true of so many of the northern breeds, was developed and nurtured as a hauling animal, as well as hunter of large animals such as bear and seal. It was the only domesticated animal that could withstand the rigors of the northern climes, snow, frigid temperatures and hard work. The breed was a diligent worker in its natural state.

TEMPERAMENT

The origin and purpose of the breed should be remembered when assessing its temperament. Current breeders stress its evident affection

Canadian Eskimo Dog

and responsiveness but also recognize that it is not suitable for all homes and individuals. It is a breed which responds enthusiastically to any stimulus, be it food, play, work or fighting.

HEALTH MATTERS

The breed is relatively free of major health problems, considering the way that the breed was re-established and the relatively small gene pool which was used. Dedicated breeders must be relied on to address any problems as they occur.

ADAPTABILITY

As a breed dependent for survival on strength, independence and a pack psychology, it is most suited to homes that can provide sufficient exercise and control. Although primarily a sled dog with an ability to pull heavy loads for long distances on minimum food, the Canadian Eskimo Dog also fits into the show ring where its natural inquisitiveness carries it

through. Natural intelligence coupled with independence of nature make it an interesting challenge for Obedience work.

ESSENTIALS OF THE BREED

In overall appearance, the Canadian Eskimo Dog resembles other northern breeds. It is a powerfully built, moderately sized dog with a medium length leg, giving the impression that it is not built for racing but for hard, sustained work. With its wedge-shaped head and erect ears, it is typical of the spitz family of dogs. Oblique eyes give it a serious expression. The coat should consist of a dense undercoat with thick straight guard hairs. Males possess a manelike growth over the neck and shoulders which emphasizes the impression of strength. Canadian Eskimo Dogs are found in a great range of colors and patterns and no particular color is preferred.

Registry: CKC

CÃO DE CASTRO LABOREIRO

This is the least known of Portugal's herding dogs. It has a reputation of being a very reliable guard dog that will announce visitors

Cão de Castro Laboreiro

with impressive barking. Its origin is not clear but this type of hardy working dog has been known in the area of Castro Laboreiro for centuries. Although the breed is unfamiliar outside Portugal it can be seen today at local dog shows.

The Cão de Castro Laboreiro's body should be decidedly rectangular with a well-developed rib cage and a broad back. The height at its withers should be about 20-24 inches/52-60 cm. The head should be quite strong with a broad skull, and the ears and tail should be left natural. The coat should lie close, be about 2 inches/5 cm long and coarse in texture. Color is usually very dark brindle, almost black, though all shades of wolf gray are also permissible.

Registry: FCI (Group 2)

CÃO DE FILA DE SÃO MIGUEL

Cão de Fila de São Miguel

This Portuguese cattle dog comes from the Azores Islands in the Atlantic. The Cão de Fila de São Miguel is said to be old and its origin comes from breeds once known only to the Iberian peninsula. The breed was recognised by the FCI in early 1995. It is said to be a tough working dog, known for its sharp temperament and instinct to guard.

The Cão de Fila de São Miguel stands about 19-24 inches/48-60 cm at its withers. It has a compact body, resembling a heavy, coarse Boxer but without a short muzzle. The tail should be docked short and the ears cropped short with rounded tips. The coat should be short and brindle in color without white markings.

Registry: FCI (Provisionally Group 1)

CÃO DA SERRA DE AIRES

The Portuguese Sheepdog is said to be closely related to Pyrenean and Catalan Sheepdogs but this has not been confirmed. It is true to the old-fashioned type of sheepdog that can be found in many European countries. It is a hardy breed that is also known to herd cattle. In recent years the breed has also gained popularity as a companion dog. It can be seen at large European dog shows.

The Cão da Serra de Aires are known to be devoted, loyal, obedient and very observant dogs. All these characteristics can describe the typical sheep dog temperament.

The height at its withers should be about 16-19 inches/40-48 cm. The dog's body should be rectangular, strong and muscular. Its head should be broad with a well-defined stop and occipital bone. The ears are usually not cropped. Its tail should be long with a slight curl at the end. The coat should be quite long and shaggy on its head, with eyebrows, whiskers and a beard. Its coloring may be any shade of fawn, yellow, brown, gray or black-and-tan.

Cão da Serra de Aires

Registry: FCI (Group 1)

CATAHOULA LEOPARD DOG

The origin of the Catahoula is lost in legend. Some speculate that it is perhaps descended from Mastiff-type war dogs, brought into the southeastern United States by Hernando de Soto, who cruelly set these dogs to attack Indians in the area and then left them to be cared for by their victims. There has obviously been hound blood mixed in as the dog does trail. Catahoula Parish, from which the breed's name derives, is in northeast Louisiana.

The Catahoula is known as a "Hog Dog." People from the bayous used to eke out a living running wild hogs in the woods. During the annual roundup, the hogs were almost impossible to drive. The Catahoula was essential to penning the pigs. The odd pig was picked out by a dog and challenged to a fight. When the enraged boar sounded its distress call the other ranging hogs ran to the rescue. The Catahoula then turned tail and ran directly into the waiting hog pens, successfully trapping the hogs and escaping their wrath by jumping the back fence. The modern Catahoula has been adapted to work with cattle as well as hogs. It is aggressive — a necessary trait for working with stock. The Catahoula is also able to hunt stock by scent.

In 1979 the Catahoula was named the state dog of Louisiana. It is a strong willed breed and is considered a herding dog. It weighs 40-50 pounds/18-22 kg, its height is 20-26 inches/ 50-65 cm. Its short, dense coat may be either merle or black-and-tan in color.

Registry: This breed is not recognized by the AKC, CKC, FCI or KC.

Catahoula Leopard Dog

CATALAN SHEEPDOG/
GOS D'ATURA CATALÀ

Spanish sheepdogs from the Catalan have been used for years to herd sheep near the Pyrenean Mountains. With its long coat, this breed bears a physical resemblance to one of the varieties of the French Pyrenean Sheepdog. The Catalan Sheepdog is considered a good guard dog. This quality has made the breed suitable for police and army work. In recent years this lively and agile breed has also been appreciated as a companion dog, although it is said to be wary of strangers.

At its withers, the breed stands about 18-22 inches/45-55 cm. Its body should be slightly longer than its height at the withers. The Catalan Sheepdog's head should be strong, slightly convex with a fairly broad skull and muzzle that should be slightly shorter than the length of the skull. Its ears should be pendulous and the undocked tail quite long — if docked it is usually to half its length. The coat should be long and shaggy, usually grayish black or pale fawn with gray shadings. The Catalan Sheepdog is not often seen outside Spain except at large European dog shows.

Registry: FCI (Group 1)

Catalan Sheepdog

CAUCASIAN OWTCHARKA/ KAVKAZSKAJA OVTJARKA

This herding dog from southwest Russia comes from the Caucasian Mountains. It resembles and shares various common characteristics with the Anatolian Shepherd Dog. A flock guardian that is often left alone to deal with thieves and predators, it is also used as a military guard dog.

Males should be over 26 inches/65 cm at the withers; females over 24 inches/62 cm. The skull should be broad and massive; the muzzle slightly shorter. Its ears are cropped to make them look torn. The tail is left long. The coat may be semi-long to long and any color although it is commonly pale fawn, red sable, parti-color or shades of gray. The breed has gained interest in several European and Scandinavian countries but is still rare.

Registry: FCI (Group 2)

Caucasian Owtcharka

CAVALIER KING CHARLES SPANIEL

ORIGIN AND DEVELOPMENT

It is impossible to discuss the origins of the hugely popular Cavalier without also mentioning the King Charles Spaniel, and in doing so one is faced with a "chicken and egg" situation. King Charles Spaniels of one type or another have existed in Britain since the sixteenth century, having been bred down from a variety of sporting spaniels which produced small specimens. These were retained out of curiosity, and then selectively interbred to produce "Toy spaniels." In the early days these would have been very much influenced by their spaniel ancestry. Whether or not it was through further selective breeding, or by the introduction of foreign blood from some of the imported oriental Toy breeds, such as the Pug, is unclear, but the breeders of Toy spaniels began to produce a much more exaggerated head, with a great dome and flatter face. This was the type which found favor and which breeders attempted to establish.

The breed takes its name from King Charles II who kept large numbers of Toy spaniels and, according to diarist Samuel Pepys, spent more time playing with his dogs than attending to affairs of state. The breed was much favored by the aristocracy and from the early nineteenth century a strain of small red-and-white spaniels were bred by the Marlborough family at Blenheim Palace. Despite their appeal as companions for ladies, it is said that they could still acquit themselves well in the field. The King Charles of the time was becoming a much more exaggerated breed, and appeared to be be straying from the type of Toy spaniel which had been depicted in many paintings by a variety of Old Masters.

When shows resumed after World War I, the only type of King Charles on the show bench had an increasingly popular flat-faced, dome-head. On a visit to the United Kingdom, a wealthy American, Roswell Eldridge, was very disappointed that he could not buy dogs reminiscent of those he had seen in the paintings of artists such as Steen, Metsu and Gainsborough. In 1926 he offered a prize of £25 (a veritable king's ransom in those days) for the best Blenheim King Charles Spaniel "of the

Blenheim Cavalier King Charles Spaniel

old type". This prize was offered for five years. Such entries were initially ridiculed by the purist King Charles fanciers, but — arguably out of entirely commercial interest — enthusiasm increased for producing a suitable recipient of Eldridge's generous prize. The prize was won in 1928, 1929 and 1930 by a dog called Ann's Son and he became the model for the first breed Standard drawn up for what was now to be known as the "Cavalier King Charles Spaniel." In 1945 the Kennel Club granted Cavaliers separate registration and the following year they received Challenge Certificates for the first time. The first Champion in the breed, Daywell Roger, was out of a bitch that was sired by Ann's Son. and out of his own daughter. The first Bitch Challenge Certificate winner was also a granddaughter of Ann's Son. Since those early days the Cavalier has mushroomed in popularity, overtaking the King Charles dramatically. It has evolved into a high-quality show dog all around the world, and its handy size and easy temperament make it the perfect pet dog.

For many years the Cavalier has been very popular in the United States, its specialty shows drawing huge entries, but the Cavalier King Charles Spaniel of America has fought long and hard to keep the breed outside the province of the American Kennel Club. From January 1, 1996 this breed will be eligible to be shown in regular class competition in the United States.

TEMPERAMENT

The breed is a born companion and it makes the perfect lap dog. It is still essentially a small sporting spaniel and enjoys great activity. Its temperament is gentle and loving, with aggression or nervousness being wholly untypical. The Cavalier is enthusiastic about everything and can be quite vocal at times.

HEALTH MATTERS

The breed is generally sound and healthy, with no major hereditary problems, but concern has been expressed at the incidence of heart murmurs in some bloodlines. Breeders are now religiously monitoring this condition with the full support of the breed clubs. Patella luxation does sometimes occur as well as eye conditions such as retinal dysplasia and hereditary cataract.

SPECIAL CARE AND TRAINING

The breed is easy to maintain and easy to train. Its coat can be kept spick and span with a

The Cavalier King Charles Spaniel comes in four colors. From left: Blenheim, black-and-tan, tricolor and ruby.

weekly grooming session, when special attention should be given to the ears. It will respond readily to basic obedience routines.

ADAPTABILITY

Cavaliers thrive in a home environment, but will also live happily in a group if kenneled. They are very undemanding as a breed, and so long as they receive plenty of company — be it human or canine — they will settle virtually anywhere.

ESSENTIALS OF THE BREED

The Cavalier is a Toy spaniel and as such should never be a heavy, coarse dog. It should be graceful and active, with an extrovert temperament, and move freely and happily. The head is important and should be almost flat between the ears with no suggestion of a dome; the stop should be shallow and the muzzle should taper without being snipy, and be moderately well cushioned. The eyes should be large, dark, round but not bolting and spaced well apart. The ears should be long, well feathered and set quite high. The Cavalier's expression must be one of softness and quality.

The Cavalier's body should be square with a level topline, well-sprung ribs and the hindquarters should have well-turned stifles. The overall dog should have moderate bones, being neither cloddy nor spindly. The tail should be carried out and upward, but not over the back. In males particularly gay tails are a problem. The breed comes in four colors: black-and-tan, ruby, tricolor and Blenheim. The Blenheim color is a rich chestnut red on a pearly white background. In Blenheims, a red lozenge centrally situated in the white facial blaze is highly prized as a breed characteristic. Both tricolors and Blenheims should have their body color well broken up with white. The ideal size of the Cavalier is between 12 -18 pounds/5.4-8 kg. The Cavalier takes time to mature fully and an interesting aspect of the breed is that they appear to develop in bone up to around eighteen months. Also, puppies which are slightly undershot up to around twelve months can invariably end up with the correct scissor bite.

Registry: AKC, CKC, FCI (Group 9), KC

CESKY FOUSEK

This Czech gun dog breed is very similar to the German Wirehaired Pointer. In fact, it takes great experience and knowledge to tell the two breeds apart. Indeed, German Pointers were used to re-establish the breed after World War II. The Cesky Fousek is a breed strictly used for hunting and is rarely seen outside what was formerly Czechoslovakia.

The breed should stand about 23-26 inches/ 58-66 cm at the withers. Its coat should be wiry, about 1 1/2-2 3/4 inches/4-7 cm long, and with a thick undercoat. The color should be liver brown, with or without speckling, or speckled with brown patches.

Registry: FCI (Group 7)

Cesky Fousek

CESKY TERRIER/CESKY TERIÉR

The Cesky Terrier was created by the Czech geneticist Frantisek Horak after World War II. Horak was a devoted hunter who had bred Scottish Terriers even before the war. In 1949 he started his experiment by crossing Scottish Terriers with Sealyham Terriers with the aim of breeding a hunting terrier that was lighter in build than the original breeds but which had the same enthusiasm to go to ground. He continued the breeding program for ten years before he started to try to get them recognized as a new breed. In 1963 the line was considered consistent enough to be recognized, and it got its breed name. The new breed was met with interest but the export prohibition in former Czechoslovakia during the 1970s was a drawback. The breed is mainly kept as a companion dog outside its country of origin and it can be seen at most European shows, although only in small numbers.

The Cesky Terrier is about 10-13 inches/27-35 cm at the withers. It should be low on its legs, have a rectangular body and a long neck. The head should be strong and fairly long, and the ears are pendulous, not too low set and rounded. The tail is kept undocked and carried up when the dog moves. The coat, which it is customary to clip, should be soft, thick and have a silky shine. The color should be bluish gray or light brown, with or without pale cream or beige tan markings. Puppies are born black, with or without tan, or deep liver brown also with or without tan. White is allowed around the neck and at the tip of the tail.

Registry: FCI (Group 3)

Cesky Terrier

CHART POLSKI

The Polish sighthound closely resembles the Greyhound and is considered a very old breed. Polish sources claim that the dog was used by nobility to course hunting hare and fox several hundred years ago. However, it was only in 1992 that the breed was recognized by the Fédération Cynologique Internationale and it is very rare outside Poland.

At its withers, the breed stands about 27-31 inches/68-80 cm. Although it is very similar to the Greyhound, it is not as racy in build. Its head should be long with hardly any stop and preferably a roman nose. The coat should be smooth with a hard texture and undercoat. All colors are permitted.

Registry: FCI (Group 10)

Chart Polski

CHIEN D'ARTOIS

This very old hound from Artois, in the Pas-de-Calais region, is a heavily built hound that has more foxhound and harrier in its blood than most French hounds. The breed was known in the fifteenth century and was revived from extinction 400 years later. After World Wars I and II, it was again thought to be extinct. However, the breed seems determined to survive. In the early 1970s several couples were found to be of true type and today fairly substantial packs are worked near the Somme. In 1977 a new Standard was drawn up and accepted. Considering the number of French breeds that are still kept as excellent working hounds it's quite astonishing that the revival of the Chien d'Artois has had such an impact in so few years.

At its withers, the breed stands about 20-23 inches/52-58 cm. The Chien d'Artois has a broad, rather short skull and its broad ears are set fairly high, hanging flat with almost no fold. The color should be white with quite big patches of tan and black. Its head and ears should be tan colored.

Chien d'Artois

Registry: FCI (Group 6)

CHIHUAHUAS

ORIGIN AND DEVELOPMENT

There are many theories about the origin of this tiny breed. Some feel that the Chinese, who were adept at dwarfing living things, were responsible for its creation. It is thought that Spanish traders, who traveled through Mexico from China, may have imported the breed to the American continent. There may also have been crosses to small native dogs. Other authorities feel the breed was developed by the Aztec Indians., while there are those who think that the Chihuahua reached Mexico in 1519, arriving with the explorer Cortes.

The true story about the breed's ancestry may never be known. However, it appears to have been named for the Mexican state of Chihuahua. Mexico City was the place where the breed first gained publicity, in about 1895, and the smooth-coated variety appears to have been the original breed. It was after the "tinies" traveled to the United States that crosses were made to other Toys — perhaps Pomeranians or Papillons — and the long-coated version was produced and

Long-coated Chihuahua

became popular. The breed soon became one of America's favorites in the Toy Group.

TEMPERAMENT

Because of its small size, the Chihuahua is a marvelous pet for the apartment dweller and the elderly. It can be left shut inside and can be easily trained to paper, so it does not have to be taken for walks in wet weather. It loves those that it knows, and can be a sharp and noisy watchdog, not realizing that its size cannot back up its threats. As this is such a small breed, it is not suitable as a pet for young or boisterous children. Care should be taken if it is kept with larger dogs because jealousies may arise — and the Chihuahua would hardly be able to put up a fair fight. The breed should be handled and socialized from soon after birth, so that it is encouraged to reach the peak of companionship of which it is capable.

HEALTH MATTERS

With a tiny dog that may weigh only 1 pound/ 0.5 kg, health matters are of grave importance. Many Chihuahuas have a soft spot in the center of their heads called a molera (this is recognized and allowed under the breed Standard). Because of this, the head should always be protected — a blow to this spot could prove fatal. The Chihuahua also has fragile bones and will easily sustain a fracture. Other health matters that owners should be aware of include slipped stifles, heart disease and a susceptibility to low blood sugar. This can cause fainting or mild seizures when the young animal is stressed (such as when teething). These turns should not be confused with epilepsy which is occasionally encountered in the breed. A Chihuahua bitch should not be bred from without consulting a reputable breeder and vet because its small size can lead to problems.

SPECIAL CARE AND TRAINING

Chihuahuas should be socialized well and early. Care must be taken not to step or sit accidentally on these little dogs. Similarly, they should not be allowed to jump off furniture. Their ears,

Smooth-coated Chihuahua

nails and teeth should be checked weekly. They should be protected in cold weather.

ADAPTABILITY

Because they are tiny, yet hardy and smart, the Chihuahua, in either coat is a wonderful house dog. However, they do feel the cold and must have a warm draft-free environment.

ESSENTIALS OF THE BREED

At under 6 pounds/2.5 kg and sometimes as light as 1 1/2 pounds/680 g, the Chihuahua is definitely the smallest of the purebred breeds. They mature at around 5 inches/13 cm tall at the shoulder and are slightly longer in body than height. They have a wonderful thick tail carried up often like a sickle, fine bones, a large very round head (in proportion) with a prominent brow, and erect pointed ears which are also large and carried standing out from the head. Its eyes are very expressive and the eye color may vary from dark to light. Two coats are permitted. A smooth Chihuahua has a shiny close-fitting sleek coat with a well-furred tail. A long-coated Chihuahua has fringed ears, as well as a longhaired tail, legs and frill under its neck and underbody. All colors are permissible.

Registry: AKC, CKC, FCI (Group 9), KC

CHINESE CRESTED

ORIGIN AND DEVELOPMENT

It is generally accepted that, over the years, hairless dogs have periodically been born to coated parents as a genetic mutation. Such hairless dogs have been recorded as far afield as Africa, the Middle East, India, Turkey, Ceylon and Malaysia. However, for some reason, the largest proportion of hairless "breeds" and variations on them are found in South and Central America.

Hairless specimens used to be kept as curiosities, but they soon proved to be well suited to a household existence. It is said that Mexican Indians kept herds of hairless dogs, the females for breeding, with the majority of males being castrated and fattened for eating.

As hairless dogs were bred together, it became apparent that it was possible to perpetuate the hairless factor and so various breeds evolved. Chinese Cresteds are recorded in China as far back as the thirteenth century, and via trade routes these curious little dogs found their way to Europe and South America.

The first Chinese Crested to be registered in the United Kingdom was called Chinese Emperor and was exhibited in 1881. However, it was not until the 1960s that the breed was reintroduced to the United Kingdom by Ruth Harris, who worked closely with Deborah Wood of Florida in the United States. Wood supplied the original imports from her Cresthaven kennel and these were followed by dogs from the famous entertainer Gypsy Rose Lee. Few American imports arrived in the United Kingdom after the early 1970s, mainly because Wood, who was then dying, refused to hand over the American Hairless Dog Club's breed register. However, a few Chinese Cresteds were imported – they had been registered with the Mexican Kennel Club and thus had acceptable documentation for the British Kennel Club.

A nucleus of breeders in the United Kingdom worked hard to establish the breed (the Chinese Crested Dog Club was formed in 1969). The original breed Standard catered for two distinct types of dog – the "Deer" and the "Cobby," but it did not refer to the coated specimens that invariably appear in most littters. This caused much dissent among breeders and exhibitors, some of whom showed coated specimens under judges who refused to place them because they were not catered for in the Standard. It was not until 1984 that the Kennel Club agreed to make provision for the hairless dogs' coated siblings – the "Powder Puffs."

Challenge Certificates were first awarded to the breed in 1982, and since then the breed has increased steadily in both numbers and degree of quality. Furthermore, its type and size have become much more stable, and several Chinese Cresteds have figured well in Group competition.

The American Kennel Club accepted Chinese Crested Dogs for full registration in 1992. Thirty-two Cresteds were entered that year at the Westminster Kennel Club's show. This figure is four times the number of German Shepherd Dogs at the 1992 show.

TEMPERAMENT

Having been domesticated for so many years, the Crested is very much a "people dog." It is full of character and loves its human family, yet it will happily live in groups with other dogs. It has almost no instinctive vices and has now risen from the role of "freak" to being an instantly recognizable companion.

HEALTH MATTERS

The breed is generally hardy, which is no surprise considering that it has survived for so many years. Hairless specimens are sometimes born with missing teeth and claws – these being related to the hairless factor. However, breeders are striving to improve both features and today many Hairless Cresteds are bred with excellent mouths and full feet.

SPECIAL CARE AND TRAINING

The Hairless Crested needs careful maintenance of its skin which is likely to become dry and scaly if it is not oiled regularly. It should also be watched in bright sunlight, because the delicate skin burns easily.

The Powder Puff's single coat needs thorough grooming at least once a week. Cresteds do not always take kindly to being overhandled by strangers, so exhibition dogs need to be trained on the table from an early age.

ADAPTABILITY

The Crested requires little in the way of exercise. Its naturally busy character will ensure that it is not standing still for long, especially on home ground. Being naturally domesticated, the breed will thrive in a one-dog family, and yet many breeders keep large numbers of Cresteds together as a pack, where they are equally happy. They do not make good kennel dogs, and will only blossom with constant companionship and home comforts.

ESSENTIALS OF THE BREED

The variation in the two different types — "Cobby" and "Deer" — is now barely visible. Most dogs exhibited and bred are very stable in their degree of substance and elegance.

The main difference between the Hairless and the Powder Puff is obviously the coat. The Hairless has a fine-grained skin, smooth and warm to the touch, with tufts of hair on the skull, feet and tail. The ears should be erect with an optional fringe of hair. The Powder Puff's coat is a soft, long undercoat which hangs like a veil on both sides of the body, and it may have dropped ears.

The Chinese Crested is reminiscent of a prancing pony and the Hairless is certainly equine in its appearance. Its head is long and smooth, with a slightly rounded skull and dark, wide-set eyes. Its neck should be lean and gracefully arched, and its body of medium

Hairless Chinese Crested

length with a broad, deep chest and moderate tuck-up. The feet are a feature of the breed, being narrow and very long, the toes almost appearing to have an extra joint. The tail should be long, high set and carried gracefully without any curl or twist. The Crested's movement should be elegant and display good reach and drive.

Any colors are allowed. Male Cresteds should stand 12-13 inches/30-33 cm at the withers (or 11-13 inches/28-33 cm in the United Kingdom), and bitches 9-12 inches/23-30 cm. Weight will vary with type to a degree, but the maximum weight should be 12 pounds/5.5 kg.

Registry: AKC, CKC, FCI (Group 9), KC

CHINESE SHAR-PEI/SHAR-PEI

ORIGIN AND DEVELOPMENT

The Chinese Shar-Pei is an ancient breed that is quite unique. It has existed for centuries in the southern provinces of China, quite probably since the Han Dynasty (202 B.C.-220 A.D.). A thirteenth-century Chinese manuscript mentions a wrinkled dog with characteristics of the present day Shar-Pei. The breed was originally recognized as a fighting breed, but it also used to help its owners by hunting, herding and offering protection. In its capacity as a fighter, it was a very difficult adversary because it was capable of turning around in its loose skin. Its tiny ears, deep-set eyes and harsh coat, made it a tough dog to beat.

The modern history of the Shar-Pei is very sketchy. Following the establishment of the People's Republic of China as a Communist nation, dogs in China were virtually eliminated. They were never seen in the cities and very few were found in the country. Fortunately a few Shar-Pei were bred in Hong Kong and in Taiwan. The breed was recognized by the Hong Kong Kennel Club and registered by it until 1968. The Hong Kong Kennel Club and the Kowloon Kennel Association established a combined dog registry and registered the Shar-Pei. Today the breed is registered by them and registries in Taiwan, Japan, Korea, the United States, Canada, Great Britain and some European countries.

The name Shar-Pei translates to "harsh sandy coat" or "sandpaper-like coat" — a reference to the two distinctive types of Shar-Pei coat (one is short and the other harsh). The Shar-Pei has a blue-black tongue, a characteristic only found in two other breeds — the Chow Chow and the Thai Ridgeback — which may indicate common ancestry.

In the United States the documented history of the breed begins in 1966 with dogs imported for breeding registered with the Hong Kong Kennel Club. A strong interest was generated in the breed when Matgo Law of Down-Home Kennels, Hong Kong appealed to dog fanciers in the United States to "save the Shar-Pei." American dog fanciers answered this call and a limited number of Shar-Pei were imported into the United States in the fall of 1973. Those interested fanciers collected together to form the Chinese Shar-Pei Club of America, Inc. and held its first meeting in 1974.

The first National Specialty was held in 1978 and since then a National Specialty has been held annually. In May 1988 the Shar-Pei was accepted into the American Kennel Club Miscellaneous Class and there were 29,263 registered dogs. The Chinese Shar-Pei was admitted to the AKC Stud Book on June 1, 1992 and was granted classification in the Non-Sporting Group on August 1, 1992.

TEMPERAMENT

Dedicated fanciers of the Chinese Shar-Pei have done a magnificent job in regard to the temperament of their favorite breed. Adorable as puppies, the Shar-Pei, which may once have been a fighting dog, used to be inclined toward a sharp and unmanageable nature. Today's carefully bred Shar-Pei shows a steadiness of temperament and a willingness to conform not only to its status as a house pet and companion, but to the rigors of dog show and Obedience competition. Puppies must be socialized early and introduced to children of the family carefully and properly. They are good watchdogs but any tendency toward aggression should be discouraged.

HEALTH MATTERS

Once again the dedicated breeders of the Shar-Pei have approached the problems inherent to the breed, which include a very loose and wrinkled skin which was prone to skin disorders. The earlier Shar-Pei had very tiny deep-set eyes that then became obscured by the heavy folds of skin about its head which caused an irritation of the eyes, thereby interfering with the Shar-Pei's eyesight. Skin problems have been held to a minimum by careful breeding practices, and the same practices are resulting more and more in clear eyes. Buyers should procure stock from well-established breeders who carefully screen for heritable defects.

SPECIAL CARE AND TRAINING

The Shar-Pei's strong personality and dominant temperament require firm training and socialization. Among all purebreds the Shar-Pei is the easiest to house train which assures its early acceptance into a household. The Shar-Pei does not kennel well. As a puppy, it has twice as much skin as it needs and it eventually grows into this. A great deal of attention must be paid to the skin to ensure that no irritations exist within its folds. The teeth must be kept clean and a small tip taken off each toenail every ten days or so in order to keep the foot from spreading out. The ears should be checked for cleanliness, although few ear problems exist. Exercise is essential as the dog is quite active and robust.

ADAPTABILITY

The Shar-Pei is better off if it is in a one-dog family. It is suited to both country and city living but does not like living in a kennel.

Chinese Shar-Pei or Shar-Pei as it is known in the United Kingdom

ESSENTIALS OF THE BREED

The preferred height for the Shar-Pei is 18-20 inches/45-50 cm to the top of the shoulder with a weight of 45-55 pounds/20-25 kg. The Shar-Pei is alert, dignified, compact and rather square in profile. The breed's large head has a hippopotamuslike muzzle shape, tiny dropped ears, dark, small almond-shaped and sunken eyes, plus a large wide nose. The lips and the top of the muzzle are well padded and may cause a slight bulge at the base of the nose. The tongue, roof of the mouth and gums are a bluish black. The teeth are strong with a scissors bite. The neck is of medium length, set well into the body with heavy folds of loose skin.

The topline should dip slightly behind the withers and then rise to the high-set, thick tail which curls over or to either side of the back. Its legs are sound and strong with good feet. The hind dewclaws must be removed. Its coat is harsh and off standing. The "horse coat" is extremely short and the "brush coat" should not exceed 1 inch/2.5 cm. The Shar-Pei is shown in its natural state. Only solid colors are acceptable: cream, fawn, red, black, chocolate, sable and silver. Its gait should be a trot and proper movement is essential. The mature Shar-Pei is regal, dignified, lordly, scowling, sober and snobbish.

Registry: AKC, CKC, FCI (Group 2), KC

CHINOOK DOG

In 1966, 1987, and 1988, the *Guinness Book of World Records* listed the Chinook as the rarest of all breeds. At the time of writing, they number only 300. A few enthusiasts are gaining more recognition through exhibition in Rare Breed Dog Shows throughout the United States and in 1994 two were shown in competition in Florida. The breed is an American creation, which dates back to 1917 and may be part Eskimo Dog. Early breeders wanted to develop a dog equal in speed to a Husky with the strength of the larger pulling breeds.

The Chinook is an incredibly hardy dog — a willing northern breed that lives from ten to fifteen years. For a breed of this size and bone, its hips are normally well formed and surprisingly free of hip dysplasia. It has a tawny, golden coat, may have drop or erect ears and is a robust and obliging worker. The members of the Chinook Owners Association in the United States have created a Standard of perfection for the breed and are working with biogeneticists to breed the Chinook along strict guidelines, with emphasis on its working qualities. Many feel that the Chinook has the heart of a dog twice its size. It certainly has great courage. It is loyal and makes an excellent family member. It has frequently performed feats pulling enormous weights. Chinooks pulled sleds for Admiral Byrd on his Antarctic trip in 1929.

Registry: The breed is not recognized by the AKC, CKC, FCI or KC.

Chinook Dog

CHOW CHOW

ORIGIN AND DEVELOPMENT

It is commonly understood that the Chow Chow owes its name to a Cantonese word for food, but there is little evidence that the breed was developed to delight Chinese gourmets. Closer to the truth perhaps is the fact that a commonly found spitz-type dog, resembling early Chow Chows, was plentiful in China, a country where dogs were indeed occasionally sources of human food. The development of the Chow Chow as it is known probably began when primitive spitz types were crossed with eastern Mastiff-type dogs, then selective

Chow Chow

breeding fixed the heavier head type to the more usual spitz features.

Chow Chow type dogs which possessed the rare blue-black tongue appear to have reached Great Britain by the late eighteenth century. These dogs also had the typical "scowl" of the breed, a feature which has frequently been misinterpreted by the layman as a sign of aggression. Although the Chow has enjoyed periods of great popularity, it remains a breed which is mistrusted by many who do not understand its inscrutable nature. Over the years, its leonine features have been in many ways exaggerated, and the scowl made so extreme that the British Kennel Club, in agreement with breeders, amended the breed Standard so that a less exaggerated head would be encouraged.

The Chow Chow's small deep-seated eyes, and loose skin on its head made entropion a regular problem in the breed. Today British breeders aim for a more moderate type of Chow Chow, perhaps less "overdone" than many American dogs which are generally heavier all round than their British counterparts. The Chow Chow has remained true to type and pure for many years, free of cross-breeding. It is this ancient lineage that remains one of the main attractions with many of its fanciers.

TEMPERAMENT

The Chow Chow has a reputation of being aggressive but this is not deserved. To its owner and immediate family it is friendly and faithful, although it is not the sort of breed to greet strangers with a wagging tail. The Chow Chow is aloof and will take its time before it condescends to pass time with a new acquaintance. Forcing one's attentions on a Chow Chow could be asking for trouble, and for this reason some judges at dog shows find the Chow Chow a difficult dog to assess — especially as it is necessary to establish the color of its tongue!

HEALTH MATTERS

The Chow Chow's major trouble has been entropion, due to the structure of its head and eyes, but as already mentioned firm attempts are being made by many breeders to eradicate this problem.

SPECIAL CARE AND TRAINING

Because of its dense coat which is very thick and plushy, regular grooming is necessary to avoid serious matting, especially when the coat is shedding. Care should be taken to ensure that the eyes are kept clean and dry and that any facial folds are kept dry.

ADAPTABILITY

The Chow Chow will follow its owner anywhere and be happy in his or her company. Relatively speaking the breed is quite sedentary and, given suitable companionship, its demands are rarely vigorous.

ESSENTIALS OF THE BREED

The Chow Chow is a short-coupled and well-balanced dog with a characteristic scowl, created by its small, deep-set almond eyes, neat, thick, small, erect ears placed quite wide and its broad muzzle. Its bones should be heavy, feet neat, and its characteristic blue-black pigment should be present in the tongue with even darker shades in the inner flews and roof of the mouth. Ideally the gums too will be black. The chest should be broad and deep, the back short, straight and strong, and the hindquarters show little angulation which helps to create its characteristic stilted gait. The tail should be set high and carried proudly over the back.

In color, the Chow can be black, red, blue, fawn, cream or white. While the back of the thighs and under the tail may be a lighter shade than the base color, the breed should essentially be self-colored with no suggestion of broken or parti-colors. All bitches measure 18-20 inches/45-50 cm at the shoulder and dogs 19-22 inches/48-55 cm. It is a little known fact that the breed comes in two coat types — rough and smooth, the rough being much more common.

Registry: AKC, CKC, FCI (Group 5), KC

CIRNECO DELL'ETNA

This ancient Italian breed looks like a small delicate sighthound, very reminiscent of a small Pharoah Hound, but it is still used in Sicily, its island of origin, for hunting rabbit. The breed is supposed to come from Egypt.

The breed is about 16-19 inches/41-48 cm at its withers. The Cirneco's slender build, long elegant neck and narrow head, with large, erect ears, fine bone structure and visible muscles do not give the impression of it being the keen efficient and ferocious worker that it actually is. Its coat should be smooth, very fine and elastic. Its color is usually a bright red but all shades of red as well as white, with or without red patches, are allowed. The pigmentation must never be black.

Registry: FCI (Group 5)

Cirneco dell'Etna

COLLIES — ROUGH COLLIE

ORIGIN AND DEVELOPMENT

All varieties of Collie hail from Scotland and it is generally accepted that they share some common ancestry. The similarity between the present-day Border Collie and Champion Rough Collies of the late 1880s is indeed remarkable, though over the years the Rough Collie's type has become more clearly defined. This can be seen particularly in its head and overall elegance.

It is claimed that, in an attempt to make the Rough Collie more distinctive, certain crosses were used including the Borzoi. This seems quite logical as even today certain Borzoi characteristics do tend to crop up in Rough Collie heads. The Rough Collie had remained a utilitarian working sheepdog until the 1860s when history relates two events which affected the fortunes of this now internationally popular breed. The Birmingham National Dog Show scheduled a class for "Herding Dogs," and this stimulated great interest in the Rough Collie as a breed. Furthermore, when Queen Victoria made her first trip to Balmoral, she encountered the breed for the first time. So impressed was she with the Rough Collie, that she took some specimens back to the royal kennels at Windsor. This in itself was sufficient to stimulate great public interest in the hitherto little-known breed. Almost overnight, the Rough Collie became fashionable. Two black-and-tan Collies from the royal kennels were exported to the United States where they aroused great interest.

At that time, tricolor and blue merle tended to be the most common colors, rather than the sables which are today much more popular. Indeed, all present-day Rough Collies can trace their ancestry back to a tricolor dog named Trefoil, which was born in 1873. The sable coloring was actually introduced through a dog called Old Cockie. Vast prices are recorded as having been paid for the finest examples of the breed in the late nineteenth century, many dogs changing hands for more than $1,000 which — at that time — would be considered an astronomical sum. The highest price reputed to have been paid for a Rough Collie was for Ch. Parbold Piccolo, sold to America having sired several Champions in Britain including the legendary Ch. Anfield Model, which is still regarded by many as a model for the breed, its head and expression being particularly outstanding and of such quality that it could more than hold its own in the ring today. On arriving at his new home in Milwaukee, Piccolo seemed such a friendly and happy animal that he was allowed freedom to roam his new surroundings. Tragically Piccolo disappeared that same day, doubtless in an attempt to find his way home.

Since those early days, the breed has refined its type through selective breeding with no cross-breeding. Gradually the Rough Collie acquired more elegance and refinement, and soon became a glamorous contender in the show ring. Much of the breed's popularity with the general public can obviously be attributed to the "Lassie" films. These films suggested that the Rough Collie was a perfect childhood companion, loyal to the very end. The Lassie stories emphasized the breed's natural homing instinct, and this is no exaggeration. It is essential that anyone buying an adult Rough Collie should keep it securely confined until it completely adjusts to its new surroundings, as it will invariably escape and try to make its way "home."

TEMPERAMENT

The Rough Collie has been immortalized as the perfect pet by the "Lassie" films, and it is true that it is an ideal family dog that enjoys the company of humans. Having said this, the dog was bred to work and enjoys both mental and physical challenge. It is gregarious and will happily get along with other dogs. Aggressive or nervous Rough Collies are totally untypical.

Rough Collie

HEALTH MATTERS

The breed has a problem with Collie eye anomaly which, through carefully screened breeding programs, diligent breeders are trying to eradicate. This apart, the breed is fairly resilient and healthy.

SPECIAL CARE AND TRAINING

Puppies should be taught basic obedience from an early age. The Rough Collie responds well to obedience and agility training, but the breed still has a natural herding instinct which should be kept in check. Because the Rough Collie has such a profuse coat, daily grooming is advisable to keep these dogs in the peak of condition, It is essential that the brushing of the coat should be thorough, going right down to the skin. Far too many owners "surface groom," oblivious to the weighty mats which are forming closer to the dog's skin. When the coat starts to "blow," it is best to give the dog a really good bath. Then all its dead hair should come away, leaving the dog's skin clean and healthy and ready for the new coat to grow.

189

Some judges and breeders have become obsessed with the Rough Collie's head and sweetness of expression.

Adaptability

Rough Collies will happily live in groups in kennels, but they should never be starved of human contact. On the other hand, one Rough in isolation will fit into an otherwise totally human environment with no problem at all. They are essentially a large working breed and therefore need ample regular exercise.

Essentials of the Breed

In recent times many breeders and judges have become obsessed with the importance of the Rough Collie's head and sweetness of expression, almost at the expense of other constructional points which should really be considered a priority in view of the breed's working ancestry. The Rough Collie should be a balanced dog of great beauty, with an impassive dignity. It should have a look of strength and activity, but show no signs of coarseness or cloddiness.

Expression is important, and the ideal will only be achieved with a correct balance between the skull and foreface, placement and carriage of the ears, and the size, shape and color of the eyes. The head is essentially like a blunt wedge without prominent cheeks or snipiness of muzzle. In profile, the top of the skull and muzzle should be parallel, with only a minimal stop. The central point between the eye-corners should also represent the middle of the head's length. There should be a strong underjaw, and the nose should always be black. The eyes should be of medium size (and not too small), almond shaped and set obliquely. They are usually dark brown, but in blue merles one, both, or part of one, may be blue or blue-flecked. The expression should be full of intelligence and always alert. The dog's ears should be small and carried semi-erect. They should not be set too wide, but neither should they be too close.

The Rough Collie is moderately boned with oval feet, its overall body shape should indicate length, and its firm back should rise slightly over the loin. The ribs should be well sprung and chest deep. There should be good turn of stifle, with the hocks well let down and powerful. One of the most important features in the overall appearance of the Rough Collie is its tail. This should be long, reaching at least to the hock joint, and it should be carried low with a slight upward swirl at the tip. There is a tendency, in males particularly, for the tail to be carried rather gaily — this can be accepted when the dog is excited but the tail should never be carried over the back. The Rough Collie moves rather close in front, but should always display a smooth action in profile. The coat should enhance the dog's outline and consist of a straight and harsh outercoat covering a soft and extremely dense undercoat. In color the breed can be sable and white, tricolor or blue merle, with white markings traditionally confined to a part or full collar, shirt-front, legs, feet and tail tip. A facial blaze is permitted. In Great Britain males tend to stand up to 24 inches/60 cm at the shoulder and bitches 2 inches/5 cm smaller, but in the United States the height limits for both sexes are 2 inches/5 cm greater.

Registry: AKC, CKC, FCI (Group 1), KC

COLLIES — SMOOTH COLLIE

ORIGIN AND DEVELOPMENT

Through recent events, actively encouraged cross-breeding and a great similarity in type, it is often assumed that the Rough and Smooth Collies are two varieties of the same breed and that they have been so since early development. It is, however, far more likely that the Smooth began life as a drover's dog, its forefathers being much less like the forefathers of the Rough than is generally assumed.

Certainly illustrations of early Smooth Collies suggest a rather more "cloddy" dog than the present-day Smooth Collie, with less height and a heavier head. It is highly probable that when dog shows began to increase in popularity, and competition took place between the various herding breeds, that it was felt by some breeders that an infusion of Rough Collie blood would enhance the Smooth in some respects and give them more of a chance in the show ring. So, for many years the two breeds were inter-bred until such time as there were few major differences other than coat. Today the Smooth's ears are larger and wider-based than those of the Rough, and its pasterns need to be rather flexible. In other respects, the requirements of the breed are much the same as those of its Rough cousin.

While never enjoying the widespread popularity of the Rough (who knows what would have happened had "Lassie" been a Smooth?), the Smooth retains a loyal band of fanciers who have managed to maintain quality in the breed on an international level. Furthermore, the Smooth has proved itself in Obedience and Agility competition, being very much an all-purpose working dog.

TEMPERAMENT

The Smooth is a naturally outgoing breed that should be happy and friendly toward other dogs and people. Its temperament should be rock-steady, never displaying aggression or nervousness.

Smooth Collie

HEALTH MATTERS

As with Roughs, hereditary eye problems can occur, and so breeding stock should always be thoroughly researched. This apart, the Smooth tends to be a hardy and resilient breed, free of major defects.

SPECIAL CARE AND TRAINING

The Smooth has less coat to manage than its Rough cousin, but the breed still needs regular grooming to maintain overall good condition. It responds well to all kinds of obedience tracking and many Smooth Collies have acquitted themselves well in the competitive Obedience and Agility rings.

ADAPTABILITY

The Smooth is a versatile and social breed. While it will happily live in a group with other dogs, it will be equally happy to share its life with a human family. Being fundamentally a large working dog, it will need regular exercise regardless of where it is housed.

ESSENTIALS OF THE BREED

Apart from having rather larger ears and specifically flexible pasterns, the Smooth shares its main essentials with the Rough Collie (see above).

Registry: AKC, CKC, FCI (Group 1), KC

COONHOUNDS

ORIGIN AND DEVELOPMENT

Although they vary in coloring, there are many similarities among the six types of Coonhound: the Black and Tan Coonhound, the Blue Tick Coonhound, the English Coonhound, the Plott Hound, the Redbone Coonhound, and the Treeing Walker. This breed has blood that can probably be traced back to an extinct hound from the eleventh century. It also has elements of Bloodhound in its heritage, as well as some blood from American and English Foxhounds.

Much credit must be given for the development of these hounds to the people in the United States who live in the mountains of Virginia, the Ozark Mountains and the Great Smoky Mountains. They bred hounds to trail and hunt not only raccoon but also bear in the rugged mountain terrain. The present Black and Tan Coonhound was bred selectively for its color, and its ability not only to trail but to "tree". This involves sending the prey up into the branches and then baying to alert the attention of the hunter. The Black and Tan hunts like the Bloodhound, not by sight but by using its scenting abilities. This color was admitted to the American Kennel Club in 1945.

Of German heritage, the Plott Hound works as a single hunter or in packs for small and large game. It is named after Jonathan Plott, an émigré from Germany who settled in North Carolina.

TEMPERAMENT

The Black and Tan Coonhound makes a good family dog and enjoys long walks with children. It is very steady in temperament and has been bred as a companion as well as a hunter for many generations. However, it tends to stray and so needs a good safe area in which to exercise and close supervision when out walking. The breed loves water and is a good swimmer when introduced to water early in life.

The Blue Tick Coonhound is similar to the Black and Tan Coonhound but it has a more aggressive nature which means that is not recommended as a house dog. It also has a loud bawling bark; the Plott Hound's bark is sharp and high-pitched. The Redbone Coonhound is also similar to the Black and Tan

Coonhound, easy going and even tempered. A favored dog in the United States, the Coonhound can be kept as a pet, but mostly out of doors. The English and the Walker, on the other hand, are very highly strung.

HEALTH MATTERS

Serious inherited health problems are not a concern for this natural breed. Of course, nails need filing or clipping and ears cleaning on a weekly basis. Hard biscuits given as treats should keep the Coonhound's teeth gleaming and free of tartar. All breeding stock should be X-rayed for correct hips at two years. Breeding stock should also be checked for progressive retinal atrophy yearly.

SPECIAL CARE AND TRAINING

Coonhounds are born natural hunters, so they have a tendency to run off and hunt if they are not kept well fenced while exercising on their own. They should be well socialized at an early age and taught simple obedience like walking on a leash. They should be kept in

Black and Tan Coonhound

clean surroundings and fed a good quality balanced diet. When they start to hunt, hounds should be checked daily for torn nails, split pads on their feet, torn ears, fleas and ticks — and given medical treatment as needed.

ADAPTABILITY

All these dogs thrive better in a rural setting than in a city apartment. They have no road sense at all so must be kept in a safe environment.

ESSENTIALS OF THE BREED

The Black and Tan Coonhound is an upstanding hound, with males about 25-27 inches/63-68 cm, and females about 2 inches/5 cm smaller. Its color is a gleaming black with rich tan points on a typical black-and-tan pattern. White is allowed on the chest — but then only a small spot. The Coonhound's coat is short, smooth and glossy. Its head is long and lean, with dark and kindly eyes that are always clear. Both the ears and tail are very long — puppies often look as if they are all ears and tail. The teeth are regular and meet in a scissors bite. The breed has a good length of neck and solid level topline. Its strong legs should be well formed with good feet. It carries its tail up and gaily when moving.

The Blue Tick Coonhound has a mottled blue coat and tan markings on its ears and lower legs. The English Coonhound generally has a solid hound color (usually red or blue) with black, white or brown ticking. The Plott Hound is always brindle or black with brindle trim. The Redbone Coonhound is always red with a small amount of white allowed on its chest and feet. The Treeing Walker is tri-color, of solid black, white and brown.

Registry: (Black and Tan Coonhound only) AKC, CKC, FCI (Group 6)

COTON DE TULÉAR

The Coton de Tuléar has probably the same origin as several other white, soft-coated Toy breeds from the Mediterranean. It is supposed to have survived hundreds of years ago from a ship that was wrecked in a storm off Madagascar, which is the breed's home. The word "Coton" in the breed name indicates the quality of coat texture; Tuléar is the old name of the city where the breed was most frequently found.

The breed is about 10-11 inches/25-28 cm at its withers. Its body should be rectangular and the backline should be slightly convex. The croup should be short and falling, and the tail should not be carried too much over the back. The head is triangular and rather small. The coat should be about 3 inches/8 cm long, slightly wavy with a fine texture, intermingled with glossy hair. It should be kept natural and never scissored. The breed should be white, although small patches of very pale lemon or gray are permissible on the ears.

Coton de Tuléar

Registry: FCI (Group 9)

CROATIAN SHEEPDOG/HRVATSKI OVCAR

Croatia (Hrvatska) in former Yugoslavia claims that its sheepdog has kept to type and has been used for herding for several hundreds of years. Its appearance is similar to the Hungarian sheepdog, the Mudi. The Croatian Sheepdog is a hardy, tough and agile breed with a keen guarding instinct. Nowadays it is considered a companion dog and is rare outside Croatia.

The dog should stand about 16-20 inches/40-50 cm at its withers. The body is square, with the topline sloping from withers to hindquarters, and it has pricked ears. The tail may be docked short, a natural bobtail or kept long. On the body the coat length is about 3-6 inches/7-15 cm long, wavy, or slightly curly giving it a shaggy look. The head and front of the legs have a short coat. Its color is black or grayish black.

Registry: FCI (Group 1)

Croatian Sheepdog

CZECHOSLOVAKIAN WOLFDOG/ CESKOSLOVENSKY VLCAK

This wolf-dog hybrid emanates mainly from crossing wolves with German Shepherds and is said to have been developed after World War II. The Czechoslovakian Wolfdog has a slightly stronger build than the otherwise almost identical wolf-dog hybrid, the Dutch Saarloos Wolfhond. Apparently the breed is a useful herder.

At its withers, the breed is about 26 inches/65 cm tall. Its appearance should resemble the Nordic wolf but it should have a broader skull, a more substantial body and stronger bone. The Czechoslovakian Wolfdog should have wolf coloring.

Registry: FCI (Group 1)

Czechoslovakian Wolfdog

DACHSHUNDS

ORIGIN AND DEVELOPMENT

Old German documents refer to predecessors of the Teckel, the name by which the Dachshund is known in its native land. From the beginning of the sixteenth century documents have recorded the existence and activities of the "earth dog," "little burrow dog," "badger digger," "badger creeper" and "dachsel." The German word "*dachs*" means 'badger" and this explains the breed's early use as a hunting dog. Its shape was designed for burrowing, going underground to hunt badger and fox, and later — with the development of the miniature types — rabbit.

The smooth-haired variety is thought to have developed in the eighteenth century with the mixing of the French Braque (a small Pointer type) and the Pinscher. The German teckels were described in the seventeenth century as "a peculiar low-crooked species." When the nobility fled France during the French Revolution in the later years of the eighteenth century, many took their French Bassets with them. The two breeds were crossed and the resulting pups became Dachsbracke (if they were long in the leg) and Dachshunds (if they were short-legged, with short ears and pointed muzzles).

The Dachshund owes much to the work of Major Ilgner, founder of many Dachshund societies, and later to Herr Fritz Engelmann; both were devotees of the breed and both used it for hunting. The first Teckel Stud Book was produced in Germany in 1890 and referred to Smooth, Longhaired and Wirehaired varieties. The German breed club has always placed great importance on the breed's working abilities. To this end, its size and structure are largely functional, low to ground, with a long

Miniature Smooth Dachshund

196

supple body facilitating ample heart and lung room, and front legs and feet designed for digging. The development of the miniature and dwarf (Kaninchen) types came later and their size is measured not in height or weight (as in the United Kingdom) but by girth, the measurement being taken from behind the withers. Miniatures must be under 13 1/2 inches/ 35 cm in girth; the Kaninchen no more than 12 inches/30 cm. The smaller type Dachsund is used in smaller burrows and usually to hunt rabbit. The German breed clubs still hold regular working tests for the breed.

While the Teckel has maintained uniformity of type in mainland Europe, imports to the United Kingdom and the breed's development there brought a divergence of type. The British breeders developed a more exaggerated dog, of greater length, heavier and lower to the ground with a considerably more developed forechest or keel. The German Teckel breeders decry these exaggerations as rendering the breed incapable of working.

In the United States, the Dachshund owes its development to bloodlines from both countries, though perhaps the type is not as extreme as found in the United Kingdom. In the United States, the breed is split into three varieties divided by coat but not by size. These different coats were developed through the use of terriers and some spaniel types. Again, the coats are functional: the Wire's coat gives more protection in thorny, rough hedges and underground. The Longhaired variety is good in water — the breed is used for tracking wounded deer — and the Smooth is good underground.

TEMPERAMENT

The breed's working instincts call for a dog which is lively, intelligent, courageous and sporting, and a dog that will enjoy tracking by scent. The Dachsund also makes an excellent family dog — but it should be noted that it has a bold, assured temperament and this should not be overlooked. Some of the Miniature varieties, popular because of their size, have become prone to nervousness, yet the Dachshund should always have a dignified and elegant carriage.

HEALTH MATTERS

Because the Dachshund has a long back, it is prone to disc problems, so it is important that owners do not let their hounds become overweight. Sometimes the Smooth can suffer from skin problems, but this problem is comparatively rare and a balanced diet should prevent dry and scaly skin. The Dachshund's large teeth tend to develop tartar so regular scaling is recommended if gnawing an occasional large bone or dry biscuit does not remedy this condition.

SPECIAL CARE AND TRAINING

Regular exercise is important so that a tendency to put on weight is discouraged. Besides, the Dachshund is essentially a sporting breed and enjoys plenty of activity. The Dachshund's coat is easy to keep in condition: the Smooth is odor-free and sheds its coat only to a very small degree — a hound glove or soft cloth will maintain a healthy shine. The Longhaired variety needs a regular brush and comb and its feet may need an occasional trim. The Wirehaired will cast its coat and needs the dead hair to be stripped out: this is easily done with a stiff brush or stripping knife, or can be performed at a reputable grooming parlor.

ADAPTABILITY

Dachshunds are active dogs that need plenty of exercise to keep them fit. Sadly because of their convenient size and attractive looks, many pet Dachshunds are turned into sedentary creatures by their owners — this is detrimental from both a mental and physical standpoint. In a rural setting, the Dachshund will swiftly show its prowess at killing vermin, yet it can happily adjust to the life of a town-dweller, provided it is given plenty of activity. The breed is known to be quite vocal, so understanding neighbors are essential for anyone intending to keep a Dachshund or two.

Standard Dachshunds with three coat types. From left: longhaired, wire and smooth.

ESSENTIALS OF THE BREED

"Long, low and level" are the key words in establishing breed type. The Dachshund is a long dog with rib cage extending well back. Its topline should be level and it should be well let down in the rear. Its front assembly is very important. The shoulder should be well laid back with an upper arm of equal length so that the dog has plenty of fore-chest or keel. The forelegs should be short and strong in bone, free from wrinkles or loose skin. A correctly placed foreleg should cover the lowest point of the keel when viewed from the side. Because of the breed's construction, the forearm is shaped to accommodate the keel and will therefore incline slightly inward. This sometimes produces feet which might turn out slightly. The dog should move with a good stride in front, driving from the rear. Its level topline should remain firm on the move, the tail being carried low or on a level with the back, but not carried too high above it.

Most frequently found colors are black-and-tan and red in the Smooth and Longhaired varieties, while badger, hare-colored and reds tend to dominate the Wires. Chocolate-and-tan is found in all varieties and dapples — usually silver or chocolate — are acceptable in all coats. Size in the United Kingdom is dictated by weight, with Standard weight being recommended at 20-26 pounds/9-12 kg, although many Standards weigh much more. In Miniatures, 11 pounds/5 kg is the maximum allowance and exhibits are traditionally weighed in the presence of the judge before class judging commences. The Standard for the Dachshund in continental Europe differs radically, with the accent on a slightly longer-legged, lighter dog and the size dictated by girth measurement.

Registry: AKC, CKC, FCI (Group 4), KC

DALMATIAN

ORIGIN AND DEVELOPMENT

The Dalmatian takes its name from Dalmatia, part of former Yugoslavia, but its origins are not very clear. Its basic roots may be the English Pointer.

The Dalmatian has had many uses: hunter, watchdog, and shepherd. A coach dog, its job was to run underneath a coach and keep at bay any dogs that might attack or frighten the horses pulling the coach. Dalmatians are also known as Firehouse dogs in the United States. Before the introduction of the fire engine, horses were used and kept under control by Dalmatians. The breed remains the mascot of many fire fighters to this day.

TEMPERAMENT

The Dalmatian is energetic and athletic. It adapts well to family life but should be exposed to children when it is very young.

HEALTH MATTERS

The Dalmatian is prone to inherited deafness. Also, urinary stones are a problem and the breed has an unsightly but not life-threatening tendency to have allergic skin reactions, hives or redness of the skin.

Dalmatian

SPECIAL CARE AND TRAINING

Short coated, the Dalmatian is easy to keep clean but it does shed, thereby necessitating a brushing and rubdown with a rough, damp towel several times weekly. It must have exercise and is a prime candidate for obedience work that exercises both its body and mind.

ADAPTABILITY

Because it is quite a large dog, in an urban situation the Dalmatian should have access to large open spaces for regular exercise.

ESSENTIALS OF THE BREED

Dalmatian puppies are born all white except for those born with a patch of liver or black coat color. Spots vary from about 3/4-1 1/4 inches/2-3 cm in diameter and should be evenly distributed. The white of the coat should be clear and very white. White must show in the ears and there must be only black or liver spots, not a combination of the two. Eyes are dark in the black spotted and a lighter brown in the livers. In both black and liver spotted Dalmatians, blue eyes are only acceptable in the United States. The Dalmatian should have normal balance and proportion, good shoulders and running gear. In the United States the breed should be about 19-23 inches/48-58 cm (with Dalmatians over 24 inches/61 cm being disqualified in the ring). In the United Kingdom, dogs should stand about 23-24 inches/ 58-61 cm, and bitches 22-23 inches/56-58 cm. The tail should be carried well but not over the back and reaching only to the hock. A gay, happy demeanor, hard muscle, good feet and a brilliant color pattern identify the Dalmatian.

Registry: AKC, CKC, FCI (Group 6), KC

DANDIE DINMONT TERRIER

ORIGIN AND DEVELOPMENT

The Dandie Dinmont is one of the oldest British terriers, having originated in the Coquet River valley in Northumberland during the eighteenth century. Its precise origin is not known, but native terriers were certainly used and some think that the old Otterhound may be part of its make-up. There are many theories but no proven detail. In those days the breed was known by the farm name where it was bred, or was called the Pepper or Mustard Terrier. The dogs were highly prized and used against small vermin, otters in ponds, and foxes, as well being a hunt terrier.

The Allan family of tinkers had many terriers, including Peppers and Mustards and one, Willie (or "Piper") Allan and his family bred many of these small dogs. It is claimed that the Duke of Northumberland once offered Piper Allan a farm, rent free, in exchange for one of his terriers, but the offer was declined. In 1814 Sir Walter Scott's novel *Guy Mannering* was published and featured these Pepper and Mustard Terriers along with a farmer who bred them, called Dandie Dinmont. The name became attached to the breed, and it is the only breed which takes its name from a literary source. A farmer named James Davidson, who lived at Hindlee Farm on Rule Water in the Borders, was nicknamed "'Dandie Dinmont" by his companions, because he had many of these terriers. Sir Walter Scott did not meet James Davidson until after the publication of his novel, but apparently thought James was very much like his character. The breed was well known in England and Scotland on both sides of the border and Sir Walter and Lady Scott kept quite a number at their home, Abbotsford.

In 1875 at the Fleece Hotel, Selkirk, a club was formed by fanciers — the Dandie Dinmont Terrier Club, which together with the Bulldog and Bedlington Terrier Clubs are the longest-established breed clubs in the world.

TEMPERAMENT

The Dandie is a dignified "mind your own business" dog, highly intelligent, and an excellent companion. Deep inside is a true terrier spirit and a roused Dandie can be a veritable demon that can tackle fox or smaller vermin. Many choose a special human companion for life.

HEALTH MATTERS

The Dandie is a very tough dog that can tolerate a great deal of pain. Often they have been ill for a few days before the owner notices that anything is wrong. They are fit dogs and suffer from few diseases or ailments in their youth. The ears and eyes should be kept clean at all times. Disc disease can affect the Dandie, so it should not be allowed to get overweight.

SPECIAL CARE AND TRAINING

The topknot should be carefully looked after and it is advisable to shampoo it occasionally. Companion Dandies should have their coats stripped by an expert at least twice a year. The training of youngsters should be sympathetic, never harsh. The Dandie is a sensitive dog and a youngster's spirit should not be broken.

ADAPTABILITY

This affectionate character of a dog thrives on human companionship. It is adaptable as a town or country dog and many still have the instinct to work.

ESSENTIALS OF THE BREED

Sir Walter Scott said that the Dandie was "the big little dog" — a marvelous description. Dandies should weigh from 18-24 pounds/8-10 kg, with lower weights preferred. The head has expressive, melting dark eyes with a beautiful topknot. The body is long, low at the withers and with a slight arch over the loin. The tail should be carried in scimitar fashion, higher than the body. The front feet are larger than the hind feet and are excellent for digging. The Dandie should move along with strong impulsion from the hindquarters. Its coat is a double one with a crisp topcoat and comes in two colors — Mustard (pale fawn to rich tan, with a creamy top knot) and Pepper (pale silver to deep bluish black with a silvery-white topknot). The United Kingdom population is around 2,000 dogs, with approximately 200 puppies born each year.

Registry: AKC, CKC, FCI (Group 3), KC

Dandie Dinmont Terrier

DEUTSCHE BRACKE

The German scenthound (Deutsche Bracke)
deviates from several local hounds that in the
early twentieth century were classified as one
breed. Strangely enough it resembles the Swiss
Hounds more than the breeds from which it
originated. It is a very efficient tracking hound,
known for its loud and clear voice. It is strictly
a hunting dog that is rarely seen outside its
native country.

The breed stands about 16-21 inches/40-53
cm at the withers. The body should be rectangular and elegant, with a long, narrow head. Its
long ears are quite low set and its tail is rather
thin and long. The coat should be smooth and
glossy and in traditional hound colors; tan with
a black mantle and white markings.

Registry: FCI (Group 6)

*This Deutsche Bracke is from the German
Saulander region.*

DEUTSCHE WACHTELHUND

The German Spaniel is thought to look very
much like old European spaniels that were
used before guns were invented. The breed
was on the verge of dying out in the late
nineteenth century but was revived. Although
it has always enjoyed a very good reputation
as a hunting dog in Germany, this hardy and
versatile breed has recently attracted more
interest in other countries as well.

At its withers, the German Spaniel should be
about 18-21 inches/45-54 cm. Its body should be
rectangular and sturdy. The coat should be of
medium length, close lying or wavy but not
curly. It should either be solid liver brown, or
white with ticking and large patches of brown
with or without tan markings. Red or liver
roan with or without patches are also allowed
even though they are rarely seen.

Deutsche Wachtelhund

Registry: FCI (Group 8)

DINGO

Australia's native dog, the Dingo is one of the most ancient dog breeds to be domesticated and, through isolation over thousands of years, one of the purest. The Australian Dingo, whose technical name is *Canis antarcticas*, was originally found throughout the whole of mainland Australia but not in Tasmania. As no evidence has yet shown that the Dingo is indigenous to Australia, it is generally agreed that the dog was developed from a domesticated version of the Asiatic wolf or the Dhole (Indian wolf dog) which accompanied the Aborigines on their earliest invasions of Australia by sea. Though many Dingoes remained close and valued companions to the natives, who sometimes called the dog a "Warrigal," the breed has existed in the wild in increasing numbers since the arrival of Europeans.

Invariably, Dingoes are reddish brown in color, with white feet and a white tip to the tail. The Dingo has great endurance and has been described as the most cunning dog known to man. It has a high degree of intelligence, strong reasoning powers and great independence.

Its vital need for security makes its keeping and training at all times a great responsibility. It must be stressed that the Dingo is not a suitable pet for the average domestic household. Indeed, in most states of Australia Dingoes are considered vermin and it is illegal to keep a Dingo as a pet. The "Dog Fence" has been built, stretching across most of Australia, to keep the Dingo out of sheep and cattle grazing areas.

Registry: Recognized only by the ANKC (Australian National Kennel Council)

Dingo

DOBERMAN PINSCHER/DOBERMANN

ORIGIN AND DEVELOPMENT

The Doberman Pinscher is a dog of relatively modern times, having originated in Apolda in Thuringen, Germany in 1890. The breed was officially recognized in 1900.

There is some disagreement as to which breeds composed the foundation stock but most authorities think that a shorthaired shepherd dog, the Rottweiler, a German smooth-haired Pinscher, and a Black and Tan Terrier were significant components. All agree that its name comes from Louis Dobermann who developed the breed in his search for the ideal guard dog and companion.

TEMPERAMENT

The requirements of an ideal companion guard dog at the turn of the twentieth century were very different from what they are today. The well-bred and raised modern Doberman is a much more family oriented dog than the animal that was developed by Herr Dobermann. Today's breed — socialized from birth to accept and trust humans, introduced to the outside world through trips in the car, and given early obedience training — has become a tractable member of the family. However, it may not be a breed for the first time dog owner and its temperament will always depend on whoever is responsible for raising it, as well as on its training, general health and proper nutrition.

In the Germany of Herr Dobermann's time, people traditionally respected the boundaries of a man's property. A fenced yard told everyone, "Stay out unless you are invited in." Therefore, those that chose to have guard dogs expected them to attack anyone who entered unannounced. The tougher the dog, the more it was prized. Eventually, to make certain those qualities were never lost, trials to test a dog's perseverance in attack work, its scenting ability and its trainability (obedience) were inaugurated. Such tests are today known

as Schutzhund trials and are still a measure of the working ability of dogs in some countries and a prerequisite in some instances if the dog is to be eligible for the highest award at a conformation show.

It it is easy to understand how the original stock, imported from Germany into the United States, proved to be a bit sharp for the less than dog-wise American public. Fortunately, two ameliorating factors operated in the dog's favor. First, breeders, through selective breeding, were able to arrive at a Doberman that was more in harmony with the environment surrounding most American homes, without sacrificing the intelligence and basic protective instinct which Herr Dobermann so zealously cultivated. Secondly, the Doberman Pinscher is most fortunate in that leadership in the parent club has traditionally been vested in people of intelligence and dedication. Their educational programs were in place years before the American Kennel Club (AKC) ever gave thought to that responsibility. Their forthright attention to Von Willebrand's disease (a bleeding disorder), their willingness to supply data and fund research is an example that other breed clubs could well emulate. Their library of available literature on the breed and their rescue program have no peer. It is no small wonder that the privilege of judging a Doberman Specialty is a cherished assignment. One is always assured of quality. The first club to hold a "Top Twenty" was the Doberman Pinscher Club of America (DPCA). This format has subsequently been adopted by other breed clubs and is always a popular event.

TEMPERAMENT

To summarize the Standard, the Doberman should be an energetic, watchful, determined, alert, fearless, loyal and obedient dog.

HEALTH MATTERS

Although Von Willebrand's disease is no longer

Doberman Pinscher or Dobermann as it is known in the United Kingdom

such a problem, two other maladies are unfortunately associated with Dobermans. One is Wobblers Syndrome (a disease of the spinal column of the neck). This causes the dog to stagger or wobble as it walks. It is thought to be a heritable disease, and it may or may not respond to surgery. The second problem is a lethal heart disorder. All breeding stock should be tested before being bred.

ADAPTABILITY

Some idea of the adaptability of the breed can be gleaned from registration figures, which reflect that Dobermans register the fourth greatest number in the Working Group. Were it not for the concerted effort of dedicated Doberman people to promote education and responsibility for each breeding, the figures would be much higher.

SPECIAL CARE AND TRAINING

The Doberman excels in Obedience with large numbers achieving degrees with frequent high placements. It is not unusual to find that a Specialty winner aside from being a Champion has an Obedience suffix tacked to its name. In fact, one such animal won Best in Show (BIS) at the Westminster Kennel Club in the United

States and after that most prestigious win went on to acquire a Utility Dog (UD) degree. To put the importance of Dobermans to obedience in perspective, it is worth supporting the claim with some figures. In 1992, the AKC recorded 7,845 Companion Dogs of which 327 were Dobermans, 2,176 Companion Dog Excellents (CDXs) of which 87 were Dobermans, 842 UDs with 38 going to Dobermans. In the same year, 450 Tracking Dogs (TDs), 84 Tracking Dog Excellents (TDXs), and 84 Obedience Trial Champions (OTCH) in total were recorded. Nine TDs, 2 TDXs, and five OTCHs were credited to Dobermans. These figures speak eloquently of the priority that American Doberman fanciers place on Herr Dobermann's original thesis demanding a dog of sound mind and body. It also speaks of the dedication of those who own them.

ESSENTIALS OF THE BREED

Reference has been made to the leadership qualities of the DPCA. No facet of a parent club's responsibility is more important than its presentation of a Standard. Typically, the Doberman Standard is a concise, well-worded, positive description of the ideal Doberman. There are no references to faults. Thus, judges, breeders, and novices are presented with a positive picture starting with a discussion of

A Doberman Pinscher with uncropped ears

general appearance which defines the medium-size, square, compactly built, muscular, alert dog they seek.

Size, proportion, and substance are addressed by indicating that measured from withers to ground an ideal dog is 27 1/2 inches/69 cm and the ideal bitch is 25 1/2 inches/64 cm in height. Males should be 27 inches/68.5 cm in the United Kingdom.

The unique qualities which spell breed type and nobility for a Doberman are always present in a beautiful head. The correct bone structure, the set of the eyes, the placement of the ears and the proper scissors bite, all contribute to the long, dry look which is so essential. The Doberman ear should be cropped in countries where this is permitted or left natural (folded over just above the skull line and falling forward).

The powerful head is properly supported by an adequately well-arched neck which is in proportion to the head and the body. The pronounced withers, the short back, muscular loins and the slightly rounded croup describe the desired topline. The broad chest, with well-defined forechest, oval rib cage reaching to elbow and the well tucked-up belly define the underline. Loosely equating the breadth of hips to the breadth of body at the rib cage and the shoulders is a very important measurement. The shoulders should be at an aproximate angle of 45 degrees.

The coat and markings should be clearly defined. A Doberman's gait should be a vigorous movement which is difficult to achieve within the confinement of an indoor show ring — luckily its walk can reveal much about the way it moves.

Registry: AKC, CKC, FCI (Group 2), KC

DOGO ARGENTINO

The all white guard dog of Argentina was developed on the large cattle farms of the Pampas. It is believed that Boxers and white Bull Terriers were crossed with local guard

Dogo Argentino

dogs to develop the Dogo Argentino. This should be a hard, tough and unbribable guard dog, especially since it was often left in paddocks with beef cattle to protect them against thieves. The breed is nowadays seen at most large dog shows in Europe, except in Great Britain and Scandinavia. In Great Britain the Dogo Argentino is one of four breeds listed under the Dangerous Dogs Act introduced in 1991.

The breed stands about 26-27 1/2 inches/ 65-70 cm at the withers. Its body should be rectangular, massive and muscular but never heavy or lymphatic. The skull should be broad and also massive with a strong, fairly short muzzle. The ears are cropped quite short, but with pointed tips and the tail should be left long. The coat should be smooth with a hard texture and always white.

Registry: FCI (Group 2)

DOGUE DE BORDEAUX

Some feel this breed originated from the Molosser that the Romans brought on their expeditions. Dogs like the "Bordeaux" were praised by Varrone in A.D. 100. Others though, believe that the breed is a cross between Mastiffs and Bulldogs. Most historians think that the breed is identical with dogs the Celts used for hunting wild cattle. In fact, the Dogue d'Aquitaine, now extinct, but existing in the Middle Ages, was also thought to originate from Celtic dogs.

The breed is fairly rare outside France. It probably attracted more attention than ever before when a Bordeaux played the leading part in the American motion picture *Turner and Hooch* in 1988. The Bordeaux is kept as a companion dog and known to be very faithful.

Although it should have a calm and tranquil disposition, it is also a good guard dog.

At the withers, the breed is about 23-26 inches/58-68 cm. The Mastiff type should be evident in the rectangular, heavy and massive body. It must never look leggy or shallow. The head should be big, rounded with pronounced cheeks, and with a rather short, deep muzzle, fairly broad with an undershot bite. The ears are never cropped. The tail is left long. The coat should be smooth, soft and glossy. Its color may be any shade of red but most common is a clear, deep red with harmonizing pigment and hazel or amber eyes.

Registry: FCI (Group 2)

Dogue de Bordeaux

DRENTSE PARTRIDGE DOG/
DRENTSCHE PATRIJSHOND

The Dutch pointing and retrieving gun dog has not changed in appearance for centuries, as paintings reveal. This is a keen hunting dog that is easily trained and used for several purposes. It is very rare outside the Netherlands.

The breed is about 22-25 inches/55-63 cm at its withers. Its body should be rectangular with a slightly rounded skull and a square muzzle in profile. The coat should be thick, slightly wavy and longer on the ears and tail. Its color is white with liver-brown or orange patches that should always cover the sides of the head and ears.

Registry: FCI (Group 7)

Drentse Partridge Dog

DREVER

The Swedish scenthound was developed from the German Bracke, and the Westfalische Dachsbracke. This breed appeared in Sweden in 1910 under the name of Westfalische Dachsbracke. Twenty years later with the increase of red deer in Sweden, the Bracke proved to be an excellent deer tracker. The demand for the breed rose rapidly. In 1947 the Swedish Kennel Club declared the breed Swedish and the breed name was decided by a newspaper contest. The winning name, Drever. comes from the Swedish word for the type of hunt (*drev*) where scenthounds drive the prey toward the hunter. The Drever is strictly a hunting dog and considered one of the best scenthounds in Sweden. The breed is little known outside Scandinavia.

The male is about 12 1/2-15 inches/32-38 cm at the withers and the female 11-14 inches/30-36 cm. The Drever is rather long in the body with sturdy, fairly short, straight legs. It should have a robust appearance and never look elegant. The coat should be short, close lying and rather coarse in texture. Most hound colors are allowed as long as they have white markings. Most common is any shade of red, with or without a black saddle. All white and liver brown are disqualifying faults.

Drever

Registry: FCI (Group 6)

DUNKER

The Norwegian scenthound takes its name from Lieutenant William Dunker who, with his dappled dog Alarm, developed the breed in the nineteenth century. The Dunker is strictly a hunting dog used for hunting hare. The merle gene used to give the breed problems with white puppies being both blind and deaf. This resulted in a change in the Standard in 1925 which permitted black and tan to be included as a color. The Dunker is only seen in Scandinavia and even there it is rare.

The Dunker is about 18 1/2-22 inches/47-55 cm at the withers. Coloring is this breed's most significant point. This should either be a dappling of faded bluish beige or a diluted black-and-tan. Both varieties also have white markings — as a blaze or on the throat, chest, feet, legs or tip of the tail.

Dunker

Registry: FCI (Group 6)

DUTCH SHEPHERD DOG/ HOLLANDSE HERDERSHOND

The Dutch Shepherd Dog closely resembles the breeds that were used to create the German Shepherd Dog. It also looks very much like the Belgian Sheepdog. The breed was saved when a breed club was formed in 1898. Although the breed comes in three varieties of coat texture, it is very much one breed in all other respects. It is still used as a herder for sheep but its ability for all types of work have made the breed very popular for military and police work in the Netherlands. It is considered a good companion and guard dog and one that needs to be kept occupied with useful tasks.

The breed is about 22-24 inches/55-62 cm at the withers and its body should be strongly built. The head should be fairly long with pricked, high-set ears. The tail is long and carried low or straight out in the same fashion as the German Shepherd. There are three different coat textures. The first is smooth with a close, flat lying, coarse-textured coat that is longer on the neck, back of the thighs and on the tail. The second type is also long, neither curly nor wavy, with a considerably longer coat on the neck, the backside of the legs and tail. The wirehaired type has a very wiry, open curled coat on the body, and a shorter one on the legs, with eyebrows, whiskers and a beard. Color in all three varieties of Dutch Shepherd should be brindle, with or without a black mask; the base is light-colored and may be anything from pale fawn to deep red or grayish with black stripes. The brindling is very dark with its broad, black stripes on the light-colored base. This type of dark brindling is usually called black-brindle. The color has, at times, been incorrectly described as black with light stripes. It is not unusual to have the pepper-and-salt effect in black-brindle dogs that have a wiry coat-texture. And if the brindling is very mixed and somewhat light the color could look steel-blue.

Registry: FCI (Group 1)

Dutch Shepherd Dog

DUTCH SMOUSHOND/ HOLLANDSE SMOUSHOND

This Dutch Schnauzer breed is said to be related to the German Schnauzers, imported into the Netherlands in the nineteenth century. The breed almost faced extinction after World War II but was revived and had its breed status restored in the 1970s. It is very rare even in the Netherlands.

The height at the withers is about 13 1/2-16 1/2 inches/35-42 cm. The body should be broad and deep, with a slightly rounded skull and not too long a muzzle. The eyes should be round and the ears triangular. The coat should be shaggy, not very long on the legs, and with a rough topcoat, and eyebrows, whiskers and a beard. The color may be all shades of pale fawn and light red, with black pigmentation.

Registry: FCI (Group 2)

Dutch Smoushond

ENGLISH TOY SPANIEL/ KING CHARLES SPANIEL

ORIGIN AND DEVELOPMENT

Small specimens of Springer Spaniel type have been in existence for hundreds of years in Britain. Small dogs, which might have been culled had their only fate been as working dogs, found that they were treasured as companion dogs and selective breeding soon ensured that Toy Spaniels were established purely as companions with true breeding. It has been suggested that red-and-white and black-and-white dogs of Toy Spaniel type arrived from China via Europe, and that dogs of both colors arrived in Great Britain with Henrietta of Orléans, Charles II's sister.

It is believed that the black-and-tan color did not appear until later, and the ruby later still. Mary, Queen of Scots was reputed to keep a pack of Toy Spaniels, and Charles II became so taken with them as a breed that they took his name. It was suggested that the monarch was much keener on playing with his Toy Spaniels than minding the affairs of the country! Following the king's overt royal patronage of the breed, the King Charles Spaniel became a firm favorite of the aristocracy, and many noblemen and women were painted in the presence of their King Charles Spaniels by the likes of Gainsborough, Rubens and Rembrandt.

Gradually the breed was developed in a slightly different direction from its working Spaniel ancestry. Possibly through the introduc-

A Blenheim English Toy Spaniel. The breed is known as the King Charles Spaniel in the United Kingdom.

tion of other long-established Toy breeds of eastern origin, such as the Pekingese, Japanese Chin or Pug, the body became wider and more cobby, and the heads rather more extreme. Their ultra-short muzzles, with lavish cushioning and very pronounced dome-skulls became highly prized. Indeed, it was the determination to create the "new" King Charles head which created something of a stigma for the breed in years to come. For a long time, King Charles breeders seemed obsessed with head qualities, at the expense of virtually all other aspects of the dog. In fact, until recently the breed Standard consisted only of "head and skull, eyes, ears, coat and color" apart from a brief description of the "general appearance." At one time it was commonplace to see exhibitors of King Charles Spaniels competing in the show ring, with the dogs held in their arms, ever keen to draw the attention of the judge to their magnificent head qualities. It is said that some dogs received top honors without ever having actually proved that they could walk.

In the 1970s, the King Charles began to attract breeders who failed to see why the King Charles should not have to walk and show like other breeds. They began to place greater emphasis on sound construction and bolder temperaments, perhaps at the expense of some of the classical heads which had hitherto been produced. In the United States, the breed is known as the English Toy Spaniel and is shown as two varieties — the Blenheim and the Prince Charles (tricolor) competing together, and the King Charles (black-and-tan) and ruby constituting the other variety.

TEMPERAMENT

Many generations as the ultimate lap dog has given the King Charles a rather "clinging" character, and they are perfectly happy to sit at their owner's side, with little exercise. This is why they are much favored by elderly dog-lovers. They are less outgoing than their Cavalier cousins and need time to get to know strangers. Group placings are now not unheard of for the breed.

HEALTH MATTERS

Generally they are trouble-free but patella luxation occurs quite often within the breed. Due to the conformation, Caesarean sections are sometimes necessary to deliver puppies.

SPECIAL CARE AND TRAINING

The King Charles is very much a pet and as such it retains a certain independence. It will not carry out orders automatically, but the social niceties of life seem to come quite naturally to it. Grooming is minimal, but the ears and eyes should be inspected regularly and the coat given a thorough brushing and combing at least once a week.

ADAPTABILITY

The King Charles was bred for the fireside rather than the farmyard and its character will only develop if it can enjoy constant human companionship.

ESSENTIALS OF THE BREED

Weighing between 8-14 pounds/3.5-6.5 kg, the King Charles should be a square, cobby dog with a well-developed rib cage, good bones and substance for its size. Height is not specified in the Standard but will usually be about 10 inches/25 cm at the withers. The coat should be long, silky and straight with a slight wave being acceptable. The head remains a major characteristic of the breed. There should a noticeable dome, the skull being well filled over the eyes. The nose should be black with large open nostrils, and well turned up between the eyes which are large, dark, set well apart and with a soft intelligent expression. The ears are set on low, further accentuating the domed skull, long, and well feathered. The standard colors are Blenheim (rich red and white), tricolor, black-and-tan and ruby. Both Blenheims and tricolors should have the color well broken up with white. Tail docking is now becoming less commonplace.

Registry: AKC, CKC, FCI (Group 9), KC

ENTLEBUCHER SENNENHUND

The Entlebucher Sennenhund was developed in Switzerland and is believed to have originated from Roman cattle dogs.

The Entlebucher Sennenhund was developed in Entlebuch in Switzerland and is believed to originate from cattle dogs left by the Romans. The modern Entlebucher was recognized in 1889, but it was hardly known. In 1913 four exhibits were shown and after World War I there were no traces of the breed. After intensive searching all over the country, sixteen dogs were found in 1927. Those sixteen are the foundation of the modern Entlebucher. The breed is used for driving cattle and guarding property.

The Entlebucher should be 16-20 inches/ 40-50 cm high at the withers. It has a rectangular body with a natural bobtail about 3 inches/ 7.5 cm. Its ears should be triangular, hanging close to the cheeks. The coat should be harsh, close fitting and black with symmetrical tan and white markings.

Registry: FCI (Group 2)

ÉPAGNEUL DE PONT-AUDEMER

The Épagneul de Pont-Audemer, near extinction after World War I, was revived with the help of Irish Water Spaniels, which it resembles.

This French gun dog originates from local Spaniels and Irish Water Spaniels and takes its name from the city of Pont-Audemer in Normandy. After World War I it was almost extinct but it was revived with the help of Irish Water Spaniels which it resembles except that it is lighter in build and usually has a docked tail. Even in France, it is very rare.

The height at its withers should be about 20 1/2-23 inches/52-58 cm. The coat should be decidedly wavy on the body, longer and curly on the ears and short and smooth on the face and front of the forelegs. Its color should be liver brown with or without slight roan markings which should be very finely speckled to give a grayish shade.

Registry: FCI (Group 7)

ÉPAGNEUL FRANÇAIS

The French Spaniel, sometimes also called the French Setter, is an old breed that is still very much used as a pointing gun dog. It has hardly changed in type since the fourteenth century when it was described by Gaston Phébus (1331-91), an authority on hunting dogs at the time. The French Spaniel is considered a gentle, calm and very thorough field working dog that also retrieves with expertise. Despite all these superlatives, the breed is rarely seen outside France.

At its withers, the breed should stand about 21-24 inches/54-62 cm high. It resembles the English Setter but is slightly heavier and more rectangular in body. The coat should be soft and silky, lie flat or be slightly wavy with a longer coat on its ears, chest, the backside of the legs and on its tail. It should be white with rather large liver brown patches and ticking but not so abundant as to form belton markings, as in the English Setter.

Registry: FCI (Group 7)

Épagneul Français

ÉPAGNEUL PICARD

The French "all-round" hunting dog from the region of Picardy is a former variety of the Épagneul Français. The first "Picards" were exhibited in 1904 and the breed club was established in 1907. The Épagneul Picard is a hardy, versatile breed that despite its many good features and an even temperament is very rare, even in France.

The height at its withers is about 22-24 inches/ 55-62 cm. Its conformation is very much like the Épagneul Français but its head is stronger with a more rounded and broader skull. The coat should be slightly wavy, lying close on the body, soft but not silky and with wavy fringes on the ears, backside of the legs and on the tail. Its color should be liver roan with brown patches on its body as well as on the sides of the skull and ears. Bright tan markings are essential.

Registry: FCI (Group 7)

Épagneul Picard

ÉPAGNEUL BLEU DE PICARDIE

The French gun dog from the region of Picardy is a variety of Épagneul Picard. The infusion of English Setters with blue belton coloring and

Épagneul Bleu de Picardie

possibly of Gordon Setters is said to be the breed's origin. It was recognized in 1921 and the breed club was established in the same year. Its speciality is working with wildfowl and it is also known for having an even temperament. The breed is very rare, even in France.

The dog is 22 1/2-24 inches/57-60 cm at its withers and females are slightly smaller. The breed is similar to the Épagneul Picard but its head resembles that of the Gordon Setter. Its coat should be slightly wavy, lying close on the body, soft but not silky and with wavy fringes on the ears, the backside of the legs and on the tail. Its color should be a dark blue roan with large black patches on the body as well as on the sides of the skull and ears.

Registry: FCI (Group 7)

ERDÉLYI KOPÓ

The Hungarian scenthound, which has been called the Transylvanian Hound in some literature, originates from east European scent-hounds. This breed is very rare and, although the Fédération Cynologique Internationale only states one Standard for the breed, it can be found in two sizes. The variety with long legs is too fast for deer hunting, but the variety with shorter legs is said to be an excellent deer hunter. The breed is also known to be tough and wild boar tracking comes naturally to the Erdélyi Kopó.

At its withers, the breed is about 22-25 1/2 inches/55-65 cm, the lower variety 18-20 inches/45-50 cm. Its coat should be smooth, harsh and thick. Coloring in the taller variety is black-and-tan with slight white markings. The smaller variety is usually red grizzle with slight white markings.

Registry: FCI (Group 6)

The Erdélyi Kopó, or Hungarian Scenthound, is very rare. It has sometimes been called the Transylvanian Hound.

ESKIMO DOG/GREENLAND DOG/ GRØNLANDSHUND

The Eskimo Dog's origin probably extends to the vast island of Greenland. Here, for hundreds of years, nomadic Eskimo tribes have traveled from the Beaufort Sea in the west to the Denmark passage in the east. Sled dogs were, and still are in many places, an essential ingredient for the Eskimos' survival. These large, Arctic spitzes had to be extremely hardy to tolerate severe cold. They are often left to sleep outside in the snow and are only fed by Eskimos during the winter period. In summer they usually have to provide for themselves.

The Eskimo dog is considered to be half wild dog. This breed is tough and has great persistence. They thrive if they have a purposeful assignment like hauling sleds. Although fairly well domesticated in some parts of the world, this breed should not be first choice for a pet, unless the owner is prepared to give it lots of time and exercise. The dogs thrive outdoors and if given the choice will opt for sleeping outside, whatever the weather conditions. The Eskimo Dog is very self-sufficient. It has been accustomed to looking after itself for hundred of years, in a climate where only the hardiest and fittest survived. This is how it acquired its temperament.

At the withers, males should be over 24 inches/60 cm and females over 22 inches/ 55 cm. The Eskimo Dog is not as heavy as the Alaskan Malamute, nor as racy as the Siberian Husky. The breed's make-up combines strength with speed. Its head should be wedge shaped with a strong muzzle, decidedly slanted eyes and small, pricked ears set well apart. The tail should be carried over the back in a loose curl. Its coat should be quite long, very thick, standing out from the body and with an almost impenetrable undercoat. All colors and color patterns are permitted.

Registry: CKC, FCI (Group 5), KC

Eskimo Dog

ESTRELA MOUNTAIN DOG/ CÃO DA SERRA DA ESTRELA

This breed comes from northern Portugal, and carries the name of the region. It is thought to have evolved mainly from Roman Mastiffs. Peasant farmers used it to guard sheep and goats.

Although of Mastiff origin, the Estrela is not a massively boned dog and it should be agile rather than cumbersome. It is supremely loyal to its owners. It is intelligent and very alert but it can be extremely stubborn.

Its head should be long and powerful, with a muzzle and skull of equal length. The skull is slightly rounded, the occiput noticeable, and although the muzzle tapers it should never be sharp or pointed. The nose and tip should be black and the roof of the mouth heavily pigmented with black. The eyes should be amber, black rimmed and oval. The eyebrows should be well developed. The ears are small, triangular and rounded at the tips.

The Estrela should be short backed with high withers and well-sprung ribs. Males should stand 25 1/2-28 1/2 inches/65-72 cm and bitches 24 1/2-27 inches/62-68.5 cm. Under the neck, especially in males, there is often a thick tuft of hair, the trace of a defense mechanism, designed to thwart attacking wolves.

The breed should move freely at a purposeful trot. There are two coat types, both with an undercoat. The color may be fawn, brindle or wolf gray. A black muzzle is highly desirable.

Registry: FCI (Group 2), KC

Estrela Mountain Dog

EURASIER

The German spitz breed Eurasier is the result of one man's work. A German breeder, Julius Wipfel, decided that he wanted to create a beautiful Euro-Asian spitz. He was a great admirer of Professor Konrad Lorenz and very impressed with the professor's work in crossing the Chow Chow with German Shepherd Dogs in order to study their behavior patterns. Wipfel set to work in the middle of the 1960s by crossing Chow Chow males (he started with two reds and one black) with four smaller female Wolfspitzes (equivalent to the Keeshond in some countries). Puppies selected for further breeding were true to type, and from somewhere in between the two breeds emerged what became known as the Wolf Chow. One Samoyed male was also part of the creation.

The breed was recognized in 1973 under the name of Eurasier. It is a wonderful family dog. It loves children, has a gentle nature and insists on being part of the family. It is considered a pleasant companion and good guard dog. The Eurasier has recently gained new interest and may be seen in most European countries, although Germany and Switzerland still have them in greatest numbers.

At its withers, the breed stands about 19-24 inches/48-60 cm. The type resembles both the Chow Chow and Wolfspitz and it has a blue, or partially blue, tongue as part of its Chow Chow inheritance. Its coat should be long but not as abundant as in the breeds that formed the Eurasier. The color is usually any shade of red or wolf gray but black or black-and-tan are also permissible.

Registry: FCI (Group 5)

Eurasier

FILA BRASILEIRO

The Brazilian Mastiff originates most probably from Spanish and Portuguese Mastiffs. It is likely to have been crossed with local dogs as

well but the Mastiff features are predominant. The breed was used both for guarding flocks and property, and the breed is best known for its reputation as a fierce guard dog. Although it can be seen at most European shows, it is considered rare. Its breed Standard states that judges should never attempt to handle the breed. In its native South America, dogs will often be seen in the ring with two or more handlers per dog for maximum control. The Fila Brasileiro is listed under the Dangerous Dogs Act of 1991 in Great Britain.

The breed is about 24-28 inches/60-70 cm at the withers. It has a heavy, rectangular body — the backline should slope behind the withers and then rise over the loins and end in a sloping croup. The ears and tail should be kept undocked. Pacing is typical of the breed. The coat should be smooth and hard. Although all colors are permitted, it is usually brindle or fawn, with or without white markings.

Fila Brasileiro

Registry: FCI (Group 2)

FINNISH HOUND/SUOMENAJOKOIRA

The Finnish scenthound originates from crosses of Swedish, Swiss and Russian hounds and Foxhounds that took place in the 1870s. The breed is a hunting dog used to hunt hare. About 3,000 puppies are registered yearly in Finland, but the breed is rare outside Scandinavia.

The height at its withers is about 20 1/2-24 inches/52-61 cm. The breed is very like the Swedish Hound, Hamiltonstövare, apart from being slightly taller and with a longer head and ears. Its coat should be smooth, hard and glossy, and tricolored with deep, rich tan, black saddle and white markings.

Registry: FCI (Group 6)

Finnish Hound

FINNISH SPITZ/SUOMENPYSTYKORVA

Origin and Development

The Finnish Spitz (or Finsk Spets), the national dog of Finland, was recognized in 1892 by the Finnish Kennel Club. It is one of Europe's most ancient breeds and, because it used to be a hunting companion to the Finns, was once called the Finnish Hunting Dog, as well as the Barking Bird Dog. Today the breed is used to hunt forest birds, squirrel and sometimes elk. In the nineteenth century, the Finnish Spitz accompanied northern bear hunters. By all accounts, the dog was always courageous and unafraid when confronting bear. In the forest, when the dog has spotted a bird, its barks loudly or yodels, to attract the hunter's attention. The dog also points at the prey, swaying its tail back and forth which has a mesmerizing effect.

Finnish Spitz

The breed is recognized by all the international kennel clubs.

Temperament

The Finnish Spitz is independent, reserved, cautious and sometimes aloof. According to some breeders, it is not a cuddly puppy that likes being petted and fondled, but is rather catlike in its reserved affections. Sensitive and strong-minded, the Finnish Spitz is very loyal to its human family.

Health Matters

Health problems are rare in this breed although some incidences of hip dysplasia, luxating patellas and weak elbows have been found. However, most breeders agree that the Finnish Spitz is relatively free of genetically inherited diseases.

Special Care and Training

As the Finnish Spitz comes primarily from a hunting dog background, it needs careful supervision when exercising. It is best to walk it on a long leash or it should be allowed to run freely in a securely fenced yard. If left to its own devices, the Finnish Spitz is likely to take off on a hunting expedition. The breed should have basic obedience training so that it will come when called. Its coat is easy to care for, and should be kept clean, brushed and free of ticks and fleas.

Adaptability

The Finnish Spitz is adaptable to both town and country as long as it has sufficient room to move and exercise. If it is a house dog, it loves to be walked. As a pet, it is a faithful friend, a guardian of the home that barks at the sounds of an intruder. It loves being with children.

Essentials of the Breed

The Finnish Spitz is a slightly off-square dog, of medium size (males are 17 1/2-20 inches/44-50 cm, bitches 15 1/2-18 inches/39-45 cm) with bright red to apricot coloring. Its small, sharply pointed ears, medium-sized dark almond eyes, and lushly coated tail give it an alert, appealing foxlike expression. Its back should be level and strong, hocks rather straight and its coat moderately harsh and short. Its movement is agile, gaiting quickly at a trot. Its striking color, bold appearance and lively gait make it an impressive dog.

Registry: AKC, CKC, FCI (Group 5), KC

FOXHOUNDS — AMERICAN FOXHOUND

Origin and Development

The American Foxhound lived on the American continent before it became known as the United States of America. Many settlers brought these handsome hounds with them when they emigrated. George Washington was a great fancier and kept a famous pack at Mount Vernon, including some imports from France.

The American hounds were developed to chase fox, coyote and deer. The English hound was developed mainly as a pack hound (large numbers hunted together and formed a pack) to be followed by hunters on heavyweight horses. American hounds were used not only in this way but also as lone hunters, turned loose to hunt a fox by itself or to work in small packs, particularly in the mountains of Tennessee and Kentucky. These original dogs were working and running hounds that were then developed as bench show hounds as well.

Temperament

Although not bred to be a family pet, the occasional hound that has been well socialized as a young pup will adapt to family life. The

American Foxhound by nature is not aggressive.

HEALTH MATTERS

The American Foxhound is a very natural breed and thus it is free of many heritable defects. The hips should be X-rayed after the hound's second birthday if the animal is to be used for breeding.

SPECIAL CARE AND TRAINING

The American Foxhound must have brisk daily exercise and diligent training. The hound must be confined and not allowed to run free without supervision, as indeed no dog should. Of course, good nutrition is always essential.

ADAPTABILITY

This breed is inclined to roam but it will adapt to any environment if it is cared for properly.

Much of the breed's adaptability depends on its early upbringing. If it is totally kennel raised, as most pack hounds are, it will always be bonded to other hounds and not humans. If it is socialized early, especially by about seven weeks when the dog-human bond is thought to be made, then it should be a good pet and watchdog throughout its life.

ESSENTIALS OF THE BREED

Distinguished from its English cousins, the American Foxhound has finer bones, more leg length, more angulation in the hindquarters and a distinctive well arched loin. The American Foxhound always has natural (not rounded) ears. Its eye expression is soft and slightly pleading and its voice or bay is always melodious.

Registry: AKC, CKC, FCI (Group 6)

American Foxhound

FOXHOUNDS — ENGLISH FOXHOUND

As its name implies, the English Foxhound originated in England where it was bred to follow fox as well as stag. It is heavy with round, rather than bladed bone, handsome in head, with hard feet, moderate angles at either end and a wonderful tail with evident brush (longer hair at the end). The breed gallops, stays and easily jumps fences and streams as necessary. The dogs have a magnificent voice when in pursuit of quarry. Designed and reared by horsemen to be followed on horseback, English Foxhounds were and remain beautiful animals.

Bred initially as workers, the tendency was to breed English Foxhounds without worrying about color, size, coat pattern or texture. As

English Foxhound

time passed, the aim was focused on a pack of hounds that were tremendous workers and that had a level of quality and resemblance in color, type and size. The coat made the pack uniform in all respects so that members of the pack could be readily identified by their appearance.

As a rule, the English Foxhound should not be relegated to being just a household pet because it is bred for a purpose. It is a good sized hound, accustomed to exercise, work and to live with other hounds. The occasional dog that is chosen as a companion must be well socialized, made to feel that its human family is its pack, and must have a great deal of exercise and attention.

The breed taken as a whole is remarkably healthy. This is mainly because breeders cull out any weak, undersized or shy specimens at an early age.

Its coat is a shiny, hard hound coat, needing normal care and brushing as it tends to shed as the seasons change. The nails of the breed need attention as do its teeth and ears. Hard biscuits usually take care of the tooth tartar problem, and exercise on a hard surface suffices to keep the nails short. Without this the nails of the English Foxhound will need monthly attention.

The breed is handsome, houndy, with great bone and substance. It should have beautiful hard cat feet and a glorious, proudly carried tail (or stern), well furnished on the back with coarse hair. The breed has an appealing head and eye.

There are many hound colors, the most popular being tan marked with black saddle and white trim, though lemon or red with white trim is found equally often. The breed always has a rich, deep mellow voice. Its ears should be left natural or "rounded" shortly after birth.

Registry: AKC, CKC, FCI (Group 6), KC

FOXHOUNDS — WELSH FOXHOUND

While not recognized by any of the major controlling bodies, and consequently not seen at dog shows, the Welsh Foxhound still exists in its native Wales, where it thrives in a small number of specialist packs. In size and stature, the breed is similar to its English cousin, with its most distinctive feature being its coarse, shaggy wire coat. This is possibly due to crossing with Otterhounds.

A free moving and unexaggerated hound, with well-developed scenting abilities and voice, the Welsh Foxhound is very much a pack hound which will resent domesticity. Its small band of *aficionados* has determined that the breed should be preserved in its natural state, performing the tasks for which it was bred.

Registry: The breed is not recognized by AKC, CKC, FCI or KC.

Welsh Foxhound

FOX TERRIERS

ORIGIN AND DEVELOPMENT

The Fox Terrier has two varieties — the Wire and the Smooth. In the United States, they are considered two separate breeds. The breed was initially developed as a hunt terrier, and the precise antiquity of the breed is difficult to resolve. Long before dog shows began in the mid-nineteenth century, there were numerous strains of terrier, some having been carefully bred to go to ground, seeking their prey — be it fox or other predacious vermin. These were commonly referred to as Fox Terriers. Their predominating color was white, because occasionally colored dogs out working were mistakenly worried by hounds.

As a pure breed, the Fox Terrier first came to the notice of the public around 1860. In the 1870 entries of Fox Terriers at dog shows were remarkably high. It is recorded that at a Nottingham show then, some 276 Fox Terriers were entered in the three scheduled classes. Up until this time, both coats of Fox Terrier had been classified as one breed, with the Smooth tending to dominate competitions. However, in 1876 the Fox Terrier Club was founded and the two coats were given separate registers. The breed club issued the first written breed Standard, initially one Standard with an added rider characterizing coats. Subsequently, separate Standards were introduced. Contempt was shown by some judges for what was considered

Smooth Fox Terrier

the "barbering" of exhibition Wires, and some were exceedingly severe in both their judgement and comment.

Today the presentation of the show Wire is the product of extreme skill. The breed has changed considerably in only a few generations, and some might suggest that the head of the Wire has become somewhat exaggerated. Nevertheless, selective breeding has enhanced their general balance and appeal. The Smooth remains very much the same type as its predecessors.

TEMPERAMENT

The Fox Terrier is eager, extremely alert, always "on the tiptoe of expectation" and yet amiable. It makes the ideal family dog and utterly trustworthy companion. Its acute hearing enables it to warn of approaching visitors long before they arrive. Being of an ideal size, Fox Terriers can easily be "gathered up" into the arms, giving further moral support should this be required. The Wire is a more precocious, spirited and sharper character than the Smooth. Both enjoy free exercise and will walk many miles without tiring.

HEALTH MATTERS

The Fox Terrier is a hardy breed, suffering few ills. It generally has a long lifespan. The Wire, because of its thicker coat, may be disposed to a form of eczema, or hot-spot skin conditions in summer, but a common cause of such a condition may simply be an incorrect diet. Lack of regular grooming may well be another cause.

SPECIAL CARE AND TRAINING

The Smooth naturally sheds twice yearly, normally in the spring and fall. Minimal trimming is required in the show dog. However, the companion Wire requires stripping to remove its dead and old coat, usually twice yearly. Clipping is not advised, nor is it acceptable to the purist, for this eventually ruins both the natural color and wire coat texture.

The degree of show preparation required in

Wire Fox Terrier

the Wire is exceedingly specialized. Grooming should be carried out on a regular basis. The Wire can be kept tidy between trims with a brush and comb and an occasional bath. The Smooth will also benefit from an occasional bath, but in between times a wipe down with a moistened chamois leather quickly achieves the desired result. A useful aid for grooming the Smooth is a dimpled rubber hound glove. This not only removes loose hair but tones the skin and muscle. The Smooth tends to be more easily trained in routine social obedience than its Wire cousin.

Teeth need regular attention — brushing will help to keep them clean and the mouth fresh. Nails need to be filed on a weekly basis to preserve the shape of the close tight foot.

ADAPTABILITY

It is often said, "Once a Fox Terrier lover, always a Fox Terrier lover," such are the endearing qualities of this smart and alert breed. It adapts to household routines very easily and makes a useful guard dog. Little escapes the attention of the Fox Terrier. It appreciates human company and thoroughly enjoys family life, but it is not a dog to be allowed loose among livestock or poultry.

ESSENTIALS OF THE BREED

The Fox Terrier is a cleverly made terrier, reminiscent of a short-backed hunter, standing over a lot of ground, and basically the same breed Standard applies to both varieties. However, the purist will recognize the infinite differences in head shape. As mentioned before, some think that the Wire head has become somewhat exaggerated. The Smooth head remains very much in the same mold as the early dogs, its head being V-shaped. The expression of any terrier is an essential characteristic, none more so than in the Fox Terrier. The shape of its head, placement, shape, size and color of eyes, and carriage of its ears determines the correct expression. The jaw should have a punishing strength with a scissors bite. The forequarters and neckline should be clean and muscular, the front legs dead straight, finishing in round, tight feet. The mature chest should be deep, not broad, the back short and showing strength without slackness. The loin should show muscular strength and be slightly arched. The hindquarters are strong and muscular, the hocks well let down with a good turn of stifle. The tail is normally docked, is of good strength, well set on and carried gaily. The gait should be straight and free flowing, with the stifles and hocks showing no inclination to turn in or out. Correct movement confirms correct conformation. Driving power from well flexed hindquarters is desirable.

In color, white should predominate — the Fox Terrier can be all white, or white with tan, black, or black-and-tan markings. Brindle, red or liver markings are highly undesirable. The Smooth has a softer undercoat and a topcoat which should be straight, flat and smooth, yet hard and abundant. The correct Smooth coat is virtually waterproof. The Wire has two coats; a softer undercoat, with a topcoat of dense hair on the back and quarters which should be harsher than that on the sides of the body. The hair on the jaw should be crisp and of sufficient length to impart the appearance of strength and character. The leg furnishings should be dense and hard. Ideally the male Fox Terrier should not exceed 15 inches/ 39 cm at the withers, with bitches measuring slightly less. In hard show conditions, the breed should weigh up to 18 pounds/8 kg, although many Fox Terriers — if not the majority — may be slightly above this stipulated limit.

Registry: AKC, CKC, FCI (Group 3), KC

FRENCH BULLDOG

ORIGIN AND DEVELOPMENT

The French Bulldog is, to some extent, a smaller version of the larger, more exaggerated English Bulldog. The Frenchie is very adaptable and has been around since the late 1800s. There is disagreement about its origin but the French claim that the breed is theirs. It is in the Non-Sporting Group in the United States.

TEMPERAMENT

The breed is happiest as a one-man or one-woman dog. It often behaves like a child and so it tends to compete with other pets as well as with children. It is a distinctive dog, well loved by Frenchie fanciers, that is best as a pet for the elderly rather than those with a young family.

HEALTH MATTERS

Since the breed has a very short nose as well as foreface, it tends to snore and has some breathing problems. It is very susceptible to heat stroke. Eye injuries are common due to the size and prominence of the eyes. Short coated, it is easily kept clean and has few skin problems. Its large erect bat ears do not usually allow inner ear problems to develop.

SPECIAL CARE AND TRAINING

The teeth should be kept clean (brushing is an option) and nails kept filed or clipped weekly. The Frenchie should be encouraged to be friendly with all members of the family and not to devote itself to just one person. Its short coat does not give much protection from the elements, so it should wear some sort of garment when walked in wet weather.

ADAPTABILITY

The Frenchie's size makes it suited to small apartments, yet it is an energetic dog that is always keen to roam in large areas, so it is suited to most lifestyles. It is a good watchdog and does just as well in the town or country.

ESSENTIALS OF THE BREED

A bulldog shape in small size, the French Bulldog is generally about 12 inches/30 cm tall with a relatively short back which rises over the loin. The head is large and square with big bat ears and round sharp eyes; the muzzle is short, broad and deep. The Frenchie has a short tail. The skin is pliable, covered with a short shiny coat of brindle, fawn, or white with brindle markings. Any pigment should be black, although lighter pigment is permissible in fawns. France and most of the FCI member countries do not accept fawn. Black-and-tan, black-and-white and liver colors are not acceptable, nor is a weight of more than 28 pounds/12 kg.

Registry: AKC, CKC, FCI (Group 9), KC

French Bulldog

GALGO ESPAÑOL

This Spanish sighthound is believed to have inhabited the Iberian peninsula since ancient times. It is still used for coursing hare and rabbit but is mainly kept as a companion dog. The Galgo can be seen in great numbers in Spain but rarely elsewhere.

The breed stands about 24-27 1/2 inches/60-70 cm at the withers. It resembles the Greyhound in appearance but is finer in build. Its coat should be smooth or semi-wired and all colors are permissible, although it is usually, brindle, fawn, red or black, with or without white markings.

Registry: FCI (Group 10)

Galgo Español

GASCON-SAINTONGEOIS HOUNDS

In the southwest of France, north of the Gironde Bay, the River Dordogne and the province of Gascogne is the old province Saintonge. This is the birthplace of huge packs of the most typical of the old, large French hounds, the Saintongeois.

Only three hounds survived the French Revolution. They came into the ownership of Baron de Carayon-la-Tour who decided to cross them with Grand Bleu de Gascognes owned by Baron de Ruble. The gentlemen continued to mix the lines because the results were so good. The mottled hounds (Bleu de Gascogne) went to de Ruble's kennels and the white with black ticking (the color of the original Saintongeois) were retained by the Carayon-la-Tours kennels where they were eventually given the name Gascon-Saintongeois.

The breed's hunting ability is said to be excellent. The Gascon-Saintongeois Hound is also meant to have a very good nose and an excellent voice.

The height of the Gascon-Saintongeois Hound at its withers is about 24-27 1/2 inches/ 60-70 cm. The head should be long and narrow with a prominent occipital bone. The muzzle is slightly convex and the lips pendulous. The ears should be set very low and be very long, fine and folded.

Its color should be white — the body is often

Grand Gascon-Saintongeois

covered in black ticking and may also have a few large black patches. Each side of the head should have a large black patch that covers the ears and goes down to the jowl. There should be pale tan markings over the eyes and on the cheeks, edging the black. Pale tan may also be found as mottles on the lower part of the legs.

In some parts of this southwestern French region packs of smaller hounds were used and they eventually became a breed of their own — the Petit Gascon-Saintongeois. Their height at the withers should be about 19-20 inches/ 48-50 cm.

Registry: FCI (Group 6)

GERMAN HUNT TERRIER/ DEUTSCHE JAGDTERRIER

The German Hunt Terrier was developed in the 1920s by a very precise method. The need for them came about because of the inefficient burrowing work that the terriers of the time were performing. Hunters generally agreed that they could do with a terrier that was hardy, keen and had sufficient toughness to go to ground to tackle badger and fox without hesitation.

Guidelines for the breeding program were set up and it turned out that they needed more of an all-round terrier. Under very systematic rules, breeds like the Welsh, Lakeland and Fox Terriers were used, and it is believed that the Pinscher as well as some Dachsbracke might have been involved in creating the new breed.

By the 1950s the type was set and it had all the working ability that the hunters could have wished for. The German Hunt Terrier is used for hunting wild boar, deer, fox, badger and even forest birds. The breed is strictly a hunting dog with a tough temperament. Although well established among hunters in Europe and Scandinavia, its numbers are not great.

The breed's height at the withers should be not less than 13 inches/33 cm and should not exceed 16 inches/40 cm. The body of the German Hunt Terrier should be rectangular and never have the reach of its British ancestors. The head should be long but not as narrow as

in the Fox Terrier; the muzzle should have very strong, punishing jaws. The coat may be either smooth or very wiry and short. It should be either black, grayish black or liver brown with tan markings. The grayish black color is often seen in dogs with very wiry coats.

Registry: KC, FCI (Group 3)

German Hunt Terrier

GERMAN POINTERS - GERMAN SHORTHAIRED POINTER

ORIGIN AND DEVELOPMENT

As its name suggests, the German Shorthaired Pointer originated in Germany — it was known as early as the seventeenth century. This manmade breed was specifically bred as a hunting dog, in an age and country where hunting was an important source of food. The old German Pointer was produced by crossing the old Spanish Pointer with the Bloodhound. This resulted in a bulky, houndlike dog that was not only used for rabbit and birds but was also useful for trailing larger game.

By 1872, breeders were able to produce litters sufficiently to type to enable them to be registered in the German Kennel Club's Stud Book. The parent club not only set physical standards on the breed, but insisted on standards of performance in the field as well. Great emphasis is still placed on the true dual-purpose of the breed today.

In 1925, Dr. Charles Thornton of Montana set up a kennel of the breed in the United States and by 1930 the American Kennel Club had recognized it. The breed was first seen at the Westminster Kennel Club dog show in 1937, when three were entered, and the first national Specialty was held in March 1941 in conjunction with the International Kennel Club of Chicago's all-breeds event. The British Kennel Club allowed the first German Shorthaired Pointer Club to be registered in 1951 and in 1953 two classes were scheduled for the breed at Cruft's dog show, when seven dogs were entered.

In Germany, the most popular hunting dog is the German Wirehaired Pointer, but in both America and Great Britain the popularity of the Shorthaired has proved greater than that of its cousin. It cannot be stressed too highly that the Shorthaired and Wirehaired are two distinct breeds. They are not simply the same breed with two different coat types. The Shorthaired should have a short, firm back and the Wirehaired a longer back. Their temperaments — indeed their whole attitude to life — tends to be different too. In Germany, emphasis is put strongly on the working side, and dogs must be qualified in both the field and the show ring to be used in breeding programs to this day.

The overall quality of the contemporary German Shorthaired Pointer is such that top awards are frequently won in both the United States and Great Britain.

TEMPERAMENT

The German Shorthaired Pointer's temperament is gentle, affectionate and even-tempered. It is alert, biddable and very loyal — an ideal family dog that loves children and thoroughly enjoys nothing more than joining in games in the garden.

As an all-purpose sporting dog, the breed will happily get out in a field and work to its owner's command, but at the end of the day it will be perfectly happy to be curled up on the sofa in front of a roaring fire. The Shorthaired may be kenneled but because of its love of the family and its need to feel that it belongs, it prefers to be with its owner and family for most of the time. It does not like being left out of things.

HEALTH MATTERS

A no-nonsense type of dog, its health problems are minimal. Cases of hip dysplasia, entropion and epilepsy have been recorded, but the quality of stock is such that these problems will only be encountered very rarely.

SPECIAL CARE AND TRAINING

The breed is highly trainable. The German Shorthaired Pointer enjoys learning, whether this means being trained for the field or in basic obedience. They are quick learners and like to please, picking up commands very

German Shorthaired Pointer

quickly. Bearing in mind their love for the family and also their hunting instincts, it is essential that they do have some formal training to ensure that their guarding instincts are kept under control.

ADAPTABILITY

The German Shorthaired Pointer prefers to live with people and if left alone for long periods can be destructive. Although very adaptable, they are obviously happier in homes with gardens rather than in apartments. They thrive on company, so if they must be kenneled they should have a mate with which they can play, though they really prefer just to fit into the family. If a German Shorthaired owner does not intend to work the dog, he or she should consider the possibility of teaching it Obedience, Agility or Working trials, as the dog will thrive on the challenge.

Essentials of the Breed

This noble breed has grace of outline and a clean-cut head, a well-muscled coat with a deep chest. When the sun shines on its gleaming coat, it shows what a truly aristocratic, ancient breed it is. In Britain, the breed's colors are solid liver, liver and white, solid black, or black and white. Black is not allowed in the United States. The size is quite specific in both the American Kennel Club and Kennel Club's breed Standards — 23-25 inches/58-64 cm for males and 21-23 inches/53-59 cm for bitches. Although the British Standard does not give a weight, its American counterpart states 55-70 pounds/25-32 kg for dogs and 45-60 pounds/ 20-27 kg for bitches.

The German Shorthaired Pointer's skull should be sufficiently broad and slightly round. Its eyes are medium sized, soft and intelligent. Their color should be in keeping with their coat, giving the gentle expression that is an essential of the breed. Unlike its Wirehaired cousin, its coat should be short, flat and coarse to the touch. A soft, silky coat is quite untypical. It may be slightly longer under the tail, which is customarily docked to prevent injury while working. The true beauty of the breed lies in its movement — true, purposeful and driving, covering the ground with an effortless gait that is synonymous with the breed.

Registry: AKC, CKC, FCI (Group 7), KC

GERMAN POINTERS — GERMAN WIREHAIRED POINTER

Origin and Development

It was in the late 1870s that German sportsmen looked for an all-round gun dog that could find game, point and then retrieve it. The Griffon and Stichelhaar were used for coat quality, and then the Pudel Pointer and German Shorthaired Pointer were added for working ability, eventually producing the German Wirehaired Pointer.

Although the German Wirehaired Club — or Verein Deutsch Drahthaar — was formed in Berlin on May 15, 1902, it was not until 1928 that the breed gained membership to the German Kartell for dogs. It was introduced to the United States in the 1920s but did not reach Britain until 1955, mainly through servicemen who had seen the dogs at work in Germany. This hunt, point and retrieve breed has the highest registration of hunting breeds in Germany, and is popular in both the United States and Great Britain where it is a strong contender at Group level..

Temperament

The German Wirehaired Pointer should be gentle, affectionate and even tempered. It is alert, biddable and very loyal. Although happiest when working, it can be just as content being part of a family group. A fun dog that likes to be involved in everything that is going on, it still has a guarding instinct and tends to be aloof with strangers.

Health Matters

The German Wirehaired Pointer is a very healthy and robust breed, but cases of hip dysplasia and entropion have been recorded. The bitches can sometimes suffer hormone problems that affect their coats. In general, however, they are a long-living breed with very few problems.

Special Care and Training

As a hunting dog, it is essential that the German Wirehaired Pointer is taught basic obedience, and early socialization with dogs and humans is vital. The coat should need the minimum of work, just a little tidying up and possibly some hand-stripping.

ADAPTABILITY

The Wirehaired Pointer thrives on human companionship and attention, but it is not really a suitable apartment dog because it likes fresh air and plenty of exercise. It can be stubborn but responds well to training.

ESSENTIALS OF THE BREED

The essence of the breed is its harsh double coat, which should be no more than 1 1/2 inches/4 cm in length. It is a medium-sized hunting dog that is slightly longer in length than in height. In the United States, males should be 23-25 inches/58-64 cm and bitches 21-23 inches/53-58 cm. In the United Kingdom, males should be 24-26 inches/60-23 cm and bitches 22-24 inches/55-60 cm. The breed's coloring is liver and white, solid liver or black and white (which is not permitted in the United States). Solid black and tricolor are both considered highly undesirable. The dog's eyes should look almost human, with a smooth skull, eyebrows and a full or half beard that is not too long. The head is always either liver or black, in keeping with its coat color, and it may have a white blaze. The tail is customarily docked to two-fifths of its natural length to prevent injury while working.

Registry: AKC, CKC, FCI (Group 7), KC

German Wirehaired Pointer

GERMAN POINTERS — GERMAN LONGHAIRED POINTER

The German Longhaired Pointer is not a longhaired variety of the German Shorthaired or Wirehaired Pointers, but is a breed with its own Standard and an almost completely different origin. It was developed at the end of the nineteenth century. The aim was to produce a gun dog with more speed than the Short and Wirehaired varieties of the time. It is probably the least known of the German gun dog breeds but is appreciated for its versatility as an all-round gun dog.

Ideally, the height at the withers should be 25-30 inches/63-66 cm for males and never under 24 inches/60 cm or over 28 inches/70 cm. Females should be 24-25inches/60-63 cm and never under 23 inches/58 cm or over 30 inches/ 66 cm. The body should be rectangular, very muscular and with a purposeful build. This breed is never as elegant as, for instance, a Setter, but it is capable of doing the same sort of work. The coat should be about 1 1/4-2 inches/3-5 cm on the body, lying flat and close, or slightly wavy and with a hard texture. It is longer on the throat, chest and under the belly, and longest on the ears, backside of the legs and the tail. The undercoat should be thick. Its color should be either liver brown, with or without white markings, and liver roan or white with brown on the head and patches on the body. Tan markings are also allowed.

Registry: FCI (Group 7)

German Longhaired Pointer

GERMAN SHEPHERD DOG

ORIGIN AND DEVELOPMENT

In the early days of their origin, the shepherd dogs in Germany did not conform to any type. Sheep herders used both large and small dogs for herding. If a dog could perform the job, they put it to the task. During the nineteenth century, some semblance of uniformity started to take place. This may have been due to the efforts of Verein für Deutsche Schaferhunde SV, now a huge organization of 50,000 members from all over Europe. This organization, formed in 1899, had the objective of molding shepherd dogs into a more uniform herding dog with a high level of intelligence and versatility.

Even in the early stages of breed develop-ment, a few demanded dogs that were useful for police work. At the turn of the century, the German Shepherd Dog as it is known today started to evolve. The Verein für Deutsche Schaferhunde SV took control of breeding and breeding practices. It molded the amorphous mass of herding dogs into a useful, uniform breed — the German Shepherd Dog. Breeders of the period favored dogs of German origin.

The first German Shepherd Dog in America surfaced in 1906 but returned to Germany without registration in the *American Kennel Club Stud Book*. From 1912-1914, the American Kennel Club registered the first two dogs of the breed, enthusiasts formed the German Shepherd Dog Club of America, and a distinctly

German Shepherd Dog

The Canadian White Shepherd is only recognized by the CKC.

correct, modern type dog appeared.

Early in 1917, during World War I, anything German became taboo. To save the breed from prejudice, the American Kennel Club changed the original name, German Sheepdog, to the Shepherd Dog. In 1931 it restored the "German" to give it back its full name. During this same period, the British knew the breed as the Alsatian Wolfdog. They soon discarded this name because of the unfavorable wolf connection. The British called them Alsatians until 1979 when the English Kennel Club renamed it the German Shepherd Dog.

Following World War I, a movement in the United States toward importing began in earnest. Fanciers brought many fine dogs over from Germany and showed them in America. These dogs and strict selective breeding practices made an invaluable contribution toward setting breed type.

The popularity of the breed sky-rocketed with the appearance from Germany of two Shepherds. One named Strongheart was used by motion picture promoters and, several years later, Rin Tin Tin came on the movie scene.

These dogs catapulted the breed into the limelight and the Shepherd became a household word. A succession of Rin Tin Tins over three decades kept the breed in the public eye. Everyone wanted a Rin Tin Tin of their very own. Registrations rose to a number one position during these years.

Hundreds of dedicated breeders in America, with careful choice of progeny, continue to improve this exciting breed. During the five decades since World War II, Americans have become more selective in their use of German dogs for breeding. There is still a need for improvement in the temperament of some. Much remains to be done before the breed reaches a zenith of popularity for the second time in recent history.

TEMPERAMENT

The German Shepherd Dogs' service as guide dogs for the blind is legendary. Society asks them to undertake this task and many others only because they have a steady, solid temperament and consistent behavior. They should display aloofness and not out-and-out friendliness. As the Verein planned so many years ago, the German Shepherd Dog has developed into an excellent utility dog with a high degree of intelligence and dependability. Its quickness to learn, self-confidence and common sense makes it a good utility breed to use.

The Standard for the German Shepherd Dog is specific, heavily penalizing poor temperament to the point of exclusion from competition. The German Shepherd Dog Club of America encourages rewarding dogs with a good temperament.

HEALTH MATTERS

Four disorders merit comment when discussing health problems in German Shepherd Dogs. Hip dysplasia (abnormal development of hip joints) is a frequent problem. More Shepherds than any other breed suffer from panosteitis, an inflammation of long bones in the legs. They do not respond well to therapy for pyoderma, bacterial infection of hair shafts or therapy for idiopathic epilepsy.

SPECIAL CARE AND TRAINING

The German Shepherd Dog requires very little special care. It should be groomed daily and bathed occasionally. Its nails should be cut with a nail trimmer and then filed. It is necessary to keep teeth clean and free of tartar. Weekly inspections should show when this is necessary. The gums and teeth should be brushed with a toothbrush or gently rubbed with a piece of gauze soaked in peroxide. Pet outlets sell suitable dental kits.

Every large dog should have obedience training to improve its social behavior. Shepherds need specialized training to meet the requirements of the owner. Dogs shown in conformation require additional ring instruction. Owners interested in Obedience competition should enroll in classes under a qualified trainer. Some require protection training for their dogs. The German Shepherd Dog, a beautiful and extremely versatile animal, easily learns any or all of these accomplishments.

The German Shepherd Dog should have a noble, clean head.

ADAPTABILITY

Adaptability is a prime attribute of German Shepherd Dogs, a quality essential for performing the tasks expected of them. It is uncertain whether natural flexibility or the need for it came first. Perhaps the many working situations in which breeders place these dogs helped them to develop their abilities.

German Shepherds perform well in sentry duty, police work, tracking, obedience, herding, and drug and bomb detection. They function equally well as guide dogs, hearing and companion dogs, and in search and rescue situations. They show good judgement, enjoy training and exhibit a willingness to learn. They excel in these qualities sometimes under stressful and dangerous circumstances.

ESSENTIALS OF THE BREED

A good temperament is at the top of the list of essentials for the breed. If this is of prime importance, it is closely followed by correct and proper movement. They should be firm of back and with no excess weight. Ideally they are well balanced, measuring 22-26 inches/ 55-65 cm at the withers. In body proportions, it should be slightly longer than its height.

The breed should have a noble, clean head, not too fine, that has strength but no coarseness. In shape and form, the male should look masculine and the female feminine. The eyes should have a keen expression, be almond shaped and as dark as possible. The ears are erect, open toward the front and pointed. The head is rather long, wedge shaped and with a moderate stop. The nose should be black.

German Shepherd Dogs should have substantial bone. They should be fit, nimble and have the ability to move with good speed. A weather-resistant coat helps them to withstand extreme climates. They should have full dentition and show no sign of overshot or undershot mouths. The tail is bushy, with the last vertebra extending at least to the hock joint and set low (rather than high) into the croup. When the dog is in motion, the tail should be slightly curved, streaming out behind and never curled up or over the back. Most colors are acceptable in this breed, although preference is given to strong rich colors and blue, liver and pale washed out shades are undesirable. White dogs are disqualified in the United States and although the white German Shepherd is not recognized by the Fédération Cynologique Internationale, twenty or so were entered at the FCI World Show in Bern, Switzerland, in 1994.

Registry: AKC, CKC, FCI (Group 1), KC

GERMAN SPITZES

According to archeological findings, German Spitzes are descended from spitz dogs that existed very much in the same form during the Stone Age. The breed is recognized in five sizes by the Fédération Cynologique Internationale (FCI): the Wolfspitz or Keeshond is 17-21 inches/ 45-55 cm and ideally 19 inches/50 cm; the Grosspitz is 16-19 inches/42-50 cm (ideally 18 inches/46 cm); the Mittelspitz is 12-15 inches/30-38 cm (ideally 13 inches/34 cm); the Kleinspitz is 9-11 inches/23-39 cm (ideally 10 inches/26 cm); and the Zwergspitz or Pomeranian is 7-8 inches/18-22 cm (ideally 20 cm). In Britain, two sizes are recognized: Klein (small, 9-11 inches/23-29 cm) and Mittel (Standard, 11-15 inches/29-38 cm), while in Australia only the Standard size is recognized.

The breed Standards only distinguish the varieties by size and color. All colors and markings are allowed in the Kennel Club's Standard, making a spectacular exhibition in the show ring with all colors competing on equal terms in the same class. However, they are not allowed in Germany, the breed's country of origin. The FCI Standard divides the colors and the dogs compete for awards within their color range. Under the FCI Standard, the Wolfspitz or Keeshond is wolf gray and the Grosspitz is black, white or liver brown. The Mittelspitz, Kleinspitz and Zwergspitz may be self-colored in black, white, orange or liver brown, or white with patches of these colors. It may also be cream with sable, orange and black-and-tan patches. The Giant variety is seen very rarely, even in Germany but it should be solid black, white or liver brown. The height at the withers should be 16 1/2-19 1/2 inches/ 42-50 cm and ideally 18 inches/46 cm.

Originally thought to be a drover's dog, the German Spitz gained popularity as a companion dog from the seventeenth century. Represented in art by such masters as Landseer and Gainsborough, the breed became very popular in Britain during the reign of Queen Victoria who owned the breed and exhibited her dogs at Cruft's dog show, though these were

Klein German Spitz

described as Pomeranians and weighed around 14 pounds/6.35 kg.

Spitzes are particularly sturdy little dogs with a compact body and square outline. They have a characteristic foxy head, pricked ears and tail curled over the back. Their crowning glory is undoubtedly the profuse stand-off coat, short on the head and legs, longer on the body with a thick ruff and well feathered legs and tail. The coat is easily maintained with regular brushing once a week. Vivacious, non-aggressive little dogs in their own home, though a little reserved with strangers, they are excellent and vocal watchdogs. Very intelligent, they are capable of achieving a high standard in Obedience and Agility. Free from health problems and vice, and well adapted for city or country living, the German Spitz is an ideal pet for today's family. Challenge Certificates were awarded for the first time at the 1995 Cruft's show.

Registry: FCI (Group 5), KC

GLEN OF IMAAL TERRIER

This fascinating and ancient terrier breed hails from southern Ireland and takes its name from the scenic if bleak area of West Wicklow. Long before it ever saw a show ring, the Glen had to hunt badger and fox, keep down the rodent population and frequently be pitted against other dogs in organized fights. It was also used to propel spit-wheels. The Irish Kennel Club first recognized the breed in 1933 but it was not until 1975 that the Kennel Club in Britain gave it recognition. While not that numerous in Britain, the breed is becoming increasingly popular in continental Europe.

The breed's general appearance is not unlike a heavyweight rough-and-ready Sealyham, though it comes in blue, brindle or wheaten. It stands some 14 inches/36 cm at the shoulder, weighs around 35 pounds/15 kg and is strong, utterly reliable, quiet and docile, yet capable of tackling any antagonist should the need arise. The breed is renowned for its stoicism.

Its coat is easily trimmed since the undercoat and topknot are soft; the topcoat has a harsher texture and this should be groomed regularly. The Glen has an extremely powerful jaw, with a vicelike grip and has heavily boned and somewhat bowed front legs. Its body is longer than the height at its withers, and it should possess great substance with well-sprung ribs. Its hindquarters are unusually powerful, well boned and noticeably muscular, with sufficient length to maintain a level topline.

Registry: FCI (Group 3), KC

Glen of Imaal Terrier

242

GRAND BLEU DE GASCOGNE

The largest and most original of the French hounds is the Grand Bleu de Gascogne, is sometimes called the "King of the Hounds" because its majestic appearance is equalled by

Grand Bleu de Gascogne

no other hound. Although used as crosses for breeds that pursue larger game, the "Blues" are only used for hunting hare. They have a rather slow gait, useful in the hot climate of the Midi in southwest France.

Its height at the withers is about 24-28 inches/62-72 cm. The coat should be smooth and glossy and the fine skin rather loose, especially on the head and throat. Color is the best-known feature in the breed. The mottling is dense to give an impression of blue. Black patches or blanket are permissible. There should always be black patches on the sides of the head and ears, and the muzzle and blaze should be mottled. The required tan markings on the head should be clearly defined. Slight tan mottling is allowed only on the lower parts of the legs. The breed is well known even though it is not often seen outside France.

Registry: FCI (Group 6)

GRAND GRIFFON VENDÉEN

The Vendée region, on the west coast of France, is the home of four rough-coated hound breeds. They are all shaggy coated and of similar type, except for the length of their legs. The largest, probably oldest and rarest is the Grand Griffon Vendéen. It is strictly a pack hound that was formerly used for hunting large prey like wolf and wild boar. The few packs that remain today are used for hunting smaller game like deer, fox and hare.

At the withers, its height is about 24-26 inches/ 60-65 cm. It looks like a small Otterhound. Its coat should be shaggy, long but not exaggerated and the color is usually any shade of red, or white with red or grayish patches.

Registry: FCI (Group 6)

Grand Griffon Vendéen

GREAT DANE

ORIGIN AND DEVELOPMENT

Many breeds make claims to have been around since the beginning of time. Certainly there is evidence of a large, powerful dog of similar build to the Great Dane living in 2000 B.C. in Assyria, and further evidence links them with the ancient Greeks and Romans. The modern Dane has its roots in a boarhound found in central Europe from the fourteenth century onward. The breed has the build to hunt boar. If you watch them at play, there are signs that this instinct is very much alive even today, so perhaps credence should be given to this theory, particularly as they were first shown in the United Kingdom under the name "Boarhound."

Wild boar used to roam the mid-European forests, and it was a favorite pastime of the landed gentry to hunt them with packs of noble dogs. To understand what the breed should look like, you need to be aware of the task for which they were used. The dog had to be able to hunt at great speed, have great stamina, but also sufficient strength and power to be able to bring the boar to a halt.

Not only were Great Danes prized hunting dogs, but with their large size and noble bearing, one can quite understand why a nobleman would want a Dane lying in front of an open fire in his castle. The name Great Dane is something of a mystery as Denmark has no real claim to be the country of origin of the breed. Germany is widely accepted as the home of the modern Great Dane; indeed it is known as the Deutsche Dogge in that country. The Germans certainly developed the breed to the Great Dane as it is known today and German dogs were among the first to be shown in Britain. The breed was first exhibited in Britain in 1875, and the first breed classes were scheduled in 1879, the English Great Dane Club being formed in 1883.

The popularity of the Great Dane increased around the world, and it can be considered a truly international dog — breeders have often sought fresh blood from each other's countries to improve certain points in their own stock. Currently dogs with a blend of British, American and Scandinavian blood are winning competitions all over the world. German breeders, having first established the breed, are still at the forefront in some of the leading "colors" (as the blues, blacks and harlequins are known).

TEMPERAMENT

In a dog standing over 32 inches/81 cm at the shoulder, temperament is of the utmost importance for obvious reasons. The Great Dane should show absolutely no sign of unprovoked aggression. It is highly intelligent and likes to feel part of the family. Danes do, however, have a stubborn streak and at times will decide that they just don't want to do what their owner wants. They can be reasoned with, and it is important that the owner is always in charge and does not allow the dog to dominate.

HEALTH MATTERS

Great Danes involve a great deal of work during rearing because their growth rate is so rapid. Unfortunately, they are not long lived, in common with many of the giant breeds. Their rapid growth rate can take its toll on bone development and it is important to get the balance of a youngster's diet just right. The muscle needs to be built up sensibly from an early age.

SPECIAL CARE AND TRAINING

Once fully grown, the Dane does not take a huge amount of special care. While a puppy may eat its owner out of house and home, the adult does not eat as much as many would think. The Dane needs plenty of exercise and sleep. Given firm but fair training, it can be trained to be a valuable member of the family. They are naturally quite clean and love to please their owners.

Black Great Dane

ADAPTABILITY

The Dane is a real family dog. But be warned: it has a great love of creature comforts and at the first opportunity is likely to take to its owner's favorite chair or sofa — or to lying in front of the fire. When fully grown, so long as it has a good gallop or two during the day, it will be quite happy to lie down and sleep in comfort, and actually adopts quite a sedentary lifestyle. With a puppy, however, there is an entirely different story. The Dane likes being with people and, if it is left alone for any length of time, it may well rearrange the house somewhat in its solitude. However, with its soft, intelligent expression, and the most mobile of eyebrows, it is almost impossible to be cross with this friendly giant!

ESSENTIALS OF THE BREED

The Great Dane is very much an international dog, with few differences in type from country to country. The German dogs are perhaps a little heavier and more stocky, and the American dogs have longer, more elegant heads. However, a good Dane should be able to win anywhere in the world. The breed traditionally has its ears cropped in the United States and in parts of Europe. The key words for the Dane are elegance, nobility, grace, substance and power. The head has that "look of eagles" about it. The dog should be remarkably light on its feet and move with a long, free stride, keeping a noble, proud outline at all times. Its head should be long with the skull and muzzle the same width. The head can take up to three years to develop fully from puppyhood and it must not look coarse or have chiseling throughout.

The Great Dane's body is more or less square in outline, with a deep chest and long legs, giving elegance and strength. A long, crested neck flows into the withers, the loin should be slightly arched and the rear full of

This fawn Great Dane has natural, uncropped ears as required by the Kennel Club in the United Kingdom.

power. Note that the Dane has strong bone which should be flat, rather than round. There are five recognized colors for the breed, and while others exist, they are unlikely to be seen in the show ring — at least, not in the winning position. In the United States, Boston-marked Danes are now accepted. These are black dogs with white trim (similar to a Boston Terrier's traditional markings — hence the term) and they are often born in harlequin litters. Fawn can range from a deep orange color to a light buff. All shades have their admirers and all are equally correct. Brindle, put crudely, is a fawn with black stripes in relief. Black is black. Blue can range from a very light gray

through steel blue to deep slate. Harlequin should have a pure white background with blue or black patches, although blue patches are not allowed under the Fédération Cynologique Internationale's Standard. The markings should be irregular; not so large that they create a blanketed effect, nor so small that they appear to be a series of dots. The overall impression should be as if ink has been flicked over a sheet of white paper — a pure white neck looks wonderful in this color. Harlequins alone are allowed to have wall eyes, and pink or butterfly noses.

Registry: AKC, CKC, FCI (Group 2), KC

GREATER SWISS MOUNTAIN DOG/ GROSSER SCHWEIZER SENNENHUND

When Caesar's legions invaded Switzerland by crossing over the Mont Jervis (St. Bernard) Pass, their dogs naturally accompanied them. Caesar's army had typical guard dogs, a mastiff type, which protected the troops' camps as well as the large herds of stock that marched with the army as a source of food. The four main Swiss mountain breeds are descended from these dogs.

The Greater Swiss Mountain Dog is perhaps the oldest and is certainly the largest of the four breeds. All four of the breeds today still have similar coloring — mainly black with white trim and tan always appearing between the black and white. The Greater is directly descended from Caesar's invading Mastiffs and has been used by the Swiss in many ways: as a butcher's dog to guard the shop and accompany the butcher on his rounds, as well as for guarding herds. It was also put to good use as a heavyweight draft dog, well able to pull a cart laden with goods to the country market.

There were once some red-and-white Swiss Mountain Dogs. However, these were not recognized as true Mountain Dogs because their color indicated cross-breeding with the St. Bernard. In fact, the Swiss Mountain Dog was probably used to strengthen the St. Bernard's gene pool during the 1800s.

In the early 1900s Greater Swiss Mountain Dogs were bred to the size and color typical of the dogs currently found in Switzerland. Two dedicated men, Franz Schertenleib and Dr. Albert Heim, who were responsible for resurrecting the Bernese Mountain Dog, came across a good example of the Greater Swiss by chance and they took it upon themselves to encourage the Swiss to renew the breed.

Everyone worked together and until the 1930s used dogs without pedigree so long as they were a true reflection of the breed with the required characteristics. All this work was successful and the breed today has earned a loyal following.

A handsome animal, the Greater Swiss Mountain Dog was first imported into the United States in 1968 and is now classified in the Working Group. It became eligible to compete in the Miscellaneous Class, Obedience Trials, and Tracking tests in the United States from October 1, 1985 and was recognized to full championship status ten years later.

TEMPERAMENT

Primarily a working dog, the Greater Swiss Mountain Dog is large and energetic. It is a good family dog, with a sense of duty to its family and home. Basically it is very even tempered.

ADAPTABILITY

Because of its size and its eagerness to work, the Greater Swiss Mountain Dog is more suited to country living than city life. Typically a draft animal, it loves farm chores, pulling carts and sleds, and children. It does well in obedience training which improves both its mind and body.

Greater Swiss Mountain Dog

HEALTH MATTERS

Generally, the Greater Swiss Mountain Dog is a large, healthy animal but some eye problems may exist. All breeding stock should be X-rayed for hip dysplasia after it is two years old.

Smooth-coated, albeit with a thick coat, the Greater Swiss Mountain Dog should be groomed regularly and bathed as necessary. Its teeth should be kept clean and hard biscuits should help with this. The nails should be looked after and trimmed regularly. The ears of this breed need gentle weekly cleaning. Any ear odor should be checked by a vet.

ESSENTIALS OF THE BREED

Large (males should be 25 1/2-28 1/2 inches/65-72 cm and females 23-27 inches/58-68 cm), powerful and alert, this breed is always a deep lustrous black with white trim on the feet, face, chest and tail tip. Tan always lies between the black and the white. The Greater Swiss Mountain Dog has a thick, short coat; it is big boned and of very good substance. The long natural tail of the breed should be carried slightly raised, never curled.

The head of the Greater Swiss Mountain Dog should be large with a good muzzle or foreface, good dentition with a scissors bite, tight lips and no dewlap. The ears of the breed are triangular, set high and hanging flat. The eyes should be dark brown and of medium size. This breed should have a good neck and shoulders and a deep, broad body slightly longer than it is tall. The bones in its legs and feet are wonderfully strong. The Greater Swiss Mountain Dog is a well set up, attractive breed that moves with reach and drive.

Registry: AKC, CKC, FCI (Group 2), KC

GREAT PYRENEES/ PYRENEAN MOUNTAIN DOG

ORIGIN AND DEVELOPMENT

The Great Pyrenees or Pyrenean Mountain Dog is one of the oldest of the natural breeds. Fossil remains of this dog found in Europe date from the Bronze Age, and the Babylonians depicted similar dogs in their art dated about 3000 B.C.

The dog as it is known today was developed in the Pyrenees for rugged mountain work, guarding flocks against wolves and bears, and drawing sleds. Its weather-resistant coat allowed it to withstand the intense cold of the mountains in Europe. It is still used with livestock, but in the United States and Great Britain it is chiefly valued as a companion and show dog.

TEMPERAMENT

The Great Pyrenees is rather quiet, ponderous and introspective. Inclined to be a one-family dog, it is wary of strangers and makes friends slowly. It is a good watchdog and should have an eye kept on it when strangers cross its turf. It will also tend to challenge other dogs.

HEALTH MATTERS

In general, the Great Pyrenees is very healthy, although it can suffer from hip dysplasia. Only dogs that have been X-rayed and found normal at two years of age should be used for breeding. The problems to look out for are hot spot skin conditions (easily treatable), possible eyelid defects and epilepsy.

SPECIAL CARE AND TRAINING

The thick double coat must be kept clean, well brushed and free of fleas and ticks. Because the coat was originally intended for outdoor living, it tends to shed, particularly in spring and early summer. The breed thrives on exercise. It requires a great deal, especially accompanying its owner on hikes and pulling carts or small sleds.

ADAPTABILITY

This beautiful, hardy dog needs a lot of human companionship and attention. The Great Pyrenean Mountain Dog is not for the apartment dweller or the haphazard dog owner.

ESSENTIALS OF THE BREED

This is a very imposing dog with heavy bones and a deep body. The males should be 27-32 inches/68.5-81 cm tall and weigh 100-125 pounds/ 45-56 kg. Bitches should be 25-29 inches/63.5-74 cm tall and weigh 90-115 pounds/ 40-52 kg.

The head should be large and wedge shaped with lovely, knowing, dark brown eyes and drop ears. The lips should be tight and black tipped; the chest quite deep but flat sided. The feet should be large and tight with double dewclaws on the lower part of the rear legs. The tail should be long, should reach below the hock and form a wheel when alert. The coat is thick, double and completely white, though gray, tan or badger markings are permissible.

The Great Pyrenees is in the Working Group in the United States.

Registry: AKC, CKC, FCI (Group 2), KC

The Great Pyrenees is known as the Pyrenean Mountain Dog in the United Kingdom.

GREYHOUND

The origins of the Greyhound can be traced back to the Egyptians. The Greyhound was traditionally used to hunt large prey such as wolf, deer and wild boar. In more recent years, it has been used for coursing or racing. The Greyhound was always raised and owned by ruling classes following the custom of the royal families in Egypt. This practice continued until very modern times. Stringent laws used to prohibit anyone owning a Greyhound unless they were of a certain high station. Today, however, the Greyhound is owned by many and racing dogs has become commercially profitable in the United States, and popular in the United Kingdom.

Greyhounds are among the most popular show dogs in the United States. The Westminster Kennel Club show catalog from 1877 lists an entry of eighteen Greyhounds. No breed can claim to have stayed so close to its original look for such a long period. To preserve the breed's stamina, several other dogs have been bred into the Greyhound's bloodlines. Some even believe that the Bulldog was infused into the Greyhound to give it more gameness and tenacity. The Greyhound is also the fastest of all breeds. It is capable of covering ground at 44 miles/70 km an hour.

The temperament of the Greyhound remains extremely stable. It is quite relaxed, poised, with a "laid back" attitude, and does not require constant attention from its owner. Amiable

Greyhound

with both humans and canines, the Greyhound is rarely tough or aggressive with anyone or any dog.

Furthermore, splendid health is a positive attribute of the breed and such soundness in body and mind is one of the reasons that the breed has existed for so long and so successfully. The Greyhound is one of the few large dogs that has been almost completely free of hip dysplasia. This fact has been attributed to the premise that the Greyhound's bones develop before its body carries a great deal of weight. As for their eyes, the Greyhound uses them well and few eye problems have developed. There have been no major concerns with the breed's vital organs: heart, kidneys, liver and so on. Deafness is one of the few health problems that has only recently been detected in a very small percentage of the breed.

As it has been bred for centuries to hunt or course, the Greyhound adapts to racing very readily. Once retired from the race track however, the breed easily adjusts to being a good all-round house dog and companion.

Essentials of the breed involve the properties which enable the Greyhound to be such a succeful coursing dog, namely stamina and speed. A great deal of this stamina comes from the heart and the mind and these characteristics can also be judged in the show ring.

In conformation classes, the Greyhound should have the qualities which will allow it to course to its best advantage: a strongly built and an upstanding posture, symmetrical in its body outline and parts. It should have a long head with long, punishing jaws, combined with large eyes that allow the dog to track down and kill its prey. A long neck, cleanly flowing into smooth well laid-back shoulders is essential. A deep chest is important, too, to allow for plenty of room for the lungs and heart. A strong, powerful arched loin is noteworthy in Greyhounds. The thighs and second thighs should be wide and muscular, showing great power. The stifles should be well bent and well let down to allow the dog to stand over a great deal of ground.

A saying describes a good Greyhound in part as having a head like a snake, neck like a drake, foot like a cat and tail like a rat.

Registry: AKC, CKC, FCI (Group 10), KC

GRIFFON À POIL LAINEUX

This very rare French gun dog breed was created by one Emmanuel Boulet in the 1880s. He used sheepdogs, Poodles and Griffons to create the breed, which has also been known as the Griffon Boulet. It has been used as a pointing dog but the few seen nowadays are said to be mainly kept as companion dogs.

The breed should stand about 19-23 inches/ 49-58 cm at the withers. Its most important feature is its coat, which also gave the breed its name. It should be long, very soft and woolly and the color should be yellowish, rather like dried leaves.

Registry: FCI (Group 7)

Griffon à Poil Laineux

GRIFFON BLEU DE GASCOGNE

Where this French hound came from is not very clear, but it is probably descended from crosses between the Bleu de Gascogne and either the Griffon Nivernais or the Griffon Vendéen, or both. The dog has a rustic appearance and is said to be a hardy breed used for smaller game and not just as a pack hound.

The height at its withers is about 17-20 inches/ 43-52 cm. Its likely ancestry from the Bleu de Gascogne (in its coloring) and the other Griffons (its coat texture) are clearly visible. Its ears are not too low set and are not as long and folded as in many other French hounds. The coat should be harsh, not abundant and lie close on the body. Its color should always be blue mottled with big black patches or a black mantle as well as tan markings. The Griffon Bleu de Gascogne is rarely seen outside France.

The Griffon Bleu de Gascogne has a rustic appearance and is used in France to hunt small game and also used as a pack hound.

Registry: FCI (Group 6)

GRIFFON FAUVE DE BRETAGNE

This breed has been known since the four-teenth century when François I had a pack. However, by the mid-nineteenth century they had become almost extinct. The breed has been slowly revived since and although still rare, it can nowadays be seen at both hound and traditional dog shows in Europe, including the United Kingdom and Scandinavia. Its temperament is considered best suited for hunting fox and wild boar.

The Griffon Fauve de Bretagne is about 19-22 inches/48-56 cm at the withers. It is coarser in build than traditional French hounds and has a long head, slightly convex nose ridge, prominent occipital bone and low-set, long and folded ears. Its coat should be harsh, almost wiry in texture but not so long as to be called shaggy. Its color may be any shade of red.

Griffon Fauve de Bretagne

Registry: FCI (Group 6)

GRIFFON NIVERNAIS

The Griffon Nivernais is believed to be very similar to the ancient Canis Segusien. Drawings of dogs in Stone Age caves bear a remarkable resemblance to this type of shaggy hound. The breed was known to be used in the fourteenth century for the hunting of wolves and wild boar. It became almost extinct after the French Revolution but was revived with help of the Grand Griffon Vendéen. It is still mainly seen in the highland area of Morvan, east of the Loire, in Nivernais, where it is hunted in packs of four to six hounds. It is regarded as the very best breed for hunting wild boar because it perseveres when in pursuit, and is brave and fearless in combat.

The breed is about 21-24 inches/53-60 cm at the withers and is longer in body than most French hounds. Its head should be long, lean and narrow with very expressive eyes and slightly low-set, long and folded ears. Its coat should be about 2 inches/5 cm long, shaggy and harsh in texture. Its color should be wolf gray, bluish gray or wild boar gray with quite pale tan markings.

Griffon Nivernais

Registry: FCI (Group 6)

HALDENSTØVER

The Norwegian scenthound takes its name from the city of Halden where it was found in the nineteenth century. Although it has been around for a long time, the breed was not recognized until 1952. It is strictly kept for hunting hare and fox. Even in Norway, the Haldenstøver is rare.

The height at its withers is about 20-24 inches/50-60 cm and its body should be rectangular. Its head should resemble that of the English Foxhound with fairly high-set, close lying ears. Its coat should be smooth and white with sparse but large black patches. The sides of the skull and the ears should be tan and there may also be tan spots on the body, very often surrounding the black patches.

Registry: FCI (Group 6)

Haldenstøver

HAMILTONSTÖVARE

The Swedish scenthound was named after Count Adolf Patrik Hamilton who founded the Swedish Kennel Club in 1889. The breed originates from East European hounds introduced to Sweden during the fifteenth and sixteenth centuries, and Swiss and English Foxhounds. Before 1921 the breed was called the Swedish Hound. It is used to hunt hare and fox, and is well known in Scandinavia. Apart from a small representation in Great Britain, the breed is rare.

The height at its withers should be within 18-24 inches/46-60 cm and its body should be rectangular, strong and well muscled. Its head resembles that of the English Foxhound. Its coat should be smooth, hard and glossy. The color may be any shade of tan with a black saddle and clearly defined white markings.

Hamiltonstövare

Registry: FCI (Group 6), KC

HANOVERIAN HOUND/ HANNOVERSCHER SCHWEISSHUND

This German, tracking scenthound is believed to originate from ancient hounds, sometimes called bloodhounds, that existed over 2,000 years ago. It is a very rare breed, strictly used for tracking on a lead – the game is usually deer.

The breed stands about 20-24 inches/50-60 cm at the withers. The body should be long, rather strong and heavy but not clumsy. The head should be broad with a similarly broad – but not too long – muzzle. Very large, broad ears should hang close to the head. The coat should be smooth, hard and glossy. It may be any shade of red or fawn. Typically, black tips on the hair give a black tinge to the coat, particularly on the head, back and tail, although the most common color is dark brindle.

The Hanoverian Hound is a very rare German breed that is believed to have originated from ancient hounds, 2000 years ago.

Registry: FCI (Group 6)

HARRIER

In about 400 B.C. the Greek historian Xenophon described hare (or rabbit) being hunted with hounds that resemble today's Harrier. English hunting records mention packs of Harriers in the thirteenth century. Since hounds were common in Europe even before this, Harriers may have traveled to England with the Normans, whose word "*harrier*" meant hound. In the seventeenth and eighteenth centuries, hunting or Harrier packs became the "poor man's" alternative to the upper class practice of hunting with packs of foxhounds. From the late eighteenth century, hunting Harrier packs became extremely popular and they are still a part of the sport today.

Friendly, gentle and responsive, Harriers make charming family companions and good house dogs. Given early socialization, the Harrier adapts well to situations. It must have exercise, companionship and training. It should not be left alone for long periods, because it has a hound voice or bay that it will use not only when hunting but also if it becomes frustrated or lonely. The Harrier is inclined to roam and must be exercised on a lead or in a safely fenced yard.

A most normal dog, the breed is quite healthy. Dental irregularities and knuckling over in the front legs are occasionally noticed. Its coat is short and sleek and easily kept clean. The Harrier should be bathed as necessary, its nails filed weekly and its teeth checked regularly.

The Harrier has a typical hound outline, mid-size between the Beagle and the English Foxhound. Male Harriers are 19-20 inches/48-50 cm tall; females are slightly smaller. Both have a typical hound head, with dropped ears and a gentle expression in their dark eyes. The Harrier holds itself proudly. It has a medium length neck, a good shoulder, hard topline and a well-set and gaily carried tail. Its chest should be deep and quite broad, and its legs very strong with good bone and superb feet. It may be any hound color and its coat should be hard, dense and glossy.

Registry: AKC, CKC, FCI (Group 6)

Harrier

HAVANESE/BICHON HAVANAIS

This Toy breed is supposed to have the same origin as the white Toy dogs from the Mediterranean area called Barbichons. Some historians are of the opinion that its brown color, Havana brown — the well known brown color of the Cuban cigar — is the reason this breed is called the Havanese. The use of "Havana brown" to describe a liver brown color is well known in several breeds of other types of pets. Although there are records that the breed existed in Cuba, its modern development is said to be centered in the United States. Although the breed was almost unknown before the early 1970s, in recent years, the Havanese has been exhibited at most large European and particularly Scandinavian shows.

The height at the withers is not given in the Standard but the breed should weigh about 13 pounds/6 kg. Its body should be rectangular, its croup decidedly sloping and its muzzle should be pointed. The tail of the Havanese should be carried over the back. The coat should be long, silky and slightly wavy but not standing out

Havanese

too much from the body. Except for tidying around the muzzle, the coat should not be scissored. This breed may be any shade of liver brown (Havana brown), gray, beige or white, with or without patches in all these colors.

Registry: FCI (Group 9)

HELLINIKOS ICHNILATIS

This very rare scenthound is only recognized in Greece. Few have seen it because it is kept for hunting hare, rabbit and fox. It is believed to be closely related to the Balkan hound breeds.

The height at its withers is about 18 1/2-20 inches/47-52 cm. Its build is like that of east European hounds but slightly more elegant, for the body of the breed is shorter with an almost square outline. The head is rounded with ears that should not be too broad or long. Its black-and-tan coat (the only color allowed) should be smooth and hard.

Registry: FCI (Group 6)

Hellinikos Ichnilatis

HOVAWART

The Hovawart takes its name from a German word that translates as "guardian of the home." Drawings from as early as the seventeenth century depict a dog similar to the old "Hofwart." It is said that such a breed had lived, as a watchdog, with humans for many years and the desired attributes of the breed included courage, intelligence and a natural discernment between friend and foe. Such dogs had weatherproof coats and had no desire to wander from their homes.

The founder of the breed as it is known today was Kurt Konig, who collected dogs which resembled the breed's original description from the Hertz and Odenwald areas. He also introduced bloodlines from various other shepherd and mountain dogs as well as the Leonberger to create a "new" Hovawart. His aim was to produce a breed which had beauty, stamina, was large but not cumbersome, and with an aristocratic bearing yet very equable temperament.

The first litter of contemporary Hovawarts was bred in 1922 and in 1937 the breed was recognized as a separate German breed. It suffered great setbacks during World War II, but in 1947 fanciers formed the German Hovawart Club and set about re-establishing the breed. Hovawarts first arrived in the United Kingdom in 1980 and the Breed Club was formed in 1982. The Hovawart is an ideal house dog, thriving on human company, and its desire to please is always evident — it constantly finds "presents" for its owners. It is also highly sociable with other dogs. To the layman the Hovawart looks rather like a lighter, more elegant and plainer-headed Golden Retriever. It also comes in black and gold, and solid black, as well as in this attractive gold color. The breed continues to increase slowly but steadily in numbers in Great Britain and at the 1995 Cruft's Dog Show, eighteen Hovawarts competed in the scheduled breed classes.

Registry: FCI (Group 2), KC

Hovawart

257

HYGENHUND

This Norwegian scenthound is named for a procurator called Hygen who developed the breed in the 1830s from an earlier known lineage of red-and-white hounds. The Hygenhund is very rare today, even in Norway, and is closely related to the Dunker.

The breed should be with 18 1/2-23 inches/ 47-58 cm at the withers. Its body should be square and compact, with a triangular head, a broad skull and a muzzle that is neither too long, nor snipy. Its coat should be smooth and glossy, and the color may be black, red or lemon, with or without white markings, or white with red or black patches or both.

Registry: FCI (Group 6)

Hygenhund

IBIZAN HOUND

ORIGIN AND DEVELOPMENT

As might be expected, the Ibizan Hound derives its name from Ibiza, a Spanish island that has been ruled by many different peoples, including Arabs, Vandals, Carthaginians, Romans, Chaldeans and Egyptians.

The Ibizan Hound can be traced back to about 3400 B.C. when it was the hunting dog of the Pharaohs. The breed's distinct features have enabled Egyptologists to identify the Ibizan as the dog depicted on artifacts that have been discovered in the tombs of the Pharaohs. The breed was also referred to as the Galgo Hound. A duplicate of today's Pharaoh Hound was discovered in the tomb of Tutankhamen.

The resemblance between the Pharaoh Hound then and the Ibizan is so close that most scholars now believe that the Pharaoh and the Ibizan may be the same breed. It is now accepted that Phoenician traders brought the Ibizan from Egypt to Ibiza. It is thought, too, that the Ibizan was the dog that accompanied Hannibal and his elephants on his difficult journey across the Alps.

It was not until 1956, however, that Colonel and Mrs. Seoane of Rhode Island brought the first Ibizan Hounds to the United States. It was from their two original imports, Hannibal and Certera, that the first American litter was born. Eight puppies were produced in the first litter. These offspring, along with several other imports, were the foundation of the breed in the United States.

Unlike other Greyhound-like dogs, the Ibizan can hunt by sound as well as by sight and scent. It is believed that, along with the Greyhound and Saluki, the Egyptian Mastiff made up the characteristics of the Ibizan. The relative isolation of ancient Egypt contributed to the purity of the Ibizan and helped the breed to remain unchanged in form through the years.

TEMPERAMENT

The Ibizan is like most Greyhound-type dogs: loyal, affectionate and generally even-tempered. The breed is not given to great bursts of demonstrated affection, but these dogs are quiet, loyal and giving.

Ibizan Hounds do have a certain sense of play and will occasionally tear around in huge circles at a dead gallop giving the impression that they are simply glad to be alive. Ibizan Hounds like their comfort (particularly a couch or bed) and they may well want to cuddle up in cold weather.

HEALTH MATTERS

Health problems are very rare in the Ibizan. For centuries they were culled from any problems and lived in a land where survival of only the fittest was the maxim. Today, fortunately, the Ibizan has not suffered from indiscriminate breeding and has stayed true to its original form, health and structure.

SPECIAL CARE AND TRAINING

The Ibizan needs a good healthy diet but requires no special care. It has a natural instinct to hunt and is very easy to train for

Shorthaired Ibizan Hound

lure-coursing, tracking, Obedience and the show ring.

ADAPTABILITY

House training should begin early and the young Ibizan should not be left unattended until it has learnt what it may or may not do — it can be very destructive. Crate training by eight to ten weeks is essential, and the young hound should always ride in a crate in the car — sudden stops and starts may result in sprains, strains and fractures if the animal is not confined. Training on a leash should also be begun at an early age. So long as it has the opportunity to exercise daily, the Ibizan Hound will adapt to both country and urban surroundings.

ESSENTIALS OF THE BREED

The Ibizan has all the qualities to make it a proper hunter. It is a moderate dog and is not extreme in any way, except for its large pointed ears which it uses to hunt with. Its clear amber eyes and very large mobile ears, set on a long narrow head give it a unique expression. A prominent occipital bone, a slight stop and a moderately convex muzzle distinguish the breed from other Greyhound-type dogs. The light pigment around its eyes and on its nose is one of the unique characteristics of the breed. It should be built to have great speed, along with splendid stamina so that it can work for long periods of time. Agility is essential and it should never appear heavily muscled. The breed displays a unique "hovering" gait where the forefoot tends to hover before being placed on the ground, quite unlike other hounds.

The Ibizan Hound comes in two types of coat: shorthaired and wirehaired, the most common being the shorthaired variety. The coat of the wirehaired varies from 1-3 inches/ 2.5-7.5 cm in length. Both types of coat should be hard, close and dense. In the wirehaired type there should be a slight feathering on the back, thighs and tail.

Registry: AKC, CKC, FCI (Group 5), KC

Wirehaired Ibizan Hound

ICELAND DOG/ ÍSLENSKUR FJÁRHUNDUR

The herding spitz of Iceland is believed to have arrived with Vikings and Norwegian settlers in about A.D. 800. In the early twentieth century, distemper almost wiped out the breed and thirty years later these dogs were supposed

Iceland Dog

to be the cause of an epidemic that struck sheep and also infected people. This resulted in legislation that banned dogs from cities in Iceland. The breed was saved by an Englishman, who had taken dogs to England in the 1950s. He managed to get the breed recognized by the Fédération Cynologique Internationale in 1956. It is a rare breed, but it has become quite popular in Scandinavia in recent years.

The height at its withers is about 15-19 inches/ 38-48 cm. The breed has typical spitz features and a rectangular body, with either a long or short coat. All colors are permissible — a golden-red with white markings is quite common.

Registry: FCI (Group 5)

INCA ORCHID DOG/ PERRO SIN PELO DEL PERÙ

The Peruvian hairless dog comes in three sizes. It resembles the Chinese Crested Dog and the Mexican Xoloitzcuintli. Archeological findings in Peru have shown that dogs of a similar type existed a thousand years ago. The breed is very rare but has gained interest in Europe.

The height at the withers varies according to the three sizes. The Standard is 20-26 inches/ 50-65 cm, the Miniature 16-20 inches/40-50 cm and the Toy 10-16 inches/25-40 cm. All sizes are elegant in build, with a long, slightly wedge-shaped head. The ears should be carried erect. The skin should be smooth and elastic and sparse hair is permissible on the skull, feet and the tip of tail. The color should be black, or any shade of gray or liver brown, with or without pink spotting on the lower part of the body.

FCI (Group 5)

Inca Orchid Dog

IRISH TERRIER

ORIGIN AND DEVELOPMENT

The Irish Terrier is possibly the oldest of the terrier breeds to have come from Ireland, but documented evidence of its early history is scarce. When dogs were first shown in 1870, there was tremendous variation in their size, shape and type — and black-and-tan and brindle specimens were not unknown. At the end of the nineteenth century, attempts were made to breed out these colors in favor of red.

During World War I, Irish Terriers were used as messenger dogs in the trenches and they acquired a reputation for being both intelligent and fearless. This fearlessness has contributed to its nickname of "Daredevil", though it still stands proudly by its early description as "the poor man's sentinel, the farmer's friend, and the gentleman's favorite".

While many may consider the Irish Terrier to be disadvantaged when competing in the Terrier Group up against the more "flashy" breeds such as the Fox Terriers, Kerry Blue and Airedale, the breed has produced many dogs on both sides of the Atlantic which have distinguished themselves in the contemporary show ring. Indeed, at the 1994 Montgomery County KC in the United States, acknowledged as the premier terrier show in the world, an Irish Terrier took on all comers and won Best in Show.

TEMPERAMENT

Renowned for loyalty to its owner, the Irish Terrier has no equal as a companion and guardian, especially of children. It is affectionate and amenable, and its courage and heedless — almost reckless — pluck knows no bounds. When attacked, the Irish will fight to the bitter end and for this reason it is essential that its owner is always in complete control.

HEALTH MATTERS

In general, Irish Terriers are healthy and hardy. Other than routine visits for inoculations, they will seldom require veterinary attention other than perhaps to repair accidental damage incurred during any confrontation.

SPECIAL CARE AND TRAINING

As with most other hard-coated terriers, the Irish Terrier's topcoat requires hand stripping, usually in the spring and fall. This is essential if it is to retain its beautifully natural color and texture of coat — clipping will ruin this coveted feature of the breed. Occasional baths, coupled with regular grooming, should keep the dog in top form.

ADAPTABILITY

The Irish will fit into most environments, and wherever it is living, it is guaranteed to protect and guard its human family well. However, caution should be exercised if it is to be kept with other dogs because if a fight occurs the Irish will never be the first to back down.

ESSENTIALS OF THE BREED

The Irish Terrier should be a substantial, long-legged, lithe dog with a racy outline. The color of its coat may be red, red-wheaten or yellow-red, and the dog should be whole-colored — black shading is undesirable. White sometimes appears on its chest and feet but this is not to be encouraged.

The head should be long and the skull flat. Its ears are V-shaped and small; they should drop forward toward the cheeks and be folded above the level of the skull. Together with its dark eyes and strong jaw, the breed has a unique expression. Its nose is black. Its neck should be a fair length, with no throatiness, and its forequarters such that the shoulders are well laid back, and the legs straight and satisfyingly boned, with sound feet and pads. The chest is deep and muscular, its back well ribbed but not full or wide. The loin should be slightly arched and muscular. An ultra-short

Irish Terriers

back, as prized in some terriers, is not a virtue in an Irish Terrier. The tail is customarily docked and set high. The hindquarters are strong and very flexible, with the hocks straight and well let down. The front and rear action should impart total freedom. The coat should be hard and wiry, with a soft undercoat. In addition, the hair on its foreface and legs should be crisp to the touch, giving an additional appearance of strength. It is important that the beard is not excessively long or soft in any way. Males stand around 19 inches/48 cm at the shoulder, with bitches about 1 inch/ 2.5 cm smaller.

Registry: AKC, CKC, FCI (Group 3), KC

IRISH WOLFHOUND

ORIGIN AND DEVELOPMENT

Irish history and literature is full of references to the Irish Wolfhound and there can be no doubt as to the ancient lineage of this particular breed. The continental Celts are known to have had great-sized hounds which have been portrayed in illustrations found in Greece and Cyprus. It is generally agreed that they took their hounds to Ireland in around 1500 B.C. Gifts of large Irish-bred hounds were then made to the invading Romans before the third century A.D.

The name Irish Wolfhound is comparatively modern. All large hounds were once known as "Cu." This term used to imply bravery and many warriors prefixed their own names with the word. Latterly the breed was known as the Irish Hound and Irish Wolfdog — the current Irish name for the breed is Cu Faoil. The name gives more than a clue to the purpose for which the breed was used but does not tell the full story. They were greatly prized as hunting dogs, being used against wolf, deer and wild boar; indeed, so good were they that for over 100 years Ireland has had no wild wolves. They were also often used as guards of both persons and property and were considered very valued gifts between noblemen. King John of England is known to have given a Wolfhound to Llewelyn, Prince of Wales in the thirteenth century. The dog — Gelert — was immortalized in a poem by William Robert Spencer (1769-1834).

Irish Wolfhounds were also used in battle to pull men off horseback. In the eighteenth and nineteenth centuries, the numbers of the breed in Ireland gradually dwindled and their ownership was restricted to the nobility. It is unlikely that a peasant farmer would have been able to feed such a dog, even if allowed to keep one, particularly since great animals of prey had largely died out. Further, great numbers of the breed had been sent to other parts of Europe

as treasured gifts. Following the famine of 1845-46, the breed had nearly died out. However, Captain Graham, a Scottish officer in the British army, set about a program to revive the breed. He managed to obtain descendants of a dog named Bran, said to be the last true example of the Wolfhound in Ireland, and by breeding them with Glengarry Deerhounds, with the occasional outcross of Borzoi and Great Dane to increase the size of the breed, he eventually achieved a dog that bred true to type. After their success at Dublin shows in the 1870s, a club was formed for the Irish Wolfhound in 1885. The breed now has worldwide popularity and can be found in numbers wherever dogs are exhibited.

TEMPERAMENT

The Wolfhound is known as the gentle giant and this really sums up its character. A perfect gentleman, the breed should show no signs of aggression nor timidity. A kindly disposition is both essential and highly typical of the breed.

HEALTH MATTERS

The breed rarely lives to a great age and, in common with many giant breeds, can suffer with heart problems. A well-reared Wolfhound should, however, give many years of pleasure to its owner. Rearing is critical because of the rapid growth rate of Wolfhound puppies.

SPECIAL CARE AND TRAINING

Rearing a Wolfhound requires great care so that the bone and muscle develop at a sensible pace. The growth rate is rapid and a young Wolfhound will need plenty of good food, sleep and play. The coat is fairly easy to maintain and, since it is an untrimmed breed, should look good with regular basic grooming. Wolfhounds are willing to please and as such are easily trained. They do, however, get bored and need to see the point of what they are being asked to do, so are unlikely to

Irish Wolfhound

endure standard obedience exercises of the "Sit, Stay" type for long.

Adaptability

The Wolfhound makes a good family dog, being both gentle in disposition and very willing to please its owners. The breed does require a fair amount of exercise and it would be unwise to leave a young Wolfhound alone in the home for long, as boredom may encourage its more destructive tendencies.

Essentials of the Breed

The Irish Wolfhound is the largest sighthound and should combine the attributes of a sighthound with great size and a commanding appearance. The outline should be made up of a series of gentle curves, with a strong, arched neck flowing through good withers to a moderately arched loin and into strong quarters with good angulation at the stifle. This, in many ways graceful, outline should be on a big, powerful, strong dog with heavy bone, a deep chest, moderate tuck-up, hard muscle and a harsh coat. While great size is highly prized, judges should not fall into the trap of putting up the tallest in the class for that reason alone. Size means build and bone as well as height, and they must be accompanied by the correct shape and make. The hound should be able to move with long, free strides, easily covering the ground.

The minimum height is 31 inches/78 cm for dogs and 28 inches/62 cm for bitches, although a good average is 32-34 inches/81-86 cm. Claims of a 38 inch/96.5 cm dog are sometimes made, but often great height can come from incorrect angulation at the front and rear. The Wolfhound should never look a great lump of a dog; it must have the power to bring down and deal with its prey, but it must obviously also have the build first to catch it. A sound hound with a long, free stride is required; it should be fit enough to hunt all day.

The head should be fairly long, with moderate width and powerful jaws. A scissors bite is required, although the breed can be prone to minor dentition faults. Judging is about weighing up faults and virtues, and an otherwise typical hound with a couple of slightly misplaced teeth should, under the majority of judges, beat an untypical dog with a perfect bite. The ears should be small and rose-shaped, and must not hang close to the face. The neck should be a good length, but must be strong — a long neck is not required. The chest should be deep and broad, with elbows set well under the dog, giving support to its body, with shoulders well laid back.

The body is long rather than short, but the length should come from the rib cage and not the loin. The length of body should not be confused with length of back; a well-constructed hound will have a fair amount of body in front of its withers. Hindquarters are well angulated but powerful. Under-angulation or over-angulation is a sign of weakness. The feet are moderately large and round with well-arched toes. The tail is long, slightly curved and never carried over the back. The coat should be rough and harsh, giving protection against all weather; a long, open coat can look glamorous but is entirely incorrect. The recognized colors are gray, brindle, red, black, fawn, wheaten, steel gray and pure white, though these days white is never found.

Registry: AKC, CKC, FCI (Group 10) KC

ISTARSKI GONIC

The Istrian Scenthound from the peninsula of Istria in former Yugoslavia is thought to be the oldest of the hound breeds in the Balkan region. It is strictly used as a hunting dog, mainly for hare and fox. There are two varieties of the breed with separate Standards. The Wirehaired "*Ostrodlaki*" should be 19 1/2-20 inches/50-52 cm at the withers and the Smooth "*Kratkodlaki*" should be just slightly smaller at 19-19 1/2 inches/48-50 cm.

The dog's body should be rectangular, well muscled and with good bone. Its type is typically east European, with a broad head, flat skull, and fairly short triangular ears hanging close to the cheeks without any folds. The Wirehaired's coat should be about 2-4 inches/ 5-10 cm long, wiry on top and with a thick undercoat. The Smooth's coat should be hard and glossy. Both varieties should be white with sparse patches of clear orange.

Smooth Istarski Gonic

Registry: FCI (Group 6)

ITALIAN GREYHOUND

ORIGIN AND DEVELOPMENT

Perhaps surprisingly, the Italian Greyhound was one of the first breeds in ancient antiquity to be bred exclusively as a companion. The breed is also the smallest of the sighthounds. "IGs," as the breed is popularly referred to, were the pets of Egyptian, Greek and Roman aristocrats. The look of the breed was recorded for posterity some 2,000 years ago in stone and pottery found in Mediterranean countries, and in a mummified state in Egyptian tombs. Later, its image was captured on canvas. By the sixteenth century, IGs were known in most of Europe and had become particularly popular in the royal courts of Spain and Italy. From the thirteenth to fifteenth centuries, European painters such as Giotto, van der Weyden, Botticelli and Bosch

Italian Greyhound

glorified the breed in oil and contemporary sculptors did the same in stone and metals. In England John Wootton painted the breed a couple of hundred years later.

These little dogs were known as royal companions to James I of England, Francis I of France, and to Frederick the Great of Prussia. All the monarchs recorded how much they admired the high-stepping gait of the IG, reminiscent of the highly bred royal horses. Catherine the Great of Russia and Queen Victoria also owned the breed. In French literature, Alphonse de la Martine, the poet, wrote many verses about IGs. And Gustave Flaubert, the celebrated French novelist, chose an Italian Greyhound, Djali, to be the companion of his quintessential romantic heroine Madame Bovary.

By the late 1880s a negative development occurred when IGs became so diminutive — only about 10 inches/25 cm tall — that they began to develop dwarfish characteristics. But by 1950, when fifty IGs were registered in the United States, and by 1957, when Great Britain registered about the same number, these unfortunate traits began to disappear. It was not until 1968 that the official Standard of the IG was written in Italy.

TEMPERAMENT

All authorities praise the breed's adaptability to indoor living and to a comfortable family situation. An IG, always lively and full of good spirits, wants to please, craves affection and returns it gladly. Particularly decorative in repose, when it crosses its elegant legs, the IG almost looks as if it is made of bone china. But although it is light in weight and easily carried, it is not a fragile little dog. Common sense should govern how it is handled.

HEALTH MATTERS

As far as the IG's health is concerned, breeders report that although there are some cases of isolated illness, the breed is quite free of major genetically inherited problems.

SPECIAL CARE AND TRAINING

The Italian Greyhound is quite easy to care for and responds fairly well to training. This dainty Italian is bred and revered as a pet. It has a justified reputation for breaking its bones, particularly those of its front legs. This may be due to the fact that it sometimes seems to lack common sense. It should be prevented from jumping off furniture and, if allowed to exercise in an enclosed yard, the fence should be too high for it to jump. Exercise is important to build up the strength in the muscles. It should always be crated when traveling in a car, or held firmly in a passenger's lap.

The IG is prone to chills and so should be kept in a draft-free environment and given a warm bed in which to snuggle. It should also wear a coat in wet or cold weather. In addition to being fed a balanced diet, it needs to eat crunchy dog biscuits to help to keep its gums and teeth healthy. Its teeth should be cleaned weekly and nails also trimmed slightly.

ADAPTABILITY

Because of its small size, the Italian Greyhound is particularly suited to living in an apartment, and can be taken wherever dogs are welcome. Its coat is short and sleek. IGs are not noisy, get along well with other pets and do not have a jealous nature. It enjoys being in the country and loves to run as befits its sighthound heritage.

ESSENTIALS OF THE BREED

All experts agree that the Italian Greyhound is a small version of the Greyhound, and the IG is ideally 13-15 inches/33-38 cm. It is just a little more slender in all parts compared with its larger progenitor. Graceful, lithe and beguiling, it is an elegant canine with a narrow tapering head with rose-shaped ears set far back on the head. Its rather prominent eyes are expressive and luminous. An arched neck with a svelte body a slight rise over the loin, along with its high-stepping gait, make the IG an enchanting Toy dog.

Registry: AKC, CKC, FCI (Group 10), KC

ITALIAN SPINONE/SPINONE ITALIANO

ORIGIN AND DEVELOPMENT

A very ancient, all-purpose working gun dog, the Italian Spinone is noted for its fast trotting gait when working in the field. Purely Italian in origin, it was first mentioned as existing as a distinct breed over 2,000 years ago. Until recently, few were found outside Italy where they are both successful show dogs and very popular hunting dogs, able to work over all types of terrain and cover in all weather. The popularity of the breed has grown rapidly since its introduction into the United Kingdom, with full Championship status granted by the Kennel Club in 1994. In the United States the breed is also gaining ground, particularly among hunters where its outstanding game-finding abilities, allied to its sociable temperament, are much appreciated. Despite its relatively short time in the British show ring, judges have been quick to appreciate the virtues of the Spinone which looks considerably

Italian Spinone

different from any of its competitors in the Gundog Group. Indeed at the Bath Championship show in 1994 the very first Spinone won a Gundog Group, thus creating breed history.

Spinone breeders are anxious that the breed should remain a versatile working gundog and the breed club is keen that the working and show fraternities should not develop different priorities which may result in two types of Spinone emerging, as has happened in several other of the gundog breeds.

The numbers of Spinone seen at British shows have escalated. Eighty competed at Cruft's in 1995. This is remarkable when one considers that Challenge Certificates were not available for the breed until 1994. Hopefully this sudden popularity will not prove to be to the detriment of the breed.

TEMPERAMENT

Tolerant and friendly, the Spinone is renowned for being utterly trustworthy with children. A very sociable breed, gentle and sensible in maturity, its well-developed sense of humor allied to its keen intelligence can lead to rather exuberant behavior when young. Be warned that if left to its own devices the breed can be very destructive.

HEALTH MATTERS

Hip dysplasia is a problem and puppies should only be purchased from parents that have had their hips X-rayed. Osteochondrosis of the shoulder, and more rarely of the elbow, also occurs and affected dogs should not be bred from. Hormone imbalance and pyometra are fairly widespread conditions in bitches. Additionally, the breed is particularly susceptible to ear infections.

SPECIAL CARE AND TRAINING

Great care must be taken not to over-feed or physically over-exercise a puppy until it is at least twelve months old. Mental exercise, however, is most important as puppies easily become bored and destructive. Adult Spinoni vary a great deal in their need for exercise, but this breed is not for the owner who does not enjoy extensive walking. The correct, shortish, single coat needs little attention, but many Spinoni have longer, soft coats which mat easily and require regular stripping and daily grooming. Daily ear care is also necessary.

ADAPTABILITY

Provided that it has constant companionship, the breed is very adaptable to all situations and environments. It is an excellent family dog with children, yet is equally adept at finding a pheasant for its owner's supper.

ESSENTIALS OF THE BREED

A fairly large country dog with strong bone, the Spinone should be well muscled and have a broad, deep chest. Its body is square, short-backed, with a distinct dip behind the shoulders. The tail is customarily docked and carried level or down. Males stand 23-27 inches/58-68 cm at the shoulder and bitches 23-25 inches/ 58-63 inches. A special characteristic of the breed is its thick, leathery piglike skin. The head should be long, with an oval skull and large fairly round eyes.

The Spinone is particularly known for the markedly sweet "human" expression of its eyes. Its single coat is thick, slightly wiry, close fitting and not more than 2 inches/5 cm long on the body. It is shorter on the head and legs, with no fringeing or feathering. Longer hair forms eyebrows, a beard and mustache, giving the typical "good natured grouch" expression. Permitted colors are solid white, white with orange markings, white speckled with orange (orange roan), white with brown markings, white speckled with brown (brown roan) or brown roan with brown markings. The pigment of its skin, eyelids, nose, lips and pads should be fleshy red in white dogs and deeper in colored dogs.

Registry: FCI (Group 7), KC

JÄMTHUND

The largest of the Swedish spitz breeds has been in existence since the country was populated. Originally it was simply regarded as being a large version of the Norwegian

Jämthund

Elkhound. People that had kept the "big ones" for generations did not care about dog breeds — they were only concerned about how good their dogs were at hunting elk and bear. However, when exhibited as Norwegian Elkhounds they caused problems because it emerged that they were not only larger but also of a different type. This was settled in 1946 when they were recognized as a specific breed. The breed name comes from the county of Jämtland where most of the dogs were found. This is strictly a hunting dog and is considered a proud "one-man dog."

The height at its withers should be within 20 1/2-25 1/2 inches/52-65 cm. Its body should be rectangular, strong and muscular. The head is long with a rather broad skull and the tail should be carried over its back in a loose curl. The coat should not be too long but thick and harsh in texture. The color should be iron gray with very light, well defined "wolf markings."

Registry: FCI (Group 5)

JAPANESE CHIN

ORIGIN AND DEVELOPMENT

Despite its name, the Japanese Chin is descended first from China and then Japan. These oriental Toy dogs were presented by Chinese emperors to Japanese royalty. Some say that Chinese Buddhist teachers undertaking missionary work in Japan also took the Chin to Japan. Yet another story tells of a Korean diplomat who brought Chins to Japan in A.D. 732. Whatever theory one believes, it is clear that the Japanese perfected the breed as it is known today. When Admiral Perry opened up Japan to international trade in 1853, he was presented with a pair of Japanese Chins which he subsequently gave as

a gift to Queen Victoria. In 1880, Chins were first shown in England and Lady Samuelson and Queen Alexandra were early British owners. In the United States, August Belmont, a financier and philanthropist, owned Chins in the early part of this century although, in fact, the breed was known as the Japanese Spaniel in the United States until 1977.

TEMPERAMENT

The Japanese Chin is an exemplary breed in that it is bright, lively, animated, and loves to cavort and play. One breeder reports that her eight Chins will chase each another endlessly, running throughout the house with such

Japanese Chin

agility and grace that they never break or upset anything.

Health Matters

The Japanese Chin has only a few minor health problems. It does suffer from some eye problems because of their size and prominence. Washing and checking the eyes daily should prevent any problems. Its teeth should be cleaned weekly. Nails should be clipped once a week.

Patella luxation is a problem in this breed — it may be heritable or caused by trauma. To avoid the latter, the dog should not be grabbed by the legs and should be prevented from jumping off high furniture. If the patella (knee cap) is allowed to become dislodged, the animal may become lame.

Special Care and Training

Gentle and affectionate, the Japanese Chin is fastidiously clean and very easy to housetrain. However, because of its somewhat independent mind owing to its Oriental background, it may be hard to train in obedience. It catches on quickly and likes to please, and yet it does not relish endless repetition and is too free-spirited for such monotony. Catlike, it often sits on furniture and becomes master of all it surveys. It is proud to be king of a household in which it is loved and appreciated.

Adaptability

The Japanese Chin is one of the most adaptable of breeds if it can live indoors — it should never be kenneled. Many consider it to be the perfect pet, particularly when it can live inside in comfortable surroundings.

Essentials of the Breed

This is a zestful little dog with a noble bearing, squarely and compactly built, with a sumptuous shining coat which is usually black and white but may also be red and white. Its large square head, rounded at the front, is balanced by a short muzzle and large, dark lustrous eyes. Moving quickly, daintily and stylishly, the Japanese Chin exhibits so much *joie de vivre*, it is a pleasure to behold and to live with.

Registry: AKC, CKC, FCI (Group 9), KC

JAPANESE SPITZ

Origin and Development

The Japanese Spitz was developed in Japan in the 1930s. Some white spitz-type dogs were found in a cargo shipment from Canada at the time of the Tokyo earthquake and it seems certain that these were American Eskimo Dogs. That breed was originally taken to America from central Europe, having been developed from the White Spitz or Pomeranian. Russian White Spitzes were also imported into Japan in about 1930, this breed having spread to Russia from central Europe. There were a few white spitz-type dogs in Japan many years earlier but it was not until after World War II that the breed was really established at the Nagoya Centre for Spitz Breeding.

The first English imports were brought over by Mrs. Dorothy Kenyon from Sweden where the breed had been recognized. Although it was possible to import the breed directly into Sweden from Japan, it was not possible to do this in the United Kingdom. The British Kennel Club recognized the breed in 1977. Today the breed is well established in Britain and the level of quality is such that the Japanese Spitz is now a serious contender at Group level.

Temperament

The Japanese Spitz has a delightful temperament, being very alert and aware of what goes on around it. These dogs are intelligent, bold and make great companions.

Health Matters

In general, Japanese Spitzes are very healthy little dogs which usually live to about twelve or fourteen years of age. There has been some incidence of patella luxation when the kneecap in the stifle joint slips out. Hopefully

Japanese Spitz

selective breeding will help to eliminate this condition.

SPECIAL CARE AND TRAINING

The breed has a typical spitz double coat which means that the undercoat is shed once a year. Regular grooming is important to keep a Japanese Spitz in prime condition. Like other breeds in this group, Japanese Spitzes take to training quite well so long as this is done gradually from when the puppy is about eight weeks.

ADAPTABILITY

Japanese Spitzes are very adaptable dogs that make excellent companions, because they are naturally very affectionate. They have acute hearing and will warn of approaching strangers. They can be kept in either a kennel or home environment, but if the dogs are kenneled they must have plenty of human contact. The breed's popularity owes much to its size, being much larger and sturdier than the Pomeranian, yet considerably smaller and less demanding than the Samoyed.

ESSENTIALS OF THE BREED

The Japanese Spitz is very eye-catching with a beautiful double coat. Its medium-sized head should be moderately broad and its skull slightly rounded, tapering to a pointed muzzle. Its small, angular ears are set on high; it has dark, oval-shaped eyes set obliquely. The breed has a broad, deep chest with powerfully sprung ribs. Small, round, catlike feet are called for with black pads and dark nails. The tail should curl over and lie along the back. The breed moves with a light, smooth action. The outer coat must stand off and a soft, dense undercoat is required; the breed has a mane on its neck. The hair is shorter on the face, ears, the front of the foreleg and on the hind legs. The coat is always pure white and this, coupled with its dense black pigment, is a major part of the breed's attraction. Dogs stand 12-14 inches/30-35.5 cm in height at the shoulder, with bitches slightly smaller.

Registry: FCI (Group 5), KC

JAPANESE TERRIER/NIHON TERIA

Japanese Terrier

The Japanese Terrier is believed to have been developed from early Fox Terriers and English Toy Terriers. They mainly resemble the American Toy Terrier in looks. The breed was recognized by the Japanese Kennel Club in 1930 but is still very rare, even in Japan.

The breed should ideally be 12 inches/30 cm at the withers. Its elegant, finely built body tends to be rectangular; its head should be wedge shaped and its ears carried in the fashion of the Manchester Terrier. The coat should be smooth, fine and silky. Its color should be white with black on the head and ears and tan markings. A smaller, black patch is allowed on its back and at the root of the tail.

Registry: FCI (Group 3)

JUGOSLAVENSKI TROBOJNI GONIC

This tricolored scenthound from former Yugoslavia has been known and true to type since the nineteenth century. The Jugoslavenski Trobojni Gonic is used strictly as a hunting dog, mainly for hare and fox. It is very rare outside the region of its origin.

The breed should be about 18-22 inches/ 45-55 cm at the withers. The body should be rectangular, well muscled and with good bone. The head should be rectangular, with the muzzle longer than the skull. The ears should be triangular, hanging close to the cheeks with no folds, and not set too low. The smooth, dense and hard-textured coat of this Gonic should be a rich tan with a black saddle and white markings.

The Jugoslavenski Trobojni Gonic is very rarely found outside its region of origin.

Registry: FCI (Group 6)

KAI/KOHSHU-TORA

The Kai, one of Japan's six native spitzes, is mainly regarded as a hunting dog. It comes from the mountains around Fuji on the island of Hon Shu and is considered one of the most ancient of the Japanese spitzes. It is said to be a hard, self-confident hunter as well as being a guard dog that is wary of strangers.

At the withers, the dog should be 18-22 inches/ 46-56 cm. The various Japanese spitzes differ mainly in size. Their common features are a wedge-shaped head with pronounced cheeks, decidedly slanted eyes and hooded ears. The coat should be short and harsh, standing out from the body except on the tail and buttocks where it should be longer. The colors seen most frequently are black, red or very dark brindle, often with white markings. The Kai is rarely found outside Japan.

The Kai is considered one of the most ancient of the six Japanese Spitzes.

Registry: FCI (Group 5)

KARELEAN BEAR DOG/ KARJALANKARHUKOIRA

This spitz breed from Finland has very close links with the Russian Laikas. It comes from the same area as the Russian-European Laika which it resembles to such an extent that even judges find it difficult to distinguish the breeds. These spitzes are known to have followed the first settlers in Finland, thousands of years ago. These early tribes of people survived on what they could hunt, which is why dogs that were hardy, brave and tough enough to tackle bear, wolf and lynx were so important.

The Karelean Bear Dog was very popular among hunters at the turn of the century when it could be found in vast numbers. It was first exhibited at a dog show in Helsinki in 1936 but after World War II the breed almost became extinct. All modern Kareleans are traced back to forty dogs found and saved after the war. Today the breed is mainly used for hunting elk, wild boar and of course bear. It is a hard, self-confident breed that is considered to be a one-man dog. Strictly kept as a hunting dog, it is rarely seen outside Finland.

The height at its withers should be about 19-24 inches/49-60 cm. It has all the features of the spitz but it may be born with a bobtail. Its coat should not be profuse but thick and harsh in texture. The color should be black — a copper tint is typical — with white markings on the muzzle, neck, chest, legs and tip of the tail.

Registry: FCI (Group 5)

Karelean Bear Dog

KEESHOND/WOLFSPITZ

ORIGIN AND DEVELOPMENT

The Keeshond is a member of the Non-Sporting Group in the United States, although it resembles the spitz or northern breeds in the structure of its head, ears, its balance and proportion, tail and coat.

The country most responsible for the development of the Keeshond is Great Britain, based on imports from Holland. The name of the breed came from Kees de Gyselaer, the leader of Dutch patriots against the monarch. It was Dutch riverboat and barge captains, and farmers, who kept the breed alive and in its original form. This required thought and planning by those interested in breeding these useful animals in order to preserve the look and the temperament of this delightful breed.

As the breed became popular in other parts of the world, that same care was taken in

Keeshond

selective breeding so that today the breed is virtually unchanged from its original form. It is depicted in a picture painted in 1794 which shows the children and dog of a burgomaster mourning his tomb. The dog clearly resembles today's Keeshonden or the German Wolfspitz.

Temperament

The Keeshond is a typical house dog, watch dog and companion. As a watch dog it has a sharp clear bark and is not afraid to give the alarm. With those who it knows, it is affectionate and loving. It makes friends easily, since it is naturally inquisitive. If raised with children, it accepts them well and is therefore a well-loved member of the family. As an Obedience dog, it learns quickly but may wish to imprint its own style on its performance.

Health Matters

As with most "natural dogs," the Keeshond is quite healthy. Its long double coat must be groomed frequently to stave off potential problems of skin trouble caused by hot spots or fleas. There have been cases of hip dysplasia, epilepsy, as well as some congenital heart problems. The best plan is always to purchase the Keeshond, whether for a pet or a show animal, from a reputable breeder who will have taken all the precautions and applied all methods in testing for health problems.

Special Care and Training

The Keeshond's crowning glory is its coat. It must be thoroughly brushed at least twice a week, and more frequently if it is to be shown. Constant grooming — with either dry shampoo that is sprinkled in and then brushed out, or a water spray, sprayed on to its coat and then brushed through — should suffice to keep it clean and well groomed. Baths should be infrequent, as they tend to soften the coat. Both the teeth and nails require weekly attention. The Keeshond is not a breed that is trimmed to excess; in fact the American Standard expressly forbids this. Trimming around the foot to neaten up the back of the

hocks is allowed and smartens the dog's appearance. The whiskers may also be removed but this is optional.

Adaptability

As the Keeshond continues today to fulfill the role for which it was bred centuries ago, that is one of companion and watchdog, it adapts readily to almost any situation. Since it is heavily coated, care must be taken in very hot, humid weather to prevent it from becoming overheated and collapsing with heat stroke. Its sharp watchdog bark may become annoying, particularly if it is left alone for long periods and starts barking from boredom. It thrives on human companionship and will relish good walks, ample playtime and good nutrition.

Essentials of the Breed

The Keeshond is a square breed, meaning that it is as long as it is high at the shoulder. The ideal height under the British and American Standards for males is 18 inches/45 cm with females 1 inch/2.5 cm shorter. The German Wolfspitz should be 17-21 inches/45-55 cm — and 20 inches/50 cm in a perfect specimen. Its coat should be long, profuse, and double. It tends to stand off from the body and to form a ruff about the head and neck. The outer coat should be a mixture of gray and black, and the undercoat light gray or cream. Lighter markings with cream-colored bands running from the shoulders to the elbows are usual.

The head is wedge shaped and in balance with the size of the dog. Its ears are small, triangular and held stiffly erect. The eyes should be dark brown or black, definitely almond in shape, and must be surrounded by dark lines or spectacles that give the characteristic expression of the breed. The tail should be tightly curled, carried up and over the back. It is barely noticeable unless it is wagging. All its legs have good feathering, which should resemble breeches on the rear ones. Taken as a whole, the Keeshond is a stylish, self-confident, attractive breed.

Registry: AKC, CKC, FCI (Group 5), KC

KERRY BEAGLE

Many are confused by the name of this breed, because the Kerry is in fact a much larger and less compact breed than the Beagle proper. In shape, it is more like the American Coonhound, a breed in whose development it has been suggested that the Kerry Beagle played a significant part. Furthermore, the long established reputation of the Kerry Blue Terrier (commonly referred to as simply "the Kerry") does the Kerry Beagle no favors, as there are no physical similarities whatsoever.

The breed claims an ancient heritage, which can be traced back to early Celtic hounds. In the eighteenth and nineteenth centuries, the breed was almost solely in the care of just one family — the Ryans of Scarteen, County Limerick.

Detailed pedigrees of the Ryan pack dating from 1784 have been passed on to this day. Packs of Kerry Beagles continue to flourish in rural Ireland and the breed has recently been seen at Irish Kennel Club Shows.

The breed may be black-and-tan, blue mottled and tan, tricolor, or tan and white. Kerries generally stand about 24 inches/60 cm at the shoulder, and are moderately long in the back, deep chested and with a fully developed dewlap. The head should also be moderately long, with a broad skull, raised eyebrows, a full muzzle and a bright intelligent expression.

Registry: Irish Kennel Club (not recognized by AKC, CKC, FCI or KC)

Kerry Beagle

KERRY BLUE TERRIER

ORIGIN AND DEVELOPMENT

The Kerry Blue Terrier is a product of south-western Ireland and its name comes from the county Kerry. In its native land, the Kerry Blue Terrier was not only a companion, but an all-round useful farm dog, a guard dog and a very good hunting dog. The Kerry was not only a dispatcher of rats and other vermin in the barnyard, but was used on rabbit and birds and was a good retriever, even fetching prey from water. It was also used to herd sheep and cattle. The Kerry Blue Terrier was purebred in that part of Ireland for well over 100 years.

Although always considered a working and sporting dog, after the formation of the Irish

Kerry Blue Terrier

Republic it began to appear at dog shows. Taken up by English fanciers and trimmed "to the nines," the Kerry Blue was provided with regular classification by the English Kennel Club. The breed became an overnight success.

The Kerry in Ireland is controlled by the Irish Blue Terrier Club of Dublin. Dogs must be shown in the rough. The English Standard is virtually the same as the American Standard and the coats are trimmed. The first important show at which a Kerry appeared was at Westminster Kennel Club in New York City in 1922. In 1924 the Kerry Blue Terrier was officially recognized by the American Kennel Club as a breed and assigned to the Terrier Group.

TEMPERAMENT

The Kerry Blue Terrier is strong willed, active and enthusiastic. It must be socialized early, raised from puppyhood with kind firmness, obedience trained and taught manners. It is a rollicking, rambunctious, Irish individualist.

HEALTH MATTERS

The breed is healthy and long lived. Kerry Blue Terriers at their middle age of seven or eight have been taken for much younger dogs. It is prone to a few heritable problems.

SPECIAL CARE AND TRAINING

The Kerry Blue has an unusual silky-soft but very dense and wavy blue coat that needs to be groomed regularly. Puppies are born black and go through varying changes in color until they are two years old. At this time the dog may be any shade of blue, from light silver gray to midnight or slate blue. The Kerry often has darker points about its head, feet and tail. The coat must be brushed and combed at least every other day right down to the skin. A monthly bath is necessary. Correct trimming with scissors and clippers should be left to professionals until an adult member of the family has learned simple trimming practices.

Because of the way its coat falls heavily, its eyes should be checked daily for unwanted matter and cleaned if necessary. The Kerry must have its nails checked from puppyhood and have a small tip of each toenail removed every ten days or so. The ears should be checked weekly, wiped out with cotton wrapped around the finger and dampened with a little baby oil. If any odor seems to be coming from the ear, veterinary advice is needed.

The Kerry thrives on daily exercise on a leash, unless a securely fenced yard is provided in which case it will happily run around by itself.

ADAPTABILITY

The Kerry will adapt to the country or the city if its need for exercise and companionship are adequately provided. The Kerry is strong willed and is best suited to an equally strong-willed assertive owner. It must have daily human companionship.

ESSENTIALS OF THE BREED

The Kerry Blue Terrier is a short backed, upstanding, vibrant terrier clothed in a soft, dense, wavy blue coat. Its head is long and rectangular, with dark eyes, a slight stop, clean cheeks and a full muzzle with strong white teeth. It has a flat skull with small V-shaped button ears carried forward close to the cheeks, and with the top of the folded ears slightly above the level of the skull. It has a long clean neck, well set and carried proudly over its short back. Its tail should be docked, well placed and carried. It has straight front legs with firm feet and well-angulated hindquarters without dewclaws.

This breed has the character of a well-developed muscular dog with definite terrier style. Great spring of rib is a feature of the breed. The ideal height for a Kerry male is 18 1/2 inches/47 cm at the highest point of its withers and slightly less for a female. Its weight should be from 33-40 pounds/15-18 kg. Carefully groomed in its eye-catching blue coat, the Kerry is stylish and dapper and, thanks to its heritage of a long active life, it carries this look well into its senior years.

Registry: AKC, CKC, FCI (Group 3), KC

KISHU

The Kishu was originally used mainly for hunting. It originates from the Japanese island of Kyushu and is considered one of the most ancient of the country's six spitz breeds. It is said to be a hard, self-confident hunting and guard dog that is wary of strangers.

The breed should stand about 17-21 inches/ 43-53 cm at its withers. Although the Japanese spitz breeds differ in size, they share some features, particularly a wedge-shaped head with pronounced cheeks, decidedly slanted eyes and hooded ears. This breed's coat should be short and harsh, standing out from the body and slightly longer on the tail and buttocks. It is most often seen in white, red or brindle. It is most unusual to come across the Kishu outside Japan.

Registry: FCI (Group 5)

Kishu

KOMONDOR

ORIGIN AND DEVELOPMENT

A rare but very old breed, the Komondor was used to protect flocks of sheep in Hungary. It appears to have the same ancestry as the long-legged dogs of the Russian steppes. Always white and covered with long cords or string-like matted hair, these huge dogs lived outdoors with flocks in all extremes of weather. Their purpose was to guard and protect sheep from any marauders be they human or animal. The Komondor is still used today throughout the American continent for just this purpose.

TEMPERAMENT

The breed is wary of strangers due to its background and because its corded coat falls over its eyes and restricts its vision. Care should be taken with children for this reason.

HEALTH MATTERS

Generally healthy, hip dysplasia is a problem and breeding stock must be X-rayed after the age of two years. Its teeth should be cleaned and nails checked routinely every week. As it is a large dog with an immense coat, the Komondor must have a nutritionally balanced diet. Two or three small meals a day, without soy products, are better than one large one. This is a simple preventative measure against gastric torsion. It is also wise not to allow the Komondor to exercise just after the dog has eaten. It does need very long walks on a regular basis, so it is not a good breed for owners who are not able or prepared to provide this. This breed must be taught not to put up a struggle early in life — it is much too big and strong to wrestle with.

SPECIAL CARE AND TRAINING

The coat of the Komondor requires much care and attention. This chore cannot be overlooked or taken lightly. The Komondor should be socialized early and obedience training is of great importance.

ADAPTABILITY

Because of its size and unique coat, the Komondor is much happier in a country setting than in the city. It should never be cramped or cooped up as this is contrary to its nature.

ESSENTIALS OF THE BREED

The breed is very large, over 25 inches/63 cm in many cases, and weighs up to 95-100 pounds/ 43-45 kg. Always white with dark pigment on its nose and eyelids, there should be no albino characteristics found in this breed. The Komondor is large, full-bodied, heavy boned, with a long natural tail, large neck and expressive eyes, . The Komondor is completely covered with long white ribbons of matted coat material that naturally parts along its backbone and covers the entire animal. This large breed has a very graceful gait.

For show purposes the Komondor is presented gleaming white and in huge coat. This is no mean feat for the Komondor requires up to two full days to dry completely after a bath! This breed is only for the dedicated.

Registry: AKC, CKC, FCI (Group 1), KC

Komondor

KOOIKERHONDJE

The Dutch Spaniel originates from a very ancient type of spaniel that was used before the invention of guns. The dogs used to attract fowl and water birds by jumping and playing around. This made the game curious and venture close enough for the hunters to throw their nets over them.

Some historians have mentioned the Kooiker as possibly playing a part in the development of the Nova Scotia Duck Tolling Retriever. Emigrating Dutch weavers are said to have brought them to North America. Certainly, the way in which both breeds perform and work to this day are very similar.

The Kooiker was almost extinct by the end of World War II but through a lot of hard work it was re-established and recognized in 1971. It is still rare and seldom seen outside the Netherlands where it is mainly kept as a companion dog.

The height at its withers is about 13-16 inches/ 35-40 cm. Its body should be slightly rectangular and its head quite broad in the skull, the same length as the muzzle. The ears should be small and fairly high set. The coat should be soft and silky, lying flat on the body and with longer hair on the ears, neck, back of the legs and its profusely coated tail. Its color is usually white with patches of bright red. The sides of the head and ears should always be red and it is very typical that fringes on the ears have black hair tips

Registry: FCI (Group 8), KC

Kooikerhondje

KRAZSKI OVCAR

The Krazski Ovcar, sometimes called the Karst, is a herding dog from Kraz, the Istrian mountains on the border between Slovenia and Croatia in former Yugoslavia. The breed belongs to the group of herding and guard dogs that are also called mountain dogs and are found in ranges all over the world. The Krazski Ovcar is best known as a herder although it is closely related to several of the mountain dogs that are used as flock guardians. In particular, it resembles the Sarplaninac.

Krazski Ovcar

At its withers, its height is about 20-24 inches/ 52-60 cm. The Krazski Ovcar's coat should be harsh, medium long on the body and longer on the neck, tail and buttocks with a thick, woolly undercoat. Its ears are small and often folded. Its color should be a dark wolf gray with a black mask except for "spectacles," and with light tan or cream on its legs, very similar to the colors of the Keeshond. The Krazski Ovcar is rarely seen outside its homeland.

Registry: FCI (Group 2)

KROMFOHRLÄNDER

This German breed was established in the 1950s through the mating of a Wire Fox Terrier to a French Griffon-type dog. After three generations the breed was recognized and named for the district around its creator's home. It is a very rare breed that shows its Fox Terrier ancestry.

The height at withers is about 15-18 inches/ 38-46 cm. Its body should be rectangular and head long and wedge shaped. The ears may be button or rose style, set high but not above skull level. Its tail is carried in a loose curl over the back. The coat is wiry and three lengths are permissible. The color should be white with a few clearly defined patches. The sides of the head and ears should always be red.

Registry: FCI (Group 9)

Kromfohrländer

KUVASZ

ORIGIN AND DEVELOPMENT

Tibet was the birthplace of this tall white working breed that was used as a guard dog. The breed spread throughout Europe. It was used in Hungary in the eighth century as a guard and hunting dog. Its name comes from the word *kawasz* which in Turkish means protector. Its aptitude showed that it could herd both sheep and cattle, so it was put to these tasks. Because of their great size and strength they were also used to hunt boar.

Today, the breed is used in North and South America to guard flocks of sheep. It is powerful enough to protect them against large marauding animals and fast enough to run down coyotes and wolves.

TEMPERAMENT

As it is inherently a working dog, the breed must be occupied or it will become bored, restless and destructive. Potential owners should remember that breed is primarily a guardian of sheep, and a powerful animal with a temperament of toughness. It must be socialized early and well. It should not be exposed to young children unless it has been brought up with them. The breed can and should be obedience trained.

HEALTH MATTERS

Although the Kuvasz is quite healthy overall, hip dysplasia is a genetic problem. X-rays of breeding stock are essential and, like all giant

Kuvasz

breeds, so is good nutrition. Teeth, ears and nails should be inspected and attended to on a weekly basis.

SPECIAL CARE AND TRAINING

The Kuvasz must have early socialization and obedience training as a young dog if it is to be a well-behaved member of the family. Its owners must be assertive in order to maintain control of this breed. It requires plenty of monitored exercise.

ADAPTABILITY

This robust and protective dog is a country dog. It must have sturdy kenelling if kept out of doors, as well as a safe fenced yard in which to exercise. Obedience training will concentrate its mind and so should be encouraged. It is definitely considered to be a guard dog with a temperament to match.

ESSENTIALS OF THE BREED

This large dog stands 28-30 inches/70-76 cm at the shoulder. The Kuvasz is always white, longhaired, with dark almond-shaped eyes. The coat is double and may be flat or wavy on the back, sides and tail. The male Kuvasz will weigh up to 115 pounds/52 kg and the female a little less. It should have a deep body, good bone and feet and dropped ears that slant forward. An absence of dewclaws on the rear legs is a characteristic of the Kuvasz.

Registry: AKC, CKC, FCI (Group 1), KC

LAGOTTO ROMAGNOLO

This old and genuine water dog has been known in the marshlands of the Romagna region of northeast Italy since the fourteenth century. The marshes have gradually been drained over the centuries and the Lagotto that was once used to hunt waterfowl lost its work. But the dogs' good nose found them a new role because they turned out to be excellent at sniffing out truffles. It is the only breed specialized in this skill. Truffles cost more per kilo than gold — which might be the reason why truffle-searchers have kept their knowledge of the breed a secret. Amazingly, the Lagotto today still fits a detailed description of its appearance and working ability that was written in the late fourteenth century.

The height at the withers should be within 16-19 inches/41-48 cm. Its weight should be within 24-35 pounds/11-16 kg. The body should be square and never look low on the legs. The head should be broad with a rounded skull, round eyes and a blunt muzzle that is not too long. It carries its tail almost erect when interested. The coat should be rather short, thick and woolly with tight curls, with looser curls on the head and ears. A long and corded coat is not permissible. The color should be off-white or white, with or without liver brown patches and ticking, liver brown or liver roan or orange. A black coat and black pigmentation is a serious fault.

Registry: FCI (Group 8)

Lagotto Romagnolo

LAKELAND TERRIER

ORIGIN AND DEVELOPMENT

The name of the Lakeland Terrier was eventually decided upon after meetings of fanciers had been held in the market town of Keswick, in Cumbria, first in 1912 and then in 1921 when devotees of "the improved working terrier" agreed to form the Lakeland Terrier Association. The original Cumbrian terrier had been known by various names depending on its immediate home locality; these included Black Fell, Fell, Westmorland, Patterdale and others. This once tenacious terrier was initially developed to dispatch the fox from its mountainous lair. Often working in extreme weather conditions, the Lakeland was required to be hardy and resolute, possessing sufficient length of leg and body to twist and turn easily in underground passages while seeking its quarry. While a variety of local terriers were involved in producing the modern Lakeland, there seems little doubt that an infusion of Fox Terrier blood was considered advisable to smarten up the breed's overall appearance.

While Lakelands have never been as numerous as some of the terrier breeds, either in the show ring or as companion dogs, the breed has for many years produced a steady stream of show dogs whose overall excellence has rendered them formidable competition.

In 1963 the Lakeland dog, Rogerholm Recruit, brought the breed considerable publicity when he won Best in Show at Cruft's. Just four years later another of the breed, Ch. Stingray of Derryabah, repeated the triumph. Stingray was to become something of a legend, for after his great Cruft's win he crossed the Atlantic having been purchased by Mr. and Mrs. James A. Farrell Jr. Having won Best in Show at the United Kingdom's most famous dog show in 1967, Stringray went on to capture the same spot at the United States' best known show, Westminster Kennel Club, the following year. 1976 saw another Lakeland, Ch. Jo Ni's Red Baron of Crofton, win Best at Westminster for

Mrs. V. K. Dickson, this dog going on to make a great name for itself as an outstanding producer.

TEMPERAMENT

The Lakeland is highly intelligent and compliant. While not naturally aggressive toward other dogs, it will stand its ground.

HEALTH MATTERS

The Lakeland is normally long lived with relatively few health problems. In some parts of the world Legg Perthes Disease, a disorder of the femoral head has been documented.

SPECIAL CARE AND TRAINING

Lakelands require grooming regularly, and twice yearly the old coat should be removed by hand-stripping. This is preferable to clipping, which eventually destroys the natural color and texture of the coat. Hand-stripping requires the minimum of equipment and can be mastered by terrier owners, but it requires great patience and tolerance.

ADAPTABILITY

The Lakeland is highly recommended as a domestic companion. It is a handy size and, being a highly efficient guardian, only barks when necessary. It will fit in well in any home situation, enjoying the freedom of the countryside as much as the indulgence of attentive owners in a more urban environment.

ESSENTIALS OF THE BREED

Noted as a smart, well-balanced and compact dog, the Lakeland comes in a variety of colors — blue-and-tan, black-and-tan, self red, red wheaten, red grizzle, liver, blue and black. Mahogany or deep tan are not typical. The black Lakeland, while not found in Britain at present, is proving highly popular in some Scandinavian countries where it is enjoying something of a revival. The head of the Lakeland is well balanced, equidistant between nose and eye as from eye

Lakeland Terrier

to occiput and flat-skulled. The eyes are dark or hazel and the jaw has a vicelike grip. The ears should be V-shaped, small, carried alertly but set neither too high nor too low. The forequarters require well laid-back shoulders, straight well-boned legs and feet that are round and well padded. The neck is reachy, the rib cage deeper than round, the back strong and moderately short coupled. The hindquarters are well developed and muscled, with hocks straight and low to ground. The tail is customarily docked. The topcoat is dense and weather-resisting, with a softer undercoat. The face and leg hair is crisp. Its movement should be true, with a strong driving action. The Lakeland's height should not exceed 14 inches (37 cm) at the shoulder.

Registry: AKC, CKC, FCI (Group 3), KC

LANCASHIRE HEELER

The Heeler is indigenous to the county of Lancashire, England, and more specifically to the western and coastal region which is largely agricultural. The breed was formerly known as the Ormskirk Heeler and evolved on the farmsteads and estates of Lord Sefton in the early part of the twentieth century. The Heeler proved to be a healthy and versatile dual-purpose dog that was as adept at controlling vermin as herding livestock. The Heeler's ancestry includes Welsh Corgi, Manchester Terrier and possibly some Dachshund blood. The Corgi influence arrived from Wales when cattle were driven by herdsmen to farms and abattoirs in the county — the local terrier from nearby Manchester was already being established in the area.

The Heeler has sharp, alert features and pricked or semi-erect, ears. It is highly intelligent, affectionate and yet still requires firm, kind handling. It is trainable but needs to be kept fully occupied because it has boundless energy despite its small stature. It has a great love of people and children.

The length of its coat may vary according to the time of year, from sleek to a longer coat showing a neck ruff. It has a strong jaw, a low-set but strong body, its front feet turning slightly outward. The topline is firm and level and the tail carried high. The show Heeler must conform to the color markings stipulated in the breed Standard — black with rich tan markings on the muzzle, cheeks, above the eyes, from the knees down (with a black thumbprint above the feet), inside the hind legs and under the tail. These markings are sometimes inclined to fade with age. The height at the shoulder should be 12 inches/30 cm for dogs and 10 inches/25 cm for bitches.

Registry: KC

Lancashire Heeler

LANDSEER

The Landseer was developed in Germany and Switzerland. During the 1930s, breeders in these countries started a breeding program by crossing black-and-white Newfoundlands with Pyrenean Mountain Dogs. The idea may well have been to produce a dog that looked like the ones that the British artist, Sir Edwin Landseer (1802-73) painted of the first Newfoundlands in Europe in 1823. As the white-and-black Newfoundland variety has always been called the Landseer, the choice of this name for a breed (that is no more than a cross between two already existing breeds) was very unlucky. It took decades of discussions before the Fédération Cynologique Internationale finally relented and recognized the Landseer as a breed.

Several points separate the Landseer from the black-and-white colored Newfoundland. The Landseer is a considerably lighter dog in build and lacks the body depth that is required in a good Newfoundland. The Landseer is kept as a companion dog and is very rare, even in its countries of origin. The height at its withers should be about 27-31 inches/67-80 cm. Its body should be rectangular with a slight tuck-up, and a waist that is neither broad, nor deep. It is rather high on its legs compared with the Newfoundland and not as massive. Its head should be big with flat cheeks and tight lips. The coat should lie flat, straight and longer on chest, buttocks and tail.

To be correct the color should really be called white and black — white with black patches and not vice versa. Black should appear on the head except for the muzzle and a blaze. Large patches of black on the body should not go beyond the neck, chest, under belly or down the legs or tail.

Registry: FCI (Group 2)

Landseer

LAPPHUNDS

The Scandinavian herding spitzes were originally guard and hunting dogs kept by nomadic tribes that came from the east thousands of years ago and settled in Scandinavia. The Laplanders descended from these ancient tribes and their dogs have played an important part in survival on the endless hills and snow-covered fields. It is only in recent centuries that these breeds have been used for herding reindeer, and in the last couple of decades their work has increasingly been taken over by the use of snow scooters. The few dogs of this breed that are still used for herding in Sweden are usually smooth-coated and of a lighter build. These dogs herd by barking intensively which is a habit that can be a drawback today if they are kept as companion dogs in cities. The breed makes an excellent farm dog, however, that will guard and announce the arrival of visitors. Lapphunds are today kept mainly as companion and show dogs. All three breeds are well represented in Scandinavia but rarely seen elsewhere.

The height at the withers varies for each type: the Finnish Lapphund should be 16-20 inches/40-51 cm, the Laponian Herder about 17-21 inches/43-54 cm, and the Swedish Lapphund about 17-19 inches/43-48 cm. The body should be rectangular, deep, compact and muscular — none of the breeds should look shallow or leggy. The head is wedge-shaped, should be strong with a broad skull and a muzzle that is not too long or pointed.

The Finnish and Swedish Lapphunds should carry the tail curled over the back. They each should have a long, profuse coat that stands out from the body; the undercoat should be thick and woolly. The coat is longest on the neck, buttocks and tail. The Laponian Herder should have a saber-like tail that is never carried

Finnish Lapphund

Laponian Herder

Swedish Lapphund

over the back. Its coat is medium short and should lie close with a harsh texture and thick undercoat. The Finnish Lapphund may be any color but it is most commonly black or liver brown with very light tan markings. The Laponian Herder is black, grayish black or mole with light tan markings — white markings are permissible.

The Swedish Lapphund tends to be black. Brown (the color of a bear) is preferred but is never seen today. In the early 1900s all white or all white Swedish Lapphunds were commonly found. In the early 1900s all-white Swedish Lapphunds were commonly found.

Registry: FCI (Group 5)

LEONBERGER

The Leonberger is a mountain dog originating from Swabia in the foothills of the Black Forest. In the 1840s Herr Heinrich Essig, Mayor of Leonberg, decided to create a breed to resemble the lion emblem on the town's crest. It is believed that Essig combined the Saint Bernard, Newfoundland and Pyrenean Mountain Dog, and added a secret ingredient! The Leonberger has inherited the Newfoundland's love of water and has a dense waterproof coat and webbed feet. Its body color may range be sand, light yellow, golden, or red-brown, and all colors may have black tips to the guard hairs. Its black mask extends to the ears, and its lips and eyes should be tight.

The modern Leonberger is a large, intelligent and affectionate breed. They make excellent companions to adults, children and other animals. Careful feeding and exercise in the first eighteen months of life is essential to ensure that the rapid bone development is healthy and sound. Hip dysplasia and bone problems are not common, but they can result. Two world wars resulted in its almost total decimation. Great Britain and the United States have imported dogs from the European continent and the Leonberger is now firmly established on an international basis.

Registry: FCI (Group 2), KC

Leonberger

LHASA APSO

ORIGIN AND DEVELOPMENT

There can be little doubt that the Tibetan breeds which are now so popular, namely the Tibetan Terrier, Tibetan Spaniel and Lhasa Apso, have common ancestors. In the land beyond the northern boundary of India, the Lhasa Apso (or at least its venerable ancestors) has existed for many years. These dogs were treasured by the privileged classes that owned them, and for many years the breed remained in Tibet, very few specimens ever leaving the country. Apparently the Lhasa was once presented by the Dalai Lhama to individual members of imperial families and dignitaries in China. It was considered a great honor to receive these dogs as gifts, because they supposedly brought good luck and health to the recipients.

The Lhasa is truly an aristocrat, having been bred in a domestic environment for generations, yet its hardy constitution, amiable disposition and convenient size for contemporary living has brought it to a level of popularity which could never have been envisaged by those who fostered its early development. There is evidence to suggest that at the beginning of the twentieth century small numbers of Tibetan dogs arrived in Great Britain, having being brought in by military personnel. Others followed in the hands of private individuals who had fallen for their charms. In those early days, however, what are now known as the Lhasa Apso and the Tibetan Terrier were imported as — and assumed to be — the same breed. This is confirmed by the fact that they were originally classified as "Lhasa Terriers."

As discussions and arguments developed over correctness of type, the breed was split into two, primarily divided by size. The more leggy animal formed the basis of the Tibetan Terrier and the lower-to-ground dogs laid the foundations for the Lhasa Apso. At the time it was registered as the Tibetan Apso the breed was first awarded Challenge Certificates at

Cruft's Dog Show in 1965. Strangely, Tibetan Terriers had been accorded Championship status many years earlier.

Meanwhile the breed had its stalwarts in the United States, where it had been developed along slightly different lines from other imported stock. In the 1970s British breeders turned their attention to the United States, and both Anne Matthews (Hardacre Kennel) and Jean Blyth (Saxonsprings Kennel) imported stock from America with a view to adding a little more "style" to the already excellent type they had established. Several key American dogs were imported to Great Britain but none proved more significant than Ch. Orlane's Intrepid. He rapidly built up a great reputation in the show ring and later earned a place in history by producing many excellent children.

In a relatively short space of time, the American style and glamor, combined with the sound breed type of the British Lhasa, proved to be a recipe for great success. Dogs which were a product of the two were highly sought after and many such dogs were imported into other countries where they, in turn, founded their own dynasties. One such country is Denmark where the breed has been developed to such a high standard that many visiting judges have concluded that this is now where the best Lhasas in the world can be found.

TEMPERAMENT

The Lhasa is a naturally alert dog, but tends to be watchful and slightly aloof with strangers. Once introduced, it has an outgoing and friendly personality with no suggestion of aggression.

HEALTH MATTERS

The breed is generally healthy and free of hereditary diseases, though breeders are keen to monitor their stock to prevent any frequently occurring condition becoming established.

Lhasa Apso

SPECIAL CARE AND TRAINING

Like many eastern breeds, the Lhasa has an independent streak and is not the sort of dog to carry out obedience exercises without question. They can be trained in basic disciplines but will think about what they are being asked to do. With their lavish coats it is vital that they are groomed on a daily basis if they are to look their best. This should take the form of a complete brushing, right through to the skin, paying special attention to the areas around the eyes and ears.

ADAPTABILITY

Lhasas have been domesticated for many years and they thrive in a household environment. Even so, they will live in the company of other dogs without question, provided they maintain regular human contact.

ESSENTIALS OF THE BREED

The Lhasa stands around 10 inches/25 cm at the shoulder and is slightly longer than its withers height. It should have a strong and well-arched neck, a firm level topline, great spring of rib and its tail should be high set, carried in a gentle curve well over the back. The skull is moderately narrow, falls away slightly behind the eyes, and is not quite flat and yet never domed. The muzzle should be straight and about one-third the head length, with a moderate stop. The nose is always black; the head is heavily furnished with a good fall over the eyes and a lavish beard. The eyes are frontally placed, oval, dark and medium in size. The mouth should show a reverse scissors bite — with the upper incisors closing just inside the lower. The hindquarters should be muscular and show good angulation; the feet should be round and with firm pads.

The Lhasa's coat has a moderate undercoat with a topcoat that is heavy, straight and rather hard. It should not be woolly or silky. In color, the breed can be golden, sandy, honey, dark grizzle, slate, smoke, black, white, brown or parti-color. Today's Standard gives all colors equal acceptance, though in the early days it was said that "lion colors" should be preferred.

The movement of the Lhasa is characteristic and is described as "free and jaunty." One of the negative aspects seen in the offspring from some of the successful American dogs is that the hind action tends to be a little extreme, with rear pads being flicked too high, a movement that is considered untypical by some purists.

Registry: AKC, CKC, FCI (Group 9), KC

LÖWCHEN

ORIGIN AND DEVELOPMENT

The name of the Löwchen translates directly from German as "little lion" (and is pronounced "Lerv-chun"). This stems from the traditional method of clipping the breed's coat into what is ostensibly a lion shape. The Löwchen is a member of the family of dogs known as the Bichons, a group that contains such breeds as the Bichon Frisé, the Maltese, the Bolognese and the Havanese. It is irrelevant as to which, if any, was the "original," suffice to say that the dogs have common roots and have been developed as separate breeds where coat types seem to be a major differentiating factor. There is debate as to why the coat was first clipped into the lion pattern. One story which seems logical is that the breed was used as a "living hot water bottle" in the beds of ladies during the Middle Ages — shaving part of the body gave ready access to a naturally warm surface area. To this day, Löwchens will eagerly crawl under the bedclothes and remain there, motionless.

While the breed has evidently existed in

Löwchen

central Europe for many years, it became very rare for reasons which are difficult to ascertain. In fact, in the late 1960s the breed was described as the rarest breed of dog in the world in the *Guinness Book of Records*. This, again, is debatable. In 1968 two English Toy breeders, Mrs. Stenning and Mrs. Banks, imported stock from Germany to Britain — since so few of the breed were to be found, all the early imports were very closely related. With time, further imports followed, still with family connections.

The very narrow genetic base on which the breed was built in Britain is proven when one looks at the pedigree of the first ever Champion Löwchen, Ch. Cluneen Adam Adamant. To begin with, he was from a mother-to-son mating, his sire being Cluneen Itzi v.d. 3 Lowen, his dam Cluneen Butzi v.d. 3 Lowen. Not only was Butzi Itzi's dam, but Itzi's sire, Adam v. Livland, was the result of a brother-to-sister mating between a dog and bitch who were full brother and sister to Butzi! In view of the dramatic in-breeding which took place to found the breed, it is quite remarkable that it has remained free of any major hereditary defects.

Some people naively believe that the Löwchen coat grows naturally in the traditional lion pattern, so it comes as a surprise when they learn that the pups are born fully coated and need to be clipped. The breed had an unexpected boost in popularity when an unclipped specimen featured in the American television series, "Hart to Hart" — Freeway was the dog that achieved universal fame.

TEMPERAMENT

The Löwchen is a typical Toy dog, naturally outgoing and happy. It is lively and intelligent and should always be even-tempered.

HEALTH MATTERS

Remarkably, particularly considering the breed's ancestry, the Löwchen remains mainly free of major hereditary problems and its natural longevity is testament to its freedom from major disease. Patella luxation and other deformities in the hindquarters are seen occasionally, and it is vital that puppy-buyers deal only with breeders who breed from sound stock.

SPECIAL CARE AND TRAINING

The Löwchen is highly trainable and responds well to basic obedience routines. They also enjoy playing household games with their owners. It is easy to maintain, but whether the coat is clipped or kept full, thorough grooming is necessary to avoid mats and tangles. Also, the area around the eyes and inner ears should always be checked for cleanliness.

ADAPTABILITY

The Löwchen is not a good kennel dog — it much prefers a home environment. So long as it has adequate human company, it will fit in virtually anywhere. Many Löwchen owners first acquire one when they have already established themselves with another breed. The Löwchen will happily join in with the other members of the canine family. Invariably the charms of the breed are such that in time the owners are won over and the number of Löwchens far outnumbers the original breed.

ESSENTIALS OF THE BREED

There is a tremendous variation in the Löwchen's size. Under the British Standard, it should stand 10-13 inches/25-33 cm, yet the Fédération Cynologique Internationale's Standard allows 8-14 inches/20-36 cm. The head is quite wide-skulled, the eyes round, dark, large and intelligent. The ears are pendant, long and well fringed so that the hair merges with that of the mane. The body is square with moderate angulation and a level topline. There is moderate tuck-up and the outline is completed with a plumed tail which is carried gaily on the move. The feet are small and round. The coat is long with a slight wave (never curly) and is silky in texture. A major attraction of the breed is that it can be any color or combination of colors.

Registry: FCI (Group 9), KC

LUNDEHUND/NORSK LUNDEHUND

This is probably one of the most singular dog breeds in the world. It developed in the Lofoten Islands off the north of Norway. The dog's make-up would be considered a bad fault in other breeds but there is a purpose for its peculiarities. The Lundehund is thought to descend from the Norwegian Buhund and small Laikas. Over many centuries, it has developed the very specialized skill of hunting and killing puffins on steep cliffs. (This type of hunting is banned nowadays.) To perform their task, the dogs had to be able to climb up vertical cliffs. They are very agile and their extra toe and very large dewclaw, as big and long as a normal toe, helped them to grip to the cliffs. As well as an ability to stretch their front legs completely from left to right, they have a very short upper arm. They also have a narrow chest and are able to bend their neck backward as well as fold their otherwise pricked ears when necessary. This was particularly useful when a dog was forced down the very narrow holes where the puffins nested. The breed was little known before the 1930s even in Norway. It was recognized in 1943 and is still very rare.

The height at the withers should be about 12 1/2-15 inches/32-38 cm. Its weight should be about 13-15 pounds/6-7 kg. The body should be rectangular, with front feet turning out and five showing toes. A very well-developed dewclaw is typical — there should also be well-developed dewclaws on the hindlegs. The head should be small, wedge shaped and with rather big, pricked ears. The eyes are quite pale with a darker brown ring around them. The absence of premolars is typical. The breed's front movement is wide with legs moving in circles and its hind action is close. The tail may be carried over its back in a loose curl or pendant. The coat should be straight and medium short with a thick undercoat. Its color may be any shade of golden-red with black tips. The forehead is grizzle-marked and the eye rims are black and well defined.

Registry: FCI (Group 5)

Lundehund

MAGYAR AGÁR

The Hungarian Sighthound resembles the Greyhound but is smaller, shorter in the back and lacks the Greyhound's elegant long head. The Magyar Agár should have a wedge-shaped head with a broad skull. It is a very old breed that is said to have arrived with the Magyars. As it is used for racing, the breed has been crossed with Greyhounds during this century to improve its speed. It was recognized by the FCI in 1966 and is still quite rare outside Hungary.

At the withers, dogs should be about 26-27 1/2 inches/65-70 cm and bitches slightly smaller. The coat should be smooth and rather harsh in texture. All colors are permissible.

Registry: FCI (Group 10)

Magyar Agár

MALTESE

Origin and Development

Without question, the most dramatic breed in the Toy Group — and frequently the most appealing to the ringside — is the Maltese. Much of its drama and appeal stems from its crowning glory: its silky white floor-length coat.

Since the time of Paul the Apostle, there have been references to the Maltese — for instance, a bitch named Issa was owned by the Roman governor of Malta. Many of these early references refer to the breed's delightful temperament and the importance of its diminutive size. The Maltese has even been compared to ferrets and squirrels.

As with many breeds popular in the United States today, the Maltese gravitated to England where it was a favorite of Elizabeth I. In 1877, a Maltese was exhibited at the first Westminster Kennel Club show in the States but it was listed as a "Maltese Lion Dog". Two years later, a colored Maltese was exhibited as a "Maltese Skye Terrier". The breed was admitted to the registry of the American Kennel Club in 1888. Despite its tiny size, the Maltese traces its origin to a spaniel type rather than to terriers.

Temperament

In some ways, the Maltese seems almost to have a split personality. As history notes, it has always been popular with ladies, who used to carry these dogs in their arms and travel with them in their carriages. In a sense, the Maltese is a quiet, docile breed, very much at home when it is cuddled by its owners. But at the same time, it is a lively, spritely breed, capable of great animation and full of fun.

Health Matters

Normally the Maltese is quite healthy, but there are a few areas of concern. Luxating patellas (the kneecap covering the joint in the rear leg) may cause lameness. This condition is heritable but may also be caused by trauma, so the dog should never be grabbed by the rear legs or allowed to jump off tall furniture. Occasionally low blood sugar may cause a Maltese — particularly a tiny one — to faint. Honey rubbed into the gums will bring it round almost immediately. Teething sometimes brings on this condition and dogs can and do grow out of it. The eyes sometimes tear excessively and if the ducts become blocked the Maltese should be taken to the vet. Its teeth should be cleaned and toenails clipped weekly.

SPECIAL CARE AND TRAINING

Because the Maltese coat is so much a part of the breed, owners should either be prepared to spend time attending to the coat or should forego the look that is the hallmark of the breed by opting for a more convenient pet trim.

Maltese coats require frequent care. The breed should be carefully trained to walk on a leash fearlessly — and to carry itself with great style. Once it has realized that it must go with its owner when on a leash, it will soon accept all manner of sights and sounds. The Maltese should have a proud carriage with its head and tail up.

ADAPTABILITY

The dual aspect of the breed's personality makes it highly adaptable and well suited to a variety of living situations with the usual limitations that are placed on many refined Toy breeds in relation to their ability to withstand rough-housing with children.

ESSENTIALS OF THE BREED

The mantle of long, silky white hair is a

Maltese

dominant factor affecting the overall appearance of the Maltese. But under the hair, the breed Standard calls for a compact, squarely built dog with its height (measured from the ground to the withers) equal to its length (measured from the withers to the root of the tail). Its neck is long enough to permit a high head carriage; its tail is a full plume carried gracefully over the back. The topline of the Maltese should be level.

The coat is single — without an undercoat. It should hang flat and silky over the sides of the body with highly conditioned show dogs wearing coats that reach the ground. Any sign of kinkiness, curliness or woolly texture is not allowed. Pure white is the preferred color, although light tan or lemon on the ears is permissible.

The Maltese head is of medium length with a moderate stop and rounded skull. The ears are low set and heavily feathered. The eyes should be very dark and round with black rims that project a gentle but alert expression. The foreface is of medium length — not snipy — and the nose is black. The bite is even or scissors.

The preferred weight is under 7 pounds/ 3 kg with 4-6 pounds/1.8-2.7 kg the preferred range. The Maltese moves with a smooth flowing gait and, considering its size, gives the impression of rapid movement.

Registry: AKC, CKC, FCI (Group 9), KC

MANCHESTER TERRIER

ORIGIN AND DEVELOPMENT

The Manchester Terrier is an elegant, smooth-coated English terrier. It was originally called the Black and Tan Terrier and it has been refined over hundreds of years. The breed can be seen in many old paintings and drawings. It is essentially a ratting terrier, bred to live in the house — hence its short, single coat — and to keep both house and yards clear of vermin. This was very necessary in the days before drains and proper rubbish disposal were introduced. The breed remains true to type, being a good guard, devoted to its owners, and clean and well mannered around the house.

TEMPERAMENT

This is a true terrier, inquisitive, alert and keen to investigate and look into everything. It does not take immediately to strangers, but when they are accepted as friends it will never forget them and will greet them enthusiastically — and probably noisily! As a breed the Manchester is generally good with children and not aggressive toward other dogs.

HEALTH MATTERS

This is a healthy breed with cast-iron digestion. Some individuals have a predisposition to a bleeding disorder called Von Willebrand's

Manchester Terrier with natural (uncropped) ears

disease, but this is rare and wounds heal quickly. The Manchester invariably lives to between twelve and fifteen years.

SPECIAL CARE AND TRAINING

The coat is single and therefore needs little attention. The emphasis is on a daily routine — soft, warm, clean bedding, fresh water, a balanced diet and a brush down once a week. They will take as much exercise as you care to give them, and respond well to Obedience, Agility and show training.

ADAPTABILITY

Above everything else, this handsome, athletic dog needs human companionship so it does not respond well to being left for long periods or if it is exclusively confined to a kennel environment. The Manchester will live quite happily as a dog about town or as the complete country companion.

ESSENTIALS OF THE BREED

This is a slender, black-and-tan dog, standing 15-16 inches/39-40 cm at the shoulder. Its head is wedge shaped, with a tight-lipped mouth. The ears are small, V-shaped and held above its dark eyes. In the United States, the ears are usually cropped to a point. The body is graceful and slightly arched over the loin. The legs are long and the feet neat with black nails. The tail should be long, tapering and held no higher than the level of the back. The tan markings should be precisely placed: tan spots over the eyes and on the cheeks, black "thumb marks" in the tan above the front feet, tanned legs and muzzle. The coat is short and very glossy, and the tan should always be rich and dark.

Registry: AKC, CKC, FCI (Group 3), KC

MAREMMA SHEEPDOG

ORIGIN AND DEVELOPMENT

Although this breed is known as the Maremma Sheepdog in Great Britain, in its native Italy it has a double name, Maremmano Abruzzese, after the two regions that have long claimed the imposing white dog as their own.

The Maremma is rolling countryside with wooded hills that reach down to the sea along the coast from Cecina to Rome. This used to be excellent pastureland for cattle, sheep and horses, and provided almost impenetrable cover where wild boar, roe deer, bears and wolves could escape destruction. For centuries, the life of the sheep, shepherds and the large white dogs that accompanied them followed a strict routine. From June to October they would all venture up into the mountains of Abruzzi, and from October to June they would retreat to the plains of Maremma. Yet a few dogs always stayed behind in both areas as watchdogs on the farms — and a Maremma could usually be found in all the fine houses of Tuscany.

History relates that in 1872 a "Roman Maremma" won a class at a dog show in Nottingham, England. In the early part of the twentieth century, various Maremmas were imported to Britain and in 1936 the Kennel Club recognized the breed as the Maremma Sheepdog. A breed club was formed in 1950 but the breed never really achieved a strong foothold until the mid-1970s when an Italian, Franca Simondetti, loaned two in-whelp bitches to breeders in Britain. The breed was first awarded Challenge Certificates in 1980 and, largely due to the efforts of a small band of enthusiasts like Gordon and Anne Latimer of the famous Sonymer Kennel, type and quality have improved steadily. In 1995 Signora Simondetti was honored with an invitation to judge Maremmas at Crufts Dog Show. There were thirty-five dogs entered under her and she must have been fascinated to see how the breed had developed in the United Kingdom since she supplied what was basically the breed's foundation. Interestingly, as Best of Breed she selected a male who was bred from two more recent Italian dogs, its dam being imported in whelp.

TEMPERAMENT

The Maremma is a proud and dignified breed, the product of the harsh solitary lifestyle that it has endured for generations. It is supremely loyal to its family, while also an excellent protector and guard. However, it is also a thinking dog and is consequently not naturally subservient. It will rationalize what is asked of it before acquiescing.

HEALTH MATTERS

The Maremma has remained an unexaggerated breed for decades and, as a result, has few health problems. As with many large dogs, some breeders feel that X-raying for hip abnormalities is advisable but generally this is not a problem with the breed.

SPECIAL CARE AND TRAINING

The Maremma needs to be trained to fulfill its

Maremma Sheepdog

role within the family. It responds well to logical training but may not prove to be the ideal Obedience competitor because it is a thinker. Once a Maremma knows who its "pack leader" is, it will become devoted to him or her. Its white coat needs thorough weekly grooming to maintain a clean, majestic appearance.

ADAPTABILITY

Despite the solitary existence that its ancestors lived, the Maremma has always been around people. It is an ideal family dog but it needs space, exercise and mental stimulation if it is to thrive.

ESSENTIALS OF THE BREED

The breed is often confused with the Great Pyrenees and Kuvasz, but the Maremma has a very distinctive head. This is conical in shape and quite large in proportion to the body. It is vaguely reminiscent of a polar bear's head — broad between the ears but not short in muzzle. The whole head is smooth and the eyes almond shaped and dark; the ears are small, high set, with pointed tips and lying flat against the skull. It is important that the pigment in the lips, eye rims and pads should be black. Males should look overtly masculine, with a very pronounced ruff, while bitches are noticeably feminine in looks and disposition.

The Maremma is powerfully built and slightly off-square with high withers. At the shoulder, males stand 25 1/2-28 1/2 inches/65-72 cm while bitches are 23 1/2-26 1/2 inches/ 60-67 cm. The tail hangs low but curves at the tip when carried out level with the back in an action that is nimble and free, giving the impression of a dog that can turn easily. The coat should be all white but a little ivory or biscuit shading is usually tolerated. In texture, it is harsh and plentiful with a thick undercoat. A little waviness — but not curl — is permitted. The tail should be well covered with thick hair.

Registry: FCI (Group 1), KC

MASTIFF

ORIGIN AND DEVELOPMENT

As the lion is to the feline species, so the Mastiff is to dogdom. The American Standard says it well: "Large, massive symmetrical and well knit frame. A combination of grandeur and good nature, courage and docility." The group of dogs known as Mastiffs is by all accounts an ancient one. With origins in Asia, Mastiffs were depicted in Egyptian monuments and also mentioned in Persian, Roman and early English literature. They were once used as dogs of war, as fighting dogs pitted against a variety of adversaries and even in packs against humans. Their primary role, however, has been as guard dogs and over the centuries, the Mastiff has developed into a guardian and much loved family dog.

TEMPERAMENT

This is a dog of such impressive size and mien that aggression is not necessary. In ancient times, Mastiffs were kept tied by day and loosed at night to protect and keep predators at bay. The modern Mastiff is a superb family dog: devoted, gentle and biddable. Its very presence imparts a feeling of companionship and security.

HEALTH MATTERS

As in most breeds of average and above average size, hip dysplasia is a concern, as well as other developmental problems associated with great and rapid growth. Gastric torsion is also a possible health risk. Problems identified with reproductive efficiency are thyroid imbalance and uterine inertia. As in so many breeds, cancer is a major cause of death. Some may describe the Mastiff as enormous and ponderous but to its devotees its greatest disadvantage is its all too short life.

SPECIAL CARE AND TRAINING

The Mastiff must be raised with care, attention, proper diet and exercise to realize its potential. Overfeeding is almost as detrimental as underfeeding and exercise should be appropriate. The Mastiff should not succumb to the vagaries of the rage that afflicts some big tough dogs. This is a noble breed, loyal and loving, but not without problems. Physically it does require considerable space. Some people do not like the way that most Mastiffs salivate and snore.

ADAPTABILITY

Generally rather sedentary, the Mastiff is unobtrusive as a house dog, despite its immense size. Out of doors, it tends to keep close to home and is disinclined to roam. It wants to be where it belongs — with its family. Although capable of considerable speed and agility, the Mastiff is a marvelous walking or hiking companion, contented to pace itself and remain close by.

ESSENTIALS OF THE BREED

The Mastiff presents a massive appearance when viewed from any angle. Its body is rectangular, being somewhat longer than high, with great depth, bone and mass throughout. The minimum height at the top of the shoulder is 30 inches/76 cm for dogs and 27 1/2 inches/ 70 cm for bitches. Its well-knit structure is muscular and powerful.

An image to conjure with when envisioning the head is a box with a smaller box for the muzzle. The length of the skull should be twice that of the muzzle, with proportionate breadth and depth. The stop should be well defined but not too abrupt. The ears are V-shaped, not houndy, set at the broadest point of the skull and lying close to the cheeks. Its medium-sized brown eyes have an alert, kindly expression. Its brows should be moderately raised, with a furrow extending up the forehead. Wrinkles appear more prominently when the dog is at attention. Its jaws are well developed and powerful. The preferred bite is a scissors one but, so long as the teeth are not visible, a moderately undershot jaw should not be faulted.

The muzzle, ears, and nose should be dark — the blacker, the better. Its slightly arched neck fits smoothly into moderately sloping shoulders. The strong topline finishes off with a slightly rounded rump and thick rooted tail, long enough to reach the hock. The tail should hang down in repose but be carried in a slight upward curve when the dog is in motion. The forechest is well defined, ribs well rounded and the deep, hind quarters broad and muscular. The heavy boned legs are straight and strong with moderate angulation in the hip, stifle and hock assembly to match the shoulders. The gait enhances the breed's image of power and strength, with the legs reaching and driving true. Its moderately short coat of fawn, apricot or brindle is set off by a black mask and ears.

Registry: AKC, CKC, FCI (Group 2), KC

Mastiff

MEXICAN HAIRLESS/XOLOITZQUINTLI

ORIGIN AND DEVELOPMENT

Xoloitzquintli is pronounced "show-low-its-queen-tlee", so the breed is usually referred to simply as the Xolo. Ancestors of the Aztecs brought the Xolo when they emigrated from Asia to Mexico 3,000 years ago. The dogs were used as pets, bed warmers and a source of food.

When the Aztec dynasty disappeared, the naked dogs survived in isolated villages. The Mexican artist Diego Rivera (1886-1957) pictured the Xolo in his murals. The Mexican Kennel Club helped establish the breed in the 1950s.

TEMPERAMENT

Xolos are calm happy dogs, generally without fear. They can be good alarm dogs. They were, and are, bred as pets.

HEALTH MATTERS

The breed is hardy but requires special care. Teeth and nails should receive attention weekly.

SPECIAL CARE AND TRAINING

Like most hairless dogs, the breed can be very uncomfortable in cold weather. In the summer,

Mexican Hairless

it must be protected from direct sunlight. There is a powder puff variety of this breed that is coated all over the body and tail and so does not need this special care.

ADAPTABILITY

Bred as a pet the Xolo must be kept as a house dog — regardless of whether it is in an urban or country environment. The breed is adaptable to all styles of living, as it comes in a size for everyone. Raised as pets, they should be well socialized and if they are going to a family with children the dogs and children should meet in a calm, unhurried way. They should get used to each other gradually. Children should be instructed to be gentle and kind with the Xolo.

ESSENTIALS OF THE BREED

The Xoloitzquintli comes in three sizes: Toy, Miniature and Standard. Toy is 11-12 inches/ 28-30 cm; Miniature 13-18 inches/33-45 cm; and Standard 18-22 1/2 inches/45-55 cm. The naked variety has only wisps of hair on its head, nape of the neck, feet and tip of the tail. The powder puff has a full coat of medium length soft hair covering the entire body, including the tail. The Xolo reveals its sighthound heritage in the shape of its head and large, elegant, uncropped, erect ears. The mouth in the powder puff variety usually has a full complement of forty-two teeth, while the naked variety generally has many teeth missing. The tail is a natural one, undocked and carried gaily, but not over the back. Any color combination is allowed in this breed.

In the United States the Toy variety is called the Mexican Hairless. The Mexican Hairless may soon be registered with the Canadian Kennel Club. The Standard and Miniature varieties are not recognized in the United States.

Registry: FCI (Group 5)

MIDDLE ASIAN OWTCHARKA/ SREDNEASIATSKAJA OVTJARKA

This Russian herding dog is mainly used to guard flocks and property. It is self-confident, tough, determined and wary of strangers. The breed resembles the Anatolian Shepherd Dog and the Caucasian Owtcharka.

The height at the withers should be over 24 inches/65 cm in males and 24 inches/60 cm in females. The body should be rectangular, well muscled and with strong bone. Its massive head should have pronounced, strong cheeks, but not too long a muzzle. The ears are cropped very close, and the tail is docked either short or to half its length. The coat may be short, straight and coarse or medium long. Accepted colors are black, gray, white with or without patches, light fawn, red or brindle.

Registry: FCI (Group 2)

The Middle Asian Owtcharka is a tough and determined Russian herding dog and it is very wary of strangers.

MINIATURE BULL TERRIER

ORIGIN AND DEVELOPMENT

Bull Terriers have always varied considerably in size, and there is still no limitation as to height or weight of the Standard dogs. Miniature Bull Terriers have existed for as long as the breed itself, and classes for "small" dogs, under 10 pounds/4.5 kg in weight, were scheduled as long ago as 1863. The type very nearly died out in the early years of this century, but in 1939 the Kennel Club was persuaded to open a separate register, with the present size limit, and the modern Miniature Bull Terrier was born.

The breed Standard remains almost exactly the same as that for the full size Bull Terrier, with the exception of a height limitation. To quote the Kennel Club Breed Standard: "Height should not exceed 35.5 cm (14 inches). There should be an impression of substance to size of dog. There is no weight limit. The dog should at all times be balanced." The word "should" in this Standard, where it refers to height, is significant; exceeding the height limit is not, under Kennel Club rules, a disqualification.

The breed has never entirely stabilized in type, almost certainly because of its origins as a

Miniature Bull Terrier

combination of the old "Toy" and "small" versions of the breed. There is some degree of polarity between the very small dogs, which to some extent may lack the quality of Standard dogs, and Miniatures whose size approaches, or even exceeds, the height limit. The quality of the Miniatures has become very good indeed.

TEMPERAMENT

Miniatures should have the same temperament as their larger cousins, although as with almost every small dog, they tend to show a need to assert themselves when the occasion demands. They are certainly no more lap dogs than any Bull Terrier.

HEALTH MATTERS

Miniature Bull Terriers are as healthy as Standard dogs, but some are known to suffer from an inherited eye problem, lens luxation. This eye problem has not been recognized in larger Bull Terriers.

SPECIAL CARE AND TRAINING

To all intents and purposes, Miniature Bull Terriers should be treated exactly the same as their Standard cousins.

ADAPTABILITY

Again, the breed does not differ from Standard Bull Terriers to any great extent; if anything their more convenient size may make them even more adaptable to modern living conditions. Many is the elderly Bull Terrier fancier who finds the prospect of a standard weight dog a little daunting, in view of its bulk and power. The Miniature variety provides the perfect solution.

ESSENTIALS OF THE BREED

These are precisely as those of the larger dogs, and the more closely a Miniature approaches the conformation of a good specimen of the Standard version of the breed, the better it will be. It would be a matter of great concern to most breeders of either type of Bull Terrier if, for whatever reason, the conformation of the Miniature was allowed to drift away from that of the Standard size Bull Terrier.

Registry: AKC, CKC, FCI (Group 3), KC

MINIATURE PINSCHER

ORIGIN AND DEVELOPMENT

The vivacious tiny show dog in the Toy Group with a short coat of black-and-tan, bright red, or chocolate and rust, erect natural or cropped ears, docked upright tail and with a look on the end of its lead that appears to communicate "Look at me and I'll look at you," is the epitome of a show-off. This breed is the Miniature Pinscher.

The breed is German in origin and is older than its larger counterpart, the Doberman. They are not, in fact, thought to be related, but the Miniature Pinscher is thought to have descended from the German Pinscher. The Min-Pin was sometimes thought to resemble the tiny red deer found in German forests. It took breeders a short time to produced the tiny, showy, toy dog that is such a stand out in the international show ring today, possibly using Italian Greyhounds and Dachsunds. It made its way to the United States in the early 1900s and became an immediate success.

TEMPERAMENT

Although it is very alert and on the go at all times, it does make a clever child's companion as well as an all-round house dog. It is at its best as a watchdog, barking being one of its favorite indoor (and outdoor) sports. It needs plenty of attention and interaction with its owners.

SPECIAL CARE AND TRAINING

Since it is very short coated, the Miniature Pinscher should sport a snappy overcoat when outdoors for exercise in cold weather. It needs vigorous exercise because it is a vigorous little dog. The males may be difficult to housetrain — they are extraordinary leg lifters — but if they are started early and taught with diligence, housetraining can be accomplished.

HEALTH MATTERS

This is a very hardy breed that is easily kept. As is true with many Toy dogs, the breed may be afflicted with patella luxation. This condition is when the kneecap covering the joint in the rear of the leg slips to one side of the legs and causes the dog to limp. It may be heritable or caused by trauma, so the dog should not jump off high furniture, in and out of cars or be grabbed by its legs. When the patella slips out, the knee can be put back in place by a vet or a

Miniature Pinscher

knowledgeable person, but it may need to be surgically corrected (in which case it would not be eligible to be shown in the United States).

Teeth should be checked regularly, particularly at teething time (four to six months) to make sure that the baby teeth are being shed correctly. When mature, the Miniature Pinscher's teeth should be cleaned with weekly brushing. Its toenails need weekly attention with a file or clippers. Its coat can be kept smooth and shiny without excessive bathing.

ADAPTABILITY

The Miniature Pinscher is fun loving and extroverted and makes a top-notch show dog because of its self-esteem. Small, hardy and portable, the breed may be taken anywhere that dogs are welcome. One possible drawback is that this is a noisy dog, so there may be a problem with

near neighbors. The breed is a good pet for an older child who understands that its legs are delicate and breakable. The Miniature Pinscher can be as active as the child but also likes to be petted and cuddled at quiet times.

ESSENTIALS OF THE BREED

The Miniature Pinscher is 10-12 1/2 inches/ 25-32 cm at the shoulder with a square erect outline, well-carried head and neck, and very short upright tail. It should have good legs and feet all the way around. Its erect ears are usually cropped but may be natural. The Miniature Pinscher is at its best on the move with well-bent pushing hindquarters and high, sound Hackney action in front (not essential in all countries' Standards) — not forgetting its great "look at me" attitude.

Registry: AKC, CKC, FCI (Group 2), KC

MUDI

This Hungarian guard and herding dog is believed to come from crossings between the Puli and the Pumi and perhaps also with some other breeds. The Mudi was first discovered during an investigation into local breeds in the early twentieth century. The type was found to be homogenous and it was recognized in 1936.

At its withers, it should be about 13 1/2-18 1/2 inches/35-47 cm. The body should be almost square, rather light in build and with a wedge-shaped head. The ears should be pointed and carried erect. The tail is low set and docked quite short. An undocked tail should be carried over the back in a loose curl. The coat on the body should be medium long, wavy or curly. On the legs and head it should be smooth — the ears should have slight fringes. It is usually black but is allowed to be white with black patches although this is rarely seen.

Registry: FCI (Group 1)

The Mudi was first discovered in the twentieth century during an investigation into local breeds in Hungary.

MUNSTERLANDERS — LARGE MUNSTERLANDER

The Large Munsterlander is of German origin — a gun dog that hunts, points and retrieves. The breed has been selectively bred to maintain natural working ability. Ideal for the rough shooter, it has an excellent nose, working equally well on land and in water. It is absolutely fearless in the thickest of cover.

Basic training such as walking to heel, entering water, retrieving and acknowledgement to the whistle may be started while it is still a puppy, but it should be understood that this is a slow maturing breed and so serious training in the field and to the gun should not be undertaken until the dog is more mature. In temperament, the Large Munsterlander is a very loyal, affectionate and trustworthy dog, a superb companion that loves human company, with a preference for living in the home as one of the family rather than kennel life. The breed is highly intelligent, alert, active and brimming with energy. It should be a strong dog with a well-muscled body. The mature dog will need ample exercise that should include road walking, free running and, if possible, swimming which is usually a firm favorite.

There are no hereditary defects in the breed, although hip dysplasia does exist to a small degree. Most breeders will check existing stock before breeding.

As far as coloring goes, it has a black head, although a small white blaze is permissible. Its body may be any combination of black and white and blue roan. Its long, dense, silky coat is well feathered and must be regularly groomed.

The height at its withers should be 24 inches/61cm for dogs and 23 inches/59 cm for bitches. The Munsterlander's head is slightly elongated but the skull is noticeably broader than the Setter breeds for example, and slightly rounded. Its minimal stop and slightly rounded lips give it a very "moderate" look, free of any extremes.

Registry: CKC, FCI (Group 7), KC

Large Munsterlander

MUNSTERLANDERS – SMALL MUNSTERLANDER

This breed can be likened to its very close relative, the Large Munsterlander, except in terms of size and color. It is also a hunter, pointer and retriever. It originates from the Westphalian area of Germany and is rarely seen other than in northern Europe. Breeding began in earnest in the latter half of the nineteenth century. The Small Munsterlander is used extensively for hunting in areas of dense woodland and rough moorland where it has been found to be most efficient in the hunting of hare and deer. After many years of controlled breeding, these dogs have developed into the ideal companion for the rough shooter. Although slower than some of the other hunting, pointing and retrieving breeds when out in the field, it is most persistent in finding game that it will point and retrieve very efficiently. It also excels at swimming and retrieving from water.

The Small Munsterlander is normally easy to train and makes an ideal family companion, being loyal and affectionate. However, it must be remembered that this is an active and intelligent breed, so naturally will require adequate exercise when fully matured. This should include road work, free running and swimming if possible.

Regular grooming is necessary, but elementary. The color of the breed is dapple brown and white with moderate feathering. Dogs stand 20-22 inches/50-56 cm at the withers; bitches 19-21 inches/48-54 cm. Generally this is a hardy breed, although cases of entropion and hip dysplasia have been recorded from time to time. To the uninitiated the Small Munsterlander may have the appearance of a working-type Springer Spaniel, being very moderate in all respects and devoid of any exaggeration.

Registry: FCI (Group 7)

Small Munsterlander

NEAPOLITAN MASTIFF

The Mastino, as it is called in its native Italy, is a relic of ancient Roman times. The breed has recently enjoyed something of a revival, with several excellent Italian specimens taking major awards at the leading shows. It is a dog of immense bulk for its height (26-29 inches/65-74 cm), with tremendous bone and substance.

The Mastino possesses a supremely powerful and quite unique head. It is large, broad across the cheeks, with a skull that is also broad and short. The skull should be two-thirds and the muzzle should be one-third of the head's length. The top of the skull is parallel to the topline of the muzzle and the stop is very pronounced. The muzzle drops off square and deep, the nose never protruding beyond the vertical line of the muzzle, and the lips are heavy and full. The nose should be large with well opened nostrils. Both skull and muzzle show distinct wrinkles and from head-on the upper lip placement resembles an inverted "V." The eyes are deep set, rounded and forward looking. The ears, set high and forward, are quite small and cropped close (when cropped).

The neck is short, thick and shows dewlap. The elbows are not set too close under the body, to allow freedom of action. The body is slightly off-square, well ribbed and with no noticeable tuck-up. The tail tapers and is set lower than the topline. In action, the Mastino has a slow, free and almost bearlike gait, making long, sedentary steps.

The breed should be self-colored in back, blue, gray or brown and brindling is allowed. A small white star on the chest and minimal white on the toes is also permissible. Despite its fighting ancestry, the breed is not naturally aggressive.

Registry: FCI (Group 2), KC

Neapolitan Mastiff

NEWFOUNDLAND

In the early 1700s, the famous Captain Bligh in his *Journal of a Voyage to Newfoundland* wrote: "I was told at Trepassy lived a man who had a distinct breed which he called an original Newfoundland dog, but I did not have the opportunity of seeing any of them." Later, in the eighteenth century, the English botanist Sir Joseph Banks acquired severable identifiable specimens. Professor Albert Heim of Switzerland described and identified the breed type in the late 1800s. There are numerous theories about the source breeds which provided the genetic make-up of the Newfoundland, and various explanations about the countries originally involved in its early development. Most agree that the Tibetan Mastiff figured in the breed's beginnings.

Whatever other breeds might have been used, they had to be large, intelligent, faithful and comfortable in water. These characteristics made this breed the choice of the Honorable Harold McPherson who governed the province of Newfoundland early in the 1900s. He has always been closely identified with the breed. Similarly, Sir Edwin Landseer (1802-73) was most intrigued by these dogs and painted them in many of his canvases. *A Distinguished Member of the Humane Society* beautifully depicts a Landseer, while *Saved* shows a child being cradled by a Landseer that has just rescued her from water in the background. Couldrey showed the true nobility of the Newfoundland head in his painting *The President*. In this century, the well-known American artist, Edwin Megargee, who specialized in dog portraits, showed its soft intelligent expression in his painting *Waseeka's Crusoe*. This breed has always been and continues to be a great subject for artists.

Both single-color dogs and Landseers have been bred for type and have been exhibited successfully at dog shows throughout the world. Most of today's Newfoundlands trace down from a very dominant male "Ch Siki"

who with his sons and daughters set head, body, temperament and coat texture type. The Newfoundland has been blessed with responsible breeders who have realized the importance of addressing both the mental and the physical needs of the breed. The essence of this working dog is its massive size, even temperament, water-resistant coat and soft, sweet expression. It is at home in the water and is able to rescue both children and adults. It can pull a loaded cart handily and distinguished itself in both world wars.

TEMPERAMENT

The Newfoundland's expressive face mirrors its equanimity. It is exceptionally patient with small children, provides wonderful companionship for growing active children, and yet also fits into a household of mature people with patience and adaptability. It is able to live in a household with other breeds. Although a quiet dog by nature, its size is intimidating enough to rout the most adventurous burglar.

HEALTH MATTERS

Through the most careful breeding by committed breeders, the Newfoundland is continuing to become more sound of limb. Constant caution must be observed to maintain advancement in eye, bite, pasterns and hips to avoid health problems. Any breed that matures to between 26-28 inches/65-70 cm and weighs from 100-150 pounds/45-68 kg requires dedication if it is to remain sound in mind and body.

SPECIAL CARE AND TRAINING

The Newfoundland's shiny coat needs care but, if healthy, does not require constant grooming. Naturally, its need for complete nutrition is great because it grows rapidly, matures with both a lot of bone and muscle, and will always be at a disadvantage if not properly fed. As with most giant breeds, life span is usually around ten years. Newfoundland puppies look

Newfoundlands

like bears. They are people oriented, respond quickly and happily to training and grow very quickly.

If their owners wish, Newfoundlands can be easily trained to pull a cart. They enjoy the challenge and respond to the praise they are given when they perform. Their willingness has led many fanciers to participate in pulling contests. Owners interested in these activities should inquire at their local Newfoundland clubs or through the parent club. Building plans for carts are available and proper harnesses may be purchased through many pet supply stores. This activity, along with any

water exercise, helps to keep this giant breed physically and mentally fit.

ADAPTABILITY

This breed does require room for exercise and thoroughly enjoys time and activities in water, to which it is attracted very early on. Its mature development continues well into its third year when it should be powerful, controlled and completely faithful to its family. Owners must accept a certain amount of drooling and some messiness when this breed enters the house, because it has webbed feet to which mud and debris will stick. Any giant breed requires vigilance in breeding, care in raising and commitment. In return, he or she gives complete devotion, constant protection and a never-ending involvement in every aspect of the family's life.

ESSENTIALS OF THE BREED

The Standard used to breed and judge Newfoundlands varies slightly from country to country. In the United States, Britain and Canada, it is placed in the Working Group. In Australia, it is placed in the Non-Sporting category. Canada mentions two colors in its Standard, the United States allows three solid and the Landseer, while other countries allow other solid colors plus the Landseer. All Standards curently used to breed and judge this dog emphasize size, temperament and coat. The basic color patterns are bronze, brown, blue, gray, lemon or black, which must be solid and is the best known. The Landseer has a basic white coat with black markings. Typically the head is solid black, or black with white on the muzzle, with or without a blaze on the top of its head. It has a separate black saddle and black on the rump, extending to a white tail. Occasionally a leg will also be black. In the United States, only blacks, browns and grays are recognized in the solid colors, and in the United Kingdom only brown and black. Variations within a certain parameter are permitted in both solids and Landseer coats.

Head type is very important in the Newfoundland and the classic Newfie expression will only be achieved with a good width of skull; small deep-set eyes; minimal stop and a short muzzle. In some instances, modern heads have stops that are far too deep or have too much drop in the lips, which creates an alien head that is more like a Saint Bernard's.

Registry: AKC, CKC, FCI (Group 2), KC

NORFOLK TERRIER

ORIGIN AND DEVELOPMENT

The Norfolk Terrier, once registered as the Norwich Terrier, is a working terrier. Its first recorded ancestors were small demon ratters, popular among sporting Cambridge undergraduates toward the end of the last century. These sought-after scrappers were a mixture of gypsies' dogs crossed with weavers' pets from Yorkshire and fiery red mites from County Wicklow in Ireland.

By 1932, two types of Norwich Terrier achieved Kennel Club recognition as one breed. While usually red in color, some were black-and-tan. Though roughly equal in height, weight and spunk, their once-cropped ears were now either erect (up) or pendant (down).

Due to the efforts of Miss MacFie, the drop-ear variety survived. During World War II, many East Anglian farms used ratting terriers. Then, when hostilities ceased, Miss MacFie made every effort to popularize drop-ear Norwich (now Norfolk) Terriers through showring and press exposure. The dogs from her Colonsay Kennels, at Steyning in West Sussex, were consistent winners. However, ultimately the rewards proved disappointing when the plainer, hard-coated, drop-ear dogs were often defeated by their prick-ear counterparts. This ring rivalry ended in 1964 with the separation from Norwich and the recognition of the Norfolk Terrier as a separate breedwith a club of its own.

In the United States, Norfolk Terriers gained American Kennel Club recognition in 1979. This is also when the American Norfolk Terrier Association (ANTA), a separate educational association, was established in the United States. Currently, with six active clubs

Norfolk Terrier

throughout the world, the future of the breed is assured.

TEMPERAMENT

Appealing, clever and portable, Norfolks are outgoing and affectionate with a passion for digging. Rarely quarrelsome, they are both sensitive and jealous and so can become stubborn or shy without an understanding owner. Norfolk Terriers have no road sense and are fascinated by rodents, wheels, water and everything that flies.

HEALTH MATTERS

Game and sturdy, Norfolk Terriers are easy to breed and whelp naturally with few problems. Three is the average litter size and the devoted dams prefer seclusion so that they can follow their own weaning and teaching schedule.

Tooth care is important as this breed has a tendency to retain both puppy teeth and to have tartar build up. Norfolks are prone to mouth faults which may impede their show careers but rarely affect their health. Heart murmurs are not uncommon and those with sensitive tracheas prefer walks in a harness or a flat, wide collar.

SPECIAL CARE AND TRAINING

Norfolks require no special care. Their natural short coats collect little dirt and are easy to tidy with thumb and forefinger. Unfortunately the show ring has encouraged breeders to produce softer coats which need trimming with a knife and scissors as many exhibitors and judges today favor a dog with furnishings. Norfolks respond well and are easily trained as ears for the deaf. They are also popular for pet therapy.

ADAPTABILITY

These adaptable family pets thrive on regular exercise, travel and town or country life. They are reliable watchdogs, seldom yappy without reason.

ESSENTIALS OF THE BREED

The Norfolk, game and energetic, is a small power-packed worker with short straight legs of good substance and bone. It should have a clean outline free of fringe or skirt. Its height should not exceed 10 inches/25 cm or its weight about 12 pounds/5 kg.

The wedge-shaped head has a well-defined stop, a slightly rounded skull and good width between the ears. The small dark eyes, placed well apart at a slight angle, give a kindly, keen expression. The muzzle, tight-lipped, wide and deep, is just slightly shorter than the distance from the occiput to the stop. The mouth has large close-fitting teeth with a scissors bite. A strong, slightly arched neck is covered by a protective mane and flows into clean close shoulders. The topline is level, standing or moving; the tail, set high, is carried erect when docked. (Docked tails should be left long enough to grasp. In 1984, optional docking was added to the Standard but in the United States a tail is still unwelcome at American Kennel Club dog shows.)

The well-sprung rib cage of the Norfolk Terrier is long and heart-shaped with the brisket below the elbow. The loin is short; the quarters wide and deep with short parallel hocks. The legs should track truly and drive in a purposeful manner. While going away, the pads should show.

The coat is a significant breed trait and in general should be harsh, wiry and straight, lying close to the body, with a short, dense undercoat. However, the coat should be longer and rougher on the neck and shoulders, The hair on the head and ears is naturally short except for slight eyebrows and whiskers. Its color may be any shade of red. Wheaten, black-and-tan, and grizzle are equally desirable. Under the American Standard, its pigment should be black.

Registry: AKC, CKC, FCI (Group 3), KC

NORRBOTTENSPETS

The small Swedish hunting spitz is mainly used for hunting forest birds. It is closely related to the Finnish Spitz, which is also thought to originate from small reddish Laikas.

Norrbottenspets

Both breeds are used for the same type of work. By the 1940s the Norrbottenspets was believed to be extinct and it was withdrawn from the Registry. Some twenty years later this proved to have been a hasty decision because the breed was found still to exist on small outlying farms in the far north of Sweden. It was re-introduced to the Registry in 1967.

The height at the withers should be about 16 1/2-18 inches/42-45 cm. Its body should be square and rather slender without any weakness. The neck should have a good reach and the wedge-shaped head should be carried high. Its pointed ears should be carried erect and the tail carried in a loose curl over the back. The coat is quite short, lying close with longer hair on the chest, buttocks and tail. All colors are permitted but white with sparse, big red patches is preferred.

Registry: FCI (Group 5)

NORWEGIAN BUHUND/NORSK BUHUND

ORIGIN AND DEVELOPMENT

For over 2,000 years dogs fitting the general description of an under middle-sized spitz breed have helped farmers eke out a living on the barren slopes and narrow pastures of the Scandinavian countryside. Lithe and elegant, yet sturdy and well boned, the Buhund was primarily used as a sheepdog, but its innate sense of territory ensured a dual purpose role as a farmyard watchdog as well. The beginning of this century saw the Buhund make its first appearance in the show ring in Norway. It was imported to Britain in the 1940s and the first American imports were made in the late 1980s. At Cruft's 1995 a Buhund won Group Two for the first time.

TEMPERAMENT

Full of character and very intelligent, the Buhund has been described as the ideal family pet. Very affectionate, it loves human company but requires firm handling. "No" must mean "no." Excellent Obedience and Agility dogs, Buhunds have demonstrated abilities in fields as diverse as working with the British Royal Air Force, police dog training and as hearing dogs for the deaf.

HEALTH MATTERS

The Buhund is one of a large number of breeds which suffer from cataracts, although this appears to have little effect on the dogs. Notwithstanding this, the breed is extremely healthy and requires surprisingly little exercise in order to maintain a high level of fitness, although long walks and rambles are undertaken with relish.

SPECIAL CARE AND TRAINING

A well-trained Buhund is a delight to own and basic obedience is a must for these intelligent dogs. Easily groomed, they shed their coats once a year. Like a cat in their cleanliness, they do not have a "doggy" smell, even when wet.

Norwegian Buhund

ADAPTABILITY

The breed adapts equally well to bungalow or mansion, town or country. However, everyday access to a garden, park or countryside is essential, as is companionship, preferably human, for the greater part of any day. An ideally sized, intelligent, active and homely dog, devoted to its family, particularly children, the Buhund is also an excellent watchdog. Whether working in its native country, as highly trained companions for the disabled, as Obedience and Agility dogs, show dogs, or quite simply as a family pet, the Buhund demonstrates exceptional loyalty and affection which is returned in full measure by its doting owners.

ESSENTIALS OF THE BREED

Standing about 18 inches/45 cm, with bitches somewhat smaller, the Buhund has a wedge-shaped, foxy head, pricked ears and a tail curled over its back. The close lying coat, consisting of a thick undercoat with longer topcoat, a thick ruff and bushy tail, comes in shades of cream to gold, with or without black tips, and black with or without symmetrical white markings on the head, chest, neck and feet. Well-balanced and elegant, the Buhund moves with a light, active gait and is particularly agile, even at full speed.

Registry: FCI (Group 5), KC

NORWEGIAN ELKHOUND

ORIGIN AND DEVELOPMENT

The Norwegian Elkhound with its pricked ears, sharp face, curled tail and harsh double weather-resistant coat is a hardy dog with great stamina. Its family can be traced back to the Vikings 6,000 years ago. They were used as watchdogs and guards to raise the alarm against wolves and bears, and to hunt elk.

When the breed reached the United States, the word "hund" was translated as "hound", rather than "dog" which is the current translation. However, because of the breed's versatility as a hunter, it was allowed to remain classified as a hound and to compete in that group.

TEMPERAMENT

The Norwegian Elkhound makes a good family pet and a good watchdog. It is an active dog, needing something to do, which makes it suitable for Obedience work, as well as Agility. It is alert, trainable and loves to go places and do things. It takes a good deal of exercise in its daily rounds and enjoys walks or roadwork behind a slowly driven car or bicycle on a quiet road.

SPECIAL CARE AND TRAINING

A relatively vociferous breed, care should be taken to try to train out some of the barking. Correct feeding is necessary because hot spots can be a problem, as can a tendency to be overweight. Elkhounds should be well socialized at an early age and will benefit from obedience training. It keeps their minds active and teaches them who is the boss.

HEALTH MATTERS

The breed suffers from hot spots and shedding problems. These will respond to warm baths with a mild soap and careful brushing while drying to remove the old loose coat. It is prone to progressive retinal atrophy, other eye problems and kidney disease. Otherwise, as a natural dog the breed is quite healthy.

ESSENTIALS OF THE BREED

This is a medium-sized breed of about 45-55 pounds/20-25 kg. It is Arctic in type, with a square build. The coat is thick, hard, weather resisting and flat lying. It is made up of soft,

Norwegian Elkhound

dense woolly undercoat and coarse, straight covering guard hairs. The coat is short and even on the head, ears and front of the legs. It is longest on the back of the neck, buttocks and the underside of the tail. The color is gray, with medium gray preferred. Any variation in shade is determined by the amount of guard hairs and by the length of the black tips on them. The undercoat is clear light silver, as are the legs, stomach, buttocks and underside of the tail. The gray body is darkest on the saddle, lighter on the chest and mane and has distinctive harness marks (a band of longer dark guard hairs from the shoulder to the elbow). The black of the muzzle shades to lighter gray over the forehead and skull. Any overall color other than gray as described above is disqualified in the United States.

The breed has pricked ears and a tightly curled tail which is carried up and over. It has just moderate angulation in front and in hindquarters, making the breed a fast trotter and very stylish. With dark eyes and a piercing expression, the Norwegian Elkhound is an attractive breed to live and work with.

Registry: AKC, CKC, FCI (Group 5), KC

NORWICH TERRIER

ORIGIN AND DEVELOPMENT

The history of the Norwich Terrier is fascinating in its diversity and obscurity. For over a century, numerous dogs and people have contributed to the development of this breed. Among other things, there seems to be an argument as to whether the drop ear or the prick ear came first. As many of the early Norwich Terriers had cropped ears, the truth may never be known. However, it is known that the first prick-ear champions bred in the United States came from drop-ear parents.

During the latter half of the nineteenth century near Cambridge, England, "Doggy" Lawrence used a small Irish Terrier, perhaps crossed with a Yorkshire Terrier, to produce small red and often black-and-tan "Cantab" Terriers. Between 1899 and 1902, a sports loving Cambridge undergraduate mated a smooth brindle bitch of doubtful origin to a Cantab and called the resulting litter Trumpington Terriers. The Master of the Norwich Staghounds picked one and named him Rags. Bred to a varied lot of small terrier bitches, Rags stamped his offspring with pricked ears and a harsh red coat. In 1901 Frank Jones, Whip to the Norwich Staghounds, eager to breed his own small sporting terriers, crossed his two Glen of Imaal Terriers and his small red Trumpington back to Rags. The results were prick-ear terriers which became known as Jones Terriers. One season while hunting with the Norwich Staghounds, Sir Alfred Munnings painted Jones and his terriers.

"Rough Rider" Jones left the Norwich Staghounds for Leicestershire in 1904 and continued to breed his sporting prick-ear terriers. They were used in Leicestershire hunt country for bolting foxes when they had "gone to ground." Hence, the Standard for the breed was to read "TAIL medium docked — long enough for a man to pull the Terrier out of a fox hole." In America the "Jones Terriers"

took the Millbrook and Virginia hunt country by storm. Their popularity spread.

In the early days it was seldom that any two "Jones" looked alike, even if they came from the same litter. In 1932, both prick and drop-ear types were recognized by the English Kennel Club as Norwich Terriers. Subsequently, English breeders through great effort and with the support of a strong breed club, stabilized the type without losing any of the sporting gameness of this delightful breed. In 1964 the English Kennel Club decreed that there would be two breeds, the drop-ear to be called Norfolk Terriers and the prick-ear to continue with the name Norwich Terrier. In 1979 the American Kennel Club followed suit and split the two breeds.

In its country of origin, the Norwich has always been mainly considered a farm dog and ratter, and its status has only been raised since it has been termed a hunt terrier in the United States.

TEMPERAMENT

As the breed is small, portable and adaptable, owners sometimes make the mistake of coddling and trying to make the Norwich toy-like. This is not in the best interest of the breed. Several may be kept together and if raised together there is seldom a grumble. The breed's lot is to beguile, amuse and entertain. With its pricked ears, it hears well and makes a good watchdog.

HEALTH MATTERS

As a general rule, this breed is very hardy and healthy. Some whelping problems do exist. The breed is not known for severe heritable problems, although some dental problems do occur. Stock should be purchased from reputable breeders who will assist the new owner in getting to know and understand the breed.

SPECIAL CARE AND TRAINING

Puppies should be purchased early, by ten weeks, and housetrained immediately since they tend to be very stubborn about this. Puppies must not be overfed. As mature dogs they have a fearsome habit of overeating — they really will try to eat anything that does not eat them first. They are active, need long walks in safe areas off the lead, but are quite happy in cities on a lead. In the United States and Great Britain, they have been known to do well in Obedience. On the whole, the breed will learn tricks, and do anything to make their owners and themselves happy.

Grooming, although not extensive, is needed regularly. A half hour or so each week is all that is required for the show dog to pull out a layer of old coat all over the head, body and tail. Before showing, clean the teeth, nip off a tiny bit on each toenail, and give the dog a good combing and brushing. Its leg coat should not be long and untidy, and stray hairs should be pulled out weekly, as should straggly hairs from the ears. Hair around the feet may be neatened with scissors. Full baths are seldom necessary.

Adaptability

The Norwich was bred to adapt. The Cambridge boys kept them in their colleges where the breed thrived in drafty halls and was fed on table scraps. These feeding habits are definitely not to be encouraged.

Essentials of the Breed

Small, hardy and game describes the Norwich, which stands about 10-12 inches/25-30 cm tall, big for their inches, with good bone substance and body. The Norwich foreface is just a little shorter than its back-skull; the ears are erect, giving a slightly foxy expression. Its neck should be long according to the British Standard, and of medium length in the United States. Whatever the length, the neck should be protected by a longer mane of rough coat; the topline should be strong and straight; the tail well set and carried up with a long enough dock. Its hindquarters are strong with good propelling power. Its expression is alert and knowing, with a dark eye set off by slight eyebrows. Its coat may be various shades of red including wheaten, as well as black-and-tan and grizzle — grizzle being a sort of mixture of black-and-tan and red. The Norwich was bred to be a companion and friend. The breed fits the bill!

Registry: AKC, CKC, FCI (Group 3), KC

Norwich Terrier

OGAR POLSKI

In type, the Polish scenthound is very much like the old east European hounds, before they were crossed with Foxhounds. It is quite a heavily built hound that is used for hunting fox, wild boar and hare. The breed is even tempered and fairly docile. It is rarely seen outside Poland.

The height at the withers should be about 22-25 1/2 inches/55-65 cm. The body should be rectangular, well muscled and with strong bone. The coat is usually short, harsh and close lying. Its color should be a rich tan with, black or grayish black saddle; slight white markings are permissible.

Registry: FCI (Group 6)

Ogar Polski

OLD DANISH POINTING DOG/ GAMMEL DANSK HØNSEHUND

This old breed was probably established in the sixteenth century. Some historians are of the opinion that the Old Danish Pointing Dog, the Portuguese and the Spanish Pointer are the gun dog breeds that look most like the gun dogs of 200 years ago, that are supposedly the basis of origin for all pointing gun dog breeds.

At its withers, these dogs should be about 19-23 inches/48-58 cm. The body is rectangular and rather heavy in build with a deep, broad and slightly rounded chest. The skull should be broad and quite short; the muzzle deep with pendulous lips. The ears of the Old Danish Pointing Dog should not be set too high, broad at the base and with rounded tips. Dewlaps are typical. The coat should be smooth and white in color with liver brown patches and ticking. This color is also thought to be the color of this breed's pointing gun dog ancestors.

Registry: FCI (Group 7)

The Old Danish Pointing Dog is said to be one of the modern-day gun dogs that most resemble gun dogs of 200 years ago.

OLD ENGLISH SHEEPDOG

ORIGIN AND DEVELOPMENT

In early times, the Old English Sheepdog used to be simply referred to as "the Shepherd's Dog" but by the mid-1800s people started to call it by its current name. Today it sometimes also goes by the fond name of "Bobtail", which came about because of its lack of tail. The practice of docking the Old English Sheepdog actually developed to avoid an excise duty levied on dogs. This duty did not apply to working dogs and so, to prove their lawful occupation, shepherds used to dock their dogs' tails.

The exact origins of the Bobtail are unclear and, as with so many breeds, there are a number of varied opinions as to its ancestry. Most popular opinion includes the early Bearded Collie among the original stock that was used to develop the breed. Certainly, early photographs of the two breeds show amazing similarities. This, coupled with possible crosses with large continental herding breeds, seems likely. However, opinion is agreed that the breed really began to develop in the hands of the farmers in England's West Country, probably around 200 years ago. It then became an extremely popular drover's dog. Although this was its primary purpose, its natural protective instinct also made it invaluable as a "minder" of the flock.

The breed was first exhibited at Birmingham in 1873 and attracted three entries. According to the judge of the day, the quality was so unimpressive that he felt justified in only awarding a Second placing. Early photographs reveal that, over the years, little physical change has taken place although the styles of presentation have altered dramatically. The consensus of opinion is that this is not necessarily a change for the better. The various fashions like backcombing, chalking and powdering were recorded as early as 1907 as, indeed, were problems that are still alluded to by breeders and judges — snipiness, excessive length of foreface and so on. Nevertheless, the "sculpting" by inordinate scissoring which is encountered in the show ring today would undoubtedly outrage the doyens of the breed. Whether due to more sophisticated presentation or in fact a deterioration of the harshness, the "break" in the coat certainly appears to have been better than is seen today, although the harshness can and definitely does vary from country to country because of climatic and environmental differences.

TEMPERAMENT

The Bobtail is an affectionately loyal dog, protective of those it loves. Sometimes boisterous, its generous personality should be free from any hint of aggression. A natural protector, it was originally the guardian of a flock and this instinct is displayed in its tendency to "adopt" young animals and children. The breed is very stoic by nature and not given to temperamental displays. It is demonstrative in its affection for family and friends, or those it chooses to be a member of its "flock.". However, despite its natural instinct to be a guardian, and the fact that it is sometimes known as the "nanny dog", ("Nana" in J.M.Barrie's *Peter Pan* was by some accounts an Old English Sheepdog), it is quite happy to share its material possessions — and yours as well. In fact, it is more likely to lead a burglar to the family silver than to become an obstacle in his way.

HEALTH MATTERS

As in many large breeds of dog, hip dysplasia, although happily on the decline, is still of concern to fanciers of the breed. Most authorities now concede that this problem can be attributed as much to environment as it can to heredity. Breed frailties are thankfully not in abundance and any common ailments are restricted to those that one would normally associate with a large, drop-eared, profusely coated breed.

Old English Sheepdog

SPECIAL CARE AND TRAINING

The Bobtail is a biddable dog and is therefore easily trained. As it is so profusely coated, its grooming requirements will obviously be greater than those of shorter-coated breeds. Under normal circumstances, a few hours of thorough "to the skin" grooming each week should be sufficient to ensure a mat-free coat.

While not a lazy dog, the breed does tend to have a casual approach to exercise. The suggestion of "walk" is not normally met with great enthusiasm, and if you put a dog on its own in a 10-acre/4-hectare paddock, when you return you will probably find it unmoved! The opportunity to accompany its owner on a leisurely stroll, however, will invariably prove sufficient motivation.

Adaptabililty

Bobtails are cute, adorable puppies. Regretfully, breed clubs worldwide all experience the problem of having to help to re-home some of these puppies when they grow up and are no longer compatible with their owners' lifestyles. However, an owner who is prepared to make a small invesetment of time, and maintain the coat which is a hallmark of the breed, will be rewarded with a lifetime of complete loyalty and devotion incomparable with any other breed.

Essentials of the Breed

The purpose for which it was bred makes it mandatory for the Old English Sheepdog to be steady, placid and totally trustworthy. It is a compact, strong-boned and sturdy dog and very elastic when at a gallop.

The Old English has a large skull with a deep, square muzzle and a noticeably large black nose. Its ears are relatively small and hang close to the sides of the head. The desired eye color is dark or wall-eyed, although blue eyes are permissible. To ensure good balance, its neck is fairly long and gracefully arched. Its shoulders are well angulated and its feet are round, but also small in comparison to its body size. The requirement for well-arched toes and thick pads acknowledges that the Bobtail works on its feet.

Its coat is abundant, especially on the thighs, and is harsh and shaggy but free from curl. Today, the most common color is gray-blue with glamorous white markings, but any shade of gray, blue or grizzle is acceptable. White "splashes" on the solid body area are to be discouraged and any brown shading is undesirable.

Possibly the most unique characteristic of the breed is its distinctive bark. Described as having a "*pot cassé* ring", it should be sufficiently deep and resonant to sound the warning of any impending danger or foe to the absent shepherd or owner.

Registry: AKC, CKC, FCI (Group 1), KC

OTTERHOUND

Otterhunting and Otterhounds were first mentioned in about 1175 during the reign of Henry II. "Otter dogges" were utilized then and throughout subsequent generations as a means of keeping the supra-abundant otter from destroying the fishing industry in England.

It was not until the reign of Edward II (1307-1327) that a huntsman, William Twici, left the earliest description of the type of dog used in packs to hunt otter as, "a rough sort of dog, between a hound and a terrier." There have been various opinions about breeds or combinations of breeds that were the foundation of the Otterhound as it is now known. Among them are the now-extinct Old Southern Hound, the Griffon Nivernais from France, the Bloodhound, the rough-coated Welsh Harrier or Foxhound, Griffon de Bresse, Griffon Vendéen, Bulldog and even the wolf. The most likely origin of the Otterhound seems to be French. Marples, an authority on dogs, described the Otterhound as being almost an exact replica of the old Vendéen Hound of France — they are alike in both conformation and coat. The English authority and huntsman, Croxton Smith, writes of the Otterhound, tracing back to the rough-coated Griffon Vendéen. The uniform "purebred" Otterhound of today was standardized to breed true to type during the nineteenth century.

While the hunting of otter began as a means for survival of the fishing industry, it is probably the oldest form of sport for which scenthounds in packs are used in the United

Otterhound

Kingdom. Almost all the British monarchs since Henry II maintained a royal Master of Otterhounds and kept several pairs of hounds to hunt the otter. Since it was the only sport available from March to October, it eventually caught on with the gentry. With the otter now on the endangered species list, many packs have been disbanded, with only drag hunts still taking place. The Bell-Irving family in Scotland of the Dumfriesshire Pack have steadfastly maintained the type necessary for hunting. Otterhounds have now found their place as pets and show dogs and have a small but enthusiastic following throughout the world.

TEMPERAMENT

Otterhounds are boisterous and amiable. Being pack animals, they are tolerant of other dogs and are warm and affectionate with people. They are naturally good natured, but if attacked, they will respond with ferocity. They are not guard dogs in the traditional sense but have a loud and melodious voice which they will use if they hear strange noises. Being hounds, they are intelligent yet independent — even stubborn. Young hounds, especially, are active and energetic and need room to exercise and explore the world. These are large dogs and they can be awkward when young. Naturally, they love water and, since they retain

Otterhounds are pack animals and like the company of other dogs.

their hunting instincts, must be kept in a fenced yard.

Health Matters

The breed is relatively healthy but it is large and hip dysplasia can occur. Dedicated breeders are working to overcome the problem. It is wise to take precautions against gastric torsion. The Otterhound needs good exercise, either taking brisk walks or romping safely in a large fenced yard. When it is mature, it will enjoy road working about three times a week behind a bicycle or slowly moving car on quiet roads.

Special Care and Training

The breed's coat is quite easy to maintain with a weekly brushing, which will keep shedding to a bare minimum. Dirt brushes out easily. The teeth and toenails need weekly attention as soon as the puppy can be easily handled. If there are any irregularities in its scissors bite, a vet should be consulted. The Otterhound may need to have its coat stripped — it should not be clipped — by having the dead loose hair pulled out in the direction of the hair growth. The ears should be looked after and kept clean. If there are any signs of odor or irritation, the vet should be consulted.

Adaptability

Even though the Otterhound has been a hunter for generations, its appealing countenance and affectionate nature have made its transition to house pet an easy one, provided that the home is run on a casual basis. Its hairy face and love of water can easily undo an immaculate living room.

Essentials of the Breed

The Otterhound should have the qualities and appearance of a hunter. It has an athlete's body, lean and well muscled, and it is covered from nose to tail and all around with a rough, crisp water-shedding outer coat and a warm undercoat. Since the Otterhound swims, it must have large webbed feet. Its face is majestic, large, fairly narrow, but long with a large, sensitive nose. It shows great strength and dignity. Its ears are long and pendulous and, like the rest of its head, are covered with hair. Its jaws have a punishing grip, with a scissors bite, and its eyes are dark.

This is a large breed: males stand about 26 inches/66 cm at the shoulders and females about 24 inches/60 cm. Its weight ranges from a minimum of 65 pounds/29 kg for a small female to 115 pounds/52 kg for a large, substantial male. The Otterhound is slightly longer than it is tall, with a strong body and a long, easy stride, rendering the breed capable of a long day's work on land and water if it is required to do so.

Registry: AKC, CKC, FCI (Group 6), KC

PAPILLON/ÉPAGNEUL NAIN CONTINENTAL

ORIGIN AND DEVELOPMENT

This energetic Toy breed dates back to the sixteenth century when it was known as the "dwarf spaniel." Many were included in ladies' portraits and Marie Antoinette was an admirer of the breed as early as 1545.

Spain deserves credit for much of the breed's popularity. Italy also played a key role although France ultimately contributed the breed's name, Papillon, which is the French for "butterfly." Many were transported from Italy to France on the backs of mules.

During the days of Louis XVI, the dwarf spaniel developed an erect-type ear that resembled the shape of a butterfly and that is how it got its name. Both the drop ear (Phalène) and erect ear are allowed throughout Europe and the United States. The Toy breed was first recognized by the American Kennel Club in 1935.

TEMPERAMENT

The breed can be quiet and affectionate and, consequently, appeals to a wide range of people. Despite its size, the Papillon is a hardy breed able to withstand the effects of both hot and cold weather. They are aggressive ratters and require no coddling.

SPECIAL CARE AND TRAINING

The Papillon is a delightful dog to have around and to bring up in the ways of the family. It is very much all dog and not at all a delicate shrinking flower.

The breed should be easily housetrained and

Papillon

is naturally very clean. Care should be taken over a puppy jumping off high furniture because although its legs are strong they can break while the puppy is young and inexperienced.

The Papillon is a wonderful little worker in the Obedience ring. It takes to it with a will and enjoys itself immensely, as it does in the show ring.

Its coat is easily cared for and should be bathed and brushed as necessary. The nails should be clipped with a professional nail clipper once a week. Similarly the teeth should be cleaned weekly — a small, hard biscuit will help to keep both teeth and gums clean.

ADAPTABILITY

This is an alert, energetic breed that is as much at home on the farm as in an apartment. Although it is small and quiet, it is a clever watchdog. The Papillon travels well and adapts to any climate. This delightful breed loves to walk and looks stylish as it prances along.

ESSENTIALS OF THE BREED

This fine-boned dainty dog with a lively action is easily distinguished by its butterfly-like ears and long, high-set plumed tail. Its head is small with the length of muzzle approximately one-third the distance from the tip of the nose to the occiput. The skull of the breed is of medium width; the muzzle is fine and tapered to the nose. Its eyes are dark, round and of medium size. The ears of The Papillon and Phalène should be large with rounded tips, set on the sides and toward the back of the head. When alert, each of the erect ears forms a forty-five degree angle with the head. Drop type ears are carried drooping and must be completely down.

The drop ear Phalène is recognized in Europe as a separate breed and is shown alongside erect-eared specimens, as Papillons in the United Kingdom and the United States.

The Papillon is not a cobby dog. Its body length is slightly longer than the height at its withers. This should range from 8-11 inches/20-29 cm. (In the United States, a dog over 11 inches/29 cm is faulted; above 12 inches/30 cm it is disqualified.) The topline should be level, ribs well sprung and the chest moderately deep. Both forequarters and hindquarters should be well developed and well-angulated. Its feet — rather harelike — should point straight ahead and the Papillon should move with a quick, free and graceful gait.

The Papillon has an abundant fine, silky coat which hangs flat on the sides and body. The hair on the head is short and close. The hair on the front of the legs and on the hind legs beneath the hocks should also be short and close. Its ears are well fringed, the chest has a profuse frill, and the hind legs are covered with abundant breeches. The backs of the forelegs are covered with feathers.

Papillons are predominantly white with patches that may be any color except liver. Tricolors are permitted. Color must cover both the ears and the eyes. A symmetrical head marking is preferred.

Registry: AKC, CKC, FCI (Group 9), KC

PARSON JACK RUSSELL TERRIER

In 1819 a young theology student at Exeter College, Oxford, strolled across Magdalen meadows and happened to meet a man delivering milk in the village of Marston. The milkman had a terrier with him and the student was Jack Russell. The terrier was, according to Russell's friend and biographer, the Reverend "Otter" Davies, such as Jack Russell had only previously seen in his dreams. The terrier was Trump from which, over a period of more than sixty years, Jack Russell was to breed a distinctive strain of Fox Terrier. Davies' description of Trump, approved by Jack Russell, records that: "In the first place, the colour is white with just a patch of dark tan over each eye and ear, while a similar dot, not larger than a penny piece, marks the root of the tail. The coat, which is thick, close and a trifle wiry, is well calculated to protect the body from wet and cold, but has no affinity with the long, rough jacket of a Scotch Terrier. The legs are straight as arrows, the feet perfect; the loins and conformation of the whole frame indicative of hardihood and endurance; while the size and height of the animal may be compared to that of a full-grown vixen fox."

In 1989 the Kennel Club gave official recognition to the terrier which had been developed by one of its first members. The Standard reflected Davies' description for enthusiasts have declared their purpose is to preserve the type of terrier which had been developed by the student who became Parson Jack Russell. This breed is generally healthy and may be short-tempered. Show entries have proved the breed's following.

Parson Jack Russell Terrier

Registry: FCI (Group 3), KC

PEKINGESE

ORIGIN AND DEVELOPMENT

That the Pekingese is a long-established breed is undeniable but being Chinese its origins are lost in the mystique of that country. However delightful, that the Pekingese is the offspring of a lion and a marmoset can be discounted as legend. This was that a lion fell in love with a marmoset and made a request to a holy man that he be reduced to a small size so that the two could live in marital bliss. The story goes that the holy man granted the request and the lion and the marmoset lived happily ever after, their offspring being the imperial Pekingese.

For centuries, there has been a sacred dog of China, quaint characters whose stone figures guard the imperial palaces and shrines of the Chinese. Their features are remarkably similar to those of the Pekingese. A massive head, short broad face, nose well up between large bold eyes, short bowed legs, a lion-shaped body, a ruff or mane and the tail carried over its back: these are all features of the Pekingese. It is almost certain that the Pekingese shares its forebears with other Asian breeds. With selective breeding, different breeds have emerged, each with their distinct characteristics.

The Pekingese was held in great esteem by the various imperial dynasties of China, some more than others. It was with the advent of the Manchus in the seventeenth century that the Pekingese took pride of place, being coveted and treasured for its quaintness and individuality. Dogs were often painted on silk and the figures depict a breed that is definitely Pekingese. One of the chief supporters of the breed was the Dowager Empress Tzu Hsi.

While the Pekingese was being bred and nurtured in the precincts of royal palaces, it was little known outside the palace walls and was so protected that any attempt to smuggle one to the outside world was met with punishment, usually death by stoning. And so the Pekingese survived and prospered, known only to the privileged few. Times were to change, however.

In 1860, goaded by punitive actions of the Emperor, troops of the western nations, led by Britian and France marched on the imperial palace in Peking. The courtiers fled taking with them their priceless possessions including the lion dogs — but five were inadvertently left behind. These fell into the hands of British officers and were taken back to England. None of the five weighed more than 6 pounds/2.7 kg which indicated that the true palace Pekingese was small in stature. Of the five, the most illustrious was Looty, which was presented to Queen Victoria. It was not known whether she became a particular favorite of the queen, but she must have been important to have her portrait painted by Keyl, a student of Landseer.

Admiral Lord John Hay secured a brace, retaining the dog, and the bitch was given to his sister, the Duchess of Wellington. Another pair was given to the Duke and Duchess of Richmond at Goodwood.

Little is known of the breed's progress in England until the 1890s. Times were changing in China. It was obvious that court officials and servants were becoming more bold as dogs were smuggled out of the royal palaces and were perhaps being bred outside. One of the first importations to be recorded since 1860 was a dog named Pekin Peter, imported by Mrs. Loftus Allen in 1893. Her husband was a sea captain who made several trips to the Orient bringing back as many Pekingese as he could lay his hands on. Pekin Peter made his ring debut at Chester in 1894, reputedly the first time a Pekingese was exhibited in the British show ring. He was entered in the Foreign Dog Class. No one knows what people thought of the dog at the time or what he was thought to be. Mrs. Loftus Allen herself must have had doubts as she placed an advertisement in the Ladies Kennel Journal where he was described as a Chinese Pug and a good dog to breed with rough-coated English Pugs. His fee was four

Pekingese

guineas to an English Pug but five guineas to a Chinese Pug. The breed progressed slowly for the next couple of years but 1896 was ultimately to be one of the most important dates in the breed's history. It was then that Mrs. Loftus Allen imported a famous pair of blacks, Pekin Prince and Pekin Princess. Yet, it was another pair, Ah Cum and Mimosa, that was to ensure the popularity of the Pekingese.

Mrs. Allen was the first serious exhibitor. There was a distinct bias against blacks but Prince became the leading winner of the day. At the time, the breed was called the Pekingese Spaniel. Ah Cum, a red, was not exhibited extensively by his owner, Mrs. T. Douglas Murray, but after a chance meeting with Lady Algernon Gordon Lennox, daughter-in-law of the Duke and Duchess of Richmond, his future was assured. Bred to bitches of the Goodwood strain, he was to become one of the leading sires of the day. Nearly every Pekingese in the show ring throughout the

world today can trace directly in the tail male line to Ah Cum. By the turn of the century, the foundation of the Pekingese breed was firmly established and its steady march to the pinnacle of popularity was soon to be achieved.

The majority of Pekingese enthusiasts were also Japanese Chin breeders, and so the Pekingese was first catered for by the Japanese Spaniel Club. This later became the Japanese and Asiatic Association. In 1898 the first Standard of Points was drawn up, and the Pekingese Club was established four years later. In 1903 the first Pekingese Champion, a dog named Goodwood Lo, was followed by the first Pekingese bitch Champion, Gia Gia. In 1908, the Peking Palace Dog Association was founded by former members of the Pekingese Club who wished to see a weight limit of 10 pounds/ 4.5 kg for the breed. For many years, no dog over this weight was allowed to be exhibited at the Association shows.

The Pekingese Club of America was formed

in 1909 but the breed had been firmly established in the United States before then. Pekingese had been imported from England, but the first Pekingese bitch Champion (a black named Chaou Ching Ur) came from China, directly from the palace in Peking. She was a personal gift from the mellowing Dowager Empress to Dr. Cotton. The first Champion dog was Tsang of Downshire, owned by Mrs. Morris Mandy.

TEMPERAMENT

The Pekingese has a mind and will of its own — it tends to want to get its own way. It can be stubborn and disobedient but it has the courage of a lion. Perhaps its independence and self-esteem are its most endearing characteristics. It is definitely neither cloying nor servile. Firmness is needed with a Pekingese. Once it knows who is the master, it is a delight and will respect authority and obey your wishes.

If it is brought up with children, it will adore them. However, if it is a companion to the elderly or to a childless couple, it will probably resent the very young. The Pekingese is intelligent and has a great air of dignity inherited from its regal ancestors. It can also be an excellent watchdog, alerting its owner to approaching strangers. It is not a breed that is prone to bark unnecessarily, contrary to the reputation that it sometimes does.

The Pekingese is a dog of great beauty but perhaps its temperament is its greatest asset. It should be fearless but never aggressive, aloof but never timid. It is a dog of great courage, bold with an air of confidence.

HEALTH MATTERS

The Pekingese is a stout-hearted individual and longevity is the norm. It is unusual for a Peke not to reach between fifteen and seventeen years without much wrong with it. Care of its coat is essential. A thorough grooming once a week will keep the skin healthy. A Pekingese generally is not a bad eater but if pandered to may become finicky.

Its eyes need to be watched because their large size and its flat face means that they may be damaged more easily than in many breeds. Keep the eyes clean by washing them in a mild saline solution and put ophthalmic treatment into the eye at the first sign of a blink or a wink. The saying "a stitch in time saves nine" applies here. Do not wait until the eye is china blue or ulcerated.

SPECIAL CARE AND TRAINING

Although the Pekingese is stubborn, so long as its owner is persistent it will quite easily train to the basics and become obedience trained. Never despair with a Pekingese. When lead training, you can take it out fifty times and it will refuse to budge. Yet on the fifty-first try, it might suddenly walk as if it has been doing so all its life. Patience is the key word when training this breed. Never give in and always remind it that you are in charge

ADAPTABILITY

A Pekingese adapts well to its environment, surroundings and circumstances. It is as much at home in a small apartment or on a large country estate. It can be a companion to a solitary elderly person or a young couple with growing children. As it is independent, it neither needs nor demands constant attention. It is somewhat catlike, yet delights in giving pleasure. It is quite comfortable being one of a crowd, but can be equally happy when it is the lone pet in a household.

ESSENTIALS OF THE BREED

The Pekingese is a Toy dog and as such should be small. The Standards make no requirements, with the exception of the American Standard which has a limit of 14 pounds/6.3 kg. The British Standard gives only an ideal weight not exceeding 11 pounds/5 kg in dogs and 12 pounds/5.4 kg in bitches but a well-proportioned Pekingese of 12 pounds/5.4 kg would stand about 7 inches/18 cm. "Small" with the Pekingese does not mean dainty. The expression "multum in parvo" in the Pug Standard can equally apply to the Pekingese. There should be a lot of dog in a small package — short, thick-set and compact, with a large head, heavy bone and great spring of rib. A Pekingese should look small but weigh heavy.

The head is an important feature of the breed. It should be large in proportion to the body. It should also be wide with the top skull flat and the ears set level with it. The ears should frame the face thus enhancing the appearance of width. The nose leather is black and broad with open nostrils set well up between the eyes which are set wide apart and are large, round, dark and lustrous. The eyes should be bold but never bolting and should show no white. The chin should be strong, firm, definite and undershot. All these head essentials plus the most important feature, a flat face, distinguish this breed from others.

As it is compact, the Peke requires a short thick neck, giving the impression that the head is set into the shoulders. The body is compact with great spring of rib, tapering to a narrow waist and hindquarters. This is often referred to as "pear shape" and is an apt description. The hindquarters are narrow and lighter in bone than the forelegs, with the hind feet facing forward. The front legs are heavy and well bowed with feet turning outward. With a proper layback of shoulder, the body is slung between the legs with a modicum of chest in front of the forelegs. This very build of body and legs creates the typical rolling action and essential feature of the breed. It should be free and flowing as well as rolling — never a trot or high stepping. A Peke should be moved at a pace to reflect its dignity and demeanor. Its tail should be set high. Anything else would diminish the compact appearance that is required in the breed. The tail should be carried well over the back.

Its coat is a Pekingese's crowning glory. This is a double coat. The fringing on the tail, ears, legs and skirtings should be long, profuse and somewhat softer in texture than that of the body. The mane or ruff should be profuse on the neck and form a cape around the shoulders. This is harsh in texture in front of the neck, and often called the bib. The mane is a characteristic of the breed but has unfortunately been slowly disappearing over the years. The coat should never be so long as to obliterate the shape of the dog.

Registry: AKC, CKC, FCI (Group 9), KC

PERDIGUEIRO PORTUGUÊS

The Portuguese Pointer looks very much like the English Pointer but has a more rounded head, a very pronounced dish face and a more rounded rib cage. It has been true to type for hundreds of years and is strictly used as a hunting dog.

The height at its withers should be within 19-24 inches/48-60 cm. Its body should be rectangular, well muscled and with strong bone. The ears are set fairly high and are broad at the base. The tail is usually docked to half its length. The coat may be smooth and all shades of fawn or red, with or without white markings.

Registry: (Group 7)

Perdigueiro Português

PERDIGUERO DE BURGOS

The Spanish pointing dog is considered one of the oldest and has a type that has kept very much the same for centuries. It was severely reduced in numbers during the two world wars but was revived after World War II. It is still rare and seldom seen outside Spain. It is strictly used as a hunting dog.

At its withers, its height should be about 26-29 1/2 inches/65-75 cm. Its body should be slightly rectangular, rather heavy but well muscled and with strong bone. The head should be massive with low-set, folded ears and decidedly pendulous lips. The tail is docked to half its length. Its coat may be smooth and colored liver brown with fine speckling and large brown patches on the body, head and ears — so-called liver roan.

Registry FCI (Group 7)

Perdiguero de Burgos

PERRO DE PRESA MALLORQUÍN/ CA DE BOU

This Spanish breed originates from the Balearic Islands where it is called Ca de Bou and is said once to have been a fighting dog. The Perro de Presa Mallorquín is used as a guard dog and is very rare, even in Spain.

The height at the withers should be about 22 inches/56 cm. Its body should be compact, well muscled and with strong bone and a slightly arched backline. Its head should be massive with pronounced cheeks, strong, broad and not too long in the muzzle. The ears are carried as in the Bulldog, the so-called rose ear. The tail is usually docked short. The coat should be harsh in texture and short. It is usually any shade of fawn, from very pale yellow to dark red or brindle.

Registry: FCI (Group 2)

Perro de Presa Mallorquín

PETIT BLEU DE GASCOGNE

The Petit Bleu de Gascogne is a smaller version of the Grand Bleu de Gascogne and was developed for hunting smaller game like hare, fox and roe deer. It is not identical to its larger relation, being shorter coupled. Also, although its head is long and narrow, the stop is not so pronounced. The ears are long but not folded as much as in the Grand Bleu de Gascogne.

The height at the withers should be about 19-22 inches/48-56 cm. The coat should be short and fine and in the traditional Grand Bleu de Gascogne colors — blue mottled with large, black patches or a black mantle, black patches on the sides of the head and on the ears plus tan markings. The breed is rare even in France.

Registry: FCI (Group 6)

The Petit Bleu de Gascogne is a small version of the Grand Bleu de Gascogne, but is shorter coupled.

PHARAOH HOUND

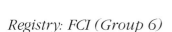

The origin of the Pharaoh Hound dates back to around 3000 B.C. Originally bred by the Egyptians to hunt gazelle, the Pharaoh was brought from Egypt to Malta by Phoenician traders well before the Christian era. In Malta, the Pharaoh was bred to hunt rabbit and only the most successful workers were kept for breeding. In 1979 the Pharaoh was declared the national dog of Malta.

The first Pharaohs were brought to the United Kingdom in the 1930s but they were not shown there until 1963. In 1967 the first Pharaoh Hound was introduced to the United States and the first American Pharaoh litter was whelped in 1970.

TEMPERAMENT

The Pharaoh Hound is much more demonstrative than other sighthounds. The breed seeks out human companionship and invites attention, making this ancient dog an excellent pet.

HEALTH MATTERS

Because only the purest and the most able Pharaoh Hounds were bred for many centuries, very few health problems are known to the breed. It has not become popular enough to suffer from indiscriminate mass breeding.

SPECIAL CARE AND TRAINING

Pharoah Hounds are eager to please and so should respond well to training, provided praise is given when a dog does well. Normal care applies as much to this breed as others. Its nails should be attended to weekly, unless the hound has worn down the tips by being exercised on sidewalks. Its teeth should be brushed regularly. Because of its short coat, the Pharaoh Hound needs protection from the cold. It should have a soft bed with something like a sheepskin pad as a cushion to provide warmth. The Pharaoh should be taught to walk quietly on a leash. It should also be trained to come when called before it is allowed to run loose, or its hunting instincts may send it off after some prey that is has seen or scented.

Adaptability

The breed adjusts well and quickly to new surroundings. It bonds readily to any and all who will give it affection and companionship. Generally a quiet dog, the hound will fit in well and make the best of situations.

Essentials of the Breed

These concentrate on the important traits that the Pharaoh needs for hunting and they are coupled with its great speed and stamina to work long hours. It should give the impression of medium size with clean-cut lines. The male should be 23-25 inches/58-63 cm and bitches 21-24 inches/53-61cm. The very alert expression comes from amber eyes, and a very mobile ear that is set high and is large and broad at the base. The skull is long and lean, with a foreface slightly longer that the skull. The mouth should be normal with strong jaws and a scissors bite. Its coat is short, smooth and glossy, and colored from a rich tan to chestnut, with various white markings. A white tip to the tail is strongly desired. A white spot on the chest (called a star), white on the toes, and a slim white snip on the center line on the face are permitted. A hound with a solid white spot on the back of the neck, shoulder or any part of the back or the sides is disqualified in the United States. The tail is long, reaching to the hock or just below. When the Pharaoh is in motion, the tail should be like a whip, well carried and curved. It should never be tucked between the legs. The breed must also be able to move easily in order to perform well in the hunt, which the Pharaoh Hound does both by scent and by sight.

Registry: AKC, CKC, FCI (Group 5), KC

Pharaoh Hound

PINSCHER

The Pinscher and the Standard Schnauzer are believed to be the origin of the Pinscher-Schnauzer varieties that are today known as different breeds — the Doberman, the Miniature Pinscher and the Giant and Miniature Schnauzers. The medium-sized Pinscher and Schnauzer were once the same breed with a smooth and a wire-coated variety. They were mainly farm dogs that were used for ratting, and they were so common that no one really paid much attention to them until dog shows and dog breeding became popular in the nineteenth century.

This type of dog is believed to have existed in Germany for thousands of years. The breed name "Pinscher" is thought to derive either from the English word "pinch" of from the French "pincer", both roughly meaning to bite or snap off. The name may have come about because the breed has a reputation as an efficient rat killer. Although the Pinscher is the most original of the breeds, it is the least known, which is quite surprising given its manageable size and easy-to-care-for coat. According to some breeders, however, the Pinscher used to have a reputation — that has been difficult to eliminate — of being a difficult guard dog that is both temperamental and cautious.

The height at its withers should be about 18-20 inches/45-50 cm. Its body should be square and compact but never look coarse or clumsy. Its elegant outlines should be combined with strength and substance, as in the Doberman and Schnauzers. It should always look alert and full of vitality. The German Standard is identical to that of the Miniature Pinscher and resembles that of the Doberman. The breed's coat should be smooth, hard, glossy and colored bright red or black-and-tan.

Registry: FCI (Group 2), KC

Pinscher

PLANINSKY GONIC

This scenthound from Slovenia is also known as the "Mountain Hound" because it hunts and tracks like the Bavarian Mountain Dog. The dog is put in harness and attached to a long leash to track both live and dead game. It is used strictly as a hunting dog and is rarely seen outside the region.

At its withers, the breed is about 18-22 inches/45-55 cm. The body should be decidedly rectangular, well muscled and with good bone. The head is quite broad with a flat skull and triangular ears. These should hang close to the cheeks without folds and be set not too high. The coat should be short, hard, glossy and black with rich tan markings.

Registry: FCI (Group 6)

The Planinsky Gonic depicted in this illustration, is a rare scenthound that is put in harness on leash to track dead game.

PODENCO CANARIO

This Spanish breed from the Canary Islands is very similar to the Ibizan Hound. Both of these breeds are considered sighthounds but are classified by the Fédération Cynologique Internationale as "primitive type" hunting dogs.

The Podenco Canario are still used for hunting rabbit, using coursing methods, in their country of origin. The breed is very rare, even in Spain.

The height at its withers should be about 21-25 inches/53-64 cm. Its body should be rectangular, slender but well muscled. The head should be long and shaped like a narrow wedge. The ears are large, high set and erect. The coat should be smooth and fine and its color may be any shade of red, with or without white markings. Black pigmentation in this breed is a fault.

Registry: FCI (Group 5)

Podenco Canario

PODENGOS PORTUGUÊS

The Portuguese Podengo is believed to descend from Egyptian Hounds along with the Cirneco dell'Etna, Pharaoh, Ibiza and Canario Hounds. Incidentally, this also applies to the Andalusian Hound, which is very similar but not yet recognized by the Fédération Cynologique Internationale. All these breeds are used for hunting rabbit — either as single dogs or in a pack. They have a specialized technique of using both scent and sight. They track the scent and when close to the prey they jump straight up in the grass, which is usually very high. Once they have spotted the rabbit, they chase, catch, kill and retrieve it to the hunter.

The Podengo comes in three sizes — Grande, Médio and Pequeno. The height at the withers varies accordingly: Grande is about 22-28 inches/ 55-70 cm, the Médio is about 16-22 inches/ 40-55 cm and the Pequeno is about 8-12 inches/ 20-30 cm. The body should be rectangular, slender but well muscled and quite upright in the shoulder and neck. The head should be triangular with a long muzzle and tight lips. The ears are set high, rather large and erect. The coat should be smooth and glossy without being soft or semi-wire. The color may be any shade of red, with or without white markings. Black pigmentation is a fault.

Registry: FCI (Group 5)

Medium-sized, smooth-coated Podengo Português

Small, wire-coated Podengo Português

Small smooth-coated Podengo Português

POINTER

ORIGIN AND DEVELOPMENT

There are records of Pointers in England as far back as 1650. Some historians believe that the breed developed in Spain and Portugal; others think that it sprang up in both eastern Europe and England at the same time. It appears to be generally accepted, however, that the first Pointers as they are known today were a result of crossbreeding the old Spanish Pointer and a lighter-boned variety of Foxhound. This cross countered the "too heavy" influence of the previous Bloodhound crosses and some of the less desirable characteristics of the Greyhound crosses — rounded croups, broken toplines, long thin curved tails and a poor underline. All crosses are not golden, however, and too much Foxhound resulted in straighter shoulders, rounder bone, occasionally longer coats and, too frequently, an improper tail carriage and a plainer head.

In 1890 William Arkwright began his book on early Pointer history and thirty years later produced a volume that is still considered the basis of the breed. The current Standard has changed little since that time.

TEMPERAMENT

For the most part, the Pointer is obedient and eager to please its owner. It can be somewhat aloof with strangers. A good Pointer is the aristocrat of all the sporting breeds. Nothing is quite as exciting as watching a Pointer coursing the ground with its tail held high and its nostrils flared, searching the wind for the scent of game.

SPECIAL CARE AND TRAINING

Like all sporting dogs, Pointer puppies should be brought up on the best possible food served four times daily, lots of fresh air and sunshine, regulated exercise, good nap times and plenty of love. They should be taken on short walks from an early age so that they become exposed to a variety of situations and acquire self-confidence.

ADAPTABILITY

The Pointer is an ideal house dog. It is of moderate size and shorthaired. When given early exposure it becomes a secure member of the family, is good with children and will sound the alarm when a stranger approaches.

Pointer

ESSENTIALS OF THE BREED

Balance and symmetry are more important than size in the Pointer. However, the most desirable size for a male is 25-28 inches/63-71 cm and 55-75 pounds/25-34 kg. Females should ideally be 23-26 inches/58-66 cm and 45-65 pounds/20-30 kg. Pointers come in four colors: liver, black, orange and lemon, usually in combination with white. However, solid colors are acceptable although rarely seen today and, in the United States, white tends to raise doubts as to the purity of the breed. Orange differs from lemon, not in the depth of the coat color, but in the difference of nose and eye pigment. Oranges should have a dark or black nose and eye pigment and lemons a lighter or flesh-colored pigment. This is important only in breeding for color genetics. As the Standard clearly states, "A good Pointer cannot be a bad color."

The Pointer has two very distinct characteristics — its head and tail are both true hallmarks of the breed. The head should be of medium width, about as wide as the length of the muzzle with a slight furrow between the eyes and the cheeks. In an adult it should be slightly chiseled. This chiseling will change constantly as the dog matures. There should be a pronounced stop. The muzzle is of good length with the nasal bone formed so that the nose is slightly higher at the tip than the muzzle at the stop. This creates the true dish face and allows for good scenting ability. The nose should be large and the nostrils wide. In the American Standard, parallel planes of the skull and muzzle are equally acceptable.

The tail should be of medium length — no longer than to the hock and shorter if possible — and should be thick at the base, tapering to a fine point on the move. The tail should lash from side to side, not in a wagging sense but as part of the actual movement. Once seen, it will not be forgotten.

Registry: AKC, CKC, FCI (Group 7), KC

POITEVIN

This breed used to be known as the Chiens du Haut-Poitou. These hounds have existed for many hundreds of years in the region of Poitiers in western France. They have been crossed with Foxhounds several times over the centuries. Fast galloping hounds, they hunt in packs in pursuit of red deer, roe deer and even wild boar.

The height at the withers should be about 24-28 inches/60-72 cm. The Poitevin should be tall, elegant and with a long, fine and lean head and a slightly pointed muzzle. The ears are shorter and higher set than in most French hounds and its skin should be fine and fit tightly to the body. The coat should be smooth, glossy and tricolored. The sides of the head and the ears are always tan.

Registry: FCI (Group 6)

The Poitevin, a fast galloping pack hound, has been used to hunt deer and wild boar for hundreds of years in France.

POLISH OWCZAREK NIZINNY

The Polish Sheepdog is called the Polish Lowland in some countries because it is used on lowlands to herd sheep. This old breed has been mentioned as part of the ancestry of the Bearded Collie. The breed gained interest as a companion dog outside Poland after the 1960s and can now be seen at dog shows in most European countries.

At the withers, the height should be about 16-20 inches/40-52 cm. Its body should be compact, almost rectangular, well muscled and with strong bone. The head should be strong with a broad skull and a strong, but not too long muzzle. The tail is usually docked short. The coat should be long, harsh in texture, shaggy and slightly wavy. All colors are permitted but the most common is white, with or without black or gray patches, or solid gray with or without white markings.

The Polish Owczarek Nizinny, an old breed, is used to herd sheep on lowlands.

Registry: FCI (Group 1), KC

POLISH OWCZAREK PODHALANSKI

The Polish herding dog is mainly used to guard flocks and property. It comes from the Carpathian Mountains in the south of Poland. Large white mountain dogs found in several European countries are thought to have the same origin which goes back thousands of years. It is a self-confident and independent breed that is considered "a one man dog."

The height at its withers should be about 24-27 1/2 inches/62-70 cm. Its body should be rectangular, well muscled and with strong bone. The head should be massive with a pronounced stop, strong, but with not too long a muzzle. The coat should be thick, slightly wavy and of medium length on the body. It should be longer on the chest, back of the legs and on the tail. The head, lower parts of the ears and front of legs should have short hair. The breed should be white with black pigmentation.

The Polski Owczarek Podhalanski is an ancient breed used as a herding and guard dog in southern Poland.

Registry: FCI (Group 1)

POMERANIAN

ORIGIN AND DEVELOPMENT

This has always been one of the most popular Toy breeds – and its outline suggests that it is a spitz breed. The breed was not known as the Pomeranian until around the eighteenth century and it is German in origin.

The Pomeranian was first introduced to Britain in the nineteenth century when it weighed around 30 pounds/13.6 kg. Then it was usually cream, biscuit or red. Blacks and whites were rare and, to quote the author of an early work on the breed: "The white ones are dreadfully bad specimens, but the blacks worse!" Queen Victoria was a great devotee of the breed.

By 1870 the breed had been given Kennel Club recognition and classes were provided at dog shows shortly afterwards. The classification at that time tended to be divided into two sections – over and under 8 pounds/3.6 kg in weight. Challenge Certificates (CCs) were awarded for each of the two categories, but the allocation was cut by half in 1908 mainly because very few over 8 pounds/3.6 kg were being shown. After several appeals from the different Pomeranian clubs, they were restored until 1915 when the Kennel Club once more withdrew CCs from the upper weight section. After some discussion the Kennel Club amended the breed Standard so that the weight was reduced to 7 pounds/3 kg. With the advent of smaller dogs being shown in numbers, the Standard was further revised to 4-5 pounds/1.8-2.25 kg and this remains today.

The breed has become popular in most countries where dog showing is commonplace, and following the purchase of many top quality dogs from leading British breeders, Japan is now considered to be the country where some of the best Poms in the world are being bred. The Fédération Cynologique Internationale does not recognize the Pomeranian as described under the British Standard. In continental Europe it is considered to be a German breed, the German Zwergspitz. The two Standards are very similar, however.

TEMPERAMENT

The Pomeranian is an extrovert, lively and intelligent dog – and very much a large personality in a small frame. It is independent up to a point, will protect its owners quite vigorously at times and can be extremely vocal. Its small but sturdy stature makes it an excellent pet.

HEALTH MATTERS

The breed is generally very healthy with no major hereditary problems, though patella luxation is seen in the Pomeranian quite often. Breeding from very small bitches may mean than Caesarean sections are unavoidable. Otherwise, with sensible basic husbandry the Pomeranian is a sturdy little dog with few health problems.

SPECIAL CARE AND TRAINING

Pomeranians are naturally intelligent and take readily to basic training. Some companion dogs will also learn learn amusing "tricks" very quickly. The coat is profuse and needs to be attended to daily if matting is to be prevented; however, all that is really necessary is a thorough brushing and combing right through to the skin. A monthly bath is also recommended.

ADAPTABILITY

Pomeranians will happily live together as a canine group, but will equally adapt to a situation where they are the only dog in an otherwise human household. They require little in the way of exercise, but being natural extroverts, need to be kept mentally occupied. Kept *en masse* the breed does tend to be rather noisy.

ESSENTIALS OF THE BREED

At first sight, the Pom looks like a fluffy ball. This is due to its overall compactness, its profuse coat and tail and its rather short neck, with its "thrown back" natural head carriage. It is a naturally busy little dog displaying great buoyancy and activity in its carriage. It should always be dainty and never cumbersome or heavy in any way.

The Pomeranian's head is essentially foxy in outline, the skull being slightly flat and quite large in proportion to the muzzle which is finely finished, clean, tight and free from lippiness. The eyes are medium in size, slightly oval, bright and dark, always showing fire and intelligence. Black eye rims are required in the most common colors. The ears are small, set relatively high and carried erect. The Pom's neck is rather short, its forelegs should be straight and finely boned, with small compact cat-feet. There should be sufficient length of leg to give the dog balance. The body is short-backed, well ribbed and the chest should be quite deep but not too wide in front. The hindquarters are fine boned, moderately angulated and with no suggestion of cow-hocks or undue width behind. The tail must be set very high, carried straight and flat (according to the British Standard) right over the back and lavishly covered with long, harsh and spreading hair.

The Pom should move briskly and with great bounciness. There is a double coat; the undercoat is soft and fluffy while the topcoat is long, straight and harsher in texture, covering the whole body. It is very profuse around the neck and shoulders, forming a definite frill. Most colors are permissible. Black and Tans are accepted in the United States and FCI countries and there is currently a move to get them accepted in Great Britain — at the moment the wording of the British breed Standard does not provide for this color. In Great Britain, when particolor and whole-colored dogs compete together, if all other points are equal, preference is given to the whole-colored specimens.

Registry: AKC, CKC, FCI (Group 5), KC

Pomeranian

POODLES

In today's world, the Poodle serves primarily as a companion animal, although the Standard variety is still used as a water retriever. In the United States, the two larger varieties, the Miniature and the Standard, are members of the Non-Sporting Group and the Toy variety is in the Toy Group. For these reasons, the breed's history is particularly important because if its form (or type) is to fit its function (or purpose), students of the breed have to look to its history to learn the purpose that the dog had during its developmental years.

Some breed authorities attribute Germany as the country of origin for the Poodle, but there are references to other dogs of similar type in Russia, France and several other countries in

Black Standard Poodle

White Standard Poodle

southwestern Europe. Germany, however, probably gave the breed its name Pudel. This roughly means to splash in water and, indeed, its original function was that of a water retriever.

The Poodle's traditional trim came about because the breed started life as a water dog.

Today's show trims are reminiscent of the trims that suit a water dog: the front part of the dog is left with long hair to protect the heart and chest; the legs are clipped to free them for swimming. Lion trims of this type are depicted in both art and literature going back as far as the 1500s.

The breed became quite popular among the French aristocracy and in fact was ultimately designated the national dog of France. France also contributed to the "fanciness" of the Poodle by adding decorative touches such as the pompons and rosettes found on Poodles in the ring today. Recognition of the Toy variety in the United States in 1943 was followed by a significant breeding effort on the part of Toy breeders throughout the States. Most breed authorities consider the progress made in Toy breeding to be one of the greatest success stories in all canine history.

At about the same time that the Poodle Club of America was established, the Poodle saw a steady growth in popularity, and by 1960 it was the most popular breed in the United States and remained so for the next twenty-three years. While no longer the "most" popular breed, it remains high on the list.

TEMPERAMENT

The Poodle is said to be one of the most, if not *the* most, intelligent of all canines. Sometimes it is too smart for its own good and figures ways to get into mischief and forgets to figure ways to get out of it!

HEALTH MATTERS

Owners should be aware of a variety of heritable problems. Many can be screened with blood tests, eye examinations, X-rays and skin punch biopsy. Hip dysplasia is known in Standards, and stifle problems and progressive retinal atrophy in Miniatures and Toys. Juvenile cataracts, skin problems and epilepsy are also considerations. Gastric torsion is not unknown in the Standard. Small meals, two or three times a day with rest periods for an hour or so following, as well as a soy-free diet, are all recommended.

Most, if not all, well-known breeders do extensive health testing and this information should be available to interested buyers. Ears must have the insides kept very clean and free of hair growth. Nails must be kept short and teeth brushed weekly. The coat must be kept trimmed, clean and tangle-free. Trimming a show coat is an art form that can be learned but is not an overnight study. Generally, pets are kept in neat short trims.

SPECIAL CARE AND TRAINING

It is said that great patience is required to obedience train Poodles as they are far more interested in hearing a crowd chuckle at their clowning than to do a perfect job. In fact a Standard Poodle can do anything that a Labrador can do in the field as a retriever. The difference comes at night when the Lab wants to dream in front of the fire and the Poodle wants to be the Fourth at Bridge and tell naughty stories! The Toy Poodle is not aware of its small size and feels it can perform as well, if not better than its Standard counterpart. They can take their own exercise within the house and fenced yard but do love walks and play time as well as learning any tricks the family has the time to teach.

ADAPTABILITY

The Standard is the Poodle for all seasons. Smart, steady and loyal, it will do anything an owner could wish, including obedience, shows, tricks, hunting and retrieving. The list is endless. The Miniature, raised as a family companion will suit all members from child to oldster and fit almost any type of lifestyle. To know, to understand, to be aware of a Poodle's abilities is a great experience, be it Toy, Miniature or Standard.

ESSENTIALS OF THE BREED

Sturdy, square, stylish, trimmed in one of the allowed trims, the Poodle is unique in the world of dogs. In the United States, the Toy is 10 inches/25 cm or less at the shoulder; the Miniature over 10 inches/25 cm but not taller than 15 inches/38 cm. The Standard is normally 21-26 inches/53-66 cm. The United Kingdom also accepts three sizes but the Fédération Cynologique Internationale regognizes four: the Standard, Miniature, Dwarf and Toy.

The Poodle's face is one of length, refinement

and beauty. Its eyes reflect intelligence and humor. It moves with its head and tail up in a light springy fashion, always with neat tight feet and an alert demeanor.

There are three allowed show trims for competition. The Lion trim with Saddle trim on the rear and the Lion Continental trim with shaven rear with rosettes over the hip bones share some features. On these two trims the face, feet and the base of the tail are shaved with bracelets on the front and rear legs and a pompon on the tail. The Puppy trim which is allowed until the Poodle's first birthday requires the face, feet, and base of tail to be shaved and the balance of the coat is left full and shaped to relieve any impression of overcoating or a bearlike look.

The breed has two distinct types of coat. The curly coat is double, thick and easily styled, while the corded coat, which was once very popular, is now rarely seen. The corded coat naturally forms into long cords or stringlike ropes when the Poodle is mature. The coat is then styled, usually in the Continental trim. In all the trims the hair above the eyes is either held in place by rubber bands or barrettes, left free or scissored into a cap. The Poodle must be a solid color in almost any shade — black, white, apricot, brown, blue, silver, café au lait or cream. With the exception of the browns, all colors should have dark pigment and dark eyes. All shades of brown should have brown pigment and brown or dark hazel eyes.

Registry: AKC, CKC, FCI (Group 9), KC

PORCELAINE

The Porcelaine used to be called the Franche-Comté Hound after its region of origin on the French-Swiss border. This hound's ancestors are said to be "the Royal White hounds" of medieval times. Years later, during the mid-nineteenth century, an infusion of Billy and Harrier took place. The Porcelaine is mainly used for hunting hare and packs can be found in several places in France.

The height at the withers should be about 21-23 inches/53-58 cm. This medium-sized hound has no structural exaggerations. Its main feature is its very fine, smooth coat with a translucent coloring reminiscent of the fine china that gave the breed its name. The skin should be pink with sparse black mottling that shows up through the white coat. From a distance, it gives an impression of pale blue glass. Any pale orange markings should be small — they are usually on the ears with perhaps an occasional patch on the body.

Registry: FCI (Group 6)

The Porcelaine originates from the French-Swiss border and is used for hunting hare in packs in several French regions.

PORTUGUESE WATER DOG

Origin and Development

A very old breed that originates in the Algarve province of Portugal, the Portuguese Water Dog has been the fisherman's friend for centuries. At home in the water, their uses were varied. They helped to set nets, herd schools of fish, carry messages between boats and dive for escaping fish. The breed was admitted to the American Kennel Club in 1983 as a member of the Working Group. Its unique Lion trim has been described in books since the 1500s.

Temperament

This is an old working breed and can have guard dog tendencies. If this is not wanted, it must be trained from the age of ten weeks to accept all comers in a friendly fashion and any guarding symptoms should be discouraged.

The breed can be and is often very friendly. It is wonderful with its family and takes well to children if it is brought up with them and if the children are taught how to treat the dog. It loves water and retrieving, and is a smart and willing worker in Obedience.

Health Matters

Health problems of the inherited kind are progressive retinal atrophy, storage disease, puppies born without an essential enzyme which leads to early death, hip dysplasia and a type of skin condition that leads to early hair loss. All of these conditions except the last may be identified by blood test, X-ray or eye examinations. Puppies must be purchased from reliable sources — breeders who are concerned with the health and well-being of the breed and can give results of all health checks to

Portuguese Water Dog with a working trim

prospective buyers of their stock.

Ears must be kept under constant supervision because they can be irritated by water that enters them when the Water Dog indulges in its favorite sport: swimming. Nails should be kept short, although the foot itself is somewhat large and spread with skin webbing between the toes to help it when in the water.

SPECIAL CARE AND TRAINING

The Portuguese Water Dog is active and will take exercise in a safely enclosed yard or on walks. It likes swimming with its owners and it thrives on obedience training. The coat must be brushed frequently to keep it free of tangles and mats.

ADAPTABILITY

The Water Dog is usually a quiet animal that only barks when it is on watchdog duty. It fits well into many lifestyles and loves to be part of the family.

ESSENTIALS OF THE BREED

The breed, with its various colors, coat options and trims is a stylish companion. It has a well-carried head, good topline and a gaily carried natural tail with a pompon on the end. It is very hardy and designed to be of moderate size (17-23 inches/43-58 cm tall). Females are slightly smaller than the males. The body is substantial with firm and elastic muscle, and is slightly longer in body than tall, with a large head for its size.

Its coat does not shed — a boon to those who suffer allergy problems. It comes in all shades of brown or black, with or without white markings. The coat must be trimmed in either the typical Lion trim where the face and the rear third of the body are shaved and the rest of the coat left long, or the working Retriever trim where a short blanket of hair covers the whole dog. The tail in both cases is shaved at the base and a pompon is left on the end. There are two types of hair coat: the curly, a harsher, tighter and fuller coat, and the wavy which is not as harsh to the touch with soft waves and a sheen to the individual hairs.

Registry: AKC, FCI (Group 8), KC

Portuguese Water Dog with a "lion" trim

POSAVSKI GONIC

This scenthound comes mainly from the area around the Sava River in former Yugoslavia. It is strictly used as a hunting dog, usually for hare. The breed is very rare outside its region of origin.

The height at the withers should be about 18-23 inches/46-58 cm. Its body should be almost rectangular, well muscled and with good bone. The head should be long, quite narrow and with a slightly convex nose ridge. The ears should be triangular, not too long and hang close to the cheeks without folds. The coat should be short, hard and glossy. It may be any shade of red with white markings.

Registry: FCI (Group 6)

The Posavski Gonic is a rare breed used to hunt hare near the Sava River in former Yugoslavia.

PUDELPOINTER

This German breed was developed in the late nineteenth century by crossing French and English Pointers, hunting Poodles and probably German Wirehaired Pointers. This work was carried out by the same men who created the German Pointer. The Pudelpointer resembles the German Wirehaired Pointer so much that the breeds are difficult to distinguish. One has to admire the skill of these men to create a homogenous conformation in the breed and maintain good working dog characteristics. It is mainly used as a gun dog and is very rare.

At its withers, the height is approximately 24-25 1/2 inches/ 60-65 cm. The body should be rectangular, well muscled and with strong bone. The tail is docked, slightly shorter than half its length. The coat should be medium long, wiry and with longer hair forming a beard, mustache and whiskers. The color should be liver brown.

Registry: FCI (Group 7)

Pudelpointer

PUG

ORIGIN AND DEVELOPMENT

There's little question that the Orient provided the roots from which today's Pug stems but, as is the case with so many breeds, it is almost impossible to be definitive about its origin. Early pieces of art depict small dogs with tightly curled tails, a typical ear and charming face complete with wrinkles, large, dark round eyes — all in all with many of the hallmarks that are so evident in today's Pug. These early dogs were known as "Pu" or "Poo" dogs and were once popular figures in statuary and paintings.

Most breed historians believe that, as the breed evolved, Holland was its home before it ultimately arrived in England. In fact, for a while, the breed was called "The Dutch Pug." But at the same time, historians agree that the breed was also evident in both France and Russia. And even then, fawns and light creams — both with black masks — were much in evidence. The now-popular black Pug came later.

Without question, the Pug's rise in popularity took place in England where the breed found great favor with the upper echelons of society. Two well-documented English fanciers, Lady Willoughby de Ersby and Mr. Morrison of Walham Green championed the breed's development. England's Kennel Club was founded in 1873 and there followed the establishment of several breed clubs. The British Pug-dog Club was created in 1882 and the British Kennel Club's first Stud Book listed sixty-six Pugs.

England became the source of seed stock for early American fanciers and history credits Dr. M.H. Cryder with being one of the very early Pug breeders in the United States. Many of his imports were descendants of two Pugs that were brought to England after they were captured from the Emperor of China's palace during the Siege of Peking. The American Kennel Club (AKC) accepted the breed in 1885, but despite an initial wave of popularity, the breed suddenly took a downward turn and by the beginning of the twentieth century had dwindled to zero. By the mid-1920s, however, the tide had turned with fifteen Pugs recorded in 1926 and 155 in 1944. In 1994, Pug registrations stood at 15,464 placing the Pug twenty-sixth in AKC registrations.

Pug authorities speculate that the fundamental characteristics of the breed have undergone as little change as any other breed of dogs in the world today. During one period the ears were cropped but that practice has been abandoned in favor of the natural ear.

TEMPERAMENT

Some people tend to assume that the thick-set body type, short nose and chuggy demeanor of the Pug means that the breed is fairly quiet and sedentary. This is one dimension of the Pug personality — but only one. While the Pug may be perfectly pleased to spend a quiet evening with its owner, at any point in the evening it may well drop down to the floor, stretch, and then frolic or race around the house — just because it can and because that is what Pugs do. To a degree the Pug is a study of diversity: quiet and docile; vivacious and teasing. But whatever the Pug's demeanor, it is most acutely attuned to its owner.

Pugs belong to the Toy Group and they are sturdy members. They are capable of hard play and take in their stride any bumps that life offers. Consequently, they are most suitable as children's pets. On the other hand, they are frequently the choice of older people who enjoy not only their quietness but also their sometimes teasing and wistful attitude. Pugs are not yappy — but they do snore.

HEALTH MATTERS

The Pug is quite a healthy breed with few problems. However, it sometimes has accidents that befall its eyes because of their large size and its "Devil may care" attitude. These may be

Pug

puncture wounds, scrapes, cat scratches or soap in the eye. All these require attention from the vet, who will check out the problem and supply medication to reduce any pain and aid the healing. The Pug should be taken to the vet as soon as possible or it will make matters worse by rubbing or scratching the damaged eye. The breed may also develop luxating patellas, particularly if it is overweight, that cause the dog to limp. The kneecap that has been put out of place may be replaced by a vet but if surgical attention is required the dog may not be shown at shows in the United States. Skin problems and epilepsy are also known to have occurred in the breed. The Pug is a good eater and will help itself to the food

of other animals and the family if given the chance, so care should be taken not to allow it to become overweight or obese.

SPECIAL CARE AND TRAINING

The only caution that the breed demands is special attention during hot, humid weather. The short nose so typical of many Oriental breeds (and the accompanying respiratory system) inclines this breed to suffer more from heat than other dogs. The Pug should not be left out in the hot sun for an extended period. It responds fairly well to basic training. Its nails and teeth need weekly attention and care. The Pug is not required to have very short nails but they should not be overly long. Pugs hate to have their mouths examined but if they get used to having dentifrice rubbed onto the teeth weekly their teeth will last longer. Pugs do shed because even though their coats are short, they have long undercoats. Warm baths, a rub down and brushing with a natural bristle brush will solve any shedding problems.

ADAPTABILITY

Because of its size, the Pug is at home anywhere from a small apartment to a farm home. The Pug is truly adaptable to any situation. It can behave perfectly but then its mischievous nature may suddenly take over and it becomes the life of the party.

ESSENTIALS OF THE BREED

The overall shape of the Pug is square and cobby. The breed is sometimes described as an awful lot of dog in a relatively small space. Its sturdiness comes from its compactness and moderately heavy well-knit muscles. It should be neither lean nor leggy, nor should it be long and low. The breed Standard does not define a height, but lists the desirable weight in the range of 14-18 pounds/6-8 kg.

The tail is distinctive and should be tightly curled with a double curl preferred. The feet are well split, neither round like a cat's nor long like a hare's. However, the head is perhaps the most distinctive feature of the Pug. It is large and massive (not apple-headed) with an indentation of the skull. The eyes are large, round, dark and lustrous, capable of both a fiery and melting expression. The muzzle is short, blunt and square, but not up-faced. The ears are thin, small, and soft, either "rose" or "button" — with the button ear preferred. The markings are clearly defined with the muzzle or mask, ears, moles and all other black indications as black as possible. A black line from the occiput to the tail is called for. Wrinkles on the forehead should be large and deep. The hair should be fine, smooth, soft and glossy in silver or apricot-fawn (both with black markings) and black.

Registry: AKC, CKC, FCI (Group 9), KC

PULI/HUNGARIAN PULI

ORIGIN AND DEVELOPMENT

The Puli is one of several herding breeds native to Hungary, including the much larger Komondor. Its most obvious breed characteristic is its long, corded coat. As far back as the mid-1750s a German author named Heppe wrote of a dog believed to be a Puli, which he termed the "Hungarian Water Dog," and which was said to hunt rabbit and duck. The breed seems to have been developed, however, as a specialized herding dog, tending and guarding flocks. The Puli was actually trained to run along the backs of sheep when they were massed together. Gradually, the breed found its way into more urban environments and became a much desired pet as its intelligence and character proved popular virtues in a companion dog.

The American Kennel Club recognized the breed in 1936, but the breed did not qualify for Challenge Certificate status in Great Britain until 1978. One of the pioneer breeders, Pat Lanz, established the highly successful Borgvaale Kennel using European and subsequently American imports. For a time American fanciers showed Pulik (the Hungarian plural form) with their naturally corded coats brushed out, but today most specimens are seen in corded splendor. Due to the length of time it takes for a dog to acquire its mature cords, many Pulik continue winning in the show ring until they are ten or more years old. Many of the breed are approaching their best at an age when dogs of other breeds are retiring from competition.

TEMPERAMENT

The Puli is a naturally busy and lively little dog that was bred to work. It should never be nervous, but neither should it display any signs of aggression. It can, however, be a little wary with strangers until they are accepted.

HEALTH MATTERS

Generally the Puli is a hardy and healthy breed. From time to time cases of retinal dysplasia have been found, but breeders can now screen puppies for the condition from as early as six weeks of age. Fortunately puppies can be cleared at this stage. Most caring breeders also screen breeding stock for hip dysplasia, but this condition is no more of a problem in Pulik than in any other working breed.

SPECIAL CARE AND TRAINING

Apart from the fact that its teeth should be kept clean and nails shortened weekly, the obvious aspect of the Puli which requires specialist care is its coat. This is naturally double, with a soft and dense undercoat and a longer topcoat. From an early age, the coat is trained to develop in the traditionally corded pattern. As the cords are not brushed out,

Puli, known as the Hungarian Puli in the United Kingdom

regular bathing is advisable, without which the breed can develop a strong odor. The Puli responds well to basic obedience training and has retained its natural tendency to herd.

ADAPTABILITY

The breed needs to be kept occupied and a Puli will be at its best when it can live with other animals in a rural home. However, given that it has plenty of company it will adapt well to an urban environment, so long as regular exercise is not neglected.

ESSENTIALS OF THE BREED

The Puli is a sturdy, but wiry breed, with bone that is finer than at first may be assumed, because of the heavy appearance created by the corded coat. Underneath the coat the head is quite small and fine with a slightly domed skull. The muzzle is one-third of the head length and bluntly rounded. The nose should be large and black, with eye rims and flews also black regardless of body color. The roof of the mouth should be darkly pigmented, either uniformly or with deeply pigmented spots on a dark base.

The Puli should have a virtually square appearance. The mature animal's coat on the head, neck and tightly curled tail should blend with that of the body. The feet should be short, round and tight and the pads springy and dark gray. The Puli's movement is quite individual, not exhibiting great reach. It is naturally short stepping, but quick and nimble. The British Standard asks that the Puli stands up to 17 inches/43 cm at the withers for males, bitches up to 16 inches/40.5 cm. The American height limits are 19 inches/48 cm and 18 inches/46 cm respectively. The breed can be black, rusty black, white and various shades of gray or apricot. Grays and apricots may have a suggestion of a black mask, but the overall impression should always be of a self-colored breed.

Registry: AKC, CKC, FCI (Group 1), KC

PUMI

This Hungarian sheepdog is believed to have been developed about 200 years ago by crossing the Puli with German and French prick-eared sheepdogs. A later cross is also said to have been made to the Wire Fox Terrier. It is said to be an efficient ratter and has been known to hunt smaller game. Nowadays it is mainly kept as a companion dog.

The height at the withers should be about 13 1/2-17 inches/35-44 cm. The body should be square, with a narrow front with moderate angulation and a long neck. The head should be long and narrow. The ears are set high and carried like the Fox Terrier's ears. The tail should be set high and carried over the back in a loose curl. The coat should be medium short, curly but never corded — it is longer and wavy on the ears and tail. The color is usually any shade of gray, but black and white are also permissible although rarely seen.

Pumi

Registry: FCI (Group 1)

PYRENEAN MASTIFF/ MASTÍN DE LOS PIRINEOS

The Pyrenean Mastiff was developed in the region of the Pyrenean Mountains that stretches from Aragon to Navarra. In fact, the breed was once called the Navarra Mastiff. The breed was at one time almost extinct but has gained new interest in recent years. It is still rare despite this.

The ideal height at the withers for males is 32 inches/81 cm and 29 1/2 inches/75 cm for females. The body should be rectangular, well muscled and with strong bone. The head should be massive, broad and with a strong,

deep muzzle. The tail should be very long with a curl at the tip. Double dewclaws on the hind-legs are typical. The coat should be abundant, thick and medium long. The color on the body should be white with the sides of the head and ears either black, badger, any shade of gray, sand, red or marbling in the mentioned colors. A few large patches on the body are permissible but not in all white or tricolored dogs.

Registry: FCI (Group 2)

Pyrenean Mastiff

PYRENEAN SHEEPDOGS

There are two varieties of this small French sheepdog from the Pyrenean Mountains. One variety is long coated, *à poil long,* and the other has a short-coated face, *à face rase.* The coat on the body in both varieties is almost the same length and looks shaggy. The texture should be coarse except on the tail, over the loin and on the thighs where the coat is very long and more woolly in texture.

The Pyrenean is one of the old type of sheepdog that used to herd flocks while their larger Mollosser-type companions kept guard with the shepherd. This combination of dogs working together has existed for hundreds of years in mountains throughout Europe and the Middle East.

It is only during the last twenty or so years that the Pyrenean Sheepdog has gained interest as a companion dog. Its active and very energetic temperament requires that it be kept occupied with purposeful activities. The breed is known for its agility and is very quick to respond to noise or any movement.

The height at the withers is approximately 15-19 inches/38-48 cm. The body should be rectangular, well muscled but never heavy or strong. The head should be triangular, not too long in the muzzle. The ears are usually cropped and the tail docked or with a natural bobtail. Double dewclaws on the hind legs are typical. The breed's accepted colors are all shades of fawn with or without brindling and harlequin. All colors of Pyrenean Sheepdog are permitted with or without slight white markings. Black pigmentation is essential.

Registry: FCI (Group 1)

Pyrenean Sheepdog

RAFEIRO DO ALENTEJO

This is the largest of the Portuguese breeds. It comes from the province of Alentejo in southern Portugal. It is believed that it owes part of its origin to the Spanish Mastiff that was developed in the plains around Madrid in the Extremadera and Castilla-La Mancha areas. It is used as a guard dog on farms and for flocks and is considered a tough, self-confident, independent dog. The breed is very rare and may occasionally be seen at major dog shows in Spain and Portugal.

The height at the withers is approximately 25-29 inches/64-74 cm. The body should be rectangular, well muscled, deep and with strong bone. The head should be bearlike with a rather short muzzle.

The coat of the Rafeiro do Alentejo should be medium short, straight and coarse in texture. Accepted colors are black, fawn, cream, red-grizzle and brindle, with or without white markings. The most typical color pattern is sometimes described as off-white

The Rafeiro do Alentejo, the largest of the Portuguese breeds, is a very rare guard dog.

with large patches. The patches, that cover the head and usually part of the back and rump, are fawn or red covered with greyish black brindling.

Registry: FCI (Group 2)

RETRIEVERS — CHESAPEAKE BAY RETRIEVER

ORIGIN AND DEVELOPMENT

The Chesapeake Bay Retriever is one of only two sporting breeds which has evolved entirely in America (the other being the American Water Spaniel). Descending from two shipwrecked Newfoundland dogs — Sailor and Canton (which were never bred to each other) — the breed was designed by judicious outcrossing with many other breeds to include spaniels, Indian dogs, pointers, setters, and Irish Water Spaniels to be wonderful retrievers, tireless hunters and guard dogs. These early days were spent in and around the environs of the Chesapeake Bay in Maryland — hence the name.

TEMPERAMENT

This is a good sized, hearty, workmanlike breed, devoted to its family. It makes a great waterfowl hunter and retriever and a trusty guard dog for homes and farms.

HEALTH MATTERS

Health is quite straightforward with a well-bred, well-raised Chesapeake. Of course breeding stock should be X-rayed for hip dysplasia and dewclaws removed at birth. The ears should be checked and medicated if inflamed. This occurs when water in the ears starts an inflammation and invites an invasion of ear mites.

Chesapeake Bay Retriever

SPECIAL CARE AND TRAINING

Puppies should be well socialized before ten weeks of age. Coats normally shed yearly and a warm bath or two helps the old hair to shed, leaving a clean base for the new coat to emerge. A working Chesapeake Bay Retriever should not have frequent baths since baths destroy the natural oils in the coat that make it shed water. The breed responds well to many kinds of training.

ADAPTABILITY

The Chesapeake must be allowed to do the job for which it was bred and, as a result, should be owned by sportsmen and women. They are generally considered as country rather than city dogs.

ESSENTIALS OF THE BREED

Strength, sturdiness and a fearless nature are just some of the many hallmarks of the unique Chesapeake Bay Retriever. At the shoulder males should be 23-26 inches/58-66 cm and bitches 21-24 inches/53-61 cm. Males should weigh 65-80 pounds/30-38 kg, bitches 55-70 pounds/25-32 kg.

Its coat should be the correct texture, color and pattern. The color may be any shade of brown, or the color of dead grass (so it blends with its surroundings when working). It may have small spots of white on its breast, on the belly or toes. In the United States, white in any other area disqualifies in the ring. The coat is a coarse, harsh outercoat with a short woolly undercoat — this texture coupled with the natural oils in the coat give a waterproof covering so that the wet dog is almost dry after just a quick shake. The coat's pattern should be as follows: thick and short (no more than 1 1/2 inches/4 cm) on the face and leg. It should also be straight with a tendency to wave on the shoulders, neck, back and loins only. A coat that tends to curl all over the body and feathering on the legs or tail that is over 1 3/4 inches/4.5 cm will result in disqualification in the United States. The breed should also have a wedge-shaped head, clear yellow eyes, tight lips, hind legs a trifle longer than front ones for greater propelling power when swimming, good legs and feet and a perfect mouth.

Registry: AKC, CKC, FCI (Group 8), KC

RETRIEVERS — CURLY-COATED RETRIEVER

ORIGIN AND DEVELOPMENT

The Curly-Coated Retriever is a cross between the St. John's Newfoundland, and descendants of the old English water dog, with a cross to the Poodle to tighten the curl, and was one of the earliest recognized retrievers. Extremely popular in the nineteenth century, particularly with English gamekeepers, the Curly was a multipurpose hunting retriever. Prized for its innate field ability, courage and indomitable perseverance, the Curly was valued equally in its role as loyal companion at home and as a hunter.

However, as the century ended, the Curly-Coated Retriever lost popularity to the newer retriever breeds. Today its greatest support and numbers occur in Australia and New Zealand, although it continues to have an increasing presence, particularly in the United States.

TEMPERAMENT

Loyal and affectionate, the Curly is intelligent and proud. A charming and gentle family companion, it can sometimes appear aloof and is one of the better guard dogs in the Sporting Group. In the field the Curly is eager, persistent and inherently courageous. At home it is calm and laid back.

HEALTH MATTERS

A healthy dog, the Curly-Coated Retriever does have some disposition to cancer. It also has coat problems that manifest in a pattern baldness — specifically bare patches on the throat and rear legs.

SPECIAL CARE AND TRAINING

The breed is an easy one to manage. Normal care, good food, and plenty of human companionship, including early socialization, will stand it in good stead.

If the Curly-Coated Retriever is to be a hunting dog, it should be introduced to water at a young age. Weather permitting, this should be in calm shallow water when the puppy is eight to ten weeks old. By this time, it should be retrieving a favorite toy at the very least, and at best a puppy bumper (this is a dummy bird that floats and may be tossed out for the puppy to retrieve from land or water).

ADAPTABILITY

The Curly-Coated Retriever is an outdoor type of dog. It needs plenty of exercise and is brilliant at retrieving wounded duck. With great stamina and water eagerness, it is also a good land worker.

ESSENTIALS OF THE BREED

The Curly must be balanced, sound, quick and agile. Uniquely upstanding, it is 25-27 inches/ 64-68.5 cm at the withers (23-25 inches/58-64 cm in bitches) and is slightly off-square. It is sturdy yet elegant with balance being of great importance. Its head is a longer than wide wedge with long strong jaws and an intelligent, alert expression.

The coat, a hallmark of the breed, is of supreme importance for all Curlies. A dense mass of small, tight, distinct crisp curls, the Curly's coat is resilient, water-resistant, and provides protection against the weather, water and punishing cover. It comes in two colors, black and liver, and is equally acceptable in either shade.

The Curly-Coated Retriever should move with strength and power, showing a level topline and carrying a straight tail that is covered in curls.

Registry: AKC, CKC, FCI (Group 8), KC

Curly-Coated Retriever

365

ORIGIN AND DEVELOPMENT

The Flat-Coated as a breed was developed in the United Kingdom from stock that probably came from the Newfoundland and Labrador. The original English Flat-Coateds were descended from a strong working strain owned by J. Hull, a gamekeeper. The breed gained tremendously in popularity because of its temperament and working ability. H.K. Cook of the famed River-side Kennels put the breed on the map and won numerous awards for field work as well as bench awards.

Toward the end of the 1800s, the breed's popularity waned and gave way to the emerging Labrador and Golden Retrievers. Never falling into the hands of commercial breeders, the Flat-Coated has retained its supporters and steadily comes to the fore because of its tractability and willingness to work. The energetic members of the Flat-Coated Retriever Society of America have worked tirelessly to promote the best interests of the breed.

TEMPERAMENT

The Flat-Coated is easy, outgoing and alert. Its hallmark is a lively spirit, demonstrated by a head held up, eyes alight and a wagging tail. It craves human companionship, is very good with children and will be a friend to the entire family.

HEALTH MATTERS

The Flat-Coated is a hardy natural breed. As with many of the retrieving breeds, stock that will be used for breeding should be X-rayed for hip dysplasia. The breed is naturally full of ambition, and eager to exercise, swim and retrieve anything. this should not be confused with hyper-activity — it is the nature of this charming breed.

SPECIAL CARE AND TRAINING

The Flat-Coated is a good natural retriever on land and water, marks well and can also be used on upland game in heavy cover. He is a natural in obedience, and thrives on training and

Flat-Coated Retriever

pleasing its owner. Obedience training is a good beginning for its field work if it is to be a hunter.

ADAPTABILITY

The breed fits well into most situations. If it is kept in the city, it will require long daily walks. The Flat-Coated is really at its best in the country where it can do what it was intended to do — run, hunt, swim and be a companion.

ESSENTIALS OF THE BREED

The Flat-Coated has a moderately racy appearance, and stands about 24 inches/60 cm tall, with all its parts in harmony. It is either black or liver, with dark brown or hazel eyes. The head is long, clean and well molded, with a slight but definite stop, and small, flat-lying ears. The neck is strong, the topline firm and the body deep but not too broad. It should have good legs and feet, a tail set on the level off the back and carried out.

The coat should consist of a healthy, flat-lying double coat, with very moderate feathering on the chest, back of the legs and tail. The Flat-coated Retriever makes a handsome unexaggerated picture of a useful bird-dog in size, symmetry and elegance. Its tail is always apparent and generally wagging.

Registry: AKC, CKC, FCI (Group 8), KC

RETRIEVERS — GOLDEN RETRIEVER

ORIGIN AND DEVELOPMENT

The evolution of the Golden Retriever as a "pure breed" of working gun dog is well documented in the handwritten records of Lord Tweedmouth. Deerhounds, Pointers and varying types of retrievers were kept as working dogs at his Scottish home, Guisachan, where, as on many other great estates in the 1800s, large shooting parties were regularly hosted. The size of the resulting "shoots" indicates the high standard of work required of the dogs — "98 grouse, 24 roes, 24 stags; Grouse very scarce, but at length healthy . . . The best stalking season hitherto, 52 stags, 1,197 grouse, 42 woodcocks". Tweed Water Spaniels were renowned on the rough coast of the River Tweed for their strength and retrieving ability. In 1868, Lord Tweedmouth mated Belle, a Tweed Water Spaniel, to Nous, a yellow retriever — and the resulting four yellow puppies were the foundation of the definitive yellow breed now known as the Golden Retriever. Two puppies, Cowslip and Primrose, were retained at Guisachan; Ada and Crocus and many subsequent puppies were given to relatives and friends throughout England and Scotland, and to keepers on neighboring estates. Breeding for performance, outcrosses were introduced: Flat, Wavy and Curly-Coats and a red Setter named Sampson were used. A sandy colored Bloodhound is also listed as producing big, powerful, ugly dogs of a darker color and savage temperament.

Lord Tweedmouth's family traveled extensively at home and abroad and interest in the "yellow retriever" spread. In 1881 Lord Tweedmouth's son, Archie Marjoribanks, went to the family's Texas ranch, taking with him two yellow retrievers, Sol and Lady. Another of Lord Tweedmouth's sons lived in North Dakota, and probably also had yellow retrievers. In the early 1900s, Armstrong of Winnipeg and Burton of Vancouver interested Colonel Magoffin in the breed and Speedwell Pluto (later to become both an American and Canadian Champion) was imported. A little later, Dr. Chas Large was imported from England. With an increasing interest in the breed, the Golden Retriever Club of America was founded. The American Kennel Club recognized the Golden Retriever breed in 1932 and the British Standard (recognized by the Kennel Club in the previous year) was adopted. This was later revised and slightly amended, and is now much more detailed than the British version.

The first British dog shows held in Newcastle-upon-Tyne and Birmingham in 1859 started an interest in the "dual purpose" Golden Retriever; a dog with working ability and character, construction and beauty of form to win in the show ring. Progressively, owners interested in "working" placed greater emphasis on the working ability of their dogs; those interested in the show ring concentrated on "beauty." However, even "show" Golden Retrievers normally retain a natural retrieving instinct.

Today the breed can be seen as a beautiful show specimen; a faithful, biddable companion; competing in Working Tests, Field Trials, Obedience and Agility; used as a guide dog for the blind, hearing dog for the deaf and a therapy dog in homes and hospitals. It is truly a breed of brains and beauty.

TEMPERAMENT

The Golden Retriever should be stable, friendly and confident. Frequently the breed has a sensitivity and an intense desire to please.

HEALTH MATTERS

This is normally a robust, healthy dog but, as with many fast-growing and relatively large breeds, hip dysplasia may be a problem in the Golden. To minimize the probability, hips are X-rayed and scored by a panel of experts. Although it is thought that the condition is only 25 percent attributable to hereditary factors, it is advisable to exclude animals with excessively high scores from a breeding program. Many companion dogs with very high scores live normal, pain-free lives. Hereditary cataract, a problem with the lens of the eye, has decreased dramatically following the policy that only dogs and bitches with up-to-date certificates of freedom from cataract should be used for breeding. Epilepsy is also considered a problem for the breed in Europe, where breeders are addressing the problem.

SPECIAL CARE AND TRAINING

Because of the predisposition to hip dysplasia, exercise in the first nine months should be carefully controlled and over-exercise avoided. The desire to please means that the dog responds more readily to praise than punishment; its biddable, intelligent character makes it highly responsive to all levels of training. The strongly in-bred retrieving instinct means that anything left lying around is "retrievable." To avoid potential problems, the dog must be taught from an early age to give up what has been retrieved. As this instinct often includes carrying or holding the owner's hand or wrist, it is far more comfortable if the dog is trained to be gentle or "soft mouthed." With this intelligence and retrieving ability, the Golden is far happier when mind and body are being suitably exercised.

ADAPTABILITY

With the company of other dogs, the Golden will adapt well to a kennel environment. However, it prefers human company and is not happy in solitude.

ESSENTIALS OF THE BREED

Developed as a "working" gun dog, an overall balance, symmetry and lack of exaggeration are important. There should be no coarseness in the well-chiseled head, which should be of sufficient length, depth and strength to carry game. There should be a regular scissors bite — the American Standard makes an overshot or undershot mouth a disqualifying fault. The nose, preferably black, should have large, open nostrils for efficient "scenting." The defined stop, dark brown, well set-apart eyes and neat ears set on level with the eyes contribute to the gentle, intelligent, biddable expression, so essentially typical of the breed. The neck needs to be of sufficient length and strength to allow the dog to scent, track and carry game. The shoulders are well angulated, the body balanced, well ribbed, short coupled and with a strong loin and firm topline. The hindquarters should be well muscled and angulated, with hock joints strongly angulated, short parallel hind pasterns, and the feet round and catlike. The tail is set on and carried level with the back. The gait is powerful, with a long, free stride.

The coat, such a beautiful feature of the breed, may be flat or wavy, but should have a water-resisting undercoat. The British Standard allows any shade of gold or cream but excludes mahogany. The American Standard requires rich, lustrous gold of various shades but penalizes extremely light or dark shades as undesirable. The American Standard asks for an untrimmed ruff, while fashion in the British show ring results in a considerable amount of coat trimming. Sizes differ between the two Standards. British requirements are for dogs to be 22-24 inches/55-60 cm and bitches 20-22 inches/50-55 cm. The American Standard asks for dogs to be 23-24 inches/58-60 cm and bitches 21-22 inches/53-55 cm, with deviation of more than 1 inch/2.5 cm from the Standard serving as a disqualification.

It has to be said that the overall type within the breed is rather different in the United States from that seen in Great Britain. Breeders in these countries believe that their type is more correct. Studies of early pictures of British dogs can be most revealing and can prompt searching questions as to which of the two is more akin to the original.

Registry: AKC, CKC, FCI (Group 8), KC

Golden Retriever

ORIGIN AND DEVELOPMENT

The Labrador Retriever is little changed from the water dog that sportsman Peter Hawker found in Newfoundland in the early 1800s. He referred to it then as the St. John's Newfoundland and as the years progressed, many others called this same dog the "Lesser Newfoundland." It is interesting to conjecture that if these names had been retained, what a different understanding of the breed would be had by today's judges.

The original Labradors were active black dogs that were bred for the water and an assortment of jobs associated with water, such as bringing in game, pulling small boats and skiffs, and generally performing a variety of tasks that involved boats and the sea. In 1899 a yellow dog, Ben Hyde, was whelped from a black sire and dam and from him all of today's yellows are descended. The chocolate Labrador as it is known today was not an original true Labrador color but the result of various crosses. One British matriarch of the breed has been credited with saying that "Labradors come in three colors: black, black, and black." Today, however, dogs of good quality can be found in any of the three allowed colors. The breed was first recognized by the Kennel Club in 1903. It is extremely popular on both sides of the Atlantic, ranking among the top ten breeds for many years.

TEMPERAMENT

The Labrador temperament is as much a hallmark of the breed as any characteristic. It should be totally non-aggressive toward man or beast. It is intelligent, genial and gregarious. The "girls" when not tending puppies of their own make wonderful "aunties" and the "boys" make wonderful "troop leaders." They also make wonderful baby-sitters for children of all ages. In groups they have a tendency to play hard and, to the uninitiated the breed may appear dangerous, although very rarely is any damage done. It should not be forotten that as shooting dogs they are required to join hunts, which will often include other dogs, so there should be no signs of aggression or jealousy.

HEALTH MATTERS

The Labrador is basically a healthy breed. Puppies are whelped easily and are looked after carefully and well by their dam, which has very strong maternal instincts. There are heritable problems to be aware of including hip dysplasia, epilepsy, progressive retinal atrophy and some tendency to allergic skin disease. It is best to buy stock from a reputable breeder who screens for these diseases.

SPECIAL CARE AND TRAINING

The Labrador requires very little special care save a good dry bed, plenty of water to drink and play in, and two good meals a day. The Labrador does not require an elaborate diet and, in fact, does much better on a good kibble mixed with meat, chicken or beef, cooked vegetables, cooked rice and warm water. Most adults do well on a two-cup mixture of this fed twice daily. Puppies, once weaned, do well on four meals a day. A top quality puppy food can be mixed with ground meat for two meals and with a milk formula for the other two meals. The number of meals can be reduced at three months to three and at six months to two per day. Growing puppies need good food, fresh air and sunshine, lots of nap time and unlimited love.

Puppy walks, starting at six weeks, are a great way to socialize and exercise, making certain that a fresh bowl of water is available upon their return. Short walks of ten minutes are a good beginning and can be lengthened to half an hour as the puppy matures. Labradors take light correction well and are usually eager to please their owners. Many have been trained to be excellent guide dogs for the blind.

Labrador Retriever

ADAPTABILITY

The breed was developed primarily as a ladies' and gentlemen's shooting dog. They appear to have an almost special bond with people which makes them good companions and excellent obedience dogs. They do well in a kennel situation but once exposed would much rather be a part of the household.

ESSENTIALS OF THE BREED

There are three essentials to the Labrador that are interchangeable in order of preference — its temperament, coat and tail. The temperament should be excellent, and the coat should be fairly short and dense, with a soft undercoat to give protection from water, cold and all types of ground cover. Finally, it should have an "otter" tail — fairly short and rounded and thickly covered with hair.

The Labrador is a large and quite substantial dog, bred for hunting and water retrieving in all types of weather. The male should be 22 1/2 -24 1/2 inches/57-62 cm at the withers and weigh 65-80 pounds/30-36 kg. Bitches should be 21 1/2-23 1/2 inches/55-60 cm and weigh 55-70 pounds/25-32 kg. In the United States, heights 1/2 inch/1 cm above or below these measurements will be disqualified, although Labradors under the minimum height that are not yet one year old will not be disqualified. Its head is broad, its mouth large enough to retrieve a Canada goose, its neck strong and powerful and its body deep and wide. The front legs and feet are well set and of good bone. The hind legs are well bent and give it good use both on land and in water. It must be either black, yellow or chocolate in color and have a weatherproof coat and a knowing, intelligent eye. It is a grand all-round dog.

Registry: AKC, CKC, FCI (Group 8), KC

RETRIEVERS — NOVA SCOTIA DUCK TOLLING RETRIEVER

The art of tolling was practiced for hundreds of years in England and on the European continent. Hunters used small dogs to frisk and leap about the mouth of a long funnel-like net in order to lure ducks into the trap. For some reason, ducks will approach a frisking dog, particularly a red one that resembles the best toller of them all, the Eastern Red Fox. More recently, tolling dogs were used up and down the eastern seaboard of North America. Over time this type of hunting became less popular until Little River, Nova Scotia became the last stronghold for these unusual bird dogs.

The basis for breed development has always been one of performance — a dog should have tolling ability, agility, playfulness and great retrieving instinct. The Chesapeake Bay Retriever, Flat-Coated, Labrador, brown Cocker and Irish Setter have all been credited with playing a part in the make-up of today's Nova Scotia Duck Tolling Retriever.

The Toller is an all-purpose dog: a wonderful companion, great playmate, a flashy show dog, and a willing and happy working bird dog. It is perhaps overly fond of playing ball, for it never tires of retrieving anything. It is a useful watchdog, but not a guard dog.

A good Toller has an extremely animated

Tollers are strong swimmers and can switch from tolling to retrieving as required.

style of movement with its full long tail in continuous motion. A strong swimmer, it changes from tolling to retrieving as soon as is necessary. This healthy working breed is starting to see some increase in popularity and with its limited gene pool a corresponding increase in some health dangers. Beside some thyroid and auto immune problems, progessive retinal atrophy is starting to show up.

Medium-sized and compact, the Toller ideally stands 19-20 inches/48-50 cm at the withers (18-19 inches/45-48 for bitches) and weighs between 45-51 pounds/20-23 kg (27-43 pounds/ 12-19.5 kg for bitches). Well-muscled and balanced the Toller has a speedy, rushing action and its often slightly sad expression changes to one of intense concentration and excitement as soon as it starts working. This alertness and animation, coupled with its luxuriant and heavily feathered, continually moving tail, are keynotes to breed type. A water-repellent double coat of medium length is a must while the feathering should be moderate. It may be any shade of red or orange with some white markings.

Its slightly wedge-shaped head and high-set ears combine with its amber to brown eyes to give the Nova Scotia Duck Tolling Retriever its friendly, alert and intelligent expression.

Nova Scotia Duck Tolling Retriever

Registry: AKC, CKC, FCI (Group 8), KC

RHODESIAN RIDGEBACK

ORIGIN AND DEVELOPMENT

Of all the dog breeds seen in the show ring today, when it comes to logical classification none seems to have had more of an indentity crisis than the Rhodesian Ridgeback. In some countries it is regarded as a hound, in others as a working breed, and elsewhere it appears in the Group ring with gun dogs! Positive thinkers may interpret this as merely emphasis of the Ridgeback's great versatility.

The breed is one of only two where a ridge of hair runs down the back in the opposite direction to the rest of the coat, the other being the recently recognized Thai Ridgeback. Despite the geographical disparity between the two

lands where indigenous ridgebacked dogs are found, it has been suggested that the ancestors of the Thai dogs originated in Africa, having been taken to the island of Phu Quoc, in what was then Siam, and left there by slave traders.

The ridge has come down through many generations directly from the African Hottentot Hunting Dog. It is said that these dogs were jackallike in type, with ridges along their backs. When the Dutch colonized the Cape in the mid-1600s, it is fairly certain that the hunting dogs which acompanied them were crossed with native ridgeback dogs.

It was the big game hunter, Cornelius van Rooyen, who helped to develop the modern Ridgeback. On his visits to the Reverend Helm

Rhodesian Ridgeback

The outstanding feature of the Rhodesian Ridgeback is the ridge that runs down its back.

in Matabeleland, he met two ridgebacked dogs that the Reverend had brought from the Cape in the 1870s. Van Rooyen arranged to breed some of his own hunting dogs with the Helm dogs, and in the resulting litters produced some smooth-coated, solid-colored dogs not unlike the present-day Rhodesian Ridgeback. It is said that the dogs that possessed ridges were the bravest in the field, fearless in front of lions. The fame of van Rooyen's dogs was such that a dog bred by him became widely sought after. Demand increased and the "breed" began to evolve.

Erroneously, some people believed that these courageous hunting dogs actually killed lions, but anyone giving minimal thought to this idea would realize that no dog, no matter how fearless, would ever triumph in combat with a lion. The Ridgeback's tactics were to harass a lion constantly, making fake attacks, until it became totally bewildered, giving the hunter a chance to move in for a shot at close range.

While many ridgeback dogs were being used in the early part of the twentieth century, their type varied considerably, the only common denominator being the ridge. In 1922, seven enthusiasts gathered in Bulawayo in an attempt to form a club — the Rhodesian Ridgeback (Lion Dog) Club — and to make the breed more uniform. Later, a Breed Standard was drawn up, evidently based on that of the Dalmatian.

Official acceptance of the Rhodesian Ridgeback as a breed was given by the South African Kennel Union in 1924. The first specimens arrived in Britain in the early 1930s and on a royal visit to South Africa in 1947, Elizabeth II (then Princess Elizabeth) was given a pair of Ridgebacks, the male of which subsequently became the sire of the first British Champion when Challenge Certificates were introduced in 1954.

TEMPERAMENT

The Ridgeback is a strong-minded dog with a character that is an amalgam of its various functional predispositions. It can hunt, guard, stand its ground and fend off intruders as required. It is imperative that it knows that its owner is in charge, because a headstrong Ridgeback can be a liability. Given fair discipline and training from an early age, the Ridgeback will prove a loyal companion. However, they can be stand-offish and are not the type of breed to bound up with a wagging tail to welcome strangers.

HEALTH MATTERS

This is a hardy breed through and through, and while conscientious breeders will X-ray breeding stock for hip irregularities, there should be no major health defects within the breed, although it may occasionally suffer from dermoid sinus problems. Also, osteochondrosis occasionally occurs in the breed. This is a condition which affects the cartilage in the growth plates and joints. Supplementing the diet too much may be a contributing factor. The problem can be identified early in life by mild lameness and it is essential to visit the vet, who will probably suggest revising the Ridgeback's diet and exercise regime.

SPECIAL CARE AND TRAINING

The Ridgeback is a relatively maintenance-free breed, being short-coated and free of physical exaggeration. Its training, from the earliest age, however, is of paramount importance. It must be taught basic obedience and any juvenile or adolescent signs of undue aggression must be checked. Properly disciplined, it will be a joy — left to have its own way and it could prove a nightmare.

ADAPTABILITY

It will live happily in an urban environment if it has company, plenty of exercise and mental stimulation. However, it will thrive in a large property where it can patrol its home ground and reassure its owner that all is well.

ESSENTIALS OF THE BREED

The breed's main feature is its ridge. This should taper, be symmetrical and have two identical "crowns" ("swirls" of hair) at its head. The ridge should start behind the shoulders and continue to the hipbones. The lower edges of the crowns should not extend further than one-third of its entire length.

Overall type in the breed is still very varied, with some specimens appearing too "bully" and others too "houndy" and light. Midway lies the ideal Ridgeback which has substance and quality. Males stand 25-27 inches/63-68.5 cm and bitches 24-26 inches/60-65 cm. The head should be fairly long, with quite a flat skull, broad between the ears. It should be wrinkle-free when relaxed — though slight furrows may appear when the dog is aroused. The muzzle is strong and the stop moderate, the lips tight and not pendulous. Black-nosed dogs should have dark eyes; brown-nosed dogs, amber ones. The ears should be wide-based, high set and tapered to a rounded point. They are held close to the head. The neck is strong, fairly long and clean. The chest is deep, moderately well ribbed and the back and loins powerful. The tail is carried in a graceful curve but never curled.

In color, the Ridgeback should be light red to wheaten, with small white markings tolerated on the chest and toes. Ideally, there should be no white, and a darker muzzle and ears are typical.

Registry: AKC, CKC, FCI (Group 6), KC

ROTTWEILER

Origin and Development

In *The Complete Rottweiler*, Muriel Freeman writes: "Reasonable supposition indicates the likelihood that the Rottweiler is descended from one of the drover dogs indigenous to ancient Rome. This drover dog has been described by various accredited sources to have been of the Mastiff type with great intelligence — rugged, dependable, willing to work, and with a strong guarding instinct."

It does not take much imagination to understand the value a dog with these qualities would have for cattle farmers in the Middle Ages. Indeed they adopted this dependable, versatile drover dog and named it Rottweiler after the thriving town of Rottweil where it had become a familiar sight driving its charges to market.

From Roman times to the middle of the nineteenth century, the Rottweiler's popularity was assured. The life of a farmer in those days was beset by the vagaries of the weather, conquering armies, pestilence and disease. When and if they did raise their cattle to marketable age, it was the Rottweiler's job to herd the cattle safely to the marketplace and, with the proceeds of the sale neatly tucked into a pouch in their collars, to return safely to the farmhouse. This entailed a two- or three-day journey over land, avoiding any human contact, with little promise of water and none of food until the safety of the farm was reached. Only survival of the fittest was assured, as all others either died by the wayside or were destroyed as superfluous.

By the late 1800s, cattle driving was outlawed and the donkey and the railroad replaced the dog cart. As a consequence the Rottweiler declined in popularity. A few were used in police work, herding and leading the blind, but only one Rottweiler was entered at the dog show in Heilbron, Germany in 1882. In 1901 a combined Rottweiler-Leonberger Club was founded. During the next twenty years several Rottweiler clubs were formed but there was constant dissent in the ranks of these organizations until 1921 when the Allgemeiner Deutscher Rottweiler Klub (ADRK) with a registry of about 3,400 dogs was formed. The Standard was accepted and the breeding precepts were inaugurated.

Temperament

Emphasis on the fact that the Rottweiler is a working dog cannot be overstated. It is never as happy as when it has a job to do. Whether it is herding, competing in Obedience, tracking, search and rescue, therapy work, or just plain retrieving the newspaper, a Rottweiler loves to be "gainfully employed." The Rottweiler's character is such that it wants to be a partner — not a slave.

Health Matters

Regarding general health, this is perhaps the breed most prone to contract parvo; it is also the breed most prone to succumb to its ravages. Hip dysplasia is of grave concern and some lines appear to have a predisposition toward cruciate ligament problems as well but proper Rottweiler breeders have addressed both these areas of concern since 1967. Hopefully, ongoing research will provide future solutions. Rottweilers, unfortunately, like most large dogs, are relatively short lived. Nine years can be expected. Many live to be eleven, but older than this is rare. Cancer, heart disease and loss of mobility (all diseases of old age) are other common causes of death.

Special Care and Training

When training a Rottweiler the best results are achieved by those who are kind, patient and consistent. A Rottweiler is not the fastest learner, but it is the most thorough, so that once it has learned a lesson it never forgets it and there is no facet of a challenge that it does not grasp.

Rottweiler

ADAPTABILITY

Depending upon the early socialization of the individual dog, a Rottweiler of proper breeding will accept strangers, but it must always be remembered that its heritage is that of a guard dog and if it perceives danger to its owner's possessions it will act to defend. Thus, anyone who owns a Rottweiler should shield the dog properly from any situations where misunderstandings might occur. One such example is the practice of allowing a dog unsupervised to be present with small children at play. A Rottweiler does not take kindly to a child pummeling and sitting on "its own child" — the owner. As a result, many children have been needlessly bitten simply because the dog thought it was doing its job.

Notwithstanding, a Rottweiler of proper temperament is a fabulous family dog. By nature they love children and tolerate their unending demands cheerfully. It is usual for the Rottweiler to be protective of the woman of the house, somewhat less so of the man. On the other hand, prompt response to his commands can be expected. They are good natured, will tolerate all manner of pets with one exception — there should not be more than one dog of the same sex. With some exceptions two bitches will get along. Two unneutered males can never be trusted together.

ESSENTIALS OF THE BREED

For the purposes of this book, it is worth making the point that Germany is the Rottweiler's "country of origin." Under the concept of the Fédération Cynologique Internationale (FCI), which allows the country of origin to write the Standard for a breed, all FCI member clubs internationally must abide by the German Standard. Thus, whether in Germany, Brazil, Spain, Mexico or wherever the show is held, if it is under the auspices of the FCI, the Rottweiler is judged by the German Standard.

Neither the American Kennel Club nor the Kennel Club subscribe to the FCI principle, nor do some other clubs which were originally under the British influence. How one views this departure depends somewhat upon the breed involved and also upon one's basic dog philosophy. But in the opinion of a Rottweiler breeder, who better than the Germans to define the "ideal" Rottweiler? Any divergence from their Standard is contamination of the ideal and must not be tolerated. Fortunately for the breed in the United States, the leadership is in accord and with each Standard revision there is closer duplication of the German Standard.

The Rottweiler is a working dog. Thus, in any discussion of the Standard it must be remembered that any departure which could affect the working ability of the dog is of a serious nature. For instance, lack of proper proportion, insufficient substance, weak bones or lack of musculature, improper angulation are all major faults. Similarly, snipy muzzles, weak backs, poor feet are serious working faults. Such deviations from the Standard must always be heavily penalized. Whereas cosmetic faults, such as incorrect markings, poor mouth pigmentation and medium eye color are deviations, the same emphasis should not be given to these problems because they do not affect

The Rottweiler's head should be large with dark, expressive and alert eyes.

the working ability of the dog.

The Rottweiler is a large working dog, with males standing about 24-27 inches/61-68 cm tall and weighing about 100 pounds /45 kg. Females are about 22-25 inches/56-63 cm in height and about 115 pounds/52 kg in weight. A correctly proportioned dog should be slightly longer in body length than it is at the withers. The body should be broad and strong, with a broad deep chest, a topline that is as hard as possible, and a short docked tail carried as an extension of the topline. Its legs should be sturdy and sound, with good feet and thick pads. The head is large with dark, expressive and alert eyes. The foreface is slightly shorter than the backskull. The mouth pigment should be dark, and the full forty-two teeth regular, closing in a scissors bite. If it is undershot or missing two or more teeth, the dog will be disqualified in the United States. The coat is short, flat and coarse. It should be black with tan markings in the typical black-and-tan pattern (on the cheeks, over each eye, the sides of the muzzle, the front of the chest, the legs and under the tail).

In the final analysis, the ideal is an animal of correct size and body proportion possessing a proudly carried head of correct dimensions.

Registry: AKC, CKC, FCI (Group 2), KC

RUSSIAN LAIKAS

The Russian Laikas are hunting spitzes that have been around for hundreds of years. There are many different varieties in its country of origin but only three of them are recognized by the Fédération Cynologique Internationale. They are rarely seen outside Russia with the exception of the Scandinavian countries. All three Laika breeds mentioned here are strictly used as hunting dogs for bear, lynx, elk, forest birds and they are also used by trappers dealing in fur.

The East Siberian Laika (Vostotjno Sibirskaja Lajka) is the largest, the height at its withers being 20-25 inches/51-64 cm. It is said to have been crossed with wolves as late as in the middle of this century. This Laika is a sturdy, strong and very hardy breed, with a similar temperament. It looks very much like a coarsely built Nordic Wolf but it may be any color. The Russian-European Laika (Russko-Evropejskaya Lajka) is mainly found in the area close to the Finnish border. It is closely related to the Finnish Karelean Bear Dog. Both breeds are usually black with white markings. The Russian-European Laika is shorter coupled and stands about 19-23 inches/48-58 cm at the withers. The West Siberian Laika (Zapadno Sibirskaja Lajka) should be 20-24 inches/51-62 cm at withers. Its head, although like a wolf, is more elongated and narrow in skull compared with the East Siberian Laika. Its body is slightly longer and its topline should slope slightly from the withers to the set of the tail. It is usually wolf-colored but it may be darker, more reddish, badger-colored or white with patches.

Registry: FCI (Group 5)

West Siberian Laika

SAARLOOS WOLFHOND

The Dutch geneticist Leendert Saarloos began to cross German Shepherd Dogs with wolves just after World War II to create what he thought would be a sounder variety of the German Shepherd. The Czechoslovakian Wolfdog also comes from crosses of German Shepherds and wolves. The last infusion with wolf is said to have taken place in 1966 and the resulting, the more elegant Saarloos breed, was recognized in 1975. It looks very much like the Nordic Wolf and is mainly kept as a guard and companion dog. It is known to be reserved toward strangers.

Consistent with being in part developed from the wolf, the Saarloos Wolfhond possesses a strong pack instinct. Most owners of the Saarloos have two or more dogs in order to create a "pack" environment for their pets.

The height at the withers should be about 24-29 1/2 inches/60-75 cm. In general appearance, the breed should resemble the wolf in

Saarloos Wolfhond

shape, coat and coloring, except that a light liver brown color is also accepted. Some people say that this exception is an indication that the Siberian Husky may have had a part in the creation of the breed.

Registry: FCI (Group 1)

SABUESO ESPAÑOL

The Spanish scenthound has been known for centuries and it has kept very much to the type that can be found in old paintings. It is strictly used as a hunting dog and is rarely seen outside Spain.

At the withers, the height should be about 19-22 inches/48-57 cm. The body should be rectangular, well muscled and with strong bone — never giving a leggy appearance. The head should be elongated and quite elegant with long, folded and very low set ears. The coat could be smooth with the skin tightly following the contours of the body. Its color may be any shade of red with white markings.

Registry: FCI (Group 6)

Sabueso Español

SAINT BERNARD

ORIGIN AND DEVELOPMENT

High in the Swiss Alps lies the Hospice of the Great Saint Bernard, the fountainhead of the most famous breed of dog in the world, the Saint Bernard. Before the construction of the Grand Saint Bernard Tunnel, travelers could start their journey in the valleys in brilliant sunshine, only to find themselves in the grip of a violent snowstorm once they reached the high pass. The monks who lived there used to keep dogs that helped to locate lost travelers, eventually producing a breed that has achieved international recognition and is inevitably linked with the brandy barrel that it carries around its neck to sustain those it finds.

Various theories have been put forward regarding the actual origin of the breed as it is known today. The most likely is that they are descendants of a large Mastiff-type of dog that was brought to the area by Roman invaders. The Valais district of Switzerland is extremely isolated, so for 400 years the monks have selectively bred from the dogs left behind. From them has resulted the modern Saint Bernard.

It is said that in the 1850s, Newfoundland blood was introduced to the Saint Bernard, in the belief that the thicker coat would give the dogs better protection against the cold. However, the result was disastrous because the dogs developed ice-balls which clogged their coats and weighed them down, so this line of development was quickly abandoned. The massive mahogany-colored dogs were bred for specific white markings which represent the stole, chasuble and scapular — parts of the religious vestments worn by the monks. Most important of all, however, was the breed's ability to find lost travelers while working in severe weather conditions.

The most famous Saint Bernard of all was a dog called Barry, which was born in 1800. One story relates how he found a small boy in the snow, managed somehow to persuade the child to climb on his back, and carried the child to safety. It is said that Barry saved the lives of at least forty people — his body is now preserved in the Natural History Museum in Berne.

During the 1800s Saint Bernards were imported from Switzerland to England. Many

Smooth Saint Bernard

Rough Saint Bernard

were crossed with the very popular Mastiffs in the hope of producing bigger, taller Mastiffs. One famous Saint of the period was Plinlimmon, which was recorded as standing 34 1/2 inches/87.5 cm at the shoulder and weighing 210 pounds/95 kg. He was sold to an actor in the United States for $7,000, who subsequently exhibited the dog in theaters.

Gradually the breed achieved popularity in Britain and, as so often happens, with this popularity came unscrupulous breeders who were attracted to the breed purely because of its reputation for commanding high prices.

In a wave of commercialism, the dogs became bigger, heavier and so gross and unsound that many of them had difficulties in getting from one end of a show ring to the other.

In the early part of the twentieth century, Dr. George Inman and Mr. Ben Walmsley established the Bowden Kennel in Cheshire, England, which was to influence the breed greatly and considerably improve its soundness. When Dr. Inman died, the kennel was dispersed and many other breeders benefited by acquiring valuable Bowden stock. Since that time, the breed has seen occasional imported dogs being used to good effect, and present-day breeders have done an excellent job of improving the breed's soundness while still maintaining type.

TEMPERAMENT

In view of the job for which it was bred, the Saint Bernard must, of course, be steady, benevolent, intelligent, courageous and totally trustworthy. Any sign of nervousness or aggression is completely alien to the breed.

HEALTH MATTERS

As with all giant breeds, there can be bone problems caused by ignorant rearing and sometimes heart defects occur. Due to its very open eye, the breed has suffered with entropion but breeders today are keen to maintain a healthy eye free of exaggeration and excess haw.

SPECIAL CARE AND TRAINING

As this is a giant breed with a tremendous growth rate, correct rearing is absolutely vital because permanent damage may be done in the precious first few months. It is essential that the breeder's advice is followed regarding diet and husbandry.

Obviously with a dog of its size, it is important that the Saint Bernard is trained to do exactly as it is asked. A disobedient Saint Bernard will prove a nightmare. Basic obedience training is essential.

ADAPTABILITY

Although the Saint Bernard does not need hours of prolonged exercise each day, it does require an amount of space so it is not the ideal choice of breed for an apartment dweller. It is a gregarious dog and will happily live with others of its species, but at the same time it is an excellent companion for the one-dog owner, provided that the owner gives it ample companionship. The fact that it invariably salivates does not endear it to the houseproud!

ESSENTIALS OF THE BREED

The Saint's large and massive head is its trademark. Its circumference is said to be more than double the length from its nose to occiput. The muzzle is short and square, the cheeks flat and deep. The lips have great depth without being unduly pendulous. The stop is well defined, the skull broad and somewhat rounded at the top, showing a prominent brow. The nose should always be large and black, together with well-developed nostrils. The eyes are set not too close together, and the lower eyelid droops slightly but not so much as to cause health problems. The British Kennel Club's Breed Standard was recently rewriten to include "eye lids reasonably tight without any excessive haw" in an attempt to eradicate unhealthy eyes. The Saint's ears are moderate in size, lie close to the cheeks and are not heavily coated.

The neck is strong and shows dewlap, and the withers are quite high, with heavy bone all through. The back is broad and straight, the ribs well sprung and the loin should be wide and very muscular. The chest should show great depth and width, but should not extend beyond the elbows. The tail is quite high set but should not be curled over the back.

There are two coat types. The rough coat is dense but flat, and more profuse around the neck and thighs. The smooth variety has a houndlike coat, close and flat with minimal feathering on the thighs and tail. As far as color goes, the Saint may be mahogany brindle, red brindle or orange with white markings on the muzzle, blaze, collar, chest, forelegs, feet and tail end. There is usually black shading on the face and ears.

In size, the British Standard says that the taller the dog the better, provided that symmetry is maintained. The American Standard gives 27 1/2 inches/70 cm as a minimum for males and 25 1/2 inches/65 cm for bitches, stressing that females are generally finer and more delicate in build. The Saint's gait should be one of easy extension — unhurried and smooth.

Registry: AKC, CKC, FCI (Group 2), KC

SALUKI

ORIGIN AND DEVELOPMENT

The Arabs were the first to breed the Saluki but it dates back to the time of the ancient Egyptian pharaohs. It is a kind of eastern Greyhound and was once used in the pursuit of gazelles and smaller game, sometimes in partnership with the falcon. These Greyhound-body type dogs, with feathered legs, tail and ears, are ancient and have shown up in carvings that date back over 8,000 years.

Some believe that when dogs are referred to in the Bible, the breed in question is the Saluki. Similarly, Muslims consider this breed as sacred because it was given to them by Allah. In ancient times, the Saluki was often mummified, and numerous specimens have been found in tombs in the upper Nile region.

Because the desert tribes were nomadic, the Saluki used to be found over a vast area which stretched across Persia, Anatolia, Syria, Mesopotamia, Egypt, Arabia and Palestine. Of

Saluki

384

course, type varied from region to region and the Arabian-bred Saluki was a smaller dog with less feathering than the Persian variety. Today, Salukis still have two types of coat: the feathered and the smooth.

TEMPERAMENT

The Saluki is more aloof than any of the other sighthound breeds. For example, it can amuse itself for hours just by watching an eagle soar. Although it is affectionate and loyal to its owners, it is not a demonstrative dog to people in general.

HEALTH MATTERS

The Saluki is fundamentally a very sound dog, having been raised for centuries according to the principle of the survival of the fittest. Because of this practice, this breed possesses very few health problems. However, like all sighthounds with low body fat, the breed is susceptible to problems with anesthesia. When the need arises great care should be taken.

SPECIAL CARE AND TRAINING

Because of its tendency to be aloof, the Saluki should have diligent socialization from puppyhood. If it does not, it will never bond to humans as it should, will become even more aloof and very independent.

Training on a leash should be done early and gently. Care should be taken not to allow the Saluki to run loose until it has been taught to respond to the owner's wishes — it can be difficult to catch and may well run off in a speedy fashion to hunt. The breed can become a charming member of the household but it takes time and patience.

The Saluki loves its comfort and should have a soft bed that is out of drafts — or it may well find a human bed that is to its liking. Feeding can somtimes be a problem since Salukis are not eager eaters and will never be otherwise. They must have nutritious food that tastes good to them. Young dogs should have three meals daily and mature dogs should have two.

ADAPTABILITY

In the past, the Saluki was constantly forced to adjust to new environments as its nomadic masters moved from one feeding ground to another. Devoted to their owners, Salukis warm up slowly to strangers. This breed does not give its heart to every passer-by.

ESSENTIALS OF THE BREED

The Saluki, a hound bred to course, catch and kill gazelle, shows the typical Greyhound outline. On average, the males stand about 23-28 inches/58-71 cm while the females are considerably smaller. They come in many and varied colors from white through cream, fawn, golden, red, grizzle and tan, tricolor, black and tan, and particolored. The body is not long, the chest is quite deep and there should be great breadth between the hip bones. The legs should have moderate angulation. The Saluki's nose should be black or liver, and its bright oval eyes dark to hazel, not prominent or too large. Its strong teeth should have a good bite. The ears are long and fringed. The coat should be a soft and silky texture with slight feathering on the back of the legs and on the underside of the long low-set tail, which is carried low with a natural curve. In the smooth variety all points are the same, except that the coat has no feathering.

A good Saluki combines a symmetry with type of outline. It should give the appearance of possessing both great speed and stamina. In fact, it should look as if it can work in deep sand or in rocky mountains. Its well-arched toes, coupled with a moderate length of foot, feathered between the toes, remain essential to the breed which must be able to work over such difficult terrain. The Saluki's expression, unlike that of other Greyhound-like breeds, has a "far-off" look. Most importantly, it should have a hard, well-conditioned body — this remains the key and is the reason why it was originally bred.

Registry: AKC, CKC, FCI (Group 10), KC

SAMOYED

ORIGIN AND DEVELOPMENT

The Samoyed is a herding dog formerly used by a nomadic tribe of the same name which lived on the tundra of northern Russia. The name was agreed by the Cynological Congress of 1892 in Sweden. The tribe was one of many ranging the vast areas between the Ural Mountains and the Yenesei River, adjacent to the Arctic Circle. They depended on reindeer herds for their livelihood, moving perpetually, seeking lichen and moss to sustain the animals. The Samoyed was a herd and guard dog, responsible for keeping the mass of reindeer compact and warning of any threat such as marauding wolves. Occasionally they pulled sleds, though more often reindeer were used for this; dogs were preferred for hauling boats along the summer streams. They lived in close contact with the Samoyed people, even sharing their chooms (tents of reindeer skin).

The modern Samoyed has great affection for people and likes nothing better than being with its human family. The upsurge in polar exploration at the turn of the century saw many intrepid adventurers taking dog teams with them. Samoyeds were easier to obtain than Eskimo Dogs and on the whole were more tractable. They were used by Nansen, Jackson, the Duke of Abruzzi, Borchgrevink and Shackleton on expeditions, after which some dogs were left in New Zealand and Australia, and others were taken to England.

It is acknowledged that Mr. and Mrs. Kilburn Scott established the breed in Britain and dogs from their Farningham Kennel were sent to the United States, Canada and many countries in Europe. Mr. Kilburn Scott's interest was aroused when he saw some Samoyed tribesmen in Archangel in 1889. He visited their homeland and bought a puppy, Sabarka, for his wife; following this an interest in the breed quickly developed in the United Kingdom. A dog called Moustan was taken to the United States by the Princess de Montyglyon in 1906, having been given as a present by Grand Duke Nicholas. Samoyeds have since become popular in both the States and the United Kingdom and adorn the show benches, not only with their arresting beauty but also their show qualities and natural "showmanship" helping to take many top awards against other breeds of dog.

British dogs have contributed to the development of the breed in the United States, but the discouraging effect of the United Kingdom quarantine laws has meant that no significant dog has been introduced to Britain from the States. English dogs have won well in the United States and some judges prefer the English type with their good heads and excellent coats. The American Samoyed probably scores in movement at present over its British counterpart.

TEMPERAMENT

Samoyeds are intelligent, very alert and show marked affection for all humans. They make good family pets and love being regarded as a member of the family. This essential contact stems from their ancestry; they are anxious to please and join in their owners' activities. Though friendly, they will warn of visitors by persistent barking, then will accept them willingly when they enter the home.

HEALTH MATTERS

Samoyeds are best kept in hard physical condition and not allowed to become soft. Their health is generally good, but they can have hip dysplasia problems. All breeding stock should be X-rayed under the relevant country's scheme. In the United States there has also been some incidence of progressive retinal atrophy but this has not appeared in British dogs.

SPECIAL CARE AND TRAINING

Samoyeds can be willful and should be well trained in early puppyhood while they are eager to please. Time spent then is well worth

Samoyed

the effort to produce a biddable adult that comes when it is called. The Samoyed coat should be groomed thoroughly, and the fact that the hair does shed may not make the breed an ideal pet for the overly houseproud. Samoyed hair has been collected and woven by some fanciers, producing warm and soft woolly garments.

ADAPTABILITY

Samoyeds will readily fit into any loving home. They will accept kennel environments, provided daily activities with people are part of their routine because they tend to regard themselves as family members. It is important to remember that their basic instinct is to herd, and they will readily respond with any reindeer substitute, such as sheep or cattle.

ESSENTIALS OF THE BREED

The Samoyed should be medium sized, strong, active and graceful but never coarse. Both sexes

should give the appearance of being capable of great endurance. There is a size difference between the Standards. The height at the withers in the United States is 21-23 inches/53.5-58 cm for dogs and 19-21 inches/48-53.5 cm for bitches. The British and Fédération Cynologique Internationale Standards state 20-22 inches/50-55 cm for dogs and 18-20 inches/46-50 cm for bitches. The head should be wedge shaped with a broad, flat skull and muzzle of medium length, not too sharply defined. The eyes are almond shaped, medium to dark brown, and set well apart. The ears are upstanding, set well apart, well furred with slightly rounded tips. The rims of the eyes and lips are black; a black nose is preferred though brown or flesh color is permitted — pigment may change on a seasonal basis. The mouth should not have heavy flews, but curve up at the corners. These points contribute to the famous "smiling" expression of the Samoyed. The neck should be proudly arched, not stuffy.

The forequarters should be straight and muscular with good, but not heavy, bone. The chest should be broad and deep with well-sprung ribs, giving plenty of heart and lung room. The back needs to be broad and muscular, neither too short nor too long, with muscular hindquarters and well angulated stifles.

The characteristic spitz breed tail should be carried over the back with long and profuse hair, dropping to one side. It should be set neither too high nor too low. The feet are important and should be long, flattish, slightly spread but not splayed. The Samoyed has long featherings extending over the ends of its feet. This gives the breed a distinctive appearance, although in the United States these tend to be trimmed, as are the back hocks. The feet should be well cushioned with hair underneath.

The gait is free moving with a strong, agile drive; it should be long reaching in front with no trace of hackney action and with power coming from the drive of the hindquarters. Its coloring is pure white, white and biscuit, or cream. It is important that biscuit should be retained as it helps to maintain harsher outercoat texture. The coat is double with a thick, soft undercoat and the harsher outercoat standing away from the body. The outer hairs should carry silver tips which glisten in the sunshine and are another valued Samoyed feature. Bitches carry a shorter coat which is often softer than the male's. It is important that Samoyed bitches should look feminine, while males should look masculine without coarseness.

Registry: AKC, CKC, FCI (Group 5), KC

SARPLANINAC

The Sarplaninac is a herding and guard dog from the vast plains of Sar in Kosovo in

Sarplaninac

former Yugoslavia. The breed belongs to a group of flock guardians that also are called mountain dogs, and as such works in mountain ranges in many parts of the world. For several hundreds of years, it was found in the Illyrian region on the Adriatic. The breed is used more as guard of the shepherd and his flock than as a traditional herder. It is a self-confident guard dog.

The height at the withers is about 23-24 inches/58-62 cm. Its coloring may vary from wolf-gray, red sable and fawn with a black mask to white, with or without sparse patches. The most common color is a dark wolf-gray with almost cream-colored tan markings. The coat should be medium long on the body, longer on the neck, tail and buttocks and with a harsh texture. The Sarplaninac can now be seen in several parts of the world, although in small numbers.

Registry: FCI (Group 2)

SCHAPENDOES

This small Dutch sheepdog has been known for centuries but although it used to be a common sight on farms, it did not attract much

Schapendoes

interest until after World War II. Then a breed enthusiast, a Mr. Toepoel, started the work that resulted in the breed's recognition in 1952. The Schapendoes is still used for herding sheep but is also a popular companion dog. The breed has gained interest in a number of countries in recent years.

At the withers, the height is about 16-20 inches/ 40-50 cm. The Schapendoes resembles several other European sheepdog breeds. Its body should be rectangular, well muscled but not heavy boned. The ears are small and pendulous and the tail long and hanging and never carried over the back. Its coat should be thick, about 3 inches/ 8 cm long, shaggy, slightly wavy and with a woolly undercoat. All colors are permissible but usually the breed is gray, bluish gray to black, with or without white markings.

Registry: FCI (Group 1)

SCHILLERSTÖVARE

This Swedish scenthound was named after its creator, Per Schiller, who at the end of the nineteenth century established the breed from different types of old hounds of mainly East European origin. It was recognized in 1909 and is still strictly a hunting dog used mainly to hunt fox and hare. It is hardly ever seen outside Sweden.

The height at the withers should be about 21-22 1/2 inches/53-57 cm. Its body should be rectangular, well muscled but never coarse or heavy in build. The coat should be short, glossy and with a hard texture. Its color should be a deep, rich tan with a jet black mantle.

Registry: FCI (Group 6)

Schillerstövare

SCHIPPERKE

ORIGIN AND DEVELOPMENT

The attractive small black dog that competes in the Non-Sporting Group in the United States is not a member of the spitz or northern sled dog breeds, although it resembles them in some regards — such as its small triangular erect ears, the proportions of its head, its thick double coat and may have a tight spitz tail. The Schipperke comes from the Flemish provinces of Belgium and is descended from the Belgian Sheepdog or Leauvenaar. In the mid-nineteenth century the old Belgian Sheepdogs used to herd sheep in the Louvain area and from those sheepdogs both the Schipperke and the Belgian Sheepdog have descended. The Sheepdog was gradually bred larger and the Schipperke was bred down in size to become the inquisitive and beguiling watchdog of today.

The Schipperke has been known for several hundred years; in fact in 1690 a show for Schipperkes was held in the grand palace of Brussels. After the Specialty Club was formed in 1888 the breed was named Schipperke The name is Flemish and means "Little Captain." (The correct pronunciation is "Sheep-er-ker," the last vowel being almost silent.) Many Schipperkes were used as guard dogs on canal boats in Brussels and Antwerp. The custom of docking the tails very short began in 1609. Today more dogs are born without tails than in the early days of the breed.

The Queen of Belgium purchased a Schipperke in 1885 and this ensured its overnight success as a fashionable pet. Three years later Walter J. Comstock imported what is believed to be the first Schipperke into the United States. The breed caused little stir and it was not until after World War I that a few fanciers got together and founded the Schipperke Club of America in 1929. Today the Schipperke is more popular than ever and entries at dog shows in both breed and Obedience, where it is often a brilliant performer, have increased steadily.

TEMPERAMENT

An excellent and faithful watchdog, the Schipperke is suspicious of strangers. It is very active and agile, very curious, and may be quick tempered and territorial, as well as quite stubborn.

HEALTH MATTERS

The Schipperke is an extremely healthy little dog with very few health problems. It is very long lived, regularly reaching fifteen or sixteen years and sometimes even older.

SPECIAL CARE AND TRAINING

Because of its curiosity and stubbornness the Schipperke must be taken in hand at an early age of eight to ten weeks. It must be house-trained early and properly. It should also be exposed to all members of the family, particularly children of whom it is extremely fond. Obedience training should be started early, too, and should continue throughout its active life. Always remember that the dog is stubborn and will think that its way is the best way.

The Schipperke's coat is thick and double and should always be clean and gleaming. A good brushing once or twice a week should suffice except in the shedding season when it must have warm baths with mild soap to provide a clean healthy skin for the new coat. Its erect ears generally pose no problem. It needs exercise, but do not trust it off the lead since it is so curious that it is likely to dart away very quickly. The Schipperke is a keen hunter and may well go kiting off after squirrels, raccoons, or cats — so a collar and lead are recommended.

ADAPTABILITY

Small, easy to care for, distinctive looking and portable, the Schipperke was bred to be adaptable and it lives up to its heritage. It is well suited to families and will adapt to either city or country living.

Schipperke

ESSENTIALS OF THE BREED

The Schipperke may weigh as much as 18 pounds/ 8 kg although most are smaller. Males usually measure about 13 inches/33 cm at the highest point of the shoulder and bitches about 12 inches/30 cm. The Schipperke has a foxy face, erect ears, small dark brown eyes, a full mouth of rather large teeth, a fairly short neck, short and firm back, and a tail which is docked and either non-existent or no longer than 1 inch/2.5 cm. The legs have bone in proportion to the size of the dog. Its feet are small, round and tight. The coat is abundant and slightly harsh, naturally short on the face, ears, front of the legs and the hocks. In the United States, it is always black but the British Standard allows other colors — cream is very popular. The longer coat around the neck begins at the back of the ears and forms a ruff and a cape; a jabot extending down between the front legs is also longer on the rear where it forms a culotte. The Schipperke is unique in its appearance and its action is always proud and jaunty.

Registry: AKC, CKC, FCI (Group 1), KC

SCHNAUZERS

ORIGIN AND DEVELOPMENT

The Schnauzer family is a group of three breeds, each of which is intelligent, adaptable and good natured. The Standard and Miniature are primarily companions and excellent as family dogs. The largest member, the Giant, however, does have a stronger inbuilt instinct to protect and has proved a highly versatile working dog.

The origins of the first of the family, the Standard Schnauzer (always referred to by some Kennel Clubs as merely "Schnauzer" — fanciers have adopted the "Standard" label to differentiate) go back over several centuries. Its actual roots are uncertain, but it is felt that the black Poodle, the wolf-spitz and a rough-coated German terrier are breeds which may have played a part in its early development. It first appeared in central Europe and centered around the Austrian Tyrol.

Giant Schnauzer

*Standard Schnauzer with
natural (uncropped) ears*

Like many breeds, the Schnauzer had humble beginnings, being developed and coming to notice as a general farm and drover's dog. Yet in addition it was always recognized and highly praised for its construction, shape and rugged appearance — and above all for its thinking mind. All of these attributes gave it an ability to apply itself to the many varied, essential and important tasks necessary in rural life during the Schnauzer's developing period of the late nineteenth century. In those days they proved to be important assets, for with its versatility and ability to cope with such a variety of jobs, a Schnauzer was as good as another pair of hands. Primarily used for herding, protecting the flocks and herds, as well as being efficient watchdogs, Schnauzers also proved excellent killers of vermin, and were even able to catch something for the pot if necessary. They would also accompany the livestock and produce to market, a journey that could often take several days and nights and be over rough terrain. They also acted as guards for money and any valuables, for in those days the purse would usually be attached to a dog's collar for safety.

With changing times and lifestyles, people's needs in relation to their dogs also changed, and consequently the Miniature with a shoulder height of around 14 inches/35 cm came into being, and then later the Giant at around 25-27 inches/65-70 cm. The Miniature became an obvious companion, but no mere lap dog, while the Giant proved a great defender and guard, but certainly not as a foolish, unreliable hothead, for with both sizes early breeders were emphatic in seeking to emulate and retain the balanced and sensible character which had become greatly admired and prized in the Schnauzer.

Schnauzers are unique in two points. The first is their agouti coat color with each individual hair banded dark/light/dark gray which gives the unique "pepper and salt" coloring. The second is that it is the only breed which takes its name from one of its own kind. This came about because the much-admired winner of the class for rough-coated dogs at the 1879 Hanover Show was named Schnauzer (which, loosely translated, means small beard). Interestingly, in Stuttgart a statue — which still stands today – of *The Nightwatchman and His Dog,* dated 1620, clearly depicts a Schnauzer-type dog. Coincidentally, the first Specialty Show for Schnauzers took place in Stuttgart in September 1890.

The Miniature has three recognized color patterns under the American and British Standards: the pepper-and-salt (shades of gray) body color with silvery beard, eyebrows, chest and leg markings; the solid black; and the black-and-silver, which has a solid black body with silvery markings and furnishings. The Fédération Cynologique Internationale also recognizes white in the Miniature. The Standards and Giants are only recognized in pepper-and-salt or solid black. Standard Schnauzers from Germany in the late 1920s were the first of the family to be introduced into Britain. They were first granted Kennel Club Challenge Certificates in 1932, some three years after the British parent club was formed. Miniatures were imported in 1928 via America where the breed had been introduced a few years earlier, and they received their first Challenge Certificates in 1935. Interestingly, Miniature Schnauzers are classified in the Terrier Group in the United States, while in the United Kingdom they remain, alongside their Standard cousins, in Utility. Giants came to Britain with the intention of their being seriously bred and promoted from Sweden in the early 1970s. They were first granted Championship status in 1977 and their own breed club formed in 1979, the Giants being classified as a Working Breed.

TEMPERAMENT

Today Schnauzers are primarily companion dogs, but temperament in all three sizes has always been important to successive generations of breeders. The breed proves to be a devoted and good-natured companion that adapts easily to its surroundings and owner's lifestyle, as well as mixing well with other dogs and domestic animals. Giants, with their larger bulk and more inbuilt protective instinct, are bolder and more assertive in their temperament. They

have been successfully trained and used for security and police work but can be just as delightful, lovable and good-natured a family pet as their two smaller cousins, provided they are sensibly trained.

HEALTH MATTERS

With its sturdy body and sensible make and shape, the breed has little in the way of health problems. Hereditary eye problems are not unknown in Miniatures, although dedicated and sensible breeders have for many years had their stock regularly checked, and the problem should not be allowed to overinfluence against this delightful breed.

SPECIAL CARE AND TRAINING

Schnauzers enjoy mental and physical activity and are responsive and easily trainable, but they do quickly become bored with mere repetitive exercises. Over the years all sizes have done well in Obedience and Trials, and Miniatures have been especially successful in Agility. When left for any period of time, Miniatures seem to be the most contented in waiting for their owners' return. Standards and more so Giants (especially when young) do not really take kindly to being left on their own.

The Schnauzer's coat requires regular grooming if it is to maintain a smart appearance. For the show ring this tends to be an ongoing process, while companion dogs can be kept looking shapely with a twice-yearly stripping session and basic daily grooming.

ADAPTABILITY

The Schnauzer is equally at home in town or country, but the two larger sizes need lengthy periods of regular exercise at least twice a day. While Schnauzers will fit into most environments, it should always be remembered that their brains need to be kept occupied if boredom is not to set in.

ESSENTIALS OF THE BREED

The working origins and background of the Schnauzer are emphasized throughout the three

Miniature Schnauzer with natural (uncropped) ears

breed Standards, especially with regard to construction, body and coat. Schnauzers should have a robust, big-ribbed, deep body with a prominent breastbone, as well as a good, hard coat and dense undercoat (although the latter is mostly removed for show competition since a full undercoat quickly detracts from the looked-for clean, smart outline). Essentially the breeds should be balanced and unexaggerated, having a sturdy, short-coupled body, good bone and strong quarters.

Although not mentioned in the breed Standards, the hocks should be short and straight. The requisite shortness in body should come only through short coupling of the loin. The head should be strong, clean, flat and elongated with a good strong foreface and broad muzzle. There should be no cheekiness as this detracts from the overall quality of the head. Correct expression is also an essential with the Schnauzer breeds and both the eyes and ears play a big part in obtaining this. The eyes should be dark, oval

in shape, and set to give a "down the nose" look. The ears, when natural, are set on the side of the head rather than on top, and although the breed Standard calls for them to be small and V-shaped, they should be in proportion to the head and fall to the temple, which means to the side of the head and not more centrally over the brows. A dark facial mask that harmonizes with the body color has always been thought essential to the Schnauzer look by old-time breeders, but this is only mentioned under color in the Giant's breed Standard. Movement should be easy and free-striding, without any high-stepping or paddling, and with good driving power from the hindquarters. Although now highly groomed and prepared for the show ring, the Schnauzer breeds (especially Miniatures) are not "pretty" dogs, but are no-nonsense, sound in temperament and character dogs, and this — along with their origins — should never be forgotten.

Registry: AKC, CKC, FCI (Group 2), KC

395

SCOTTISH DEERHOUND/DEERHOUND

ORIGIN AND DEVELOPMENT

The history and lore of the Scottish Highlands going back to the Middle Ages attests to the presence of hounds that were developed to chase and bring down wild deer in the glens. By the early eighteenth century, changing times and sport had brought the breed perilously close to extinction. It is recorded that, through the efforts of Archibald McNeill and his brother Lord Colonsay, a concerted attempt was made to assemble the best bloodlines still available and to start the Colonsay strain which would prevail as working hounds until the early twentieth century.

TEMPERAMENT

Scottish Deerhounds are unique in the contradictory terms that can be used to describe them, such as gentleness, staying power, strength, sensitivity, indomitable courage and docility. Yet all of these are key to the breed that exists for its family and the chase, with the former always the more important. Known for its docility in the home as much as for its courage in the field, the Scottish Deerhound makes a superb pet for adults and children who recognize this unique and interesting blend of characteristics.

HEALTH MATTERS

The Scottish Deerhound is relatively unaffected by specific genetic health problems but does share some of the health problems common to larger dogs. Included in these must be gastric torsion (bloat) and bursa. Owners must always be on guard for broken toes and damaged tails which both may result from its desire to course freely.

SPECIAL CARE AND TRAINING

Because the Scottish Deerhound is a very large hound that grows very quickly, care should be taken in many ways. From the age of six weeks, a puppy should be given at least fifteen minutes of undivided attention away from its siblings. The young hound will have coordination problems during its physical growth. It should not be allowed to overextend itself in running or play and although it can be left to exercise itself in an enclosed yard, it should be taken out for walks of fifteen to twenty minutes daily.

The Scottish Deerhound that is to become a house dog, show dog or a companion should have early training that exposes it to all sorts of outside stimuli. Ten weeks is not too early an age to begin housetraining the young dog, to walk it on a lead, to take it on trips in the car, to begin to clip its nails and to check its teeth for proper shedding. The puppy should be allowed to meet new people and other dogs and cats and housepets, so that nothing it may encounter later in life will be startling. Talking to the young dog will teach it the sound of its owner's voice and the young Deerhound will quickly learn the meaning of often-repeated words.

ADAPTABILITY

Any home considering a Scottish Deerhound should ensure that it has the necessary space and time for exercise and must appreciate the breed's sensitivity to even the smallest of changes. In particular, the owner should recognize the introspection which any change might produce and which frequently does cause seriously damaging results in regard to the dog's health.

ESSENTIALS OF THE BREED

The Scottish Deerhound, with the graceful outline of the Greyhound and its rough coat, immediately gives the impression of power and speed. With its height ranging from 28-32 inches/71-81 cm, coupled with graceful curves and a powerful overlay of muscles, this breed presents the picture of a formidable adversary

The Scottish Deerhound is known simply as the Deerhound in the United Kingdom.

in the hunt. Its strong neck and powerful jaw are those of an effective hunter, while its keen eye gives the impression of being good at searching out its quarry. On the hearth all this power is transformed into the picture of domesticity and its expression becomes soft and gentle.

The Scottish Deerhound ranges from dark blue-gray to sandy red and red fawn in color. White is strongly discouraged, although white on the toes, on the tip of tail, or a small patch on the chest are all accepted. Well-sloped shoulders, a well-muscled loin, and powerful drooping hindquarters complete the image of power and grace of the Deerhound. The tail of the breed should be dropped down or slightly curved, but never lifted out of line with the back.

Registry: AKC, CKC, FCI (Group 10), KC

SCOTTISH TERRIER

ORIGIN AND DEVELOPMENT

Scotland has been the home of various terrier breeds for many years. In the main they were small, active rough-haired dogs of strong character. Perhaps due to the geography of Scotland, different types were traced to particular areas. This led to selective breeding and the development of the five Scottish breeds, as they are known today. The similarities are still there — short legs, low-to-ground bodies and harsh, shaggy coats. The Scottish Terrier type was favored in the Aberdeen area, so for several years they carried the title of Aberdeen Terrier. "Exports" to England and America soon took place and devotees of the Scottish Terrier were to be found in both countries. Early British Champions, Ch. Dundee (born in 1882) and Ch. Alister, were responsible for many Champion offspring on both sides of the Atlantic. Many of England's top dogs and bitches since that time have made similar journeys and the

Scottish Terrier is now as popular as ever.

The heyday of the breed, however, seems to have been in the years following World War II. Clever fanciers were able to maintain a nucleus of sound breeding stock and so were able to continue the high standards seen before the war. The breed, like many others, has passed through fashions and fancies. Breed type, however, has been paramount. The craze for excessive body coat (furnishings) has thankfully become, like all fashions, outdated and now a more practical, sensible appearance is required in the show ring.

At one time the United States seemed to favor a taller, lighter animal than the breed's native country, but recently type and build have become more uniform. Exports from America and Canada can and do compete with great success in shows throughout the world. American presentation is still slightly different from the British style, with the dog in a shorter, closer trim, thus accentuating its construction and shape.

Scottish Terrier

TEMPERAMENT

The original Standard for the Scottish Terrier asked for a dog which was willing to go anywhere and do anything, and today this still holds true. It should be bold, dignified and upright. It should be willing to stand its ground but not be aggressive without reason. It is at home with adults and children alike, and many Scotties have played both guard and nanny over the years.

HEALTH MATTERS

Usually the Scottish Terrier is sound in mind and limb. Pre-war problems included skin troubles, but thankfully these have to a large extent been eliminated. However, Scottie cramp is still a problem. It resembles a slight seizure and for a few moments the Scottie is unable to walk. Stock should be bought from families where this has not been a problem. A healthy appetite with plenty of activity tends to provide a happy and contented dog.

SPECIAL CARE AND TRAINING

Like most dogs, a Scottie needs training from an early age. An uncontrolled dog is an unhappy dog, having to fight for its rights. It needs basic training and socializing to bring out the best of its character. Scotties should be stripped twice yearly to maintain a healthy coat.

ADAPTABILITY

Scottish Terriers can turn up in the most unlikely of places — for instance, President Roosevelt had a Scottie named Fala in the White House and Hitler gave two to his mistress Eva Braun, while numerous other celebrities have given their affection to the breed. This demonstrates their ability to adapt. Scotties are equally at home wherever their owner happens to be, whether in an apartment, airplane or mansion. It must be remembered that the Scottie is not a "gushing" breed, but needs time to make its own introductions. It will usually sit back and survey the scene before committing itself.

Once your friend, the Scottie is your friend for life. Loyalty, to a Scottie, is all important.

ESSENTIALS OF THE BREED

The Scottish Terrier should be a sturdy, thick-set dog of a size suited to going to ground. A balance must be reached between these characteristics: too big and it would never get down a crevice to catch its prey. The height at the shoulder should be around 11 inches/28 cm, and its weight should be approximately 21 pounds/9.5 kg. The Scottie's head, which perhaps seems rather long for its size, is carried proudly — characteristically its nose appears to slope backward. The planes of the head should be parallel and show quality. The eyes are dark and deep set under prominent eyebrows. Fine, neat ears are pointed, carried erect and set on top of the head at the corners of the flat skull. The neck should be moderately thick, not too long and lead to well-laid shoulders. The forearm slopes well back, which allows for a good overhang or forechest, and the short legs are then placed well under the body. This is slung between the well-boned front legs. The well-rounded ribs flatten to a deep chest. The "rule of thumb" in Scotties is that a man's clenched fist held upright should fit beneath the Scottie's chest and the ground, and that the chest should be wide enough to accommodate the same man's open hands with fingers together.

The Scottie's body is short and well muscled, the hindquarters creating great power in action. The undocked short tail is carried erect and should be clothed with enough coat to have a carrot shape. The Scottie should always be seen to be moving with purpose and drive. The coat color may be black, brindle or wheaten of any shade. Unfortunately fashion took its toll in Britain when black coats were given preference. Wheaten is very popular in the United States and hopefully there will now be a resurgence of interest in the country's homeland for this most attractive color.

Registry: AKC, CKC, FCI (Group 3), KC

SEALYHAM TERRIER

ORIGIN AND DEVELOPMENT

During the middle and late nineteenth century, various areas within Great Britain saw the development of a number of "go to ground" breeds of dogs designed to meet the perceived needs of the sportsman. Captain Edwardes who lived at his estate of Sealyham in Pembrokeshire was no different. He wanted a plucky, tenacious dog which would be powerful and yet small enough to go into the badger sett and prevent the badger from tunneling away before the sportsman could dig it out. The dog needed to be able to hunt by sight and scent and to "give tongue" when the quarry — be it badger or fox — had been cornered. Most importantly, having witnessed the fate of brown dogs which emerged from forest earth at the jaws of the pack hounds, he determined that it should be mainly white.

To achieve his new terrier, Edwardes combined a number of breeds and, although there are no specific records, it seems that the Welsh Corgi, the Cheshire Terrier, the Dandie Dinmont Terrier, the Fox Terrier and the West Highland White Terrier all had a role to play. Given this background there was great diversity in type and color in the early years but by the twentieth century, the low slung, big-headed, strong-boned dog which is now expected had emerged. Body color was still evident, but by the period between the wars white bodies predominated, although tan, lemon and badger head markings remained. The fascination of the American buyer for all-white dogs had its effect on the breed but, for many exhibitors today, head markings are part of the breed's appeal.

TEMPERAMENT

The need for a terrier to hold a badger or fox has basically disappeared but the Sealyham Terrier has instead gained a firm metaphorical hold on owners through the many other attributes which Captain Edwardes imparted

Sealyham Terrier

into it. Sealyham Terriers are devoted and faithful companions, while at the same time remaining independent personalities. They have unflagging tenacity and remain the sworn enemy of rabbits and mice. Bred to be quiet while working but to give tongue once the quarry was sighted, this terrier is far from quiet and yet barks only when it sees the necessity.

HEALTH MATTERS

The breed is generally healthy although eye problems are known to occur. Sealyhams are particularly prone to skin allergies, and should be kept free of fleas. Deafness is also known in the breed. Stock should be bought from breeders of good reputation who test for heritable defects.

SPECIAL CARE AND TRAINING

The Sealyham Terrier's true hard white coat requires regular maintenance and constant grooming is essential if it is to look its best. This may require professsional attention. The breed should not be clipped on its body but should be plucked, like all hard-coated terriers.

ADAPTABILITY

The breed's relatively small size and large personality make it an ideal dog for the urban dweller who wants a large dog in a small package. The Sealyham must have good walks on a leash if kept as a city dog and good exercise off a leash in the country, once it has learned to come when called. It enjoys exercise and this is very necessary for its well-being.

ESSENTIALS OF THE BREED

The Sealyham Terrier is the embodiment of power and determination and should communicate a sense of power in a relatively small package. It should not form the square picture so desired in many terrier breeds but rather should appear oblong. An average height of 10 1/2 inches/26 cm with a weight of between 23-25 pounds/10-11 kg is typical. However, a sense of power comes not from its height or weight but from its bone and strength of jaw.

The head should be long, broad and powerful without coarseness. The long lean head so prized in some other terriers is not a characteristic of this breed. Powerful, square jaws with a full and well-boned muzzle are essential. A black nose, dark eyes and at least some pigment around the eyes is important to the proper expression. The variety of markings which are acceptable on the head add to the charm and individuality of this breed, but extensive body markings or undercoat ticking is to be discouraged.

The body should be strong, substantial and well-muscled but without any indication of coarseness. This is a sporting terrier, strong and agile enough to do its work. Good legs and feet are necessary to the breed to ensure that it retains the characteristics for which it was bred. Its action should be strong, quick and free. There should be a good reach of neck which is about two-thirds the height at the withers blending smoothly into the shoulders at the withers. Shoulders are well laid back and sufficiently wide to permit freedom of action. The forelegs are short and as straight as is consistent with the chest that is well let down between them.

The Sealyham is a working terrier which should always be able to carry out its original purpose in life — although today its quarry is more likely to be a small rodent than a badger.

Registry: AKC, CKC, FCI (Group 3), KC

SEGUGIO ITALIANO

The Italian scenthound retains much of the noble appearance illustrated in paintings of hunting scenes centuries ago. The Segugio is not hunted in packs. It has a very good reputation for hunting hare.

The height at the withers should be about 19 1/2 - 23 1/2 inches/50-60 cm. Its body should be almost square, fairly deep, well muscled and with good bone. The head should be long, elegant and with a convex nose ridge. The ears are long, with a slight fold and low set. The coat may be either smooth and glossy or wiry and medium long. Accepted colors are any shade of fawn and red or black-and-tan.

Registry: FCI (Group 6)

Segugi Italiani

ORIGIN AND DEVELOPMENT

The English Setter is one of the oldest breeds of gun dog. It has been mentioned in European literature since the fourteenth century as a setting dog, and has been defined and registered at the Kennel Club in London since 1873. However, the breed had become established many years before this. Many noble families in Britain kept their own kennels of setters for private hunting and shooting. Famous kennels include the Featherstone's, the Edmond Castle's, Lord Lovat's breed, the Earl of Southesk's, the Earl of Derby's and the Welsh or Llanidloes Setter.

The first recorded breeder of English Setters who initiated tabulated pedigrees as they are known today was Mr. Edward Laverack, whose pedigrees go back to around 1860, seventeen years before the Kennel Club was founded in England. One of the Kennel Club's founders, and later its Chairman, was an English Setter enthusiast, Mr. S. E. Shirley. Following the line

of great early breeders was Mr. R. Purcell Llewellin, who purchased his original stock from Laverack and introduced various outcrosses. The "Llewellin Setter" has a separate register in the United States with its own Field Stud Book. Although Laverack and Llewellin aimed to produce their individual ideals of English Setters for show and work combined, each had a different way of working towards this goal; Laverack practiced inbreeding within his own strain, while Llewellin experimented with crosses. He was only interested in shooting and had no interest in his dogs' appearance. These two breeders' stock and specialization led to the main division in the breed of today, between show dogs and working dogs, although it must be remembered that both types originated with the Laveracks. Edward Laverack indeed produced the first book on the breed, *The Setter,* published around 1875, and the Standard which he then compiled for the breed is the

English Setter

one used, with almost identical wording, to the present day.

The breed has evolved in slightly different directions. In some Scandinavian countries they favor the old working setter type, a rather lighter build of dog than what is popular in the show ring in the breed's homeland. English (working) Setters and Scandinavian English Setters look very similar. The differences really affect only show dogs and there can be problems for judges who have to assess whether dogs would be considered of Championship quality in the breed's native country.

TEMPERAMENT

As in so many breeds today, there are English Setters which do not have the normal totally reliable temperaments of their ancestors. Careless breeding from unreliable stock means that the breed as a whole cannot now be guaranteed. There are enthusiasts with very high standards, however, who only breed from affectionate, kind and gentle dogs. A large dog, with lively spirits, deserves a loyal owner or family, who will attend to its needs in return for its unswerving devotion to the whole family.

HEALTH MATTERS

In general, the English Setter remains a robust and healthy breed. As with many large dogs, the occasional case of hip dysplasia has been found, but not to such an extent that this constitutes a major hereditary problem.

SPECIAL CARE AND TRAINING

Being a particularly affectionate and gregarious breed, English Setters thrive best in human company as family companions, or kenneled with other dogs, but never alone. They are not difficult to rear and feed if provided with ample food of good quality. If kenneled, English Setters need ample comfortable bedding to keep them clean, warm and content. Daily grooming with a coarse steel comb and stiff brush is essential to keep the coat in good condition, and special care should be taken to comb out the feathering on the legs and tail to prevent knotting.

ADAPTABILITY

The English Setter will fit into most environments, be they rural or urban. In the house, they must have a bed or rug of their own where they know that they can rest. For such an active dog, road work and free exercise are both essential — every day from about three to four months, when ten minutes twice a day is ample. This should be increased to an hour or more when adulthood is reached.

ESSENTIALS OF THE BREED

One of the chief attractions of the breed is the variety of colors: blue belton (black and white), orange or lemon belton (orange or lemon and white), blue belton and tan (black, white and tan or tricolor) and liver belton (liver and white). The origin of the word "belton" comes straight from Laverack's book, which describes the ticking or roaning, which varies from light to dark, so giving the light or dark blue beltons, and the other combinations of this "color." Belton is the name of a village in Northumberland, one of the many places where Laverack rented shooting land. Puppies are usually born white except for those with solid black, orange or liver patches, which are generally less popular in the show ring, although they can be most attractive.

The English Setter Standard is an international one, with minor variations. The head should be long and reasonably lean, with a well-defined stop. The skull is oval shaped from ear to ear. The muzzle is moderately deep and fairly square; from the stop to the point of the nose should equal the length of the skull from the occiput to the eyes; the nostrils should be wide and the jaws of nearly equal length; flews should not be too pendulous. The mouth should have a scissors bite. The eyes should be bright, mild and intelligent, in dark or hazel — the darker the better. Ears are of moderate length, set low and hanging in neat folds close to the cheek. The neck should be rather long, muscular and lean, slightly arched at the crest and not throaty nor pendulous, but clean and elegant in appearance. The body should be of moderate length, the back short and level, with good round, widely sprung ribs and deep in the back ribs, i.e., well ribbed up. The hindquarters should be wide, slightly arched, strong and muscular, with a defined second thigh. The stifles should be well bent and the thighs long from hip to hock. The shoulder should be well set back; the chest deep and of good width between the shoulder blades. The pasterns are short, muscular, round and straight, and the feet close and compact. The tail should be set on almost in a line with the back, to be slightly curved but with no tendency to turn upward.

The feathering should start slightly below the tail root and increase in length to the middle, gradually tapering off toward the tip.

The coat should be slightly wavy, long and silky, but never curly. Those without heavy patches of color on the body, but evenly flecked all over, are preferred. The British Standard calls for males to stand 25-27 inches/ 63-68.5 cm and bitches 24-25 inches/60-63 cm, whereas the American version asks for dogs to be around 25 inches/63 cm and bitches 24 inches/60 cm

Registry: AKC, CKC, FCI (Group 7), KC

SETTERS — GORDON SETTER

ORIGIN AND DEVELOPMENT

It appears quite possible that there were black-and-tan setters in Scotland well before there even was a Duke of Gordon, but it is a well-known fact that the Fourth Duke of Gordon is considered to be the first person to make a strong effort to stabilize the breed in its native land.

It was in the late 1700s that the Duke's kennels, which were known as the Gordon Castle Setters, came into prominence. A sportsman writer at the time described the dogs as easy to train. They naturally point well and, although they are not fast, they have great stamina. They seldom make a false point and when they make a find you may be sure that they are "on birds." The Fourth Duke was keen on performance and inclined to breed for the best working dogs in the field. When the kennels passed on to the Sixth Duke of Gordon in about 1835, more of an attempt was made to keep the good working ability and to pay attention to standardizing appearance and type.

In 1842, the Americans George Blunt and Daniel Webster imported the first Gordons, attracted by the breed's ability, good looks and conformation. More imports to the United States followed from Great Britain as well as the Scandinavian countries. Today's American breeders, backed by a strong breed club, strive to keep the working ability of the Gordon strong and its appearance uniform. There is a latitude offered in size, however, as the breed has fanciers who wish a bigger, more rugged setter and those who, because of the type of terrain and country hunted, prefer a more moderate size.

TEMPERAMENT

The devotion of the Gordon to its owner and family is legendary. The Gordon, however, does not make a friend of every passing stranger or unwanted intruder. It is good with children if raised with them as part of the family and will be protective to them. These protective traits may make it aggressive with other dogs.

HEALTH MATTERS

All breeding stock should be X-rayed at two years for possible hip dysplasia. It should also be screened for progressive retinal atrophy. Epilepsy has occasionally occurred in the

Gordon Setter

breed. Stock should be bought only from reputable breeders who screen on an ongoing basis for heritable diseases.

SPECIAL CARE AND TRAINING

The Gordon Setter is a fairly large hunting dog, bred for that purpose for many years, so the new owner must provide it with space in which to grow up and a secure yard in which it may exercise. It also needs a loving family that it can protect and love in return. Obedience training will direct its energies into a learning situation and will serve it in good stead if it is to continue training for the field or for bench shows. It does grow a fairly heavy coat which will require professional attention until the knack of keeping it groomed is learned by a member of the family.

Its ears need to be wiped out with a bit of cotton wrapped around the finger and dipped in baby oil on a weekly basis. Any odor noticed coming from the ear should be brought to the notice of a veterinarian. Nails should have just

a bit taken off the tip and the teeth should be brushed on a weekly basis. A dry dog biscuit daily will help to keep the teeth clean but they still need to be brushed. Its long feathering should be combed and brushed weekly and it should be given a bath as necessary. If used for hunting, the Gordon must be carefully groomed to remove anything that it may have picked up in the fields, including ticks.

ADAPTABILITY

The Gordon thrives on companionship, which it needs in addition to training, care and comfortable quarters to call its own. This may be either a snug outdoor kennel and yard or its own place in the house, be it somewhere in the kitchen or a rug by the fire. It must have exercise, good food and a family to look after.

ESSENTIALS OF THE BREED

The Gordon Setter is the largest and most substantial of the three setters. It is always black-and-tan in color, that is a gleaming black base coat with mahogany red markings over the eyes, on the muzzle, throat, chest, feet, inside of the hind legs and under the tail. The coat on the head, back of neck, top of body and the front of the legs should be trimmed to be smooth and lie flat. The ears, chest, belly, back of legs and tail should have flowing feathers of longer hair.

The males may weigh 55-80 pounds/25-36 kg, while the females are 45-70 pounds/20-31 kg. Its size, measured at the shoulder, should fall within 23-26 inches/58-66 cm for bitches and 24-27 inches/60-68 cm for males. The British Standard calls for males to be 26 inches/66 cm and bitches 24 1/2 inches/62 cm. A smooth, free movement with high head carriage is typical. The eyes should be dark although some very worthy specimens have paler ones. The neck should be long and strong, the back firm in topline and the tail carried out and waving. Its bone should be flat rather than round. The front legs should be straight with good feet, the hindquarters well angulated with good propelling power. The Gordon Setter is a handsome animal, at home, in the show ring or in the bird field.

Registry: AKC, CKC, FCI (Group 7), KC

SETTERS — IRISH RED AND WHITE SETTER

Origin and Development

The Irish Red and White Setter is an elegant, eye-catching dog that should not be confused with its close relation, the Irish Setter (which is all red). The Red and White is a medium-sized dog of substance descended from the Land Spaniel. The earliest records of the breed are from the mid-seventeenth century, although there are paintings of similar dogs in terms of size, type and color that date from a century earlier.

When Irish Setters first appeared in the show rings of Ireland, just beyond the middle of the nineteenth century, there was a good deal of confusion about the correct color. Some showed traces of black in their coats; others patches of white. At early Irish shows there were occasionally separate classes for Red and White and the all-red. At other times they were shown together, but by the end of the nineteenth century the popularity of the all-reds had virtually eclipsed the Red and White which became a great rarity, so much so that some believed the breed to be extinct. During the 1920s, efforts to revive it by the Rev. Noble Huston, of County Down, proved highly successful and by 1944 the club had re-established itself to such an extent that the first specialist breed club was formed. Today it is a very popular breed across the whole of Britain. At the 1995 Cruft's Dog Show well over a hundred Irish Red and White Setters were entered, proving conclusively that this dog found a firm foothold as one of the most popular gundog breeds. Its vibrant coloring and smart markings have appealed to many enthusiasts from foreign lands and there is a steady demand for the breed from overseas. Already several enthusiasts in the United States have acquired foundation stock.

Temperament

The Red and White is a very alert dog, intelligent and friendly with an excellent scenting ability. This makes it an ideal shooting companion as well as a family pet.

Health Matters

In general, the Red and White is a remarkably healthy breed and happily has not succumbed to some of the prevalent hereditary conditions seen in its all-red cousin. Having said this, prudent breeders should keep a watchful eye

Irish Red and White Setters

on breeding stock, checking in particular for any eye or hip abnormalities.

SPECIAL CARE AND TRAINING

The Red and White needs regular grooming to keep its feathering free from knots and tangles. The breed is easy to keep clean, its coat being naturally silky in texture and when bathed it dries very quickly. It thrives on human companionship and requires plenty of regular exercise once adulthood has been reached. Early regular training is advisable and should be persisted with. The Red and White's high hearing perceptibility makes it very responsive to whistle-training.

ADAPTABILITY

The Red and White is really more of a country dog than an urban dweller. However, given regular exercise and the chance to work with its owner, it will settle in any family environment.

ESSENTIALS OF THE BREED

The Red and White is a well-proportioned, medium-sized dog that is well muscled and powerful without being in any way coarse. It is rather more athletic than the racy all-red breed. A desirable height for dogs is 24-26 inches/ 60-65 cm, with bitches 2 inches/5 cm smaller. The head should be broad in proportion to the body with a good stop and clean, square muzzle. While the skull should be domed, there should be no noticeable occiput as with the all-red Irish. The eyes are dark hazel or dark brown, round, quite full and without haw. The ears are set well back, on a level with the eyes and should lie close to the head. The body is deep-chested with well-sprung ribs and the back should be muscular and powerful. The Red and White should be well boned with tight feet, and the tail should be of moderate length and strong-rooted, carried on a level with or below the back.

The breed's crowning glory is the exquisite color of its straight, flat coat. The base color is a pearly white, with clear islands of red, both colors showing the maximum of life and bloom. Flecking, but not roaning, is permitted around the face and feet and up the foreleg as far as the elbow and up the hind leg as far as the hock. Roaning, flecking or mottling on any other part of the body is most objectionable and should be heavily penalized in competition. The ideal proportion of white to red is 60 percent white to 40 percent red.

Registry: FCI (Group 7), KC

SETTERS — IRISH SETTER

ORIGIN AND DEVELOPMENT

Dogs were used to set birds as early as the fourteenth century. These setting spaniels were undoubtedly the ancestors of the Irish Setter. However, there is considerable difference of opinion as to the various crosses used thereafter — Bloodhound, Pointer, Gordon Setter or English Setter — or all of these. All probably did play a part.

The early Irish Setter was a white dog with red patches but gradually the solid red dog became more common. As early as 1812 the Earl of Enniskillan would have only self-colored dogs in his kennel.

Still, the color controversy continued through most of the nineteenth century. Indeed, for many years there were three colors in Ireland: red in the north, white and red in the south and west, and "shower of hail" along the northwest coast. A "shower of hail" dog was described as sprinkled with uniform 1/4 inch/ 5 mm white spots 1 inch/2.5 cm apart.

However, by the 1870s the red dog had won and the Irish Setter came to mean a solid red dog with small, if any, areas of white on its chest and/or toes. Several of the early imports to the United States were registered as various colors including lemon, black, or black and white. The most dominant Irish Setter in the 1870s was Champion Palmerston, said to be in the pedigree of almost all Irish Setters.

Bred for work as a hard performing bird dog, the Irish Setter was a capable shooting dog and the early imports to the United States were brought over by avid hunters who had admired the breed's work in Ireland and England. The Irish Setter lost out as a dramatic field trialer to the Pointer and Llewelin Setter — its color was a problem in cover and while it had a fair intensity it lacked the high style demanded in field trial competition.

Still, the Irish Setter maintained a loyal following among the hunting fraternity and

Irish Setter

began to build up a further entourage of admirers among those fanciers who appreciated the breed for its beauty and its gay devil-may-care personality. As time passed, however, the breed's beauty became its undoing. It was bred less and less for its hunting skills rather than for its showmanship. Today there is a strong movement to demonstrate that the Irish Setter still has all its old field abilities and more of these dogs are now to be seen in hunting tests.

TEMPERAMENT

The Irish Setter has a great desire to please members of its human family and is an affectionate, joyful companion. It is good with children although perhaps too boisterous for little ones. This breed makes an excellent watchdog and even, if pushed, a guard dog.

HEALTH MATTERS

Two major health problems affect the Irish Setter today. These are epilepsy and gastric torsion (bloat). Feeding several small meals is suggested and soy products should be avoided. Progressive retinal atrophy, long a problem in the breed, is now being brought under control with a newly developed test.

SPECIAL CARE AND TRAINING

Although not the easiest of dogs to train, the Irish Setter is responsive and loyal and, in the hands of the right owner, is an excellent Obedience dog. The Irish Setter needs a fair amount of exercise and a large amount of human attention.

ADAPTABILITY

The Irish Setter likes to be the center of attention and is flamboyant enough to hold that place, thus making it an outstanding show dog. The breed can be kept as either a city or a country dog.

However, it is difficult to exercise the Irish Setter adequately in a city situation because walking the dog is generally not enough to give this bold, big trotter a proper workout.

Even in a country setting, unless there is an area that can be safely fenced to give the dog space in which to trot and stretch its legs, it will need road work on a quiet road behind a car or bicycle to get the exercise that it needs. If it does not get sufficient exercise, it may become hyperactive , not eat correctly or may go to the other extreme and become obese, lazy and soft.

The Irish Setter's coat is fairly profuse and needs brushing, combing, bathing and trimming on a regular basis. It will enjoy hunting in the bird field and, if this is to be one of its pursuits, it must be carefully brought along and trained for this work. Most Irish Setters have instinctive noses for bird hunting, but this innate ability must be properly developed and focussed in each dog. Early obedience training is good preparation for this sport.

ESSENTIALS OF THE BREED

The Irish Setter should be substantial yet elegant, ideally standing 27 inches/68.5 cm at the withers (25 inches/63 cm for bitches) and weighing 70 pounds/31 kg (60 pounds/27 kg for bitches), although Ireland, the country of origin, does not state a specific height in its Standard. Overall balance is of great importance in creating the beautiful lines of the Irish Setter. Its slightly sloping topline and good angulation fore and aft give it the big, graceful and efficient trot that is so characteristic of its flamboyant personality.

The Irish Setter's head should be long and lean, delicately chiseled and framed by its long, low-set ears. The mouth should have a scissors bite and its eyes should be dark, and neither large and round nor small and sunken. They should show intelligence and good humor. It should be mahogany or rich chestnut red with no black and at most only a small amount of white on its chest, throat, or toes, or have a narrow center streak on its skull. Without doubt, a good Irish Setter is indeed a thing of beauty and a joy to behold.

Registry: AKC, CKC, FCI (Group 7), KC

SHETLAND SHEEPDOG

ORIGIN AND DEVELOPMENT

Hutchinson's Dog Encyclopedia devotes ten full pages of text and photographs to the Shetland Sheepdog. It is depicted as "a smaller species of one of the most beautiful of British breeds, the Collies of Scotland." Through the early years, there was great debate about whether the working (herding) type or the show type miniature Collies should be advanced. Small sheepdogs from the Shetland Islands arrived on England's mainland before World War I. All that could be completely verified about their beginnings is that these little dogs had been a vital part of the islands "as long as man could remember." The Shetland Sheepdog Club was formed in Lerwick, the capital of the Shetlands, in 1908. Within a year, the Kennel Club in the United Kingdom recognized the show type 12 inch/30 cm herding breed.

The mainland immediately adopted this bright, beautiful, small herding breed and through the first half of the twentieth century, type tightened, its adaptability was nurtured, and the essence for which it was bred was always addressed as the written Standard evolved.

In the British Standard, head and expression are of prime importance. Now, after almost one hundred years, it is still the choice of people who wish to have a small, beautiful, biddable companion. The Shetland Sheepdog of the British Isles continues to be a smaller, lighter boned dog than its American offspring. Breeders throughout the United Kingdom worked to preserve the soft sweet dark eye, molded skull, correct stop, and magnificent double-textured coat so vital to this breed. Its colors have varied from golden to mahogany sable, tricolor (black, tan, and white) to blue merle. There has been little color interbreeding.

After World War II, when Americans traveled to England to purchase dogs either as pets, show dogs or for breeding purposes, the Shetland Sheepdog was often the breed of choice. Some very knowledgeable breeders became involved in "Shelties." Mrs. Dreer's Anahassit, Nate Levine's Page's Hill Shelties and Betty Whelen's Poconos were all bred and exhibited extensively. Everyone worked hard to maintain the best of this beautiful hardy breed. Through the late 1940s and up to the present time, Shelties have held their own in both conformation and Obedience competition.

When Scott and Fuller embarked on their scientific research that would lead to the definitive book, *Genetics and the Social Behavior of the Dog,* the Sheltie was one of four breeds chosen. In exhaustive, lengthy tests, the Shetland Sheepdog was found to be intelligent, slightly shy and biddable. It appeared that human contact was necessary at a very early age and should continue steadily to ensure that the talents of this breed are maximized. Praise and encouragement had a much more positive effect on the dogs than food rewards.

TEMPERAMENT

Shetland Sheepdog puppies are beguiling and exhibit a desire to please from a very young age. Shelties can be trusted in a home situation very early.

SPECIAL CARE AND TRAINING

As with any coated breed, Shelties should start standing to be groomed early in life. It not only keeps the beautiful coat in condition but assists in the bonding to its human. Leash training should start before eight weeks with patient encouragement and should take place several times each day. When the puppy is well acclimatized to the lead, trips outside, visits to new surroundings and handling by family members and friends should become part of each day. Shetland Sheepdogs are easily housetrained. As with any dog, it should be

Shetland Sheepdog

given its own place in which to rest.

In Obedience competitions, Shetland Sheep-dogs score extremely high. Their desire to please, their naturally inherited herding behavior (watch the shepherd, respond to sound and hand signals, endurance, knowledge of the stock to be herded), and their agility all contribute to these high scores. This is a breed that needs interaction and motivation.

A whole different area of competition is open to Shetland Sheepdog fanciers through herding trials held by associations in the United States. Here, dogs bred for very specific competition compete with Border Collies and other herding breeds to demonstrate highly specialized skills inherent in all herding breeds.

The innate ability aready exists, of course, but a long process of training and conditioning (much like any athlete) is required to ensure both the success and safety of competing dogs.

HEALTH MATTERS

This breed is long lived and ages of fourteen through sixteen are not uncommon. Owners need to address health care, exercise and mental stimulation in order to make the most of its wonderfully long lifespan.

ADAPTABILITY

The Shetland Sheepdog will adjust to small living quarters if its owners provide daily, sustained exercise. Trips to parks, jogging or accompanying a bicycle can provide the exercise needed.

ESSENTIALS OF THE BREED

The American Shetland Sheepdog Association is the parent club in the United States. The Standard by which Shelties are judged has evolved over many years and continues to be the guideline for breeders in their quest for perfection. Three colors are recognized: sable, black and blue merle with varying amounts of white and/or tan. In the United States, the size should be between 13-16 inches/33-40.5 cm, with dogs measuring under or over being disqualified in the conformation ring. Dogs that do not fall within the size limits may still be shown in Obedience competition. Under the British Standard the breed should be 14-14 1/2 inches/35-36 cm, with dogs 1 inch /2.5 cm

above or below this "highly undesirable" but not automatically disqualified.

The head properties count for twenty points on a scale provided by the governing body and the areas mentioned are expression, eyes, ears, skull and muzzle. Each quality stresses moderation and molded beauty. Body and leg qualities account for fifty-five points on the scale and again stress moderation and balance. Because these are the areas where the purpose of the breed must be considered, it is wise that they play a very important part in the Standard, even when the head is the feature that defines the beauty of the breed. Each area — neck, top-line, body, forequarters and hindquarters — has clearly defined demands that must be fulfilled to keep this breed sound.

Registry: AKC, CKC, FCI (Group 1), KC

SHIBA INU

ORIGIN AND DEVELOPMENT

The Shiba is probably one of the oldest native dogs of Japan, dating back to the third century B.C. when it was used as a versatile hunting dog. Its traditional spitz features and lack of exaggeration render it typical of ancient breeds that have existed for many centuries. The breed has gradually reduced in numbers and almost became extinct thanks to World War II and an outbreak of distemper in 1952.

A breeding program was resumed, combining the stocky, heavier-boned hunting Shiba of the mountainous regions with the more elegant and "leggy" type found in other parts of Japan. The fact that the two types have been combined still manifests itself today, with some variation in the puppies produced.

TEMPERAMENT

The Shiba is not a dog for the faint-hearted: it is a large animal in a small body, wonderful

with people it knows but quite aggressive toward other dogs of the same sex. It never feels intimidated by a larger opponent. If necessary, it will take on the whole world and never back down. This natural instinct is used to advantage by the Japanese who exhibit the Shiba "terrier style." Two dogs stand in their own circle "eye-balling" each other, coming up on their toes, leaning forward and standing their ground. This spirit is much admired by Japanese judges. The bolder dog becomes the winner in a close decision between two otherwise equal dogs.

The Shiba is very territorial and faithful to its owners. An excellent watchdog, it will sound off if all is not well. It is very vocal and will "yodel" when it requires attention, especially at meal times. It is easily excited and, on seeing its owner after an absence, will demonstrate its total exuberance by leaping high into the air on its hind legs while emitting a high-pitched scream. This scream is also used as a self-defense

Shiba Inu

mechanism, especially when lead-training as a young puppy. In fact, the Shiba could collect an Oscar for its performance of over-reaction! Its philosophy is, "If I scream loud enough, they will think that I am hurt and will stop pulling the lead." The noise is blood-curdling and is often followed by a pretense of being turned to stone. The Shiba will stand rigid, tail tightly held, and give an unrivaled display of stubborness. However, once it has gained its confidence and is fully lead-trained, it will never want to keep still again but will be keen to examine everything in life.

A male Shiba demands respect and, like a

Samurai warrior, is bold, courageous and never shy or nervous. The fascination of the Shiba is the way that it investigates people. Once it decides that it likes you, it craves affection, climbs on to your knee and stares into your eyes, as if it is trying to discover the secrets of your soul.

HEALTH MATTERS

In general the Shiba is a very healthy breed. In the United States and Europe, X-raying for hip dysplasia and patella luxation is a matter of course. In the United Kingdom this is not considered a normal practice, keeping in line with other small breeds.

The temperament of the parents should be considered before buying a puppy. Nervous dogs and bitches should not be bred from, since obviously no one wants a cringing wreck as a show dog or companion. A fear-biter in any breed is a danger.

The Shiba has very large teeth for such a small mouth, and when its adult teeth are growing it may hang on to its milk teeth. This must be carefully monitored because retained baby teeth can misalign the adult teeth, pushing the bite out of line. If milk teeth are not shed naturally, they should be removed so that the correct scissors bite can develop. This may require veterinary assistance.

SPECIAL CARE AND TRAINING

The Shiba has a thick double coat with a soft woolly undercoat and a strong, straight, harsh outercoat. This creates a really dense and plush look. It requires grooming once a week with a stiff "slicker" brush and will usually shed twice a year, when the coat lifts off from the body in clumps. The coat needs a good raking at this point to strip out all the wool. An amazing amount of coat can be removed for such a small dog.

A show dog must be taught to be "tabled" and groomed from a very early age. It must be trained to stand still on the grooming table and to accept a noisy hair dryer. Its plush stand-off coat must be bathed and groomed the day before every show.

The Shiba should be fed on a high-fat diet and bathed and blown dry regularly, especially through its shedding period. The quicker the old dead coat is removed, the sooner the new coat will appear. If the dog is well fed and regularly groomed, the coat will "rotate," in that a new coat will grow as soon as the old coat is shed.

The Shiba needs plenty of mental stimulation; lock it up all day and it will become bored, noisy and try to escape. Some Shibas can use a mesh pen like a ladder and be away in seconds. Training should begin at an early age. As it is a spitz breed, obedience does not come easy, but with patience it can become quite biddable. Shibas still retain the acute hunting instinct of a primitive breed. They are aware of their surroundings and never miss an opportunity for a "bid for freedom." The breed is extremely fast and agile and could be miles away before its owner has blinked. Consequently, teaching a Shiba to "come" is vitally important. Similarly, an extending lead is an absolute must.

ADAPTABILITY

The Shiba is very catlike in its habits, being extremely clean, very affectionate and good with children. It likes nothing better than being a much-stroked lap dog.

A crate is invaluable for traveling in a car, staying in hotels and so on, especially if your particular Shiba is an escape artist. It needs a secure garden or yard where it can race around and chase its toys, and do not be surprised if it proudly trots up to you with a bird in its mouth. It is quite capable of catching a bird on the wing — it is a hunter after all!

ESSENTIALS OF THE BREED

The Shiba is a very sturdy, compact and robust dog with proportions of 9 inches/23 cm high to 10 inches/25 cm long in males and females being 1 inch/2.5 cm longer in body. Males should stand about 15 1/2 inches/39.5 cm and females 14 inches/36.5 cm. There should be a very clear distinction between dogs and bitches, with sexual differentials quite obvious.

A typical Oriental spitz, the Shiba is strong bodied, muscular and powerful. When picked up, it should feel "all dog." Its neck should be strong and broad, leading into quite high withers and a level topline.

The front should be straight with a good forechest, the depth of brisket representing at least 45 percent of the height. The loins are broad and strong with slight tuck-up, the hindquarters just moderately angulated and well muscled. The tail is strong rooted and curled. When standing, the Shiba should have plenty of rear behind the tail.

The head carries the essence of the breed. The ears are small, well padded and leaning slightly forward. The eyes are deep set and slanting upward, dark with well-pigmented tight rims, all helping to create an Oriental yet foxy expression. The forehead should be flat with a slight groove leading into a minimally sloping stop. The full cheeks of the Shiba give it a "moon head," framed under the chin with cream or white "ghosting" that should not extend over the nose or above the eyes. Overmarking will give a "clown" effect that is deemed incorrect.

The Shiba's colors are red, red sesame and Aka Goma (red with a black overlay), and black-and-tan (which is technically a tricolor). White, cream and Kuro Goma (red with a predominance of black) are colors which are not considered correct in Japan and yet are accepted in many other countries.

The coat is double with a soft, dense undercoat of gray or red, with a hard and straight topcoat, longest on the breeching and tail. However, the coat length should never be such that it has a "plumed" effect. A long-coated Shiba shuld not be used for breeding because a true coat is one of the breed's main attributes.

Registry: AKC, FCI (Group 5), KC

SHIKOKU/KOHCHI KEN

The Japanese spitz breed Shikoku is mainly a hunting dog. It originates from the island of Shikoku and is considered one of the most ancient of the Japanese spitz breeds. It is said to be a tough, self-confident hunter and a guard dog that is wary of strangers. It is rarely seen outside Japan.

The height at the withers should be about 17-21 inches/43-53 cm. Japan has six native spitz breeds and the main difference between them is their size. The common features that they share are a wedge-shaped head with pronounced cheeks, decidedly slanted eyes and hooded ears. The coat should be short and harsh, standing out from the body and slightly longer on the neck, buttocks and tail. The colors most frequently seen are red or brindle.

Registry: FCI (Group 5)

Shikoku

SHIH TZU

ORIGIN AND DEVELOPMENT

Although only recognized by the American Kennel Club in 1969, the Shih Tzu — a name meaning "lion" — has existed since as long ago as A.D. 624. Some theorize that the breed stems from a cross between the Tibetan Mountain Dog and the Pekingese. One theory suggests that the Chinese court received a pair of dogs from the King of Vigur during the Tang Dynasty. Yet another theory proposes that they were introduced to China from Tibet in the mid-seventeenth century. Whatever the story, it is known that the dogs chosen for court breeding were selected with great care, and it was from this foundation that the dog now known as the Shih Tzu developed. These early dogs were small, intelligent and extremely docile. Those most favored by the Emperor were portrayed in various Chinese paintings.

The first Standard for the breed was developed in 1938, four years after the Peking Kennel Club was formed. Madame de Breuil, a Russian refugee, was instrumental in the development of this first Standard. English interest in the breed stemmed from the arrival of two pairs: one owned by Madelaine Hutchins and the other by General and Mrs. Douglas Brownrigg. These dogs were brought to England in 1930 (when they also arrived in Norway) and, during the early years, the breed was classified as "Apsos." A ruling by the Kennel Club changed that, however, and the Shih Tzu Club of England was established in 1935. Soon after this, interest in the breed developed in Scandinavia, Austria and several other European countries. But it was not until after World War II, when members of the military stationed in England returned home, that the breed was introduced to the United States.

Many importations followed — from both England and the Scandinavian countries — as interest in the breed flourished. The Shih Tzu was granted recognition by the American Kennel Club in March 1969. The breed has been in the regular show classification in the Toy Group at American Kennel Club shows since September 1, 1969.

TEMPERAMENT

In the show ring the Shih Tzu appears proud and arrogant but its personality is actually most playful and, despite the breed's robustness, in many ways it is as gentle as a cat. The breed is well able to withstand the rough treatment to which many children might subject it. Shih Tzus also serve as loyal and gentle house pets for older people. The breed really does have a gentle yet upbeat attitude that should suit most people.

HEALTH MATTERS

The breed is known to suffer from a kidney disorder (familial nephropathy), which is also found in Tibetan Spaniels, Lhasa Apsos, Tibetan Terriers and English Cocker Spaniels. This is a fatal disease and the way in which it is inherited is the subject of investigation by several American universities. In other respects, the breed should not have major health problems.

SPECIAL CARE AND TRAINING

In the traditional coat called for by the breed Standard, considerable daily care is required. Some management of the topknot is also necessary to keep the hair out of the dog's face and eyes. However, many breeders keep pets and older breeding animals in a short terrier-like trim and, if coat care is going to be time-consuming, these trims offer an attractive alternative. Shih Tzus should be given basic training as soon as puppies are brought into the home.

ADAPTABILITY

The Shih Tzu was bred to be a pet and nothing else. Its size, shape, temperament, the fact that

Shih Tzu

it eats well and is a strong sturdy dog with a friendly disposition all stand it in good stead in this respect. This breed will adapt to any family situation but it is definitely an indoor dog that should not be left outside in kennels.

ESSENTIALS OF THE BREED

Shih Tzus are among the least delicate members in the AKC's Toy Group. (They are in the KC's Utility Group.) They are intended to be a big-ribbed breed with a broad head and, in general, are substantial from stem to stern. The ideal Shih Tzu is neither high-stationed nor dumpy and should be 9-10 1/2 inches/23-26 cm. In the United States it should never be less than 8 inches/20 cm or over 11 inches/28 cm. It is slightly longer from the withers to the tail than its height at the withers. Its high head carriage and level topline, flat croup and high set tail — carried well over but not flat on the back — makes the overall picture that of a proud, aloof dog. When moving, its smooth, effortless gait, with both reach and drive, makes an exciting picture.

The dense, flowing double coat — almost without any curl — contributes to the overall appearance. A modest amount of trimming is permitted for neatness and to tidy the pads of the feet, but dogs in top condition have coats that sweep the ground.

The Shih Tzu's head is one of its most appealing attributes — broad with dark round eyes that do not protrude. The stop is very definite with no more than 1 inch/2.5 cm permitted from the tip of the nose to the stop. Wrinkles are also not called for. The bite may be undershot and should be wide. Misaligned or missing teeth are not a major concern.

Shih Tzus should be well angulated both in front and in the rear, and the angulation should match or balance. The hocks should be parallel and rear pads should be evident when the dog is moving. All coat colors are permitted. In the show ring, the topknot hair is generally set in a rubber band to control the hair about the face, and to add to the overall expression and attractiveness of the breed.

Registry: AKC, CKC, FCI (Group 9), KC

SIBERIAN HUSKY

ORIGIN AND DEVELOPMENT

A true Northern breed, the Siberian Husky was nurtured and developed by the Chukchi tribe of northeastern Asia about 3,000 years ago. These semi-nomadic people developed the Siberian to pull lightly loaded sleds for many miles.

The tribe became famous for its ability to breed very good dogs that were well suited to the needs of its people. Although nomads, the Chukchis lived inland and hunted along the coast. The Siberian was used to pull their felled game home, sometimes over incredible distances. The Chukchis maintained purity of their sled dogs through the nineteenth century and these dogs are the direct ancestors of the breed known today as the Siberian Husky.

In the early 1900s, when Americans in Alaska heard of the super sled dogs in Siberia they began to import this famous breed. A race to supply Nome in Alaska with a diphtheria anti-toxin was won by a Siberian Husky team and this focused attention on the delightful breed. Similarly, the Byrd Antarctic expeditions were made possible because of the use of the Siberian Husky. The American Kennel Club recognized the breed in 1930.

TEMPERAMENT

The Siberian Husky is friendly, eager and mischievous. Thanks to the Chukchi people who bred the Siberian wisely and well, it is ideal as a house dog. The women and children of the Chukchi tribe were responsible for tending to the dogs and raising the puppies. As such, the breed is well known for its sweet temperament. The breed as a whole is suited for family living. Males are not aggressive but they are inclined to roam, so proper attention must be paid to their housing and exercise must be supervised. The breed is very people oriented and therefore does not make a good guard dog.

Siberian Husky

HEALTH MATTERS

A natural breed, the Siberian is usually quite healthy. Hips should be X-rayed for hip dysplasia on breeding animals. They are subject to some heritable eye problems. As with all dog purchases, only buy from a reputable breeder.

SPECIAL CARE AND TRAINING

The Siberian is basically a working dog and it thrives on pulling a sled or a light wheeled vehicle. Exercise is a must, for if it has nothing to do it will become bored and destructive. Its coat is unusual, a double coat that is soft and plush. It will shed in warm weather. Brushing weekly is a necessity. It may also be given a bath as needed but in fact its coat and skin are virtually free of odor. Weekly attention to cleaning teeth and trimming nails is essential.

ADAPTABILITY

The Siberian is a moderate sized dog and though it is a worker and happiest in the country, it will adapt to city living if given plenty of attention. It makes an amusing pet for the entire family.

ESSENTIALS OF THE BREED

Males should be 21-23 1/2 inches/53-59.5 cm tall; females 20-22 inches/51-56 cm and slightly longer than tall. They have a wedge-shaped head and a good stop. The eyes are almond shaped and have a quizzical, mischievous glint. They may be dark or blue, or one of each color. The ears should be small and erect. The breed may be all colors and hues including white and pied with striking head markings.

There should be moderate angulation of fore and hindquarters, with a long tail carried trailing like a fox's or carried over the back, but not snapped flat on the back or curled. The coat is double and plush. The Siberian's trot is sound and ground covering and the dog should not carry excess weight.

Registry: AKC, CKC, FCI (Group 5), KC

SILKY TERRIER/ AUSTRALIAN SILKY TERRIER

ORIGIN AND DEVELOPMENT

The origins of the Australian Silky Terrier are clouded in obscurity, with few actual records in existence of any concentrated effort to establish the breed. Whether the earliest breeders were attempting actually to develop a new breed, or whether the Silky Terrier was simply a chance by-product, it seems clear that the breed evolved mainly from crossing the Australian Terrier with the Yorkshire Terrier, with perhaps a sprinkling of other Scottish Terrier-types.

Although most of the Australian dog breeds are derived primarily from the bush country, it appears that the Silky Terrier was developed principally as an urban pet and a house com-panion. The breed, however, is a good ratter, and is adept at killing snakes which are numer-ous in Australia.

Shortly before 1929 efforts were made to establish a correct weight classification for the three related breeds (Australian, Yorkshire and Silky) and revised Standards were published in 1926. In 1932 canine legislation was introduced to prohibit further cross-breeding and to protect the three individual breeds.

Silkies have been known by a variety of names including Australian Terrier (Soft Coat) and Sydney Silky. In 1955 they became known as Australian Silky Terriers, and in 1958 the breed Standard was set by the Australian National Kennel Council. The ideal Silky Terrier combines the glamour and size of a Toy dog

The Silky Terrier is called the Australian Silky Terrier in the United Kingdom.

with the character and spirited action of a terrier. It should appear to have a refined and elegant outline, and is a compact and moderately low set, alert dog with a level topline and strong sound movement. The Silky Terrier's crowning glory is its straight, soft, well-groomed silky hair.

The head must be strong and of Terrier character, set on a somewhat long, fine and elegantly arched neck which fits gracefully into sloping shoulders. The muzzle should not be as heavy as the Australian Terrier's where the skull and muzzle are of equal length, nor should it be as short as that of the Yorkshire Terrier. The Silky should stand around 9 inches/ 23 cm at the withers and weigh 8-10 pounds/ 3.5-4.5 kg.

The Silky Terrier's coat must be straight, of silky texture, glossy and gleaming, and should hang flat to the sides of the body; there is no undercoat. Its color ranges from a gray-blue to a deep rich blue, with rich tan points and a silver-blue or fawn topknot. Puppies are born black-and-tan and between the ages of two and twelve months change color; the black

fades into blue or gray-blue but the tan remains. The earlier the change, the lighter the mature coat color.

The care of a Silky is very straightforward; it requires regular bathing and brushing to give its coat the desired silky look. The only trimming necessary is of any long or untidy hair on the feet, ears, tail and muzzle.

The Silky is a real one-family dog, a keen watchdog, very obedient and a very adept pupil. It is wary of strangers until they are approved by a member of its family, after which it will immediately accept them. It is not a fighter, so many of the breed may be permitted to run together but, should it have to defend itself, it can become a bundle of fur and acquit itself creditably.

As a house dog it is very easily trained and scrupulously clean. Its loyalty, coupled with a great sense of humor, affection and gentleness make it an asset to any home and very competitive in both conformation and Obedience rings.

Registry: AKC, CKC, FCI (Group 3), KC

SKYE TERRIER

ORIGIN AND DEVELOPMENT

In the first book written on dogs, *De Canibus Brittannicis* (1570), Dr. Johannes Caius describes the early Skye as "brought out of barbarous borders fro' the uttermost countryes northward...which, by reason of the length of heare, makes showe neither of face nor of body." The breed is named after its ancient homeland, the Isle of Skye, which lies off the coast of Scotland. This land is rugged and threatening and required a dog which was equal to the environs.

Known variously as the Clydesdale Terrier,

Skye Terriers

the Paisley Terrier, the Fancy Skye Terrier, the Glasgow Terrier and the Silky Skye Terrier, the breed has moved from humble beginnings into the heart of style and fashion. Its elegant demeanor and proud carriage early on made it a favorite of aristocrats.

None less than Queen Victoria herself was a devotee of the Skye which she bred and which were maintained in the royal kennels. Some have been immortalized in the paintings of Sir Edwin Landseer but the most famous is Rona II, the Skye featured in the William Nicholson portrait, *Queen Victoria and Skye Terrier*.

The first stud book of the Kennel Club includes Skyes and they competed at the first dog show ever held, the Birmingham Dog Show of 1860. In the United States, the first of the breed to be registered was a bitch named Romach that was whelped in 1884.

TEMPERAMENT

The breed is agile yet strong, loving of its family and select friends but wary and stand-offish with strangers. The Skye Terrier always remembers a friend and *never* forgets an enemy.

HEALTH MATTERS

The Skye is generally healthy and appears to have no hereditary problems. The breed matures very slowly and young dogs do not have big robust bodies until they are three or four years old. The Skye often finds it difficult to see because its hair falls over its eyes, so many fanciers hold the hair back in a barrette or rubber band.

SPECIAL CARE AND TRAINING

Since the Skye's front legs are slightly bent to curve around the deep chest, the legs require some care. The young Skye Terrier should not be allowed to go up and down stairs or to jump off furniture or any high place, as this could put strain on the immature bones of the front legs. It is sensible to hold back the long hair from the eyes with a rubber band and to

brush the coat carefully each day. It is best to start training the Skye in basic obedience while it is still young.

ADAPTABILITY

The Skye will happily settle in any surroundings provided that it has human companionship and should not be isolated in a kennel. Similarly, Skye Terrier puppies cannot be raised successfully in a kennel situation and they must be handled from birth. Special attention should be paid to the forty-ninth day of life when it is thought that the human-dog bond is formed. Each puppy should spend time with a human away from its siblings if it is to develop into a mature dog that loves company.

ESSENTIALS OF THE BREED

The words "long, low, lank and level" describe the essence of the breed. With a shoulder height of 10 inches/25 cm and a body length twice that, plus a tail which is correctly carried as an extension of its topline, the desired signature proportions of this unique breed are maintained.

The Skye's ears may be held pricked or dropped — both are equally acceptable. The prick ear is erect, not large, high on the head and slightly wider at the peak than at the skull. In the drop ear the leather is larger, lies flat against the skull, and is capable of only slight forward movement when attracted, not unlike a proper Beagle ear.

Covered from head to toe with a heavy, weather-resistant, protective coat, the Skye Terrier's ancestors hunted among the crags and cairns of their homeland. The proper coat is made up of long heavy outer hairs and a soft, blanket of undercoat. The breed's allowable colors range from black through gray and silver to cream. Black points on the ears, muzzle and tip of the tail are correct and, while shading of the same color is the norm, no patterning is allowed.

Registry: AKC, CKC, FCI (Group 3), KC

SLOUGHI

The Sloughi is closely related to the Saluki and Azawakh and is like a type of hound that existed thousands of years ago. The Sloughi ("*slughi*" in Arabic means "fast as the wind") was once known all over Middle Asia but is now regarded as a North African breed. Morocco is its country of origin. The Bedouins use the hound for hunting.

Since the 1950s, the Sloughi has established itself as a show and companion dog outside Africa, particularly in France and Germany. It is still a rare breed that is wary of strangers and considered a one-man dog.

The height at the withers is about 24-28 inches/61-72 cm. Its appearance should be very elegant with a short back, a decidedly sloping croup and long legs. Its muscles and tendons should be visible under the very thin, tightly attached skin. The head should be long with a slightly rounded skull that is fairly broad. The ears should be high set, broad at the base, hanging flat close to the cheeks and with rounded tips. The coat should be smooth and fine and any shade of sand, red or brindle.

Registry: FCI (Group 10), KC

Sloughi

SLOVAK CUVAC/SLOVENSKÝ CUVAC

The Slovakian herding dog is closely related to the Hungarian Kuvasz and Polish Owczarek

Slovak Cuvak

Podhalanski and it probably shares the same origin as the Italian Maremma Sheepdog. It is used as a guard and herding dog but in recent years has also gained interest as a companion dog, although it is still a very rare breed.

The height at withers should be about 23-27.5 inches/59-70 cm. Its body should be rectangular, well muscled and with strong bone. The head should be strong with a broad skull, strong, but with not too a long muzzle. The ears are high set and carried close to the cheeks. The tail should be long and well plumed. The coat on the body should be thick, about 2 3/4-6 inches/7-15 cm long and with slight waves and a woolly undercoat. The coat should be white and any pigmentation jet black.

Registry: FCI (Group 1)

SLOVENSKÝ HRUBOSRSTY STAVAC

This Slovakian gun dog has been known since the nineteenth century but it became almost extinct in the early part of this century. It has been revived with the help of German gun dog breeds, and particularly the German Shorthaired Pointer and the Weimaraner. It is strictly used as a working dog and is said to be an excellent tracking and retrieving breed. It is rarely seen outside Slovakia.

At its withers, it stands about 22-26 inches/ 57-68 cm. Its body should be almost rectangular, well muscled and with strong bone. The tail is docked to half its length. The coat should be hard and wiry, lying quite close and with no leg fringing, although it may have slight eyebrows and whiskers on its face. In color, it is similar to the Weimaraner being a silvery gray with a nougat tinge.

Registry: FCI (Group 7)

The Slovenský Hrubosrsty Stavac is a very rare gundog that is said to be an excellent tracker and retriever. It is rarely seen outside Slovakia.

SLOVENSKÝ KOPOV

In type, this Slovakian scenthound is very much like the old east European scenthounds and resembles the more strongly built Polish hound, the Ogar Polski. The breed is extremely common in former Czechoslovakia but is rarely seen outside this part of Europe. It is strictly used as a hunting dog and its prey is usually wild boar. This is a strong, hardy breed with a temperament to match.

The height at the withers should be about 15-20 inches/40-50 cm. The body should be rectangular, well muscled and with strong bone. The head should be strong with broad, rather high set, pendulous ears. The coat should be short, glossy, straight and lying close with a hard texture. This is a black-and-tan breed — the tan markings should be a deep rich color.

Registry: FCI (Group 6)

The Slovenský Kopov, used to hunt wild boar in the former Czechoslovakia, is rarely seen outside this part of Europe.

SMÅLANDSSTÖVARE

This Swedish scenthound is descended from a mixture of old East European hounds and local farm and hunting dogs. As the breed is often born with a bobtail, other breeds are also thought to have played a part in its ancestry. It is only used as a hunting dog and is considered an all-round dog that is equally effective with hare, fox, elk and forest birds. It is very rarely found outside Sweden.

The height at the withers should be within 16 1/2-21 inches/42-54 cm. The body should be almost square, well muscled and with good bone but must never look coarse or heavy. The coat should be short, straight, lie close and be quite a hard texture. The color should be black-and-tan, with the tan markings well defined, particularly the spots over the eyes.

Registry: FCI (Group 6)

Smålandsstövare

SOFT COATED WHEATEN TERRIER

ORIGIN AND DEVELOPMENT

In Ireland, their country of origin, terriers with soft coats have existed for centuries. However, there is nothing written as to the exact origin of the Wheaten. Many believe that it was an ancestor of the Kerry Blue Terrier, but this is supposition. The Wheaten evolved as a dog of moderation. It was used to guard the house, farm and its animals, hunt game, sometimes as a water retriever, and also simply as a companion. The earliest Wheatens, in their Irish setting, were tough, hardy dogs, for they lived in a time of the survival of the fittest.

The Soft Coated Wheaten Terrier was admitted to registration in the Irish Kennel Club, and was first exhibited at the Irish Kennel Club's Championship Show in March of 1937. In order to become a Champion in Ireland at that time, the Wheaten had to compete not only in the show ring, but also in field trials against rat, rabbit and badger. This has been discontinued. The English Kennel Club recognized the Wheaten in 1943. On November 24, 1946, seven pedigreed Wheaten pups arrived in the United States via the freighter *Norman J. Colman*. As far as anyone knows, these were the first to be imported to the United States. The breed

An American Soft Coated Wheaten Terrier

A Soft Coated Wheaten Terrier from the United Kingdom

attracted several breeders who took great interest in the new arrival; however it was not until October 3, 1973 that the Wheaten was accepted into the Terrier Group in the United States. So popular have they now become that there are close to 200 Wheatens entered and shown at the Montgomery County All Terrier Show held annually in October in Pennsylvania.

TEMPERAMENT

Normally non-aggressive, the Soft Coated Wheaten Terrier will get along with other pets in the household. Playful and good with children if raised with them correctly, it makes a good companion to any member of the family, regardless of age. It is a dependable, sensible watchdog.

HEALTH MATTERS

The breed is prone to some heritable health matters. These include progressive retinal atrophy, an eye disease, as well as colitis and an allergic skin problem. It is always best to purchase stock from a reputable breeder who screens for heritable disorders.

SPECIAL CARE AND TRAINING

The Soft Coated Wheaten has a long flowing coat that will need constant care. This comes down to careful brushing, at least twice weekly, as well as slight trimming to remove the fringe from its ears and to create a terrier outline. The feet should be kept trimmed around the edges, as should the long hair under the tail — using shears, not scissors or clippers. Its teeth require weekly brushing, and its ears should be checked for cleanliness. A small tip of the toenails should be taken off with nail nippers every ten days or so. The Wheaten should be bathed as necessary and dried carefully with a hair dryer while brushing.

ADAPTABILITY

Wheatens will settle down happily anywhere be it city or country. They need companionship, long walks on a lead, and a fenced, safe yard.

for free frolics. Obedience is always a good idea. Naturally, correct feeding is most important. Should the Wheaten be of a quality to be shown, discuss the correct show trimming with its breeder or with a professional show groomer.

ESSENTIALS OF THE BREED

As the name of the breed is the Soft Coated Wheaten Terrier, it goes without saying that the breed should have a soft flowing coat of a wheaten color! At birth the puppies are quite a dark apricot which lightens as they mature; at two years the mature Wheaten should be a clear golden wheaten color. The ears and muzzle may be shaded yet not solid black. There should be no other colors present in the mature coat, which is a single coat without an undercoat. Also, the coat should be flowing (not curled), cottony and slightly waved.

The breed is moderate in size: 17-19 inches/ 43-48 cm at the top of the shoulder. The ideal size for males is 18 1/2 inches/47 cm and 35-40 pounds/16-18 kg; for females it is 17 1/2 inches/ 45 cm and 30-35 pounds/13.5-16 kg. The head is rectangular in appearance with dark reddish brown or brown eyes, well hidden under the eyebrows. The nose is large and black, the teeth large and clean with a scissors or even bite. The ears are small to medium in size, folding level at the skull and drooping forward with the tip of the ear pointing toward the ground.

The Wheaten should have good neck and shoulders, compact well-knit body, and a tail that is docked, well set and carried up. Its legs are soundly made and carry the Wheaten in a happy and confident manner. The feet should be round and firm; dewclaws may appear on front legs but not on the rear. A carefully cared for Wheaten is an attractive dog in all respects.

Registry: AKC, CKC, FCI (Group 3), KC

SOUTH RUSSIAN OWTCHARKA/ JUZJNORUSSKAJA OVTJARKA

This herding dog from south Russia is mainly used to guard and herd flocks of sheep. It is self-confident, tough, hard and wary of strangers. The type resembles that of the Bearded Collie

South Russian Owtcharka

and the two breeds are likely to share the same origin.

The height at the withers should be over 26 inches/65 cm in males and 24 inches/62 cm in females. Usually both sexes are much taller and there is no upward limit. The body should be rectangular, well muscled and with strong bone. The head should be elongated with a broad skull. The ears are small and carried close to the cheeks. The tail is long, often with a kink at the tip. The coat should be abundant, long (about 6 inches/15 cm) and give a shaggy appearance. Its texture should be coarse. This breed is usually white or cream, pale lemon or shades of gray. White markings are allowed but not required. All the pigmentation should be black.

Registry: FCI (Group 1)

ORIGIN AND DEVELOPMENT

Despite its name, the ever-popular American Cocker Spaniel is in fact originally a breed of Spanish blood. The Spanish Spaniel is considered to be the oldest of the recognized land spaniels. From these beginnings the spaniel found its way to England where it was developed into a hardy worker that followed closely under the gun to flush game birds, primarily woodcock, grouse and pheasant. The spaniel would retrieve the bird to hand and move on to the next find.

The Cocker's name came from the use of these dogs to hunt woodcock. In 1892 the Cocker Spaniel was recognized as a breed in England. Before this, Cockers and Springers were from the same litter — only size at maturity separated the breeds. In fact, in the early days of breeding Cockers in England, crosses were made to English Setters to lengthen the neck and make a more streamlined modern animal. From these crosses came the parti-colored and roan patterns found in so many of the early specimens.

The English Cocker and the American Cocker share the same backgrounds. When the Cocker Spaniel was brought to the United States in the late 1870s the breed was developed along quite different lines from the English Cocker. The two breeds were shown in conformation classes in the United States as separate varieties until 1946. As only one Cocker Spaniel was permitted to compete in the Sporting Group, the one that was judged Best American Cocker was judged against the Best English Cocker. The winner was then eligible to compete in the Group. In 1946 the two varieties of Cocker became two separate Cocker breeds — the American Cocker Spaniel and the English Cocker Spaniel. Interbreeding was no longer allowed and the two breeds competed against each other in the Sporting Group.

After the separation, because of the huge numbers of entries at the shows and because the black Cocker was unbeatable by any other color, breeders of the American Cocker applied for and were granted permission to have the breed represented in the Sporting Group in three different colors: the Black American Cocker (which includes black with tan points), the Parti-colored American Cocker, and the ASCOB (Any Solid Color Other than Black to include those with tan points). In its heyday there were huge numbers of Cockers exhibited. Ch. My Own Brucie, a black dog owned and handled by Herman Mellenthin, was Best In Show at the Westminster Kennel Club's Show in 1940 and again in 1941 — an unprecedented feat in Cockers.

TEMPERAMENT

The merry Cocker is how it was known and merry it is. Cockers became the darlings of the show world and charmed themselves into many households in the United States and throughout the world. They became America's most popular dog; however, the breed's popularity nearly became its undoing.

The Cocker was promoted and bred indiscriminately, with little attention paid to the very thing that had made it such a hit: its temperament. Additionally, at the time there was no knowledge of heritable problems. Fortunately, intelligent breeders with the foresight and diligence to apply themselves to the problems at hand took control of the situation.

Today there is a concerted effort to breed only animals cleared of heritable defects and to concentrate on the basic strengths of the breed. Its temperament is not only heritable but is secured by raising puppies carefully and socializing them early. There is now a preponderance of the merry Cocker temperament in the show ring and at home — but it was very nearly lost.

A pale buff American Cocker Spaniel

HEALTH MATTERS

So long as it is carefully bred, the Cocker is quite hardy. Health problems are apparent in various inherited disorders. These may be eye problems of several kinds, hip dysplasia, slipping stifles and epilepsy, as well as ear problems. The American Cocker Spaniel's main heritable problems have been addressed by serious breeders who constantly screen all of their breeding stock.

Skin and ear problems can be coped with if the American Cocker Spaniel is kept scrupulously clean and trimmed and, of course, brushed and combed thoroughly several times a week. Its nails should be kept trimmed, either filed or cut weekly. If the ears are kept trimmed at the top, checked weekly and cleaned when necessary with a little baby oil on a piece of cotton wrapped around your finger, most kinds of potential ear problems will be checked before they start. At the first sign of any odor from inside the ear, get a vet's advice.

The American Cocker Spaniel is hardy in all types of weather but may be susceptible to tonsillitis. Drying the Cocker very carefully, even with a hair dryer, should the dog become soaked in the rain, may save a trip to the vet. Always buy from a reputable breeder and then keep your Cocker in a clean, comfortable condition.

SPECIAL CARE AND TRAINING

It is important with this breed that training begins when the Cocker is only a pup. The young American Cocker Spaniel should be taught to allow an examination of its teeth to be sure the teeth are shedding properly. This early weekly training will prepare the pup for the brushing of its teeth to keep them clean and to avoid mouth odors as the dog gets older. The Cocker always has a heavy coat. It should learn very early to lie quietly on a table to be groomed with a brush and a comb. Grooming is best left to an older child or an adult, and it must be done regularly. Professional attention will be needed from a groomer even if the Cocker will not be shown since its coat growth is heavy and constant. It is important to housetrain this breed early and carefully.

Top quality food should be provided, particularly as the puppy is growing, but you should never let an American Cocker Spaniel get too fat. This breed quickly learns to beg from the table and its antics are irresistible, particularly to children. Children should be taught never to lift Cocker puppies by the back or front legs. Similarly, puppies should not be allowed to jump off furniture as this may damage the legs. Good walks on a lead or free running in an enclosed, safe yard is fitting exercise for this breed.

ADAPTABILITY

The American Cocker Spaniel is adaptable to most situations and lifestyles. It does need exercise, but is perfectly happy being walked in a city. This breed is good with children and should be raised with them. Children should be taught to be kind and gentle to the Cocker.

ESSENTIALS OF THE BREED

The American Cocker is the smallest member of the Sporting Group. The male must never be over 15 1/2 inches/39 cm in height and the female no more than 14 1/2 inches/37 cm. The breed is merry, active and able to do a day's work in the field if shorn of its very heavy coat. Bred primarily to retrieve woodcock or pheasant, these dogs can be used to hunt rabbit as well.

The head is the hallmark of the American Cocker Spaniel with its slightly rounded dome, well-pronounced stop and square lip. The American Cocker should have long, low-set ears and large, round, expressive dark eyes. A long neck, well laid-back shoulders, short, hard topline, good legs all the way around and a short docked, merry tail are required of this breed.

The American Cocker comes in colors of solid black or black with tan markings. The Parti-colored variety requires two or more colors with the base color being white. There are many color combinations with the white including black, red, chocolate with or without tan points, and also patterns of roaning in all the above colors. In the ASCOB variety the color buff may range from Setter red to a pale silver blonde. Liver, more correctly called chocolate, is provided for in this variety and this color may have tan points. Tan points may be dark or light in color. They are found in the following areas: a clear spot over each eye, on the sides of the muzzle, on the cheeks, on the underside of the ears, on all four feet and/or legs and under the tail. Markings on the chest are optional. The American Cocker looks smart and attractive if well groomed and cared for.

Registry: AKC, CKC, FCI (Group 8), KC

A black and white American Cocker Spaniel

ORIGIN AND DEVELOPMENT

There is very little in the record book to define the origins of the American Water Spaniel. It apparently descended from many different small spaniel types, probably including the Irish Water Spaniel, that were brought to the United States by immigrants and settlers. It was bred at first for the size, color and ability of a water retriever, but little or no attention was paid to stabilizing this water spaniel as a recognizable breed. It was used to retrieve ducks and geese that had been downed by hunters from both land and lakes. It was also used to retrieve rabbit.

Late in the nineteenth century, Dr. F.J. Pheifer took the breed in hand, created a written Standard and applied for recognition by the American Kennel Club. The American Water Spaniel was admitted to the registry in 1940. It is thought to be an ancestor of the Boykin Spaniel.

Primarily a hunting dog, the American Water Spaniel makes an ideal family pet and interacts well with the entire family, including children. It definitely thinks of itself as a water dog and is known for its barking. The breed willingly adapts to any circumstance, but should have good human companionship and exercise on a regular basis.

The American Water Spaniel must have something to do because it is in its heritage. Hunting comes naturally to this breed and it makes an ideal dog for Obedience work. The dog seems free of most common health problems but its skin and coat should be kept clean and well brushed.

A medium-sized working male Water Spaniel weighs 30-45 pounds/13-20 kg and a bitch weighs 25-40 pounds/11-18 kg. Both sexes are 15-18 inches/38-45 cm at the withers. The breed is always dark brown with a closely curled or marcelled coat, with short hair on the face and the end of the tail. The head is broad in the skull with a muzzle that is long enough for the dog to carry a bird as large as a Canada goose. It has hazel eyes and typical spaniel ears. The American Water Spaniel is very muscular, and sturdy in build, with sound legs and an honest disposition.

Registry: AKC, CKC, FCI (Group 8)

American Water Spaniel

SPANIELS — BOYKIN SPANIEL

This is a small liver or brown spaniel that has a great following among the bird hunters in the southern United States. The original Boykin was a stray with wonderful bird sense and was owned by Whit Boykin. The breed has evolved from this one dog, with crosses to American Water Spaniels, Springers and Chesapeake Bay Retrievers. It is used as a hardy retriever of upland birds as well as water fowl. The Boykin is an intelligent and loyal companion.

This breed is small, weighing 25-40 pounds/ 11-18 kg, with a dark brown or liver colored coat, docked tail and spaniel-type head. The coat is usually flat to slightly curly but a smooth coat is also acceptable.

Registry: The breed is not recognized by the AKC, CKC, FCI or KC.

Boykin Spaniel

SPANIELS — CLUMBER SPANIEL

ORIGIN AND DEVELOPMENT

Named for the Clumber Estate of the Duke of Newcastle, the Clumber Spaniel is believed to have originated when the Duc de Noailles moved his kennel to England for sanctuary during the French Revolution. This explains the differences between the Clumber and other English spaniels and its connection with the Alpine Spaniel. A 1788 painting by Francis Wheatley R.A. called *The Return from Shooting* shows the 2nd Duke of Newcastle with three Clumbers that look remarkably like today's dog.

The Clumber soon became known as the retired gentleman's shooting dog, due in part to its popularity with the retired military and civil servants. Slow paced and easily handled, the Clumber worked well in small areas where abundant game made speed unnecessary and thoroughness a plus. The breed became even more fashionable with the Sandringham Kennels of Edward VII and the continued use of Sussex Spaniels by his son George V.

First shown in England in 1859, the Clumber Spaniel arrived on the North American continent in Nova Scotia in 1844. By 1878 the first Clumber was registered in the United States in one of the stud books that became the basis of the American Kennel Club in 1884.

TEMPERAMENT

The Clumber is a gun dog first and foremost. Inclined to be lazy if left to its own devices, it will always join in a walk or go hunting. It is steady and reliable, kind and dignified, although perhaps a little more aloof than other spaniels. It is a great-hearted dog, stoical, highly intelligent and with a determined attitude to life. The Clumber is an excellent house pet if a little cumbersome at close quarters.

HEALTH MATTERS

Areas of concern in the health of the Clumber Spaniel include hip dysplasia, although it is usually still very functional, and disk disease. Entropion has also caused concern but there has been some improvement recently.

SPECIAL CARE AND TRAINING

As the Clumber has a large body and is a heavy-boned spaniel, care should be taken so that it does not become obese. Puppies should be socialized, trained on a leash, housetrained and trained to come when called as early as possible. Mentally and physically, the Clumber grows and matures slowly.

ADAPTABILITY

The breed makes an ideal country companion. Friendly and affectionate and sometimes reserved, it is never timid or hostile with strangers. Its size means that it must have good space inside the house and a fairly large yard in which to exercise. The Clumber may be kept in the city although its white coat may be a drawback, because it will attract grime and require extra time spent on grooming.

ESSENTIALS OF THE BREED

The Clumber is a heavy, solid dog standing 19-20 inches/48-50 cm at the withers (bitches 17-19 inches/43-48 cm). In the United States, males should weigh between 70-80 pounds/32-36 kg (bitches 55-70 pounds/25-32 kg). A dog's weight in the United Kingdom should be 55-70 pounds/25-32 kg with bitches 45-60 pounds/20-27 kg.

The Clumber has a long, heavy body, a deep chest and well-sprung ribs. Massive but agile it looks aristocratic with a large intelligent head. Its heavy brow, marked stop, and the slight furrow up the center skull add to its dignified look. The dense, straight coat is soft and of good weather-resistant texture. Its white color with lemon or orange markings enable it to be seen easily by the hunter. The Clumber Spaniel moves easily, with good reach and drive and a tendency to roll slightly.

Registry: AKC, CKC, FCI (Group 8), KC

Clumber Spaniel

SPANIELS — ENGLISH COCKER SPANIEL/ COCKER SPANIEL

ORIGIN AND DEVELOPMENT

The present day English Cocker Spaniel was originally one of the smaller members of the working spaniel family that was often classified into breeds according to what use the breeder thought the pup might adapt to in the field. Little consideration was given to the pup's background or parentage and its size and substance were often the only determining factors in classifying it into a "breed." Literary references to sporting spaniels go back to the twelfth century, and the works of Chaucer and Shakespeare have many spaniel references.

However, it was not until the middle of the nineteenth century when dog shows began to gain popularity that more definition was brought to the spaniel family. Spaniels over 25 pounds (11 kg) were referred to as Field Spaniels, and those under this weight were classified as Cockers. Selective breeding from the end of the 19th century has produced the Cocker as it is known today. An important dog on both sides of the Atlantic was the dog Obo — the forerunner of both the English and American Cocker Spaniel. Although referred to at that time as a Field Spaniel, Obo and his progeny featured in more than half of the Cocker pedigrees for the next twenty years in Britain and the United States. His American influence came by the importation of the bitch, Chloe II, in whelp to Obo, one of the male progeny being named Obo II.

In Britain the Cocker Spaniel was classified as a separate breed by the Kennel Club in 1892 and the Cocker Spaniel Club was formed in 1902. In the United States the Cocker was divided by two types and resulted in the formation of the English Cocker Spaniel Club of America in 1936. Ten years later the American Kennel Club recognized the two types of Cocker — the English and American. Since the formation of the Cocker Spaniel Club there have been several noticeable changes in the appearance of the breed as a study of early photographs will reveal. Type and size are now more unified, with a squarer outline and a shorter back being developed. Coats are more abundant — often unfortunately taken to excess with some, blacks in particular. Quality and competition in the breed is intense because of its maintained popularity.

TEMPERAMENT

"The merry Cocker" is an epithet traditionally given to the breed, earned by the Cocker's reputation for its happy, outgoing nature, its ever-wagging tail and its devotion to its owner. It is always willing to please, inquisitive but biddable and its soulful expression is a real asset. However, the English Cocker retains its sporting instincts and many still enjoy work in the field. The English Cocker remains one of the most popular breeds because of its happy nature. Sadly, in recent years there have been cases of unprovoked viciousness in some red animals which has led to research into a condition known as "rage syndrome". These cases are in the minority: all responsible breeders would steer clear of using any dogs of suspicious temperament in their breeding program. The true temperament of the English Cocker is one of its greatest characteristics, valued by all, and must be preserved.

HEALTH MATTERS

The old myth that all spaniels suffer from ear canker is now, thankfully, well exploded. Regular grooming and cleaning of the ears with one of the many readily available preparations keeps ear canals clear, clean and healthy. The Cocker is a largely sound, healthy breed, though there are occasional cases of hereditary cataract, progressive retinal atrophy and familial nephropathy (shrunken kidneys), but these are relatively rare and all serious

English Cocker Spaniels or Cocker Spaniels, as they are known in the United Kingdom

breeders research pedigrees thoroughly to avoid using suspect bloodlines.

SPECIAL CARE AND TRAINING

The English Cocker is a sporting breed; it is active and energetic. It needs and enjoys exercise. Like most dogs, the English Cocker thrives on human company. It should not be left for long periods of solitary confinement as its inquisitive and energetic nature could lead to destructiveness. It is also biddable and easily trained. The English Cocker does grow abundant feathering and needs regular careful grooming; this should become a regular feature in its life and should be enjoyed by both dog and owner. A periodic visit to a grooming parlor is recommended to keep it in trim. Show dogs need more specialized trimming to suit the demands and expectations of the show ring.

ESSENTIALS OF THE BREED

The English Cocker Spaniel should be an unexaggerated, squarely built and balanced dog, males standing no higher than 16 inches/ 40.5 cm and bitches with an upper height limit of 15 inches/38 cm. The American Standard allows for 17 inches/43 cm for dogs and 16 inches/40.5 cm for bitches as upper limits. The beautiful head of the Cocker is a prime characteristic, with its balanced skull and foreface, its square muzzle, its cleanly chiseled skull, low-set ears and full, medium-size dark eyes all contributing to the overall effect. The back should be short, with the body having a good spring of rib. The legs should be well boned and the feet round, thick and catlike. The hindquarters should be well rounded, the stifles well bent and the hocks low to ground.

The tailset is important and one of the major variations with the American Cocker. The English Cocker's tailset is slightly below the level of the back and the rump is rounded. The tail should be carried below, or on a level with, the back. The Cocker should have a strong, driving, reaching gait with incessant tail action. It is essentially an unexaggerated animal and comes in a variety of colors, both solid and parti-color. Unfortunately there has been a tendency to seek exaggeration as a way of giving the English Cocker more show-ring impact with the accent on more neck, more coat, more streamlining — this "modernization" of the breed moves away from true breed type and should be avoided.

Registry: AKC, CKC, FCI (Group 8), KC

SPANIELS — ENGLISH SPRINGER SPANIEL

ORIGIN AND DEVELOPMENT

The English Springer Spaniel was first granted a separate place in the Kennel Club Stud Book in 1902, separating it from its Welsh counterpart. Yet long before this time the breed had been evolving from the larger sporting spaniel family. For a long time the breed was popularly known as the Norfolk Spaniel after one of the Dukes of Norfolk in the nineteenth century who kept the strain. They were liver-and-white, long headed and with ever-working tails when in pursuit of game. They gained their "springer" title because of their usefulness in "springing" game for the gun, the net, the hawk or the hound. The breed was most popular with sportsmen because of its versatility in the field — being adept at hunting, retrieving and going to water. It was the highest on the leg of all the land spaniels and some Springer blood was used to prevent the over-long, over-low tendencies in the Field Spaniel.

While liver-and-white remains the most popular color, often with tan markings, the black-and-white has also gained ground. The breed in its native England remains an unexaggerated working spaniel, the show dogs often also achieving honors in field trials. The working fraternity do, however, favor a much lighter type than that found on the show bench. The breed in America has, it must be said, diverged markedly from its English counterpart, so much so that in 1993 the English Springer Spaniel Club voiced its desire for separation from its American counterpart, feeling that it was now, to all effects, a different breed in the same way that the American Cocker had separated from the English Cocker.

The debate continues, but the reasons for the English club's wishes are there for all to see. The American type has evolved with shorter backs, sloping toplines, higher tailsets and a tail often carried above the level of the back — anathema to the English purist. Head type, eye and expression also differ and the American variety has greater rear angulation and a more flamboyant style of moving. Its coat is longer, with more feathering on both leg and body, and very little ticking in the white. It has been developed into a glamorous, stylized show dog in the short-back, long-neck mold so popular in the show ring in the United States. This type has achieved much show ring success and exports have gone to many European countries where they compete with the English type, often causing a great dilemma for judges of the breed.

English Springer Spaniel on its native shore

TEMPERAMENT

Biddable, intelligent, faithful and devoted and yet active, energetic and always willing for work and exercise, the English Springer makes an excellent family companion as well as a working dog. Its temperament can be seen in its expression, a hallmark of the breed, and was described very aptly by an interested show visitor who, looking at a Springer bitch on her bench, remarked "Look at that ... she looks at you like a Christian." It is a little disconcerting to hear that some American lines are experiencing aggression in Springers, a totally unacceptable trait in any gun dog.

HEALTH MATTERS

Being an unexaggerated breed, the English Springer is usually sound and healthy. In fact, it should be one of the hardiest of breeds, with few serious commonly occurring ailments. The odd case of eye abnormality has been recorded but generally problems are rare. Some breeders in the United States have been concerned that untypical vicious temperaments are increasingly emerging in the breed. This fault should be viewed with great seriousness as it is totally alien in any spaniel.

SPECIAL CARE AND TRAINING

While the English Springer makes a devoted family pet, it should not be forgotten that it is a sporting dog that needs and enjoys exercise. It can be headstrong but is intelligent and learns easily. It is active, energetic and needs outlets for this. Its coat requires regular grooming and the occasional trim of ears and feet.

ADAPTABILITY

The breed is happy in any situation but it must have human company and the freedom to take regular exercise running off a lead. It was bred to be a working gun dog, kept active for much of the day, and because it needs to exercise its mind and body it does not make a good "couch potato." An outdoor environment is ideal for this breed. It will not take kindly to a restricted existence in an apartment or town house, unless it can be guaranteed plenty of exercise and company.

ESSENTIALS OF THE BREED

With a good length of leg, the English Springer stands at around 20 inches/51 cm high. Its conformation is conventional, functional and free from exaggeration, well angulated at both ends, with medium length of back, good ribs and depth of body. The head stamps breed type with balanced skull and foreface, fluting between the eyes and toward the back of the skull, the soft expression from its dark eyes and low-set ears all contributing to the overall picture.

It comes in a variety of colors, liver-and-white being the most popular. Its movement is a forward swing straight from the shoulder, coupled with strong driving action from the hocks. Its tail should not rise above the level of his back. Springer type is very much confirmed by head quality and unexaggerated, functional conformation. Only time will reveal whether there is to be a transatlantic split into two separate breeds.

Recognition: AKC, CKC, FCI (Group 8), KC

SPANIELS — FIELD SPANIEL

ORIGIN AND DEVELOPMENT

William Arkwright writes in an introduction to H.W. Carlton's *Spaniels* that "the spaniel is the most generally useful to the sportsman — being able to understudy, in an emergency, all the other members of the family, be they pointers, setters or retrievers, while none of these can fully return the complement." This certainly applies to the Field Spaniel, one of the oldest of land spaniels and the epitome of the basic spaniel.

Few breeds can boast such an interesting and dramatic history as the Field Spaniel. At one stage all the sporting spaniel family were loosely classified as Field Spaniels — this meant spaniels which were useful for work in the field. After 1892 the family was divided by a 25 pound/11 kg demarcation, with the bigger dogs being known as Field Spaniels, the smaller ones Small Fields — later Cockers. The large Field Spaniel used Cocker, Sussex and English Water Spaniel blood as its roots and was black. Of course from the mixed roots, colored spaniels cropped up but these were discarded.

The repeated use of Sussex Spaniel blood brought to the breed in the late nineteenth century a new shape of length and lowness which for a time found popularity in the show ring. However, there was a swing against this with a reversion to a higher-on-leg type, and an infusion of Irish Water Spaniel blood. Dr. Spurgin, a successful breeder of solid-colored Fields campaigned to popularize the colored Field with the use of his liver roan and tan dog, Alonzo. There was thought to be some use of the Basset Hound in the colored Field, but colored specimens have achieved recognition, acceptance and success — although numerically far fewer than the livers and blacks. By the turn of the century the Field had been bred to a grotesque exaggeration of its former self — overweight, over long and lacking sufficient length of leg to allow any semblance of being useful in the field.

The breed went into a dramatic decline in the 1930s and during World War II, and after a short revival in the 1950s was almost lost at the end of that decade, so much so that all modern Field Spaniels are directly descended from four dogs — the litter brothers Ronayne Regal and Gormac Teal, and two bitches, Colombina of Teffont and Elmbury Morwena of Rhiwlas. A great contribution to the preservation of the breed was made by Mrs. A. M. Jones M.B.E. and her Mittina Kennel, her son Mr. Roger Hall Jones (Elmbury) and Mrs. Peggy Grayson (Westacres). These and a handful of other stalwart Field supporters have brought the Field to its present day numbers and relative popularity, with over one hundred dogs entered at the Cruft's show in 1995.

Field Spaniel

TEMPERAMENT

The Field Spaniel is a medium sized hunter-companion, and combines independence and intelligence with a great affinity for human companionship. It is a devoted family member, although sometimes reserved with strangers. It is an excellent bird dog, easily trained, and a tireless worker with great perseverance and an excellent nose.

The breed Standard mentions "unusual docility" but it should be remembered that the breed is a sporting spaniel which is active, enjoys exercise and it will get bored if left alone for too long. The Field is energetic and affectionate and needs outlets for both of these qualities.

HEALTH MATTERS

The Field Spaniel is a generally sound animal. Like all spaniels its ears need regular cleaning, but it is generally free from hereditary problems which is remarkable considering the frequent in-breeding which was practiced to preserve the breed. Most good breeders check for hip dysplasia and eye problems. Some instances of thyroid problems do crop up.

SPECIAL CARE AND TRAINING

The usual care of coat, with regular grooming, is required. Regular cleaning of the ears will keep them healthy. The Field is intelligent and biddable and retains its working qualities to enjoy activity in the field. Despite its docility and sweetness of expression, the Field is very athletic and energetic. Many Field Spaniel owners are keen to preserve the breed's working abilities and a number of dogs have been successfully trained to work to the gun.

ADAPTABILITY

The Field Spaniel needs plenty of outdoor exercise and enjoys nothing more than gamboling in fields — it will not be deterred by rain or mud. Given that it needs an active and typical life, it might not be the best choice of breed for the houseproud because it is likely to bring in mud and debris when it returns from a country walk.

ESSENTIALS OF THE BREED

The Field Spaniel is a substantial, moderately sized dog. It combines beauty and utility and should show none of the exaggerations of an earlier age. The Field's head is a hallmark of the breed, conveying character and nobility with a well-developed skull, pronounced rounded occiput and low-set ears. The muzzle is long and lean, especially beneath the raised brown and eyes which are almond shaped, dark or hazel and show no haw.

The breed is somewhat longer than it is tall. The ideal height at the withers is 18 inches/46 cm for dogs and 17 inches/43 cm for bitches. The Field is a substantial, big-bodied dog with moderate bone, a rib cage two-thirds of its body length and smooth muscles. Its tail is set and carried on a level with its back, or slightly below it. Its movement should be a long, slow, low stride covering a lot of ground. In fact, the Field Spaniel looks its best when moving at its own natural endurance trot with the head carried alertly and tail not above the line of the back. The coat is single, silky in texture, glossy, flat or with a slight wave. A moderate amount of feathering is desirable but an excessive or cottony coat is incorrect.

Liver (including golden liver) is much the most seen color with black next in popularity, but roans are permitted. Tan markings are allowed with all colors. Clear black-and-white or liver-and-white coloring is considered a fault.

There can be no denying that the Field is very much a specialist breed and those who choose to judge it should be well aware of the important differences distinguishing a Field Spaniel from a Cocker. Careful study is vital to appreciate the subtle differences in head type, as an obvious example.

Registry: AKC, CKC, FCI (Group 8), KC

SPANIELS — IRISH WATER SPANIEL

Origin and Development

It is generally believed that the Irish Water Spaniel as it is known today is the survivor of two varieties of water spaniel found in Ireland at least from the early nineteenth century. Today's dog was once known as the Southern Irish Water Spaniel, and was developed by Justin McCarthy.

In the north another variety of Water Spaniel was found, often brown and white in color and with short ears — similar to the breed known then as the English Water Spaniel. It was respected for its working abilities rather than its uniformity of type or appealing appearance.

The Southern Irish Water Spaniel, also known at the time as McCarthy's Breed, bred remarkably true to type and was admired and kept for its excellent working abilities, especially in water. It also attracted the attention of breeders and exhibitors in England from the mid-nineteenth century and appeared on the show benches in England from then on, with two classes being given to the breed at the Birmingham Show in 1862.

In 1906 Claude Care in *The Sporting Spaniel* wrote: "and although their best friends could not accuse them of being exactly beautiful to look at from an aesthetic point of view, still there is something very attractive in their quaint expression and appearance which always gives me the idea that if they were endowed with the faculty of speech, they would be found to be full of the same wit and humour which is popularly credited to the human inhabitants of their native isle." This is interesting from two points of view. The writer captures perfectly the somewhat clownish quality of the breed, but who knows what he might say if he saw the breed in the show ring today where modern trends in presentation, particularly in the United States, have glamorized the Irish Water Spaniel to make it a force to be reckoned with in its Group.

The Irish Water Spaniel maintains a constant band of unswerving devotees on an international basis, and it has been noticeable how cooperation between breeders in different countries has resulted in great strides being made by the breed in Great Britain, the United States and Scandinavia. Leading breeders have worked together to introduce new bloodlines to supplement existing breeding stock with very positive results, by the export of both mature dogs and semen. Never a commercial breed, the Irish Water Spaniel remains the province of the connoisseurs in whose hands its future is assured.

Temperament

The Irish Water Spaniel's great sense of fun makes it an ideal all-purpose sporting and companion dog. The breed is never boring but like all sporting dogs needs regular exercise and to be kept occupied. It is an excellent "people dog" but does need firm handling from an early age. Males in particular can become headstrong if they are not sensibly disciplined. Consequently the breed may not be an ideal first-time buyer's dog.

Health Matters

The breed is naturally hardy but in common with some other mainly brown colored dogs, coat and skin problems do occur, particularly in some strains. Regular monitoring can prevent such instances becoming too severe. Otherwise the breed remains relatively free of hereditary problems.

Special Care and Training

As a gun dog the breed has proved its great versatility and some have suggested that the Irish Water is more of a hunting, pointing and retrieving breed than a spaniel as such. It loves water, as its name suggests, and will often take a flying leap into any pond it

Irish Water Spaniel

encounters. Its coat, a special feature of the breed, needs care. The Irish Water Spaniel will lose its coat with seasonal changes and if not regularly groomed the coat will form mats and cords.

ADAPTABILITY

Whether based in a town or country situation, the Irish Water will adapt well to varied living conditions. However, it should always be remembered that it is an active sporting dog with great thinking power, and so needs to be kept occupied.

ESSENTIALS OF THE BREED

The Irish Water Spaniel is a smart, upstanding, strongly built dog standing no more than 23 inches/58 cm at the shoulder. Its body is square with barrel ribs which account for its rolling gait, a unique feature in a breed of this type. Its head is high in dome, of good length and brain room. Its muzzle should be long, strong and quite square. The breed's eyes are comparatively small and dark brown is preferred, although the liver gene allows for a slightly lighter color. The Irish Water Spaniel's head has a topknot of long, loose curls, growing down into a well-defined peak between the eyes. The quality and color of the coat of this breed is all important: it should be covered with a rich puce liver coat of tight, crisp ringlets which have a natural oily quality. There should be no woolliness about the coat, although when changing coat or exposed to long periods of bright sunshine, it will lose both coat color and texture.

Registry: AKC, CKC, FCI (Group 8), KC

443

SPANIELS — SUSSEX SPANIEL

ORIGIN AND DEVELOPMENT

The Sussex Spaniel is so named because it originally flourished in that English county. The breed can be traced back to at least the eighteenth century to Rosehill Park, near Hastings. In 1803, John Smith writing about spaniels for *Sportsmen's Cabinet* stated, "The largest and strongest are common in most parts of Sussex and are called Sussex Spaniels." Seventeen years later, *Sportsmen's Repository* described the spaniels of Sussex as good working dogs.

Bred and perfected by a number of Sussex landowners, the Sussex Spaniel was ideal to work the heavy clay soil, dense undergrowth and thick hedgerows through a long day of hunting. In these conditions its habit of "speaking" is useful in informing the guns when they have hit the right line in the cover. In 1859, Stonehenge (J.H. Walsh) wrote, "the Sussex differs from other Spaniels in his questing, the note being full and bell-like." These dogs were deep through with well sprung ribs, longer in the back than the Cocker Spaniels of the day, but short and strong in the couplings and with wide thighs and powerful hindquarters. Their coats were thick, dense, seallike and waterproof. Although the small gene pool meant much close breeding, and there was frequently a necessary infusion of Field Spaniel blood, the breed's rich golden liver coat has always been a prized hallmark of the pure Sussex.

By the end of the century the Sussex had lost popularity and if it were not for the efforts of two dedicated breeders, the Sussex could well have been lost. Working separately, Moses Woolland and Campbell Newington both did much to save and even to improve the breed. In the 1920s Joy Scholefield (who later became Mrs. Freer) began her work with the Sussex — for sixty years she was to shepherd and save the breed. Without her efforts the Sussex would have died out during World War II. Indeed her stock forms the basis of today's Sussex. The breed is now gaining increased popularity on the show bench while others prove their maintained capabilities in the field.

TEMPERAMENT

A good house dog and family pet, the Sussex is soft and affectionate with a placid outlook on life. Like all sporting dogs, the breed should be even-tempered and as much at ease with people as other dogs. Prone to give tongue, this has proved less popular with field trialers, but as more and more game preserve hunting becomes popular, the Sussex is likely to come into its own again. The heavy build and frowning expression of the Sussex often belie its energetic and sporting character.

HEALTH MATTERS

The extremely small gene pool has caused difficulties in avoiding some health problems including both heart and joint problems. The eye formation, showing some, but not excessive, haw has been the cause of some entropion in the breed. This is the painful condition of ingrowing eyelashes.

SPECIAL CARE AND TRAINING

An excellent and ardent hunter with great endurance and high intelligence, the Sussex possesses an outstanding nose and in spite of being somewhat slow and massive, is a lively worker with a good spaniel tail. Easily trained, it loves to hunt and is an accomplished bird dog. The Sussex coat does acquire profuse feathering when mature, so regular grooming is required, but this is rewarded by the glorious sheen and sealskin texture unique to the breed. Many Sussexes still work in the field and take readily to basic gun dog training. Dogs kept as companions should be trained in elementary obedience.

ADAPTABILITY

The breed adapts well to family life, enjoying companionship. Like all sporting spaniels, the

Sussex Spaniel

Sussex is always ready for vigorous exercise, so it should not be allowed to become bored or isolated.

ESSENTIALS OF THE BREED

The Sussex Standard has gone through several changes over the years, mostly to accommodate the dogs of the day. Consistent throughout, however, is the abundant flat coat of rich golden liver hue. The Sussex is the lowest to ground of all the spaniel family. Allied to this lowness is immense substance on a frame of good, but not exaggerated, length. It is rectangular, long and somewhat massive, but not so extreme as to hinder its active, energetic free movement. It moves with deliberation, in a typically distinctive rolling Sussex action which is, nevertheless, of good ground-covering ability. Its rib cage is long, well sprung and should show no sign of a waist when it is mature.

The Sussex is a balanced dog with its head not carried too high just above its backline. It has a good length of neck, well frilled down to its chest. It has a somber, serious appearance and often a frowning expression produced in part by its fairly heavy brows. Its head has good brain room and a square muzzle with well-developed lips. It should have a scissors bite but this has been a problem in recent years, happily now much improved. Its legs are short and strong, its hindquarters not overangulated or "Settery." Its feet are large and round. Its tail set is low and the tail is carried on a level with, or below the level of, the back.

Today the Sussex is a moderate dog standing 13-15 inches/33-38 cm at the shoulder in the United States and 15-16 inches/38-40 cm in the United Kingdom; it weighs 35-45 pounds/15-20 kg in the United States and about 50 pounds/ 22.5 kg in the United Kingdom.

Registry: AKC, CKC, FCI (Group 8), KC

SPANIELS — WELSH SPRINGER SPANIEL

ORIGIN AND DEVELOPMENT

The Welsh Springer Spaniel was acknowledged by the Kennel Club as a separate breed in 1902, but there are reports of dogs being worked in Wales for some years before that. In Wales, the Welsh is still known and referred to as a "starter." One theory suggests that the breed's forefathers arrived with the Gauls in pre-Roman times, and the Welsh Springer's closeness in many ways to the Brittany lends credence to this.

TEMPERAMENT

In general, the Welsh Springer has a good temperament, although a few are occasionally wary of strangers. Welsh puppies are extremely boisterous, thrive on human companionship and must have early socialization. They are certainly not an ideal breed for the household where they might need to spend hours alone each day.

HEALTH MATTERS

Normally the breed is very healthy, but can suffer from hip dysplasia. Ideally, only dogs that have had their hips X-rayed and have scores lower than the breed average should be bred from. There is a small incidence of epilepsy. A list of animals that have produced "fitting" progeny is published by the parent club of the breed in the United Kingdom. Breeding should be researched and undertaken with care. Advice from responsible breeders should be sought.

SPECIAL CARE AND TRAINING

The Welsh Springer always has a rich red and white coat, which is flat, straight and silky to the touch. Its coat must be kept clean and well brushed. The breed thrives on exercise and, although generally thought of as a dog for the country, is now often found in the town where two or three long walks each day seem to suffice. It can, of course, be trained as a working gun dog and its natural instincts in this field are still very evident.

ADAPTABILITY

The original use for the Welsh Springer was as a gun dog, where it startled game, making it fly up in the air for the guns. Today it is even more acclaimed as a family pet, with a kindly disposition and ever-ready eagerness to get up and go.

Welsh Springer Spaniel

ESSENTIALS OF THE BREED

The general appearance of the Welsh Springer is that of a symmetrical, compact dog that is obviously built for endurance and hard work. It is a fast and active worker with hindquarters showing plenty of drive. It has a kindly expression and should never show aggression or be nervous. The muzzle should be of medium length and the nostrils may be from brown to dark, mirroring the eyes which may be hazel or dark, but must not show any haw. The ears should hang close to the cheeks and be shaped somewhat like a vine leaf, much smaller than those of the English Springer. The jaws are strong, and the teeth set in a perfect scissors bite. The neck is set into sloping shoulders and the front legs should be straight and well boned. The body of the Welsh needs to be strong and muscular with a deep brisket and well-sprung ribs. It should have catlike feet, round with thick pads. It is important that its movement is ground-covering with plenty of drive from powerful hindquarters.

Color is the characteristic that most identifies the Welsh Springer. It is only ever a very rich red and white. In size, the dog measures about 19 inches/48 cm at the shoulder, while the bitch stands about 18 inches/46 cm. There is no weight requirement.

Registry: AKC, CKC, FCI (Group 8), KC

447

SPANISH MASTIFF/MASTÍN ESPAÑOL

The Spanish Mastiff is believed to originate from the ancient Molosser dog, that can be traced back to 2,000 years B.C. These dogs were probably introduced to the Iberian peninsula by Phoenician tradesmen who had brought them from Syria or India. Although mastiffs have been known to exist in Iberia for thousands of years, and the Spanish Mastiff was shown regularly at dog shows early this century, no Standard for the breed was drawn up until 1946.

The Spanish Mastiff was developed in the plains around Madrid, in the areas of Extremadura and Castilla-La Mancha, which is why the breed has also been called the Extremadura or La Mancha. It has been used to guard estates and farms and also to guard — but not herd — flocks of cattle. Self-confident and brave, it is mainly kept today as a companion dog. The breed may be seen in great numbers at Spanish dog shows but is still rarely seen outside the Iberian peninsula.

The height at the withers should be over 30 inches/77 cm in males and 28 inches/72 cm in females, but heights over 31 1/2 inches/80 cm and 29 1/2 inches/75 cm respectively are preferred. The body should be rectangular, well muscled and with strong bone. The head should be massive, with a long, deep muzzle, pendulous lips and well-pronounced dewlaps. Although a very heavy breed, its movement should be free and elastic.

The coat could be thick, soft and not too long with a fine, almost woolly, texture. The skin should be abundant and loose on the body. Its color is usually any shade of fawn and red, wolf gray, grizzle with cream tan markings or brindle.

Registry: FCI (Group 2)

Spanish Mastiff

SPANISH WATER DOG/ PERRO DE AGUA ESPAÑOL

The Spanish Water Dog has recently been accepted by the Fédération Cynologique Internationale although it is a very old variety of the Barbet or water dog family. It

Spanish Water Dog

should not be mistaken for either the French Barbet or the Italian Lagotto. Although all three breeds are Water dogs with a curly coat, they have distinctive differences in type. Although primarily a retrieving water dog, the Spanish Water Dog has been known to herd sheep. It is very rare but is exhibited in Europe.

At the withers, its height is about 15-19 1/2 inches/38-50 cm. Its body should be rectangular, well muscled and with strong bone. The head should be elongated, and the skull and nose ridge should have parallel lines. The neck should be short and muscular. The tail is docked very short or a natural bobtail. The coat should be decidedly curly and of a woolly texture, either clipped short or, if left long, corded in thin corkscrew-curls. Accepted colors are black, liver brown or white, with or without patches in black or liver brown. Tricolor is not permissible.

Registry: FCI (Group 8)

STABYHOUN

This Dutch gun dog is used for pointing, flushing and retrieving game. It is of ancient origin. It is known to have an even, friendly temperament.

The ideal height at the withers is 21 inches/ 53 cm for males and 19 1/2 inches/50 cm for females. The body should be fairly broad in front, rectangular, well muscled and with strong bone. The head should be strong with rounded, not pronounced cheeks, and not too long in the muzzle. The coat should be soft, long on body and usually slightly wavy. It should be white with large patches and ticking in black, brown or tan.

Registry: FCI (Group 7)

Stabyhoun

STAFFORDSHIRE BULL TERRIER

Origin and Development

The development of the Staffordshire Bull Terrier was not recorded in its early stages. However, it is generally accepted that the breed evolved in the British Isles as a direct result of a cross between a Bulldog and a smooth-coated terrier. The implementation of the Cruelty to Animals Act of 1835, which made the baiting of animals illegal, gave ample protection to the bull and bear, but did little to safeguard the welfare of the dog. Men previously involved with the brutal baiting "sports" then transferred their attention to the dog pit. The fighting dog they required was to have limitless endurance, courage and agility. The relentless qualities displayed by the Bulldog combined with the speed and cutting bite of the terrier proved to be an ideal blend for the pit.

The first crosses were all shapes and sizes, some cloddy in appearance favoring the Bulldog, others having the much lighter bone structure of the terrier. Further research on the origin of the Stafford has produced some evidence to show that the breed may have a longer history then previously summarized — substantiating claims of an ancient lineage. Bear baiting was an extremely popular pastime supported by English monarchs. The Calendar of State Papers, dated May 30, 1559, tells of Elizabeth I giving presents of Mastiffs, great and small. Without doubt a small, agile type of fighting Mastiff not dissimilar to the Staffordshire Bull Terrier would have been ideal to face the bear. Erasmus records in 1506 that in England many herds of bears were maintained for the purpose. Illustrations of the 1825 lion baits show dogs with physical characteristics identical to the Stafford of today.

From the mid-1800s the fighting canines of the dog pit were dubbed with a variety of titles: Pit Bulldog, Pit Dog, Pit Bull, Staffordshire Bull, Patched Pit Dog and Bulldog Terrier. Public opinion eventually made dog fighting and associated "sports" disreputable pastimes. The fighting dog gradually disappeared from many parts of England, Staffordshire being the noted exception. Dog fights continued in that county for many years — a haven for fighting breeds. During the 1850s the American dog fighting "fancy" imported great numbers of fighting dogs from the Midlands. In London during the 1880s a desire materialized to reintroduce the old-fashioned fighting dogs. Show classes for "Bull Terriers other than white" were provided at one or two shows. The exhibits taking part were not bred to type and the experiment was deemed to be a failure. It was in the 1920s that the men of Staffordshire began to advertise their dogs solely as Staffordshire Bull Terriers. The 1930s saw a renewal of interest in the breed — the pit dog was about to be transformed into a show dog. In 1935 the Staffordshire Bull Terrier Club was formed and the Kennel Club accepted the Staffordshire Bull Terrier as a recognized breed in the same year.

Temperament

The Staffordshire Bull Terrier has unique qualities: its reputation purely as a tough guy is deceptive, for when at home it makes a great nurse for children. It will generally tolerate any amount of mauling, never tires of games and awaits the next move of a child with patience and a continual wag of its tail. The breed is an excellent choice for show purposes or companionship. It also makes an excellent sporting companion, undertaking any task demanded in the field. A rough diamond it may be, but for all that it is a diamond — a wonderful addition to any household.

Health Matters

The Stafford is naturally healthy — the historical background of the breed has contributed to the well-being of the modern dog. It heals rapidly and usually consents readily to treatment — visits to the veterinarian should be minimal.

Staffordshire Bull Terrier

SPECIAL CARE AND TRAINING

As a show dog the Staffordshire is easily prepared for competition; a quick brush of the coat and a rub-down with a chamois leather will enhance the coat's natural shine. A polish to the traditional brass decorations adorning the leather collar — and you are ready to go. The Stafford possesses high intelligence, easily accepting any form of obedience training. Its determined temperament makes the breed ideal for competition. Trained to guard, it has no equal and it will be the first in line to defend people and property from any danger. As a rule the breed is not quarrelsome; however, a

451

display of canine aggression toward a Staffordshire may arouse dormant propensities — care should be taken to anticipate a situation of this nature.

ADAPTABILITY

The Stafford is an everyman's dog whose surroundings it will consider very much secondary to the care and attention it receives from its owner. With its high intelligence and love of companionship, it is unwise to leave it languishing alone for prolonged periods.

So stable is the character of the Staffordshire Bull Terrier as a companion dog, be it with adults or children, that it has become firmly established as the ultimate "people dog" with thousands of enthusiasts who cannot imagine life with any other breed of dog. Stafford lovers can be found in all walks of life, classes and income levels, all sharing a love — which borders on obsession — of the breed. The Stafford will adapt to any environment whatsoever provided it has human companionship. In view of its fighting ancestry it is not an ideal kennel dog, kept in large numbers, and it is no coincidence that at any British Championship show, the vast majority of Stafford exhibitors will be just one or two-dog owners.

Bearing in mind the special place which the Stafford has carved in the heart of the British dog owning public, it seems tragically ironic that the breed should have become the victim of so much adverse publicity, most of which is inaccurate and ill deserved. The breed is frequently mistaken for a Pit Bull Terrier, and public reaction to the Stafford is now rather guarded. Many British Stafford owners have been harrassed by the ignorant who believe they are harboring a dog that is outlawed by the Dangerous Dogs Act, and Stafford clubs and owners are currently working very hard to maintain the breed's true image. It is increasingly sad that the breed has had to cope with this unfair tar-and-feathering. In truth, a human being could find no more versatile and loyal friend.

ESSENTIALS OF THE BREED

The Staffordshire is of medium size, muscular in build and has a short, smooth coat. In 1948 the Kennel Club approved a new Staffordshire Bull Terrier Breed Standard, which replaced the original version created in 1935. The most important change was to the desired height and weight of the breed, which decreased the height of "about 15-18 inches [38-46 cm] at the shoulder" to "14-16 inches [35-40 cm]." Significantly, no alteration was made to the weight clause. It was considered the original greater height to weight ratio produced too many terrier physical characteristics. The modern dog should give an overall impression of balance and power for size, with no exaggeration to any area of physical make-up.

The head of the Stafford should be wide, deep, with obvious temporal muscles and a defined stop. Pronounced masseter muscles should give the impression of cheekiness. There should be a powerful muzzle, clean lips and a scissors bite. The ears should be small, neat and held tightly folded backwards. The eyes are of moderate size, round and dark. When the mouth is open, the expression is of a laughing, comical appearance. The neck is muscular, short to medium in length, and the topline is level, with a tail which is thick at the root, tapering to a point and finishing in the locality of the highest joint of the hocks. There should be great spring of rib, and the dog should be close coupled. The forelegs should be straight and of ample bone with upright pasterns, and there should be good width of forehand. The thighs should be muscular, and there should be good turn of stifle. The feet are medium sized and thickly padded. The pigment should be black throughout. In color the Stafford may be brindle, blue, red, smut, white and pied. The secret of a top-class Stafford is that it should display a balanced blend of "bull" and "terrier."

Registry: AKC, CKC, FCI (Group 3), KC

STUMPY TAIL CATTLE DOG

The Stumpy Tail Cattle Dog descended from the original cross of the black-and-white bobtail dogs called Smithfield Cattle Dogs (these dogs were so-called because they used to herd stock to Smithfield meat market in London) with the dingo by a drover in New South Wales named Timmins. This produced red bobtail dogs known as Timmins' Biters since they were headstrong and quite severe with their biting. The effort was made to breed out the vicious bite of these dogs so that they could heel cattle more effectively. They were mated to Smooth Collies imported from Scotland and produced red, blue and blue mottled bobtail dogs. By selective breeding of mating bobtail to bobtail, the absence of the tail became fixed. Puppies are born with tiny stumpy tails which, according to the Standard, may not exceed 4 inches/10 cm in the fully grown adult. The breed possesses a natural aptitude for the working of cattle and is also very loyal and courageous.

At first glance, the Stumpy Tail Cattle Dog resembles its longer-tailed cousin but closer scrutiny reveals that the Stumpy Tail has a squarer build and does not have any tan in its coloring as the black-and-tan Kelpie was not used in the Stumpy's creation. The height at the withers for males should be 18-20 inches/ 46-51 cm and 17-19 inches/43-48 cm for bitches. Although the breed is now rarely seen, the Australian National Kennel Council has recognized these dogs for some years.

Registry: Australian National Kennel Council

Red (left) and blue Stumpy Tail Cattle Dogs

SWEDISH VALLHUND/VÄSTGÖTASPETS

The Swedish Vallhund's origin has been a matter of discussion for many years. The question has been did the Vikings bring their little farm dogs with them to the British Isles on their plundering expeditions to form the origin of the Corgi, or did they take back the Corgi to form the Västgötaspets? This will never be satisfactorily answered but an interesting discovery is that bowsprits from Viking ships have been found on the Irish coast with ornaments in the shape of Swedish Vallhunds.

The Swedish Vallhund lived its life unnoticed on farms in the west of Sweden for hundreds of years. They were and are still used for herding cattle or whatever animals may be kept on farms; they are also very efficient watchdogs. As with many other breeds, they used to be such a common sight that no one thought much about them. But by the 1940s they had become rare and their decline and absence was then noticed, whereupon an investigation took place that actually saved the breed from extinction. The Swedish Kennel Club recognized the breed in 1943 and it is now well represented as a companion dog, not only in Scandinavia but also in Great Britain.

Two types of Swedish Vallhund still exist. One type is heavier, usually with a slightly off-standing coat that is longer on the neck but not so long as to form a mane. The other type is more slender, more elegant, with a longer neck and a coat that lies closer to the body.

The height at the withers should be within 12-13 inches/30-34 cm. The body should be rectangular, well muscled and with strong bone. The head should be wedge shaped with a strong muzzle that is not too long or pointed. The ears should be pointed and carried erect. The tail is either a natural bobtail, docked short or, if left long, will curl over the back. The coat should be short, lie close to the body, with a hard texture and soft, thick undercoat. It should be wolf colored with light wolf markings — slight white markings are allowed.

Registry: FCI (Group 5), KC

Swedish Vallhunds

SWISS HOUNDS

The Swiss Hounds are among the most genuine when it comes to ancient origin. They have been used for centuries to improve other scenthound breeds. The West European Hounds, to which the Swiss Hounds belong, are distinguished by their long heads with a narrow skull, low-set and folded ears, long, narrow muzzle often with convex nose ridge and a large nose. The body is elegant with the skin hanging quite loosely.

Since ancient times they have been known to be excellent hunting dogs that track hare, fox and wild boar by scent. Today they are not hunted in packs but they are still strictly kept as hunting dogs. Yet their friendly temperament also makes them good companion dogs. Swiss Hounds are divided into two breeds, with separate Standards.

In the medium-sized breed, the height at the withers should be 18 1/2-23 inches/47-59 cm. It is shorter in back and more elegant in build than the smaller variety. The smaller breed stands at 13-16 inches/33-41 cm. The smaller variety is longer in the back. All varieties in each size group are distinguished by colors and named for the region in which they can be found.

The Berner hound variety comes from the region around the Swiss capital Bern. The color should be white with large black patches and rich tan markings. The sides of the head and

Medium Luzerner Swiss Hound

Small Wirehaired Berner Swiss Hound

ears should always be black. The coat should be smooth and glossy in both sizes but the smaller Berner Swiss Hound may also have a wiry coat.

The Jura variety (which is also called the Bruno by French-speaking Swiss) comes from the Jura region bordering France. Juras are mainly seen in the smaller size, but can also be found among the larger hounds. It should be black-and-tan or tan with a black saddle. The coat should be smooth and glossy; the smaller size may occasionally have a coarser topcoat with a woolly undercoat.

The Jura used to come in two varieties — a very old variety called St. Hubert was decidedly

heavier with a particularly heavily boned head, a broad skull and a general lack of elegance, particularly in the head structure. The St. Hubert, which is never seen today, is said to have had black-and-tan coloring, with a lighter tan color than is seen in general today in the Jura, and with black coloring the body as a mantle. One still today finds this type of tan marking in really elegant Jura specimens, although the most common color seems to be jet black with deep tan markings like the markings seen in Rottweilers.

The Luzerner comes from the region of Lucerne and its very spectacular coloring resembles that of the old French hound, Grand Bleu de Gascogne. It should be blue-mottled, from white with fine black speckling to dark bluish-black with large black patches that should cover sides of the head and ears and may also form a mantle. It has clearly defined light to rich tan markings. The coat should be smooth and glossy in both varieties.

The Schwyzer comes from the northwest of Switzerland. It must always be white with large orange patches that should cover the sides of the head and ears. Orange covering the back and sides like a mantle is permissible. The coat should be smooth and glossy in both sizes.

Registry: FCI (Group 6)

Large Jura Swiss Hound

Medium Schwyzer Swiss Hound

THAI RIDGEBACK DOG

The Thai Ridgeback Dog has recently been recognized by the Fédération Cynologique Internationale. It has a ridge on its back, formed by hair growing in opposite directions, forming whorls and circles. The ridge may also be in the shape of a guitar.

The breed was first noticed 360 years ago on the island of Dao Phu Quoc on the border of Cambodia and Vietnam. It can also be found in eastern Thailand. It is believed that the breed came to Asia with tradesmen from Africa 400 years ago and that it might be a descendant of the now extinct Hottentot dog, also believed to be part of the Rhodesian Ridgeback's ancestry. It was used as a guard and watchdog and is still a good guard although today it is mainly kept as a companion dog. It is very rare outside its country of origin.

The height at its withers should be about 23-26 inches/58-66 cm. Its body should be rectangular, well muscled and with good bone. The head is wedge shaped with hooded ears. The tongue should be blue or bluish gray. The coat should be smooth, fine and glossy, and the skin very fine. It should be loosely attached to the body — this is particularly noticeable in puppies. Its color should be black, gray, blue or shades of clear red.

Registry: FCI (Group 5)

Thai Ridgeback Dog

TIBETAN MASTIFF/DO-KHYI

The Mastiff of Tibet is believed by many cynology historians to be the origin of most mastiffs, mountain dogs and large herding breeds. It used to be a fierce guard dog that was kept in zoological gardens when imported to Europe in earlier centuries. Tibetan guard dogs are mentioned in Chinese documents dating from 1121 B.C. A more detailed description of the Tibetan dog was written by the Greek historian Megasthenes in 327 A.D.

This is one of the most genuine breeds, which has been kept to type for literally thousands of years. The black guard dog with a terrifying bark that was kept by the nomadic Tibetan tribes has been mentioned by many explorers over the centuries. In modern times they were hardly known until the breed was imported to the United States, Germany and Switzerland in the 1970s. Today its temperament is not a problem though this is a dog that will protect its family and home and is wary of strangers.

Although the Tibetan is called a "mastiff", it should not be as heavy and deep in body as many of the other traditional mastiff breeds. The Tibetan Mastiff should give an impression of having the strength and stamina to live in high altitude mountain ranges. The height at the withers should be over 26 inches/66 cm in males and 24 inches/61 cm in females. Its body should be rather deep, almost rectangular, well muscled and with strong bone. The head should be massive with a pronounced stop, strong, but with not too long a muzzle. The ears are rather high set and carried close to the cheeks., the tail carried in a loose curl over the back. The coat should be medium long with very thick undercoat; males in particular should have longer coat around the neck to form a mane. Accepted colors are black, brown and bluish gray, with or without tan markings. Red or golden are also allowed.

Registry: FCI (Group 2), KC

Tibetan Mastiff

TIBETAN SPANIEL

ORIGIN AND DEVELOPMENT

This ancient breed is rooted in the isolated Himalayan monasteries and villages of Tibet where the dogs were bred by Buddhist monks. They served as companions and watchdogs, were much prized and only given away very rarely. They love to watch from a high viewpoint; because many monasteries were isolated, they used to sit on walls and bark to warn of approaching strangers. They first appeared in England in the 1890s and became popular after 1950. The American Kennel Club recognized the breed in 1984.

TEMPERAMENT

The Tibetan Spaniel is highly intelligent, slightly aloof with strangers, but very affectionate with family and friends. It is a good companion, sensitive and responsive to its owner's moods and feelings. It is an alert, happy little dog that enjoys life but has a mind of its own. The breed is fastidious in it habits and will spend many hours preening itself in an almost catlike fashion.

HEALTH MATTERS

Generally the Tibetan Spaniel is very healthy — advanced ages of fifteen to sixteen years are quite common. It does, however, have general-

Tibetan Spaniel

ized progressive retinal atrophy — an affected case will progressively go blind — so all breeding stock should be regularly checked for this. There are testing schemes in the United Kingdom, United States and many other countries. There have also been a very few cases of juvenile kidney disease.

SPECIAL CARE AND TRAINING

Tibetan Spaniels have a double coat which requires grooming, especially when the undercoat is shed. The dogs usually accept this if done regularly from puppyhood. Puppies need early training to the lead and general household behavior. They learn quickly but do not always display instant obedience.

ADAPTABILITY

While many breeds will adapt to kennel or home, the Tibetan Spaniel is definitely a breed that needs its creature comforts and does not make a good kennel dog. Given comfortable surroundings and constant companionship, it will blossom in a country manor or city apartment. These little dogs should ideally live as part of the family. They think that they are gracing your home by being part of it! They thrive on company, whether human or canine, and will not do well if they are left alone for long periods.

ESSENTIALS OF THE BREED

The Tibetan Spaniel is very natural looking, has great quality with overall balance and alertness, without exaggeration. Its height is about 10 inches/25 cm at the withers and its weight 9-15 pounds/4-7 kg. The head should be rather small in relation to the dog's overall size, with a slightly rounded skull. The ears are pendant, but set fairly high with a slight lift from the skull. The eyes are oval in shape, set well apart, but forward looking and dark brown in color. The medium-length muzzle is rather blunt and free from wrinkle but should show a degree of cushioning. The mouth is undershot, but no teeth should be visible when the mouth is closed, and full dentition is desired.

The Tibetan Spaniel's body is slightly longer than the height at its withers and a rectangle of daylight should be visible underneath. The tail should be well plumed, curving over the back and falling to one side. The feet are hare-feet with feathering extending beyond the toes. The gait should be quick-moving, straight and positive. The coat is double, silky-textured, lying rather flat on the body with longer hair on the mane with feathering on the ears, feet, tail and buttocks. The breed should not be overcoated and all colors and mixtures of colors are permissible.

There was a time, not that long ago, when Tibetan Spaniel owners seen out walking their dogs were assumed to have a rather indifferent quality Pekingese. Thankfully those days are long since gone, but it should always be borne in mind that the two breeds do have similarities, and therefore individual breed characteristics should always be given priority, and any aspect of a Tibetan Spaniel which creates a Pekingese-type appearance should be avoided. There are several areas where Tibetans deviate from true type into the realms of Pekingese: too much length of body, coupled with insufficient height of leg; too full and round an eye; too low and heavy ears; too short and wrinkled muzzle, are such examples.

It is vital for those who judge the breed to look at the Tibetan Spaniel as a unique breed and not a distant relation of the the Pekingese. The essence of type will only be achieved when there are correct proportions of height to length, the ideal dog being slightly longer than its height at the withers. The head and expression are also vitally important — the Pekingese head is massive, the Tibetan's relatively small — and if a Tibetan Spaniel moves with action which would be acceptable in a Pekingese, it has to be totally untypical for a Tibetan.

Registry: AKC, CKC, FCI (Group 9), KC

TIBETAN TERRIER

ORIGIN AND DEVELOPMENT

The boiling desert, precipitous mountain inclines, high plains covered with grass in summer and snow in winter are all natural turf to the Tibetan Terrier. Native to remote sections of the high Himalayas, in its present form the dog is the result of 1,000 or more years of natural adaptation to some of earth's harshest, most variable climate and geography. The Tibetan people have never purposefully bred dogs, and so it was evolutionary necessity — sheer survival — that contributed to the development of the breed's traits such as its compact size, a balance of substance with agility, its double coat and its specialized feet.

The Tibetan Terrier fits well into the group of breeds categorized by the British as Utility Dogs for it has never been ornamental in form or function. It traditionally served its master in a variety of ways: as companion, caravan dog, herder and guardian of the flock, occasional

Tibetan Terrier

retriever and participant in the everyday routine of a monastery, peasant village or nomad encampment. Its solid and balanced moderation in all aspects of size, structure, manner of movement and character enabled it to withstand privation, to endure and thrive where more massive, delicate or specialized breeds could not.

In particular, the moderation of the Tibetan Terrier in all things and exaggeration in none may best exemplify the reasons how this ancient, evolved breed has successfully made the transition from isolated ancient Tibet to the contemporary world. In the United Kingdom, the Tibetan Terrier and the Lhasa Apso were originally classified as one breed — the Lhasa Terrier.

TEMPERAMENT

The Tibetan Terrier has a pleasing disposition. It makes a fine companion and watchdog, is neither hyperactive nor destructive and is not an incessant barker. The disposition of the breed ranges from a puppy's exuberance to amiable mature reserve, but the Tibetan Terrier clearly prefers human companionship to all else in life. It is a charming, generally sensible, sturdy dog.

HEALTH MATTERS

The Tibetan Terrier is fairly long lived and has overall good health. Canine hip dysplasia is occasionally seen, but it is rare for the disease to disable or limit the affected dog. Hereditary eye diseases, including progressive retinal atrophy, lens luxation and juvenile cataract are also reported, but the rate of incidence in the breed is low.

SPECIAL CARE AND TRAINING

Attention must be paid to the Tibetan Terrier's heavy double coat. The coat is not meant to be trimmed and thorough brushing once or twice weekly is important. Bathing with mild shampoo, thorough rinsing, and then careful drying with a hair dryer on a warm setting while brushing the coat to the skin will render the coat more manageable. The drop ears of the breed should be kept clean. Beyond its grooming requirements the Tibetan Terrier is an "easy keeper" that remains healthy and active to its thirteenth or fourteenth year on average and often well beyond.

ADAPTABILITY

The Tibetan is not at all a terrier in mind or body, despite the misnomer given to the breed — because of its size — during the 1920s. Young dogs need daily exercise and all, young or old, crave a daily period of attention from their owners. Innate curiosity and great speed for its size make the Tibetan Terrier a bad risk in an unfenced yard. To provide both exercise and personal attention, increasing numbers of owners are training their dogs in Obedience, Agility and similar activities. The dog's enjoyment may stem as much from interaction with its owner as from love of the sport, but it works enthusiastically and can do well. A properly trained Tibetan Terrier is a sensitive, responsive therapy visitor and the breed really loves this work. It will easily adapt to many kinds of environment and lifestyles.

ESSENTIALS OF THE BREED

The male Tibetan Terrier is about 15-16 inches/ 38-40 cm (the female is slightly smaller) at the withers, and it is slightly longer in length than in height. Its head is divided into two equal parts: from nose to the stop, and from the stop to the occiput. It has a proud head carriage, dropped ears, bright dark eyes, black pigment, level topline, and a long tail carried well up and over the body drooping to one side. Its legs are strong and feet rather large and spread. Its coat is luxurious, long and double, parting naturally down its spine and in many hues and colors (both solid as well as particolors — there are no preferred colors or combinations of colors). Its nose must be black and the eye rims are preferred black. The Tibetan Terrier is an attractive pet, show dog or obedience worker.

Registry: AKC, CKC, FCI (Group 9), KC

TOSA INU

The Japanese fighting dog, the Tosa Inu, is of ancient origin but has had several infusions of other breeds. After World War II only a few

Tosa Inu

were left. Although still rare, the breed was re-established with the help of Mastiffs, Bulldogs and several other breeds. The Tosa is listed under the Dangerous Dogs Act of 1991 in Great Britain and is rarely seen outside Japan.

The height at the withers should be over 24 inches/60 cm in males and 21 inches/54 cm in females. The body should be rectangular, well muscled and with strong bone. The head should be massive with pronounced lips and dew laps. The ears should be carried close to the cheeks and the tail left undocked. The coat should be short, lie close and be of a hard texture. It should be clear red, with or without a black mask; slight white markings are permissible.

Registry: FCI (Group 2)

TOY MANCHESTER TERRIER/ ENGLISH TOY TERRIER

ORIGIN AND DEVELOPMENT

A "black and tan terrar" was written about in 1570 but this was probably a rough-coated, short-legged dog. Today's English Toy Terrier evolved during the 1880s. Poor sanitation in the 1880s led to plagues of rats, so the sport of rat-killing became popular, with contests in public pits. A painting from 1850 shows the diminutive "Tiny the Wonder", which was reputed to have dispatched 200 rats in under an hour. In the sport of hunting, this small terrier was carried out in a leather pouch on horseback and used to flush out the fox when it had gone to ground.

The breed was recognized by the Kennel Club in 1938 as the Miniature Black and Tan Terrier. This name was changed in 1960 to the English Toy Terrier (Black and Tan) to give a

truer description of its size and type. In the United States, the Toy Black and Tan Terrier was first recognized in 1926, with the name changed to the Toy Manchester in 1934.

TEMPERAMENT

The breed is essentially a Toy, but with definite terrier characteristics. It makes a devoted pet, is totally faithful to its owner but only accepts strangers slowly. Its ratting instincts are still very much to the fore.

HEALTH MATTERS

Usually fit and active, some Toy Manchester Terriers are greedy, while others are fussy eaters — none should be overfed. There are no particualar hereditary diseases. If left out in the sun for long periods, heat bumps may appear along its back.

Toy Manchester Terrier. In the United Kingdom this black and tan terrier is called the English Toy Terrier.

SPECIAL CARE AND TRAINING

The Toy Manchester has a thin coat and so it needs plenty of warm bedding — it is definitely not a good kennel dog. Good nutrition is essential for a good coat. Thin covering of coat, scratching and dull colors in both the black and the tan can be caused by improper feeding. In general, however, the coat needs little maintenance and there is no definite shedding cycle. The teeth need weekly attention and the nails should be kept shortened. The breed likes a good walk daily but can manage without. A very biddable though independent dog, it loves to learn and will work neatly in Obedience or Agility.

ADAPTABILITY

Its small size and short coat means that the Toy Manchester can live happily almost anywhere and is relatively maintenance-free. It will fit into any lifestyle, from apartment to country estate, but it needs to be with people and makes an ideal companion for the elderly.

ESSENTIALS OF THE BREED

The ideal height and weight should be 10-12 inches/25-30 cm at the shoulder and 6-8 pounds/2.5-3.5 kg in the United Kingdom. In the United States and Canada, the top weight is 12 pounds/5 kg.

The head should be like a long wedge. The "candle flame" ears are set high on the skull and the eyes are small, dark, sparkling and almond shaped. The feet are compact, with the middle toes on the front feet longer than the others. The narrow tail should taper to a point, be low set and should not be carried above the backline. The coat is short, glossy, dense and ebony black, sharply divided from rich chestnut tan. The muzzle is tanned and there are tan spots above the eyes, on the cheeks, and rosettes on either side of the chest. The front legs are tan from the knee down, with black penciling on each toe and a distinctive thumbprint in the center of the pastern.

Registry: AKC, CKC, FCI (Group 3), KC

VIZSLAS/HUNGARIAN VIZSLAS

ORIGIN AND DEVELOPMENT

The Vizsla or Hungarian Pointer was admitted to the registry in the United States in 1960; in the United Kingdom it is known as the Hungarian Vizsla. The breed may trace its ancestry back to the Magyars who invaded Hungary from the east. Etchings that date back to the tenth century depict a huntsman with a falcon accompanied by a dog that slightly resembles today's Vizsla. The breed was once used with great success to hunt the vast plains of Hungary where game birds and hare flourished. The Vizsla does not range far, works close to the gun and though swift is cautious so it does not scare up the game. Hungarians who fled their country between the two world wars took their beloved pointers with them all over the world. The Vizsla has become popular as a worker, show dog and companion wherever it has settled.

TEMPERAMENT

The name Vizsla means alert and responsive in the Hungarian language. The breed is robust but not large and is a willing worker and companion. It does not train well under force or harsh measures. Puppies must be well socialized at an early age. The proper temperament in a puppy is alert and responsive, never shy or aggressive.

HEALTH MATTERS

All breeding stock should be X-rayed at two years of age for hip dysplasia. There are some skin problems that exist in the breed. Stock should be purchased from blood lines that are free of epilepsy.

SPECIAL CARE AND TRAINING

As with all sporting dogs, the Vizsla is a worker and is happiest when it has something to do.

Shorthaired Vizsla or Hungarian Vizsla as it is known in the United Kingdom

Obedience training is ideal as are all forms of bird work, including water retrieving. Teeth should be brushed weekly and a hard biscuit fed daily to help to keep them clean. Nails also require weekly attention. The coat is smooth, short and easily cared for. A young puppy should be raised with children so that the mature dog will tolerate and accept them.

ADAPTABILITY

If kept in a city situation, the Vizsla will require long daily walks. As its coat is thin, the Vizsla does not do well outside without adequate protection in cold weather. Human companionship is essential.

ESSENTIALS OF THE BREED

Color is the hallmark of the Vizsla. It must be a shade of golden rust — from rusty gold to dark sandy yellow. Its nose, lips and eye rims are brown, never black. Its eye color should harmonize with its coat color, the darker the better, and be very expressive. In size, the male is not much over 24 inches/61 cm and the female is 21-23 inches/53-58 cm. If the male is above 25 1/2 inches/65 cm or under 20 1/2 inches/52 cm or the female is above 24 1/2 inches/62 cm or under 19 1/2 inches/49 cm, the dog will be disqualified from show rings in the United States.

The head should be lean, foreface of good length, ears thin, low and hanging, and teeth have a scissors bite. The neck should be strong, the back short, and the legs sound, of medium bone and with tight feet. The tail is often docked by about one third shortly after birth. The tail carriage should be light and either level with the back or slightly above it. The gait is strong, light-footed and free, covering a lot of ground with only a few steps.

There is also a Wirehaired Vizsla (the Drotszoru) which has exactly the same Standard as the more common Smooth-haired variety, except that it has a close wire coat all over its body. The Wirehaired, like the Longhaired, is not recognized in the United States.

Registry: AKC, CKC, FCI (Group 7), KC

VOLPINO ITALIANO

The small Italian Spitz — Volpino means "little fox" — is considered very old and a genuine native of Italy. It resembles the German Spitz and might possibly share the same origin although it is not a direct descendant.

The height at its withers should be about 10-12 inches/25-30 cm. Its body should be square and its head wedge shaped with a rather pointed muzzle and pricked ears. The coat should be abundant, long and standing out from body. It should be long enough to form a mane around the neck. The Volpino Italiano should be pure white; cream is not desirable although it is accepted. The pigmentation should be jet black.

Registry: FCI (Group 5)

Volpino Italiano

WEIMARANER

ORIGIN AND DEVELOPMENT

The Weimaraner made its first appearance about 125 years ago in the German court of Weimar, the capital of the province of Thuringia. The breed was partly developed from the old red Schweisshunde, a breed that was responsible for so many German hunting dogs. It is probable that crosses were made to the German Short-haired Pointer and several indigenous German hunting breeds. The Weimaraner was bred to stalk deer and to trail and hunt bear and wild boar.

In 1897 the Weimaraner Club of Germany was formed at Erfort, Thuringia. As time passed, less big game was hunted in Germany. At this point, the Weimaraner was developed into the "perfect all-round gun dog" as it showed a marvelous aptitude for birds in the field in part because of its excellent nose. The German Weimaraner Club was started by a few amateur sportsmen, who bred the dog for sport rather than profit. No one was allowed to buy a Weimaraner without first becoming a member of the club. The breed was nurtured very carefully by these sportsmen.

In 1929 an American sportsman, Howard Knight, of Providence, Rhode Island, was made a member of this exclusive organization. Knight hunted with Weimaraner owners in Germany. He joined the German club, was permitted to bring back two specimens, and he ultimately founded the Weimaraner Club of America. The American Club has tried to follow the lead of its German counterpart in guiding the career of the Weimaraner in the United States. The "Gray Ghost" as it is fondly called has proved itself to be a grand all-round hunting companion rather than a field trial competitor. The breed was recognized by the American Kennel Club in 1943.

Smooth Weimaraner

TEMPERAMENT

The Weimaraner is demanding — and it needs obedience training and good steady exercise. It also needs human companionship and insists on being a member of the family.

HEALTH MATTERS

Breeding stock should be X-rayed for hip dysplasia. Gastric torsion (bloat) is known in the breed. Some mast cell tumors are found and the breed is subject to bleeding disorders. Always buy from a reputable breeder.

SPECIAL CARE AND TRAINING

The Weimaraner's sleek coat is easy to care for. However, its nutrition must be good quality, because its energy level is quite high, and to maintain its sleek coat.

ADAPTABILITY

The Weimaraner does not do well as a kennel dog. It does better in a country setting where it has the freedom to range and exercise.

ESSENTIALS OF THE BREED

This is a tall, aristocratic, intelligent looking hunting dog. Its trademark is its distinctive coloring — a gray color ranging from mouse gray to silver. Dark blue and black coats are not allowed in the Weimaraner. Males weigh up to 85 pounds/38 kg and may be as tall as 27 inches/ 68 cm. Females are about 70 pounds/ 32 kg and measure up to 25 inches/63 cm high. The breed has a long head, long high-set hanging ears, a strong neck and a hard topline. The tail is docked to about 6 inches/15 cm and carried level at the back. The gait of the Weimaraner should be light and floating. Its eyes are very expressive and are light amber, gray or blue gray.

The longhaired Weimaraner is not permitted in the show ring in the United States but is, in other countries. It has a longer, silky coat with longer hair on the ears, back of the legs and under the body.

Registry: AKC, CKC, FCI (Group 7), KC

The longhaired Weimaraner, an interesting variation, is not recognized by the AKC but is shown in other countries.

ORIGIN AND DEVELOPMENT

The origins of the Cardigan Welsh Corgi are unclear. However, what is known is that it has been a well-established and vital part of the Welsh pastoral scene for many hundreds of years. It is also called the "Yard Long Dog," or in Welsh "Ci Llathaid," meaning a yard long. The length from the tip of the nose to the tip of the tail was meant to be 40 inches (the equivalent of a Welsh yard — or just over one meter).

Popular belief is that the Cardigan descended at least in part from early Dachshunds. In the 1880s Cardiganshire farmers were believed to have crossed the Cardigan with the old Welsh Collie, and many think that this was responsible for the introduction of the blue merle gene.

In the early days of exhibition and until 1934, both the Cardigan and Pembroke were shown as one breed and were in fact thus registered by the Kennel Club. This permitted interbreeding and must have allowed certain characteristics from each breed to become integrated in the other. It is said that this wholly unsatisfactory situation brought about a lessening of the emphasis which was placed on the Pembroke being born tail-less. Previously great store had been placed on the breeding of litters without tails, but the change introduced a more widespread option to dock puppies born with tails. Not all were in accord with this action and vigorous objections resulted in the Kennel Club banning the docking of Pembrokes in 1931. This ban stayed in force for only three years. Today the subject remains still very much a sensitive one.

In 1925 Corgis were first recorded as being shown in the United Kingdom. Fittingly it was at the South Wales Kennel Association Show in Cardiff where Mr. J. M. Symmons as judge awarded the first ever Challenge Certificates (CCs) to Fairmay Fondo and his litter sister, Shan Fach, whose dam was an unregistered bitch. Their sire, Bowhit Pepper, won the Open Dog class that day. His paternal grandparents were also unregistered and his dam recorded as "pedigree unknown." It was not until 1934 that Cardigans and Pembrokes competed for a different set of Certificates, and strangely in that year seven sets of Challenge Certificates were awarded for "Any Variety Welsh Corgi," but at the last two shows of the year, Cardigans and Pembrokes had separate sets. Interestingly, at Cruft's dog show that year, the Open class was won by Glantowy (a Cardigan) while Rozavel Red Dragon (Pembroke) stood Second. Later in the year these two became the first CC winners in their own breeds.

TEMPERAMENT

The Cardigan makes an excellent pet and is extremely intelligent, loyal, affectionate and good with children. Seldom quarrelsome, it can however be possessive of its owner's property. Frequently suspicious of strangers, it may require this characteristic to be kept firmly in check.

HEALTH MATTERS

Generally healthy, the major concern to all owners is the Cardigan's propensity towards obesity. Adopting a delicate balance between diet and exercise should help to keep this problem under control.

SPECIAL CARE AND TRAINING

Its natural desire to please, coupled with firm but fair training, should reward the Cardigan's owner with a lifetime of friendship based on trust, loyalty and devotion. The herding instinct remains strong in the Cardigan and it can be easily trained to carry out its original job, as well as proving itself in Obedience. The Cardigan requires little special care other than a thorough weekly grooming with a brush and comb. Its nails should be checked

Cardigan Welsh Corgis

regularly and not allowed to grow too long — adequate road walking should keep them at a sensible length.

ADAPTABILITY

The Cardigan is extremely versatile. It should be remembered that it was bred for its working ability and it still possesses great stamina and agility. While it enjoys nothing better than working, at the end of a long day it will be more than happy to share a place beside the fire with its human family.

ESSENTIALS OF THE BREED

Sturdy, mobile and capable of endurance, the Cardigan's appearance belies its capabilities. It is alert, active and possesses a steady temperament. Its height should be as near as possible to 12 inches/30 cm at the shoulder, with weight in proportion.

The head is foxy in appearance but with eyes that give a kindly, alert and watchful expression. The ears tend to be set a little wider than the Pembroke's, and the Cardigan's ears are larger and more rounded. The Cardigan also tends to have a definite, if slight, bow of the well-boned forelegs and the feet are quite large and round — unlike the Pembroke's neater, more oval feet. The chest is moderately broad and the body fairly long, the tail resembling a fox's brush. The coat is short or medium in length, weatherproof and may be any color with or without white markings.

This is by way of a stark contrast to the Pembroke which has much more specific color requirements, and can be taken as testimony to the breed's more checkered ancestry. The blue merle coloring is extremely popular in the Cardigan, and dogs of this color may have one or two pale blue eyes.

Registry: AKC, CKC, FCI (Group 1), KC

WELSH CORGIS—PEMBROKE WELSH CORGI

ORIGIN AND DEVELOPMENT

Indigenous to southwest Wales, it is widely believed that the forefathers of the Pembroke were introduced by Flemish weavers, brought to Britain in the 1100s by Henry I. Now accepted as being of spitz origin (as opposed to the original Cardigan variety which is alleged to be of Dachshund descent), it has been suggested that its origins are a combination of primitive spitz types such as the progenitors of the Keeshond, Pomeranian, Schipperke and Swedish Vallhund.

Precisely when the Welsh adopted the Pembroke as a working dog is obscure. However there is certainly no ambiguity that it was a highly valued associate of the Welsh drover in years gone by and, indeed, is still worked today as a sheep and cattle dog in many countries. It will instinctively herd — anything! The name "Corgi," as applied to the Pembroke, also has a somewhat shrouded origin. It means "cur dog" — "Cur" being simply a working dog rather than a derogatory term — or "dwarf dog." It has been suggested that all small working dogs in Wales were once referred to as "Corgi." Logically this suggestion has some merit and can be confirmed by the situation of the Cardigan and Pembroke — both small Welsh dogs, originally of no relation, but still both Corgis. Since the two breeds were distinguished as separate, they have remained pure and their own respective breed types have become much more clearly defined.

The Pembroke as a pure breed has now evolved to a very high level of quality world-wide. Perhaps its greatest claim to fame, and no hindrance to its achieving the present level of popularity, has been its favoritism with the British royal family. In 1933 the then Duke of York obtained for his daughters a Pembroke puppy, Rozavel Golden Eagle, who won a special place in the heart of Princess Elizabeth (later Elizabeth II). To this day the breed remains the royal favorite.

TEMPERAMENT

Known for its bark, which is worse than its bite, this is a small dog that thinks big. By nature it is not a squabbler; nevertheless it is a doughty little dog and respected by many considerably larger than itself. It should be outgoing to the point of being pushy, but not precocious and never, ever, shy or aggressive. It is intelligent enough to allow you to think that you are the boss, but there are times when you will realize that it has outsmarted you. This intelligence, combined with a wicked sense of humor, frequently makes Pembroke owners wonder whether their dog is laughing with or at them!

HEALTH MATTERS

Like many humans, the Pembroke requires life-membership to a slimming club! It is more than happy if it can finish its own meal and then help you out with yours. Its tendency toward obesity can lead to spinal problems. Its food intake must be controlled to keep it in trim. In all other respects the Pembroke is remarkably healthy.

SPECIAL CARE AND TRAINING

The Pembroke will train you with ease to its way of thinking and doing things if you are not careful. It will fit in and will happily be part of your daily routine. It can easily be obedience trained and some Pembrokes have been known to acquit themselves well at competitive Obedience and Agility. Given the chance to do what it was bred for, the Pembroke will take to herding like a duck to water. Most of the year its grooming requirements are minimal. However, seasonal shedding brings with it the bane of the Pembroke-lover's life. Like no other, the Pembroke coat works its way into carpet pile and the weave of fabrics and stubbornly resists the most concerted efforts to remove it.

Pembroke Welsh Corgi

ADAPTABILITY

As an urban dweller the Pembroke requires companionship. Without this, it may devise an undesirable method of seeking attention. Being active of mind and body it is best to keep it busy if it is in a one-dog situation. Few of its peers equal its flexibility both in the sense of what it was bred to do, and the role it can play as a member of the family.

ESSENTIALS OF THE BREED

The Pembroke is low to ground and epitomizes substance and stamina in a small space. Its temperament must be impeccable. The Pembroke has a head which is foxy in shape but this is not to be confused with its expression which is alert and intelligent. Its round eye and short muzzle, which tapers only slightly, precludes any similarity to that of a fox. Its skull is fairly wide and flat between its pricked ears. A moderate amount of stop separates the muzzle from the skull. To balance with its body, the Pembroke requires a fairly long neck which runs down into a level topline.

Only medium length of body is required as it must be agile and nimble to enable it to avoid the hooves of the kicking cattle it was bred to herd. Its size of 10-12 inches/25-30 cm at the withers enables it to control cattle by nipping their heels, then dropping to the ground. If it were bigger than this, it would connect all too easily with an avenging hoof. Again designed to contribute to its agility, its feet are oval with strong pads and well-arched toes.

It must have a dense undercoat to keep it warm. Its topcoat must lie straight and flat. To do the job that is required of it, the Pembroke must be a sound mover. Its fluid action must incorporate plenty of reach from the forelegs with equivalent drive and push from the hind legs. For a dog of its size it should cover a great deal of ground in a single stride. The most common color of red (with or without white markings) can range from a light honey gold to a deep mahogany red. The red may have black tips to it, this coat pattern being known as sable. The Pembroke may also be a very glamorous tricolor of black, red and white.

Registry: AKC, CKC, FCI (Group 1), KC

WELSH TERRIER

ORIGIN AND DEVELOPMENT

It would perhaps be a shade simplistic to simply state that the Welsh Terrier originates in Wales, although there can be no denying that the principality has played a major part in its development. In truth the nineteenth century saw broken-haired terriers, similar in type and color to the primitive Welsh Terrier, evolving in several areas of the United Kingdom, notably North Wales and the north of England. Such terriers were worked against foxes and used in conjunction with hounds. Particularly significant in the breed's history is the Jones family who lived for many years in mountainous North Wales where they bred black-and-tan terriers which were used with packs of Otterhounds. While the Joneses did not breed for exhibition, gradually specimens of their breeding found their way into early dog shows, with local enthusiasts forming the Welsh Terrier Club whose first show took place in Pwllheli in 1885.

Meanwhile, in the north of England, a similar terrier was being bred which was known as the "Old English Broken-Haired Terrier". When Kennel Club recognition was sought, both types were initially classified together as "Welsh Terriers or Old English Wire-Haired Terriers". This solution did not please either faction, and eventually the Welsh Terrier Club convinced the Kennel Club that the breed should be known as Welsh Terriers, regardless of their ancestry.

The breed today has changed considerably from the distinctly rugged original. Early breeders and exhibitors obviously sought a more "fancy" type of dog, and Wire Fox Terriers were doubtless introduced to produce a more elegant dog with a cleaner head. To this day, puppies are born with small white markings. In many ways the breed today is reminiscent of a miniature Airedale, with perplexing similarities to Lakeland Terriers to the uninitiated. Type differentials are only appreciated by the discerning.

TEMPERAMENT

While still a terrier at heart, the Welsh is not as hot-headed as some breeds in the same group. Basically obedient, easily disciplined and an affectionate dog, it still has its terrier gameness, but its biddable yet outgoing nature make it an ideal family dog. It is not as quarrelsome as some terriers and should mix in well with other dogs.

HEALTH MATTERS

The breed is free of major hereditary health problems, largely due to its very moderate appearance and lack of exaggeration. In addition the fact that it has never been a "commercialized" breed has meant that its welfare has been left in the hands of dedicated breeders.

SPECIAL CARE AND TRAINING

Basic obedience training is all that is required to make an ideal companion of a Welsh Terrier.

Its coat, if it is to be kept smart and neat, should be regularly trimmed — preferably by hand-stripping performed by an expert if it is to look its best.

ADAPTABILITY

The Welsh Terrier is a very adaptable dog. It will happily play King Pin in a one-dog family, but at the same time it will happily mix in well with other dogs. Regular, but not excessive, exercise renders this breed a quite undemanding dog that is equally at home in town or country.

ESSENTIALS OF THE BREED

The Welsh is always black-and-tan or black grizzle-and-tan. It should not exceed 15 1/2 inches/39 cm in height. Its skull is wider between the ears than in the Wire Fox Terrier and should be flat. The whole head of the Welsh Terrier should look more "blocky" than the more streamlined Fox Terrier head. Its eyes are small, dark, keen and expressive. Its small V-shaped ears tip forward and are carried close to the cheek. Its neck is moderately long and thick, yet elegantly arched. The back is short and the Welsh should be well ribbed. Its hindquarters are strong, and its feet small, round and tight. The tail is set high but not carried gaily. Its coat is hard, wiry, abundant and very close. A thin, open coat is quite untypical.

Registry: AKC, CKC, FCI (Group 3), KC

Welsh Terrier

WEST HIGHLAND WHITE TERRIER

ORIGIN AND DEVELOPMENT

Neither the thistle plant nor kilts, not even bagpipes themselves, are any more Scottish than this wonderful terrier breed. It was developed high in the mountains of the west of Scotland, a mixture of a great many root ancestors to other breeds now well developed. The common ancestor was the old Scotch Terrier which was hard coated, determined and fierce enough to be used for the toughest of local game. It was found in colors running the range from black to white and included tans, browns and even pied dogs.

Terriers were common and favored by the Scottish people who used them for hunting fox, badger and otter. Others fancied them for their ability to dispatch rats and mice quickly and willingly, as well as any other vermin that stumbled on to their paths. The dogs were selectively bred for their hunting or ratting prowess. Distinctions were evident within different countries, different regions, different cities and even different estates. Sameness was much desired and the up and coming stock would be put to the test. Frequently this involved dropping a dog into a barrel containing a young badger or other foe of equal ferocity. It was a quick way to determine "heart" and those that were especially adept got to pass on their strength in this regard to the next generation, while those that did not were not missed.

The Cairn, Scottish, Dandie Dinmont and Skye Terriers are all linked with the "Westie" of those early days. There was crossbreeding among Cairns, Scotties and Westies because their similarities were strong and the divergence of type had not yet occurred. Frequently, therefore, dogs from solid black to solid white, plus all shades in between as well as pieds, were found in the same litter. It has been reported that interbreeding of the West Highland White Terriers and Cairn Terriers continued until about 1917 when the American Kennel Club ruled that no Cairn would be registered if it carried Westie blood in its first three generations. The English Kennel Club took a similar stand and the interbreeding of the two effectively ceased. The results, however, may still be experienced in Cairn litters where odd occurrences of white on the chest, feet, under the tail or on the head do arise.

There is much evidence tracing the breed back in Scottish history. The heirs of Colonel E.D. Malcolm, who lived in the mid-nineteenth century, claim that dogs of this type were bred and valued in their family for a century. Indeed the Colonel and the Duke of Argyll were two of the strong early breeders.

The Breakfast Party painted in about 1831 by the Victorian artist Sir Edwin Landseer portrays a lad feeding his hound along with several Highland Terriers of varied types. More famous is his 1839 *Dignity and Impudence* which clearly portrays an early Westie. Since Landseer's love of the region is well known and his visits there frequent, and since his ability to capture faithfully both canine attitude and structure is legendary, this painting alone is strong evidence of the existence of the Westie as a recognizable breed.

Early on, the breed was known variously as the Highlander, the White and Lemon Terrier, the Pittenweem Terrier, the Roseneath Terrier, the Poltalloch Terrier and the West Highlander. The first known use of today's name for the breed is found in L.C.R. Cameron's book, *Otters and Otter Hunting*, published in London in 1908. In this book he says, "Col. Malcolm of Poltalloch has a kennel of these terriers, that his family has bred for generations, and to which he recently applied the name of West Highland White Terrier."

It is known that the Colonel preferred the white dogs because one day while hunting hare he shot and killed one of his favorite dogs, a reddish-brown terrier, mistaking it for a hare as it worked the heavy cover. From that point on

West Highland White Terrier

he decreed that only white terriers would be bred in his kennel for the purpose of hunting.

In the United States, the breed was exhibited as Roseneath Terriers at the 1906 Westminster Kennel Club show. The first dog show classes for the breed under their present name was at Cruft's in 1907. They were admitted to the American Kennel Club registry in 1908. Today Westies are among the larger terrier entries at the shows and at many shows they are the largest.

TEMPERAMENT

The popularity of the West Highland White Terrier is understandable. It is fun loving and will play with its family indoors or out and will anxiously await the next car ride or mountain hike. It finds joy in sniffing the flowers, lying on the patio, or climbing the season's highest snow bank. The Westie is respectfully quiet but lacks the dour attitude of some of its non-canine countrymen. Its jaunty self-assured attitude, its intelligence and love of life continue to win it more friends as each day passes.

HEALTH MATTERS

The Westie is generally very healthy and quite robust. They do have problems with skin allergies, usually caused by fleas. There are also cases of patella luxation, hernias, Legg-Perthe's disease and cranio mandibular osteopathy

(CMO or lion jaw), a painful though temporary inflammation of the jawbones in juveniles. With this heritable disease, the malformation of the jaw means that the young Westie cannot close its mouth or eat properly. If lion jaw is noticed early, the dog may respond to treatment with steroids under strict veterinary supervision. As a precaution, only buy a Westie from a reliable breeder.

SPECIAL CARE AND TRAINING

The Westie is well behaved and has good manners. An intelligent breed, it is quick to learn and always looks as if it understands exactly what is being said to it. It is a dog that likes to be cleaned up if it has been on a muddy walk. Because it is white, no matter where it lives it will require extra time and effort to keep it looking good. Its hard coat will need plucking or stripping (never clipping) and its head and ears trimmed to show off its unique expression.

ADAPTABILITY

The Westie is the perfect size for an apartment, home in the country or a castle. It is a breed that enjoys human company and people of all ages.

ESSENTIALS OF THE BREED

The breed is all white and no other color, with a double coat — a hard, straight, wiry outer coat and a soft, warm undercoat close to the body. In show shape the body coat is about 2 inches/5 cm long with longer hair slowly blending into the legs, chest, sides and rear. Any suggestion of softness or silkiness to the outer coat is shunned as it loses its desired ability to protect and to be maintained. The hair on the head stands away and forms a frame to accentuate the desired expression.

The breed today is moderate of size, being about 11 inches/28 cm at the withers. Its body is compact, the back level, the ribs well sprung and deep, and the chest is deep and extends to the elbows. The skull is slightly domed and fairly broad with a well-defined stop. The muzzle is powerful and a little shorter than the skull. The jaws are powerful and the teeth, which meet in a scissors bite, are very large for the size of the dog. The ears are erect, widely set, pointed and never cropped. The Westie's eyes are dark and wide apart.

Registry: AKC, CKC, FCI (Group 3), KC

The hair on the West Highland White Terrier's head stands away and forms a frame that accentuates the expression.

WESTPHALIAN DACHSBRACKE/ WESTFÄLISCHE DACHSBRACKE

The German, low-legged Bracke from Westphalia is a variety of the German Bracke. It is also the breed that the Swedish Drever derives from. This dog is strictly used to hunt hare, fox, deer and wild boar. It is rarely seen outside Germany.

The height at its withers should be 12-15 inches/30-38 cm. The body should be long, well muscled and with strong bone. The head should be wedge shaped with ears hanging close to the cheeks. The coat should be short, lie close and be a hard texture. The color should be red with a black mantle and white symmetrical markings — so-called hound colors.

Registry: FCI (Group 6)

Westphalian Dachsbracke

WETTERHOUN

The Dutch water dog has been known since the Middle Ages, particularly in the Freesian part of the country where it was often used to hunt water fowl. It is also known as good guard and watchdog. It is rarely seen outside the Netherlands.

At the withers, the males are about 21 inches/55 cm with females slightly smaller. The body should be compact, deep and almost rectangular, well muscled and with strong bone. The head and muzzle should be strong and of equal length. The ears are carried close to the cheeks and the coat should be wavy and not exceed the tips. The tail should not be set too high but curl over the back. The coat should be thick, curly and with an oily texture. This breed should be white with very fine black or liver-brown speckling that gives a gray, blue or café au lait tone and with black or brown large patches on the sides of the head and ears as well as on the body.

Wetterhoun

Registry: FCI (Group 8)

WHIPPET

ORIGIN AND DEVELOPMENT

The Whippet is a medium-sized, shorthaired sighthound similar in conformation to a Greyhound. While there is general agreement on the origins of the Greyhound, which has existed as a breed for thousands of years, opinions vary as to those of the Whippet. Some authors endeavor to prove from early paintings and pottery that Whippets have existed as a recognizable breed from the fifth century A.D., while others will state, equally categorically, that the breed only came into being in the late nineteenth century when small Greyhounds were crossed with various terrier breeds to produce a fast little dog for hunting rabbit and later for racing.

Toward the end of the eighteenth century, the medium-sized running dog acquired a name of its own — the "Whippet" or "Snap dog" — and was a popular breed among the working men in the north of England. These dogs were first used for rabbit coursing and would be expected to run twenty-five or thirty times a day, so Bull Terrier or Manchester Terrier crosses were introduced to achieve greater strength and stamina. After rabbit coursing had fallen into disrepute, the sport of rag racing became popular. Then, as now, there was a handicapping system in Whippet racing based on weight, which gave an advantage to the smaller, lighter-boned dog. The favored weight for a racing Whippet was around 16-17 pounds/ 7-8 kg, whereas the rabbit coursing Whippet had weighed in at about 25 pounds/11 kg.

Whippets became known as "the poor man's Greyhound" and were highly prized possessions, living curled up by the fire. It is said they were often fed rather better than the human members of the family. Whippets were expected to earn their keep at race meetings where much betting took place, so a dog that lacked speed would not be considered of any value. Only the best bitches were bred from and only the fastest dogs used at stud so, once more, the Greyhound type of animal predominated.

By 1890, the Whippet had become sufficiently popular as a show dog to be officially recognized by the Kennel Club, and in 1896 the first Challenge Certificates were granted. Although the modern Whippet emerged in England, the first Whippet ever to be registered with a Kennel Club was a dog named Jack Dempsey, registered with the American Kennel Club in 1888 in the Miscellaneous Category. Although a pure-bred Whippet is a Whippet in whatever country it is bred, each country favors a slightly different type, and these differences can be traced back to the variations in the breed Standard laid down by the respective kennel clubs.

While there may exist certain subtle type differentials in Whippets from country to country, breeders in the main still maintain a rather international outlook on the breed and the true afficianados are always anxious to explore new bloodlines if they feel they may complement their existing stock.

British Whippets continue to be exported to the United States, Europe and Scandinavia, South Africa and Australasia on a regular basis. Incorporated judiciously into well thought out breeding programs, Whippets from the breed's homeland still have much to offer.

In 1992 a Whippet won Best in Show at Cruft's, Great Britain's most famous dog show, for the first time. Morag Bolton's Ch. Pencloe Dutch Gold was the victorious hound and, interestingly, the judge of Best in Show that year was the late Ann Argyle, herself a Whippet breeder and owner of the noted Harque affix. Dutch Gold was retired from active competition after this great win, but he proved to be an exceptional producer and his offspring were keenly sought after in many countries. Indeed, at the 1995 prestigous Sydney Royal Show in Australia, a daughter of Dutch Gold, namely United Kingdom Ch. Silkstone Jewel In The Crown, won Best in Show for Frank and

Whippet

Lee Pieterse who had the foresight to import her from her breeder Roma Wright Smith.

TEMPERAMENT

The Kennel Club Standard in the United Kingdom describes the Whippet as having a "gentle, affectionate and even disposition." Its medium height and light build rarely frightens small children by overwhelming them with size, and its length of leg and short coat makes it a very clean and easy dog to have in the home. Though very quiet and non-aggressive dogs, Whippets will bark a warning if strange people or cars approach the house. They are very affectionate dogs and like to be with their owners, so that a single Whippet is happiest in the house,

though several Whippets together may be content in warm, well-insulated kennels, given enough human companionship and exercise.

HEALTH MATTERS

The Whippet Standard was originally drawn up by the Whippet Club with the belief that, as a running hound, any fault which would detract from the dog's ability to work should be discouraged, and that all forms of exaggeration should be avoided. This has meant that they have remained free from many of the hereditary defects which have beset other breeds. Most visits to the vet, apart from booster injections, will be as a result of some sort of injury sustained while in full pursuit of a rabbit or squirrel, rather than any illness.

SPECIAL CARE AND TRAINING

Whippets, although very hardy, feel the cold and need a warm and draft-free sleeping place. They also need a windproof coat when exercising on the lead in cold weather. Breed owners should remember that Whippets are sighthounds and that the instinct to run is always there. Whereas one Whippet might come when called, two or more will find the temptation to chase more difficult to resist, so it is essential that puppies are taught to come when called.

A Whippet can still have its chasing instincts encouraged by tying a piece of fur or rag to the end of a pole and swinging it around (this type of game should be separated from formal training). Whippets should not be raced or coursed in competition until they are at least one year old, though they may be introduced to courses and traps from nine months. As Whippets chase by nature, the main difficulty for an owner is teaching them to differentiate between legitimate quarry and that which is strictly forbidden.

ADAPTABILITY

There are few breeds with the versatility of a Whippet. An elegant show dog will spend a very happy day running around a race track or out on the coursing field in winter conditions.

ESSENTIALS OF THE BREED

The American Standard varies from that of the United Kingdom in several ways. The main divergence is in the height, front and shoulder construction, and in the eye color and pigmentation. The American Standard has as its height specification 19-22 inches/48-56 cm for dogs and 18-21 inches/46-53 cm for bitches, with a disqualification for any dog that is 1/2 inch/2 cm above or below these heights. The British Standard lays down an "ideal" height of 18-20 inches/46-50 cm for dogs and 17-18 inches/ 43-46 cm for bitches, with no disqualification clauses at all, any decisions being left to the discretion of the judge. The American Standard also calls for a dark eye with the pigmentation around the eye complete, and lists upright ears as incorrect and to be severely penalized. The British Standard asks only for bright, oval-shaped eyes with an alert expression and for ears to be small, fine in texture and "rose shaped."

As it is a running hound developed to catch smaller game, the characteristics which lend themselves to speed, stamina and agility are very important. The Whippet should combine strength with elegance, and should present a balanced appearance with no form of exaggeration. The head should be lean, with a slight stop and small fine ears, carried folded back close against the head. When alert, the ears should fold over.

The American Standard calls more attention to the head as upright ears are severely penalized, and eye color and pigmentation must be dark. With this emphasis on dark pigment, there are fewer of the pale hound colors in the United States than in Europe, where any color or mixture of colors is permissible. The neck should be long and strong enough to pick up quarry at speed, there should be good layback of shoulder enabling the dog to stretch out at full gallop and the forelegs should be straight with good flat bone and well-knuckled feet with thick pads. A slight spring of pastern is essential to prevent injury when running. The body should have a deep brisket; the back should be firm with plenty of length and yet without exaggeration; the strong loin should have a slight arch and the long tail should reach to below the hock joint when pulled straight. The tail should be carried in a delicate curve when moving, but not over the back. The hindquarters should be strong and muscular, with a good second thigh and low set hocks. The stifles should be well bent— excessive angulation should be avoided. The Whippet's movement should show effortless driving power—long and low in front; the hind legs coming well under the body for propulsion.

Registry: AKC, CKC, FCI (Group 10), KC

ORIGIN AND DEVELOPMENT

The Wirehaired Pointing Griffon is a versatile hunting dog that was developed in the nineteenth century by Edward K. Korthals. Although from Holland, Korthals did most of the development of the breed in France. In Europe the breed is still officially called the Korthals Griffon.

Starting with a bitch, Mouche, who was a Griffon of Barbet origins and with various crosses to Small Munsterlanders, Braque Français, and various setters and pointers, Korthals developed the Griffon to be a methodical close worker in all types of terrain. Excellent in swampy country, the Griffon handles fur and feathers equally well. Not fast enough to compete successfully in field trials, the Griffon is at its best as a meticulous hunting companion, doing well as a pointer in the field and as a retriever in the water.

Wirehaired Pointing Griffon

The Griffon's profuse mustache and eyebrows, extensions of the undercoat, give the breed its characteristic unkempt appearance.

TEMPERAMENT

The Griffon is an excellent family dog, trustworthy and with a tremendous willingness to please. In fact its devotion to family and its friendly temperament endear it to all who know it. It has a delightful character and will entertain and amuse its owner from puppyhood on.

HEALTH MATTERS

A healthy working dog, the Griffon has few problems except a tendency to some skin allergies and occasionally a thyroid problem. The breed also suffers from a certain frequency of entropion and ectropion.

SPECIAL CARE AND TRAINING

The Griffon has a quick, intelligent mind and is easily trained. Like all breeds that are to become pets and work for a living, the puppies need early socialization. Housetraining, obedience training and an introduction to the bird field should start at eight to ten weeks of age.

ADAPTABILITY

The Griffon likes to be out working in the fields and water. It is therefore much better suited to living in the country than being confined to a city apartment. However, the Griffon could divide its time quite happily between the city and the country. It will adapt to any place so long as it is with its owner.

ESSENTIALS OF THE BREED

The ideal height for a Griffon is between 22-24 inches/56-60 cm at the withers (20-22 inches/51-56 cm for bitches). Size is a major characteristic of the breed and oversize should be severely penalized. It is longer than it is tall in proportions of ten to nine and is of medium substance with an efficient tireless movement.

The Griffon's color ranges from chestnut brown, steel gray with brown markings, roan or white to brown. All brown, all white, orange and white are less desirable. Black is a disqualification. The coat of the Griffon is a distinguishing feature of the breed. The outercoat is straight and wiry; the undercoat consists of a thick fine down. Its profuse mustache and eyebrows are extensions of the undercoat and give the Griffon its characteristically unkempt appearance. The Wirehaired Pointing Griffon is a dog of medium speed and at the trot shows good extension and a smooth ground covering ability.

Registry: AKC, CKC, FCI (Group 7)

483

YORKSHIRE TERRIER

ORIGIN AND DEVELOPMENT

The delightful breed now known as the Yorkshire Terrier is a manmade creation and the exact ingredients used in its formation are a little uncertain. It is likely that the now extinct Paisley Terrier played a major part in the breed's development. The Paisley was not unlike a Skye Terrier, but was shorter-backed and weighed around 16 pounds/7 kg. Documented evidence is scarce, but in 1861 reference was made to the breed as the Halifax, Blue Fawn or Broken-Haired Terrier. Back in the 1860s, Mary Ann Foster, an indomitable Tipperary woman married to a Yorkshireman, began to popularize the Yorkshire Terrier through the length and breadth of Great Britain and Ireland, and one of her dogs was the famous Huddersfield Ben. He is still referred to as the "father of the breed."

As it began to stabilize through selective breeding, the breed soon won many admirers because it had both an undisputed terrier character and yet was a small size. From the early days, its coat became one of its major characteristics, so much so that breeders for many generations have attached almost supreme importance to this aspect of the dog, greatly prizing correct color and texture. The fact that, traditionally, in Great Britain Yorkshire Terriers are still shown standing on their individual boxes so that the uninterrupted coat length may be studied by judges, gives testament to this.

The Yorkshire Terrier has continued to maintain its position as an international favorite companion breed, but generally those dogs that are purely pets tend to be a little larger than the average show specimen. In some European countries, the Yorkshire has been transferred from the companion or Toy Group into the Terrier Group. While it may look a little out of place because of its lack of size, its character is such that it can more than hold its own when up against larger breeds.

In many Toy breeds it is true that breeders often tend to produce two different types of bitches: the larger, more solid examples are kept exclusively as "brood bitches" and their smaller, and generally, more refined, sisters are the show specimens. However, the more dedicated and determined Toy breeders aim to produce bitches which are capable of both top level winning and self-whelping. It is no easy task, as larger specimens lurking in the background of a pedigree may produce the occasional "throwback" in the form of a rather large puppy.

Every Yorkshire Terrier breeder's aim is to establish a line which produces consistently even type and quality, in both bitches and dogs, so that size varies as little as possible.

A remarkable example of a Yorkshire Terrier breeder who has succeeded in this aim has to be Osman Sameja whose Ozmilion Kennel, based in Battersea, London, England, has become something of a legend in contemporary Yorkie history.

Through a regime of intense line-breeding, Sameja has produced generations of Champions, and the emphasis has always been on breeding only from the highest quality bitches.

In the late 1980s Sameja's Yorkshire Terrier male, Ch. Ozmilion Dedication, was Dog of the Year All Breeds in Great Britain, winning the Toy Group at Cruft's the following year. He also holds the record for the Yorkie to have won more Challenge Certificates than any other. In 1995, Sameja won the Toy Group at Cruft's with Ch. Ozmilion Mystification, a descendant of Dedication whose pedigree is indeed a work of art. Mystification is not only the fourteenth generation homebred male Champion in direct line — itself an incredible feat — but his Champion dam comes from five generations of home-bred Champion bitches.

Yorkshire Terrier

This long line of success for Sameja's breeding program is proof positive that it is quite possible to establish a highly successful line of dual-purpose bitches in even the smallest of dog breeds.

TEMPERAMENT

Despite its diminutive size, the Yorkie is still very much a terrier at heart and game to the last. To this day the breed never ceases to amaze its owners with its prowess as a killer of small rodents. Brave and spirited, the Yorkie should at all times be even tempered, making it an ideal companion breed. It is not quarrelsome with other dogs and frequently coexists happily with other breeds.

HEALTH MATTERS

Like its larger terrier cousins, the Yorkie remains a hardy and healthy breed with few major problems. Patella luxation is seen quite often, and its teeth should be regularly cared for in case they become prematurely diseased and cause problems in old age.

SPECIAL CARE AND TRAINING

The Yorkie is easily trained in basic Obedience routines and some have been known to prove their worth as keen Agility dogs too.

One of the breed's major characteristics is its full and flowing coat, and so this is not the breed for the faint-hearted. Grooming must take place each day — and it is a time-consuming process. Exhibition Yorkies tend to have their coat tied up, long strips of hair being rolled up in paper "crackers," which are then maintained in small bobbles over the body. These crackers are renewed on a daily basis and special oils are often applied to the coat to improve texture and encourage growth. Companion Yorkies do not need to have such intricate grooming, but if they are to look representative of their breed and be kept clean and smart, their coats should be brushed and combed right through each day. Customarily the hair on the forehead is tied up in a rubber band or bow, keeping the coat away from the eyes. It would appear rather futile to acquire a Yorkie if the intention is to clip off the coat — its crowning glory — but if the dog is not to be shown, it is often quite practical and advisable to keep the coat fall a little shorter than floor-length with a little judicious scissoring. More ruthless trimming destroys the breed's marvellous coat.

ADAPTABILITY

Yorkshire Terriers will live a rugged outdoor life as befits their terrier ancestry. At the same time,

they will be happy to live the life of a pampered pet. Provided they are given sufficient attention and company, they will fit in anywhere.

ESSENTIALS OF THE BREED

The Yorkie's head is rather small, not too prominent or rounded in skull, with not too long a muzzle and a black nose. The eyes should be medium size, dark and sparkling, with dark eye rims. They should create an intelligent and keen expression, placed to look directly forward. The ears are small, V-shaped, carried erect and not too far apart. The breed has good reach of neck, a level topline, compact body with average spring of rib and straight forelegs. The feet are round with black nails, and the hindquarters should exhibit moderate turn of stifle. The tail is carried a little higher than the level of the back.

The Yorkie's coat is a major ingredient of its overall breed type, and color and texture are extremely important. The hair on the body is long, perfectly straight, fine and silky. The coat fall on the head is long, and of rich golden tan, deeper in color at the sides of the head, around the base of the ears and on the muzzle where it must be very long. The tan color of the head should not intrude on to the neck, nor should there be any sooty or dark hairs in the tan. The dark, steel-blue (not to be confused with silver-blue or black-blue) color of the mature adult should run from the occiput to the root of the tail, and should be free of fawn, bronze or dark hairs. The hair on the chest is rich, bright tan, and all tan hairs should be darker at the roots than the middle, shading to a still lighter shade at the tips. Yorkshire Terriers may continue changing color until they are two years of age, so judges tend to be a little forgiving of darker colors in youngsters which have yet to mature. Ideally the Yorkshire Terrier should weigh no more than 7 pounds/ 3 kg. None of the breed Standards includes a height for the dog, but a well-proportioned Yorkie is about 7 inches/ 18 cm at the withers.

Registry: AKC, CKC, FCI (Group 3), KC

DOG CLUBS, REGISTRIES AND ASSOCIATIONS

Throughout the world the relationship of dog registeries, breed clubs and animal welfare societies in general is one of cooperation. Listed below is information for the four main kennel clubs whose fully recognized breeds we have included in the breed section of this book starting on page 69.

FCI has federated associations in thirty-nine countries and associated members in thirty countries in Europe, Asia, Africa, the Far East, Australia, New Zealand, the Carribean and Central and South America. Details of the affiliated associations, specialist dog clubs and welfare associations in each country can be obtained from the Secretary General of FCI. Please write to the address below.

For information about individual breed clubs and welfare organizations please contact the registry organization in your country for information, addresses and phone numbers:

The American Kennel Club
51 Madison Avenue
New York, New York 10010
phone: 212-696-8200

Canadian Kennel Club
89 Skyway Avenue
Suite 100
Etobicoke, Ontario
Canada M9W 6R4
phone: 416-675-5511

Fédération Cynologique Internationale
14, rue Leopold II
B-6530 Thuin,
Belgium

The Kennel Club of Great Britain
1 Clarges Street
London W1Y 8AB
phone: 0171-493-6651

GLOSSARY

Affix: a word granted to a breeder by the registering body for his or her exclusive use when registering dogs. The word is generally attached to the end of the dog's name. A prefix serves the same purpose and is always the first word of the dog's name.

Almond eye: an eye set in surrounding tissue of almond shape.

Amble: 1) a relaxed gait in which the legs on either side move in unison, i.e., front left and rear left move forward together. 2) a slower version of "pacing" – often the transitional movement between walking and trotting.

Angulation: the angle formed at a joint where bones meet, most often used in describing the forequarters and hindquarters.

Apron: longer hair below the neck on the chest, forming a profuse frill.

Back: the portion of the topline between withers and croup.

Balance: proportion of the whole animal, or integral parts thereof. A balanced dog indicates that it has harmony of outline where head, neck, body etc. are all in proportion.

Barrel ribs: ribs which are overly sprung to create a barrel effect.

Bat ear: an erect ear, broad based, rounded at the top and fully open in front.

Beard: thick, long hair on the muzzle and underjaw.

Belton: a white color with very tiny spots, usually all over the body in colors of black giving the impression of a blue color (hence called blue belton), lemon, orange or liver.

Benching: individual stalls in which all entered dogs must be displayed during a show or benched exhibition.

Best in Show (BIS): the final winner at a dog show.

Bitch: a female dog.

Bite: the relative position of the upper and lower teeth when the mouth is closed.

Blaze: a white stripe running between the eyes.

Blenheim: the red-and-white variety of the English Toy Spaniel and the Cavalier King Charles Spaniel.

Blue merle: blue and gray mixed with black; a marbled effect.

Bobtail: a dog born with a naturally short tail or no tail at all.

Brace: two dogs, usually of the same breed or variety.

Bracelets: trimmed hair left on the legs of some breeds.

Breeching: hair on backs of thighs and buttocks. Also describes tan hindquarters markings in some black-and-tan breeds.

Breed Standard: written ideal of a breed and yardstick by which all dogs are judged.

Breeder: one who breeds dogs. Officially, the British KC and most FCI countries regard the breeder of a dog as the person who owns its dam at the time of whelping. The AKC deems the person who owns a dog's dam at the time of mating as the breeder.

Brindle: a coat pattern where black hairs create the impression of stripes on a lighter background or vice versa.

Brisket: the forepart, below the chest between the forelegs.

Broken-down ears: deformed, misshapen ears or lacking correct carriage.

Brood bitch: a bitch used for breeding, often used to describe a strongly made bitch that may be lacking overall refinement.

Brush: a thick, bushy tail, well coated with hair.

Burr: the inside of the ear.

Button ear: a small, neat ear which drops forward lying close to the skull and pointing toward the eye.

CAC: the national Certificate which counts toward a Championship in member countries of the FCI.

CACIB: the international Certificate which counts toward an International Championship in member countries of the FCI.

Canine teeth: the two upper and lower "fangs" found at each side of the incisors.

Carpals: the bones of the wrist.

Challenge Certificate (CC): a key award offered at British Championship shows, one for the best in each sex. Three CCs must be won under three different judges, at least one when the dog is a minimum of one year old, to qualify for the title of Champion.

Champion: a dog which has met the requirements in competition to qualify for the title.

China eye: a clear blue eye.

Chippendale front: a front which is wide at the elbow, close at the pasterns with feet turning outward.

Chiseled: cleanly cut and delicately worked so that the bone structure can be seen, normally used to describe the foreface.

Chops: jowls – the pendulous flesh of the lips and jaw.

Close coupled: short in the loin.

Cobby: short bodied, compact and square with substance.

Compact: closely coupled and in no way rangy.

Condition: the level of healthy appearance as indicated by a fit body, coat, general appearance and deportment.

Conformation: the physical construction of a dog, essentially refering to its skeletal assembly.

Corded: a coat pattern where the top and undercoat twists and becomes matted in such a way that long cords develop.

Corkscrew tail: a twisted tail.

Coupling: the area between the ribs and pelvis; the loin.

Coursing: the sport of chasing hare, usually with sighthounds.

Covering ground: the relative position of fore- and hindlegs when standing, Alternatively, the amount of ground covered in action with one stride due to correct construction.

Crest: 1) the uppermost part of the neck, often used in the context of "crested" meaning elegantly arched. 2) a plume of hair found in breeds such as the hairless Chinese Crested.

Crook: part of the forelegs in breeds such as the Basset Hound where the leg bends to afford support to the chest.

Cropping: cutting the ear leather to afford erect carriage. Cropping is forbidden in the UK and some European countries.

Croup: the rump; the area that lies over the pelvic region i.e., from the hip joints to the buttocks.

Crown: 1) the uppermost part of the head. 2) the circles of hair found at the head of the ridge in the Rhodesian Ridgeback.

Cryptorchid: a male dog whose testicles are not descended into the scrotum or which are absent.

Culottes: Long hair on the back of the thighs.

Cut-up: noticeable upward turn of the underline toward the rear; tuck-up.

Dam: the female parent of a dog.

Dappled: mottled markings of different colors creating a marbled effect.

Dewclaw: the fifth digit on the inside of the legs, normally found on only the forelegs, but occasionally on the hindlegs.

Dewlap: loose pendulous skin under the throat.

Dock: to remove a portion of the tail.

Dog: used to describe the male of the species.

Domed: noticeably rounded in the skull.

Double coat: an outer coat of guard hairs, coupled with a usually denser and softer undercoat.

Dry: used to describe a skull or neck which is free of loose skin, i.e., the skin is taut and close-fitting.

Ectropion: a condition in which the eyelids are turned outward.

Entropion: a condition in which the eyelids are turned inward.

Even bite: the level bite of a mouth in which the incisors meet edge-to-edge when the mouth is closed, with no overlapping of the upper and lower teeth.

Ewe neck: a concave neckline – opposite of well-arched neck.

Eye teeth: the upper canine teeth.

Fall: great length of hair.

Fall away: the slope of the croup.

FCI: the Fédération Cynologique Internationale, which was founded in 1911 as a coordinating body between national governing bodies within the dog world.

Feathering: longer hairs on legs, ears, tail and underline.

Field trial: a competition where dogs, especially gun dogs, are judged only on their ability to find and/or retrieve game.

Filbert ear: ear in the shape of a rounded-off triangle, like a filbert (hazelnut).

Finish: a dog's overall look of maturity. In the US the term "finish" is often used to describe a dog's completion of its Championship title.

Flange: a projecting edge of rib.

Flank: the side of the body between the last rib and the hip.

Flat bone: bone, usually in the forelegs, which is flattened so that it is more oval than round.

Flat sided: used to describe a rib cage which is insufficiently sprung as the ribs approach the sternum.

Flecked: 1) a coat which is lightly ticked with another color, 2) a flawed but otherwise normal eye.

Flews: pendulous upper lips.

Floating rib: the last and thirteenth rib which is unattached.

Fluffy: describes dogs which require medium coats that are excessively full and soft, usually with exaggerated furnishings.

Flying ears: ears that are wholly erect or that stand away from the face in a breed requiring dropped or semi-erect ears.

Flying trot: an action in which all four feet are off the ground momentarily during each stride; also called a suspended trot.

Forechest: the frontal part of the chest, which is properly seen projecting in front of the foreleg.

Foreface: the muzzle; the part of the head in front of the eyes.

Forehand: the front part of the whole dog, usually used to describe the overall animal head on, from the shoulders forward.

Foxy: a sharp expression reminiscent of a fox, usually created by a pointed foreface, pricked ears and keen, small eyes.

Frill: apron.

Fringes: as feathering, referring to the ears on a Pekingese.

Frog face: expression created by an extending nose combined with a receding jaw, often accompanied by an overshot mouth.

Frontal bone: the skullbone over the eyes.

Frosting: white hairs intermingled with the base color around the muzzle, usually due to age.

Furnishings: longer hair on the head, legs, breechings and tail.

Furrow: a slight indentation or median line between the stop and the occiput.

Gay tail: a tail carried too high or over a dog's back.

Globular: describes an eye shape which is round and slightly prominent without bulging.

Grizzle: a mixture of colors including gray, red and black.

Group: 1) selection of breeds classified together e.g., Hounds, Terriers; 2) competition of Best of Breed winners in a Group.

Guard hairs: longer, stiffer hairs that grow through and often conceal the undercoat.

Hackney action: an exaggerated forehand action where the front feet are lifted very high, as in a hackney horse.

Haloes: skin with a dark pigmentation surrounding the eyes.

Ham: great muscular development of the hind leg above the stifle. Also used in the sense of "hammy hindquarters."

Handler: a person who handles a dog in the show ring.

Hard expression: a severe, staring expression.

Harlequin: a color pattern of black and white, or blue and white, where irregular colored patches appear on a clear white background.

Hare foot: an elongated foot, as that of a hare.

Harness: markings around the shoulders and chest, usually in a lighter color than the base color, in the pattern of a harness.

Harsh coat: a stiff, wiry coat texture.

Haunch: buttock or rump.

Haw: third eyelid or membrane in the inside corner of the eye, usually meaning one or both haws are unpigmented.

Heat: the estrus of the bitch.

Herring gutted: denoting acute lack of rib spring.

Hip dysplasia: abnormal formation of the hip joint where the femoral head does not fit correctly in its socket.

Hock: the collection of bones in the hind leg forming the joint between the second thigh and the metatarsus.

Hound marked: a color pattern of white, black and tan.

Inbreeding: the mating of closely related dogs.

Incisors: the upper and lower front teeth between the canines.

Interbreeding: the mating of dogs which are of the same breed but different varieties.

Jowls: the flesh of the lips and jaws.

KC: British Kennel Club.

Keel: the pronounced curvaceous outline of the brisket between the prosternum and end of breastbone.

Keen expression: deep-seeing, penetrating expression; also alert ear carriage.

Knuckling over: malformation of the wrist, allowing it to double forward under a standing dog's weight.

Landseer: originally described the white-and-black color pattern in the Newfoundland. Subsequently, and confusingly, adopted by a breed developed from the Newfoundland.

Layback: most commonly the angle of the shoulder blade and the upper foreleg viewed from the side; also the degree of recession of the Bulldog's nose.

Leather: the ear flap.

Leggy: too long on leg for correct, typical balance of the breed.

Level bite: when the front incisors of both the upper and lower jaws meet without any overlap.

Line breeding: the mating of related dogs within a line or family, or in such a way that a specific ancestor appears several times in the resulting progeny's pedigree.

Lion clip: traditional clip of the show Poodle where hair is clipped short from the last rib backward, on the legs, face and tail; also called the English Saddle Clip in the US. This is also a correct clip for the mature Portuguese Water Dog.

Liver: a dark brown color also referred to as chocolate.

Loin: the region of the body on either side of the vertebral column between the last ribs and the pelvis.

Long coupled: being long in loin.

Low set: 1) usually describes a tail which is set below the level of the topline; 2) may describe ear placement.

Lower thigh: second thigh.

Lozenge: the small spot of color found in the center of the facial blaze in the Blenheim phase of the English Toy Spaniel and Cavalier King Charles Spaniel.

Maiden: a bitch which has not produced puppies.

Mane: long and profuse hair found on the neck and shoulders.

Mantle: dark shading to be found in the coat of some breeds.

Mask: dark shading on the foreface and around the eyes.

Median line: a central line running from the top of the skull toward the muzzle, due to bone formation or muscular development. Also sometimes referred to as fluting.

Merle: color pattern, usually in gray-blue, with black flecks.

Merle eye: a flecked eye, brown or blue, with a black iris.

Molera: a small opening on the upper part of the skull due to the bones failing to merge, typically found in the Chihuahua.

Monorchid: a male dog which has only one testicle descended into the scrotum.

Multum in parvo: Latin expression meaning "much in little," to describe dogs which have great substance for their size.

Muzzle: the head in front of the eyes; the foreface.

Oblique shoulders: shoulders which are well laid back.

Occiput: the upper back point of the skull.

Occipital protuberance: a noticeably raised occiput.

Open coat: a sparse coat lacking density and texture.

Open hocks: outward-turning hocks appearing bowed.

Otter tail: a thick-rooted, relatively short tail which tapers to a blunt end, covered with short thick hair.

Outbreeding: mating of unrelated dogs of the same breed.

Over-reaching: faulty action caused by excessive rear drive and angulation, causing the hind feet to be placed beyond and to the side of the forefeet.

Overshot: a mouth where the upper incisors project beyond the lower incisors, affording no contact when the mouth is closed.

Pads: the soles of the feet.

Parti-color: a white base color with darker patches.

Pastern: the region of the foreleg between the wrist and toes.

Patella: the bone to the fore of the stifle joint.

Peak: the occiput.

Pied: unequal patches of white and another color.

Pigeon chest: a chest with a short, protruding breastbone.

Pig jaw: an overshot mouth.

Pin bones: bony protruberances of the pelvis, below the tail.

Pinto: dark markings on a white background, with markings on the head and the major part of the body.

Plume: long, profuse coat on the end of the tail.

Points: colored areas in distinct relief to the base color, usually found on the face, ears, legs and tail.

Poking: moving with the neck stretched forward and the head carried unusually low.

Pompon: rounded tuft of hair left on the end of the tail.

Prick ear: a totally erect ear, usually pointed at the tip.

Punishing jaw: a strongly developed underjaw.

Racy: creating the impression of speed and agility without any loss of substance.

Rangy: slenderly built; often used when describing a young dog that is going through "gangly" adolescence.

Rat tail: a tail which is thick-rooted, tapering to a fine point and partially or totally lacking in hair.

Reachy: usually used to describe a long, elegant neck.

Referee: a judge appointed to make a final decision when two judges have each judged one sex of a breed and failed to agree on Best of Breed. A referee is never used in AKC and FCI shows. There is only one judge in the ring at any time.

Register: to record with the appropriate governing body a dog's breeding and ownership details.

Ribbed up: with ribs reaching well back toward the hindquarters, and consequently with little length of loin.

Ridge: hair growing in the opposite direction to the main coat.

Ringer: a dog which closely resembles another, and illegally substituted for it in exhibition.

Roach back: a convex curvature of the back beginning behind the withers and continuing toward the loin.

Roan: a fine mixture of colored hairs alternating with white hairs, creating a mottled or speckled appearance often with large flecks of solid color.

Rolling gait: an ambling action.

Roman nose: a nose where the bridge is rather high and the profile curves downward in a convex line toward the nose tip.

Rose ear: a small, neat ear which folds over and back, revealing the inner burr.

Ruff: thick, longer hair growing around the neck.

Rump: croup.

Sable: a coat pattern in which black-tipped hairs are overlaid on a background of gold, silver, gray, fawn or tan.

Saddle: variation of either coat color or coat type over the back.

Scissors bite: the bite most normally found in the dog where the upper incisors closely overlap the lower teeth and are set square to the jaws.

Screw tail: a naturally short tail, twisted almost in a spiral.

Season: estrus.

Second thigh: the section of the hindquarter from the stifle to the hock; also referred to as the lower thigh.

Self color: one color; a whole color with no markings other than possibly slightly lighter shadings of the base color.

Set on: the angle at which the tail joins the body.

Set up: a dog posed in a traditional show position.

Shawl: a pronounced development of long hair around the neck.

Single tracking: an action where all four footprints fall in a single line of travel.

Sire: the male parent of a dog.

Snipy: a weak, pointed muzzle.

Socks: the hair on the feet up as far as the pasterns usually white in a colored dog.

Sooty: used to describe an ideally clear coat where black hairs intermingle with the base color.

Soundness: the state of physical and mental well-being, usually applied to movement.

Spay: the surgical removal of a bitch's reproductive organs.

Splashed: irregularly marked with white on a base color, or a color on a white ground color.

Splay foot: open-toed foot, lacking tightness, compactness.

Spring of rib: degree of curvature of the rib cage.

Stallion: a male dog who displays overt masculinity.

Standard: the breed Standard; the written description of the ideal specimen of any breed.

Stand-off coat: a coat which stands away from the body.

Stern: the tail.

Stifle: the joint of the hind leg between the thigh and the second thigh. Equivalent to the human knee.

Stop: the indentation between the eyes where the nasal bone and skull meet.

Stud dog: a male dog used for breeding purposes.

Substance: solidity of body with the requisite musculation and condition.

Supercillary ridges: projection of the frontal bones over the eye; the brow.

Sway bones: concave curvature of the back between the withers and hipbones, usually indicating weakness.

Thumb marks: black shaded spots on a contrasting ground color in the region of the pastern.

Ticked: used to describe small flecks or colored hairs on a white background color.

Tipped ears: erect ears with just the tips falling forward.

Topknot: long hair on the top of the head.

Topline: the upper outline from the withers to the tailset.

Tricolor: three colors, usually black, tan and white.

Trim: the style of coat produced in grooming.

Tuck-up: concave underline of the body where the belly appears to be well drawn up.

Tulip ear: a wide ear carried with a slight forward curve.

Turn up: upward sweep of the foreface or underjaw.

Type: the overall appearance created by the collection of characteristic features which distinguish a breed.

Undercoat: dense, soft, short coat concealed by a topcoat.

Undershot: describes a mouth where the lower jaw projects beyond the upper, when the mouth is closed, so that the lower teeth protrude beyond the upper and have no contact.

Up-faced: having a short nose and turned-up muzzle.

Upper arm: the humerus; the bone of the foreleg between the shoulder blade and elbow.

Upright shoulder: a shoulder lacking in angulation.

Veiled coat: a single coat of fine, wispy long hair.

Wall eye: an eye which is wholly or partly light-blue in color.

Wedgy: usually describes a head which lacks chiseling and has the overall appearance of a uniform, straight-edged wedge.

Well laid: having the ideal shoulder angulation.

Well sprung: having good curvature of the ribs.

Wheaten: a pale yellow or fawn color.

Whip tail: a tail which is carried out straight and stiffly.

Withers: highest point of the body, behind the neck.

Zygomatic arch: the arch of bone forming the lower borders off the eye socket reaching to the base of the ear.

PHOTO CREDITS

© John Adlercreutz 3, 51 top right, 57, 73, 127, 128, 144 top, 177 bottom, 190, 239, 330, 355 bottom, 483
Animals Unlimited 35, 113, 254 top, 269, 345
Courtesy of The Australian Government 203
Boyer, Pamela 432
Brace, Andrew 259
Brady, Lynn and Townsend, Connie 286
Brown, Fran 400
© Stephe Bruin 209 top, 449 bottom
Bruni, Tom 365
© Callea Photography 47 right, 62, 67, 91, 93, 94
Campbell, Terry and Gail 387
Canine Control Council (Queensland) 453
courtesy Anne Rogers Clark 56, 59, 60, 65 left, 65 right, 101, 121, 160, 205, 223, 224, 272 (photo © Reynolds Photography), 305, 350, 354, 467
Conner, Meghan F. 363
Creel, Mike 433
© David Dalton 80, 106, 151, 243 top, 252 top, 252 bottom, 257, 293, 300, 343 bottom right, 346 top, 373, 391, 459
© 1994 Tara Darling 70
© Kent and Donna Dannen (courtesy AKC) 440
Dobrovolney, Gert 97 bottom
Dog Ink 145 bottom, 251
Ekdahl, Barbara and Thomas 221
Falconer, Amy C. 474
Dr.D.Fleig 83, 161
Foster, Vicky 482
Foxboro Studios 102 bottom
courtesy Franckh Kosmos Verlag 342 top
© Gay Glazbrook, courtesy Sergio Balcazar and Gabriel Rangel 226
Glodek, Jaimi 476
Gottinger, W. and C. 17
Ha'Aretz Canaan Dog 166
©1984 HAGA, courtesy S. Weiss 477
Hammarstrom, Sylvia 392, 393, 395, 397
© Paula Heikkinen-Lehkonen 81, 169 bottom, 173, 292 top and bottom left, 362 bottom

© Marc Henrie 21, 37 right, 44, 49 bottom, 51 bottom, 52, 105, 138, 183, 331, 333, 349, 398, 405, 413
Het Laatste Niews Brussels 137 bottom
© F. Hinsch, courtesy Animal Photography 45
Hooks, Karen 465
Hooper, Louise 164
Irish Kennel Club, © P. J. Gilmore 279
Johnson, Carol Ann 61, 173
Johnson, Douglas A. 434
Jones, Connie 184
Kennel Club of Greece 256 bottom
Kish, Sue 372 top
© Eva-Maria Kramer 71, 77, 85, 88 bottom, 99 top, 109, 135 (Kocbek photo), 139, 143, 146 top, 168, 169 top, 202 bottom, 216 top, 230 bottom, 253 bottom, 261 bottom, 338 top, 338 bottom (Kotulla photo), 342 bottom, 355 top (Kocbek photo), 381, 401, 466, 478
courtesy Kynos Verlag 13 bottom, 23, 174, 138, 382
Lavizza, Michael 335
© Kathe Lehner, courtesy Osterreichischer Kynologenverband 96
Lindgren, Gunnar 319
Longo, Joe and Tootie 245
Louisiana Office of Tourism 170
Mathard, Liz 329
Meads, J. 225
Metier, Anne 408
Montcombroux, Michael 167
Monteleone, Stephany 420
Nakashima, Mari 74, 275 bottom, 415
Panther Photographic International 87
Pessina, Barbara 359
© Perry Phillips, courtesy Penny Hanigan 110
Powderhorn/Wencrest Rottweilers Inc. 377, 378
Reilly, Ruth Anne 280
Roslin-Williams, Ann (courtesy AKC) 340
Sammet, Wendell J. 199
Schonheyder, Sofie 298
Schor, Dr Saul 14
Seeman, Kate 132
Siner, Gregory M. 443

Sorenson, Steve 117 top and bottom
Stang-Westerlea, Alison 372 bottom
Stanton, Paul 457
Stuckey, Brenda (courtesy AKC) 140
© Sallie Anne Thompson 1, 8, 13 top, 25, 26, 27, 28, 29 bottom, 30, 32, 37 left, 38, 48 left, 51 top left, 56 bottom, 69, 75, 78, 86, 88 top, 97, 99 bottom, 102 top, 103 top, 108, 112, 116 top and bottom, 118, 119, 120, 122, 124, 125, 130, 134, 136, 142, 144 bottom, 145 top, 149, 153, 154, 157, 158, 159, 163, 171, 176, 177 top, 179, 181, 185, 187, 189, 191, 193, 194, 196, 198, 201, 202 top, 206, 207, 208, 209 bottom, 211 top and bottom, 212, 214 top and bottom, 216 bottom, 217, 218, 219, 220 top and bottom, 227, 229, 230 top, 231, 235, 237, 243 bottom, 246, 249, 250, 253 top, 254 bottom, 255, 260, 261 top, 263, 273, 275, 277, 282, 283, 284, 285 top, 289, 290, 292 bottom right, 295, 296, 299, 301, 303, 306, 308, 312, 313, 318, 320, 322, 324, 327, 332, 337, 339, 341, 343 top and bottom left, 344, 346 bottom, 348, 352, 357, 360, 362 top, 366, 371, 374, 379, 380 top and bottom, 388, 389 top, 402, 407, 411, 417, 418, 423, 424 top, 425 top, 426, 427, 428, 438, 445, 447, 448, 449 top, 451, 458, 464, 468, 470, 480, 485
Unden, Per 258, 425 bottom, 463
Volz, Elizabeth, © Perry Phillips 353
Ward, Catherine 10, 11, 12
© Soren Wesseltoft 7, 29 top, 148, 267, 316, 384 (courtesy AKC), 436, 454, 472, 496
© Torsten Widholm 146 bottom, 147, 150, 172, 175, 195 bottom, 210, 236, 247, 256 top, 271, 285 bottom, 287, 291, 307, 310, 311, 314, 325 top and bottom, 389 bottom, 424 bottom, 455, 456 top, bottom left and bottom right
© R. T. Willbie 5, 36, 43, 48 right, 49 top, 54, 55, 64, 66, 82, 90, 98 top and bottom, 115, 137 top, 233, 361, 369, 421, 461, 478 bottom
Williams, A. Roslin (courtesy AKC) 178
Wright, Jeff 430, 431

ACKNOWLEDGMENTS

The publishers and editors would like to acknowledge the contributions to this book of the following:

The American Kennel Club, Australian National Kennel Council, Margaret Barnes, Pam Blay, Damara Bolte, Thomas H. Bradley III, Roberta Brennan, Vi Buchanan, Michael B. Camac, The Canadian Kennel Club, Lesley Chalmers, Delbert Dahl, Dr. Samuel Draper, Liz Dunhill, Peter Eva, Mrs. Bernard Freeman, Stanley Gonic, Beryl Grounds, Meriel E. Hathaway, Dr. and Mrs. Samuel Hodesson, Mike Homan, Jeff Horswell, Muriel Iles, Jean Jackson, Frank Jones, Frank Kane, The Kennel Club of Great Britain, Jenny Kennish, Ruth Kitson, Constance Stuart Larabee, Peter Larkin, Dorothy M. Macdonald,

Edna K. H. Martin, Kenneth M. McDormott, Desmond J. Murphy, Peter Newman, Stuart Plane, Gina Pointing, Shirley Rawlings, Mrs. Curtis Read, James G. Reynolds, John David Savage, John Sellers, Lorraine Smart, Lawrence Stanbridge, Gael Stenton, R. William Taylor, Christopher Thomas, Elizabeth Tyson, Seymour Weiss, Dorothy Welsh, Malcolm Willis.

A special thanks to Renée Sporre-Willes for her text contribution, her photo research and checking of the FCI aspect and to Sean Frawley for providing the inspiration for this book.

BIBLIOGRAPHY

Alston, George G. and Vanacore, Connie. *The Winning Edge: Show Ring Secrets*. New York/London. Howell Book House, Maxwell Macmillan International, 1992.

The American Kennel Club. *The Complete Dog Book*. New York. Howell Book House, 1992.

Bauman, Diane L. *Beyond Basic Dog Training*. New York/London. Howell Book House, Maxwell Macmillan International, 1991.

Benjamin, Carol Lea. *Mother Knows Best: The Natural Way to Train Your Dog*. New York. Howell Book House, 1985.

Blogg, Rowan & Allan, Eric. *Everydog: The Complete Book of Dog Care and Health*. New York. William Morrow, 1987.

Caras, Roger, ed. *Harper's Illustrated Handbook of Dogs*. New York. Chanticleer Press/Harper Collins, 1988.

Carlson, Delbert G., D.V.M. and Giffin, James M., M.D. *The Dog Owner's Home Veterinary Handbook*. New York/London. Howell Book House, Maxwell Macmillan International, 1992.

Carvell, David. *All About Mating, Whelping and Weaning*. New York. Penguin, 1988.

Christiansen, J. *Reproduction in the Dog and Cat*. New York. Saunders, 1984.

Darling, Kathy. *In Praise of Dogs*. New York. Howell Book House, 1995.

BeBitetto, James, D.V.M. and Hodgson, Sarah. *You and Your Puppy*. New York. Howell Book House, 1995.

Elliott, Rachel Page. *The New Dogsteps*. New York. Howell Book House, 1983.

Evans, Howard E. and Christensen, George C. *Miller's Anatomy of the Dog*. New York. Saunders, 1979.

Farley, Pat. *Dog About Town: Keeping a Dog in the City — Myths, Facts and Advice*. New York. Simon and Schuster, 1988.

Fletcher, Walter. *Dogs of the World*. New York. Bantam Books, 1977.

Fogle, Dr. Bruce. *The Dog's Mind: Understanding Your Dog's Behavior*. New York. Howell Book House, 1990.

Gannon, Deidre E., Esq. *The Complete Guide to Dog Law*. New York. Howell Book House, 1994.

Frauling, Eleanor. *Practical Dog Breeding and Genetics*. New York. Random Century, 1988.

Frye, Federic L. *First Aid For Your Dog*. New York. Barron, 1987.

Fuller, Clarke. *A Beginner's Guide to Dog Care*. New Jersey. TFH Publications, Inc., 1986.

Gilbert, Edward M. and Brown, Thelma. *K-9 Structure and Terminology*. New York. Howell Book House, 1995.

Gerstenfeld, Sheldon L. *Taking Care of Your Dog*. Boston. Addison-Wesley, 1979.

Harris, Beth J. Finder. *Breeding a Litter: The Complete Book of Prenatal and Postnatal Care*. New York. Howell Book House, 1993.

Hart, E. *Encyclopedia of Dog Breeds*. New Jersey. TFH Publications, Inc., 1995.

Klever, Ulrich. *The Complete Book of Dog Care*. New York. Barron, 1989.

Loeb, Jo and Loeb, Paul. *Good Dog!: Improve Your Pet's Health and Behavior Through Diet and Exercise*. New York. Putnam Publishing Group, 1984.

Pfaffenberger, Clarence J. *The New Knowledge of Dog Behavior*. New York. Howell Book House, 1963.

Reader's Digest Editors. *The Reader's Digest Illustrated Book of Dogs*. Pleasantville, New York. Reader's Digest Association, 1985.

Richards, Herbert. *Dog Breeding for Professionals*. New Jersey. TFH Publications, Inc., 1978.

Saunders, Blanche. *The Complete Book of Dog Obedience: The Guide for Trainers*. New York. Howell Book House, 1978.

Schwartz, Charlotte. *The Howell Book of Puppy Raising*. New York. Howell Book House, 1987.

Seranne, Ann. *The Joy of Breeding Your Own Show Dog*. New York. Howell Book House, 1980.

Sife, Wallace, Ph.D. *The Loss of a Pet*. New York/London. Howell Book House, Maxwell Macmillan International, 1993.

Simmons-Moake, Jane. *Agility Training: The Fun Sport for All Dogs*. New York. Howell Book House, 1991.

Strickland, Winifred G. *Expert Obedience Training for Dogs*. New York. Howell Book House, 1987.

Taylor, David. *Ultimate Dog Book*. New York. Simon and Schuster, 1990.

Taylor, David. *You and Your Dog*. New York. Knopf, 1986.

Tortora, Daniel F. *The Right Dog For You: Choosing a Breed That Matches Your Personality, Family and Lifestyle*. New York. Simon and Schuster, 1983.

Vanacore, Connie. *Dog Showing: An Owner's Guide*. New York. Howell Book House, 1990.

Volhard, Wendy and Brown, Kerry, D.V.M. *The Holistic Guide for a Healthy Dog*. New York. Howell Book House, 1995.

Whitney, Leon F., D.V.M. *Dog Psychology: The Basis of Dog Training*. New York. Howell Book House, 1971.

Wilcox, Bonnie and Walkowicz, Chris. *Atlas of Dog Breeds*. New Jersey. TFH Publications, Inc., 1989.

Wilcox, Bonnie, D.V.M. and Walkowicz, Chris. *Old Dogs, Old Friends*. New York. Howell Book House, 1995.

Willis, Malcolm B., B.Sc., Ph.D. *Genetics of the Dog*. New York. Howell Book House, 1995

INDEX